Hakikat Kitabevi Publications No. 4

Se'âdet-i Ebediyye

Endless Bliss

FOURTH FASCICLE

Hüseyn Hilmi Işık

Seventeenth Edition

Hakîkat Kitâbevi
Darüşşefeka Cad. 53/A P.K.: 35
34083 Fatih-ISTANBUL/TURKEY
Tel: 90.212.523 4556–532 5843 Fax: 90.212.523 3693
http://www.hakikatkitabevi.com
e-mail: bilgi@hakikatkitabevi.com
SEPTEMBER-2014

NOTE

This book is a translation of **Se'âdet-i Ebediyye,** which was originally written in Turkish.

The Turkish original of the book **Se'âdet-i Ebediyye** consists of three parts, all of which add up to well over twelve hundred pages.

We have translated the entire book into English and published our translations in six individual fascicles.

Se'âdet-i Ebediyye is a book prepared according to the Hanafî Madhhab. There is not a single bit of knowledge or a word which contradicts the creed of Ahl-i Sunnat wa'l Jamâ'at in this book.

This is the fourth fascicle. We invoke Allâhu ta'âlâ for help, so the book may reach our dear readers.

Publisher's note:

Anyone who wishes to print this book in its original form or to translate it into any other language is granted beforehand our permission to do so; and people who undertake this beneficial feat are accredited to the benedictions that we in advance offer to Allâhu ta'âlâ in their name and also our best wishes of gratitude and we thank them very much. However, permission is subject to the condition that the paper used in printing be of a good quality and that the design of the text and setting be properly and neatly done without mistakes.

A Warning: Missionaries are striving to advertise Christianity; Jews are working to spread out the concocted words of Jewish rabbis; Hakîkat Kitâbevi (Bookstore), in Istanbul, is struggling to publicize Islam; and freemasons are trying to annihilate religions. A person with wisdom, knowledge and conscience will understand and side with the right one of these choices and will help to spread it for salvation of all humanity. There is no better way and more valuable thing to serve humanity than doing so.

TYPESET AND PRINTED IN TURKEY BY:
İhlâs Gazetecilik A.Ş.
Merkez Mah. 29 Ekim Cad. İhlâs Plaza No: 11 A/41
34197 Yenibosna-İSTANBUL Tel: 90.212.454 3000

CONTENTS

Chapter		Page
	Preface	4
	Islam	9
1–	The five daily prayers (namâz)	17
2–	The fards of namâz	19
3–	Masah (wiping) on mests (special socks or shoes); having an excuse	33
4–	Ghusl (ritual washing) haid, nifâs, darûrat, haraj	40
5–	Tayammum	79
6–	Tahârat from najâsat (Purification from uncleanliness)	87
7–	Water and its kinds	102
8–	Satr-i awrat and women's covering themselves	109
9–	Qibla: its direction	125
10–	Prayer times	135
11–	Azân (or adhân) (announcing and call to prayers) and iqâmat	197
12–	First Volume, 303rd letter	208
13–	Importance of namâz (prayer)	209
14–	How do we perform namâz (prayer)	217
15–	Namâz during long-distance journeys	232
16–	Wâjibs of namâz, Sajda-i sahw	247
17–	Things that nullify namâz	255
18–	Mekrûhs of namâz	266
19–	The namâz of tarâwîh and reverence due to mosques	281
20–	Namâz in jamâ'at	291
21–	Friday (Jum'a) prayer	311
22–	The namâz of 'Iyd	329
23–	The qadhâ namâzes [omitted prayers]	333
24–	Taghannî (singing) and music	369
25–	Second Volume, forty-sixth letter	402
26–	Second Volume, thirty-seventh letter	412
27–	Second Volume, thirty-ninth letter	415
Appendix I – FINDING THE FIRST DAY OF AN ARABIC MONTH		418
Appendix II – ULUĞ BEY'S TABLE FOR LUNAR (QAMARÎ) MONTHS		419
Appendix III – FINDING THE MÎLÂDÎ YEAR COINCIDING WITH THE BEGINNING OF THE HIJRÎ YEAR		420
Appendix IV – **TABLE** EQUATION OF TIME and DECLINATION OF THE SUN		421
Appendix V – TABLE of TAMKINS		423
Appendix VI – SUN'S ALTITUDES at TIME of LATE AFTERNOON PRAYER		424
	GLOSSARY	425

PREFACE

Saying the **A'ûdhu** (A'ûdhu billâhi min-ash-shaytânirrajîm) and **Basmala** (Bismillâhirrahmânirrahîm), I begin writing my book.

Al-hamd-u lillâh! If any person thanks another person in any manner for any reason at any place or time, all this hamd and thanks will in fact have been paid to Allâhu ta'âlâ. For, Allâhu ta'âlâ alone creates and developes everything and renders every favour done. He, alone, is the owner of might and power. Unless He reminds, no one can wish or ever think of doing good or evil. Whatever happens is only what He wills.

May the best of prayers and favours be upon Muhammad Mustafâ 'sall-Allâhu 'alaihi wa sallam', who is His Prophet and most beloved slave, the most beautiful, the most superior of mankind in every respect. Also, may Allâhu ta'âlâ be pleased with the Prophet's family and companions, and all those who love and follow them!

Every man, and even every living being, wants to live in comfort, without sorrow and without trouble or pain. Savants, scientists, and governments have all been trying to establish these conditions for the world's people. To attain this, various ideas and methods have been developed, and everyone is defending the way he thinks is better and more useful.

As unanimously declared by hundreds of thousands of Islamic savants, who have lived throughout the last fourteen centuries, and as well by all the correct religions which guided people to the way of comfort and peace in all parts of the world before Islam, there is one single way that will lead people to happiness and comfort. This unique way is through Îmân, which means to believe in the existence of one single creator, who created everything from nothing, who alone always makes everything, and who is almighty, such that what He wishes happens. The name of this single owner of power is **Allah**. Every goodness, every superiority belongs to Him only. There is no weakness or deficiency in Him. He has always existed. He never ceases to exist. He, alone, keeps everything in existence every moment. If He ceased to exist for one moment, everything would immediately cease to exist, too. To have belief in Him, it is necessary to believe and accept all His declarations, commandments, and prohibitions. Hence, there are a number of things to believe in. Islamic savants have summarized them into six groups. They are called **Principles of Îmân**. To believe in these six principles means to believe in everything that is necessary. The following are the six principles of îmân:

1 - To learn Allah's five **Sifât-i dhâtiyya** and His eight **Sifât-i thubûtiyya** and to believe in them.

2 - To learn and believe in the teachings that are necessary to believe in, about **Angels**.

3 - To learn the names of the four heavenly books sent by Allâhu ta'âlâ and to believe that they are Allah's word. Allâhu ta'âlâ sent each book to a prophet through an angel. He sent the Qur'ân to Hadrat Muhammad 'sall-Allâhu 'alaihi wa sallam'. It is permissible to translate or interpret the Qur'ân in any language and to learn the meaning of the Qur'ân as well as possible by reading such translations and interpretations. But reading the translations is not the same as reading the Qur'ân. For, not only the meanings of the words of the Qur'ân are called the Qur'ân, but also the words together with their meanings represent the **Qur'ân**.

4 - To believe in Prophets. The first of the Prophets was Hadrat **Âdam** 'alaihis-salâm'. The last and the highest Prophet was Hadrat **Muhammad** 'sall-Allâhu 'alaihi wa sallam'. The number of Prophets who came between the two is not known.

5 - To believe in the **Last day**. That day is Doomsday. That is when every living thing will be annihilated. Afterwards they will all be resurrected, men will rise from their graves and, after being called to account, some of them will go to Paradise and others to Hell.

6 - To believe in **Qadar**. Allâhu ta'âlâ knows in advance the things He will create. This knowledge of Allâhu ta'âlâ is called **Qadar**. Everything is created in accordance with this knowledge when the time comes. Men cannot change Allah's qadar.

Today, the earth has only one book revealed by Allah that has not undergone human interpolation. This undefiled and perfect book is the **Qur'ân al-kerîm**. He who believes in the six principles of îmân as declared by the Qur'ân al-kerîm becomes a **Mu'min** or **Muslim**. Only Hadrat **Muhammad** 'sall-Allâhu 'alaihi wa sallam' understood the meaning of the Qur'ân correctly, and he explained it to those Muslims who were with him. Each of these explanations of Hadrat Muhammad is called **Hadîth-i-sherîf**. Muslims who saw Hadrat Muhammad's beautiful face are called the **Sahâba**. Islamic savants who came later learned the meanings of the Qur'ân from the Sahâba, and they wrote them in their books. They are called the **Savants of Ahl-as-sunnat**. Hadrat Muhammad 'sall-Allâhu 'alaihi wa sallam' informed us that they were the true **Islamic savants**. Working day and night, the higher ones of those savants learned the various methods of worshipping within the context of what had newly happened and of what would arise later. They always adapted their methods of worshipping in accordance with what they had learned from the Sahaba, and they in turn taught them to their disciples. The highest ones among the **Ahl-as-sunnat** are called **Mujtahid imâms**. And some other savants who preferred their own minds and opinions gave new meanings disagreeing with the knowledge concerning the Qur'ân conveyed to them by the savants of the Ahl-as-sunnat. Thus they deviated from the teachings of îmân communicated by the savants of the Ahl-as-sunnat. If this deviation of theirs does not involve the clear declarations of the Qur'ân, those who hold that belief are still Mu'mins, Muslims. But they are **Bid'at holders** (heretics). If their deviation involves matters declared clearly, such misbelievers lose their îmân and become disbelievers. They, and also those who believe as they do, are called **Mulhids**. Their thinking of themselves as Muslims and declaring that they are on the right way will not absolve them from being disbelievers. It is written in all the books of fiqh, and especially in Ibni 'Âbidîn, under the chapters dealing with iman: "It has been unanimously said (by savants) that if a person disbelieves in one of the facts that are necessary for one to know to be a Muslim, he becomes a kâfir (disbeliever), even if he is **Ahl-i qibla**, that is, performs the prayers in jamâ'at[1] and does all kinds of worship throughout his life." If a belief disagreeing with the savants of the Ahl-as-sunnat is not a result of interpreting the Qur'ân erroneously, but by following one's own short mind, understanding, opinion or the day's scientific knowledge, one who believes so becomes a **kâfir**. Such disbelievers are called **Religion reformers**. For example, a person who disbelieves in the torment in the grave and in the shafâ'at (intercession) that will take place in the next world is either a heretical Muslim who is **Ahl-i bid'at**, or a disbeliever who is a religion reformer. A **religon reformer** thinks of himself as a Muslim, too. An enemy of Islam who is not a Muslim but who gives wrong meanings to the Qur'ân by pretending to be a Muslim in order to defile and demolish Islam from within is called a **zindiq**. It is difficult for youngsters to distinguish between these three types of disbelievers.

Each of Allah's commandments is called a **Fard**. His prohibitions are called **Harâm**. The mujtahid imâms, who were

---

[1] See chapter 20 for prayers in jamâ'at.

the highest of the savants of the **Ahl-as-sunnat**, in their search for documents in order to decide about certain matters, disagreed with one another in some matters. Thus, various **Madhhabs** emerged. Among them, the books of the famous four Madhhabs spread everywhere, and the other Madhhabs were forgotten.

He who wants to attain happiness in this world, in his grave, and in the Hereafter must, after adapting his îmân to the Ahl-as-sunnat, live in obedience to one of the four Madhhabs. In other words, all his worships and actions must be suited to one Madhhab. Of the four Madhhabs, he must choose the one that is the easiest for him to learn and follow; after learning it, he must act in accordance with it in everything he does. Savants of the Ahl-as-sunnat declared unanimously that when doing a certain deed it is not permissible to mix the four Madhhabs with one another. That is, it is never permissible to do one part of a deed or worship according to one Madhhab and another part according to another Madhhab. Anyone who does so will have disobeyed the unanimity of the savants and will have followed none of the Madhhabs. To follow one Madhhab means to learn it and to intend to follow it. It is not acceptable to follow it without intending to do so.

Hadrat Abdulghanî Nablusî wrote in his book **Khulâsat-ut-tahqîq fî-bayân-i hukm-it-taqlîd wat-talfîq**: "Admitting someone else's word or proof without understanding it, is called **Taqlîd** (imitation, following). A Muslim who is not a mujtahid has to do his every act of worship and everything by imitating a mujtahid. It is permissible for him to imitate one mujtahid when doing one thing and to follow another mujtahid when doing another thing for the first time. But, after having done one thing according to one Madhhab, he has to do that thing by imitating continuously the same Madhhab, except when there is a **darûrat** (strong necessity)[1] not to do so. During the times of the Sahâba and the Tâbi'în, the newly converted Muslims would do so. Likewise, Muslims who imitate only one Madhhab in everything they do, cannot imitate another Madhhab unless there is a strong necessity." As is seen, when there is a darûrat, it is permissible to do worships and everything else according to another Madhhab. But, in that case, it will be necessary to learn that Madhhab well and to observe its conditions.

A person who does not follow a Madhhab, (i.e. one of the only four valid **Madhhabs**,) is called a lâ-madhhabî. A lâ-madhhabî

---

[1] The meaning of darûrat is explained in the fourth chapter.

person cannot be **Sunnî**[1]. His worships are not sahîh (correct, valid). It is harâm to change one's Madhhab for worldly advantages in order to obtain the desires of one's nafs[2]. Each Muslim must learn at least one Madhhab and to adapt his daily life to it.

To annihilate Islam, the enemies of Islam attacked the Ahl-as-**sunnat** by state and financial forces. In all parts of the world they prevented the educating of Islamic savants. They annihilated the schools of the **Ahl-as-sunnat** and the books of the **Ahl-as-sunnat**. This onslaught was led by the British. Today, as it can be seen, there are no books of the **Ahl-as-sunnat**, nor any savants of the **Ahl-as-sunnat** left in many countries. Brought up ignorant, the youth are easily being deceived, misled, and swept into perdition by mulhids, lâ-madhhabîs, and religion reformers. I have deemed it necessary to spread all over the world in English the teachings of fiqh by way of my Turkish book **Se'âdet-i Ebediyye**. I prepared this book as a service to innocent younger generations. Thus, the fourth fascicle of my book **Endless Bliss** (English version of a considerable portion of the aforesaid peerless epitome, Se'âdet-i Ebediyye,) has been formed. I prepared this book, (Se'âdet-i Ebediyye,) by translating fiqh books of the Hanafî Madhhab. If those youngsters who are in another Madhhab or who have not been able to learn the teachings of **dîn** (religion) read this book and adapt themselves to these teachings in all their manners and acts of worship, they will have imitated the great Islamic savant Hadrat Imâm-i a'zam Abû Hanîfa Nu'mân bin Thâbit, the leader of the savants of the **Ahl-as-sunnat**, the great imâm and mutlaq mujtahid. Thus, their worships will be sahîh, they will escape the calamity of having deviated from the **Ahl-as-sunnat**.

May Allâhu ta'âlâ protect us all from being deceived by the insidious enemies of Islam, from being trapped by lâ-madhhabî people and by religion reformers who bear Muslim names! Âmin.

Husayn Hilmi bin Sa'îd Ishiq (Işık) 'rahmatullâhi ta'âlâ 'alaih', (1329 [1911 A.D.], Vezîr Tekkesi, Eyyûb Sultân, Istanbul-1422 [2001], Istanbul.)

---

[1] Our Prophet 'sall-Allâhu 'alaihi wa sallam' stated: "**My Ummat (Muslims) will part into seventy-three groups** (in matters of creed). **Only one of these groups will be in the correct path.**" This single correct group of Muslims is termed '**Ahl as-sunnat wa'l jamâ'at**', and a Muslim who is in this group is called '**Sunnî Muslim**'.

[2] A malignant power in the human nature which urges the human being against the commandments and prohibitions of Allahu ta'âlâ.
Husayn Hilmi bin Sa'îd Ishiq (Işık), 'quddîsa sirruh', a great Islamic scholar and a Walî, stated: "The Nafs is the most idiotic creature, for everything it wishes is something against it and harmful to it, (and everything it detests is something for its own good.)"

ISLAM

[Allâhu ta'âlâ created all creatures. Everything except Allâhu ta'âlâ was nonexistent. He always exists. There is not a beginning of His existence. If He had been nonexistent, a power already existing before Him would have been necessary to create Him. To have something come into being requires work. And it is a fact being taught in all high schools and faculties of science that doing work requires having power. If there is no power to create something previously nonexistent, that thing remains nonexistent and never exists. If the owner of power always existed, Allah is this powerful eternal being. But if it is determined that this owner of creative power is also a recent occurrence, then it must have a creator, too. If it is not accepted that one creator has existed since eternity, then an infinite number of creators will be necessary. And this, in turn, means that these creators do not have a beginning. The nonexistence of the first eternal creator means the nonexistence of other creators it could have created. If there is no creator, this universe of matter and souls, which has been created from nothing, cannot exist, either. Since substances and souls exist, they must also have only one creator, and this creator must have existed eternally.

Allâhu ta'âlâ created simple substances, which are the constructive materials for everything, and souls and angels first. Simple substances are called elements now. Today's knowledge reveals the existence of one hundred and five different elements. Allahu ta'âlâ created and is still creating everything from these one hundred and five elements. Iron, sulphur, carbon, oxygen gas, and chlorine gas are all elements. Allâhu ta'âlâ has not informed us of how many millions of years ago He created these elements. Nor has He declared the time He began to create the earths, the heavens, and the living things which came into being from these. Living or lifeless, everything has a life cycle. When the time comes, He creates it, and when its time is up, He annihilates it. He creates things not only from nothing, but also from other things, gradually or suddenly, and as one being ceases to exist a new one comes into being.

Allâhu ta'âlâ made up the first man from lifeless substances and a soul. There had been no man before him. Animals, plants, genies and angels had been created before that first man. That first man's name was Âdam (alaihis-salâtu wa-s-salâm). Later He created a woman named Hawwâ (Eve) from him. The earth's population finds its source from these two. And from each animal its own species multiplied.

Today, the enemies of Islam disguise themselves as scientists in order to deceive Muslim children. "Men were created from monkeys," they say. "A British doctor named Darwin said so," they say. But they are liars. Darwin did not say such a thing. He related the struggle for survival among the living. In his book **Origin of the Species**, he wrote that the living adapted themselves to their surroundings, and, in doing this, underwent some insignificant changes. He did not say that one species changed into another. In a conference organized in Salford in 1980 by the British Unity of Science, Prof. John Durant, a member of the teaching staff in the University of Swansea, made the following speech, in summary: "Darwin's views on the the origin of man has become a modern legend. The contribution this legend has made to our scientific and social progress has been sheer harm, and no more. The tales of evolution have had a destructive effect on scientific research. They have given rise to distortions, unnecessary disputes and serious scientific abuses. Now Darwin's theory has come apart at the seams, leaving behind itself ruins of erroneous conceptions." These statements, which Prof. Durant made about his compatriot, are the most interesting answers given in the name of science to Darwinists. Today's attempts to imbue people of various cultural backgrounds with the theory of evolution originate from ideological determinations. They have nothing to do with science. The theory has been exploited as a means for the inculcation of materialistic philosophy. It is not scientific to say that man has originated from the monkey. It is never a scientific statement, either. Nor is it Darwin's statement. It is a lie told by ignorant enemies of Islam who know nothing of knowledge or science. A man of knowledge or a scientist simply could not say such an ignorant, absurd thing. If a person who has received a university diploma begins to indulge in useless things, does not study his branch of knowledge, even forgets what he has learned, that person cannot be a man of knowledge or a scientist. If in addition he becomes an enemy of Islam and attempts to sow and broadcast his mendacious and wrong words and writings in the name of science and knowledge, he becomes a harmful, base and treacherous microbe in society. His diploma, status, and rank become an ostentation, a trap to hunt the youth. But the most pathetic people are those who are swept into endless perdition by the deception of these fraudulent and fanatical scientists who sow and broadcast their lies and slanders in the name of knowledge and science.

Allâhu ta'âlâ wants people to live in comfort and peace in the world and to attain endless happiness in the Hereafter. It is for this reason that He has commanded useful things that cause happiness and forbidden harmful things which cause calamity. The better a person adapts himself to the rules taught in Qur'ân al-kerîm and obeys the commandments and prohibitions of Allâhu ta'âlâ, regardless of whether he does so on purpose or by chance, the more peace and comfort will he attain in his worldly life and this rule has no exceptions dependent on the person's being religious or irreligious, a Believer or a disbeliever. It is like a person's taking medicine, which will cure him anyway. The reason why many irreligious and atheistic people and nations achieve success in most of their enterprises today is their working compatibly with the principles taught in Qur'ân al-kerîm. However, attaining eternal felicity by following Qur'ân al-kerîm requires first of all believing in it and following its rules intentionally.

The first commandment of Allâhu ta'âlâ is to have **Îmân**. And His first prohibition is **kufr**. Îmân means to believe the fact that Hadrat Muhammad 'sall-Allâhu 'alaihi wa sallam' is Allah's last prophet. Allâhu ta'âlâ revealed His commandments and prohibitions to him in Arabic and in a manner termed **Wahy**. That is, He declared them to him through an angel. And the Prophet, in turn, communicated them to mankind. What Allâhu ta'âlâ declared in Arabic is called the **Qur'ân al-kerîm**. The book in which the entire Qur'ân al-kerîm is written is called a **Mus'haf**. The Qur'ân al-kerîm is not the word of Muhammad ''alaihis-salâm'. It is the Word of Allah. No human being could have managed such an immaculate wording. Everything that is declared in the Qur'ân al-kerîm is called **Islam**. A person who believes all of it is called a **Mu'min** (Believer) and **Muslim**. Denying even one of the facts in it is called disbelief, that is, **Kufr**. It is only the business of the heart to believe the facts concerning the happenings in the next world, the existence of genies and angels, and the Prophet Âdam's ''alaihis-salâm' fatherhood over all people, and the fact that he is the first prophet. These are called knowledge of **I'tiqâd** (belief) and **Aqâid** (tenets). Both the commandments and the prohibitions pertaining to heart and body must be accepted and observed. An aggregate of these injunctions is called knowledge of **A'mâl** or **Sharî'at** (Islamic law). It is **Îmân** to believe in them, too. And it is **Worship** to observe them. As is understood, he who disbelieves or ignores the fact that worships are duties, becomes a **kâfir** (disbeliever). He who believes them but does not do them, will not become a kâfir. He is called a **fâsiq** (sinner). A Believer who has îmân in the knowledge of Islam and observes it as well as he can is called a **Pious Muslim**. A Muslim who strives to earn the love and the approval of Allâhu ta'âlâ is called **Sâlih**. One who has earned the love and the approval of Allâhu ta'âlâ is called **'Ârif** or **Walî**. A Walî who is instrumental in other's attaining this love is called **Murshid**. **Sâdiq** is the common appellation of these distinguished people. All of them are Sâlih. A pious Mu'min will never go to Hell. A kâfir will certainly go to Hell. Never leaving Hell, he will suffer eternal torment. If a kâfir becomes a Believer, all his or her sins will be pardoned. If a fâsiq repents of his sins and starts doing 'ibâdat (and begs Allâhu ta'âlâ for forgiveness), he will never go to Hell, but he will go to Paradise directly like a pious Believer. If he does not do his **Tawba** (begging Allâhu ta'âlâ for forgiveness), he will be forgiven through **shafâ'at** (intercession) or without any mediation and go directly to Paradise, or, after burning in Hell to the extent determined by his sins, caused by his sins, he will then go to Paradise.

The Qur'ân al-kerîm descended in a language suitable with the Arabic grammar spoken by the people of that time, and it is in poetic form. That is, like poetry, it is harmonious. It is replete with the subtleties of the Arabic language. It has all the subtleties of the literary sciences such has bedî, bayân, me'ânî and belâghat. It is, therefore, very difficult to understand. A person who does not know the subtleties of the Arabic language cannot understand the Qur'ân al-kerîm well even if he reads and writes Arabic. Even those who knew these subtleties could not understand it. As a result, our Prophet explained most of its parts. These explanations of our Prophet 'sall-Allâhu 'alaihi wa sallam' are called **Hadîth-i sherîf**. The Sahâbat al-kirâm 'rıdwânullâhi ta'âlâ 'alaihim ajma'în' communicated to younger generations what they had heard and learned from our master the Prophet. As time elapsed, hearts became darker and darker, and Muslims, especially the newly converted ones, attempted to interpret the

Qur'ân with their deficient minds and short sights, and inferred meanings that contradicted those which our Prophet 'sall-Allâhu 'alaihi wa sallam' had communicated. The enemies of Islam incited this faction and gave birth to seventy-two different, wrong, and heretical beliefs. People who bear such heretical beliefs are called the **Ahl-i bid'at** or **Ahl-i dalâla**. All the people who belong to the seventy-two groups of bid'at will certainly go to Hell, but, being Believers, they will not remain in Hell eternally. They will eventually be allowed out and enter Paradise. If the belief of a person belonging to one of these seventy-two heretical groups disagrees with something clearly declared in the Qur'ân al-kerîm or in the hadîth sherîfs, he will lose his Îmân. Such a person is called a **Mulhid**. A mulhid thinks of himself as a Muslim. But his îmân has left, and he has become a disbeliever.

Islamic savants who learned correctly the teachings of **i'tiqâd**, i.e., the teachings of Islam that must be believed in, from the Sahâba 'ridwânullâhi ta'âlâ 'alaihim ajma'în' and who wrote them in books are called savants of the **Ahl-as-sunnat** 'rahmatullâhi ta'âlâ 'alaihim ajma'în'. These people are scholars who have attained the grade called Ijtihâd in one of the four Madh-habs. The savants of the Ahl-as-sunnat did not attempt to understand the meaning of the Qur'ân al-kerîm with their own minds, but they believed what they learned from the Sahâba. They did not follow what they themselves understood. Thus, they wrote and taught the right way declared by our Prophet 'sall-Allâhu 'alaihi wa sallam'. The Ottoman Empire was a Muslim state, and held the belief of the Ahl-as-sunnat.

As is understood from the information above and as is written in many valuable books, escaping disasters in this world and the next and living in peace and happiness first requires having îmân, which means to learn and believe everything as communicated by the savants of the Ahl-as-sunnat 'rahmatullâhi ta'âlâ 'alaihim ajma'în'. A person who does not hold the belief of the Ahl-as-sunnat has become either an Ahl-i bid'at, a heretical Muslim, or a mulhid, a disbeliever. The second duty of a Believer with correct îmân, i'tiqâd, is to become sâlih (pious), that is, to learn the teachings of the Sharî'at (Islamic law), that is, to do 'ibâda. In explaining the teachings of how to worship, the savants of the Ahl-as-sunnat 'rahimahum-Allâhu ta'âlâ' parted into four groups. Hence, the four **Madhhabs** appeared. They disagreed on a few insignificant matters, but they agreed with one another on îmân; they loved and respected one another. Each Muslim has to worship as shown by one of these four Madhhabs. The fact that a person who does not adapt himself to one of these four Madhhabs has deviated from the Ahl-as-sunnat, is written in the Zabayih section of **Durr-ul-Mukhtâr**, an explanation of **Tahtâwî**. If a disbeliever captured in war, or during the time of peace, says that he has become a Muslim, he is to be believed. But he has to learn and believe the **six principles of îmân** immediately. Gradually, when he has the opportunity, he should learn the fards (obligations) and the harâms (prohibitions) and adapt himself to what he has learned. If he does not learn them, he will have slighted Allâhu ta'âlâ's religion and his îmân will perish. A person who has lost his îmân in such a way is called a **murtadd**. It is written in the hundred and sixteenth page of the translation of **Sharkh-i-Siyar-i-Kebîr** and at the end of the chapter about a disbeliever's marriage in the book **Durr-ul-mukhtâr** that if a person who is wise enough to earn his living and to pursue his advantages successfully reaches the age of puberty without knowing Islam, he is a murtadd (renegade, apostate) (according to Islam's evaluations). It is stated at the end of the chapter about a disbeliever's marriage in the book **Durr-ul-mukhtâr**: If a married Muslim girl does not know Islam when she reaches the age of puberty, her nikâh (marriage contract made in accordance with Islam) becomes null and void; [she becomes a murtadd.] She must be taught the Attributes of Allâhu ta'âlâ. She must repeat and confirm what she hears. Explaining this, Ibni 'Âbidîn 'rahima-h-Allâhi ta'âlâ' says: "A small girl is a Muslim because her parents are Muslims. When she reaches the age of puberty, the rule of her being in the same religion as her parents lapses. So when she reaches the age of puberty without knowing Islam she becomes a murtadd. If she heard the tenets of belief and did not believe them, she will not become a Muslim by saying the Kelima-i-tawhîd, that is, when she says the word '**Lâ ilâha il-l-Allah Muhammadun Rasûlullah**'. A person who believes the six tenets in the credo 'Âmentu billâhi...' and says that he accepts the commandments and prohibitions of Allâhu ta'âlâ, becomes a Muslim." It follows from what has been said so far that every Muslim has to have his children memorize this credo and teach them its meaning well: "Amentu billâhi wa Melâikatihi wa Kutubihi wa Rusulihi wa'l Yawm-il-âkhiri wa bi'l Qaderî khayrihi wa sher-rihi min-Allâhi ta'âlâ wa'l ba'su ba'dal mawt haqqun Esh-hadu an lâ ilâha il-l-Allah wa esh-hadu anna Muhammadan 'abduhu wa Rasûluhu." If a child does not learn these six tenets and does not say that it believes them, it does not become a Muslim when it reaches the age of puberty; it becomes a murtadd. There is detailed information on these six tenets in the (Turkish) book **Herkese Lâzım Olan Îmân**, (and also in the English book **Belief and Islam**.) Every Muslim has to read this book and have his children read it and do his best that all his acquaintances read it, too. We must spare no effort in doing this lest our children should grow up as renegades. We must teach them Îmân, Islam, ablution, ghusl, namâz before sending them to elementary school! The first duty of parents is to raise their children as Muslims.

It is stated in the book **Dürer ve Gürer**, "An apostate man is first told to become a Muslim. Religious tenets in which he has doubts are explained to him. If he asks to be given some time he is imprisoned for three days. If he makes tawba, it is accepted. If he refuses to make tawba, the (Islamic) judge is to have him killed. If the renegade is a woman, she is not killed. She is kept in prison until she makes tawba. If she flees to (a country of disbelievers called) the Dâr-ul-harb, she does not become a jâriya in the Dâr-ul-harb. If she is captivated (by Muslims) she becomes a jâriya. When she becomes a murtadd, her nikâh (if she is married) becomes void. She loses all her rights to her own property. If she becomes a Muslim again, it becomes her property again. If she dies or flees to the Dâr-ul-harb [or if she becomes a murtadd in the Dâr-ul-harb], the property she leaves behind is to be given to her Muslim inheritor(s). [If she has no inheritors, her property will by rights belong to those people who are entitled to the benefits of Bayt-ul-mâl]. A murtadd cannot inherit property from another murtadd. What is left behind a murtadd becomes a (sort of property called) 'fay' for Muslims. All sorts of trade and rental contracts (made by a person who has become a renegade) and the presents given on his part become void. If he becomes a Muslim again, these things become valid again. He will not have to make qadâ of his former acts of worship. However, he will have to make hajj again. What must be learned first after îmân is how to make an ablution and ghusl, and how to perform namâz (prayer).

The six essentials of îmân are to believe in the existence and the oneness of Allâhu ta'âlâ and His Attributes, to believe in angels, Prophets, the Heavenly Books, the events to take place in the Next World, and Qadâ and Qadar. Later on, we shall explain them separately.

In short, we should obey Islam's commandments and prohibitions with our heart and body, and our heart should be wide awake. If a person's heart is not wide awake, [that is, if a person does not meditate on the existence and greatness of Allâhu ta'âlâ, on the blessings in Paradise and the vehemence of Hell fire], it will be very difficult for his body to obey Islam's commandments. Scholars of Fiqh communicate fatwâs (explanations on how to do Islam's commandments). It devolves on men of Allah to facilitate the practice of these commandments. The body's obeying Islam willingly and easily requires the heart's being pure. However, if a person attaches importance only to purification of the heart and beautification of morals and ignores physical adaptation to Islam, he becomes a **Mulhid**. His extraordinary skills, [such as giving information about the unknown, curing his patients by breathing on them], which result from the shining of his nafs, are (called) **Istidrâj** and will drag him and those who follow him to Hell. What signifies a pure heart and a nafs which is mutmainna [docile] is the body's willingly obeying Islam. Some people who do not adapt their sense organs and bodies to Islam say, "My heart is pure. The important thing is the heart!" These are empty words. By saying so, they are deceiving themselves and people around them.]

ENDLESS BLISS
FOURTH FASCICLE

1 – THE FIVE DAILY PRAYERS (termed namâz)

Every Muslim has to know by heart the thirty-three binding duties which are called fard (farz). They are:

Essentials (fards) of îmân	: SIX
Pillars of Islam	: FIVE
Essentials of namâz (prayer)	: TWELVE
Essentials of ablution (wudû, abdast)	: FOUR
Essentials of ghusl (ritual bath)	: THREE
Essentials of tayammum	: THREE

There are also scholars who say that tayammum has two essentials. In that case, there are thirty-two of them. The fifty-four fards (commandments) are another matter and are written in my Turkish book **Islâm Ahlâkı**[1]. Performing Amr-i ma'rûf and Nahy–i munkar and not uttering any bad and ugly words (such as invectives) are not included in the thirty-three fards, but they are in the fifty-four fards.

It is fard for every Muslim who has reached the ages of puberty and discretion to perform the five daily prayers. When a prayer time comes, it becomes fard for him/her the moment he/she begins performing the prayer. If it has not been performed and if there is time left enough to make an ablution and begin the namâz before the prayer time is over, it becomes fard to perform it. If the prayer time is over before it has been performed without a good excuse[2] not to do so, he/she will have

---

[1] The seventh edition of its English version, **Ethics of Islam**, was accomplished in 1429 A.H. (2008).

[2] By 'a good excuse' we mean 'an excuse which Islam recognizes as an excuse that will absolve a Muslim from the responsibility of not performing an Islamic commandment. An excuse of this sort is termed 'udhr. The third chapter of the current book gives examples of such 'udhrs (excuses) pertaining to (the prayer termed) namâz.

committed a grave sin. Whether he/she has had a good excuse or not, qadâ will be necessary. The same applies to situations such as when a child reaches puberty, when a disbeliever or a renegade becomes a Muslim, when a woman becomes clean, (i.e. immediately after the cessation of the menses at the end of a menstrual or lochial period,) when an insane or unconscious person recovers, and when a sleeping person wakes up. It is fard for a new Muslim to learn the essentials of namâz first. After learning them, it becomes fard to perform namâz. Sleep is not a good excuse if it begins after the prayer time has begun. If a person does so, it is fard for him to make sure that he will wake up before the prayer time is over, while it would be mustahab for him to make sure to wake up before the end of the prayer time if he were to go to sleep before the beginning of the prayer time. These five daily prayers add up to forty rak'ats (units), out of which seventeen are fard, three are wâjib, and twenty are sunnat, as follows:

1 - Morning prayer **[Salât-ul-fajr]** consists of four rak'ats. First the sunnat prayer, which consists of two rak'ats, is performed. Then the fard prayer, of two rak'ats, is performed. The sunnat (the first two rak'ats) is very important. Some scholars classify it as wâjib.

2 - Early afternoon prayer **[Salât-uz-zuhr]** consists of ten rak'ats, the initial sunnat consisting of four rak'ats, the fard consisting of four rak'ats, and the final sunnat consisting of two rak'ats. The early afternoon prayer is performed in this order.

3 - Late afternoon prayer **[Salât-ul-'asr]** consists of eight rak'ats. First the sunnat, which consists of four rak'ats, and then the fard, which consists of four rak'ats, are performed.

4 - Evening prayer **[Salât-ul-maghrib]** contains five rak'ats. First the fard, which is composed of three rak'ats, then the sunnat, consisting of two rak'ats, are performed.

5 - Night prayer **[Salât-ul-'ishâ]** consists of thirteen rak'ats. The initial sunnat contains four rak'ats. The fard also contains four rak'ats. But the final sunnat has two rak'ats, while the Witr prayer has three rak'ats.

The initial sunnats of the late afternoon prayer and night prayer are **Ghayr-i muakkada**. When sitting during their second rak'at, after reciting the Attahiyyâtu.., the prayers of Allahumma salli alâ... and... bârik âlâ... are recited completely. After standing up for the third rak'at, the prayer Subhânaka... is recited before saying the Basmala. But the first sunnat of the early afternoon prayer is **Muakkad**. That is, it has been recommended emphatically. There are more thawâbs (blessings) for it. During its second rak'at, as in the fard prayers, only the Attahiyyâtu is said and then we stand up for the third rak'at. After standing up, we first recite the Basmala and then the sûra (chapter) of Fâtiha.

It is mustahab to perform four more rak'ats after the fard of early afternoon and night prayers and six more rak'ats after the fard of evening prayer. In other words, it is very blessed. One can perform all of them with one salâm or by saying the salâm after every two rak'ats. In either case the first two rak'ats are deemed to be the final sunnat. These prayers, which are mustahab, can be performed separately after the final sunnats of the two prayers of namâz as well.

The first rak'at commences with the beginning of the prayer and the other rak'ats begin as soon as you stand up, and each rak'at continues until you stand up again. The final rak'at continues until the salâm. No prayers can have less than two rak'ats. All prayers contain an even number of rak'ats, except the fard of the evening prayer and the witr prayer. After the second sajda (prostration) of each second rak'at we sit.

Each rak'at of prayer contains its fards, wâjibs, sunnats, mufsids (things or acts which spoil a prayer), and makrûhs (actions, words, thoughts avoided and disapproved by the Prophet). On the pages ahead, we shall explain these in accordance with the **Hanafî** Madhhab.

2 – THE FARDS OF NAMÂZ
(PERFORMING ABLUTION [WUDÛ, ABDAST])

Namâz has twelve fards, seven of which are preconditions, i.e., they are before beginning namâz; these conditions must exist in order for the namâz to be valid. They are called **essentials of namâz**. They are: **Tahârat** (purification) **from hadas** (state of being without abdast or ghusl), **tahârat from najâsat** (substances which Islam prescribes as unclean), **satr-i awrat** (covering parts of the body that are called awrat), **istiqbâl-i qibla** (facing the qibla), **waqt** (prescribed time), **niyyat** (intention), **takbîr of tahrîma** (beginning)[1]. All sorts of existence are contingent on some functional fulfilments so that they should exist. There are five positional types of this dependence: If an action to be fulfilled is

---

[1] Later in the text, all these new terms will be explained in detail.

within the essence of something to come into existence, i.e. if it is one of its particles, the action is called **Rukn**. If it affects the existence externally, it is called **'illat**. **Nikâh** (marriage contract prescribed by Islam.) is an 'illat of marriage. If doing something particular requires the existence of something else although there are no effectual relations between them, the existence required is called **Sabab**, the cause (reason). Waqt (appointed time for namâz) is the sabab, the cause (reason) of namâz. If doing something particular does not require the existence of something else, and yet if the latter ceases to exist in case the former should not be done, then the former is called **Shart** (condition). However, if the latter does not cease to exist in this case, it is called **Alâmat** (sign, property). **Adhân** (calling to prayer) is the alâmat of namâz. Five of the fards of the namâz are inside the namâz. Each of these five fards is also called **Rukn**. [Some Islamic scholars have said that takbîr of tahrîma[1] is inside the namâz. According to them, the rukns of namâz, as well as the sharts (conditions) of namâz, are six in number.] In the chapters ahead, we shall explain all these in accordance with the Hanafî Madhhab.

There are two kinds of tahârat from hadas:

1 - Performance of an ablution by a person who does not have an ablution.

2 - Performance of a ghusl by a person who does not have a ghusl.

Wudû' means ablution; **tawaddî** means to perform an ablution; **ghasl** means to wash something; **ightisâl** means to perform a ghusl ablution, and **ghusl** means the ablution of ghusl (in Arabic). A Muslim who does not have an ablution is called **muhdis**. A Muslim who does not have a ghusl ablution is called **junub**.

It is written in the book **Halabî-yi saghîr**: "There are fards, sunnats, adabs, and harâms in an abdast (ablution). If a person performs namâz without an ablution though he does not have a good excuse for doing so and though he knows that he does not have an ablution, he becomes a disbeliever. He who loses his ablution while performing namâz, performs the salâm (Assalâm-u alaikum wa rahmatullah) to one side right away and stops his namâz. Re-making an ablution before the prescribed time period is over, he begins the namâz again."

---

[1] The takbîr, i.e. the expression, "Allâhu akbar", which we say to begin performing namâz.

There are four fards of ablution in the Hanafî Madhhab: To wash the face once; –the face is the part between the ear-lobes (horizontally), and between the hairline and chin (vertically)– to wash both arms together with the elbows once; to apply masah on one-fourth of the head, that is, to rub a wet hand softly on it; to wash the feet, together with the ankle-bones on both sides, once each. [According to the Shafi'i and Malikî Madhhabs **niyyat** (intention) is fard. Niyyat means to intend (to make ablution) through the heart. It is not fard (obligatory) to say it orally. In the Mâlikî Madhhab it is obligatory to make niyyat when beginning to make ablution. A disbeliever's niyyat is not sahîh. The skin on the area bordering on the ear-lobes, and the hair on it as well are within the face, according to the Hanafî Madhhab; so it is fard to wash those areas. In the Mâlikî Madhhab they are (outside the facial region and belong to the rest) of the head. They should therefore be included in the masah, (since it is fard in the Mâlikî Madhhab to make masah of the entire head. In the Shâfi'î Madhhab, the niyyat should be made while washing the face. The ablution will not become sahîh if one intends before the water touches the face.] It is fard to wash the beard on the face and chin. Washing the hanging part of the beard is fard in the other three Madhhabs. The Shî'ites do not wash their feet, but only apply masah on their bare feet.

There are eighteen sunnats in an ablution:

1 - To recite the Basmala before entering the restroom and when beginning to make an ablution. He who cannot find a lonely place can relieve himself near others if he is taken short and provided he will cover himself.

2 - To wash the hands including the wrists three times.

3 - To rinse the mouth three times by using new water each time. This is called **madmada**.

4 - To wash both nostrils three times, taking fresh water each time. This is called **istinshâq**.

5 - It is sunnat, not fard, to wet the invisible parts of the skin under the eyebrows, the beard and the moustache. It is fard to wash their exterior surfaces. If the hairs are scarce and the skin can be seen, it will be fard to wet and wash the skin.

6 - To wet the section under the two eyebrows when washing the face.

7 - To apply masah on the hanging part of the beard. In the Hanafî Madhhab it is not fard to wash it. In Shâfi'î, it is fard to

wash the skin below the chin.

8 - To comb (takhlîl) the hanging part of the beard with the wetted fingers of the right hand.

9 - To rub and clean the teeth with something.

10 - To apply masah on the whole head once.

11 - To apply masah (to wipe) both ears once. It is fard to wash the parts between the ear and the cheek. (Please see the previous paragraph explaining the four fards of ablution.)

12 - To apply masah on the neck once with three adjacent fingers of both hands.

In order to perform the last three procedures together, both hands are moistened. The three thin adjacent fingers of both hands are joined together; their inner surfaces are placed on the beginning of the hair right above the forehead. The ends of these three fingers of both hands must be touching one another. Thumbs, pointing-fingers and palms must be in the air, not touching the head. The two hands are drawn backwards, thereby applying masah on the head with those three fingers of each hand. When the hands reach the end of the hair in the back, the three fingers of each hand are detached from the head and the palms of both hands are then slightly pressed against the hair of both sides of the head and drawn forward, applying masah on the sides of head. Then, putting the pointing-fingers of both hands in the ears and the inner surface of the thumbs on the back of the ears, we apply masah on the ears by drawing the thumbs downwards. Then the outer surface of each three thin fingers is put on the back of the neck and masah is applied on the neck by drawing them from the middle of the neck towards the sides. [This manner of masah is fard in the Mâlikî Madhhab.]

13 - To wash **(takhlîl)** between the fingers and the toes. For washing between toes, the little finger of the left hand is inserted between the toes from under them in succession, beginning with the little toe of the right foot and, after finishing with the right foot, carrying on with the big toe of the left foot.

14 - To wash three times, every limb to be washed. At each washing every part of the limb must be moistened. It is sunnat not only to pour water three times but to wash it completely three times. It is makrûh to wash more than three times. If you become confused counting, you may complement the counting to three. If in this case the washing is done more than three times it will not be makrûh.

15 - In the Hanafî Madhhab, to intend through the heart when beginning to wash the face. [It is written in Ibni 'Âbidin's book that it is sunnat, mustahab or bid'at to intend orally. And it is written in Berîqa and Hadîqa as well as in Ibni 'Âbidin's book that when something is said to be sunnat or bid'at, it is better not to do it. For this reason we must not intend orally. It is fard to intend for every worship ('ibâda) in the beginning, and it is also permissible to say 'in shâ-Allah.' It is not a necessity to intend for an oath, tilâwat [reading the Qur'ân al-kerîm], dhikr or adhân; and it is not necessary to make a separate intention (niyyat) for each of the stages of a certain act of worship, (when they are performed at one time,) such as abdast and ghusl.]

16 - Tartîb. In other words, to wash the two hands, the mouth, the nostrils, the face, the arms, then to apply masah on the head, on the ears, on the neck, and then to wash the feet successively, and not to change this order. Tartîb is fard in the Shâfi'î Madhhab.

17 - Dalk, to rub the limbs washed. Dalk and muwâlât are fard in the Mâlikî Madhhab.

18 - Muwalât, to wash the limbs one right after another quickly.

Adabs of an ablution: In this context adab means something which causes blessings when done but incurs no sin if omitted. But to do the sunnat is a great blessing and not to do it is tanzîhî makrûh. Adabs are called mandûb or mustahab, too. The adabs of an ablution written in the book Halabî-yi saghîr are as follows:

1 - To make an ablution before it is time for namâz. Those who have excuses[1] must make it after the time (of the prayer to be performed) has begun.

2 - When cleaning yourself in the toilet, the qibla must be on your right or left-hand side. It is tahrîmi makrûh to turn your front or back to the qibla when relieving yourself or urinating. It is an adab to squat yourself down with the feet wide apart.

3 - If the private parts have not been smeared with najâsat, it is an adab to wash them with water. If the najâsat is less than one dirham [which is equal to one mithqâl: four grams and eighty centigrams], it is sunnat to wash it off. If one has been smeared with one dirham of it, it is wâjib, and if more than that it is fard to wash. There is not a prescribed number of washing. It is

---

[1] These special excuses, called 'udhr, are prescribed by Islam.

necessary to wash until you become clean. You do the cleaning with the inner surfaces of one or two or three fingers of your left hand.

4 - To wipe yourself dry with a piece of cloth after washing. If there is no cloth available you must do the wiping with your hand.

5 - To cover yourself immediately after the cleaning is completed. It spoils the adab to uncover unnecessarily at isolated places.

6 - Not to ask for help from anybody, but to perform the ablution by yourself. If someone pours water for you without being asked, it will be permissible.

7 - To turn towards the qibla when making an ablution.

8 - Not to talk while making an ablution.

9 - To recite the kalima-i shahâdat while washing each limb.

10 - To recite the prescribed prayers (du'â) of ablution.

11 - To put water in the mouth with the right hand.

12 - To put water in the nose with the right and to clean the nose with the left hand.

13 - When washing the mouth, to brush the teeth with a **miswâk**. While the fingers of the right hand are stretched, the thumb and the little finger hold the miswâk on the lower side and the other three fingers hold it on the upper side, then the miswâk is rubbed gently on the teeth, three times on the teeth on the right side and three times on the ones on the left side. It should not be rubbed hard lest it will damage the teeth. When rubbed softly it strengthens the teeth and the gums. Miswâk is a span-long piece of stick cut from a branch of a tree of Erâk (Peelo), which grows in Arabia. In case an erâk branch is not available, branches of olive trees or others can replace it. But not a pomegranate branch because it is bitter. Your food and drink should not have a bitter taste. In case a miswâk is not available, a brush can be used. If a brush is not available, either, you must clean your teeth with your thumb and second little finger; for doing this, the former is rubbed on the teeth on the right hand side and the latter is rubbed on the ones on the left hand side, three times each. It is not shar'an (canonically) makrûh to use someone else's miswâk or comb with his permission, but it is tab'an[1] makrûh. Also, smoking is tab'an makrûh.

---

[1] That which is repugnant to the human nature.

14 - When washing the mouth, to rinse it if not fasting. A light gargling in the throat is sunnat during abdast as well as during ghusl. Yet it is makrûh to gargle when you are fasting.

15 - When washing the nostrils, to draw the water almost up to the bone.

16 - When applying masah on the ears, to insert each little finger into each earhole, respectively.

17 - To use the little finger of the left hand when washing between the toes by inserting (takhlîl) from the lower sides of them.

18 - To shift the ring when washing the hands. It is necessary and fard to shift a tight ring.

19 - Not to waste the water though it may be plentiful.

20 - Not to use too little water as if you were applying an ointment. During each of the three washings, at least two drops of water must fall from the part washed.

21 - After using a container for ablution, to leave the container full of water. You should put the ewer in its place with its mouth pointing towards the qibla. Any other traveller who wants to perform namâz can easily determine the direction of the qibla by way of the ewer's mouth.

22 - To recite the prayer (du'â) "Allahummaj'alni minattawwâbîn..." after or during the ablution.

23 - To perform two rak'ats of namâz called **Subhâ** after an ablution.

24 - To make an ablution even though you have an ablution. In other words, after performing one namâz, to renew your ablution for the next namâz though you may have an ablution.

25 - To clean the inner corners of the eyes and clear away the dried mucus in the eyelids when washing the face.

26 - When washing the face, the arms and the feet, to wash a little more than the compulsory amount. When washing the arms, we must fill our palm with water and then pour it towards our elbow.

27 - When performing an ablution, not to let the water used splash back on your body, your clothes, etc.

28 - **Ibni Âbidîn**, while listing the things that nullify an ablution, writes that if something that is not makrûh in your Madhhab is fard in another Madhhab, it is mustahab to do it.

Imâm-i Rabbânî wrote in his 286th letter that since rubbing the limbs (dalk) is a fard of ablution in Mâlikî, one should certainly rub them. While explaining the rij'î talâq **Ibni Âbidîn** wrote that it is better for a Hanafî Muslim to imitate the Mâlikî Madhhab because Imâm-i Mâlik was in the position of a disciple to Imâm-i A'zam[1].

There are twelve prohibitions in performing an ablution. Doing them is either harâm or makrûh; they are as follows:

1 - When relieving oneself or urinating in the toilet or outdoors, one should not turn one's front or back towards the qibla.

It is makrûh also to stretch one's feet towards the qibla or the Qur'ân. If the Qur'ân is above your level, it will not be makrûh. One can enter the toilet with the Qur'ân or an amulet that is wrapped up with a separate cover.

2 - It is harâm to open one's private parts in company in order to make tahârat.

3 - One should not make tahârat with one's right hand.

4 - When there is no water, it is makrûh to make tahârat (to clean oneself) with food products, manure, bones, animals' food, coal, someone else's property, a piece of flowerpot or tile, reeds, leaves, a piece of cloth or paper.

5 - One must not spit or throw mucus into the pool where one makes an ablution.

6 - One should not wash more or less than the prescribed limit of one's limbs of ablution, nor wash them more or fewer than three times.

7 - One must not wipe one's limbs of ablution with the same cloth used for tahârat.

8 - While washing the face, one must not splash the water on one's face, but pour it from the upper forehead downwards.

9 - One must not blow on or over the surface of the water.

10 - One must not close one's mouth and eyes tightly. If even a tiny part of the outward part of the lips or the eyelids is left dry, the ablution will not be acceptable.

11 - One must not expell mucus from one's nose with one's right hand.

12 - One must not make masah on one's head, ears or neck

---

[1] It should go without saying that this suggestion must be saved for such cases as you need to imitate a Madhhab other than your own.

more than once after moistening the hands each time. But it can be repeated without moistening the hands again.

An important note: Unless there is a strong necessity (darûrat), the following eleven rules must be obeyed:

1 - A person with both hands paralysed (or no hands at all) cannot make tahârat. Instead he makes tayammum by rubbing his arms on some soil and his face against a wall. If there is a wound on his face, he performs namâz without an ablution in order not to miss namâz.

2 - If a person is sick, his wife, jâriya, children, sisters, or brothers may help him perform his ablution.

3 - Making tahârat with stones and the like is the same as making it with water.

4 - If a person who went mad or fainted did not recover within twenty-four hours, he would not have to perform (qadâ) his missed prayers of namâz when he recovered. He who loses consciousness by taking alcohol, opium or medicine must perform each omitted prayer. A person who is so heavily ill that he cannot even perform namâz by moving his head while lying down, even if he is conscious, is exempted from performing namâz. However, this state must have continued for more than twenty-four hours.

5 - It is mustahab (a source of blessings) to use special baggy trousers and to cover the head when entering the toilet.

6 - When entering the toilet one must not hold something in one's hand containing Allah's name or pieces of writing from the Qur'ân. It must be wrapped up with something or it must be in one's pocket. The case is the same with an amulet.

7 - One must enter the toilet with one's left foot and go out with one's right foot.

8 - In the toilet one must open one's private parts after squatting and one must not talk.

9 - One must not look at one's private parts or at the waste material or spit in the toilet.

10 - In the toilet, one must not eat or drink anything, sing, whistle, [smoke] or chew gum.

11 - One must not urinate into any water, on a wall of a mosque, in a cemetery, or onto any road.

THINGS THAT NULLIFY AN ABLUTION: It is written in the book **Halabî**: "In the Hanafî Madhhab, seven things nullify an ablution: Firstly, eveything excreted from the front and rear organs, for example breaking wind, breaks an ablution. Only the wind coming out of a man's or woman's front does not break an ablution. This happens with very few people. The worms coming out of the mouth, ears or a wound on the skin do not break an ablution. When the point of an enema or a man's finger is inserted into one's back and taken out, if it is moist it breaks an ablution. If it is dry, it would still be better to renew the ablution. The case is so with everything that is partly inserted into the anus. If something is inserted and taken out wholely, it breaks both an ablution and a fast. If a person's hemorrhoids come out and he drives them back in with his hand or with something like a cloth, his ablution will be broken.

When a man puts some oil in his urethra and it flows out, it does not break his ablution according to Imâm-i a'zam. When a woman applies vaginal lavage, the liquid that flows out breaks her ablution.

It is permissible for a man to insert into his urethra a small natural cotton wick lest he will release urine inadvertently. In case there is suspicion of leakage, it is mustahab for a man to do this. But if he sees that it prevents leakage, it will be wâjib for him to use it. Synthetic cotton is not advisable. Unless part of the cotton remaining outside is moistened, his ablution will not be broken. And if the cotton is dry when it is taken out, the ablution will not be broken, either. So is the case with the piece of cloth called kursuf which women insert in their front. But if a woman puts it on the crevice instead of inserting it, it breaks her ablution when its inner surface is moistened. If the cotton is put in wholely it breaks the ablution if it is wet when it is taken out. A piece of natural cotton that has been inserted into the back and which is lost breaks an ablution even if it is dry when it comes out. It is mustahab for virgins to use kursuf only during menstruation and for those who are married or widows to always use it. If a person finds feces or urine stains on his underwear after istinjâ (cleaning oneself after urination or defecation) he must put a long piece of cotton between the buttocks and thus cover the anus, and, before performing an ablution, he must look at the cotton and put it back in its place if it is clean or change it if it is dirty.

He who suffers from enuresis (involuntary urination) should be extra careful lest his underwear will become dirty. For this, you need a square piece of cloth fifteen centimetres in length. Tying a piece of string about fifty centimetres in length to one of the corners of the cloth, you tie the other end of the string to a safety-pin attached to the pants. Next the cloth is wrapped around the end of the penis and secured with the string wound on it and fastened with a knot. If the leakage of urine is too much, it must be reinforced with a piece of cotton, which should be thrown away whenever it is found wet with urine. If the cloth is wet, too, it must be removed, washed and dried so as to be used again. Thus a piece of cloth can be used for months. As the penis tapers off with old age, it becomes impossible to wrap a piece of cloth round its end. A way to resolve this difficulty would be to get a small waterproof pouch, with a piece of cloth in it, place the penis and the scrotum in the pouch and tie it up with a piece of string. In need of urination, the string is untied and the contents are taken out. If the cloth is wet it must be disposed of. People who practise this hygienic cleanliness will never suffer prostatic ailments.

The second group of things breaking an ablution consists of unclean things coming out of the mouth. Of these; vomit and thick blood, blood, food and water coming out of the stomach break an ablution when they amount to a mouthful. They all are **qaba najs** (grossly impure). Matter vomitted by a suckling child is qaba najs. Vomitting phlegm will not break an ablution. Vomiting thin blood coming down from the head does not break an ablution if it is less than the spittle. Inside the mouth, in terms of an ablution, is deemed an inner limb, but it is considered an external limb when one is in a state of fasting. That is the reason why the blood issuing from a tooth or a wound inside the mouth does not break an ablution as long as it stays in the mouth. But after coming out of the mouth, if the blood is more than the spittle it breaks an ablution. Thick blood coming down from the head does not break an ablution even if it is more than the spittle. If the blood issuing from the stomach or from the lungs is thin it breaks an ablution even if it is less than the spittle, according to Shaikhayn (imâm-i a'zam Abû Hanîfa and imâm-i Abû Yûsuf 'rahmatullâhi 'alaihimâ'. If any oil dropped into the ear goes out through the ear or the nose, it does not break an ablution. But if it goes out through the mouth it breaks an ablution. If something sniffed into the nose comes back, even if several days later, it does not break an ablution.

Third; blood, pus, or yellow liquid issuing through the skin, and colourless liquid issuing painfully break an ablution in Hanafî. The fact that these do not break one's ablution in Shafi'î and Mâlikî is written in the Persian book **Menâhij-ul-ibâd**. If the blood or the yellow liquid issuing from a person with small-pox or from an abscess, ear, nose, wound, or colourless liquid that issues with pain or because of an ailment, spreads over the places that must be washed in a ghusl ablution, it breaks one's ablution. For instance, if blood coming down the nose descends beyond the bones it breaks an ablution. And if blood coming through the ears comes out of the ears it breaks an ablution. If one sponges the blood or the yellowish liquid on one's wound or boil (abscess) with cotton it breaks one's ablution. Colourless liquid issuing and flowing from them without pain or ailment does not break an ablution [according to **Tahtâwî**][1]. If one sees blood on something one has just bitten into, one's ablution will not be broken. If one sees blood on the miswâk or on the tooth pick, this will not break one's ablution if the inside of the mouth has not been smeared with blood. On the other hand, it will break one's ablution if one puts one's finger on the suspected part in one's mouth and then sees blood on one's finger. If a person who suffers from sore eyes sheds tears all the time he is one who has an excuse. (The meaning of the phrase having an excuse will be explained later on). However, except when one has a sore, weeping for some other reason, such as because of onions, smoke and other kinds of gases, does not break an ablution. In the Shâfi'î Madhhab an ablution is not broken in either case. A woman's suckling her child does not break her ablution. Sweating, no matter how much, does not break an ablution. Liquid coming out of the ears, navel or nipples because of some pain breaks an ablution. A leech sucking much blood breaks an ablution. Harmful insects such as flies, mosquitos, fleas and lice do not break an ablution even if they suck a great deal. A little blood on the skin that does not spread, blood which is formed in the mouth and which is not a mouthful, and a little vomit that is thrown up do not break an ablution; therefore they are not najs.

The fourth cause that breaks an ablution is to sleep, in all four Madhhabs. In Hanafî, sleeping in a position that will leave the anus loose, such as by lying on one's flank or back or by leaning on one's elbow or on something else, will break an ablution. If one does not fall down when the thing on which one leans is taken away suddenly, one's ablution is not broken. Sleeping in namâz

---

[1] Ahmad bin Muhammad bin Ismâ'îl Tahtâwî 'rahmatullâhi 'alaih' (d. 1231 [A.D. 1815] was the Muftî of Cairo representing the Hanafî Madhhab.

does not break an ablution. Sleeping by drawing up the legs and putting the head on the knees, or by sitting cross-legged or on the knees, does not break an ablution. Sleeping by sitting with the feet on one side does not break an ablution. [This kind of sitting posture, which women do as they perform namâz, is called **tawarruk**.] If a person sleeps by erecting one of his shanks and sitting on the other thigh, his ablution will break. Sleeping on a bare animal does not break an ablution, provided the animal is going uphill or on a level road. Sleeping on a saddle and panel does not break an ablution in any case.

Fifth; fainting, going crazy, or having an epileptic fit breaks an ablution. Being as drunk as to waver when walking breaks an ablution.

Sixth; laughter during namâz with rukû's and sajdas breaks both the namâz and the ablution. But it does not break a child's ablution. When a Muslim performing namâz smiles, their namâz or ablution will not be annulled. When heard by others present, it is called a laughter. When one does not hear one's own laughing it is called smiling. If no one but the person who laughs hears it, it is called **dahk**, which breaks the namâz only.

The seventh cause is **Mubâsharat-i fâhisha**; that is, when a man and woman physically rub their private parts (saw'atayn) on each other. In this case, the ablution of both the man and woman is broken. In Hanafî, touching a woman's skin, lustfully as it may be, does not break a man's ablution.

Cutting one's hair, beard, moustache or nails does not break one's ablution. It is not necessary to wash the limbs whereon the cutting took place. It is written in the Persian explanation of **Fiqh-i-Ghidânî:** "Cutting the nails does not break an ablution. It is mustahab to wash the hands after the cutting." A scab that falls off a wound or sore does not break it, either.

Any slashes on the skin must be washed when making an ablution. If one cannot put water on it, one makes masah. If masah is not possible, either, one may omit it. If one has put some ointment on a slash on one's foot, one washes over the ointment. If washing will harm the slash, one makes masah over it. If the ointment drains off after washing, one washes under it if the slash has healed. If it has not healed one does not wash it. [See chapter 5]. If one has wounds on both hands, and if washing will be harmful, one makes tayammum. If one hand is healthy, one uses it for ablution. If one's hand has been cut off from the elbow or if one's foot is cut off by the heel, one washes the place of the cut.

Halabî-yi kebîr writes; "If a person knows that he has performed ablution and doubts if it has been broken later, it is judged that he has an ablution. If he knows that his ablution has been broken and doubts whether he has performed an ablution again, he has to perform an ablution. If he doubts whether he has washed a certain limb while performing an ablution, he washes the limb. If he has the doubt after finishing the ablution it is not necessary to wash the doubtful limb. If a person who notices some wetness on himself after performing an ablution doubts whether it is urine or water, he performs ablution again if this happens to him for the first time. If it often happens to him, it will be understood that it is a doubt caused by the satan; therefore, he will not renew the ablution. In order to eliminate such doubts, he must sprinkle water into his pants or underwear [**Kimyâ-yi sa'âdat**], or use a cellulosic cotton wick. If a person doubts whether his pots, pans, garments, body, water, well, pond, or whether butter, bread, clothes, food and others prepared by the ignorant or by disbelievers are dirty, they are to be judged clean."

It is harâm for a person without an ablution to hold the Qur'ân al-kerîm. It is permissible to recite it without an ablution. It is sunnat to go to bed with an ablution. It is written in the explanation of **Shir'at-ul-islâm:** "It is permissible and blessed to recite the Qur'ân al-kerîm without an ablution while lying in bed. But, one must hold one's head out of the blanket and put one's legs together."

In case of (one of) exudations called wedî and medhî, ablution is broken according to all four Madhhabs. In fact, ghusl is necessary in the Hanbalî Madhhab [**Inâya**]. It is harâm to enter a mosque when you are junub or during menstruation, and it is makrûh without an ablution [**Durar Gurar**]. If frontal or anal emissions which normally break an ablution take place because of an illness and there is haraj [difficulty] in making an ablution for such reasons as extremely cold weather, illness or old age, one's ablution will not be broken according to the Mâlikî Madhhab.

It is stated in **Kitâb-ur-rahma**: "Continuous involuntary urination is termed 'silis-ul-bawl (enuresis).' One cup of chick-peas and two cups of vinegar are put in a container. Three days later, three chick-peas and one teaspoonful of vinegar are taken three times daily. Or, one spoonful of seeds of rue and ginger and cinnamon and blackpepper are pulverized and mixed. One teaspoonful of the mixture is taken with water, once early in the morning, without having eaten anything, and once before going to bed at night. The medical book entitled **Menâfi'-un-nâs** (and written in Turkish in the hegiral year 986 [A.D. 1578] by Dervish Nidâî) contains various medical formulas devised and recommended for the treatment of incontinence of urine. One of them is this: Two dirhams of frankincense is mixed with two dirhams of black cumin and four dirhams of honey and the mixture is consumed piecemeal, one piece as big as a walnut in the morning and another in the evening. Frankincense is an aromatic gum resin from trees (called Boswellia). It is like chewing gum. It is known by its smell.

3 – MASAH (wiping) ON MESTS; HAVING AN 'UDHR (EXCUSE)

MASAH OVER MESTS - While performing an ablution, it is permissible both for a man and for a woman to make masah over their mests once with wet hands instead of washing the feet, even if there is no excuse or obligation for doing so. Our Prophet 'sall-Allâhu 'alaihi wa sallam' put mests on his blessed feet, made masah on them and said that it was permissible. Masah on mests is not applicable in tayammum. When making tayammum it is not farz to make masah on the feet.

A mest is a waterproof shoe covering that part of the foot which is fard to wash (in ablution). When the mests are so big that the toes do not reach the ends of the mests and masah is made on the vacant sections, masah will not be acceptable. If the mouths of the mests are so wide that the feet can be seen when looking down from above, this will not mar the soundness of the masah performed. The mests must be strong and fit well enough so that the feet would not go out of them if you took an hour's walk. Mests cannot be made of wood, glass or metal. For one cannot walk for an hour in something hard. Masah is permissible on any socks whose soles and parts on the toes or only soles are covered with leather or which are so tough that they will not fall down when walked in. [In the Mâlikî Madhhab, the mests have to be of leather.] When a person wearing mests loses his ablution, whatever the means, the state of being without an ablution spreads throughout the limbs of ablution and the mests, but not the feet. To retain the state of ablution upon the mest, we simply make masah on them. This indicates that the mests prevent the state of hadas (being without an ablution) from reaching the feet. Therefore, if a person washes his feet only, puts on his mests, and then completes his ablution, and loses his ablution afterwards, he can make masah on his mests when he performs his ablution later.

For it is not necessary to have completed the ablution when putting on mests[1]. However, an ablution that was somehow nullified must have been re-performed fully. For example, if he has put on his mests after making a tayammum, his ablution which will become null and void when he finds water was not an ablution performed fully; therefore, he cannot make masah when he re-performs the ablution with water. In this case, he washes his feet, too. If a person with an excuse performs a full ablution and puts on his mests before the excuse (e.g. blood) issues, he can make masah for twenty-four hours even if his ablution is broken by the excuse. But if he puts them on after the excuse has issued, he can make masah only within the time of that namâz.

The duration of time one can continuously make masah on mests is twenty-four hours for a settled person and three days plus three nights, i.e. seventy-two hours, for someone on a long-distance journey (termed safar). This duration begins not when one puts on the mests, but when one's ablution is broken after putting on the mests. It is written in **Fatâwâ-i Khayriyya** that the duration of time for masah for a person with an excuse is until the end of each prayer time. If a person with an excuse performs an ablution when the cause of his excuse is over and puts on his mests before the cause begins again, he will have put them on with tahârat-i kâmila (precise purification), and he can make masah for twenty-four hours. [In the Mâlikî Madhhab, masah is permissible until one has to take off the mests for ghusl.]

In the Hanafî Madhhab, masah is done on the upper faces of the mests, not under the soles. To perform the masah in accordance with the sunnat, the entire five moistened fingers of the right hand are put in their full length on the right mest and fingers of the left hand on the left mest, then they are drawn up

---

[1] In other words, the condition to be observed before putting on the mests is to make sure that you have washed your feet; once you have washed your feet and put on your mests, you may then complete your ablution and from then on utilize the benefit of making masah on your mests till the end of the prescribed period of time, (unless something to break an ablution happened between the time you put on your mests and the time you completed your ablution.). This convenience cannot be utilized by Muslims in the Shâfi'î Madhhab or those who imitate the Shâfi'î Madhhab, since it is fard in the Shâfi'î Madhhab to wash the limbs in the prescribed order, or by Muslims in the Mâlikî Madhhab or who imitate the Mâlikî Madhhab, since it is fard in the Mâlikî Madhhab to wash the limbs of ablution in an unbroken succession.

towards the legs beginning from the ends (of the mests) right on the toes. The palms of the hands must not touch the mests. It is fard that masah cover an area as wide and as long as three fingers of the hand. To do this, it will be enough to put three fingers or the ends of the fingers which are so wet as water should be dropping from them or the palm of the hand together with the fingers, or only the palm on the toe end of the mest and to draw them towards the leg. It is also permissible to put the fingers on the outer side of the mest and to rub them gently across its width. Though masah with the back of the hands is permissible as well, it is sunnat to make masah with the inner parts of the hands. It is not permissible to make masah under the mests, on the sides of the heels or on the parts towards the legs. [In the Mâlikî Madhhab, the right hand is moistened and the lowest parts of the fingers are placed on the upper end of the right mest. Then, the tip of the thumb being on the left side and the tips of the other fingers being on the right, the hand is drawn up towards the mouth (of the mest). Then the moistened (left) hand is put likewise under the mest and drawn via the back of the heel towards the mouth. Next, the same procedure is followed with the left mest, yet this time the right hand will be used for the sole of the mest and the left hand for the upper part. This practice is mustahab (causes blessings)]. After washing a limb, you can make masah on the mests with the wetness remaining on your hands. But you cannot make masah with the wetness remaining from the masah of a limb, e.g. the head or the neck. If a person who has performed an ablution puts on his mests and does not make masah but instead puts his feet with the mests on into water when he performs ablution again, this will replace the masah, if one of their feet or more than half of it has not been moistened. If water penetrates and moistens the feet, they will have to take off their mests and wash their feet, too. If the outer surface of the mests are moistened by walking on damp grass or by rain, this replaces the masah, for which intention is unnecessary. If a person wearing mests sets out for a journey within twenty-four hours after the breaking of his ablution, he can make masah on his mests for three days plus three nights. If this person were making a long-distance journey (when his ablution was broken) and became settled twenty-four hours or longer later (after the breaking of his ablution), he would (have to) take off his mests and wash his feet when he needed to perform an ablution. In the Mâlikî Madhhab there is no time limit for masah on mests. If a person puts on another pair of mests, wellingtons, gloshes, plastic or nylon shoes on his mests before his ablution is broken, he can make masah on the outer footwear if they are waterproof. Even if they allow considerable water through, he can make masah on them, too. For, in this case the inner pair will get moistened and he will have thereby made masah on the inner pair. If he has put on the outer pair after his ablution has been broken, he can make masah on the inner pair only. If one of the outer shoes goes off his foot after he has made masah on them, he must immediately take off the other one, and make masah on the inner mests. It is permissible as well not to take off the other one and to make masah on it also. It is not permissible to make masah on any mest which has a rip large enough to let three toes through. It is permissible if the rip is smaller than this. [In the Mâlikî Madhhab, if the rip is smaller than one-third of the foot, masah is permissible. In Mâlikî, again, whereas it is sunnat for the body and the clothes to be clean, it is fard for the mests to be clean.] If small rips at several places on a mest amount to three toes if they were put together, it is not permissible to make masah on it. If one mest has a rip through which two toes can be seen and the other has a rip which would allow two toes or one to be seen, one can make masah on them. For (the limit of) three toes covers one mest, not two. However, the amounts of najâsat or the awrat parts[1] that are seen on a person's various limbs are combined and his case is judged accordingly. The size of the rip that makes masah unacceptable is large enough to let the whole of the three toes, not only the three tiptoes, to be seen. If the rip happens to be on the toes, the toes (that are seen) will be counted. But if it is at some other part, it must not be large enough to allow three small toes to be seen. If the rip is longer than three toes, but if its opening is smaller than three toes, masah is permissible. If a mest is torn by the seam, and yet if it does not open and the toes cannot be seen, masah is permissible. If the rent or rip opens and three toes can be seen as one walks, although it may not open when one stands still, masah cannot be made. If vice versa, masah is permissible. Any rent above the heel bones does not prevent masah no matter how large it is. For, it is not necessary for the mests to cover these parts. It is permissible to make masah on any mests or shoes that are buttoned, fastened, zipped on the tops or sides. [The mest

---

[1] Parts of a person's body that a person has to keep covered are called awrat parts. This subject, which is rather detailed, will be dealt with later in the text.

should not have any rips or holes according to the Shâfi'î Madhhab.]

When the heel of a foot goes out of the mest, it must be judged that the mest has gone off the foot. Yet the majority of books state that unless more than half of the foot has left that part of the mest which is level with the heel bone, the mest will not be judged to have gone off the foot. Accordingly, the masah of a person is permissible whose mests are over-sized and whose heels move in and out of the mests as he walks. His ablution is not broken when walking.

If a mest has a rip wider than three toes, and yet if its lining is strong and sewn on the mest so that the foot is not seen, masah on it is permissible.

When one or both of a person's feet go out of the mests, his ablution is not broken for that moment. The breaking of his ablution has now spread on the feet. If he, therefore, washes only his feet, he will have completed the ablution during which he made masah. Also, when the duration of masah is over he washes his feet only. However, it has been declared (by Islamic scholars) that it would be better to perform a new ablution in either case. For, muwâlât, (i.e. washing the limbs one immediately after another,) is sunnat in the Hanafî Madhhab and fard in the Mâlikî Madhhab.

It is not permissible to make masah on a turban or skullcap, on a headgear, on a veil or mask, or on gloves.

It is permissible to make masah on splints, that is, on strips of wood bound to a broken bone on both sides. The ointment, the cotton, the wick, the gauze, the plaster, the bandage or the like, which is put on or in a wound, boil, or cut or crack on the skin, if it will be harmful to untie it or to take it off, or if after taking it off washing or masah will harm the wound, we pour water on it if it is waterproof, e.g. covered with an ointment or rubber. If it lets water through we make masah on it. If cold water will do harm to a wound, warm water must be used. If warm water will be harmful it is necessary to make masah on it. If masah will be harmful, too, we make masah on what is on it. We can make masah on that part of the bandage coinciding with the healthy part of the skin as well as on the skin under the bandage. It is acceptable to make masah on more than half of it. If even this masah will do harm to the wound, we do not make masah. If it will not be harmful to make masah on it, it is necessary to make masah. If it will not be harmful to take it off and wash the healthy part of the skin under it, it is necessary to do so. [As is written in the book **Al-fiqh-u 'alal-madhâhib-il-arba'a,** the four Madhhabs are unanimous in the fact that the permissibility of making masah on a bandage or ointment applied on a wound is dependent on the condition that washing the wound or making masah on it would aggravate the wound. Aggravation means a delay in recovery or an exacerbation of pain.] If, after the masah, it is taken off or falls off before the wound heals, the masah does not become null and void. If it falls off after the wound heals, it becomes necessary to wash under it. Masah on any of all these things (which are mentioned above) replaces washing under it. He who makes masah on one of them is not a person with an excuse. He can be an imâm for others. Any part which a specialist Muslim doctor has said must not be washed is like a wound. In making masah on it a man, a woman, a muhdis and a junub are all in the same category. Intention is not necessary for any of them. Ibni Âbidîn 'rahmatullâhu 'alaih', after explaining the fards in an ablution, writes: "If a person who has a wound or cut on his hand cannot use water, that is, if he cannot wash his hands with water or put his face, head, ears or feet in the water he makes tayammum. A person one part of whose arm or foot has been cut away washes the surface of the remaining part." If a prisoner who is fastened by the hands and feet cannot perform tayammum, without an ablution he makes the rukû' and sajda without reciting the sûras. If he cannot do this, either, he performs the namâz standing by making signs. When he becomes free he performs it again.

A person **WITH AN 'UDHR (EXCUSE)** performs an ablution whenever he likes. With this ablution he performs as many fard and supererogatory prayers of namâz as he likes and reads the Qur'ân as much as he likes. When the prescribed time of namâz is over, his ablution is broken automatically. Performing a new ablution after each prayer time arrives, he does any kind of worship until the time is over. He cannot perform a prayer of namâz with the ablution he made before the time of the prayer has arrived. With the exception of early afternoon prayer, he cannot perform any of the other four prayers with an ablution he has made before the beginning of that prayer time. For, the beginning of early afternoon prayer is not at the same time the end of another prayer time. The continuous excuse of a person does not break his ablution within a prayer time. However, it will be broken by another cause. When the prayer time is over it will be broken by the excuse, too.

Having an excuse requires that something is breaking the ablution continuously. A person who, within the duration of any prayer of namâz which is fard to perform, would fail to keep his ablution even as long as to perform only the fard namâz if he made an ablution at any time from the beginning till the end of the time of the namâz, becomes an excused person at the moment he notices his excuse. For example, if one of the causes breaking an ablution exists continuously, such as the blood of istihâda (see the following chapter), urine and other issues, diarrhoea, incontinent wind-breaking, the issuing of blood and pus from a wound, the oozing of blood or any liquid from the nipples, navel, nose, eyes, or ears because of some pain, that is, if from the beginning till the end of any prescribed prayer time one could not stop it as long as to make an ablution and perform only the fard part of a prayer, one becomes a person with an excuse. If the excuse begins long enough to perform the fard prayer after the arrival of the prayer time, one waits until it is nearly the end of the prayer time and, if it has not stopped, makes an ablution at the end of the time and performs the namâz of the time. After the time of the namâz is over, if it stops within the time of the next prayer of namâz, one performs one's former namâz again. If it never stops from the beginning until the end of the time of the next prayer time of namâz, this means that one has become a person with an excuse and will not have to perform one's former namâz again.

[It is stated in (the book) **Al-fiqh-u'alal madhâhib-il-arba'a**: "According to a second report in the Mâlikî Madhhab, for having an 'udhr (excuse), it will be enough for the involuntary emission that is a result of some illness and which breaks an ablution to occur only once. It does not need to continue throughout the duration of time allotted for a prayer of namâz. Those invalid or old people who suffer involuntary urination or windbreaking before or during namâz, in case of haraj and difficulty, are permitted to imitate the Mâlikî Madh-hab lest they should lose their ablution, which would consequently cost them their namâz; in this case, it will be sahîh for them to be imâm (and conduct the namâz in jamâ'at)."]

If the excuse of a person who has an excuse oozes once and only for a little while during the time of each following prayer of namâz, his excuse will be considered to be going on. If it never oozes within the time of any namâz, that is, if any time of namâz elapses without an excuse from the beginning to the end, the person will no longer be in the state of having an excuse. If his excuse stops while making an ablution or while performing namâz and does not begin again until the end of the time of the second next prayer of namâz, he re-performs the ablution and the namâz which he performed when he had the excuse. Yet if it stopped after the namâz had been completed, or after having sat as long as the tashahhud (in the last rak'at), he would not perform the namâz again. As well, a person who sees water after having performed the namâz with a tayammum (he made instead of making an ablution for some reason the Sharî'at approves of), does not perform his namâz again. It is wâjib to stop the excuse by means of medication, by binding it or by sitting and performing the namâz with signs. If it is expected that one dirham of blood or the like, when washed, will not spread again until the namâz is performed, it is wâjib to wash it. [An excuse includes only the things that break an ablution. A person who cannot perform an ablution or ghusl is not a person with an excuse. Depending on the situation, he makes masah or performs tayammum and performs his namâz like a healthy person].

In the explanation of namâz in jamâ'at, (which will be explained in detail in Chapter 20), it is stated that a person with an excuse cannot be an imâm for healthy people. In this context, in addition to being without an ablution continuously, having more than one dirham of najâsat on you and being naked and being unable to read the Qur'ân al-kerîm correctly are counted as excuses. Therefore, a person with one of these excuses cannot be an imâm for those who do not have these excuses. Also, it is explained in the section on ghusl ablution, (which will be dealt with in the next chapter,) that a person with a filled or crowned tooth should imitate (follow) the Shâfi'î or Mâlikî Madhhab in order to conduct a namâz in jamâ'at as the imâm for the Hanafîs who are without filled or crowned teeth. [Please see chapter 20.]

A person who is ill and has an excuse can make up his debt of prayers which he did not perform when he did not have an excuse. Alms or any other kind of charity can by no means replace an omitted prayer of namâz. Heresies written by Ibni Taymiyya should not be taken for granted.

4 – GHUSL ABLUTION

An acceptable namâz requires a correct ablution and a correct ghusl. Ibni 'Âbidîn wrote in his explanation of **Durr-ul-mukhtâr**: "It is fard for every woman or man who is junub and for every woman after **haid** (menstruation) and nifâs (puerperium) to perform a ghusl ablution when there is enough time to perform the time's namâz before that prayer's time expires."

There are uncountable blessings for those who do the fard. And those who do not perform the fard are gravely sinful. Rasûlullah 'sall-Allâhu 'alaihi wa sallam' states in a hadîth-i sherîf written in the book **Ghunyat-ut-tâlibîn: "A person who gets up in order to perform a ghusl ablution will be given as many blessings as the hairs on his body** [which means very many], **and that many of his sins will be forgiven. He will be promoted to a higher rank in Paradise. The blessings which he will be given on account of his ghusl are more useful than anything in the world. Allâhu ta'âlâ will declare to angels: 'Look at this slave of Mine! Without showing any reluctance, he thinks of My command and gets up at night and performs a ghusl from janâbat. Bear witness that I have forgiven the sins of this slave of Mine.' "**

A hadîth-i sherîf written on the ninety-first page of the Turkish book entitled **Hujjat-ul-islâm** declares: **"When you become impure, hasten to perform a ghusl ablution! For, the angels of kirâman kâtibîn are hurt by the person who goes about in a state of janâbat."** It is written on the same page: "Hadrat Imâm-i Ghazâlî said he had dreamt of a person saying, 'I remained junub for a while. As a result, they have put a shirt of fire on me. And I am still on fire.' " A hadîth-i sherîf existing in the books **Zawâjir** and **Risâla-i unsiyya** declares; **"Angels of (Allah's) compassion do not enter a residence that contains a picture, a dog, or a junub person."** It is written in **Zawâjir** that if a person, regardless of whether he performs his daily prayers of namâz regularly, spends a prayer time junub, he will be tormented bitterly. For example, a person who becomes junub after the adhân of early afternoon (Zuhr) has to perform a ghusl before late afternoon ('Asr) prayer if he has not performed his early afternoon prayer, and before evening (Maghrib) prayer if he has performed his early afternoon prayer. If he cannot take a bath with water he must make a tayammum.

According to the Hanafî Madhhab there are three fards in a ghushl:

1 - To wash the entire mouth very well. Drinking a mouthful of water will do, yet some (savants) said that it would be makrûh.

2 - To wash the nostrils. A ghusl will not be accepted if one does not wash under any dried mucus in the nostrils or under any chewed pieces of bread in the mouth. According to the Hanbalî

Madhhab madmada and istinshâq are fard both in ablution and in ghusl. (See the previously explained eighteen sunnats of ablution).

3 - To wash every part of the body. It is fard to wash every spot on the body if there is no **haraj** (difficulty) in wetting it. It is not necessary but mustahab to rub the parts gently. Imâm-i Mâlik and Imâm-i Abû Yûsuf said that it is necessary. It is fard to wash inside the navel, the moustache, the eyebrows and the beard as well as the skin under them, the hair on the head and the vulva. It is not fard, but mustahab to wash the eyes, the closed ear ring holes and under the foreskin. When a woman washes the skin under her plaited hair it is not necessary to wash the plait. If the skin under the hair cannot be washed it becomes necessary to undo the plait. It is fard to wash all parts of the hair that is not plaited. If a person gets a haircut, it is not necessary to wash the hair cut [or other hairs or nails cut]. It is written on the two hundred and seventy-fifth page of the fifth volume of **Ibni 'Âbidîn** 'rahmatullâhi 'alaih': "It is makrûh to shave the groin when you are junub." [Hence it is makrûh also to get a haircut or to cut one's nails when you are junub.] It is not fard to wash under the dirt caused by fleas and flies, under henna, under the skin's natural dirt or under any fluid oil or mud. It is necessary to wash under the waterproof things stuck to the skin such as dough, wax, gum, solid oil, fish scale, a chewed piece of bread [and fingernail polish]. If water does not soak through the food remains in the teeth or cavities, or if the parts under them are not washed, the ghusl will not be acceptable. If a ring is tight it is necessary to take it off or to shift it. So is the case with earrings. If there are no rings in the ring holes, and if the holes are open, when washing the ears, it will be enough to moisten the holes. If they do not get wet you must wet them with your fingers. In doing all these it will be enough to believe strongly that they have become wet. If a person forgets to wash his mouth or some other part and performs namâz and then remembers that he has not washed it, he washes the part and performs the fard part of the namâz again. If you cannot find a secluded place when you need to check a part of your body that (you should not let other people see and which) is (called) your awrat part, you should wait until others leave the place instead of exposing your awrat part in company. If the time of namâz becomes short you should not make tahârat (clean yourself) when others are present; you should perform namâz with najâsat on your pants instead of cleaning your pants, since it is more blessed

to abstain from the harâm than doing the fard. When you find a secluded place later, you make tahârat, wash your pants and perform that namâz again.

An ablution and a ghusl do not have wâjibs. The sunnats of a ghusl are like the sunnats of an ablution. Only, in a ghusl it is not sunnat to wash in the same sequence as done in an ablution. Their mustahabs are the same, too, with the mere difference that in a ghusl one does not turn towards the qibla or recite any prayers. If a person who has gotten soaked in a pool, a river or the sea or drenched by rain washes his mouth and nose too, he will have performed an ablution and a ghusl.

To perform a ghusl as prescribed in the sunnat, we must first wash both of our hands and private parts even if they may be clean. Then, if there is any najâsat on our body, we must wash it away. Then we must perform a complete ablution. While washing our face we must intend to perform a ghusl. If water will not accumulate under our feet, we must wash our feet, too. Then we must pour water on our entire body three times. To do this, we must pour it on our head three times first, then on our right shoulder three times and then on the left shoulder three times. Each time the part on which we pour water must become completely wet. We must also rub it gently during the first pouring. In a ghusl, it is permissible to pour the water on one limb so as to make it flow onto another limb, which, in this case, will be cleaned, too. For in a ghusl the whole body is counted as one limb. If in performing an ablution the water poured on one limb moistens another limb, the second limb will not be considered to have been washed. When a ghusl is completed it is makrûh to perform an ablution again. But it will become necessary to perform an ablution again if it is broken while making a ghusl. Those who imitate the Shâfi'î and Mâlikî Madhhabs should remember this point. It is permissible to perform it at some other place even if it has not been broken or to perform it again after performing namâz.

In an ablution and a ghusl it is extravagant, which is harâm, to use more than the necessary amount of water. With eight **ritl** of water [which is equal to one thousand and forty dirham-i shar'î or three and a half kilograms], one can make a ghusl compatibly with the sunnat. Rasûlullah 'sall-Allâhu 'alaihi wa sallam' would perform an ablution with one **moud** [two ritl or 875 gr.] of water, and he would make a ghusl with water the volume of one **Sâ'**, [One Sâ' is 4200 grams of water. According to an experiment conducted with lentils by this faqîr –Husayn Hilmi bin Sa'îd Istanbûlî 'rahmatullâhi 'alaih' means himself–, one Sâ' is 4.2 litres, that is, four litres plus one-fifth a litre.]

[In the Hanafî Madhhab, if the area between the teeth and the tooth cavities do not get wet a ghusl will not be acceptable. Therefore, when one has one's teeth crowned or filled without **darûrat** one's ghusl will not be **sahîh** (acceptable). One will not get out of the state of **janâbat**. Yes, it is permissible according to Imâm-ı Muhammad to fasten one's loose teeth with gold wires or to put gold teeth in place of one's extracted teeth. Yet Imâm-i a'zam was of the ijtihâd that gold was not permissible. Imâm-i Abû Yûsuf, according to some reports, said as Imâm-i Muhammad said. It is said (by savants) that the permission given to Arfaja bin Sa'd, one of the Sahâba, so that he could use a gold nose, is, according to Imâm-i a'zam, peculiar to Arfaja only. As a matter of fact, Zubayr and Abdurrahmân 'radiy-Allâhu ta'âlâ 'anhumâ' were permitted to wear silk garments, and this permission is said (by savants) to have been peculiar only to them. But the fatwâ is based upon the word of Imâm-i Muhammad, which gives permission to wear gold teeth, ears or nose that can be taken out when performing a ghusl. This difference between our imâms is on whether or not artificial teeth and the wires fastened to the loose teeth may be of gold, and it is in cases when they can be removed so as not to prevent the performance of a ghusl. But in a ghusl all the imâms of the Hanâfî Madhhab say that the teeth must be wetted. In other words, when water does not go under the artificial teeth, which may be made of gold, silver, or any other substance that is not najs, a ghusl ablution will not be acceptable according to all the savants of Hanafî Madhhab.

It is written in **Halabî-i kebîr**: "If food remains are left between the teeth and one cannot wash under them a ghusl will be acceptable. For water is fluid and can infiltrate under the remains. But if the remains have been chewn and become solid, a ghusl will not be acceptable. This is the truth of the matter. For, water cannot infiltrate under them. There is no **darûrat** or **haraj**[1] in this." **Qâdî Khân** writes referring to Nâtifî: "If there are food remains between the teeth a ghusl will not be valid. It is necessary to pick them out and to wash the places under them."

It is written in **Al-majmû'at-uz-zuhdiyya**: "Whether little or much, if the food remains between the teeth become solid like

---
[1] For definition see the following pages.

dough and thereby prevent water from filtering through, they will prevent the ghusl."

It is written in **Durr-ul-mukhtâr**: "There are those (scholars) who have given the fatwâ that anything between the teeth or in any tooth cavity would not harm a ghusl ablution, but if the stuff is solid and does not let water through, a ghusl ablution will not be acceptable. This is the very truth itself." In explaining this Ibni 'Âbidîn 'rahmatullâhi 'alaih' wrote: "The reason why the fatwâ was given that it would do no harm was because water would infiltrate under it and wet the part beneath it." The book **Khulâsat-ul-fatâwâ** writes the same. As is understood from the fatwâ, if water does not go under it, a ghusl will not be accepted. The same is written in the book **Hilya**. The same is also written in the book of annotation **Minyat-ul-musallî**, which adds: "The present matter involves a situation in which water does not reach the tooth, and in which no darûrat or haraj is involved."

Tahtâwî, explaining **Marâqil-falâh**, wrote: "If water goes under the food remains between the teeth and in the tooth cavities a ghusl will be accepted. If they are too solid to let water through, a ghusl will not be accepted. The same is written in **Fath-ul-qadîr**.

Allâma Sayyid Ahmad Tahtâwî wrote in his explanation of **Durr-ul-mukhtâr**: "Because water will infiltrate under the food remains between the teeth and in tooth cavities, they do not prevent the performance of a ghusl. If you doubt whether water infiltrates under them you must take them out, wash in between the teeth and the cavities."

In acts and manners of worship and in acts, thoughts and manners that are harâm, every Muslim should follow the words of the scholars of his Madhhab, such as, **"This is the fatwâ", "This is the best," "This is the truest word."** If something he has done of his own accord hinders him from following the word of the scholar(s) he has adopted as his guide, and if there is haraj, difficulty, in eliminating that hindrance, he must follow another word which is declared to be right in his own Madhhab. For example, it is harâm to put the date of payment on the promissory-note of a person to whom you lend money; it involves interest. But by transferring it to someone else it will be permissible for either of them to pay it on a certain date. If you cannot do so, either, supposing you are in the Hanafî Madhhab, you act following those **daîf** words of the scholars of the Hanafî Madhhab which have not been chosen as a fatwâ. (See Endless Bliss II, chapter 33.) If you still cannot find a way out, you will have to act by imitating, i.e., following one of the other three Madhhabs. Hanafî scholars report that it is wâjib for you to imitate another Madhhab. For example, **Ibni 'Âbidîn**, while explaining **ta'zîr** on page 190, vol. III wrote: "Great 'âlîm **Ibni Âmîr Hâj** says in the book **Sharkh-i Tahrîr**: 'It is necessary to act upon the word of a certain mujtahid and to imitate another mujtahid when the necessity arises; this fact is clearly shown by a **Shar'î dalîl** (proof-text).' The Shar'î dalîl is the âyat-i kerîma **"Ask those who know."** When you come upon a certain new situation, you inquire into ways of dealing with this situation. If you know that a mujtahid has prescribed how to deal with this situation, it becomes wâjib for you to accept that mujtahid's prescription." Hence, it is wâjib to imitate another Madhhab (in that case). If it is impossible to follow another Madhhab, you should see if there is a darûrat to do the thing which causes the haraj.

A - If there is a darûrat to do something that causes haraj, it will be permissible for you not to do that fard at all, or to commit a harâm to the extent that the darûrat forces you to. The same is valid if the haraj is still present when the darûrat is over.

B - If the thing causing haraj has been done without a darûrat or if there are a few alternatives that can be done with a darûrat and you choose the one in which there is haraj, you are not permitted to omit the fard. Following this rule, scholars of fiqh have solved many problems. For example:

1 - Imâm-i Muhammad said, "When a loose tooth is tied with a silver wire, the silver will cause a noxious scent, but a gold wire will not cause it. Because there is a darûrat, it is not harâm to tie it with gold." And Imâm-i a'zam said, "A silver wire will not cause a noxious scent, either; so there is not a darûrat; consequently, it is harâm to tie it with a gold wire." In this case, Imâm-i Muhammad's 'rahmatullâhi ta'âlâ 'alaih' solution is to be acted upon. There is no need to follow another Madhhab.

2 - If a man finds out (later) that his wife is his milk-sister by way of one or both having been suckled (even if) only once by the same mother, their nikâh will become void according to Hanafî Madhhab. They will either get divorced or follow the Shafi'î Madhhab. If their walîs (guardians, protectors, parents) were not present during their nikâh, they have to renew their nikâh as prescribed by the Shafi'î Madhhab. If suckling from the same mother took place five times and both children were fully satiated, it will not be possible to follow the Shâfi'î Madhhab and the pair will have to part. (Please see the seventh chapter of the sixth

fascicle for kinship through the milk tie.)

3 - If a person on board a long-distance bus cannot persuade the driver to make a brief stop for evening prayer, he gets off at a convenient place and performs the prayer on the ground and within the prescribed time. Thereafter he takes another bus going in the same direction. Another way Islam approves of is to follow the Shâfi'î Madhhab and perform it after its preseribed time, i.e., together with the night prayer. If the prayer in question were late afternoon prayer and his destination were too far for him to perform the prayer within its time after arriving there, he would have to stop the bus, get off, and perform the prayer outside the bus. For, late afternoon prayer cannot be performed together with evening prayer in the Shâfi'î Madhhab, either.

4 - If a woman sues her husband for a divorce because he is too poor to provide her **nafaqa** (sustenance, living), a Hanafî qâdî (judge) is not authorized to grant a divorce. But a Shâfi'î qâdî is. The wife in the Hanafî Madhhab must apply to a Shâfi'î qâdî. That judge will divorce her. The **hukm** (judgement) of this judge will be **nâfiz** (carried out). See the chapter on **nafaqa** in the sixth fascicle!

A **samâvî** (involuntary) reason that forces one to do something, that is, a situation which arises beyond one's will, is called a **darûrat**. Examples of darûrat are a commandment or prohibition of the Shârî'at, an incurable vehement pain, danger of losing one's limb or life, and a compulsory choice without an alternative. When it is difficult to prevent something from hindering the doing of a fard or from causing a harâm to be committed, the case is called **haraj**.

As has been mentioned earlier, according to the unanimity of the scholars of the Hanafî Madhhab 'rahmatullâhi 'alaihim ajma'în' the ghusl of a person who has had his teeth filled or capped for some reason will not be sahîh (valid). Scholars of the Hanafî Madhhab do not have another statement (on this subject) that a person could follow in order to make his ghusl sahîh. Some people say that it is permissible for him to perform a ghusl before having his tooth crowned or filled and then make masah on the crowning or the filling every time they make a ghusl, but they are wrong. For, masah on mests is peculiar to the feet and is done not in a ghusl but in an ablution. Nor would it be right to liken the crowning or the filling to a bandage on a wound; this subject will be elaborated on several pages ahead.

When there is haraj in performing an act of worship or in avoiding something that is harâm, it is necessary to imitate another Madhhab which affords a solution without haraj; this fact is written in many books, e.g. in the fifty-first and the two hundred and fifty-sixth pages of the first volume and the five hundred and forty-second page of the second volume and in the one hundred ninetieth page of the third volume of **Ibni 'Âbidîn**, and in the eighteenth page of **Mîzan**, as well as in the final pages of the books **Hadîqa** and **Berîqa** and in **Fatâwâ-i hadîthiyya** and in the final pages of the section "Adab-ul-Qâdî" of **Fatâwâ-i Hayriyya**, in the 22nd letter of the third volume of **Maktûbât** of Imâm-i Rabbânî[1]. It is also written in **Ma'fuwwât** and in its explanation by Mollâ Khalîl Si'ridîs 'rahmatullâhi ta'âlâ 'alaih', a Shâfi'î scholar, and in its annotation. If the person who intends to imitate (another Madhhab) performed the present time's namâz before intending to imitate, the namâz will be sahîh (valid). But he will have to perform again his previous prayers of namâz which he performed before that. Tahtâwî writes as follows in the ninety-sixth page of his explanation of **Marâqil-falâh** and also in its Turkish version **Ni'mat-i Islâm**: "There is no harm in a Hanafî's imitating the Shâfi'î Madhhab for doing something which he cannot do in his own Madhhab. The same is written in the books **Bahrurrâiq** and **Nahrulfâiq**. But to do this he has to fulfill the conditions of the Shâfi'î Madhhab, too. If he imitates without haraj and does not observe the conditions he will be called a **Mulaffiq**, that is, one who looks for and gathers facilities. This is not permissible. A travelling person's performing late afternoon **('Asr)** prayer together with the early afternoon **(Zuhr)** prayer and night **(Ishâ)** prayer together with evening **(Maghrib)** prayer by imitating the Shâfi'î Madhhab requires that he will recite the Fâtiha (sûra) when he performs these behind an imâm (in jamâ'at), and that he will perform an ablution again if his palm touches his own **Saw'atayn**, that is, his two most private parts, or if his skin touches a woman's skin, except the eighteen women who are eternally harâm (forbidden) for him to marry. And he must intend for an ablution and avoid even a little najâsat." It is also permissible for him to imitate the Mâlikî Madhhab.

For imitating the Mâlikî or Shâfi'î Madhhab, it will suffice to remember that you are following the Mâlikî or Shâfi'î Madhhab when performing a ghusl or an ablution and when intending to perform namâz. In other words, the ghusl of such a person will be acceptable if, at the beginning, he passes this thought through his

---

[1] See the 34th chapter of Endless Bliss I.

heart: "I intend to perform ghusl and to follow the Mâlikî (or the Shâfi'î) Madhhab." When a person in the Hanafî Madhhab who has a crowned or filled tooth intends in this manner his ghusl will be sahîh. He will extricate himself from the state of being junub and become pure. When this person needs to perform namâz or to hold the Qur'ân he has to have an ablution that is valid also according to the Mâlikî or the Shâfi'î Madhhab. For those who imitate the Shâfi'î Madhhab; when the skins of two people of opposite sexes between whom a marriage would be permissible touch one another, an ablution of namâz, (not ghusl, that is,) becomes obligatory for both of them; for the same matter, when a person of either sex touches with their palm one of the two organs used for relieving nature on their own or someone else's body, they will need an ablution for namâz. Being elderly or not having reached the state of puberty, if the child in question is attractive enough, provides no exemption from this rule in the Shâfi'î Madhhab. Moreover, (if you are to follow the Shâfi'î Madhhab,) you should recite the sûra of Fâtiha at every rak'at of a namâz even if you are performing it in jamâ'at, and you should be very scrupulous in avoiding najâsat. When you are late for the jamâ'at (for the first rak'at of the namâz, for instance), you bow for rukû' together with the imâm and do not recite a part or the whole of the Fâtiha. Imitating Shafi'î or Mâlikî Madhhab is not taqwâ; it is fatwâ, rukhsat (permission). Taqwâ is to replace the crowned and filled teeth with false teeth.

To attain the compassion expressed in the hadîth-i sherîf, **"Differences among the mujtahids of my Ummat are Allah's compassion,"** which signifies the four Madhhabs, those Hanafîs who have filled or crowned teeth can extricate themselves from the state of being junub by following the Mâlikî or Shâfi'î Madhhab. For, it is not fard in the Madhhabs of Shâfi'î and Mâlikî to wash inside the mouth or the nostrils while performing a ghusl. But it is fard to intend to perform a ghusl. As a person imitates another Madhhab (on account of a haraj that makes it impossible for him to follow his own Madhhab in a particular matter), if a second haraj arises preventing his performance from being sahîh according to the Madhhab he has been imitating but not according to his own Madhhab or according to a third Madhhab, he maintains his performance by exploiting an eclecticism of the three Madhhabs. The kind of talfîq (unification) which scholars such as Izz-ad-dîn bin Abd-is-salâm Shâfi'î and Imâm-i-Subkî and Ibni Humâm and Qâsim say is permissible is this kind of imitation compelled by two different excuses. In case it is impossible to imitate the third Madhhab, his excuse in his own Madhhab becomes a darûrat and his worship becomes sahîh (acceptable). If the second excuse is not a continuous one, the worship he performs during the suspension of this excuse becomes sahîh according to this (second) Madhhab. As is seen, when a person imitates a third Madhhab because of an excuse making it impossible to follow the second Madhhab, this does not mean talfîq (unification of Madhhabs).

Since the ghusl of a person who is in the Hanafî Madhhab will not be sahîh (valid) as long as his teeth are crowned or filled, his prayers of namâz will not be sahîh, either. He has to perform his prayers again which he had performed until he began to imitate the Shâfi'î or Mâlikî Madhhab. Later on we shall explain how to perform the omitted fard prayers instead of the sunnat of each prayer. (See chapter 23).

Some people have been asking if there are any âyats or hadîths on the washing of the teeth. It should be known quite well that the **Adilla-i shar'iyya** are four. It is a lâ-madhhabî's attitude to recognize only two of them. Today there seem to be no qualified scholars on the earth who can derive meanings from âyats and hadîths. Having chosen one of the great scholars who understood the meanings of âyats and hadîths well and explained them in books of fiqh, we have made him our imâm, guide, leader, and have been performing our acts of worship in a manner shown by him. Our leader is Imâm-i a'zam Abû Hanîfa, 'rahmatullâhi ta'âlâ 'alaih'. To imitate one of the four Madhhabs means to follow the Qur'ân al-kerîm and the hadith-i sherîfs.

There are eleven kinds of ghusl, five of which are fard. Two of them involve a woman performing a ghusl to get out of the states of **haid** (menstruation) and **nifâs** (puerperium.)

Haid means to flow. It is the blood that starts to flow from the genital organ of a healthy girl a few days or months or a number of years after she has passed eight years of age and reached her ninth year, or of a woman after a period of **Full purity** directly succeeding the last minute of her previous menstrual period, and which continues for at least three days, i.e. seventy-two mean hours from the moment it was first seen. This is also called **Sahîh Catamenia**. If no blood is seen within the fifteen or more days after a bleeding period, and if this duration (of purity) is preceded and followed by days of haid, these days of purity are called **Sahîh Purity**. If there are days of fâsid bleeding, (which is also called istihâda bleeding,) within the fifteen or more days of purity, all these days are called (days of) **Hukmî purity** or **Fâsid purity**. Sahîh purity and Hukmî purity are called **Full Purity**. Bleedings that are seen before and after a period of full purity and which continue for three mean days are two separate periods of haid. Any coloured liquid, except for a white (colourless) liquid, is called the blood of haid, and so is any turbidity. When a girl begins haid, she becomes a **bâligha**, (an adolescent), that is, a woman. A girl who has not yet experienced the menses and a boy whose genitalia does not yet produce spermatozoa are Islamically bâligh (in a state of puberty), once they are beyond the age of fifteen. This fact is written in the annotation to the book **Durr-i Yektâ**. The number of days beginning from the moment bleeding is seen until the bleeding comes to an end is called **'âdat** (menstruation period). A period of haid is ten days maximum and three days minimum. According to the Shâfi'î and Hanbalî Madhhabs, it is fifteen days maximum and one day minimum. In the Mâlikî Madhhab it is fifteen days maximum, and yet the bleeding that is seen first is haid. If the bleeding of a woman who is in the Hanafî Madhhab and who is imitating the Mâlikî or Shâfi'î Madhhab goes on for more than ten days, she will have to make qadâ of the prayers of namâz she has omitted during this time of excess, after she becomes purified.

Menstrual bleeding does not have to be continuous. If the initial bleeding stops but more bleeding is seen again three days later, the days of purity in between are days of fâsid purity and are unanimously considered to be menstrual. According to a report Imâm-i Muhammad transmits from Imâm-i a'zam Abû Hanîfa, if bleeding is seen again before the tenth day, it will be concluded that the bleeding has continued throughout these ten days. There is also another report transmitted by Imâm-i Muhammad. According to Imâm-i Abû Yûsuf, and also in the Madhhabs of Shâfi'î and Mâlikî all these days of purity are considered menstrual if bleeding recurs before fifteen days have passed (since the cessation of bleeding). Suppose a girl bleeds for one day and then does not bleed for another fourteen days; however, she then bleeds again for one day. And suppose another woman bleeds for one day and does not bleed again for ten days, but again bleeds for only one day. And a third woman bleeds for three days and does not bleed again for five days, but when she bleeds again, it is only for a day. According to Imâm-i Abû Yûsuf, the girl's first ten days are haid; the former woman's days of haid are the same as her âdat (previous or usual menstrual period), and all the remaining days (of bleeding) are istihâda; the latter woman's nine days are all haid. According to Imâm-i Muhammad's first report, only the latter woman's nine days are haid. According to Imam-i Muhammad's second report, only the latter woman's first three days are haid, and none of the other days exemplified are haid. Translating the subject of haid from the book **Multaqâ**, we have written all the following information according to Imâm-i Muhammad's first report. One day is (a duration of) exactly twenty-four mean hours. It is mustahab for married women, all the time, and unmarried (virginal) women, during their menstrual period only, to put a piece of cloth or pure organic cotton called **kursuf** on the mouth of their vagina, and to apply perfume on it. Synthetic cotton is unhealthy. It is makrûh to insert the entire kursuf into the vagina. A girl who sees bloodstains on the kursuf every day for months is considered to be menstruating during the first ten days and having istihâda for the remaining twenty days. This will go on until the (continuous) bleeding, called **istimrâr**, stops.

If a girl sees blood for three days but does not see it for one day, and then sees it for one day but again does not see it for two days, and later sees it for one day but then does not see it for one day, and finally sees it again for one day, all these ten days are menstrual. If she sees blood one day but does not see it the next day, and if this alternating process goes on for ten days every month, she does not perform namâz or fast on the days she sees blood. But she makes ghusl and performs namâz on the following days. [Translated from the book **Masâil-i sharkh-i wikâya**.][1]

---

[1] [In the Mâlikî Madhhab, red, yellowish or turbid blood that issues from the front of a girl that has reached the age of nine is called **blood of haid** (menorrhoea). It is haid as soon as the bleeding starts. As the bleeding continues, it is menstrual until immediately before the fifteenth day, and its continuation thereafter, (as it may be the case,) is judged to be istihâda (menorrhagia). If her âdat changes the next month, her new âdat is the longest period of âdat she has so far had plus three days. Bleeding that continues thereafter, as well as bleeding that continues after the fifteenth day in any case, becomes istihâda. When the kursuf (pad, tampon, sanitary towel) is found to be dry, or colourless although it may be wet, this case must be taken as the end of the menstrual period. Bleeding that a woman past the age of seventy undergoes is not haid; it is istihâda. In case a woman's bleeding continues intermittently, the days spent without bleeding are to be taken as days of purity. The number of running days of purity is

Bleeding that goes on for less than three days, or, seventy-two hours, even if it is five minutes less, or, for a newly pubescent girl, bleeding after the tenth day when it goes on more than ten days or, for one who is not new, bleeding that happens after the âdat when it both exceeds the days of âdat and continues for more than ten days, or bleeding of a pregnant or **âisa** (old) woman or of a girl below nine years of age, is not menstrual. It is called **istihâda** or **fâsid bleeding**. A woman becomes âisa around the age of fifty-five. Supposing a woman whose âdat is five days sees blood after half of the Sun has risen and the bleeding stops as two-thirds of the Sun rises on the eleventh morning, in which case the bleeding has exceeded ten days for a few minutes, the blood that comes after five days, her âdat, is istihâda. For, it has exceeded ten days and ten nights for as long as one-sixth of the Sun's time of rising. When the ten days are over, she makes ghusl and makes qadâ of the prayers of namâz which she did not perform on the days following her âdat.

A woman undergoing the days of istihâda is categorized as a person who has an excuse ('udhr), like someone whose nose frequently bleeds or someone who is not able to control the bladder; hence, she has to perform namâz and fast, and sexual intercourse is permissible despite the bleeding. The bleeding of istihâda (menorrhagia) is a sign of a disease. If it continues for a long time it may be dangerous, so the person concerned must see a gynaecologist. A red gum powder called sang-dragon (dragon's blood) may stop the bleeding when taken orally with water, one gram in the morning, and the same amount in the evening. Up to five grams may be taken per day.

According to a report on the authority of Imâm-i Muhammad, if a girl over nine years old sees bloodstains one day for the first time in her life and does not see it the following eight days but

---

fifteen minimum. Bleeding that recurs before these fifteen days is istihâda. Such days of purity are infinite, (i.e. there is not a maximum limit.) If a bleeding stops and recurs fifteen days later, it is haid. Bleeding undergone before a childbirth is haid. If the baby is lifted out of the woman's womb through an opening cut in her abdomen, the bleeding that occurs in the immediate aftermath is not nifâs (puerperal discharge). Puerperal period is sixty days maximum. If the puerperal bleeding stops and does not recur within the following fifteen days, (the puerperal period has ended and) the woman undergoing nifâs has become tâhir (clean, purified). Bleeding that occurs thereafter is haid.]

sees it again on the tenth day, all the ten days are menstrual. However, if she bleeds the first and eleventh days only and undergoes no bleeding during the nine days in between, neither of them is menstrual. Bleeding on both days is istihâda, since the days of purity preceding the bleeding after the tenth day, as described above, are not considered to be the days of haid according to Imâm-i Muhammad. If she saw bloodstains on both the tenth and eleventh days, the first ten days, including the days of purity in between, would make up a menstruation period, while the bleeding undergone on the eleventh day would be istihâda.

A woman's haid, as well as her time of purity, is usually a period of the same number of days every month. In this sense, one 'month' (also a 'menstrual cycle') is the period from the beginning of a menstruation period to the beginning of the next period. When a woman with a certain period of âdat sees sahîh bleeding for a different number of days, her âdat changes. Likewise, the number of the days of purity changes when a different period of purity is experienced once. Fâsid bleeding or fasid purity does not change the âdat.

If the duration of bleeding of the new haid exceeds ten days and if its three or more days do not concur with the time of the former âdat, the time the âdat spans shifts, but the number of days does not change. If they (three or more days) concur with the time of (the former) âdat, the number of days concurring with it becomes haid and the rest becomes istihâda. If a woman whose âdat is five days of bleeding and fifty-five days of purity sees five days of bleeding and then forty-six days of purity and thereafter eleven days of bleeding, the time that her âdat covers shifts, but the number of days does not change. If she sees five days of bleeding and then fifty-seven days of purity but thereafter three days of bleeding followed by fourteen days of purity and then one more day of bleeding, the number of the days (of the new haid) becomes three. But the time it covers does not move. The fourteen days of fâsid purity here means continuous bleeding. If the duration of bleeding for the new haid does not exceed ten days and if it is followed by sahîh purity, all the days of bleeding make up a new haid. If it is not followed by **sahîh** purity, the number of the days of her former âdat does not change. In this case it is mustahab for her to wait until it gets quite close to the end of the time for namâz within which the bleeding stopped and which follows her âdat and precedes the tenth day (after the onset of bleeding). Then, after making a ghusl, she performs the time's namâz. Also **waty** (intercourse) becomes permissible for her. However, if she misses the ghusl and the namâz as she waits, intercourse before making a ghusl becomes permissible when the time of the prayer is over.

If the first bleeding of a girl, (menarche,) or a bleeding that begins fifteen days after the previous haid of a woman stops before three days are over, she waits until the end of the time of the namâz is quite close. Then, making wudû (ablution) only without a ghusl she performs the namâz of that time and those which she did not perform (during the bleeding). If bleeding reoccurs after she has performed that namâz, she discontinues namâz. If it stops again, towards the end of the time of the namâz she makes a wudû only and performs the time's namâz and those which she did not perform, if there are any. She acts likewise until the end of the third day. But waty (intercourse) is not permitted even if she has made a ghusl.

If bleeding continues for more than three days and stops before the end of her âdat, waty is not permitted before the end of her âdat, even if she has made a ghusl. However, if no bloodstains are seen until it is quite close to the end of the time of the namâz she makes a ghusl and performs the namâz. She does not perform those prayers of namâz which she omitted (in the meantime). She performs her fast. If bleeding does not reoccur for fifteen days after the day it stops, the day it stops becomes the end of her new âdat. But if bleeding reoccurs she discontinues namâz. If it is the month of Ramadân, after Ramadân, she makes qadâ of the fast which she performed. If bleeding stops she makes a ghusl again towards the end of the namâz-time and performs her namâz and fast. She follows the same procedure for ten days. After the tenth day she performs namâz without making a ghusl even if she sees bloodstains, and waty before a ghusl is permissible. But it is mustahab to make a ghusl before waty. If bleeding stops before the breaking of dawn and if she has only time enough to make a ghusl and dress up but not enough also to say "Allâhu ekber" before dawn, she fasts that day, but she does not have to make qadâ of the namâz of the previous night which she missed. But if the time were long enough also to say "Allâhu ekber," she would have to make the qadâ, (that is, she would have to perform the previous night's namâz.) If haid begins before iftâr (time for breaking a fast), her fasting becomes invalid, and she performs its qadâ after Ramadân. If haid begins while performing namâz, her namâz becomes invalid. When she becomes clean she does not perform qadâ for that namâz if it is fard, but she performs it if it is supererogatory. If a woman sees bloodstains on her kursuf when she wakes up after dawn, she becomes menstruous at that moment. If a woman sees that the kursuf (sanitary napkin) that she inserted before going to bed is clean when she wakes up, her haid stopped while she was asleep. It is fard for both to perform the (previous) night's namâz. For, a namâz's being fard for a woman depends on her being clean at its last minute. A woman whose haid begins before she has performed the time's namâz does not make qadâ of that namâz.

There must be **full purity** between two periods of haid. It is declared unanimously (by Islamic scholars) that if this full purity is **sahîh purity**, the bleedings before and after it are two separate periods of haid. Days of purity intervening the days of bleeding within the ten days of haid are judged to be menstrual, and the days of istihâda after the tenth day are judged to be within (the days of) purity. If a girl bleeds for three days and then does not bleed for fifteen days and then bleeds for one day and then does not bleed one day and then bleeds again for three days, the first and the last three days of bleeding are two separate periods of haid. Since her âdat is three days, the second haid cannot begin with the one day of bleeding in between. This one day makes the previous full purity fâsid. Molla Khusraw 'rahmatullâhi ta'âlâ 'alaih' wrote in his annotation to **Ghurar**: "If a girl sees one day of bleeding and then fourteen days of purity and thereafter one day of bleeding and then eight days of purity and then one day of bleeding and then seven days of purity and then two days of bleeding and then three days of purity and then one day of bleeding and then three days of purity and then one day of bleeding and then two days of purity and then one day of bleeding, according to Imâm-i Muhammad, of these forty-five days only the ten days following the fourteen days (of purity) are menstrual, and the rest are istihâda." Since there is not a period of full purity following these ten days, the new haid does not begin. Because the latter days of purity are not within the duration of her normal haid, these days are not added to the days of bleeding. (According to Imâm-i Abû Yûsuf, the first ten days and the fourth ten days with purity on both sides are menstrual.) For, according to Imâm-ı Abû Yûsuf, the following days of fâsid purity are considered to be menstrual. According to the first of the following (four) cases, the ten days of haid are followed by twenty days of purity and then ten days [the fourth ten days] of haid.

If **istimrâr** (see above) occurs, (i.e. if bleeding continues,) without any intervening days of purity for fifteen days, the calculation is based on her âdat. That is, beginning with the end of her âdat, the duration of purity is considered to be the same as that of the previous month's and the period of haid is the same as her âdat (that she experienced the previous month).

If istimrâr occurs on a girl, (who experiences menstruation for the first time,) according to the book **Manhal-ul-wâridîn** and the Turkish book **Murshid un-Nisâ**, it may be classified in one of the four cases:

1 - If the bleeding that is experienced for the first time makes istimrâr, the first ten days are considered menstrual and the next twenty days are considered days of purity.

2 - If istimrâr occurs after a girl has experienced a menarche[1] consisting of sahîh bleeding followed by sahîh purity, this girl has become a woman with a certain âdat. Supposing she experienced five days of bleeding and forty days of purity; from the onset of istimrâr five days are judged to be menstrual and forty days are days of purity. The case is valid until the bleeding ceases.

3 - If she undergoes fâsid bleeding and fâsid purity, neither of them must be judged to be her âdat. If the purity is fâsid because it is shorter than fifteen days, the bleeding which is seen first is considered to have made istimrâr. If she undergoes eleven days of bleeding and then fourteen days of purity and thereafter istimrâr, the first bleeding is fâsid because it exceeds ten days. Its eleventh day and the first five bleeding days of istimrâr are (within) the days of purity, and, after the fifth day (of istimrâr), ten days of haid and then twenty days of purity keep recurring. If the purity is full purity and is fâsid because there are days of bleeding within it, and if the sum of the days of such fâsid purity and the days of bleeding does not exceed thirty, again, the first bleeding is considered to have made istimrâr. An example of this is istimrâr after eleven days of bleeding and fifteen days of purity. Because there is bleeding on the first of the sixteen days, it is a period of fâsid purity. The first four days of the istimrâr are (within) the period of purity. If their sum exceeds thirty days, the first ten days are menstrual and all the following days until the istimrâr are considered days of purity, and after the istimrâr, ten days of haid

---

[1] Onset of first menstrual discharge.

and twenty days of purity continue to reoccur. An example of this is istimrâr after eleven days of bleeding and twenty days of purity.

4 - If she undergoes sahîh bleeding and fâsid purity, the days of sahîh bleeding become her âdat. Their deficieney from thirty days make up the days of purity. Suppose istimrâr occurs after five days of bleeding and fourteen days of purity, the first five days are days of bleeding and the following twenty-five days are days of purity. To complete these twenty-five days, the first eleven days of the istimrâr are appended to the days of purity. From now on five days of haid and twenty-five days of purity will continue reoccurring. Likewise, if istimrâr occurs after three days of bleeding and fifteen days of purity and one day of bleeding and fifteen days of purity, the first three days are days of sahîh bleeding and all the following days until the onset of istimrâr are days of fâsid purity; hence, three days are menstrual and the next thirty-one days are days of purity. During the istimrâr, however, three days of haid and twenty-seven days of purity reoccur. If the second period of purity were fourteen days, according to Imâm-i Abû Yûsuf it would be considered a period of continuous bleeding. So its first two days also, (along with the previous one day of actual bleeding,) would be menstrual, and the next fifteen days would be days of purity, and so on. For, the first three days of bleeding and the next fifteen days of purity are to be accepted as her âdat because they were sahîh.

A woman who has forgotten the time of her âdat is called **Muhayyira** or **Dâlla**.

Nifâs means lochia. Puerperal bleeding that occurs after a foetal miscarriage is also nifâs, so long as the hands, feet and head of the foetus have been formed. There is not a minimum duration for nifâs. On the day the bleeding stops, she performs a ghusl and resumes namâz. But she cannot have sexual intercourse before the period equalling her previous nifâs is over. The maximum is forty days. After forty days she performs a ghusl and begins namâz even if her bleeding continues. Bleeding after the fortieth day is istihâda. The nifâs of a woman whose bleeding lasted twenty-five days after her first pregnancy is twenty-five days. Therefore, if blood flows for forty-five days after her second pregnancy, the first twenty-five makes up the nifâs and the remaining twenty days are istihâda. She has to perform qadâ of those prayers of namâz that she did not perform during these twenty days. This rule entails that a woman make a mental note of her puerperal period as well. If her bleeding stops before the fortieth day, e.g. in thirty-five days, during the second childbirth, all the thirty-five days are nifâs; therefore, her nifâs changes from twenty-five to thirty-five days. In Ramadân, if haid or nifâs stops after dawn (fajr), she fasts during that day, yet after Ramadân she will still have to make up for that day by fasting for an extra day. If haid or nifâs begins after dawn, she resumes eating and drinking even if it begins during late afternoon.

Namâz, fast, entering a mosque, reading or holding the Qur'ân al-kerîm, visiting the Ka'ba, and sexual intercourse are all harâm (forbidden) in all four Madhhabs during process of a haid or nifâs. Later she performs the qadâ' of those fasts, but not the prayers of namâz that she did not perform. She will be forgiven for not performing namâz. If at each prayer time she performs an ablution and sits on a sajjâda (prayer-rug) and dhikrs and performs tasbîh for as long as it would take her to perform namâz, she will be given as many blessings as she would receive if she actually performed namâz in the best manner.

[When a girl is over eight years old, it becomes fard for her mother or, if she does not have a mother, her grandmothers, elder sisters, paternal and maternal aunts, respectively, to teach her about haid and nifâs. Negligence of this duty despite the presence of at least one of these next of kin, (cited above in order of priority,) will incur grave sinfulness on the negligent as well as on their husbands.]

It is written in the book **Jawhara**: "A woman must let her husband know when her haid begins. In fact, she will be gravely sinful if she does not tell him when he asks. It is an equally grave sin if she says that her haid has begun while she is pure. Our Prophet 'sall-Allâhu 'alaihi wa sallam' stated: **'A woman who conceals the beginning and the termination of her haid from her husband is accursed.'** It is harâm, a grave sin, to have anal intercourse with one's wife, during haid or otherwise." He who does so is accursed. Pederasty is even more sinful. The Sûrat-ul-Anbiyâ' states that pederasty is an **"extremely vile deed."** A hadîth quoted in Qâdîzâda's commentary to **Birgiwî** states, **"If you catch in the act those who commit pederasty as did the tribe of Lût[1], kill them both!"** Some Islamic scholars have said that they both must be burned alive. It has been discovered in America that the horrid disease called AIDS, which has been

---

[1] Inhabitants of the ancient towns of Sodom (and Gomorrah), who were famous for their immoralities.

spreading with great speed among those who practise pederasty, is more fatal with those who eat pork. No medicine has so far been developed to cure this disease, whose virus was diagnosed in 1985.

The third type of ghusl that is fard concerns a person who has become junub. Such a person must wash himself (make a ghusl) when he has to perform namâz. There are three ways of becoming junub: When the tip of the penis (its roundish part under the prepuce) enters the vulva; when the man's viscous white semen or the woman's yellowish ovum fluid is thrown out lustfully; or by nocturnal emission, i.e., when he or she has a lustful dream and sees that semen or **mazy** has issued when he or she wakes up; in such a case, both the man and the woman become junub. In the Hanafî and Shâfi'î Madhhabs, one does not become junub by the discharge of **mazy** or **wadî**. But the semen that has issued may become fluid with the effect of heat and be mistaken for mazy.

To make a ghusl for Friday, for the prayers of the Bayrams ('Iyds) of Fitr and Qurbân, and while on the mount of Arafât (which is near Mekka) on 'Arafa day is sunnat-i zawâid. If a person who has forgotten that he has been junub makes a ghusl for the Friday prayer, he becomes pure. But he will not attain the blessings for performing an act that is fard.

It is wâjib-i kifâya to wash a Muslim when he is dead. Before a dead Muslim is washed (the special prayer of namâz that Islam commands Muslims to perform collectively before the interment of a dead Muslim and which is termed namâz of janâza) cannot be performed[1].

When a disbeliever becomes a Muslim, it is mustahab for him to make a ghusl.

Besides these eleven, it is mustahab to make a ghusl before putting on the ihrâm for hajj and 'umra; when entering Mekka or Medîna; when standing for waqfa at muzdalifa; before washing a dead Muslim; after cupping; on Qadr, 'Arafa and Barât nights; when a mad person becomes sane; and for a child who reaches fifteen years of age. If a woman has sexual intercourse when her haid is over, one ghusl for both is enough. When a person makes a ghusl for some other reason on a Friday or on a day of 'Iyd, he will also be given the same blessings as he would be given if he performed (another) ghusl for these prayers of namâz.

---

[1] Salât (namâz) of janâza is explained in detail in the fifteenth chapter of the fifth fascicle of **Endless Bliss**.

When the sticky liquid called semen issues forth because of being thrashed, lifting something heavy, or falling down from a high place, a ghusl is not necessary in the Hanafî and Malikî Madhhabs. But it is necessary in the Shâfi'î Madhhab. A Hanafî person who imitates the Shâfi'î Madhhab has to take this into consideration.

If the semen that leaves its place lustfully remains in the urethra and does not go out, a ghusl is not necessary. But if it comes out later, even without lust, it will be necessary to make a ghusl. If a person who has a nocturnal emission, that is, who ejaculates semen in his dream, wakes up and squeezes his penis so that the semen is prevented from coming out, then experiences later on, after his lust has subsided, semen leaking from his organ, a ghusl becomes necessary for him. If a person who has become junub makes a ghusl without urinating and if later on the rest of the semen issues without lust, he has to make another ghusl. If he has performed namâz with his first ghusl, he does not have to reperform the same namâz. For this reason, in the Hanafî and Hanbalî Madhhabs it is necessary to urinate and thereby wash out the semen that has remained in the urethra and afterwards make a ghusl. A Muslim in the Shâfi'î Madhhab must make a ghusl again even if he has urinated. However, a Muslim in the Mâlikî Madhhab does not have to make a ghusl again even if he has not urinated.

When the tip of the penis goes into the vulva or into a woman's or man's anus, a ghusl is necessary for both persons, regardless of whether or not semen was discharged. Inserting a penis into an animal **(sodomy)** or into a dead person **(necrophilia)** does not necessitate a ghusl if semen was not discharged, according to the Hanafî Madhhab. An animal thus abused must be killed (by jugulation) and the carcass must be burned. It may be eaten as well, (if it is an edible animal.) These two acts are done by psychopaths called **sadist**. Such acts are utterly abominable and grave sins.

If a person who has a nocturnal emission notices some wetness on his bed, on his underwear, or on his legs and judges it to be the white, fluid liquid called **mazy**, or if mazy issues from him while awake, a ghusl is not necessary. If he notices some semen without remembering a nocturnal emission, a ghusl is necessary as unanimously stated (by scholars). If he thinks it may be mazy, as a precaution a ghusl is necessary. If a person remembers that he had a nocturnal emission, but does not see any wetness anywhere, a ghusl is not necessary. After a woman makes a ghusl, if some of her husband's semen comes out, a ghusl is not necessary. If a drunk person sees some semen on himself after he recovers, a ghusl is necessary. The case is the same with a person who has fainted. If both the wife and the husband see some semen in their bed when they wake up, a ghusl is necessary for both, even though they do not remember having a nocturnal emission. If a genie disguised as a human being has sexual intercourse with a person, a ghusl is necessary for that person. If the genie does not come in a human figure, the person who has an experience from this does not make a ghusl. If the man's semen, which was discharged by rubbing his penis on a part of the woman's body except her vulva, goes into the vulva, the woman does not have to make a ghusl. However, if she becomes pregnant as a result, she has to make a ghusl and perform the prayers of namâz again which she has performed since the incident occurred.

When such things as a child's penis, an animal's penis, a dead person's penis, or anything like a penis, such as a finger or a penis with a condom on it is inserted into the vulva, a ghusl is necessary if she is aroused by it. If she does not enjoy it, making a ghusl is preferred. **Merâqil-felâh** says: "Semen or an ovum released while looking at or daydreaming about the opposite sex causes one to become junub. A woman's husband pays for the water she uses when making a ghusl, an ablution and for her bath. The husband has to meet his wife's needs even if she is rich. If a man's semen is released while urinating, he makes a ghusl if his penis is erect.

If a woman begins menstruating while she is junub, she makes a ghusl immediately if she likes[1], or she may wait until the menstruation is over and then make one ghusl for both.

Durr-ul-munteqâ says: "It is permissible for men to go to public baths for men, and women also are permitted to go to public baths for women. Covering their awrat parts with thick and oversized towels is fard; looking at someone else's awrat parts[2] covered with a thin and tight towel is harâm (prohibited). It is permissible for hamâm (public bath) attendants to scour down the skin on the thighs of their customers (by using a rough cloth mitt)

---

[1] If she chooses to do so, she will have to make another ghusl when her period is over.
[2] Parts of a person's body that should be under cover in company, (and/or during certain acts of worship,) are termed awrat parts. Please see chapter 8 for details.

and to look at those parts of their body, provided they are covered. It is harâm, however, for them to touch their awrat parts under the towel (with bare hands) or to look at their bared awrat parts. People of the same sex are permitted to look at or touch one another's body, with the exception of their awrat parts and with the proviso that the sight or the contact should be secure against any likelihood of lust. On the other hand, it is prohibited (harâm) for a man to look at a woman who is a disbeliever, even without any lust." He who flouts a harâm (prohibition) conveyed by nâss or ijmâ' will lose his îmân (faith) and become a murtadd (renegade, apostate).

If a person who is junub has not performed the namâz of the current time, they will not be sinful for delaying their ghusl till the end of the current time. Yet it is a grave sin for him to delay it any longer. It is not sinful to sleep or to have sexual intercourse when one is junub. It is permissible to make a ghusl by using the same basin or container together with one's wife. It is tenzîhî makrûh for a person who is junub to eat or drink before washing his hands and mouth. For, the water touching his mouth and hands becomes **musta'mal**[1]. And it is makrûh to drink water which is musta'mal. The case is not so with a woman in haid. For she has not been commanded to make a ghusl while menstuating. [A woman in haid can suckle her baby without washing her breasts. But it is makrûh for a woman who is junub to suckle her baby without washing off (her nipples).] A woman's suckling her baby will not break her ablution.

It is makrûh to read the Qur'ân al-kerîm when one's awrat parts are exposed or in the presence of people whose awrat parts are exposed. Therefore, a Muslim who is to read (or recite) the Qur'ân al-kerîm while lying in bed should keep their head outside of the blanket as they do so, if they are wearing something not covering all their awrat parts.

If a person who becomes junub at a house where he has been a guest fears that making a ghusl may cause slander or suspicion, he does not make a ghusl. And since it is not permissible for him to make a tayammum while there is water, it is permissible for him to be pretending to perform namâz while he is junub, without intending, without saying the tekbîr of iftitâh, without reciting anything while standing, but only acting as if he were doing the rukû' and sajda. [Also, he who has to perform namâz behind an

---

[1] Please see chapter 7 for kinds of water.

imâm who is a lâ-Madhhabî reformer, does likewise.]

It is harâm to enter a mosque or to even walk through a mosque when one is junub and when a woman has haid. If one has no other way than the one leading through a mosque or if one becomes junub in a mosque or if one cannot find water anywhere but in a mosque, one makes a tayammum and then one can go in and out of the mosque. It is harâm in all four Madhhabs for one to read (or recite) the Qur'ân al-kerîm, to hold a Mus'haf and to visit the Ka'ba while one is junub. It is harâm also to hold the Qur'ân al-kerîm, or anything on which âyats are written, without an ablution. It is permissible to carry the Qur'ân al-kerîm in something not attached to it, e.g. in a bag. It is not harâm to recite the Fâtiha or the âyats which are said to be the prayer ayâts, with an intention to make a prayer, (not as the Qur'ân) or to say any prayer, yet it is mustahab to say any prayer with an ablution. **Tafsîrs** (explanations of the Qur'ân) are like the Qur'ân al-kerîm. Other books of dîn are like prayers. It is not permissible to wrap something in any piece of paper on which information of fiqh is written. If Allâhu ta'âlâ's Name or names of Prophets ''alaihim us-salâm'' are written on some paper, things can be wrapped in it only after erasing the names. But it is more honorable not to use such things as wrapping papers, for the letters of the Qur'ân are also sacred. It is written in the books **Hadîqa** and **Latâif-ul-ishârat**: "The Heavenly Book revealed to Hadrad Hûd ''alaihis-salâm'' was in Islamic letters." It is written on the six hundred and thirty-third page of the second volume of **Hadîqa**: "It is makrûh to lay carpets, mats, or prayer-rugs carrying sacred writings woven or painted on them, on the floor, or to sit on them or to use them for any purpose whatsoever. It is also makrûh to write sacred writings on coins, mihrâbs and walls. But it is not makrûh to hang them on walls." [This interdiction applies also to pictures of the Ka'ba-i-mu'azzama. Prayer-rugs without pictures or embroideries on them must be preferred.]

We repeat that it is fard in the Hanafî and Hanbalî Madhhabs to wash inside the mouth while making a ghusl. Then, those who are Hanafî should not have their teeth filled or crowned unless they strongly need to do so. We must not let our teeth decay. To avoid this, we must take care of our teeth as commanded by our religion and we must use miswâks. France's valuable medical book entitled **Larousse Illustré Medical** writes the following about dental care: "All kinds of tooth paste, powder or liquid are harmful. The best method for cleaning the teeth is with a hard brush. In the beginning it makes the teeth bleed. You should not be inhibited. It will strengthen the gums, so that they will no longer bleed." Like everybody, I had been using toothpaste. Two of my teeth began to decay. When I read the French book I began using a miswâk. My teeth stopped decaying. It was more than sixty years ago. Ever since then I have had no complaints about my teeth or stomach. Ibni 'Âbidîn wrote in **Radd-ul muhtâr**: "It is sunnat-i muakkada to use a miswâk when performing an ablution. A hadîth-i-sherîf states: **'A namâz which is performed after using a miswâk is seventy-fold superior to a namâz without a miswâk.'** A miswâk must be straight, as wide as the second small finger, and a span long. The miswâk is derived from a branch of the erâk (peelo) tree growing in Arabia. [Shaving it about two centimetres from the straight end, you keep this part in water for a couple of hours. When you press it, it will open like a brush.] When the erâk tree cannot be found, a miswâk can be made from an olive branch. You should not make it from a pomegranate branch. If an erâk or olive tree cannot be found or if one does not have teeth, the sunnat must be carried out with one's fingers. The miswâk has more than thirty advantages, which are written in Tahtâwî's **Khâshiyatu Marâq al-falâh**. Firstly, it causes one to die with îmân. It is makrûh for men to chew gum without any 'udhr (strong necessity), even when they are not fasting. Women must use chewing gum when they are not fasting instead of a miswak with the intention of performing the sunnat."

Question: It is said that all the fuqahâ and mujtahids agree that our religion gives permission to have one's teeth repaired. If they disagree on whether the repairs must be of gold or silver, does this affect their agreement?

Answer: Having one's teeth repaired means putting a false tooth that can be taken out whenever one wishes in the place of a missing tooth, fastening a tooth which is about to fall out, or having one's teeth filled or crowned. To change the fatwâ of Hanafî scholars 'rahmatullâhi ta'âlâ 'alaihim ajma'în' wherein they state that "it is permissible to fasten a loose tooth with gold" into "There is unanimity about it being permissible to have one's teeth repaired. It is permissible to have one's teeth filled or crowned," means either not to understand the declaration of the **fuqahâ** or to adapt these declarations to one's own insidious and base desires, either of which is both shameful and sinful. Our mujtahids disagreed on whether it would be fastened with gold or silver. In fiqh books of the Hanafî Madhhab tying a loose tooth is called

shad or **tadbîb**. Shad (in Arabic) means to soundly fasten with wire. For example, **shadd-uz-zunnâr** means to fasten a priest's girdle. It is written in the paragraph about sitting on a sofa made by tadbîb in the books entitled **Tahtâwî** and **Hindiyya**, which are annotations to the book entitled **Durr-ul-mukhtâr**, and also in the books **Durr-ul-muntaqâ** and **Jâmi'ur-rumûz** that tadbîb means to wind a band around something wide and flat like the sliding iron bar of a door. It is written in **Bezzâziyya** and in **Hindiyya**: "It is permissible to eat and drink from containers engraved with gold and silver designs. Yet you must not touch the silver or the gold with your hands or mouth. The Imâmayn (Imâm-i-Abû Yûsuf and Imâm-i-Muhammad) said that it is makrûh to use such containers. So is the case with a container that has been made by tadbîb. It is permissible to apply tadbîb on a sofa or the saddle of an animal, but you must not sit on those parts of it consisting of gold and silver. It is permissible to apply tadbîb on the cover of a volume of Qur'ân al-kerîm. But the gold and the silver on it must not be touched." Hence, tadbîb does not mean to cover the entire surface of something, but it means to place a metal band around something. It is written in books of fiqh: "It is permissible to apply tadbîb of gold on a loose tooth." This statement means that it is permissible to fasten a loose tooth with a gold wire or band in order to prevent it from falling. This is because water penetrates under such teeth. In fact, as today's prostheses can be taken out while making a ghusl, the tying wires and bands can be removed, cleaned, and replaced after a ghusl. Otherwise, the food that remains between them would cause stench and damage in the mouth. To say that the scholars of fiqh said that it was permissible to crown a loose tooth is to slander those great people. For, a loose tooth cannot be crowned, but it can be tied. As seen, a real man of religion would not concoct the fatwâ: "It is permissible to crown teeth," by interpreting the word **"tadbîb"** as "crowning." The assertion that books of fiqh contain statements acceding to "filling or crowning decaying teeth with gold or silver" begs the question whether they contain a single allusion that could be interpreted as a "permission to have your decaying teeth filled or crowned," which they do not.

People who have little information on matters of fiqh and who do not understand mujtahids' statements, cannot differentiate between the expression "having an artificial tooth made or fastening a loose tooth" with the expression "having one's teeth filled or crowned." They attempt to stretch mujtahids' statements so as to conflate them all into an aggregate of conveniences offered in case of a darûrat (strong necessity, inevitable situation). These poor people do not realize that there is no need for searching for a darûrat concerning tying a loose tooth or having a movable tooth mounted in place of a missing tooth. A darûrat is searched for when you have to do something that is not permissible to do. Since it is not prohibited to fasten one's tooth or to mount a false tooth, why should one look for a darûrat? In an attempt to rationalize the fillings and crownings in their own mouths and convince Muslims that their ghusl is properly performed, some people seized upon the word 'necessity' in the "necessity for fastening the teeth with gold instead of silver wires," brandished it, so to speak, as if it were the ultimate weapon, and clamoured: "It has been declared unanimously that it is a necessity to have one's teeth repaired." Thus they confused the Muslims in the Hanafî Madhhab and blocked the way leading to the grace of Allâhu ta'âlâ. These people point as a proof to the declaration that the tottering teeth can be fastened unconditionally. However, the wires tying the teeth tightly and false teeth can be taken out, cleaned and put back in their places. The unanimous declaration by Islamic savants 'rahmatullâhi ta'âlâ 'alaihim ajma'în' refers to the wires and the teeth that can be taken out when making a ghusl. It would be an abominable slander against those great scholars to say that they permitted such obstacles as crowns and fillings, which do not let water through, while there is the fact that they also declared: "It is fard to wash tooth cavities and in between the teeth when making a ghusl." Those scholars said not only that it was permissible to use a gold false tooth, but also that it was permissible to wear a silver ring. Permission to wear a silver ring does not mean that the skin under it will be exempt from being washed. They said that it was necessary to moisten the skin under the ring by taking it off or by shifting it. They said that an ablution or a ghusl would not be sahîh if the skin under a tight ring was not moistened. Having a tooth crowned is like wearing a ring. Since the tooth under a filling or crown is not moistened, the ghusl will not be acceptable.

Question: It is not a requirement to make water reach very difficult parts while making a ghusl. It is for this reason that washing inside the eyes, inside the foreskin, and for women under their plaits, is excused. If a person with a headache cannot make a masah on his head, making masah on his head is not obligatory for him. When the teeth are repaired because of a darûrat, doesn't the obligation of washing the teeth become null and void?

Answer: The Islamic rule stating that "if a certain part of the body cannot be wetted because of some **haraj** to wet it, the ghusl so performed will be accepted," is not an allinclusive rule. It applies to predicaments resulting from a darûrat, i.e. a natural situation in which you have been physically involved, or something you have had to do in order to perform an Islamic commandment. Difficulties that a Muslim has run into as a result of their own doings are excluded from the absolvement offered via that rule.

When a haraj (difficulty, predicament) arises as a result of your own doings, you are to imitate one of the other three Madhhabs, i.e. the one in which you will not encounter the same haraj. A severe headache is a darûrat which occurred involuntarily. Not being able to touch one's head in this case is haraj. Therefore, one will be exempted from washing or making masah of one's head. As is explained in the third chapter, in its eleventh paragraph dealing with making masah on splints, it is declared (by scholars) that after a wound has healed it is not permissible to make masah on the medicine, ointment, or bandage put over it, and that it is necessary to remove them and wash (the skin) under them. It is said (by fiqh scholars) that if there is haraj in removing these things, since these things are not included in the category of darûrats that occurred involuntarily, the person concerned imitates another Madhhab. According to another statement made by mujtahids; in case the same haraj exists in the other three Madhhabs, too, one is absolved from having to wash under them, since they were placed there due to some darûrat, that is, to cure the wound. As a matter of fact, since washing the whole body, including a wound or sore that is immune to water, when making ghusl is fard (obligatory) in all the other three Madhhabs as well, it is impossible to imitate one of the other three Madhhabs, i.e. a difficulty or predicament coexists with the darûrat that has caused it, one is absolved from having to wash the parts concerned. It is fard for a woman with plaits to moisten only the bottom of her hair. Ibni 'Âbidîn 'rahmatullâhi ta'âlâ 'alaih' writes: "Because women are prohibited from shaving their hair, they have been excused from undoing their plaits. Men are immune from this darûrat. The fact that haircut is sunnat for men is written in the fifth volume of Ibni 'Âbidîn. For this reason men have to undo and wash their plaited hair." Women's not undoing their plaited hair does not absolve men from having to undo their plaited hair. The difference is beause there is darûrat and haraj for the former. However, there is no darûrat, though there is haraj, concerning men's hair.

There is no haraj (difficulty) in removing artificial teeth when making a ghusl. They can easily be removed and the skin under them can be washed. It is permissible to have such artificial teeth made. It is unnecessary for Muslims who use them to imitate one of the other three Madhhabs.

Question: Imâm-i a'zam said that the darûrat of having one's teeth repaired could be met by using silver. I read this in a preacher's book. The same book writes that Itqânî says that Imâm-i-Muhammad may have said as follows: "We do not admit that the necessity of having one's teeth repaired will have been met by using silver. For, silver, which causes a noxious scent on the nose, would cause it on the teeth, too." So, it is quite obvious that having one's teeth repaired is a darûrat, the book adds. What do you say about this?

Answer: It must be untrue that the book you have read was written by a preacher. A person who conveys the books of fiqh so incorrectly is either a very ignorant man or an abject liar, a falsifier. Note what **Radd-ul-muhtâr** writes in its section called **Al-hazar wal-ibâha**: "Imâm-i-a'zam discriminated between tying a tooth and making an artificial nose. He stated that it is permissible to have an artificial nose made of gold because a silver nose would constitute a darûrat on account of the stench that silver causes, for something which is harâm can be permissible (mubâh) only when there is a darûrat. However, when silver is used for the teeth, the darûrat will no longer exist. There will no longer be a need for using gold, which is more valuable. Itqânî said that in order to help Hadrat Imâm-i Muhammad a person might say: "We do not admit that the darûrat in tying the teeth with gold is eliminated by using silver. For silver will cause a stench on the teeth as well as on the nose." As is seen, neither Imâm-i a'zam nor Imâm-i Muhammad 'rahmatullâhi ta'âlâ 'alaihimâ' uttered the expression, "the darûrat concerning having an artificial tooth made." A person who had had crowned teeth should have fabricated this darûrat lest he would be lowered in the eyes of the Muslims and so that he would have the sympathy of those who had had their teeth crowned. Concerning the tying of teeth our imâms (the mujtahids in our Madhhab) said: "When silver causes a stench, the darûrat of fastening with gold occurs. If using silver does not cause a stench, this darûrat will no longer exist." It is not for us laymen in religious matters, who are not mujtahids, to say whether or not there is a darûrat. Islam authorizes mujtahids to talk on this matter. Those men of religion who are not mujtahids do not have the right to talk on this matter. If they talk, their words will have no value. Our scholars have declared unanimously that after the four hundredth year of the Hegira there have not been any scholars educated in the grade of ijtihâd. Finding mujtahids' fatwâs, our scholars have written them in books of fiqh. It is written clearly in books of fiqh that a ghusl will not be acceptable when water does not penetrate under the food remains within tooth cavities and that there is no darûrat or haraj in this. We have explained this above. For, it is possible to remove the remnants of food in tooth cavities and between the teeth when you are making a ghusl, and there is no haraj, difficulty in doing this. It is written in the translation of **Qâmûs**: "Darûrat, which causes haraj in doing a fard, i.e. hinders its performance, either arises from compulsion, e.g. women growing their hair long – the Sharî'at has prohibited them from cutting their hair – or it is intended to cure an ailing limb or to feed the body and protect it against dangers. Or, it is because there is no other way." In case there is a haraj and it is impossible to imitate any one of the other three Madhhabs, the policy to be followed is to see whether the present haraj has arisen out of a darûrat. There is a haraj in women's undoing their plaited hair. Since it is impossible for them to imitate another Madhhab and thereby get over the haraj and growing their hair long is consequent upon a darûrat, they have been absolved from having to undo their plaited hair.

A person with a decaying or aching tooth must go to a pious Muslim dentist. The dentist relieves him from his vehement pain by putting cotton with medicine into his tooth. Later, the cotton will be taken out; the tooth with the pain has been relieved. The dentist then will suggest two options to their patient: The first way, he will say, is to extract the decaying tooth and replace it with an artificial one; the second way is to kill the nerve attached to the decaying tooth and then fill or crown it. If the decay in the tooth is new, it is filled in and the decaying is halted for some time. Depending on the dentist's skill, this tooth can be used very well for many long years. In advanced cases filling is impracticable. In such cases, only the tooth root is utilized by way of crowning. In case the root also has decayed, the tooth is extracted and a prosthesis is used. A prosthesis is not as pratical as a crowning, and so is the case with a crowning when compared with a filling. Crowning or filling does not cure an ailing tooth. Nor does it restore it to its former healthy condition. It only helps to use the ailing tooth without suffering pain. When a person with a tooth filled or crowned imitates the Mâlikî or Shâfi'î Madhhab, he or she attains the same thawâb as gained by people without any excuse. If it were impossible to imitate these Madhhabs, filling or crowning would become a darûrat and his or her prayers of namâz would be sahîh. Yet, because he or she would have an excuse, his or her thawâb would be less. As is seen, imitating another Madhhab not only causes much thawâb, but also saves the teeth from being extracted.

It would be wrong to assert that filling or crowning your teeth is a darûrat by saying, "A tooth is a limb, too. Isn't it a darûrat to have a decaying tooth cured? You yourself said that it was a darûrat to tie a loose tooth." In fact, to crown or fill a tooth does not mean to cure it. It means to remove the nerve from the decaying tooth and to use the dead tooth like a prosthetic or artificial tooth. The artificial tooth is permissible since it is movable, whereas crowns and fillings are not permissible since they are not movable. Today, making prostheses for aching teeth is not very painful or difficult. By contrast, killing the nerve of a tooth causes a lot of pain and trouble. Imitating the Shâfi'î Madhhab is permissible also for one who says, "There is haraj in using an artificial tooth, but there is no haraj in using a crowning or filling." In the process of time the root of a crowned or filled tooth becomes a home for toxins and causes various diseases in the other organs. False teeth, on the other hand, do not produce any toxins.

Those who have gotten their teeth crowned as ornamentation or their teeth filled without (the cause of) a tooth-ache or decay should imitate the Shâfi'î Madhhab when performing a ghusl. It is written clearly in **Ibni 'Âbidîn** at the end of the chapter on prayer times that when there is a haraj, imitating one of the other three Madhhabs does not depend on the condition that there should also exist a darûrat. As a matter of fact, as we have noted above, it is not a darûrat to have your tooth crowned or filled on account of an ache or decay. Therefore, we should not look on those Muslims who had their teeth repaired as dirty people; nor should we harbour a suspicion about them.

It would be quite wrong to think that the fact that it is mubâh to use gold on the teeth though gold is harâm for men to use otherwise will show that crowning or even tying the teeth is a darûrat. Though men have been prohibited from using silver utensils, they have been permitted to wear silver rings. As it would be quite wrong to think that wearing a ring is necessary because silver rings have become permissible or to think it is necessary to use gold or silver noses and ears because it is permissible to use them, likewise it would be wrong, slanderous and sinful to say that Islamic scholars agreed on the fact that crowning the teeth was necessary[1].

As the last and most irrefutable proof, we shall inform you that this faqîr[2] has the original copy of the (Turkish) **Booklet of Namâz** which the profound scholar Sayyid Abdulhakîm Arwasî 'rahmatullâhi ta'âlâ 'alaih', who was an expert in the four Madhhabs along with their subtle particulars, wrote with his blessed hand. He states in the booklet: "In the Shâfi'î Madhhab a ghusl has two fards. The first one is intention. That is, one must think, 'I intend to make a ghusl in order to purify myself of janâbat,' as water first touches each limb, i.e. the hands, the face, etc. In other words, it is to keep this intention in one's heart while washing each limb. This intention is not compulsory in the Hanafî Madhhab. The second fard is to wash the whole body with water. It is also fard to remove all najâsat, if there is any, from the body. It is not fard in the Shâfi'î Madhhab to wash inside the mouth and nose, that is, to make water reach these parts. But in the Hanafî Madhhab, it is fard to make water reach these parts. For this reason, those who are in the Hanafî Madhhab cannot crown or fill their teeth because in that case water will not reach these parts. Those who have already crowned or filled their teeth will have to imitate the Shâfi'î Maddhab."

[It is stated in **Al-muqaddamat-ul-izziyya**: "In the Mâlikî Madhhab, if some najâsat falls into clean water in a container, and yet if it has not changed one of the three properties (colour, smell, and taste) of the water, it is sahîh to use it for ablution or ghusl, yet it is makrûh. So is the case with mâ-i musta'mal (water used for ghusl or ablution). One should enter a toilet taking the first step with one's left foot and with something covering one's head. Urine and excrement of animals with edible flesh are clean. The carcass[3], bones, nails, horns, skins of these animals,

---

[1] For the sake of fluency and simplicity in the delivery of our argument, we have used the word 'necessity' for the technical word 'darûrat', which in turn is explained at various places in the text.

[2] The blessed Islamic scholar, Husayn Hilmi bin Sa'îd Işık 'quddisa sirruh', means himself.

[3] What is meant by the word 'carcass' is 'lesh' (or lash), which means an edible animal that has not been killed in a manner dictated by Islam.

(i.e. those that are from that carcass,) as well as a human corpse, semen, mazî, alcoholic drinks are all najs (dirty, foul). Namâz on a thick cloth laid on a najs place or when you are smeared with blood or pus covering an area smaller than a palm, is sahîh (valid)[1]. It is fard to make a niyyat before beginning a ghusl, to make **dalk** of the whole body [to rub gently with the palm of your hand or with a towel], to observe the **muwâlât** [to wash the limbs one immediately after another], to make **khilâl** of the hair and beard (to comb them with your fingers), to undo the tightly plaited hair and to make khilâl of it thoroughly. It is sunnat to wash inside your mouth, nostrils and ears, and to wash your hair. If you remember later that you forgot to wash a certain part on your body, be it a month later, you wash that part immediately. If you do not wash it immediately, your ghusl becomes null and void. An ablution is made before or after each ghusl.

"Also, it is fard (farz) to make a niyyat before beginning an ablution or when washing the face, to make masah on the entire head, on the hanging parts of the hair, on the beard when it is so scarce that the skin under it can be seen, to wash the beard that is thick, to observe muwâlât, that is, to wash the limbs one immediately after the other, and to make dalk on the limbs washed before they dry. It is unnecessary to undo plaited hair. It nullifies the ablution to touch one's penis with one's palm or with the inner parts of the fingers, to doubt whether one has made an ablution or whether one's ablution has broken, to touch a boy's or a nâ-mahram young woman's skin or hair with lust. [If one touches them without having a sexual appetite and does not feel any lust when one touches, one's ablution will not be broken. Muslims who are in the Shâfi'î Madhhab and who live in a mixed society, so that touching women is inevitable during their daily life, such as while walking, commuting, shopping, ought to imitate one of the Hanafî and Mâlikî Madhhabs.] Bleeding or other exudations from the body will not break an ablution. A masah is made on the inner and outer parts of the ears with newly moistened fingers. Cutting one's nails or having a haircut will not break one's ablution. There are disagreements on whether cutting or shaving one's beard will

---

[1] According to a second authentic report in the Mâlikî Madhhab, najâsat, regardless of its kind and amount, is not a hindrance to namâz. It is sunnat, not fard, to wash it off.

break one's ablution. Manual istibrâ[1] is wâjib. Masah made on the mests put on after making a tayammum is not acceptable. There is not a limit for the duration within which masah is permissible. The time for late afternoon prayer lasts until the time called isfirâr. (Please see chapter 10, which deals with prayer times, for time of isfirâr.) The latest time for the night prayer is the (end of the) first one-third of the night. It is necessary for a person staying in Mekka to turn towards the Ka'ba and for a person outside of Mekka to turn to the direction of Ka'ba. It is fard to say 'Allâhu ekber' when starting to perform namâz, to recite the Fâtiha (while standing in namâz), to stand upright at qawma (after a rukû'), to sit upright at jalsa (between the two sajdas), to make the salâm to one side in the sitting posture, and to say 'As-salâmu 'alaikum' when making the salâm. It is a sunnat to recite the zamm-i-sûra in the first two rak'ats, to sit in the two tashahhuds (sitting postures), to recite the tahiyyat and salawât, and to make the second salâm. It is mustahab to silently recite the (prayers termed) Qunût in the second rak'at of morning prayer, and to raise the pointing finger during the tashahhud (sitting posture)[2]. When something which is sunnat (to do or say during namâz) is forgotten, it is necessary to make sajda-i-sahw. It is sunnat to perform the namâz of 'Iyd and the namâz of janâza. A fâsiq[3] cannot be an imâm. It is permissible to follow an imâm who is in another Madhhab or who has an excuse ('udhr).

"The distance of safar in the Mâlikî Madhhab is the same as it is in the Shâfi'î Madhhab; that is, it is eighty kilometres. In a safar (journey) that is not sinful, it is sunnat to perform two rak'ats of those farz prayers that have four rak'ats. One becomes muqîm

---

[1] Lexical meaning of 'istibrâ' is 'to exert yourself, to free yourself from something disagreeable or impure'. In the Islamic branch of Fiqh, it means 'after urination, to make sure that there is no urine left in the urethra lest it should drop into your pants afterwards and dirty them and break your ablution'. Istibrâ is done by gently squeezing urine drops out of the penis (manual istibrâ), by walking up and down for a while (about twenty minutes), or by lying on your left-hand side for a while. Istibrâ has yet another meaning in the branch of Fiqh, used in matters pertaining to conjugal relationships. It is extraneous to the subject being dealt with.

[2] Please see the thirteenth chapter of the third fascicle of **Endless Bliss**.

[3] Fâsiq means a Muslim who commits sins habitually and frankly. Please see the tenth chapter for a more detailed definition.

(settled) at a place where one intends to stay for four days. It is makrûh for a musâfir and a muqîm to be an imâm for each other. Those Hanafîs who imitate the Mâlikî Madhhab, can be an imâm for one another whether they are muqîm or musâfir. It is better not to make jem' of the two prayers of namâz, (i.e. not to perform them one right after the other within the time allotted for either one of them)[1]. It is sunnat to say the Takbîr-i-teshrîk[2] after the Witr prayer and after the farz of each of the fifteen prayers of namâz during the Bayram ('Iyd)." To imitate another Madhhab while performing a certain act of worship does not mean to leave your own Madhhab. It means to observe the fards and mufsids in that Madhhab, (i.e. to obey the rules that the second Madhhab you are to imitate has established concerning that act of worship and to avoid doing whatsoever the second Madhhab has pronounced to be detrimental to that act of worship.) In wâjibs, makrûhs, and sunnats, you follow your own Madhhab. Suppose a Hanafî Muslim imitating the Mâlikî Madhhab makes a long-distance journey[3] with the intention of spending four days at his destination (and he stays there for four days). He performs all four rak'ats of those fard prayers, (the fard parts of early and late afternoon prayers and that of night prayer,) which consist of four rak'ats, since it is fard to do so (in the Mâlikî Madhhab, which he has been imitating, when his sojourn exceeds three days). Because it is makrûh in the Mâlikî Madhhab, and sunnat in the Hanafî Madhhab, for a musâfir, (i.e. Muslim making a long-distance journey,) to perform a namâz in jamâ'at conducted by an imâm who is muqîm, (i.e. who is not a musâfir,) or to conduct, as the imâm, a namâz in jamâ'at joined by Muslims who are muqîm, in either case he may follow his own Madhhab and perform the so-called prayer (in jamâ'at). Performing a certain act of worship by imitating one of the other three Madhhabs is conditional on there being a haraj (difficulty, predicament) in your own Madhhab. Such imitation is not allowable in the absence of a difficulty.]

It is not taqwâ for those who have had their teeth crowned or

---

[1] This statement does not mean that they must not be performed at all. It means that it is better to perform each prayer in its prescribed time.

[2] To say, "Allâhu ekber, Allâhu ekber, lâ ilâha il-l-Allâhu wallâhu ekber, Allâhu ekber wali-llâh il hamd." Please see chapter 22.

[3] Please see chapter 10 for the definition of 'making jem' of two prayers.

filled to imitate the Mâlikî or Shâfi'î Madhhab in ghusl, in ablution, and in namâz. Imitating another Madhhab is a way of fatwâ, a method to surmount a difficulty. The statement, "Islam is a religion of conveniences, not difficulties," has been distorted, by some (false Muslims called) zindiqs, so as to exploit it as a weapon to sabotage the performance of acts of worship that are fard and thereby to decriminalize their own reluctance to perform them. The true meaning of this statement is: It is easy to do all the commandments of Allâhu ta'âlâ; He has not commanded anything difficult. Contrary to what those with weak îmân say, it does not mean that Allâhu ta'âlâ will forgive the things that come difficult to the nafs or that everybody must do what comes easy to him or that He is so compassionate that He will accept anything. Imitating one of the Shâfi'î and Mâlikî Madhhabs in order to resolve a difficulty that you have run into for the sake of your teeth is not a difficulty; it is a convenience.

Calcifications called tartar are formed spontaneously by glandular emissions around the roots of the teeth, and as yet no medication has been found to prevent this unpleasant situation; hence a darûrat comes into play. In all four Madhhabs, it is not necessary to wash under the tartar that is impossible or hard to remove because it is considered similar to a boil on the skin, or a crust or pellicle formed on a wound. There is no need to imitate another Madhhab.

They say, "The problem of crowning and filling the teeth has been solved, the fatwâ has been given that they are permissible. It has been stated that they are not harmful." They have been giving the name fatwâ to subversive propaganda which those politicians and turban-wearing freemasons who had infiltrated into the religious sphere and interfered with the religious matters during the Party of Union spread in order to slander great religious scholars and to defile religious knowledge. The fatwâ book entitled **Majmû'a-i jadîda** writes in its second edition, which was printed in Istanbul in 1329 A.H. [1911]: "If while making a ghusl water does not reach a tooth cavity of a person whose tooth cavity has been filled, and if a ghusl is a darûrat in this manner, the ghusl becomes accepted." It adds that this fatwâ was given by Hasan Khayrullah Efendi, the 113th Shaikh-ul-Islâm. But the fatwâ does not exist in the first edition [in 1299] of the book. And Khayrullah Efendi, in his turn, became Shaikh-ul-Islâm for the second time on 18 Rabî-ul-awwal 1293, coinciding with May 11, 1876, and retired on Rajab 15, 1294, which coincided with December 26,

1877. If he had given the so-called fatwâ, it would have existed in the first edition of the book. It is written in the preface of the second edition: "Commanded by the time's Shaikh-ul-Islâm, Mûsâ Kâzım, we have added several fatwâs that are not in the first edition." Although the name of the fiqh book from which each fatwâ is derived, together with what it states, is appended to the fatwâ, no such references are given with the abovementioned fatwâ alleged to have been given on teeth. We must be vigilant lest our true knowledge of Islamic credal and practical systems should be undermined; otherwise we will not know enough to regret our having so gullibly believed such parvenus, their articles and false fatwâs, which they have prepared insidiously in order to mislead Muslims.

We are not trying to say that the ghusl and the namâz of those who have had their teeth crowned or filled will not be sahîh. We are trying to say that by imitating the Mâlikî or Shâfi'î Madhhab the ghusl and the namâz of some Hanafî Muslims will be sahîh even though they may have had their teeth crowned or filled. We are trying to show the easy way, the right way to our brothers in Islam who are in this situation. We do not say you should not crown or fill your teeth. We do not advise you not to perform namâz behind an imâm who has crowns or fillings, either. See also Chapter 23. We are informing Muslims who have crowns and fillings of the convenience taught by Islamic scholars. All these meticulous details we have gone into are intended for the sake of Muslims who are in the Hanafî Madhhab and who want to worship as prescribed by their Madhhab; that is, for those who esteem the Madhhabs highly. We do not write for those who slight the books of the Madhhabs and who want to worship according to their own minds, opinions and thoughts. Ibni 'Âbidîn 'rahmatullâhi 'alaih', while explaining Ramadân's crescent, states: "Many of the ahkâm change with changing times (conditions). When there is haraj, daîf riwâyat is acted upon." It is understood from this (statement) that the changing of ahkâm (rules of Islam) with time means that when one is in a difficult situation one can act upon the **non-mashhûr** (not widely known) ijtihâds of the scholars of one's Madhhab. It does not mean that everyone should do what comes easy for them. It is written on the hundred and ninetieth page of the third volume of **Durr-ul-mukhtâr**: "A person who goes out of his Madhhab is to be punished with **ta'zîr**; that is, he is thrashed and imprisoned." The

Fatwâ of Sirâjiyya states the same. Ibni 'Âbidîn writes on this subject: "It is feared that a person who abandons his Madhhab for worldly advantages may die without îmân."

For those who have had their teeth crowned or filled to imitate the Shâfi'î or Mâliki Madhhab does not mean to leave the Hanafî Madhhab or to change their Madhhab. They obey the conditions and mufsids in the Shâfi'î or Mâliki Madhhab along with the Hanafî Madhhab only in ghusl, ablution, and namâz. It is stated in the chapter about ablution in Ibni 'Âbidîn and in the two hundred and eighty-sixth letter of Imâm-i-Rabbânî's **Maktûbât** that it is mustahab for those who do not have an excuse to observe the fards and mufsids of another Madhhab. A Hanafî Muslim cannot do something impermissible in the Hanafî Madhhab on the grounds that it is permissible in one of the Shâfi'î or Mâlikî Madhhabs, without a darûrat and a haraj to compel him to do so. For example, a healthy person, or someone who is in the Hanafî Madhhab and is imitating the Mâlikî Madhhab because he has a crowned tooth, has to renew his ablution in case of a bleeding on his skin or if he discharges (even a drop of) urine. He performs the namâz of Witr as wâjib. He cannot be considered a musâfir at a place less than 104 kilometres away, and he cannot make jem' of his prayers at a place where he will be a musâfir for less than four days. On the other hand, a Hanafî Muslim who suffers from involuntary urination (enuresis) because of illness or old age, that is, as a result of a darûrat, is up against a haraj, a difficulty because he has to renew his ablution (each time he discharges urine); therefore he begins to imitate the Mâlikî Madhhab, which in turn will immediately make him a person with an 'udhr and save him from the state of having lost his ablution. (See the last part of the ninth chapter.) Ibni Emir Hajj, who explained the book **Tahrîr**, says, "The forty-third âyat of Nahl sûra and the seventh âyat of Anbiyâ sûra declare: '**Ask men of dhikr**,' which means: When you encounter an event ask those who know what you are to do. This âyat-i kerîma shows that it is wâjib to follow a mujtahid and to imitate another Madhhab. If, while doing something in accordance with the Madhhab you have been following, a haraj arises, this thing must be done by imitating one of the other three Madhhabs, and of course, the one in which the same haraj does not exist. An example of this is a Hanafî Muslim's imitating the Shâfi'î or the Mâlikî Madhhab because he has a filled or crowned tooth. If the same haraj exists in all the other three Madhhabs as well, the next step is to see if there is a darûrat. If there is a darûrat as well, it will be permissible not to do that thing at all. For instance, since it is impossible to imitate another Madhhab in a case such as when it would be harmful to take off the bandage on a wound and wash the wound, one will be absolved from having to wash the wound and it will be permissible to make masah on the bandage (when making an ablution or a ghusl). It is not permissible for us who are not mujtahids but muqallids to interpret âyats and hadîths and act upon our own understanding by saying that the Sahâba did so." When beginning to explain the tahârat, Ibni 'Âbidîn states: "It is not necessary for a muqallid to inquire about the proof-texts and documents for the information coming from a mujtahid."] [See Endless Bliss II, Chapter 34].

5 – TAYAMMUM

Tayammum before the beginning of a prayer time is sahîh in the Hanafî Madhhab, (which means that the new prayer can be performed, when its time begins, with a tayammum that you made before its beginning.) According to the other three Madhhabs, it is not sahîh before the beginning of a prayer time, (so that you cannot perform one of the five daily prayers with the tayammum you make before its prescribed time begins. Incidentally, 'tayammum' means a 'simple procedure that you follow as a substitute for an ablution and which is permissible in want of water'.

There are seven kinds of being unable to find water, or, to use it, to make an ablution or ghusl:

1 - He who is one mile away from a source of water makes a tayammum, provided he should make an intention (niyyat). One mile is equal to four thousand zrâ', which equals 1920 metres. It is always fard to look for water when you are in a city.

2 - If a Muslim is unwell and knows, from his personal experiences or upon the advice of a specialist doctor known to be a Muslim who does not openly and publicly commit sins, that making an ablution or ghusl or moving would exacerbate or prolong his illness, then he is accredited to make a tayammum. Also among 'udhrs (excuses that make a tayammum permissible) is the enervation felt on the hands and feet during the period of convalescence. [So is the case with the feebleness felt at old age. Such people (are permitted to) perform the daily prayers sitting.]

3 - If a person is too ill to make a ghusl or ablution or cannot find anybody to help him even for money, he will make a

tayammum. He who cannot make a tayammum even with help does not perform the namâz, but he performs it, (i.e. makes qadâ of it,) when he recovers. It is not wâjib for a husband and wife to help each other to make an ablution.

4 - If there is the danger that a person would die or become ill because of cold in case he made a ghusl, and/or if he does not have enough money to go to a bath and has no other alternative, even if he is in a city, he makes a tayammum instead of a ghusl and makes an ablution with water.

5 - If water is close but there is an enemy, a wild or poisonous animal, a fire or a guard near the water, or if he is imprisoned, or if someone threatens him with death or would take away his belongings as he made an ablution, he makes a tayammum instead and performs the namâz. But since these are caused by creatures, he has to perform his namâz again after he makes a ghusl and ablution.

6 - If a traveller has extra water which he and his comrades need to drink, to clean themselves of najâsat or to give to their animals, he makes a tayammum. If he drains the water making a ghusl and then has to perform the namâz with najâsat on himself, it will be accepted, but he will be sinful. If he first makes a tayammum and then removes the najâsat, he will have to make a tayammum again. For one cannot make tayammum while there is water. If a person who is junub finds water enough to wash his body partly or to make an ablution, he makes one tayammum for both ablution and ghusl. If his ablution breaks after the tayammum, he makes an ablution with the water. When the water poured on the body in an ablution or a ghusl falls down somewhere [not on one's clothes], it becomes foul and one cannot drink it. But it can be given to animals to drink. A person who is about to die from thirst buys water from someone who has extra water. If the latter will not sell it, the former takes it by force, by fighting or threatening. Water to be used for an ablution cannot be taken by force.

7 - If a person cannot find a bucket or a rope to lift water out of a well, or a person to go down the well for money, he makes a tayammum, and does not have to perform his namâz again when he finds water.

Halabî writes at the end of the subject concerning masah: "If a person has chaps, eczema or some other wound on one or both of his hands so that it is harmful to moisten them, he cannot make an ablution. According to Imâm-i a'zam, it is mustahab for someone else to help for friendship's sake or for money a person to make an ablution who cannot make an ablution for the reason mentioned above. If he makes a tayammum and performs the namâz without asking someone else for help, his namâz will be accepted. If he cannot get help or find money, it is permissible for him to make a tayammum according to the Imâmayn, too." Hence, it is necessary for him to make an ablution by wearing, if he can, a glove on his wounded hands.

In case one makes a tayammum for one of the reasons written above, the tayammum expires when the reason ceases to exist. If another reason arises before the first reason ceases to exist, the first tayammum again expires when the first reason ceases to exist. One has to make a tayammum again.

A person without an ablution or ghusl can make a tayammum even when there is water lest he will miss the prayer of Bayram ('Iyd) or janâza. If there is the fear that he may miss Friday prayer or any of the five daily prayers, he cannot make a tayammum when there is water. Ghusl and/or ablution is necessary. If the time of prayer is over he performs it later. For example, a person wakes up and sees that he or she is junub, or that her menstrual or puerperal period is over, and sunrise is close at hand, he or she makes a ghusl hastily. If the sun rises in the meantime, they perform their morning prayer together with its sunnat after the karâhat time is over. (Times of Karâhat are explained in the final part of the tenth chapter.) **Tayammum** means to purpose something.

Tayammum has three fards:

1 - To intend to purify oneself from janâbat or from the state of being without an ablution. If a person without an ablution makes a tayammum in order to teach his disciple, he cannot perform namâz with it.

Intending solely for tayammum will not make the tayammum adequate for performing the namâz with it. It is also necessary to intend also to do something which is an 'ibâdet (worship); e.g. to intend to make a tayammum in order to perform janâza namâz, to make sajda-i tilâwat, or to intend only to make a tayammum as a substitute for an ablution or a ghusl.

When intending for a tayammum it is not necessary to separate ablution and ghusl from each other. By intending (to make a tayammum) for an ablution, one becomes purified from janâbat, too. One can perform namâz with the tayammum one has made in order to be purified from janâbat. A second tayammum for an ablution is unnecessary.

2 - It is stated as follows in the book **Manâhij-ul-'ibâd**, (by Sa'îda-d-dîn Ferghânî 'rahmatullâhi 'alaih': "According to the Shâfi'î and Hanbalî Madhhabs, a tayammum can be made only on soil. (For making a tayammum compatible) according to the Hanafî and Mâlikî Madhhabs, both sleeves should be rolled up to above the elbows and the two palms, with the fingers opened, should be rubbed and moved up and down on clean soil, stone or on a wall plastered with clay or lime. Then one must make masah on the face with both palms once, that is, rub them on the face gently in such a manner as an area at least as large as the sum of three fingers on each palm should contact the face."

[To make a perfect masah on the face, the two open-hand palms, with four fingers of each hand closed together and with the tips of the two long fingers of both hands touching each other, are put on the forehead in such a way as they should abut on the hairline, and moved slowly down towards the chin. The fingers, in a level line, must be rubbed on the forehead, on the eye-lids, on both sides of the nose, on the lips, and on the facial part of the chin. Meanwhile the palms will be rubbed on the cheeks.]

3 - After putting both hands on the soil for a second time and clapping the hands so as to shake the surplus dust and soil off, first rub the inner parts of the four fingers of the left hand on the outer face of the right arm from the tip of the fingers to the elbow, then rub the left palm on the inner face of the right arm from the elbow down to the palm; in the meantime the inner part of the left thumb should be rubbed on the outer part of the right thumb. According to an authentic report (riwâya), it is unnecessary to remove the ring you may be wearing or to make masah on the sides of the fingers of each hand with the inner parts of the fingers of the other hand. Then rub the right hand likewise on the left arm. The palms must be rubbed on the soil, but the dust and soil need not be left on the hands. The tayammum will not be sahîh in case any area as large as the point of a pin on your face or arms is left untouched by your palms.

The Tayammum for an ablution and for a ghusl is the same.

A Tayammum has twelve sunnats:

1 - To put the palms on the soil.

2 - To move the palms back and forth on the soil.

3 - If there is soil left on the palms, to clap the hands together

with the thumbs until there is no soil left.

4 - To open the fingers while putting the hands on the soil.

5 - To start in the Basmala (in the name of Allâhu ta'âlâ).

6 - To make masah first on the face, then on the arms.

7 - To perform it in the quick manner of an ablution.

8 - If a person on a long-distance journey termed safar (, i.e. a musâfir,) knows that there is water within a mile, it is fard for him to look for it; if he is only estimating, it is sunnat to do so.

9 - To make masah first on the right, then on the left arm.

10 - To put the hands on the soil strongly as if you were hitting it.

11 - To make masah on the arms as described above.

12 - To make masah between the fingers.

A person who does not have water is permitted to become junub.

Tayammum can be made with any sort of clean earthen thing even if there is no dust on it.

Things that burn and turn into ashes or that can be melted by heat are not earthen. Therefore, tayammum cannot be made with trees, grass, wood, iron, brass, painted walls, copper, gold or glass. It can be made with sand. It cannot be made with pearls or corals. It can be made with lime, plaster of Paris, washed marble, cement, unglazed faience, porcelain, earthenware pans, or mud. If there is mud only, tayammum can be made with it, if the water in it is less than fifty percent. If the water is more than fifty percent, a piece of cloth must be soaked with it, dried against the wind, and then tayammum can be made with the dusty cloth. Tayammum cannot be made with muddy water. An ablution should be made with it. A tayammum can be made on a wall whitewashed with lime. When you put your hands on things with which a tayammum is not permissible, such as wheat, tissue, clothes, cushions; if your hands become dusty with the dust or ashes (that should have come) from things with which a tayammum is permissible, or if the dust or ashes fly about in the air when such things, (i.e. the aforesaid things that cannot be used for tayammum,) are shaken, a tayammum can be made with them. The case is not so with the organic dusts resting on household things. Several people can make a tayammum on the same soil. For, soil and the like do not become musta'mal when they are used for tayammum. The dust that falls from the hands and face after a tayammum is musta'mal.

When something is the mixture of something that can be used for tayammum and something which cannot, it will be named after the component that is more than half. In the Hanafî Madhhab, it is permissible to make a tayammum before any prayer time and to perform various prayers with one tayammum. In the other three Madhhabs, a tayammum becomes void when the prayer time is over. When a musâfir (traveller) strongly believes through certain indications, or after being informed by a Muslim who is 'âdil[1] and has reached the age of discretion and puberty, that he will find water at a distance less than a mile [1920 metres], less than two miles in the Mâlikî Madhhab, it is fard for him to look for water by walking or sending somebody for one hundred zrâ' [two hundred metres] in each direction, or if feasible, by only looking. If he does not have a strong expectation, he does not have to look for water. If a person who has an 'âdil friend with him makes a tayammum without asking about water and starts to perform the namâz and then is told that there is water, he makes an ablution and performs the namâz again. It is permissible to perform the namâz with a tayammum while water is more than a mile away. A person who forgets that there is water among his provisions can perform the namâz with a tayammum if he is not in a city, a village [or in any inhabited place]. If a person who thinks his water has run out finds that he does have water after the namâz, he performs the namâz again which he performed with a tayammum. Likewise, when a person who (thinks that he has an ablution although he does not and thereby) performs a namâz without an ablution remembers afterwards that he did not have an ablution (when he performed that namâz), he performs the namâz again.

It is wâjib for a musâfir, (i.e. a Muslim on a long-distance journey,) to ask for water from their company. If they decline to give him water, he performs namâz with a tayammum. In case a musâfir's friend sells water for its current price, the musâfir has to buy it if he has the extra money to do so. If its owner sells it by **ghaban-i fâhish**, that is, by heavy overcharge (exorbitant price), or if the musâfir does not have the money to buy it for its current price, he is permitted to perform the namâz with a tayammum. **Ghaban-i fâhish** means more than twice its current market value. So is the case with a naked person buying some cloth to cover his

---

[1] The term ''âdil Muslim', along with its antonym, 'fâsiq Muslim', is defined by way of a footnote in the tenth chapter.

awrat parts. But a thirsty person is permitted to buy high priced water to drink. In a desert, one must ask for a rope and a bucket from one's comrade. One can make a tayammum while there is water placed on the way especially for drinking. Ibni 'Âbidîn 'rahmatullâhi ta'âlâ 'alaih' writes in the fifth volume: "It is not permissible to make an ablution with the water set aside for drinking. One should make a tayammum."

If there is little free [mubâh] water, a person who is junub takes priority over a woman whose menstrual period has newly ended, over a person without an ablution, over a dead Muslim, in the utilization of the water for the performance of washing, (which is compulsory in all four cases.) The owner of the water has priority over others. When amounts of water belonging to different owners are brought together, the corpse of a dead Muslim must be washed first.

The way for a hadji [Muslim pilgrim] to avoid using up the zamzam water he has with him for ablution is to change its name from pure water by flavouring it with an additive such as sugar or roses. Or he must give it to a person whom he trusts as a present that cannot be returned. If the person given the present gives a small present in response, the former owner cannot demand his present back.

If a person who is junub makes a tayammum and then loses his ablution, he does not become junub in the Hanafî Madhhab, but he becomes junub in the Mâlikî Madhhab. If there is little water he makes an ablution only.

When water more than is needed for drinking, washing off najâsat, and making bread is found, the tayammum becomes annulled. If one finds it while performing namâz, one's namâz becomes annulled, too. If one passes by the water while sleeping in a vehicle, one's ablution by way of a tayammum becomes annulled because one has slept. If one cannot get off the vehicle to make an ablution though one has been awake, the tayammum does not become annulled.

If more than half of the surface of a junub person's body has a disease, such as a wound, small-pox or scarlet fever, he makes a tayammum. If a major part of his skin is healthy and if it is possible to wash himself without moistening the diseased parts, he makes a ghusl with water and makes masah on the diseased parts. If masah would cause harm, he puts one or several pieces of cloth on the diseased parts and makes masah on them. A person whose hands are diseased puts his feet and face into water. If he cannot do this he makes a tayammum. A sick person who can get help from someone in order to make an ablution does not make a tayammum. If a person cannot prostrate himself or raise his head after prostration on account of old age or illness, he does so by leaning on something such as a chair. Or, (if possible,) someone helps him to manage these actions. If it is impossible for him to wash without moistening the wounded parts, in that case also he makes a tayammum. If more than half of his limbs of ablution or two of his four limbs of ablution are healthy, he makes an ablution and applies masah on the wounded parts or limbs. If direct masah would be harmful, he makes masah on the bandages (that he has put on the wounds). If more than half of all his limbs of ablution or three or all four of his limbs of ablution are wounded, he makes a tayammum. If a tayammum would cause harm he does not have to perform the prayer. If the amount or number of the healthy parts or limbs is equal to that of the wounded ones, he must not make a tayammum. It is not permissible for a person who makes a tayammum to wash some of his limbs. There are thirty-four such things that cannot be done at the same time. Although there is an authentic report in which some Islamic scholars are quoted to have stated, "He who has such a headache that he cannot make masah on his head can make a tayammum in place of an ablution, and he who cannot wash his head can make a tayammum in place of a ghusl," this statement must not be acted upon, since the matter had already been solved by way of a fatwâ that had been issued before the statement quoted above was made, and thereby the conclusive answer to the question had been given: "In both cases the obligation concerning the head, (i.e. applying masah on it when making an ablution and washing it when making a ghusl,) is no longer an obligation."

Think of the endless world, do not adore a shadow,
Read the Sunnite book, do not be obstinate,
Wake up as you can, do not miss the chance,
Do not form habits that will burn eternally.
Be mustaqîm, hadrat Allah will not embarrass thee!
Seeing this unawareness, the devil will mock thee,
Come to yourself, my dear, do not let the accursed ape thee.
Do not be mundane, give up pomp and fame,
Beautiful morals is what most becomes to thee.
Be mustaqîm, hadrat Allah will not embarrass thee!

6 – TAHÂRAT FROM NAJÂSAT

Ibni Âbidîn writes at the beginning of the chapter on **Essentials for Salât (namâz)**: "There must be no najâsat or impurity on the body, on the clothes of a person making salât (prayer) or on the place where he prays. A kerchief, a headgear, a skull-cap, a turban, mests and nalins (clogs) are to be considered clothings. Since the hanging part of a scarf wrapped around one's neck moves as one moves when performing namâz, it is included with the clothes, and the namâz will not be accepted if this part of the cloth is unclean. When those parts where one steps and puts one's head on the cloth spread on the ground are clean, the namâz will be accepted even if there is najâsat on its other parts. For, the cloth, unlike the scarf, is not attached to the body. A child with clothing smeared with **najâsat**, a cat, a bird, or a dog salivating from its mouth does not nullify one's namâz when they sit on one's lap. For, they stay there themselves. But if one holds them on one's lap, shoulder or so on, one has carried them, and this nullifies one's namâz. One's namâz is not nullified by holding a wild animal that does not produce saliva, a clean animal such as a cat, or a child on one's lap, if their outer parts are clean. For, the najâsat in them is contained where it is produced. Likewise, the najâsat and blood of a person who is performing namâz are contained wherein they are produced. So is the case with carrying blooded eggs in one's pocket. Because the blood in the eggs is encased where it is produced, it does not nullify one's namâz. But the namâz of a person carrying urine in a closed bottle is not accepted. For, the bottle is not the place where the urine is produced. This is also written in **Halabî-yi Kebîr**. [Hence it is not permissible to perform namâz while one has a closed bottle of blood or tincture of iodine or a closed box containing a bloody handkerchief or a piece of cloth smeared with najâsat equaling more than a dirham in one's pocket.] The places where one's two feet step and where one puts one's head must be clean. Even if the piece of cloth on which one prostrates oneself is small, the namâz will be accepted even if its other parts are foul. Namâz performed on cloth, glassware [or nylon] spread or put on najâsat is accepted. It is not deleterious to namâz if the hanging ends of one's garment touch some dry najâsat when prostrating. If one raises one of one's feet because there is najâsat under it and performs the namâz on one foot, the namâz will be accepted if the place where one stands is clean. There are many Islamic scholars who say that the places where the hands and knees are put need not be clean. If one prostrates on one's hand, the place where one puts one's hand must be clean."

Any solid najâsat on one's skin or clothes and fluid najâsat such as urine and blood, even if it is on the mests, can be cleaned only by washing. Soil smeared with some fluid najâsat, such as blood, wine [alcoholic liquids], urine, is equated with solid najâsat. When solid najâsat is on a belt, a bag, mests or shoes, it can be cleaned by crumbling, wiping.

Solid or fluid, any najâsat on things not absorbent, but smooth and shining, such as glass, mirrors, bones, nails, knives, painted or varnished furniture, becomes clean when it is rubbed with the hands, soil or anything clean until it loses three peculiarities (colour, odour, taste). When a bloody knife or a sheep's head is held over a fire until the blood disappears, it becomes clean. When any soil on which some najâsat has fallen is dried by the wind and loses its three peculiarities, it becomes pure and one can perform namâz on it. But it cannot be used for tayammum. If any cloth, mat, clothes or one's skin were on the soil, these will not become clean when they dry. When these are smeared with najâsat, they must be washed before the namâz. Bricks, faience paved on the ground, grass, trees growing in soil, rocks, like soil, become pure when they dry up.

When dried semen is rubbed off its place the skin becomes clean. If the semen is wet, or if it is blood, whether wet or dry, the clothes or the skin (on which it is) must be washed. Depending upon the kind of the najâsat and the place smeared with it, there are over thirty different ways of cleaning.

When soap is made from oil mixed with najâsat or from the oil of a carrion, a foul animal or a pig, it becomes clean. So is the case with all chemical changes. Bread can be baked in an oven that was made with foul water. Things made from najs [foul] earth, such as jugs and jars, become clean when they are taken out of the furnace.

If the qaba najâsat is not so much as one **dirham** or more on one's skin or clothes or on the place where one performs namâz, the namâz performed thereby will be accepted. However, if there is as much as a dirham it is tahrîmî makrûh and it is wâjib to wash it off. If it is more than a dirham it is fard to wash it off. If it is less than a dirham it is sunnat to wash it off. Some scholars say that it is fard to wash out even a drop of wine. According to the other three Madhhabs, it is fard to wash out even a mote of any qaba najâsat completely. [In the Mâlikî Madhhab, according to a second authentic report, najâsat is not a hindrance to the performance of

– 88 –

namâz. Cleaning it is sunnat. It is written in **al-Ma'fuwât** that najâsat left after istinja is allowable in the Shâfi'î Madhhab.] The aforesaid criteria pertaining to the amounts of najâsat are to be applied as of when a person is to perform a namâz, not when he is smeared with the najâsat.

A **dirham** is a weight of one mithqal, that is, twenty qirat, that is, four grams and eighty centigrams, of solid najâsat. With fluid najâsat it is an area as large as the surface of the water in the palm of one's open hand. When solid najâsat less than one mithqal is spread over an area larger than the palm of a hand on one's clothes, it does not nullify the namâz.

THERE ARE TWO KINDS OF NAJÂSAT: 1- Qaba (ghalîz) najâsat: All things that necessitate an ablution or ghusl when they exude from the human body, flayed but not tanned skin, flesh, excrement and urine of those animals whose flesh cannot be eaten [except a bat] and of their young; excrement, urine and a mouthful of vomited matter of a sucking baby; blood of man and of all animals; wine, carrion, pork, excrement of domestic fowls, excrement of pack animals and sheep and goats are ghalîz, that is, qaba. Blood is qaba najâsat in all four Madhhabs. Semen, mazy and the turbid white, thick liquid called wadî that issues after urination are qaba najâsat in the Hanafî and Mâlikî Madhhabs. Only semen is clean in the Shafi'î Madhhab, and all three of them are clean in the Hanbalî Madhhab.

A cat's urine, only on one's clothes; a martyr's blood, as long as it remains on him; blood that exists in and does not flow out of edible meat, offal, such as livers, hearts and spleens; blood of fish; excrement and blood of lice, fleas and bed-bugs are all clean. In other words, it is said (by scholars) that namâz can be performed even when one is smeared with a great deal of the above. All intoxicant drinks, like wine, are qaba najâsat. The words of those who say that they are khafîf (light) najâsat are daîf (weak). It is written in **Halabî-yi kebîr**, in **Marâq-il-felâh**, and in **Ni'met-i islâm** (in Turkish) that raki [and spirit] are najâsat-i ghalîza.

2 - **Khafîf najâsat:** When one of your limbs or a part of your clothes is smeared with khafîf najâsat, it does not negatively affect your namâz unless it covers more than one-fourth of the limb or the part smeared with it. The urine of edible quadruped animals and the excrement of those birds whose flesh is not edible are khafîf. The excrement of such edible fowls as pigeons and sparrows is clean. Even if a small amount of a mouse's excrement or its urine falls into water or oil, although it has been forgiven, it

will be better to cleanse it. If a small quantity of it gets mixed with wheat and becomes flour, it has been forgiven. With respect to their being cleansed, and their fouling a liquid they have fallen into, (i.e. their making it najs,) there is no difference between qabâ najâsat and khafîf najâsat.

Drops of urine and blood splashing on your clothes equalling the point of a pin, drops of mud and vapours of najâsat splashing on you in the streets, gases coming on you after they have touched some najâsat, wind or steam that is formed in stables and baths, and drops that are formed on walls are all excusable when they touch your clothes or wet skin. Because it is difficult to avoid them, they have been judged to be darûrats. However, liquid obtained from distilled najâsat is najs. For, there is no inevitability (a darûrat) in using it. For this reason, raki and spirit (alcohol) are qaba najâsat and, like wine, it is harâm to drink them. [The fact that raki and spirit are najs and harâm is written in **Merâq-il-felâh** and in its **Tahtâwî** annotation. Hence, when performing namâz, the alcoholic drinks and medicines, such as lotion, spirit and tincture of iodine, which have been used without a darûrat, must be cleansed from one's clothes and skin. Please see chapter 42 in the First Fascicle of Endless Bliss!] Food cooked on a spiritcooker does not become najs.

[It is written at the end of the chapter on **Istinjâ** in **Durr-ul-mukhtâr:** "In a mixture of soil and water, if either of them is clean the mixture, i.e. the mud, becomes clean. The fatwâ is likewise." The same is also written in the fourth rule in **Ashbâh**. Ibni 'Âbidîn, while explaining **Durr-ul-mukhtâr**, writes: "It is written in **Fath-ul-qadîr** that most of the 'ulamâ (scholars) stated so. It is written in **Bezzâziyya** that they gave a fatwâ in compliance with this. Imâm Muhammad Sheybânî said the same. There are also some 'ulamâ who said that the mud becomes najs. According to them, the mixture of clean soil and fertilizer is clean because there is a necessity in it." As it is stated in **Terghîb-us-salât**, [according to some scholars], plaster mixed with dung is considered clean if it is made with clean water and the amount of dung is less than the amount of mud. Please see the sixth paragraph of the section borrowed from Ibni Âbidîn in the nineteenth chapter.

Suppose one of the two substances in a mixture prepared to obviate a necessity is clean and there is a haraj in substituting the najs component of the mixture with a clean equivalent; in this case the mixture is to be judged to be clean in view of the ijtihâd reached by the former group of scholars. Medicines with spirit, eau de cologne, varnish, ink or paint are in this category. It is written in **Al-fiqh-u 'alal-madhâhib-il-erba'a** and in the Kamışlı edition of the annotation by Sulaymân bin 'Abdullâh Si'ridî 'rahmatullâhi ta'âlâ 'alaihimâ' to **al-Ma'fuwât** by mollâ Khalîl Si'ridî, (1368 [1949]), that the najs liquids used as additives to medicines and perfumes are forgiven in the Shâfi'î Madhhab. It is written in both of these books and in Endless Bliss II, chapter 21, that it is permissible to adopt a daîf (weak) report when there is a haraj. Therefore, in case of a predicament, it is permissible for Hanafîs and Shâfi'îs to perform namâz with those mixtures on them in excess amounts. It is written at the end of the chapter about Tawakkul[1] that a medicine considered to be clean cannot be taken without a darûrat.]

An ammonia compound formed from ammonia gas issuing from najâsat is clean. If dust and flies land on some najâsat and then leave it and then land on one's clothes or on water, they do not make them foul.

It is sahîh that the mud that a dog steps on does not become najs. [It is written at the end of the book **al-Hadîqa**: "If a person's clothing is stained with najâsat and he forgets the site of the stain and washes the part he supposes to be stained, his clothing is judged to have been cleaned. If a person walks on a najs surface while his feet are wet, his feet do not get najs on condition that the najs surface is dry; but if the surface is wet and his dry feet get wet, they become najs. If the place where a dog has lain in a mosque is dry, that place is not najs; if it is wet yet no trace of najâsat is seen, it is not najs, either. The thawâb for the namâz performed with shoes on is far more blessed than that performed with bare feet. So is the case with shoes worn outdoors if no najasat is seen on them. One should disignore doubts. Garments, carpets, and similar things bought from a seller of alcoholic drinks are accepted as clean. After making a ghusl in company, the bath cloth becomes clean by pouring water over it three times without taking it off and wringing it out. Tahârat is essential in everything. Unless it is known for certain that something is stained with najâsat, it cannot be considered najs upon supposition. The meat of animals butchered by Ahl al-kitâb in the dâr al-harb is regarded as clean unless otherwise proven. Eating the food with meat prepared by Magicians or disbelievers without a heavenly book is makrûh tanzîhî since it is not known for certain that (the meat in the food

---

[1] Please see the thirty-fifth chapter of the third fascicle of **Endless Bliss**.

is from) the animal (that) was killed by them. So is the case with the meat bought from today's butchers."]

Najâsat can be cleaned out with any clean water, with water that has been used for an ablution or a ghusl or with nonviscous liquids, such as vinegar, rose-water, and saliva. It cannot be cleaned with milk or oil.

Water that has been used for an ablution or a ghusl is called **musta'mal** water. This water is qaba najâsat (najâsat-i-ghalîza) according to Imâm–i a'zam. It is khafîf najâsat according to Abû Yûsuf. And it is clean according to Imâm-i Muhammad 'rahmatullâhi ta'âlâ 'alaihimâ'. The fatwâ conforms with this final report. Najâsat can be cleaned with it. One cannot make another ablution or ghusl with it. This rule applies in the Shâfi'î Madhhab as well. It is makrûh to drink it or to knead dough with it. If it splashes on one's bath-towel, clothes or into the bath basin, or if any water used for cleaning out some najâsat splashes on an area as large as the point of a pin, it does not cause them to be najs [foul]. If water used for cleaning out najâsat forms a small pool somewhere, things smeared with that water become najs. If a person without an ablution or without a ghusl, a menstruating woman, a polytheist, or disbeliever dips his or her hand or arm not smeared with najâsat into any water and takes some water or picks up a bowl in it, the water does not become foul in any of the four Madhhabs. If more than half of the water flowing over some najâsat touches the najâsat, the water becomes najs. If a small quantity of the water touches it and if the three peculiarities of the najâsat do not exist in the water, it does not become najs. When najâsat burns its ashes become clean. Bread can be baked in an oven heated by burning dried dung. If a donkey, pig, or any carrion falls into salt and turns into salt, it becomes clean. If dung falls into a well and turns into mud in process of time, it becomes clean. In the Mâlikî Madhhab, musta'mal water is both clean itself and can (be used to) clean other things. Hence, (according to the Mâlikî Madhhab,) musta'mal water can be used for making an ablution or a ghusl [**Manâhij-ul-'ibâd**].

Grape juice is clean. It becomes najs when it turns into wine. Wine becomes clean when it changes into vinegar. If najâsat splashes on one's clothes or body and if one cannot locate the area smeared with the najâsat, it will become clean if one washes the area that one guesses to be the smeared one. If one discovers the correct area after namâz, one does not perform the namâz again. When a threshing animal urinates on some wheat, if any part of the wheat is washed, given as a present, eaten or sold, the remainder becomes clean.

Likewise, when any dirt or blood noticed after it has dried up is cleaned out in the aforesaid manner till it, as well as its remains, is completely gone, the place where it was found becomes clean. There is not a prescribed number of washings. Once will be enough if it is removed by washing once. If the najâsat is removed, existence of a colour and odour is not harmful. It is unnecessary to use hot or soapy water.

Tissue or body dyed with a najs substance becomes clean when it is washed three times. It is better to wash it until colourless water drops from it. If najâsat, such as some alcoholic medicine, is syringed under the skin, it will become clean when the syringed spot is washed three times. It is not necessary to raise the skin in order to clean under it. If one's flesh is smeared with a najs medicine which one has put on one's skin or on a wound on one's skin, or if one has put najs eyesalve on one's eyes, one does not have to wash one's flesh or eyes. The outer part, as well as the dried blood remaining on any wound, must be washed out so as not to cause any harm. If it will be harmful, it should not be washed. However, a person who has najâsat on himself equalling one dirham cannot be an imâm. One's belongings smeared with invisible najâsats, such as alcohol (spirit) and urine, should be washed in a basin or washing machine with clean water several times until one guesses they have become clean. If they become clean after washing once, it will be enough. The water and other things in the machine will not become najs during the washing. Those who are over-scrupulous and dubious must wash them three times and wring the water out after each washing. It is enough for every person to squeeze as hard as he can. Things that cannot be wrung because they are fragile, thin or big, such as carpets, body, leather that absorbs najâsat, must be dried after each washing. That is, you must wait until the water stops dripping. It is not necessary to dry or squeeze jugs, bowls and copperware that do not absorb najâsat or anything washed in the sea or in a river [or in a wash-basin.]

It is written in **Halabî**: "Najâsat is cleaned out with mutlaq water or with muqayyad water[1] or with any clean liquid. If a baby licks its own vomit on a breast or if a person whose hand has been smeared with blood or wine licks it and then spits it out, both the

---

[1] Please see chapter 7 for kinds of water.

hand and the mouth thereby involved become clean. Clothings will not be clean by licking. They must be washed. Each animal's bile is like its urine. Hairs, bones, nerves, and teeth of a dead human being or an animal, with the exception of swine, are not najs. It is makrûh to have a cat lick your hand. When a person with wet pants on breaks wind, the pants will not become najs. When the skin of a carrion is tanned with a chemical that is not najs, it becomes clean. If it is tanned with a najs chemical, such as the oil of a carrion, it will become clean when it is washed and wrung out three times. When an inedible animal is slaughtered as prescribed by the Sharî'at, only its skin is clean. The skin of a pig, a snake or a human will never become clean. A naked person cannot cover himself with the untanned skin of a carrion. Such a skin cannot be sold. For, it is foul in essence. Not so is the case with fouled tissue. If a mouse falls into solid fat, the fat that has contacted the mouse must be dispensed with. The remaining fat becomes clean. If a mouse falls into fluid oil, all of it becomes najs. When any leather rubbed with najs grease or pig's grease is washed, it becomes clean.

"Among sea animals, those that are not permissible to eat are clean, too. If a camel's excrement falls into wheat and the wheat is ground into flour afterwards, or if it falls into liquid oil or milk and is taken out later, it is permissible to eat the wheat and drink the oil or milk unless one of the excrement's three peculiarities is observed in the wheat, oil, or milk. One can perform namâz on the clean side of a foul material. If a person wearing clean shoes, socks and mests performs namâz on a najs place, his namâz will not be accepted. If he takes them off and steps on them, it will be accepted. So is the case when their soles are foul." If a fowl, after being killed, is scalded in boiling water for easy plucking before it is pulled, it becomes najs. [It is stated on the fourth page of Ebussu'ûd Efendi's fatwâ: "If a fowl is killed by jugulation and then boiled in water before it is eviscerated and then plucked, it is not halâl; it is harâm to eat it. If it is killed, boiled after being disembowelled with the insides being washed, it is halâl to eat as long as its feathers have not been smeared with najâsat." It is written in **Radd-ul-muhtâr**: "Only the skin of a fowl not disembowelled becomes najs when it is put in water that is not boiling; if the fowl is washed three times with cold water after being plucked and disembowelled, the entire fowl becomes clean again. Also, the tripe becomes clean when washed three times in the same manner."]

When any meat is boiled in wine or liquor, it becomes najs. It cannot be cleaned by any means. Some Islamic scholars said that it would become clean when boiled three times in clean water, and cooled after each boiling. To clean milk, honey or boiled grape juice tainted with najâsat, some water must be added to it and the mixture must be boiled until water has evaporated. To clean fluid oil it must be churned with water and the oil that rises to the surface is skimmed off. Solid fat must be boiled with water and then taken out.

In the Shafi'î Madhhab, the **maytas** (carcasses) of animals living on land are najs and likewise, all their parts – their feathers, hairs, bones, and skin – and every bit that comes from them except their eggs are najs. Fluid blood issuing from man and animals living on land, and all kinds of intoxicating (alcoholic) beverages are najs. Also among the kinds of najâsat-i-ghalîza according to the Shâfi'î Madhhab are swine and dogs, their entire bodies and anything that has physically contacted [the wet hairs on] their body. Anything with which the contact has taken place, whatsoever, has to be washed seven times to clean. One of the washings should be done with a water-soil mixture. Adding soil into water, it is washed with turbid water; or the thing smeared with najâsat is first dipped into water and then soil is sprinkled onto it and it is washed; or first soil is scattered and then water is poured onto it. It is necessary to remove the najâsat before washing with the water-soil mixture. If the place of the najâsat is wet, we should not put the soil onto it first, but wash it using one of the other two methods. If the removal of the najâsat is achieved only after several washings, all of them is considered as one washing. Hence, six more washings including one with soil should be done. Each of the washings done to remove the odor, color or taste is counted separately. Except for the aforesaid two animals, it is enough to wash with mutlaq water only once in order to clean away the najâsat. In the Shafi'î Madhhab, the urine of a suckling boy is khafîf najâsat. After wringing out or drying and thus removing the wetness, we sprinkle water onto it; as a result, it becomes clean even if the water does not flow. The urine of a boy who has eaten something besides milk, even once, or whose age is above two and the urine of a suckling girl, invariably, should be cleaned out only by washing with water.

[Muhammed Maz-har Efendî, one of the scholars of (the city of) Van (in Eastern Turkey), states in **Misbâh-un-najât**: "The najâsat seen is washed until the three peculiarities signifying its existence are removed and then it is washed once again [with mutlaq water]. Never mind if the signs of najâsat can still be observed slightly. When the najâsat is not visible, pouring water over it once will do. If a container licked by a pig or a dog, or its own hairs licked by itself, touches one's clothes or other things as it is still wet, these things must be washed six times with clean water and once with muddy water. In the Shâfi'î Madhhab, tayammum is not permissible before the prayer time comes. Tayammum is made when one is ill or making a long-distance journey. There should not be any holes on the mests and both of them should be put on at the same time after the ablution is finished. Carcasses of all land animals are najs. With the exception of dogs and pigs, their hides become clean after tanning; however, hides of inedible animals do not become clean, and namâz cannot be performed on them."]

ISTINJÂ – Cleaning one's front or back after discharge of najâsat is called istinjâ. Cleaning, that is, tahârat, is not necessary when gas or a stone has issued. Istinjâ is sunnat-i muakkada. In other words, after urinating or emptying the bowels in a restroom it is sunnat for a man or woman to clean his or her front or back (private organs) with a stone or with some water so as not to leave any urine or excrement. The number of washings needed has not been prescribed by the sunnat. After cleaning with a stone, it is sunnat to wash again with water. However, in case istinjâ with water would be impossible without opening one's awrat parts in company, one gives up the istinjâ with water even if a large amount of najâsat is left. One does not open one's awrat parts, and performs namâz in this state. If one opens them, one will become a sinner who has committed a harâm. When one finds a secluded place, one makes istinjâ with water and performs the namâz again. The statement, "When there is a darûrat involving relieving oneself or performing a ghusl a man can open his awrat parts in the presence of other men and a woman can do it in the presence of other women," is based on a report that is weak (da'îf). Under such conditions it is necessary to make a tayammum instead of a ghusl. For, **Ibni 'Âbidîn** says on the hundred and fourth page: "If doing a commandment will cause you to commit a harâm, you must omit the commandment lest you will commit the harâm." [Since a fard is omitted lest you should commit a harâm, then *a fortiori* it will be necessary to omit a sunnat lest you should commit a harâm (**Ibni 'Âbidîn**, page 105). It is written in the book **Uyûn-ul-basâir** that a sunnat must be omitted even lest one should commit a makrûh.]

It is tahrimî makrûh to make an istinjâ with bones, food,

manure, bricks, pieces of pots or glass, coal, animal food, others' possessions, costly things such as silk, things thrown away from mosques, zamzam water, leaves, and paper. Even a blank piece of paper must be respected. It is permissible to make an istinjâ with pieces of paper or newspapers containing secular names or writings that have nothing to do with religion. But you must not make an istinjâ with any paper containing Islamic letters. It is permissible to clean semen or urine with a piece of cloth and then wash the cloth. A seriously ill person without a husband or wife does not have to make an istinjâ. But they have to have someone help them make an ablution. It is makrûh to urinate or empty the bowels with one's front or back towards the qibla, standing or naked without any excuse. A ghusl is not permissible at a place where urine has accumulated. It is not permissible to urinate in a place used for making ghusl. Yet it is permissible if the urine will not accumulate and will flow away. Water used for istinja becomes najs. It must not be allowed to splash on your clothes. Therefore, when making an istinjâ you must open your awrat parts and do it in a secluded place. Istinjâ cannot be made by inserting one's hand into one's pants in front of the wash-basin and thereby wash one's organ by making it touch the water in one's palm. When smeared with drops of urine, water in one's palm becomes najs and causes the pants which it drops on to become najs. If the areas which this water drops on to amounts to more than the palm's width, the namâz will not be sahîh. If the person, (who has so much urine on his pants) is an imâm, others cannot perform namâz behind him. If a person without hands does not have a mahram relative to help him/her to make istinjâ (clean him/herself after urination or defecation), (obligation of) istinjâ lapses from him/her (**Qâdî-Khân**).

It is wâjib for men to make an **istibrâ**, that is, not to leave any drops in the urethra, by walking, coughing or by lying on their left side. Women do not make an istibrâ. One must not make an ablution unless one is satisfied that there are no drops of urine left. One drop oozing out will both nullify the ablution and make one's underwears dirty. If less than a palmful oozes onto the pants, it is makrûh for one to make an ablution and perform namâz. If more oozes, the namâz will not be sahih. Those who have difficulty with istibrâ must put a cellulosic cotton wick as big as a barley seed into the urinary hole. The cotton will absorb the urine oozing out, which will prevent both the ablution from being broken and the pants from getting najs. Only, the end of the cotton must not jut out. If the cotton wick is long and its end remains outside and gets wet with urine, the ablution will break. Muslims in the Shâfi'î Madhhab should not put cotton there during the blessed month of Ramadân; it will nullify one's fast according to the Shâfi'î Madhhab. [When a Hanafî Muslim imitating the Shâfi'î Madhhab in ablution and namâz uses cotton wick likewise, it will not nullify his fast. With old and invalid people, the organ becomes smaller and the piece of cloth wound around it becomes loose. A person with this problem puts a piece of cloth as large as a handkerchief in a small nylon bag and places the organ and the testicles in the bag. He ties the mouth of the bag. If the amount of the urine dripping onto the cloth is more than one dirham, the cloth must be replaced before making an ablution. If a person who cannot control his urine but who does not have an excuse notices wetness on the piece of cloth that he tied clean, and if he does not know when the urine oozed, it must be judged that it oozed at the moment he noticed it, like in the example of the blood of haid, dealt with in the fourth chapter. A person who feels doubt checks the cloth before starting to perform namâz. If he sees wetness he makes a new ablution. If he feels doubt during namâz, he checks as soons as he makes the salâm and, if he sees drops, he performs the namâz again. If he sees wetness one or two minutes after the salâm, it will be concluded that he has performed the namâz with an ablution]. After istibrâ, istinjâ is made. After istinjâ with water, the organ is wiped dry with a piece of cloth. Every woman must always put **kursuf** (some cotton or cloth) on her front [see chapter 4.]

[The fact that those who suffer from enuresis or uncontrollable bleeding and those who have difficulty in purifying themselves of najâsat should imitate the Mâlikî Madhhab is written in the annotation to **al-Ma'fuwât**. It is written in the book **Al-fiqh-u-'alal-madhâhib-il-erba'a**, "(The following principles must be observed by Muslims who intend to imitate) the Mâlikî Madhhab: Urine, semen, mazî, wadî, blood of istihâda (menorrhagia), excrement or wind issuing from a healthy person breaks an ablution. Yet an ablution will not be broken when the body emits stones, worms, pus, yellowish liquid or blood through the anus or any other part. When those things emission of which would normally break an ablution issue because of some illness and it cannot be prevented, one of the following two ijtihâds is to be followed: According to the first ijtihâd, involuntary urination that continues for more than half of the period of time prescribed for a certain prayer of namâz, when it is not known when it (the urination) started, does not break an ablution. According to the second ijtihâd, it does not break an invalid's ablution anyway, not even in the absence of the three conditions. It is mustahab for that person to make an ablution whenever the urination stops. When sick or old people have difficulty making an ablution, they are approved of availing themselves of this second ijtihâd. If it is known when the urination stops, it is preferrable for the person concerned to make an ablution then. Those Hanafîs and Shâfi'îs who have to wait rather long for istibrâ or whose urine goes on dropping afterwards and who cannot be excusable because their involuntary urination does not continue as long as a period allotted for a namâz, must imitate the Mâlikî Madhhab. Ibni 'Âbidîn says in the subject about Talâq-i-rij'î:[1] "Our scholars gave their fatwâ in accordance with the Mâlikî Madhhab in case of a darûrat. If a matter has not been explained in the Hanafî Madhhab, the Mâlikî Madhhab must be imitated." The skin over the ears is included in the area of the head. So it is fard to make masah on them. It is not written in Hanafî books that this part of the skin is included in the area of the face and must be washed. It breaks an ablution to touch lustfully the skin or hair of a woman who is permissible for one to marry[2]. In ghusl, it is sunnat, not fard, to wash (inside) the mouth and the nose. A tayammum is necessary for each prayer time. (At each prayer time the tayammum that you made for the previous prayer becomes null and void.) The dog is not foul; nor is the pig. However, it is harâm to eat their meat. Blood is foul, even if it is that of a fish. Tahârat from najâsat is fard according to one authentic report (ijtihâd), and sunnat according to another. Drops from haemorrhoids and drops of urine and excrement on one's underwears are forgiven. Human and animal blood and pus from an abscess or wound are forgiven when they cover an area as large as (and no more than) the palm of a hand. It is fard to recite the Fâtiha (sûra) in every rak'at of namâz and to remain motionless for a while (which is called **tumânînat**) after the rukû' and between the two sajdas. In rak'ats where the imâm says the (the Fâtiha sûra and the other prescribed) sûras silently, it is mustahab for the jamâ'at to say the Fâtiha (silently); and where the imâm recites the sûras aloud, it is makrûh for the jamâ'at to say the Fâtiha, (not even silently). At qiyâm (standing position in namâz), it is mustahab to place both hands on somewhere between the chest and the navel,

---

[1] Please see the fifteenth chapter of the sixth fascicle of **Endless Bliss** for kinds of talâq (divorce).
[2] The wife is no exception from this rule.

the right hand on the left hand, or to let them hang down on both sides. It is makrûh to say the 'A'ûdhu...' in prayers of namâz that are fard. Finishing the (recital of) Fâtiha after (having begun) the rukû' will nullify the namâz."

Second edition of the Mâlikî book of fiqh **az-Zahîra li-l Qurâfî** was printed in Egypt in 1402 [A.D. 1982]. It says, "Imâm-i-Mâlik said that it is wâjib for the awâm (common people, laymen) to imitate the mujtahids. The (four) Madhhabs are ways leading to Paradise. He who follows any one of them will attain Paradise."

Last edition of the book **al-Mudawwana**, which consists of narrations coming from Imâm-i-Mâlik through Ibn ul-Qâsim 'radiy-Allâhu anhumâ', was printed in Beirut. It is written in this book: "When a woman's palm touches her genital organ, her ablution is not broken. If mazî oozes continuously because of cold or illness, an ablution is not broken. Yet if it oozes as a result of a lustful thought, it will be broken. If blood of istihâza or urine oozes, an ablution is not broken; yet in this case it is mustahab to make an ablution for each prayer of namâz. Khilâl of the beard (combing the beard with fingers) is not made during an ablution. One should not perform namâz behind (an imâm who is) a holder of bid'at (a heretical or aberrant belief or conduct)." It is fard to wash (the skin) under eye-brows and eye-lashes, and also under the scarcely-haired beard, and to wash the upper part of the beard which is thickly haired. It is mustahab to probe between the toes (by using the small finger). It is permissible to dry oneself after an ablution. Seven actions are fard (compulsory) in an ablution, and five are fard in a ghusl. In case of such fears as losing one's life or property or becoming ill or one's illness becoming worse or one's healing being delayed, it is permissible to make a tayammum. If one cannot find a Muslim doctor, one will have to trust a doctor who is a disbeliever or (others') experiences.] When something washed with the hands become clean, the hands become clean, too.

It says in the subject concerning using gold and silver in the fifth volume of **Durr-ul-mukhtâr** that men's dealing with one another is called **Mu'âmalât**. In mu'âmalât, a fâsiq Muslim's or a disbeliever's word is to be accepted. A discreet child and a woman are like men (in this respect). If one of them says, "I have bought this meat from a disbeliever believing in a heavenly book," the meat will be halâl to eat. [For, formerly meat was sold by the person who had butchered the animal.] One's property does not become invalidated by one person's word. If a Muslim buys some meat and another devoted (sâlih) Muslim says that the animal (to which the meat belongs) was killed by a disbeliever without a heavenly book, the meat cannot be returned to the seller; the buyer has to pay for it. For, since he bought the meat without knowing that it belonged to a carrion, it has become his property. Information to invalidate property has to be given by two men or by one man plus two women. There are three kinds of mu'âmalât. The first kind comprises dealings that neither party has to fulfil. Examples of this are being a deputy, being a mudârib (one of the partners in a kind of joint-ownership)[1], and being granted (by a person to do something on his behalf). The second kind consists of dealings that both parties have to fulfil. Examples of this are the rights that can be subjects for law-suits. The third kind includes dealings that one of the parties has to fulfil while the other party does not have to fulfil. In this kind are dismissing a deputy and withdrawing the permission one granted to another person. In this case the deputy and the granted person can no longer act on behalf of the person they are representing. But the person who takes back his permission or authority from his deputy is free to use his own rights. We have already explained the first one. In the second, the informers must have the conditions prescribed by Islam for witnesses. In the third, the number of the informers and whether they have the quality of 'adâlat (being 'âdil Muslims) will be taken into consideration.

Matters between Allâhu ta'âlâ and man are called **Diyânât**. In diyânât, the word of an 'âdil[2] Muslim who has reached the age of puberty will be trusted. A woman is like a man in this respect. If he (or she) says, "This water is najs," one cannot make an ablution with the water. One will have to make a tayammum. If a fâsiq Muslim or a Muslim whose conduct is not known for certain says so one inquires about it personally and acts upon one's own assurance. If a disbeliever or a child says that the water is najs and if one believes them, one must pour the water away and then make a tayammum. In giving a present or a permission, a child's word can be accepted. When a child says, "Come in, please," one can enter the place. But whether a child is permitted to buy something depends upon the seller's conviction.

In diyânât, information that will invalidate one's property must be given by two men or one man plus two women. For example, if

---

[1] Sleeping (Silent or Dormant) partnership, explained in the forty-fifth chapter of the fifth fascicle.
[2] Terms such as 'âdil and fâsiq are explained in chapter 10.

an 'âdil Muslim says, "This man and wife are siblings through the milk-tie,"[1] it will not be admitted, and the nikâh (marriage as prescribed by Islam) will not be cancelled.

Ibni 'Âbidîn says at the end of the chapter about istinjâ: "If an 'âdil person says that some meat is carrion, e.g., "**a murtadd** killed it," and another 'âdil person says that it is not carrion, e.g., "a Muslim killed it," it will be judged as carrion. If the former says that some water or any sort of sherbet or any food is najs and the latter says that it is not najs, it will be taken as clean. If there are several informers, the majority's consensus will be accepted. If clean and najs clothes come together and the clean ones are in the minority, or a number of pots are together and the clean ones are in the majority, one should search for the clean ones and use the ones one supposes to be clean. If the clean pots are equal or fewer in number, all of them will be taken as najs.

7 – WATER AND ITS KINDS

It is written in **Durr-ul-mukhtâr**, and also in **Radd-ul-muhtâr**, which is a commentary to the former:

A minor ablution [an ablution for namâz] and a major ablution [ghusl] require using **mutlaq water**. In other words, mutlaq water is both clean and a cleaner. Mutlaq water is water that takes no other word besides its name and which is solely called water. Water from rain, brooks, streams, springs, wells, seas, and snow is mutlaq water. (Kinds of water such as) musta'mal water (explained earlier in the text), najs water, flower essence, grape juice and the like, which are mentioned together with their kinds and properties, are not mutlaq water. These cannot be used for making an ablution or ghusl. They are called **Muqayyad water**. Zamzam water can be used for an ablution or a ghusl. It is not even makrûh. It is permissible also to use water that has stayed for some time under the sun. Yet is tanzîhî makrûh.

Water issuing and dropping from trees, grass, fruit or from any climbing plant is clean. Yet an ablution or ghusl is not permissible with it or with any juice extracted from these plants.

When something clean is mixed with mutlaq water, if the amount of the substance mixed with the water is more than the water, the water becomes muqayyad. The substance mixed with

---

[1] Please see the seventh chapter of the sixth fascicle of **Endless Bliss**.

water may become the greater part in four ways. Firstly, something solid, such as a sponge or grass, absorbs the water completely. Secondly, something which is not used in cleaning like soap is heated in the water. Meat juice and bean juice are of this sort. In this case the water becomes muqayyad water even if its three properties did not change and even if it did not lose its fluidity. Water heated with some cleaner such as soap becomes muqayyad if it loses its fluidity. Thirdly, a solid substance gets mixed with cold water. If the substance changes the name of the water after it is mixed with it, the water becomes muqayyad even if it has not become viscous. Two examples of this are water containing saffron or sulphate of iron and water containing oak apple, if the amount of the substance dissolved in it is such that it can be used in dying, in the former example, and in tannery, in the latter. Another example is the **nebîz** made from dates. Dates or dried grapes are kept in cold water until their sugar is transferred into the water, the water is then heated until it boils. After getting cold, it is filtered. This liquid is called **nebîz**. If it is filtered without being heated it becomes **naqî'**[1]. When the name of the water does not change; it becomes muqayyad if it has lost its fluidity and become viscous; and it remains pure if it is still fluid even if all three of its properties have changed. Examples of these types are water dyed by saffron that has fallen into it and cold water whose colour, odor or taste has been changed by beans, chick-peas, leaves, fruits or grass that has remained in it for some time. It is not permissible to make an ablution or ghusl with saturated solutions of salt.

Fourthly; when a liquid substance gets mixed with water. When a clean substance in liquid form flows into a small pool, if all three properties of the substance are unlike those of water and if two properties of the mixture have changed, it becomes muqayyad. If only one has changed, it does not become muqayyad. Water mixed with vinegar is an example of this type. When one or two of its properties are like those of the water, and if a property of the water which is unlike that of the substance has been changed in the mixture, it becomes muqayyad. Milky water is an example of this type because being odorless is common in both of them. And so is water mixed with melon juice because, being colourless and odorless is common in both of them. If all three of its properties are like those of water, or if the amount of the liquid mixed with

---

[1] Please see the third chapter of the sixth fascicle of **Endless Bliss**.

water is more than the water or equal to the water, the mixture becomes muqayyad and it is not permissible to perform an ablution or ghusl with it. So is the case when musta'mal water [that which has been used in an ablution or ghusl] gets mixed with the water. This is so, inasmuch as musta'mal water is thought to be clean. So is the case when musta'mal water flows into a small pool or into a bath-tub or when a person without an ablution dips his hand or foot into it or he himself takes a dip in it. So long as it is not known that the amount of water touching the skins of those who perform an ablution at a small pool is half the total amount of the water in the pool, into which no water flows, or that any najâsat, though little, has fallen into the pool, then it is permissible to perform an ablution at the pool. If a lot of people perform an ablution at a small pool whose water is changed daily and if their musta'mal water falls back into the pool, it is permissible. But if very little najâsat falls into the pool, it is not permissible to perform an ablution there. According to some scholars, if any limb is dipped and washed in a small pool, the whole pool becomes musta'mal water. For that reason, at places rich with water, taking some water with the palms and washing the limbs outside the pool must be preferred to washing the limbs in the pool. At places with scarce water, acting upon those scholars who say that it is permissible, an ablution and/or a ghusl can be be made in the pool.

It is sahîh, but it is harâm, to make an ablution with usurped water.

It is permissible to make an ablution or ghusl with mutlaq water in which an animal without fluid blood has died. For example, it is permissible with water in which there is a dead bee, scorpion, bed-bug or mosquito. It is not permissible if there is a dead leech that has sucked blood. A silkworm and its eggs, those worms living in excrement, tapeworms and fruit worms are clean. But the najâsat smeared around them is najs.

When an aquatic animal dies in some water, such as fish, crabs, frogs, it is permissible to make an ablution or ghusl with that water. Also, of toads and snakes living on land, when those without fluid blood die in the water, it is permissible. If all such animals die after being taken out of the water and their dead boodies fall into the water, it is still permissible. Also, if a frog gets broken to pieces in the water, it is still permissible. But the water cannot be drunk. For its flesh is harâm (to eat). When an animal that is born on land and lives in water, such as a duck or a goose, dies in a small pool, the pool becomes najs.

When little najâsat falls in a small pool, according to Hanafî Madhhab, or in any pool of water that is smaller than one qullatayn, according to Shâfi'î Madhhab, the water becomes najs even if its three properties did not change. Men cannot drink it, nor can it be used in cleaning. If its three properties change, it is like urine and cannot be used in anything. A qullatayn is five hundred ritls. One ritl is 130 dirhams, and one dirham 3.36 grams. Hence, one qullatayn is 220 kilograms.

Water whose three properties have changed as a result of staying too long does not become najs. If the reason for any smelling water is not known, it must be considered to be clean. There is no need to inquire, to ask others. In order to oppose the (heretical group) of Mu'tazîla, it is sometimes advisable to make an ablution at a pool which is beside a river.

If some najâsat, whether it can be seen or not, falls in a river or a large pool, in the Hanafî Madhhab; or in an amount of water equal to one qullatayn, in the Shafi'î Madhhab; or in any amount of water, in Malikî Madhhab; it is permissible to make an ablution or ghusl at any side of it where any one of the three signs of the najâsat; colour, odour or taste; is not evident. For example, when there is a carrion, when a man or an animal urinates or when a beast of prey drinks water (from a stream), if there is no sign of them at its lower parts, it is permissible, (to make an ablution or ghusl). According to some scholars, the permissibility stipulates that the amount of water in contact with the najâsat be less than the amount of water clear of it. The water does not have to flow continuously. When any water poured on some najs place flows for one metre, so that its three properties are gone, it becomes clean. When clean water in one container and najs water in another container are poured from a level one metre above the ground and get mixed with each other in the air, the water that falls on the ground will be clean.

Water that can sweep along a chaff of straw is called flowing water. A square pool with each side measured as ten zrâ' [about 4.8 meters] is called (large pool), which covers an area of a hundred square zrâ', that is twenty-three square metres. A circle whose circumference is 17 metres covers an area of 23 square metres. Its being shallow does not detract from this specification. If a person digs a ditch from a hollow and makes an ablution as the water in the hollow flows through the ditch and the musta'mal water (used by him) accumulates in another hollow from which someone else digs another ditch and makes an ablution with the flowing water and the musta'mal water accumulates at some other place and from there another ditch is dug and so forth, the ablutions of all these people will be accepted. The flowing water is clean until any sign of najâsat is noticed. This example is based on an assumption that musta'mal water were najs. A small pool or a bath basin into which water flows continuously and which overflows continuously, [or from which water is consumed continuously and the duration between two consumptions is not so long as to let motion of the water stop], is categorized as flowing water. An ablution can be made at any side of such things. Musta'mal water must flow over the brim. If it flows through a hole at the bottom, it will differ from flowing water. It is not a condition that the pool be so small that all the musta'mal water can flow away. The surface of a frozen pool is the surface of the water in the pool below the frozen layer, if (it is seen when the ice is pierced that) the water does not touch the frozen layer covering it; and it is the surface of the water in the hole dug in the layer of ice, if the water touches the frozen layer. If clean water flows into najs water from one side and causes it to overflow from the opposite side, its sides where there are no signs of najâsat left are clean. When water equal to the amount it contained has overflowed, it becomes clean in its entirety. The overflowing water is clean so long as signs of najâsat are not noticed. So are such containers as bowls and buckets. For instance, if a najs bucket is filled and overflows, when none of the three signs of najâsat is evident both the water and the bucket become clean.

Musta'mal water, i.e., water used in an ablution or in a ghusl, and water used in (a commendable act termed) qurbat[1], e.g. water used in washing your hands before and after meals as it is sunnat to do so, become najs the moment they leave the limbs washed. According to some scholars, they become najs after they fall on other limbs, on your clothes, or on the ground. They do not dirty the place on which they fall first.

Hadrat Abû Nasr Aqta', 'rahmatullâhi 'alaih' says in his commentary to **Qudûrî**[2]: "When clean things get mixed with some water, it can be used for an ablution so long as the name of

---

[1] Qurbat is an act, a behaviour that you do in order to attain the grace of Allâhu ta'âlâ.
[2] Mukhtasar Qudûrî, by Ahmad bin Muhammad Baghdâdî (362 [973 A.D.]–428 [1037 A.D.], Baghdâd, a Hanafî Fiqh scholar and a mufti of Bukhârâ. The valuable book has various commantaries, and a Turkish version as well. Two other commentaries to Qudûrî were

the water does not change even if its colour changes."

If one finds water on one's way and knows well or has strong conviction that it is clean, one can perform an ablution with it. In fact, if the water is little, one makes an ablution or ghusl with it unless one knows well that it has been mixed with najâsat. One can not make a tayammum. It is because water is supposed to be clean essentially. Supposition does not make it najs; on the contrary, it remains in its essential state by supposition, that is, it is accepted as clean. Worships are (considered to be) pure and correct by strong conviction. But îmân, faith, cannot be correct by strong conviction; it can be correct by knowing well. If a person entering a bath sees that the basin or the pool is full, he can make an ablution or ghusl with the water unless he knows that it has been mixed with najâsat. It is not necessary to make the basin overflow by letting water flow into it.

LEFTOVERS (of food): If a living being drinks from a container or a small pool, the water left is called 'leftover'. Cleanness of liquid and food remainings takes after the cleanness of the saliva of the one who left the remainings. Every person's saliva and leftover are clean. A disbeliever's and a junub person's leftovers are clean, too. When a junub person dives into the sea and drinks water afterwards he becomes clean. In other words, his drinking water stands for his washing his mouth. If it is propounded that water left over by him becomes musta'mal and there are scholars who say that musta'mal water is najs, the musta'mal water is not the water left but it is the water he drank. It is permissible for a junub person to take water by dipping his hand into the basin instead of using a bowl; the water in the basin will not become musta'mal; likewise, water left over by a junub person, who had been drinking it, has not been considered to be musta'mal. It is makrûh for a man to drink the water left over by a woman nâmahram[1] to him lest he will enjoy its taste, so too for a woman to drink the water left over by a man nâmahram to her. Also, it is makrûh for boys to be barbers or to massage other men's bodies with hair-gloves at public baths since there is the fear that it may cause lust. So is the case with someone else's saliva.

---

written by Yûsuf bin 'Umar 'rahmatullâhi 'alaih', (d. 832 [1429 A.D.],) and Mukhtâr bin Mahmûd Zâhidî 'rahmatullâhi 'alaih', (d. 658 [1259 A.D.].)

[1] Not one of the eighteen women whom Islam has prescribed as a man's close relatives. The following chapter gives detailed information on this subject.

Leftovers from animals with edible flesh are clean, provided their mouths are not smeared with najâsat. A horse is among such animals. And so too are animals without fluid blood, whether they live on land or in sea. Leftovers from all these can be used for an ablution or ghusl or for cleaning najâsat. Milk of a horse is clean and can be drunk.

Foods left over by pigs, dogs, beasts of prey, a cat that has newly eaten a mouse, their flesh and milk are all ghalîz najâsat. It is harâm to eat or drink them. It is not permissible to use leftovers from them in an ablution, in a ghusl or in cleaning. They cannot be used as medicine, either. In the Mâlikî Madhhab pigs and dogs are clean. But, it is harâm to eat them in the Malikî Madhhab, too. [It is stated in the daily Turkish newspaper named "Türkiye" dated June 27, 1986 that: "the specialists of Ottowa University have determined after a research carried out in sixteen countries that pork causes the fatal disease of cirrhosis"]. Elephants and monkeys are beasts of prey, too. They tear their preys with their teeth. So is the food or drink left over by a person who has newly taken wine [or any other hard drink]. If a drunk person, after taking alcohol, licks his lips with his tongue three times and spits or swallows his spittle each time, the leftover from the water he drinks thereafter is not najs. In other words, there must be no smell or taste of alcohol left in his saliva. Flesh and leftovers from a hen, a sheep or a camel whose flesh smells because of going about freely in the streets and eating najâsat all the time, are makrûh. If one of these animals is not allowed to go out for a certain length of time, which is three days with a hen, four days with a sheep, and ten days with a camel or a cow, it will no longer be makrûh to eat its flesh or any edible food it had been eating and left unfinished. If it is not known that they eat najâsat, leftovers from them are not makrûh. While there is clean water, it is tanzîhî makrûh to make an ablution with leftovers that are makrûh, with water remaining from birds of prey, with water remaining from a cat which it is not known to have newly eaten a mouse or with water remaining from a mouse or a snake with fluid blood. If the beak of a bird of prey is clean, water remaining from it is not makrûh. Flesh of mice and cats is najs, but remainings from them have exceptionally been judged to be not qaba najâsat. Drinking and eating leftovers from these two have been judged as makrûh for the rich. But they are not makrûh for the poor. Water or food leftovers remaining from an ass or a mule is clean. But it is doubtful whether it is a cleaner or not. It is permissible to eat a zebra, and water or food leftovers remaining from it is clean. It is not makrûh to make an ablution with remaining water that is makrûh at a place where there is no other water. One does not make a tayammum while there is such remaining water. If there is no clean water, one makes an ablution with water remaining from an ass or a mule, and then makes a tayammum. Water into which a small child has dipped its hand is like leftover remaining from a cat's drink. That is, if it is not known that the child's hand is clean, it is tanzîhî makrûh to make an ablution with the water or to drink it. It is makrûh to begin performing a namâz while mounted on an animal whose leftover is makrûh. An animal's sweat is like the water leftover remaining from its drink. For instance, a donkey's sweat is clean.

8 – SATR-I AWRAT and WOMEN'S COVERING THEMSELVES

Those parts of a discreet and pubescent[1] person's body that are harâm for him (or her) to leave uncovered during the performance of a namâz and/or whenever in company, and which are equally harâm for others to look at, are called **awrat parts**. Men and women were commanded to cover their awrat parts through the sûra-t-ul-**Ahzâb**, which was revealed in the third year of the Hijrat (Hegira), and the sûra-t-ul-Nûr, which was revealed in the fifth year. In the Hanafî and Shâfi'î Madhhabs a man's awrat parts during the performance of a namâz are between his navel and lower parts of his knees. The navel is awrat in the Shâfi'î Madhhab, whereas the knees are awrat in the Hanafî Madhhab. Namâz performed with these parts exposed is not sahîh; (in other words, it is null and void.) When performing namâz, it is sunnat for men to cover their other parts [arms, head], [and to wear socks if a long robe or a gown is not available]. It is makrûh for them to perform namâz with these parts exposed.

All parts of free women, except their palms and faces, including their wrists, outer parts of their hands, hanging parts of their hair and under their feet are awrat (and therefore they must be covered) during a namâz, according to the Hanafî Madhhab. There are also quite a number of valuable books saying that outer parts of hands are not awrat. According to them, it is permissible for women to perform namâz while outer parts of their hands up to wrists are

---

[1] When a girl reaches the age of 9 and when a boy is 12 years old, they become discreet and pubescent and are therefore called **mukallaf** (responsible) **Muslims**. Please see the twenty-third chapter of the fifth fascicle of **Endless Bliss**.

bare. However, it is better for women to perform namâz wearing a gown with sleeves long enough, or a head cover large enough, to cover their hands, and thereby to pursue a course of action compatible with all the written sources. There are savants who said that women's feet were not awrat in namâz, but the same savants said that it was sunnat to cover and makrûh to open them when performing namâz and when going out. [It is written in the book **Fatâwâ-i-Qâdikhân**[1] that hanging parts of hair are like feet]. If one-fourth of one of a man's or woman's awrat parts remains bare as long as one rukn, the namâz becomes annulled. If a smaller part remains exposed, the namâz does not become nullified, but it becomes makrûh. For instance, the namâz of a woman one-fourth of whose foot has remained bare will not be sahîh. If she herself uncovers it, her namâz becomes annulled immediately. [See second chapter!]. It is written in **Umdat-ul-islâm**[2]: "A woman's namâz which she performed with bare heelbone, ankle, neck or hair is not sahîh. Thin tissue that lets the shape or colour of the thing under it be seen is equal to none." [Please see seventeenth chapter!] In the Shâfi'î Madhhab, a woman's whole body, other than her two hands and her face, is always awrat.

Hadrat Ibni 'Âbidin 'rahmatullâhi 'alaih' says in **Radd-ul-muhtâr**[3]:

---

[1] Also known as **Fatâwâ-i-Khâniyya** and **Majmû'a-i-Khâniyya**, Fatâwâ-i-Qâdikhân is a valuble book of fatwâs written by Qâdî Khan Hasan bin Mansûr Ferghânî "rahmatullâhi ta'âlâ 'alaih', (d. 592 [1196 A.D.],) and was printed on the page margins of the book **Fatâwâ-i-Hindiyya**, by Shaikh Nizâm Mu'înuddîn Naqshibandî, and printed in Egypt in 1310 Hijrî.

[2] A highly valuable book written in the Fârisî language by Abd-ul-'Azîz bin Hamîd-ad-dîn Dahlawî, (d. 741 [1341 A.D.], India,) 'rahmatullâhi ta'âlâ 'alaih'. In 950 [1543 A.D.] it was translated into Turkish by Abd-ur-Rahmân bin Yûsuf, and the Turkish version was printed with the title **Imâd-ul-islâm** in 1290 [1822 A.D.]. The original version was reproduced in 1989 under the auspices of Hakîkat Kitâbevi in Istanbul, Turkey.

[3] Ibni 'Âbidin Sayyid Muhammad bin Amîn bin 'Umar bin Abd-ul-'Azîz 'rahmatullâhi 'alaih', (1198 [1784]-1252 [1836 A.D.], Damascus,) was a profound scholar in the branch of Fiqh. **Radd-ul-muhtâr**, of five volumes, is a commentary which he wrote for the purpose of explaining the book **Durr-ul-mukhtâr**, by Muhammad bin Alî Ala'uddîn Haskafî 'rahmatullâhi ta'âlâ 'alaih', (1021, Haskaf, – 1088 [1677 A.D.]), Muftî of Damascus. Radd-ul-muhtâr is the source of most of the teachings of Fiqh in the Turkish book **Seâdet-i ebediyye**, also of the six fascicles of **Endless Bliss**.

It is fard to cover one's awrat parts outside of namâz as well as when performing namâz. It is tahrîmî makrûh to perform namâz by covering oneself with silk or with usurped or stolen clothes. However, since a person has to cover himself, a man can use something made of silk, if he cannot find something else. It is fard to cover oneself when one performs namâz alone, too. A person who has clean clothes is not permitted to perform namâz naked in the dark even when he is alone. When alone and not performing namâz, it is fard for women to cover between their knees and navels, wâjib to cover their backs and bellies, and adab to cover other parts of their body. When alone in the home they can busy themselves around with their heads bare. When there is one of the eighteen men that a woman can show herself to, it is better for her to wear a thin headdress. When alone, one can open one's awrat parts only when necessary, e.g. in a toilet. Authentic scholarly reports vary on the statutory latitude of opening one's awrat parts; accordingly, it may be makrûh, or permissible, or permissible only at a small place, to do so when one is alone and making a ghusl. When not performing namâz, it is necessary to cover yourself even if the only clothes readily available for the purpose have been smeared with najâsat.

It is written in **Kitâb-ul-Fiqh-u-alal-madhâhibil-erba'a**[1]: "The four Madhhabs do not exactly agree on the parts of body men and women have to cover when they perform namâz or on the parts which are harâm for men to show one another, for men to show women, and for women to show their mahrams. However, it is harâm in all three Madhhabs for women to show men and female non-Muslims their bodies other than their faces and inside and outside their hands, and for these people to look at them." In the Shâfi'î Madhhab, on the other hand, their faces and hands are awrat (and therefore must be covered) in the presence of men

---

[1] The following information is given about that valuable book in the eight hundred and seventh (807) page of the tremendous work, **Seâdet-i ebediyye**, by Husayn Hilmi bin Sa'îd Işık 'rahmatullâhi ta'âlâ 'alaih', an ageless wealth of knowledge, a beloved Walî, and a pearl of beautiful manners and behaviour: "Prepared by an Egyptian scholarly council presided by Allâma 'Abd-ur-Rahmân Jarîrî, one of the professors of **Jâmi'ul-az-har**, the book **Kitâb-ul-fiqh-'alal-madhâhib-il-erba'â**, which consists of five volumes, was reproduced in Egypt in 1392 [1972 A.D.], and was translated into Turkish by Hasan Ege and published in seven volumes by Bahar Kitâbevi in 1971-1979."

who are nâmahram to them, at times when doing otherwise would cause fitna. Permissible as it is for women to expose their faces and palms to men who are nâmahram to them, men are not permitted to look lustfully at faces or palms of those women who are nâmahram to them, no matter whether they are Muslims or disbelievers. When there is no necessity, it is makrûh to look without lust at those parts of women that are permissible to look at, e.g. at faces of nâmahram women, at pictures of their awrat parts, at awrat parts of children that have learned to speak. Awrat parts of those children that have not started to talk yet are only their saw'atayn [private parts]. It is not permissible to look at the private parts of boys until they are ten years old and of girls until they become attractive, and later, to look at any of their awrat parts. Animals do not have awrat parts. Also, it is harâm to look lustfully at boys' faces, yet it is permissible to look at them without lust even if they are beautiful.

It is written in **Fatâwâ-i Khayriyya**: "When there is the danger of fitna, a father can keep his beautiful discreet son who has reached the age of puberty in his own home and under his own discipline. He may not let him go out on a long-distance journey or for education or on hajj (pilgrimage) without a beard. He protects him like a woman. But he does not veil him. In streets each and every woman is accompanied by two devils, whereas a boy is accompanied by eighteen devils. They try to mislead those who look at them. It is fard for a boy to obey his parents' Islamically licit instructions. When there is no danger of fitna, a father cannot force his discreet son who has reached puberty to stay at home."

[It is written in the second volume of **Majma'ul-anhur**[1] that our Prophet 'sall-Allâhu ta'âlâ 'alaihi wa sallam' stated: **"On the day of Judgment molten hot lead will be poured into the eyes of those who look lustfully at the faces of women who are nâmahram to them."** Stating the afflictions incurred by the eyes, **Kâdizâda**[2], who explained the book **Birgivî Vasiyyetnâmesi**, says

---

[1] The book **Majma'ul-anhur** was written by Abdurrahmân bin Muhammad Shaikhîzâda 'rahmatullâhi 'alaih', (d. 1078 [1668 A.D.], Baghdâd,) as a commentary to the book **Multaqâ**.

[2] Kâdî-Zâda Ahmad 'Amîn bin Abdullah 'rahmatullâhi ta'âlâ 'alaih', (1133-1197 [1783 A.D.],) wrote a commentary to the book **Birgivî Vasiyyetnâmesi**, which in turn had been written by Imâm Birgivî Zayn-ud-dîn Muhammad bin Alî 'rahmatullâhi ta'âlâ 'alaih', (928 [1521 A.D.], Balıkesîr – 981 [1573 A.D.], Birgi.)

in his discourse about the kinds of ruination incurred by one's eyes that Allâhu ta'âlâ declares in the thirtieth âyat of Sûrat-un-Nûr: "**O My Messenger, 'sall-Allâhu 'alaihi wa sallam'! Tell the Believers not to look at harâms and to protect their awrat parts against harâms! Tell those women who have îmân not to look at harâms and to protect their awrat parts from committing harâm!**"

It is written in **Riyâd-un-nâsihîn**[1] that Rasûlullah 'sall-Allâhu 'alaihi wa sallam' declared in his wadâ' (valedictory) hajj: "**The eyes of a person who looks at a nâmahram woman lustfully will be filled with fire and he will be flung down into Hell. The arms of a person who shakes hands with a nâmahram woman will be tied around his neck and then he will be sent down to Hell. Those who talk with a nâmahram woman lustfully without any necessity will remain in Hell a thousand years for each word.**" Another hadîth declares, "**Looking at one's neighbour's wife or at one's friends' wives is ten times as sinful as looking at nâmahram women. Looking at married women is one thousand times as sinful as looking at girls. So are the sins of fornication.**"

It is written in the book **Berîqa**[2] that the hadîths "**Three things (when looked at) put varnish on the eyes: Looking at a verdure, at a stream, at a beautiful face**" and "**Three things strengthen the eyes: Tinging the eyes with kohl, looking at verdure and at a beautiful face**", state the use of looking at people who are halâl to look at. In fact, looking at nâmahram women and girls weakens the eyes and darkens the heart. As informed by Hâkim, Bayhakî, and Abû Dâwûd, a hadîth-i marfû conveyed by **Abû Umâma** 'radiy-Allâhu 'anh' declares: "**If a person, upon seeing a nâmahram girl, fears Allah's torment and turns his face away from her, Allâhu ta'âlâ will make him enjoy the taste of worship.**" His first seeing will be forgiven. A hadîth declares, "**Those eyes that watch the enemy in a jihâd made for Allah's sake or that weep for fear of Allâhu ta'âlâ or that do not look at harâms will not see Hell fire in the next world.**"]

Seven or ten year old attractive girls as well as all girls who have reached the age of fifteen or the age of puberty are equivalents to women. It is harâm for such girls to show

---

[1] A valuable compilation consisting of a sampler from four hundred and forty-four books prepared by Muhammad Rebhâmî 'rahmatullâhi ta'âlâ 'alaih', one of India's scholars of Fiqh.

[2] It was written by Muhammad bin Mustafâ Hâdimî 'rahmatullâhi ta'âlâ 'alaih', (d. 1176 [1762 A.D.], Hâdim, Konya).

themselves with bare head, hair, arms and legs to nâmahram men, or to sing to them or to talk to them softly and gracefully. Women are permitted to talk to nâmahram men seriously in a manner that will not cause fitna when there is necessity such as buying and selling. So is their opening their faces when among men. It is gravely sinful for women to go out with bare head, hair, arms and legs, to let their voice be heard by nâmahram men without necessity, to sing to them, to let them hear their voices through films or records or by reading Qurân-al kerîm or by reciting the mawlid or the adhân. [It is harâm for women and girls to go out with dresses that are thin or tight or of fur, wearing their ornaments such as ear-rings and bracelets without covering them, clad like men, with their hair cut short like men. Therefore, it is not permissible for them to wear trousers, not even ample ones. Trousers are men's clothing. In hadîth-i sherîfs, which exist in **Terghîb-us-salât**:[1] **"Those women who dress themselves like men and those men who ornament themselves like women are accursed."** In fact, tight trousers are not permissible even for men. For, in this case the shapes of those parts of their body called qaba awrat can be seen from the outside. Furthermore, it has not been an Islamic custom, neither of old nor now, for women to wear trousers. It has come from the irreligious, from those who do not know the Islamic way of attirement. Harâms cannot be Islamic customs even if they have spread and become settled. It is declared in a hadîth that he who makes himself resemble disbelievers will be on their side. Trousers can be worn under a mantle, yet the mantle must cover the knees as if there weren't trousers under it. Baggy trousers, being very ample, can be good dressings for women, too, at places where they are customary. If they will cause fitna at places where they are not customary, it is not permissible to wear them. Great Islamic scholar **Qâdî Sanâullah-i Pânîputî** 'rahmatullâhi ta'âlâ 'alaih' (1143 [1730 A.D.] – 1225 [1810 A.D.], Pânî-put, India), in explaining the seventh piece of advice at the end of the book **Tafhîmât** by **Shâh Waliyyullah-i Dahlawî** 'rahmatullâhi ta'âlâ 'alaih', (1114 [1702 A.D.] – 1176 [1762 A.D.], Delhi), says: "Of old, it used to be an Islamic custom to go out wearing a long shirt, wrapping oneself up with a large towel, wearing clogs or things like that. But now it would be ostentation to go out with such things on at places where they are not

---

[1] It was written by Muhammad bin Ahmad Zâhid 'rahmatullâhi ta'âlâ 'alaih', (d. 632 [1234 A.D.], India.)

customary. Our Prophet 'sall-Allâhu 'alaihi wa sallam' prohibited ostentation and making fame. We must dress ourselves with things that are customary among Believers. We must not keep ourselves aloof." So is the case with a woman's going out with a dress with a veil at places where it is customary for women to wear ample mantles. In addition, causing an Islamic attirement to be mocked at, she will be sinful. See also the last five pages of the fourteenth chapter of the fifth fascicle of Endless Bliss.]

Whether in namâz or outside of namâz, it is fard to cover one's awrat parts lest others will see from the sides, but it is not fard to cover them from oneself. If one sees one's own awrat parts when one bends down for rukû' one's namâz does not become annulled. But it is makrûh for one to look at them. Something transparent like glass or nylon that lets colour of the thing under it be seen cannot be a covering. If the covering is tight or, though ample, if it sticks to one of one's awrat parts so that it resembles its shape under the covering, it does not harm namâz. But it does not cover one from others. It is harâm to look at someone else's qaba awrat that can be seen in this manner. Men's private parts on their front and in their back, termed saw'atayn, and their buttocks are their **Qaba awrat**. When a sick person who lies naked under a blanket performs namâz by signs with his head inside the blanket, he has performed it naked. If he performs it keeping his head outside the blanket, he will have performed it covering himself with the blanket, which is acceptable. For it is compulsory not to cover oneself but to cover one's awrat parts. For this reason, it is not permissible to perform namâz naked in the dark, in a lonely room or in a closed tent.

A person who is not able to cover his awrat parts sits like sitting in namâz, or stretches his feet side by side towards the qibla, which is better, covers his front private part with his hands, and performs namâz by signs. For, covering one's awrat parts is more important than the other precepts of namâz. [As is seen, even a person who is naked has to perform namâz in its proper time and must not omit it. Hence it must be understood that those who do not perform their namâz because of laziness and who do not pay their debts of omitted namâz are under a great sinful responsibility]. A person who is naked asks for something to cover himself from others who are with him. If they promise him, he waits until nearly the end of prayer time. Also, when there is no water, a person who expects water has to wait for water until nearly the end of prayer time, and can make a tayammum only after waiting that long. He who has the money must buy water and something to cover himself. A person who cannot find anything besides a covering less than one-fourth of which is clean is permitted to perform namâz with the covering or by signs sitting; however, with a covering one-fourth of which is clean he has to perform it standing, in which case he will not perform the namâz again later.

If a Muslim on a long-distance journey[1] can find water only for drinking within one mile, (if there are no clean chothes available,) he performs namâz with the covering that has najâsat on it, in which case he will not have to perform it again later. It is not permissible for a settled person, i.e. a person who is not a musâfir, to perform namâz in a najs covering. It is possible and necessary for him to clean it. For it is strongly probable to find water in a city. If it is known for certain that there is no water in the city, the settled person also can perform the namâz with a covering with najâsat on it and can make a tayammum. It is written as follows in the fifth volume of **Radd-ul-muhtâr**:

There are four cases concerning people's looking at one another and seeing one another.

A man's looking at a woman; a woman's looking at a man; a man's looking at a man; and a woman's looking at a woman. And there are four kinds of a man's looking at a woman:

A man's looking at a nâmahram free woman; at his own wife and jâriyas; at his eighteen relatives who are permissible for him to look at; and at others' jâriyas.

It is harâm in all four Madhhabs for men to see nâmahram women's bodies, with the exception of their faces and inner and outer surfaces of their hands. It is harâm also for men to look lustfully at the faces of girls (nâmahram to them). So, girls ought to cover their faces as well. This prohibition pertaining to seeing applies to castrated, sterilized men, too. It is harâm to castrate a man. Castrating an animal is permissible only when it is intended to fatten it.

It is harâm for men to look at the part of a man's body between his navel and knees. It is permissible for them to look at his other parts without lust. It is permissible for a man to look at his wife and at his own jâriyas from head to foot even with lust, and also for them to look at him likewise.

---

[1] What a long-distance journey is, is explained in the fifteenth chapter.

[A man's awrat parts are between his navel and his knees in three Madhhabs. In the Hanafî Madhhab the knees are awrat. The navel is not awrat. In the Shâfi'î Madhhab the navel is awrat and the knees are not. In the Mâlikî Madhhab none of them is awrat. It is stated in **Mizân-ul-kubrâ**[1] that according to an authentic report in the Mâlikî and Hanbalî Madhhabs a man's awrat parts are only his saw'atayn. This nonexistence of ijmâ' (consensus among the four Madhhabs) delivers male Muslims who expose their thighs nonchalantly from the danger of disbelief[2]. Also, the Shiites' awrat is their saw'atayn only].

A man, if he feels secure of lust, can look at the heads, faces, necks, arms, legs below the knees of the eighteen women who are harâm for him to marry by nikâh and of others' jâriyas. He cannot look at their breasts, at spaces under their arms, at their flanks, thighs, knees or upper parts of their back. These parts of women are also called (ghalîz), i.e. **Qaba awrat**. Women should wear garments ample enough to cover these parts of their body in such a way as their shapes will not be discernible during namâz and in mixed company. Jâriyas can perform namâz without covering their parts that are permissible to be seen.

There are two kinds of women's dressing in Islam. Firstly, free Muslim women cover all their bodies completely except their faces and hands. It is written in **Halabî-i-kebîr**, in the section dealing with the shrouding of the dead: "Men cover themselves with an outergarment termed a 'qamîs', and women with a 'dir'. Both these garments cover the body from the shoulders to the feet. The qamîs has a collar with a slit from the shoulder to the foot and the dir is open between the breast and the foot." As is seen, Muslim women wore coats as they do today. Wearing (black outdoor overgarments called) charshaf became the vogue afterwards. An ample and long mantle, a thick headcover, long stockings cover better than today's charshaf. It is written in the fourth page of **Durar-ul-Multaqita**, by 'Abd-ul-'Azîz Dîrî (d. 694):

---

[1] Explaining the teachings of Fiqh in all four Madhhabs, the book is an epitome of compact erudition written by Abd-ul-Wahhâb-i-Sha'rânî 'rahmatullâhi ta'âlâ 'alaih', (d. 973 [1565 A.D.],) a profound scholar well-versed both in the knowledge of Hadîth and in the teachings of Fiqh in the Shâfi'î Madhhab.

[2] Otherwise, i.e. if all four Madhhabs agreed on that it was harâm for male Muslims to expose their thighs when in company, those who violated and slighted this injunction would outright become unbelievers.

"Islam has not commanded a certain type of covering for women." The second one is the dressing of a jâriya (the woman servant captured in war), who does not have to cover her head, hair, neck, arms or legs (below knees) when among men. It has been observed with regret that some women who bear Muslim names have abandoned the Islamic lady's dressing and fallen for the habiliment for jâriyas or servants.

In order to mislead Muslim women, disbelievers and zindîqs say: "In the beginning of Islam women did not use to cover themselves. In the Prophet's time Muslim women used to go out with bare heads and arms. Later, jealous men of religion ordered women to cover themselves. So women began to cover themselves afterwards, and became like ogres." Yes, women used to go out without covering themselves. Yet, later the sûras of **Ahzâb** and **Nûr** were revealed in the third year of Hegira, whereby Allâhu ta'âlâ commanded them to cover themselves. It is written in **Mawâhib-i ladunniyya**[1]: "On the way back from the Ghazâ (Holy War) of Khaiber, one night Rasûlullah 'sall-Allâhu 'alaihi wa sallam' admitted Safiyya 'radiy-Allâhu ta'âlâ anhâ', one of the captives, into his tent. The Sahâba did not know if Safiyya was honoured as a wife or served as a jâriya. But they felt ashamed to find it out by asking Rasûlullah so that they could do the reverence and service due to (the Prophet's) blessed wives. 'We'll understand that she has become a wife if she goes out of the tent in a covered manner and is escorted behind a curtain tomorrow morning,' they said. So, seeing that she was escorted out behind a curtain, they realized that she had been honoured as a wife." As is seen, in Rasûlullah's time free women used to cover all their bodies. It would be known that a woman was not a slave but a free lady by her covering herself all over.

It is permissible for a person who is secure of lust to touch someone's part which he is permitted to look at. A hadîth sherîf declares: **"Kissing one's mother's foot is like kissing the threshold of the doorway to Paradise."** On the other hand, whereas it is permissible to look at a nâmahram young woman's hand and face, it is not permissible to touch her or to shake hands with her even if one is secure of lust. Committing fornication with a woman or touching any part of her with lust, even if by forgetting or by mistake, according to the Hanafî and the Hanbalî Madhhabs

---

[1] Written by Imâm-i-Ahmad bin Muhammad Shihâb-ud-dîn Qastalânî 'rahmatullâhi ta'âlâ 'alaih', (821 [1418 A.D.] – 923 [1517], Egypt).

causes **hurmat-i-musâhara**. In this case, it becomes eternally harâm for the man to marry this woman's daughters or her mother by blood or in virtue of nursing and also, for the woman to marry the man's son or father. [If hurmat-i-musâhara takes place between a man and his daughter the nikâh between the girl's mother, that is, the man's wife, and the man does not become annulled. The woman cannot marry someone else. The man has to divorce the wife. It becomes an eternal harâm for him to remain married with the woman. If hurmat-i-musâhara happens between a man and his mother-in-law, the son-in-law will have to divorce his wife. The son-in-law cannot marry this woman again eternally **(Bezzâziyya)**[1]]. It is not permissible for girls to touch nâmahram men even if they confidently rely on themselves. If they touch with lust hurmat-i-musâhara takes place. Girls' and old people's lust is their hearts' inclination. It is permissible for a person who trusts himself to shake hands with an old woman or to kiss her hand if she is old enough not to arouse lust, but it is better not to do so.

It is permissible for men to stay together at a lonely place (halwat) and to go on a travel [e.g. on hajj] with their **eternal mahrams**[2]. According to the **tarafayn**[3], **halwat** [staying together at a lonely place] with a woman who is not one's eternal mahram is harâm. If one stays with her along with another mutteqî man or one of his eternal mahrams or one's wife, it is not harâm. Hurmat-i-musâhara does not happen by staying in halwat or by looking at any part of hers with lust except when it is at the front. While telling about being an imâm, **Ibni Âbidîn** writes: "Halwat happens also when there are more than one nâmahram women. A very old woman and an old man can go on a travel and can stay alone **[Eshbâh]**[4]. Halwat with one of the eighteen women who are one's eternal mahram is permissible, yet it is makrûh with one's milk[5]

---

[1] Written by Ibn-ul-Bezzâz Muhammad bin Muhammad Kerderî 'rahmatullâhi ta'âlâ 'alaih', (d. 827 [1424 A.D.],) this book of fatwâs was combined with **Fatâwâ-i-Hindiyya**, another book of fatwâs, and the two books were printed in Egypt in 1310 and were reproduced there in 1393 [1973 A.D.].

[2] Eternal mahrams are close relatives by blood, in virtue of nursing or through nikâh (marriage) with whom one cannot marry at all.

[3] Imâm-i a'zam Abû Hanîfa and Imâm-i Muhammad.

[4] It was written by Zeynel'âbidîn bin Ibrâhîm ibni Nujaym-i-Misrî 'rahmatullâhi ta'âlâ 'alaih', (926-970 [1562 A.D.], Egypt).

[5] Please see the seventh chapter of the sixth fascicle of **Endless Bliss** for the 'Milk-Tie'.

sister, with one's young mother-in-law or daughter-in-law when fitna is likely. It is not permissible to talk with a young nâmahram woman without necessity." It will not be halwat staying alone in a transportation wagon, shops, and places that are open to public like mosques, since the insides of such places can be seen from the outside. Two different rooms of one house are not counted as one place. Who the women that are eternally mahram are is written in the twelfth chapter of the fifth fascicle of Endless Bliss.

According to imâm-i Abû Yûsuf 'rahmatullâhi ta'âlâ 'alaih', those needy, enslaved, lonely women [employees and civil servants] who have to work for a living at such jobs as baking bread, laundering [and others that require uncovering their parts that are not their qaba awrat] can bare their arms and feet as much as their work requires. It is permissible for men to see them or to look at them without lust when work requires. And it is written in **Ni'met-i Islâm**[1] (in chapter on hajj), in **Bahr al-fatâwâ**[2], and in **Ali Efendi's fatwâ**, that wife's sister and uncle's or brother's wife are nâmahram women, too. It is harâm also to look at their hair, head, arms and legs. During mutual family visits it is not permissible for the men and women to sit in the same room, to behave cordially towards one another, to joke with one another or to make merry. At places where men's and women's sitting in the same room is customary and where this harâm is slighted, in order to prevent offence and hostility among relatives, women can sit in the same room or eat with their male relatives for a short time, but they must be covered. The talks must be serious. Utter care must be taken that the talk should last short and be rare and especially that they should not be alone in the same place. True and well learned Muslims who know and obey Islam should never sit together like that. We should not dispute with ignorant people or insist that Islam commands so, but we should try to abstain from harâms by making excuses pertaining to worldly matters, by talking softly not to offend our relatives. A male slave also is a nâmahram man to his female possessor.

Seeing once is permissible for a judge when deciding a case in the court of justice, for witnesses when giving evidence, for a

---

[1] It was written by Muhammad Zihnî 'rahmatullâhi ta'âlâ 'alaih', (1262-1332 [1914 A.D.].)

[2] It was written by Kâdî-Zâda Muhammad 'Ârif 'rahmatullâhi ta'âlâ 'alaih', (d. 1173 [1759 A.D.].)

person who is to marry a girl, even if lust is likely to happen, and for a doctor, for a nurse, for a circumciser, for a person who does enema (clyster), as long as necessary. It is permissible for a sick person to have himself clystered. It is written on the four hundred and seventy-eighth page of the fifth volume of **Durr-ul-mukhtâr**: "It is important sunnat to have one's son circumcised. It is Islam's symbol. If the people of a city do not have their sons circumcised, the Khalîfa fights them. There is not a certain age of circumcision for a child. The best time is between seven and twelve years of age." When performing circumcision, it is customary to repeat the **Takbîr-i 'Iyd** together loudly. Those who are not circumcised catch various diseases. French books describe them under the name 'Affections du prépuce'. On the five hundred and fifty-eighth page of **Hadîqa**[1] and in its chapter about afflictions incurred by one's eyes, it is written that it is permissible for girls to learn and teach science and medicine on condition that they will observe the Sharî'at. Girls must be educated and trained as obstetricians and gynaecologists. Women must be shown to women doctors. If a woman doctor cannot be found one must take one's wife to a male gynaecologist, if her illness is dangerous or very painful.

The awrat parts of Muslim women to one another are like the awrat parts of a man to another man.

If a woman is secure of lust, her looking at a nâmahram man is like a man's looking at another. The book **Jawhara**[2] says that it is like a man's looking at those women who are his mahram. But it is harâm for her to look at him lustfully. Non-Muslim and renegade women's looking at Muslim women, (as well as their paternal and maternal uncles, if they are renegades), that is, muslim women's showing themselves to them, is, like their showing themselves to nâmahram men, harâm in three Madhhabs. They cannot look at Muslim women's bodies. It is permissible in the Hanbalî Madhhab.

When those parts of the body that are not permissible to look

---

[1] It was written by Abd-ul-Ghanî Nablusî 'rahmatullâhi ta'âlâ 'alaih', (1050 [1640 A.D.] – 1143 [1731 A.D.], Damascus.)

[2] **Jawhara-t-un-nayyira**, by Abû Bakr bin 'Alî Haddâd-i-Yemenî 'rahmatullâhi ta'âlâ 'alaih', (d. 800 [1397 A.D.].) The book is an abridged version of of **Sirâj-ul-wahhâj**, which he wrote as a commentary to the book **Mukhtasar-i-Qudûrî**, by Ahmad bin Muhammad Baghdâdî 'rahmatullâhi ta'âlâ 'alaih'.

at leave the body, it is still not permissible to look at them even if the body is dead. After a woman's hair and other hairs, toe-nails [not finger-nails] and bones leave her body, they cannot be looked at.

It is not harâm to look without lust at the reflections on mirrors or on water of those parts of women that are harâm to look at. For, in this case not they themselves but their visions are being seen. [Their reflexions or pictures are not they themselves. Seeing them (their reflexions or pictures) does not mean seeing them. Looking at their pictures or at their visions in movies or on television is like looking at their images in mirrors. They are all permissible to look at without lust, but harâm to watch lustfully or to look at those visions of theirs that will arouse lust. Also, it is harâm to listen to their voices. Surely, there are people who look at them lustfully. It is harâm to draw, to publish, to take pictures that arouse lust and are harâm.] It is not permissible but harâm to look at the awrat parts of women, even without lust, behind glass, with any kind of spectacles, through water or at a woman in water.

The voice of an imâm or a hâfiz or a muazzin heard through a loudspeaker or on the radio is not his own voice, but it is its likeness. A namâz performed by following a voice heard likewise is not sahîh. It is bid'at to read or recite the Qur'ân al-kerîm or to call the azân through a loudspeaker. For, lifeless objects that are used to produce sound are called **mizmâr**, i.e. musical instrument. Thunder, cannons, rifles, owls, parrots are not musical instruments. Instruments that produce sounds for pleasure, such as drums, tambourines, cymbals, reeds, flutes, loudspeakers are all musical instruments. A musical instrument will not produce sound by itself. They have to be used so as to produce sound, i.e. with the drum you have to strike the tightly stretched skin with a stick, with the reed you have to blow, and with the loudspeaker you have to articulate sounds. The sound that comes out from them is their own production. It is not the voice of the person blowing them or talking to them. Voices reading or reciting the Qur'ân al-kerîm or calling the azân through loudspeakers are sounds produced by the loudspeakers. They are not the voices of the imâms or muazzins producing the original sounds. The muazzin's own voice is the azân. From both scientific and religious points of view, the sound coming out of the instrument is not the muazzin's own voice, which, in turn, means that it is not the azân. Because it is like the azân, it is supposed to be the azân.

What is termed the azân is the muazzin's own voice; in fact, it should be the voice of a pious (sâlih) male Muslim, not the voice of a woman or a child or a sound produced by a loudspeaker, despite the similarity. Voices and sounds of this sort belong to others. Different musical instruments produce different sounds. The sound produced by a loudspeaker is not a human voice despite the quite close resemblance. A watermelon seed sown in soil turns into a big watermelon. The watermelon is not the seed any longer. The seed is rotten, gone. Likewise, the words uttered to the microphone are gone, and other sounds come out of the loudspeaker. Some hadîth-i-sherîfs read as follows: **"As the end of the world approaches, the Qur'ân al-kerîm will be read (or recited) through mizmârs." "A time will come, wherein the Qur'ân al-kerîm will be read (or recited) through mizmârs. It will be done not for the sake of Allah, but for pleasure." "Many a reader (or reciter) of the Qur'ân al-kerîm is accursed by the Qur'ân al-kerîm he reads (or recites)." "There will be a time when the most wretched Muslims will be the muazzins." "There will be a time when the Qur'ân al-kerîm will be read (or recited) through mizmârs. Allâhu ta'âlâ will accurse them."** Mizmâr means any kind of musical instruments, e.g. reeds. A loudspeaker also is a mizmâr. Muazzins should fear the admonitions conveyed in these hadîth-i-sherîfs and should not call the azân through loudspeakers. Some people, who are ignorant in religious matters, say that loudspeakers are useful because they carry sound to distant places. Our Prophet 'sall-Allâhu 'alaihi wa sallam' stated: **"Perform your acts of worship in the manners that you have seen me and my Sahâba do them! A person who makes changes in** (the prescribed manner of) **an act of worship is called a man of bid'at. Men of bid'at shall definitely go to Hell. None of their acts shall be accepted."** It is not right to say, "We are making useful amendments to religious practices." These fibs are invented by enemies of religion. It is the Islamic scholars' business to know whether certain changes are useful. These profound scholars are called **Mujtahids**. Mujtahids do not make any changes on their own. They know whether an amendment or a change is an act of bid'at. There is a consensus (of Islamic scholars) on that it is an act of bid'at to call the azân through mizmârs. The path that will lead human beings to the grace and love of Allâhu ta'âlâ is (the one that goes through) the human heart. The heart is like a mirror by creation. Acts of worship add to the heart's cleanliness and lustre. Sins blacken the heart, so that it will no longer receive the fayds[1] and nûrs (radiance, lights) coming to it through love (of Allah or of those people loved by Allah). Sâlih (pious) Muslims recognize this state and feel sad. They do not want to commit sins. They wish to do more and more acts of worship. In addition to doing the five daily prayers of namâz, for instance, they wish to perform other prayers of namâz. Committing sins tastes sweet and sounds useful to the nafs. All sorts of bid'ats and sins feed and strengthen the nafs, who is an enemy of Allâhu ta'âlâ. An example of this is calling the azân through a loudspeaker. It is like a picture of an imâm in a book or an image on a television screen, which is not the imâm himself although it is very much like him. Even if one sees all the actions of an imâm (performing a namâz) on television and hears his voice, one cannot perform a namâz by following him.

It is permissible to look without lust at a woman dressed in clothes not so scanty as to stick on her body. It is harâm to look at a woman even without lust who is clad in a dress the qaba awrat parts of which are scanty. It is harâm to look lustfully at a nâmahram woman's underwears. It is harâm to look lustfully at those parts of hers that are not her qaba awrat and which are covered tightly, scantily.

As it is harâm for women to go out without covering themselves and by decking themselves out, likewise it is harâm for them to enter likewise any place where there are men not mahram to them. And it is even more sinful to enter a mosque with their awrat parts exposed. A place where there are people with open awrat parts or where harâm is committed is called **majlîs al-fisq** (sinning party). It is written in **Bezzâziyya** that it is not permissible for Muslims to attend or to allow their wives to a majlîs al-fisq, that is, a place where sinners gather together, without necessity. Women who have îmân must cover those parts of theirs that are not qaba awrat, such as head, hair, arms, legs, for Muslims must dread harâms lest they will lose their îmân.

---

[1] If a Muslim performs the acts of worship commanded by Islam properly, avoids those acts prohibited by Islam, subdues his nafs to full obedience to Islam, and attaches his heart to an Islamic scholar or Walî, he will attain a spiritual state wherein inexplicable pieces of subtle Islamic knowledge will begin to flow into his heart. This knowledge is called fayd. Naturally, it goes without saying that the first and the basic condition is that he should learn Islam from true, dependable sources. Otherwise, his heart may be lured away from Islam by some fatal delusions in the name of fayds.

[Some people, whose sole interest is pleasure and entertainment, do not hesitate to mislead others into mischiefs and disasters in order to attain their pleasures; they say for instance, "It is something annoying to see a woman who has covered herself like an ogre. On the other hand, it gives relief and pleasure to look at an ornamented, beautiful girl or woman in free attire. It is sweet, like watching or smelling a beautiful flower." Looking at a flower or smelling a flower is sweet to the soul. It causes the soul to recognize the existence and the greatness of Allâhu ta'âlâ and to obey His commandments. Looking at a nice-smelling, ornamented and freely-dressed girl, on the contrary, is sweet to the nafs. The ear does not take any pleasure from colours, nor does the eye from sounds. For, they do not sense these things. The nafs is the enemy of Allâhu ta'âlâ. It will not hesitate to do any sort of evil whereby to attain its pleasures. It will violate human rights and laws. Its pleasures do not have an end. Looking at a girl will not satisfy it. It will desire to meet her and to practise all its pleasures. It is for this reason that all civil codes curb the eccentricities of nafses. Excessive desires of the nafs drift people into misery, diseases, family disasters and afflictions. In order to prevent these disastrous situations, Allâhu ta'âlâ has prohibited girls' dressing freely and being close to men not related to them, alcohol and gambling. People who have been enslaved by their nafs flout these prohibitions. So they censure the books of 'ilm-i-hâl written by scholars of Ahl as-sunna and prevent young people from reading these books and attaining salvation. As is understood from all the aforesaid facts, it is sinful for women and girls to go out shopping (without properly covering themselves) and to wander likewise at market-places and stores. Muslims have to protect their daughters against these sins. Otherwise, they will lose their îmân and become disbelievers. Enemies of Islam misrepresent whatsoever is destructive to îmân as national customs in order to spread disbelief.]

9 – ISTIQBÂL-I QIBLA

It means to perform namâz towards the Qibla; it does not mean to perform it for the Qibla. Formerly the Qibla used to be **Quds** (Jerusalem). Seventeen months after the Hegira, at the third rak'at of the early afternoon or late afternoon prayer of a Tuesday in the middle of Sha'bân, Muslims were commanded to turn towards Ka'ba. According to Hanafî and Mâlikî Madhhabs, namâz will be sahîh if the opening between the crosswise directions of the optic nerves includes Ka'ba. This angle is approximately 45°. Istanbul's Qibla direction is approximately 29° east of south. This angle is called the **angle of Qibla**. The straight line drawn on a map and running between a certain city and the blessed city of Mekka is termed the **khatt-i-Qibla** (line of Qibla) of that city. This line indicates the direction of Qibla. The time when the Sun is overhead (an observer imagined to be standing on) this line is the **Qibla hour** (at that location). The angle between this line and the longitudinal circle of that city is the **angle of Qibla**. A city's Qibla direction depends on its longitude and latitude. In the northern hemisphere, the south is approximately the direction to the Sun at zawâl or, when the face of a clock adjusted to the local zawalî time is held horizontally towards the sky and its hour-hand towards the sun, bisector of the angle between the hour-hand and number twelve. The nearer the declination of the Sun and the equation of time to zero, the more precise is the result. Istanbul's Qibla direction can be determined by using one of the following two elements: 1- By using the angle of Qibla. 2- By using the Qibla hour. 1- If you first face due south by aligning yourself with the circle of longitude overhead your location and then turn eastwards by the angle of Qibla, the direction you will be facing now is the Qibla. Angle Q is calculated as follows: Longitude of the blessed city of Mekka from Greenwich is, $\lambda'=39°50'$ or 39.83° and its latitude is $\varphi'=21°26'$ or 21.43°. Since Istanbul's longitude is $\lambda=29°$ and its latitude is $\varphi=41°$, the difference between their longitudes is 10°50' or 10.83°, and the difference between their latitudes is 19°34' or 19.57°. If Istanbul's approximate angle of Qibla, as measured from the direction of south, is, say, Q, the following approximate equation, obtained utilizing the geometrical explanation in the book **Ma'rifatnâma**, can be written,

$$\tan Q = \frac{\sin (39.83° - \lambda)}{\sin (\varphi - 21.43°)} = \frac{\sin 10.83°}{\sin 19.57°} = \frac{0.18795}{0.33490} = 0.56121$$

∴ Q = 29°18'

Note: Since the difference, d, between the longitudes of Istanbul and Mekka mukarrama is less than 60°, Q is almost the same as the result obtained with the following exact formula. If d is greater than 120°, Q can be found using ($\lambda'=-140.17°$ and $\varphi'=-$

21.43° instead of 39.83° and 21.43°, respectively) for the place symmetrical to Mekka with respect to the center of the earth by means of the approximate formula. By subtracting the result from 180°, Q is found. AN represents the meridian.

S= The point where the plumb-level of the location intersects the earth's surface; N= Point of Zawâl, when the sun is at culmination.

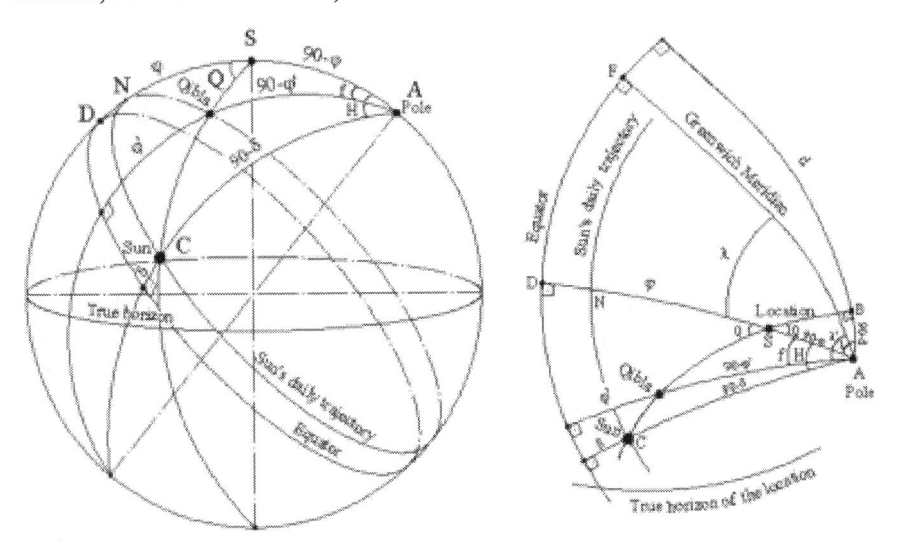

The following formula based on the spherical triangle yields the exact angle of Qibla.

$$\tan Q = \frac{\sin(39.83° - \lambda)}{\cos(39.83° - \lambda)\sin\varphi - 0.3925\cos\varphi}$$

where λ and φ are the longitude and latitude, respectively, of the location for which Q is to be found. The sign of λ is (+) in the east, and (−) in the west of Greenwich (London). φ is (+) in the northern hemisphere, and (−) in the southern hemisphere. The Q found is the angle between the two directions from that location, one to the south and the other to the qibla (Mekka).

To find the direction of Qibla, we turn Q degrees from the geographical south of the earth divided into two regions by the great circle passing through Mekka (λ'= 39.83°) and through its symmetrical point (λ'=−140.17°), to the west at locations to the east of the Qibla and vice versa at locations to its west. The Q found with this formula should have a (−) sign for the eastern regions and (+) sign for the western regions. In case of opposite

– 127 –

results, the angle of Qibla is found by adding (+ 180°) or (-180°). For example, for Karachi with λ =67°, φ=25°, the following keys are depressed on a CASIO calculator:

39.83-67 = cos x 25 sin - 25 cos x 0.3925 = Min 39.83-67 = sin ÷ MR = INV tan

Hence Q is obtained as -87° 27' for Karachi.

Q for is Istanbul +28° 21', (which may be rounded up to +29°.)

In the following, some Q values calculated by the exact and (approximate) formulas are given. The last three values are obtained by the symmetrical approach:

Munich   : 50°(47°)   New York: 122°(134°)
London   : 61°(52°)
Basel   : 56°(50°)
Frankfurt : 52°(47°)
Tokyo   : 113°(130°)   Kumasi : 115°(125°)

In the figure on the right hand side of the previous page, the point B is the point at which the Qibla direction CS is perpendicular to a declination circle or meridian AB. In the right angled spherical triangle ABS, using the Napier equations, cos (90°-φ) = sin φ = cot i x cot Q, and as tan A x cot A=1, sin φ = (1/tan i) x (1/tan Q). Hence, tan i =(1/sin φ) x Q. For example, on February 2, if the keys E/C 1 ÷ 41 sin÷ 28.21° °,,,→ tan = arc tan are depressed, we obtain i=70.5°. The equation i=70.5° is constant for Istanbul. In the right angled spherical triangle ABC, cos(i+H) = tan δ x cot d. In the triangle ABS, cos i = tan φ x cot d and, therefore, cot d = cos i / tan φ, and hence, cos(i+H) = tan δ x cos i ÷ tan φ . Keying in E/C 16.58 °,,,→ +/− tan x 70.5 cos ÷ 41 tan=arc cos -70.5=÷15= °,,,→ , the hour angle H, i.e., the arc CN, is obtained as 1 hour 45 minutes. Kadûsî notes in his annotation to Rub'-i-dâira: "The cursor set (for the date), when moved to the line of qibla, the complement of the angle indicated by the string on the arc of altitude is the supplement of the hour angle of İstanbul's time of Qibla. When it is divided by 15, the result is the hour angle H." The daily standard **time of Qibla** at which the Sun is on the direction of Qibla of a given location can be calculated by subtracting from 12:00 hours the time corresponding to the hour angle and combining the result with the Equation of Time and the difference of longitude from the Standard Meridian. In the example given above, (the standard time of Qibla) is 10 hr 33 min. The adhânî Qibla time is calculated to be 5 hr 6 min by subtracting the time corresponding to the hour angle and one Temkin from the time of dhuhr-i-adhânî (the adhânî time for early afternoon prayer). If you turn to the Sun at this time, you will face the Qibla. If the Qibla is to the east of the south, the Sun is also in the east, the time is before noon, and the H in the time equation will have a (-) sign. δ=the sun's declination. When $δ = φ$ (of Mekka) = 21.43°, the Sun will be exactly overhead the Ka'ba, which takes place twice a year. Anyone who turns towards the Sun at this time, (at the time of Qibla, that is,) regardless of their location worldover, will at the same time have turned in the direction of the Qibla.

Ahmed Ziyâ Begh found Q=29° for Istanbul by taking somewhat higher values for the longitudes and latitudes and using tables of logarithms of trigonometric functions. The mihrâb of the mosque at the Kandilli quay in Istanbul was calculated by him in this way during the restoration of the mosque.

By turning approximately thirty-one degrees eastward from the direction of south found by a compass, Qibla will be faced in Istanbul. However, the needle of a compass points to magnetic poles, which, in fact, are not the poles of the Earth's axis. And the locations of magnetic poles change in the course of time. They complete one rotation around true poles in a period of some six hundred years. The angle between the magnetic direction and the true polar direction is called the **magnetic declination**. Every location has a different angle of declination. There are populated areas where the needle of the compass even deviates 30° from the south to the east (+) or to the west (-). And a place's angle of declination changes yearly. Then, if the direction **of Qibla** is found with a compass, the angle of magnetic declination has to be added to or subtracted from the angle of Qibla. Istanbul's angle of magnetic declination is approximately +3°. When we turn eastward for 28° +3°=31° from the south direction found with a compass in Istanbul, we will face the Qibla.

If the south direction is found with the help of the Pole-Star or with a clock or by means of the meridian line drawn on the ground, it is not necessary to add the angle of declination to the angle of Qibla. The direction of Qibla is found by turning 28° eastward (from south) in **Istanbul.** For doing this you place your clock (or watch) on a table horizontally and turn the figure 6 towards south. When the minute-hand is moved to the position over 5 it points to the Qibla.

It is permissible, even when performing a namâz that is fard, to deviate from the direction of Qibla when there is the fear of illness, enemy or thieves, or by mistake, but it is a must to turn towards the Qibla when performing it on a ship or train.

A musâfir travelling on a ship or train must begin the fard namâz standing towards the Qibla and put a compass somewhere near the place he will prostrate. He must turn towards the Qibla as the ship or train changes direction. Or someone else should make him turn right or left. If his chest deviates from the Qibla when performing the namâz, his namâz becomes nullified. For a ship or a train is like one's own home. It is not like an animal. Since the fard namâz of those who cannot turn toward the Qibla on buses, on trains, on ships when the sea is rough will not be acceptable, they can imitate Shâfi'î Madhhab as long as they travel, and perform the late afternoon prayer together with the early afternoon prayer and the night prayer together with the evening prayer, one immediately after the other. Likewise, if a person in Hanafî Madhhab will not be able to turn towards the Qibla on the way after starting the journey, he must perform the late afternoon prayer immediately after performing the early afternoon prayer at the time of the early afternoon prayer when they halt somewhere for some time during the day, and perform the evening prayer and the night prayer together at the time of the night prayer when they halt somewhere during the night, and when intending to start each of those four prayers he must intend, that is, pass through his heart the thought: "I am performing it by imitating Shâfi'î Madhhab." According to Shâfi'î and Mâlikî Madhhabs, when a travelling person goes to his hometown or to a place where he intends to stay more than three days excluding the days when he enters and goes out of the city, or when he stays more than eighteen days at a place where he went for some business which he thought would take him less than four days, he becomes muqîm (settled). As he leaves the place he will not become safarî unless he intends to travel to a place at a distance of not less than 80 km. Hadrat Ibni Hajar-i Makkî[1] states in his book **Fatâwâ-i Fiqhiyya**: "If a travelling (safarî) person postpones his early afternoon prayer in order to perform it together with his late afternoon prayer but becomes muqîm (settled) after the time for early afternoon prayer is over before he performs his early afternoon prayer, he makes qadâ of his early afternoon prayer

---

[1] Shihâb-ud-dîn Ahmed bin Muhammad Hiytamî 'rahmatullâhi ta'âlâ 'alaih', (899 [1494 A.D.] – 974 [1566], Mekka.)

(performs it) first. He does not become sinful for having postponed his early afternoon prayer until its time is over. Anyone who imitates Mâlikî or Shâfi'î Madhhab because he has a crowned or filled tooth in his mouth, must not make qasr (shorten) the fard prayers where he stays more than three and less than fifteen days; he must perform all four rak'ats of those prayers. Otherwise, his fard prayers which he performs as two rak'ats will not be sahîh according to the Mâlikî and Shâfi'î Madhhabs. If he prays four rak'ats, it is sahîh, although it is makrûh in the Hanafî. Similarly, one's namâz is sahîh (valid) according to Mâlikî Madhhab if one's skin comes in contact with that of a nâmahram woman or if one's ablution (wudu') is broken during namâz. As is written in the final paragraph of the fourth chapter, this person cannot combine (perform by jem') his prayers where he stays as safarî (traveller) unless there is a haraj.

Although it is not permissible to determine the beginning of Ramadân-i sherîf beforehand by using calendars or by calculation, it is permissible to find the direction of the Qibla by calculation, pole star [compass], etc. or to ascertain the prayer times by using a calendar prepared by astronomical calculations. For, though they will not be found out accurately by sole calculation or instrumental observation and analysis, they will be guessed strongly. Finding out the Qibla or prayer times by strong conviction is permissible.

At places where there is no mihrâb and where the Qibla cannot be found by calculation or with the help of the Pole-Star [a compass], true Muslims who know which direction the Qibla is must be consulted. We should not ask disbelievers, fâsiqs, or children. Disbelievers and fâsiqs can be believed in **mu'amalât** (business transactions and social dealings), but not in **diyânât** [worships]. When you have no one with you who knows about the Qibla, you need not look for one. You must search for it yourself and then perform namâz towards the direction you have decided to be the Qibla. If later you find out that it was the wrong direction you do not have to perform the namâz again.

The Qibla is not the building of Ka'ba; it is its building plot. That is, that space from the Earth to the 'Arsh is the Qibla. For this reason, a person who is down in a well, [under the sea], on top of a high mountain [or on a plane] can perform namâz in that direction. [For being a hadji[1] a Muslim visits not the building of

---

[1] Please see the seventh chapter of the fifth fascicle of **Endless bliss** for **Hajj.**

Ka'ba but its building plot. He who visits another place cannot become a hadji].

Hadrat Ibni Hajar-i Makkî says in his book **Fatâwâ-i-fiqhiyya**: "It is not permissible to change today's shape of the building of Ka'ba. It is harâm. Today's building was constructed by Hajjâj. When the Khalîfa Hârûn-ur-Rashîd wanted to have it changed in order to put it in the right shape given by Abdullah Ibni Zubayr, Imâm-i Mâlik 'rahmatullâhi ta'âlâ 'alaih' dissuaded him, saying, "If from now on anybody changes it, it is wâjib for us to demolish the changes, provided we will not cause fitna or give damage to the original building. Otherwise it is not wâjib."

If you are ill or when there is the danger that your belongings may be stolen or it may cause the ship you are on board to sink or if there is the danger of a wild animal or of being seen by the enemy or if you will not be able to mount your animal without help in case you get down from it or if your companions will not wait for you in case you make your animal stand towards the Qibla, you combine (jem') two salâts. If jem' is impossible, you perform even the fard namâz standing toward any direction you can manage, and do not perform it again later. For, you have not caused these excuses yourself, but they have happened willy-nilly. If a person who does not know the direction of Qibla performs namâz without looking at the mihrâb or asking someone who knows or trying to find out, his namâz will not be accepted even if he has found the Qibla by chance. But if he finds out after the namâz that he has found the right direction it will be accepted. If he finds it out during the namâz it will not be accepted. If he has inquired for the Qibla but has not performed the namâz in the direction which he has decided to be right, he has to perform it again even if he understands that he has found the right direction by chance. Likewise, a person who performs namâz though he thinks that he does not have an ablution, that his clothes are najs, or that it is not prayer time yet, and who finds out later that his thought has not been correct, performs the namâz again.

[To determine the direction of Qibla, a rod is erected at a place taking sunlight. Or a key or piece of stone is tied to the end of a piece of string and let to hang loosely. At (the time of Qibla) read on the daily calendar, the shadow of the rod or the string shows the direction of Qibla, as the Sun is overhead the direction of Qibla. The Sun is on the Qibla side of the shadow.]

Thy love has infatuated me;
O my Allah, I love Thee!
Thy love is so sweet, really;
O my Allah, I love Thee!

Neither wealth pleaseth me,
Nor do I worry about property.
Thy love, alone, makes me happy;
O my Allah, I love Thee!

Thou hast commanded us to pray,
And advised to keep in the right way.
Thine blessings to enjoy in endless way.
O my Allah, I love Thee!

The nafs I have is so teacherous;
Poor me, with this being so lecherous!
I've found the real delight, so gorgeous:
O my Allah, I love Thee!

Doing the prayers properly,
And also earning the worldly,
Is what I do daily and nightly.
O my Allah, I love Thee!

Love is not only words, O Hilmi!
Thy Allah commandeth drudgery;
Let your manners testify to thee;
O my Allah, I love Thee!

Islam's enemies are so many,
Attacking the religion insidiously;
How could one ever sit idly!
O my Allah, I love Thee!

A lover simply will not sit lazily,
Lest his darling should be hurt slightly.
Silence the enemy, and then say honestly:
O my Allah, I love Thee!

Qibla angles for places with various latitudes and longitudes

	Longitudes (in degrees)		
1	145 150 155 160 165 170 175 180 175 170 165 160 155 150 145 140 135	Lati tu des	130 125 120 115 110 105 100 95 90 85 80 75 70 65 60 55 50 45 40
2	140 135 130 125 120 115 110 105 100 95 90 85 80 75 70 65 60 55		50 45 40 35 30 25 20 15 10 5 0 5 10 15 20 25 30 35
	180 175 170 165 161 156 151 146 141 136 131 127 122 117 112 107 102 97	84	92 87 82 77 72 67 62 57 52 47 42 36 31 26 21 16 10 5 0
	180 175 170 166 161 157 152 147 143 138 133 129 124 119 115 110 105 101	74	96 91 86 82 77 72 67 61 56 51 45 40 34 29 23 17 12 6 0
	180 175 171 166 161 157 152 147 143 138 134 129 124 120 115 111 106 101	72	97 92 87 82 78 73 68 62 57 52 46 41 35 30 24 18 12 6 0
	180 175 171 166 161 157 152 147 143 138 134 129 125 120 116 111 107 102	70	97 93 88 83 79 74 69 64 58 53 47 42 36 30 24 18 12 6 0
	180 175 171 166 161 157 152 148 143 138 134 130 125 121 116 112 107 103	68	98 94 89 84 80 75 70 65 59 54 49 43 37 31 25 19 13 6 0
	180 175 171 166 161 157 152 148 143 139 134 130 125 121 117 112 108 103	66	99 94 90 85 81 76 71 66 61 55 50 44 38 32 26 19 13 6 0
	180 175 171 166 161 157 152 148 143 139 134 130 126 121 117 113 108 104	64	100 95 91 86 82 77 72 67 62 57 51 45 39 33 27 20 13 7 0
	180 175 170 166 161 157 152 148 143 139 134 130 126 121 117 113 109 105	62	100 96 92 87 83 78 73 68 63 58 52 47 41 34 28 21 14 7 0
	180 175 170 166 161 157 152 148 143 139 134 130 126 122 118 113 109 105	60	101 97 93 88 84 79 75 70 65 59 54 48 42 35 29 22 15 7 0
	180 175 170 166 161 156 152 147 143 139 134 130 126 122 118 114 110 106	58	102 98 93 89 85 80 76 71 66 61 55 49 43 37 30 23 15 8 0
	180 175 170 166 161 156 152 147 143 139 134 130 126 122 118 114 110 106	56	102 98 94 90 86 82 77 72 68 62 57 51 45 38 31 24 16 8 0
	180 175 170 165 161 156 152 147 143 138 134 130 126 122 118 114 111 107	54	103 99 95 91 87 83 79 74 69 64 59 53 47 40 33 25 17 8 0
	180 175 170 165 161 156 151 147 143 138 134 130 126 122 118 115 111 107	52	103 100 96 92 88 84 80 75 71 66 60 55 48 42 34 26 18 9 0
	180 175 170 165 160 156 151 147 142 138 134 130 126 122 119 115 111 108	50	104 100 97 93 89 85 81 77 72 68 62 57 50 43 36 28 19 9 0
	180 175 170 165 160 156 151 147 142 138 134 130 126 122 119 115 112 108	48	105 101 98 94 90 87 83 79 74 69 64 59 52 46 38 29 20 10 0
	180 175 170 165 160 155 151 146 142 138 134 130 126 122 119 115 112 108	46	105 102 98 95 92 88 84 80 76 71 66 61 55 48 40 31 21 11 0
	180 175 170 165 160 155 150 146 142 137 133 130 126 122 119 115 112 109	44	106 102 99 96 93 89 86 82 78 74 69 63 57 50 42 33 23 12 0
	180 175 169 164 159 155 150 146 141 137 133 129 126 122 119 116 112 109	42	106 103 100 97 94 90 87 83 80 75 71 66 60 53 45 36 25 13 0
	180 175 169 164 159 154 150 145 141 137 133 129 126 122 119 116 113 110	40	107 104 101 98 95 92 89 85 82 78 73 68 63 56 48 39 27 14 0
	180 174 169 164 159 154 149 145 140 136 133 129 125 122 119 116 113 110	38	107 104 102 99 96 93 90 87 83 80 76 71 66 59 52 42 30 15 1
	180 174 169 164 159 154 149 144 140 136 132 129 125 122 119 116 113 110	36	108 105 102 100 97 94 91 89 85 82 78 74 69 63 55 46 33 17 1
	180 174 169 163 158 153 148 144 139 135 132 128 125 122 119 116 113 111	34	108 105 103 101 98 96 93 90 87 84 81 77 72 67 59 50 37 20 1
	180 174 168 163 158 153 148 143 139 135 131 128 125 121 119 116 113 111	32	108 106 104 101 99 97 94 92 89 87 83 80 76 71 64 55 42 23 1
	180 174 168 162 157 152 147 142 138 134 131 127 124 121 118 116 113 111	30	109 106 104 102 100 98 96 94 91 89 86 83 79 75 69 61 48 28 1
	180 174 168 156 151 146 141 137 133 129 127 124 121 118 116 113 111	28	109 107 105 103 101 99 97 95 93 91 89 86 83 79 74 67 56 35 1
	180 173 167 161 156 150 146 141 137 133 130 126 123 121 118 116 113 111	26	109 107 106 104 102 100 99 97 95 93 91 89 87 84 80 75 65 45 2
	180 173 167 161 155 150 145 140 136 132 129 126 123 120 118 116 113 112	24	110 108 106 105 103 102 100 99 97 96 94 92 91 89 86 82 76 61 4
	180 173 166 160 154 149 144 139 135 132 128 125 122 120 118 115 113 112	22	110 108 107 105 104 103 101 100 99 98 97 96 94 93 92 90 88 84 16
	180 173 166 159 153 148 143 138 134 131 127 125 122 119 117 115 113 112	20	110 109 107 106 105 104 103 102 101 100 99 98 98 98 99 101 108 174
	180 172 165 159 153 147 142 137 133 130 127 124 121 119 117 115 113 112	18	110 109 108 107 106 105 104 103 102 102 102 102 102 104 106 112 128 177
	180 172 165 158 152 146 141 136 132 129 126 123 121 119 117 115 113 112	16	111 109 108 108 107 106 105 105 104 105 105 106 107 109 113 122 141 178
	180 172 164 157 150 145 140 135 131 128 125 122 120 118 116 115 113 112	14	111 110 109 108 108 107 107 106 106 107 107 108 109 111 114 120 130 149 179
	180 171 163 156 149 143 138 134 130 127 124 122 119 117 116 114 113 112	12	111 110 109 109 108 108 108 108 108 109 109 110 112 115 119 126 136 155 179
	180 171 162 155 148 142 137 133 129 126 123 121 119 117 115 114 113 112	10	111 110 110 110 109 109 109 109 110 110 110 112 113 115 119 123 131 142 158 179
	180 170 161 153 146 140 135 131 128 124 122 120 118 116 115 114 113 112	8	111 111 110 110 110 110 110 111 111 112 114 116 118 122 127 135 146 161 179
	180 170 160 152 145 139 134 130 126 123 121 119 117 116 114 113 113 112	6	111 111 111 111 111 111 111 112 113 114 116 118 121 125 131 139 149 164 179
	180 169 159 150 143 137 132 128 125 122 120 118 116 115 114 113 112 112	4	111 111 111 111 111 112 112 113 114 116 118 120 124 128 134 142 152 165 179
	180 168 158 148 141 135 130 126 123 120 118 117 115 114 113 113 112 112	2	111 111 112 112 113 113 114 116 118 120 122 126 131 137 144 154 167 180
3	35 30 25 20 15 10 5 0 5 10 15 20 25 30 35 40 45		50 55 60 65 70 75 80 85 90 95 100 105 110 115 120 125 130 135 140
4	40 45 50 55 60 65 70 75 80 85 90 95 100 105 110 115 120 125		130 135 140 145 150 155 160 165 170 175 180 175 170 165 160 155 150 145

Longitudes are printed in rows at the top and bottom of the table in 5° intervals and Latitudes in the middle column in 2° intervals. Longitudes with a dashed line under them are to the west (-) and the rest are to the east (+) of London. Longitudes in the lines 1 and 2 are for the northern and 3 and 4 for the southern hemisphere. The figure on the cross-section of the column including the longitude and the line including the latitude for a place gives the angle of Qibla Q for it. The Qibla will be faced by turning Q degrees from the south to the west for lines (1 and 4) and to the east for lines (2 and 3). These Q angles are measured from the geographical south found by either the Sun or the Pole-star. If the measurement is made with a compass, the magnetic deviation (of the location) must be taken into account.

10 – PRAYER TIMES

A hadîth-i sherîf quoted in the books **Muqaddimet-us-salât, at-Tefsîr-al-Mazharî** and **al-Halabî al-kebîr** states: **"Jabrâîl 'alaihis-salâm'** (and I performed [the prayer termed] namâz [or salât] together, and Jabrâîl 'alaihis-salâm') **conducted the prayer as the imâm for two of us, by the side of the door of Ka'ba, for two days running. We two performed the morning prayer as the fajr** (morning twilight) **dawned; the early afternoon prayer as the Sun departed from meridian; the late afternoon prayer when the midday shadow of an object increased by the length of the object; the evening prayer as the Sun set** [its upper limb disappeared]; **and the night prayer when the evening twilight darkened. The second day, we performed the morning prayer when the morning twilight matured; the early afternoon prayer when the shadow of an object increased again by the length of the object; the late afternoon prayer immediately thereafter; the evening prayer at the prescribed time of breaking fast; and the night prayer at the end of the first third of the night. Then he said 'O Muhammad, these are the times of prayers for you and the prophets before you. Let your Ummat perform each of these five prayers between the two times at which we performed each'."** This event took place on the fourteenth of July, one day after the Mi'râj, and two years before the Hegira. Ka'ba was 12.24 metres tall, the solar declination was twenty-one degrees and thirty-six minutes, and Ka'ba's latitudinal location was twenty-one degrees and twenty-six minutes. Hence its midday (shortest) shadow (fay-i zawâl) was 3.56 cm.[1] Thereby performing prayers (salât) five times a day became a commandment. This hadîth-i sherîf clarifies that the number of (daily) prayers is five.

It is fard (obligatory duty) for all Muslims, male and female alike, who are 'âqil and bâligh, that is, who are discreet and have reached the age of puberty or, in other words, the age for marriage, to perform the five daily prayers called salât (or namâz) within their correct times. If a salât is performed before the beginning of the time prescribed (by Islam) for it, it will not be sahîh (valid). In fact, it is a grave sin to do so. As it is fard to perform a salât in its correct time for it to be valid, it is also fard (or farz) to know for certain and without any feeling of doubt that

---

[1] It was (–3.56), i.e. the shadow pointed southwards, since the Sun's declination, on that day, is ten minutes greater than the location's latitude, so culmination took place north of the observer's zenith.

you have performed it in its correct time. A hadîth-i sherîf in the book **Terghîb-us-salât** states: "**A prayer time has an earlier version and a later version.**" The earlier version of a prayer time at a certain location begins when the Sun reaches a certain height with rescept to the apparent horizon of that location. The earth on which we live rotates around its axis in space. Its axis is an imaginary straight line going through the earth's center and intersecting the earth's surface at two symmetrical points. These two points are termed the (terrestrial) Poles. The sphere on whose inner surface the Sun and the stars are imagined to be moving is termed the **celestial sphere**. Because the earth revolves around the Sun, we get the impression as if the Sun were moving, although it is not the case. When we look around, the earth and the sky appear to meet on the curved line of a tremendous circle. This circle is termed line of **apparent horizon**. In the morning the Sun rises on the eastern side of this horizon. It moves up towards the middle of the sky. Culminating at noontime, it begins to move down. Finally, it sets at a point on the western side of the line of apparent horizon. The highest point it reaches from the horizon is the **time of noon** (zawâl). At this time, the Sun's altitude from the (line of apparent horizon) is termed the **meridian altitude** ('ghâya irtifâ'='culmination'). A person (supposed to be) gazing at the sky is called **observer** (râsid). The earth's radius intersecting the earth's surface at a point exactly under the observer's feet is at the same time the observer's **plumb level**. The observer is at point M, which is some distance above the earth's surface. ME is the observer's plumb level. Planes perpendicular to this plumb level are termed the observer's **horizons**.

There are six planes of horizon: 1– The plane MF, termed (mathematical horizon), which goes through the observer's feet, (and which is numbered 3 in figure 1-A, a few pages ahead.) 2– The plane BN, termed (tangential horizon), which is tangent to the earth's surface. 3– The plane LK, termed (mer'î=[visible, observed] horizon), whereby the (line of apparent horizon) surrounding the observer, (i.e., the circle marked LK,) is determined, (and which is numbered 5 in figure 1-A.). 4– The plane, termed (true horizon), which goes through the earth's centre, (number 1 in fig. 1-A.). 5– The plane P, termed (shar'î horizon), which coexists with the apparent horizon belonging to the highest point of the observer's location; the circle q around which this plane intersects the earth's surface is termed (line of shar'î horizon, and is numbered 6 in fig. 1-A.) These five planes are parallel to one another. 6– The plane of tangential horizon passing through the observer's feet is termed the **surface** (sathî) **horizon**, (which is not parallel to the other five horizons and is numbered 4 in fig. 1-A.) The higher the observer's location, the wider and the farther away from the tangential horizon is the apparent horizon, and the closer is it to the true horizon. For this reason, a city's apparent prayer times may vary, depending on the altitudes of its various parts. On the other hand, there is only one prayer time for each prayer of namâz. Therefore, apparent horizons cannot be used for the determination of prayer times. Shar'î altitudes are employed because they are based on shar'î horizons, which in turn will not admit of any further changes contingent to increase of height. Each prayer of namâz has three different prayer times for three of the six different horizons of every location: True; apparent (zâhirî); and shar'î times. Muslims who (live at such a location as they possess the conditions wherein they can) see the Sun and the horizon perform (each prayer of) namâz at its shar'î time, which is when the Sun's altitude from the shar'î horizon attains its position which Islam ascribes to the prayer time. Muslims who do not see them are to perform their prayers of namâz at their shar'î times determined by calculation. However, altitudes based on shar'î horizons are longer than apparent altitudes based on apparent horizons. These horizons cannot be used because prayer times are after noon. There are mathematical as well as mer'î (observed) times for each of the (daily) three prayers of namâz. Mathematical (riyâdî) times are determined by calculation based on the Sun's altitude. Mer'î times are obtained by adding eight (8) minutes and twenty (20) seconds to mathematical times, because it takes the Sun's rays eight minutes and twenty seconds to come to the earth. Or it is determined by observing that the Sun has reached a certain altitude. Namâz is not performed at mathematical or true times. These times help to determine the mer'î times. Altitudes relating to sunrise and sunset horizons are zero. Altitudinal degrees with respect to apparent horizon begin as the Sun rises, before noon; and after true horizon, after noon. Shar'î horizon is before true horizon, before noon; and it follows true horizon, after noon. The Sun's altitude at the time of fajr-i-sâdiq is −19° according to all four Madhhabs[1]. Its altitude to initiate the time of night prayer is −19° according to Imâm-i-a'zam (Abû Hanîfa, the leader of Hanafî Madhhab), and −17° according to the two Imâms (called 'Imâmeyn', namely, Imâm Muhammad and Imâm Abû Yûsuf, two

---

[1] These four Madhhabs are Hanafî; Mâlikî; Shâfi'î; and Hanbalî.

of Imâm-i-a'zam's most eminent disciples), and also according to the other three Madhhabs. The altitude to indicate the beginning of early afternoon is the meridian altitude (ghâya irtifâ'), which, in its turn, is the algebraic addition of the (Sun's) declination and complement of latitudinal degrees. Mer'î-haqîqî **noon time** (zawâl) is when the center of the Sun is observed to have culminated, (i.e., to have reached the elevation called ghâya irtifâ',) with respect to true horizon. The altitudes for the times of early afternoon and late afternoon ('asr) change daily. These two altitudes are determined daily. Since it is not always possible to determine (by observation) the time when the limb of the Sun reaches the altitude from the apparent horizon for a certain prayer, books of fiqh explain the signs and indications of this mer'î time, which means to say that the apparent times of namâz are the mer'î times, not the mathematical times. Muslims who are unable to see these indications in the sky, and calendar-makers as well, calculate the mathematical times when the limb of the Sun reaches the altitudes with respect to the lines of surface horizon after noon; since timepieces will show the mer'î times when they reach the mathematical figures thereby calculated, these people will have performed their prayers of namâz at the so-called **mer'î times**.

An important note: By calculation, the mathematical times when the Sun reaches the prescribed altitudes from the true horizon are determined. That the Sun has reached a certain mer'î time (or altitude) is observed eight minutes and twenty seconds after the time thereby calculated; this time (of observation) is called **mer'î time.** In other words, the mer'î time is eight (8) minutes and twenty (20) seconds after the mathematical time. Since the time of true noon and that of adhânî sunset according to which timepieces are adjusted to begin are mer'î times, the riyâdî times indicated by timepieces are mer'î times. The times printed on calendars, mathematical as they are, change into mer'î times on timepieces. For instance, if a certain time determined by calculation is, say, three hours and fifteen minutes, timepieces demonstrate this moment of three hours and fifteen minutes as the mer'î time. First the **haqîqî mathematical times,** when the center of the sun reaches the altitudes prescribed for the prayers of namâz from the true horizon, are determined by calculation. Then these times are converted into **shar'î mathematical times** through a process performed with the period of time called **Tamkin**. Hence, there is no need for also adding 8 minutes and 20 seconds to the riyâdî times represented on timepieces. The difference of time between true time and shar'î time for a certain prayer of namâz is termed the time of **Tamkin**. The time of Tamkin for each prayer time is approximately the same.

The time for morning prayer at a certain location begins, in all four Madhhabs, at the end of **shar'î** (canonical) **night,** which in turn is when the whiteness called **fajr sâdiq** is seen at one of the points on the line of apparent horizon (ufq-i-zâhirî) in the east. This time is also the beginning of fast. Chief of Astronomy Department Ârif Bey reports: "Because there are weak reports saying that the fajr sâdiq begins when the whiteness spreads over the horizon and the altitude of the Sun is -18° or even -16°, it is judicious and safe to perform the morning prayer 15 minutes later than the time shown on calendars." To determine the Sun's altitude at the time of dawn, the time of dawn is determined by observing the line of apparent horizon and in the meanwhile directing our attention to our timepiece, in a night when the sky is clear. The time determined thereby will match one of the times calculated to correspond with various altitudes, and the altitude wherewith the matching time corresponds is the altitude of dawn (fajr). An identical method is used to determine the altitude of shafaq (disappearance of evening twilight). Throughout centuries Islamic scholars have adopted the altitude for fajr as −19°, rejecting any other values as 'incorrect values'. According to Europeans, dawn (fajr) is the spreading of the whiteness[1], and the Sun's altitude is −18° at dawn. Muslims' religious tutors are not Christians or people who have not adapted themselves to any of the (four) Madhhabs; our tutors are Islamic scholars. The time of morning prayer ends at the end of **solar night**, which is when the preceding [upper] limb of the Sun is observed to rise from the line of apparent horizon.

The **celestial sphere**, with the Earth at its centre like a point, is a large sphere on which all the stars are projected. Prayer times are calculated by using the **arcs of elevation**, which are imagined to be on the surface of this sphere. The two points at which the axis of the Earth intersects the celestial sphere are called **celestial poles**, (which are directly above the poles of the Earth). Planes passing through the two poles are called **planes of declination.** Circles that these planes form on the celestial sphere are called **circles of declination.** Planes containing the plumb-level of a location are called **azimuth planes** (or vertical planes). The circles formed by the imagined intersection of planes containing the plumb-level of a location and the celestial sphere are called the

---

[1] This is the time when **Astronomical twilight** begins.

azimuth or **altitude circles** (or **verticals**). The azimuth circles of a given location are perpendicular to the location's horizons. At a given location, there is one plane of declination and an infinite number of azimuth circles. The plumb-level of a location and the axis of the earth (may be assumed to) intersect at the centre of the earth. The plane containing these two lines is both the azimuthal and the declination plane of the location. This plane is called the **meridian plane** of the location. The circle of intersection of this plane with the celestial sphere describes the **meridian circle**. A location's meridian plane is perpendicular to its plane of true horizon and divides it by half. The line whereby it cuts through its plane of true horizon is termed the meridian line of the location. The arc, (GN), between the point, N, where the azimuth circle (vertical) passing through the Sun intersects the true horizon, and the centre of the Sun, G, is the **arc of true altitude** of the Sun at a given location at a given time. The angular value of that arc is the Sun's true altitude at that place at that moment. The Sun crosses a different azimuth circle every moment. The arcs measured on an azimuth circle between the point, Z, at which the circle passes through the Sun's (upper) limb, and the point at which it intersects the tangential, apparent, mathematical and surface horizons are called the Sun's **apparent altitudes** with respect to these horizons. Angular values of these arcs represent the Sun's **apparent altitudes** with respect to the so-called horizons. The Sun's surface altitude is greater than its true altitude. At different times the Sun is at an equal altitude from these horizons. The true altitude is equal to the value of the geocentric angle subtended by the celestial arc of true altitude. The angular values of an infinite number of arcs of a variety of lengths that are bounded by the sides of this angle and which are parallel to the so-called celestial arc as well as to one another, are equal to one another and to the true altitude. Every pair of straight lines that describe the other altitudes originate from the point where the plumb level of the place of observation intersects the horizon. The plane passing through the centre of the earth perpendicular to its axis is called the **equatorial plane.** The circle of intersection of the equatorial plane with the Earth is called the **equator.** The place and the direction of the equatorial plane and those of the equatorial circle never change; they divide the Earth into two equal hemispheres. The value of the arc of declination between the Sun's center and the equatorial plane represents the **Sun's declination.** The whiteness before the apparent sunrise on the line of apparent horizon begins two degrees of altitude prior to the redness; in other words, it begins when the Sun ascends to an altitude of 19° below the apparent horizon. This is a fact stated in a fatwâ[1]. Non-mujtahids do not have the right to change the fatwâ. It has been reported in Ibn 'Âbidîn (Radd-ul-muhtâr) and in the calendar by M.Ârif Bey that some 'ulamâ have said that it begins when the Sun is a distance of 20° (from the apparent horizon). However, acts of worship that are not performed in accordance with the fatwâ are not sahîh (valid).

The Sun's daily paths are circles on the (imaginary inner surface of the) celestial sphere and which are parallel to one another and to the equatorial plane. The planes of these circles are (approximately) perpendicular to the earth's axis and to the meridian plane, and intersect the horizontal planes of a given location obliquely, which means that the Sun's daily path does not intersect the line of apparent horizon at a right angle. The azimuth circle through the Sun is perpendicular to the line of apparent horizon. When the Sun's centre is on the observer's meridian, the circle of declination going through its center and the location's azimuthal circle coexist, and its elevation is at its daily maximum from the true horizon, (the event termed culmination).

Muslims who (possess the conditions wherein they can) observe the Sun are accredited to avail themselves of the **time of apparent zuhr**, i.e. the **apparent time of early afternoon prayer**. This mer'î time begins as the Sun's following (trailing) limb departs from the apparent region of zawâl. The Sun rises from the surface horizon, i.e., from the line of apparent horizon, which we see, of a given location. First, the **time of apparent-mer'î zawâl** begins when the preceding (leading) limb of the Sun en route for its culmination with respect to (the eastern arc of) the surface horizon, which is the **line of apparent horizon** that we observe, reaches the celestial (circle of apparent) zawâl region relating to this maximum altitude. This moment is determined when decline in the length of the shadow of a rod (erected vertically on a horizontal plane) is no longer perceptible. Thereafter the **time of true-mer'î zawâl** is when the centre of the Sun rises to the location's celestial meridian circle,

---

[1] Fatwâ is a conclusive explanation wherein an authorized Islamic scholar answers Muslims' questions. Conditions to be fulfilled to be an authorized Islamic scholar are explained in our publications, **Belief and Islam**, **The Sunni Path**, and **Endless Bliss** (chapter 33 of second fascicle and chapter 10 of third fascicle).

[i.e. when it has traversed the mid-day arc peculiar to that location,] or, in other words, when it culminates with respect to the true horizon. Thereafter, when its following limb descends to the point of culmination with respect to the western arc of the surface horizon of the location, the **time of apparent zawâl** ends, the shadow is observed to begin gaining length, and hence the beginning of the time of **apparent-mer'î zuhr**. The motion of the Sun and that of the tip of the shadow are imperceptibly slow as the Sun ascends from the apparent zawâl time to true zawâl time, and as it descends thence to the end of the apparent zawâl time, because the distance and the time involved are negligibly short. When the following limb descends to the point of culmination with respect to the shar'î horizon on the western arc of the line of surface horizon of the location, the **time of apparent mer'î zawâl** ends and the **time of shar'î mer'î zuhr** begins. This time is later than the time of true zawâl by a period of **Tamkin**, because the difference of time between the true and the shar'î zawâls is equal to the difference of time between the true and the shar'î horizons, which in turn is equal to the period of time called **Tamkin**. The zâhirî (apparent) times are determined with the shadow of the rod. The shar'î times are not found with the shadow of the rod. The true time of zawâl is found by calculation, (length of) time termed **Tamkin** is added to this, hence the riyâdî (mathematical) shar'î time of zuhr. The result is recorded in calendars. The shar'î time of zuhr continues until the **'asr awwal,** which is the time when the shadow of a vertical rod on a level place becomes longer than its shadow at the time of true zawâl by as much as its height, or until **'asr thânî,** which is the time when its shadow's length increases by twice its height. The former is according to the Two Imâms [Abû Yûsuf and Muhammad ash-Shaybânî], and also according to the other three Madhhabs, and the latter is according to al-Imâm al-a'zam.

Although **the time of late afternoon prayer** begins at the end of the time of early afternoon prayer and continues until the following limb of the Sun is observed to set below the line of apparent horizon of the observer's location, it is harâm to postpone the prayer until the Sun turns yellow, an event that takes place when the distance between the Sun's lower [preceding] limb and the line of apparent horizon is a spear's length, which is five angular degrees. This is the third one of the daily three times of kerâhat (explained towards the end of this chapter). Calendars in Turkey contain time-tables wherein times of late afternoon prayers are written in accordance with 'asr awwal. For (performing late afternoon prayers within times taught by Imâm a'zam and thereby) following Imâm a'zam, late afternoon prayers should be performed 36 minutes, (in winter,) and 72 minutes, (in summer,) after the times shown on the aforementioned calendars. In regions between latitudes 40 and 42 a gradational monthly addition of the numerical constant of 6 to 36 from January through June and its subtraction likewise from 72 thenceforward through January, will yield monthly differences between the two temporal designations termed 'asr, (i.e. 'asr awwal and 'asr thânî).

The time of evening prayer begins when the Sun apparently sets; that is, when its upper (following) limb is seen to disappear below the line of apparent horizon of the observer's location. The shar'î and the solar nights also begin at this time. At locations where apparent sunrise and sunset cannot be observed, and in calculations as well, the shar'î times are used. When (the first beam of) sunlight strikes the highest hill at one of these locations in the morning, it is the shar'î time of sunrise (at that location). Conversely, in the evening, when sunlight is observed to withdraw from there, it is the mcr'î-shar'î time of sunset. The adhânî timepieces are adjusted to twelve (12) o'clock at this moment. The time of evening prayer continues until the time of night prayer. It is sunna to perform the evening prayer early within its time. It is harâm to put it off till the time of **ishtibâk-i-nujûm**, which is when the number of visible stars increase, or, in other words, after the following limb of the Sun has sunk down to an altitude of 10° below the line of apparent horizon. For reasons such as illness, long-distance journeys[1], or in order to eat food that is ready, it might be postponed until that time.

The time of night prayer begins, according to the Imâmeyn[2], with **'ishâ-i-awwal**, that is, when the redness on the line of apparent horizon in the west disappears. The same rule applies in the other three Madhhabs. According to Imâm-al-a'zam it begins with **'ishâ-i-thânî**; that is, after the whiteness disappears. It ends at the end of the shar'î night; that is, with the whiteness of fajr-i-sâdiq according to the Hanafî Madhhab. The disappearing of

---

[1] What is meant by long-distance journeys, and also how a Muslim travelling a long distance is to perform his daily prayers termed namâz (or salât), is explained in full detail in the fifteenth chapter.

[2] 'Imâmeyn' means 'Two Imâm's'. In 'Fiqh', one of Islam's main scientific branches pertaining to acts of worship, **'Imâmeyn'** means **'Imâm Muhammad and Imâm Yusûf'**, two of the highest disciples of

redness takes place when the upper (following) limb of the Sun descends to an altitude of 17° below the surface horizon. Thereafter, the whiteness disappears when it descends to an altitude of 19°. According to some scholars in the Shâfi'î Madhhab, the latest (âkhir) time for night prayer is until the shar'î midnight. According to them, it is not permissible to postpone the performance of night prayer till after the shar'î midnight. And it is makrûh in the Hanafî Madhhab. In the Mâlikî Madhhab, although a night prayer that has been performed by the end of the shar'î night is sahîh (valid), it is sinful to postpone it till the end of the initial one-third of the night and perform it thereafter.[1] Muslims who have somehow failed to perform the early afternoon or the evening prayer of a certain day before the end of the time prescribed by the Two Imâms should not make the worse choice by (putting off the prayer till the unanimously definite end of the prayer time, which is widely expressed by Muslims in Turkey as) 'leaving the prayer (namâz) to qadâ'; they should perform them according to al-Imâm-al-a'zam's prescription; and in that case, they should not perform the late afternoon and the night prayers of that day before the times prescribed for these prayers by al-Imâm-al-a'zam. A prayer is accepted as to have been performed within its prescribed time if the initial takbîr has been uttered, according to the Hanafî Madhhab; and if one rak'a of the namâz has been completed, according to the Madhhabs named Mâlikî and Shâfi'î; before the end of the prescribed time.

A. Ziyâ Bey notes in his book **'Ilm-i hey'et**:

"The further ahead in the direction of the poles, the farther apart from each other are the beginning of morning prayer, i.e. the breaking of morning twilight, and sunrise; and for the same matter, the beginning of night prayer, i.e. the (end of) evening dusk, and

---

Imâm a'zam Abû Hanîfa, the leader and founder of the Hanafî Madhhab, one of the only four valid Madhhabs in matters pertaining to Islamic practices; **'Tarafeyn'** means **'Imâm a'zam Abû Hanîfa himself and his blessed disciple Imâm Muhammad'**; and **'Shaikhayn'** means **'Imâm a'zam himself and his blessed disciple Imâm Abû Yûsuf'**. In another register of Islamic nomenclature, e.g. when matters concerning the Sahâba (the blessed companions of Muhammad 'alaihis-salâm') are being dealt with, **'Shaikhayn'** means **'Hadrat Abû Bakr as-Siddîq** and **Hadrat 'Umar ul-Fârûq'**.

[1] It goes without saying that it must definitely be performed if it has been delayed till thereafter. What is sinful is to delay it till thereafter.

sunset, and, also incidentally, the closer to each other are the initial times of (a certain day's) morning prayer and the night prayer (of the previous day). Prayer times of a location vary depending on its distance from the equator, i.e., its degree of latitude, φ, as well as on the declination, δ, of the Sun, i.e., on months and days." [At locations whose latitudinal value is greater than the complement of declination, (i.e. when $\varphi>90-\delta$, or when $\varphi+\delta>90$,) days and nights never take place. During the times when the sum of latitude and declination is $90°-19° = 71°$ or greater, i.e., $90°-\varphi\leq\delta+19°$ or $\varphi+\delta\geq71°$; for example, during the summer months when the Sun's declination is greater than 5°; fajr (dawn, morning twilight) begins before the shafaq (evening dusk, evening twilight) turns into complete darkness. So, for instance, in Paris which is on latitude 48°50', the times of night and morning prayers do not start from 12 through 30 June. In the Hanafî Madhhab, the time of a certain prayer is the reason (sabab) for performing that prayer. The prayer does not become fard unless the reason arises. Therefore, these two prayers (salâts) do not become fard at such places. However, according to some scholars, it is fard to perform these two salâts at the times they are performed in nearby countries or places. [During the periods of time (12 to 30 June) when the times of these two prayers of namâz do not virtually begin, it is better to (try and determine the times that these two prayers were performed on the last day of the period during which such conditions existed as their prescribed times virtually began, and to) perform them at the times determined.]

The time of **Dhuhâ** begins when one-fourth of nehâr-i-shar'î, i.e., the first quarter of the canonically prescribed duration of daytime for fasting, is completed. Period of time half the nehâr-i-shar'î is called the time of **Dhahwa-i-kubrâ.** In adhânî time (reckoned from shar'î sunset) Dhahwa-i-kubrâ=Fajr+(24-Fajr)÷2=Fajr+12-Fajr÷2=12+Fajr÷2. Hence, half the time of Fajr gives the time of Dhahwa-i-kubrâ reckoned from 12 in the morning. (For example), in Istanbul on the 13th of August, the time of dawn (fajr) in standard time is 3 hours 9 minutes, the standard time of sunset is 19 hours 13 minutes, and therefore, daytime lasts 16 hours 4 minutes and the standard time of Dhahwa-i-kubrâ is 8:02+3:09=11 hours 11 minutes. In other words, it is equal to half the sum of times of imsâk and iftâr in standard time.

Since the amount of refraction of light by the atmospheric layers increases as the Sun draws near the line of apparent horizon,

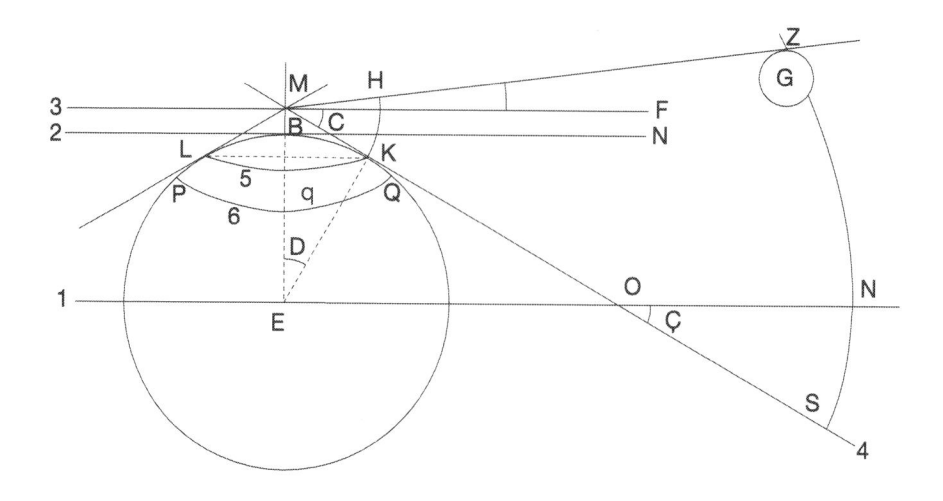

Fig. 1–A

K = The point at which the azimuthal plane through the Sun intersects the line of apparent horizon.

MS = The plane ufq-i hissî (tangential horizon) tangent to the Earth at point K, perpendicular to the plumb-line at K, is termed the observer's **surface horizon**.

HK = The altitude of the (upper) limb of the Sun with respect to point K, which is on the line of apparent horizon. This altitude is equal to the altitude ZS of the Sun with respect to the surface horizon.

D=C=Ç=Angle of dip of horizon.

M = A high place of the location.

ZS = The arc of azimuthal circle giving the altitude of the Sun with reference to the surface horizon. This angle is equal to the angle subtended by the arc HK.

NS = Dip of horizon.

O = A point on the straight line of intersection of planes of true and surface horizons.

1, 2, 3, 4, 5, 6 = Planes of horizon (1. True horizon; 2. Tangential horizon; 3. Mathematical horizon; 4. Surface horizon; 5. Line of apparent horizon; and also Plane of mer'î horizon. 6. Line of Shar'î horizon; and plane of Shar'î horizon.

G = The Sun as observed from the Earth.

GN = True altitude of the Sun.

B = Lowest place of the location.

at level places such as sea surfaces and planes it appears to have risen as the upper (preceding) limb of the Sun is still below the line of apparent horizon by about 0.56 angular degrees (33.6'). Conversely, its disappearing below the horizon in the evening takes place after its upper (following) limb has descended to an equidistant position below the horizon.

Planes perpendicular to the plumb level of a location, i.e., to the Earth's radius through that location, are called the **ufqs=horizons** of the location, the Ufq-i-sat-hî (surface horizon) being the only exception. Six types of horizon may be defined. **Ufq-i-haqîqî=True horizon** is the one passing through the Earth's centre. **Ufq-i-hissî=Tangential horizon** is an infinite plane passing through the lowest point B of the location, that is, a plane tangent to the Globe at point B. The angle formed at the Sun's centre by the two straight lines, one from the Earth's centre and the other from the Earth's surface, is called the Sun's **horizontal parallax=ikhtilâf-i-manzar**. Its annual mean value is 8.8 angular seconds. It is the difference between the altitude of the Sun's centre with respect to two different horizons, the true horizon and the riyadî (mathematical) or tangential horizon. Parallax results in a delay in the sighting of lunar and solar risings. The horizontal plane passing through the point M of a certain height where the observer is located is called the observer's **ufq-i-riyâdî=mathematical horizon.** The **khat ufq-i-zâhirî=line of apparent horizon** is the circle LK described as the line of tangency of the cone formed by the revolution about the plumb level through M, of the straight line MK, projecting from the observer's eye at M and tangent to the Globe at K. The plane containing this circle and perpendicular to the plumb level through M is called the observer's **ufq-i-mer'î=visible horizon**; and the surface of this cone is the observer's **ufq-i-sathî** (surface horizon). The **line of apparent horizon** appears to the observer, who stands at a certain height, as a circular line around which the sky and the lowest points, such as sea surfaces and meadows, on the Earth's surface intersect. This circular line is formed by the points of intersection between the visible horizon and the Earth's surface. There is a plane of azimuth containing every point of this circle. The plane of tangential horizon going through point K, which is intersected by the plane of azimuth containing the Sun, intersects the plane of azimuth at a right angle and along line MS. This tangential horizon, plane MK, is called the observer's **ufq-i-sathî=surface**

horizon. There are various surface horizons for various altitudes at a location. The points K, whereat each of these horizons is tangent to the earth's surface, make up the (circular line termed) line of apparent horizon. The direction of the ray projecting from the observer's eye, i.e. the line MS, is called the **line of surface horizon**. The vertical (azimuthal) arc, ZS, is the altitude of the Sun with respect to the surface horizon. The arc ZS subtends the angle inscribed between the two straight lines projecting from the observer's eye to the two ends of this arc. As the Sun moves, the point of tangency K of the surface horizon MS glides on the line of apparent horizon and, thereby, the surface horizon changes momently. The observer will see the Sun when he looks at the point H at which the straight line MZ from the observer to the Sun intersects the arc HK, drawn parallel to ZS, the arc of altitude. He will perceive this arc as the altitude of the Sun with respect to the line of apparent horizon. The angle subtended by this arc HK is identical with that subtended by ZS, the altitude of the following (upper) limb of the Sun with reference to the surface horizon. Therefore, the **apparent altitude** HK is used for the altitude with respect to the surface horizon. The Sun sets when it is at point S in the sky. The observer perceives as if it sets at point K on the Earth. Once the Sun and the stars go below the surface horizon of a location, i.e., when their altitude with reference to this horizon becomes zero, all the observers who share this horizon see them set. The observer at point M sees the Sun set at point K of the surface horizon. In other words, the time of sunset for the observer at point M is when the altitude of the upper limb of the Sun attains zero with respect to the surface horizon. Likewise, the other prayer times for the observer are determined on the basis of shar'î altitudes with respect to the surface horizons. Since the shar'î altitude of the Sun with respect to the surface horizon is perceived by the observer at point M as the altitude HK with respect to the line of apparent horizon, the **apparent altitudes** measured with reference to the apparent horizon are used for determining the prayer times. These altitudes are greater than those with respect to the observer's mathematical, tangential, visible and true horizons. The difference between the altitude ZS with respect to the surface horizon and the arc ZN with respect to the true horizon is called the **zâwiya inhitât-i ufq=the angle of dip of horizon** for the height of point M. The arc of azimuthal circle equal to the angle of dip of horizon, i.e. the arc NS, is the **dip of horizon. Shar'î times**, which are recorded in calendars, are used in mountainous places where the apparent horizon cannot be observed.

Mathematical, tangential, and mer'î (observed, visible) horizons are identical for an observer at the lowest point. At this lowest point, B, there is not a surface horizon, the line of apparent horizon being a small circle around B, and the altitude with respect to this line and the altitudes with respect to all the other horizons being the same. As the point of observation gains elevation, so does the observer's mathematical horizon; thereby their tangential horizon changes into their surface horizon; and their line of apparent horizon descends towards their true horizon and widens. Radius of each of thereby widening circles formed by the descending lines of apparent horizon demarcates an arc to subtend angle D, which in turn is equal to the angle of dip of horizon. The arcs ZS, which represent the Sun's altitudes with respect to the surface horizon, are higher than the true altitude by the same angular value as that of the dip of horizon.

The Sun's reaching the time of zawâl with respect to a horizon means its culmination with respect to that horizon. When the observer is at the lowest place of a location the Sun's regions of zawâl with respect to all horizons and to the line of apparent horizon converge at one point, and the diurnal arc of the Sun's daily path intersects the meridian at point A, –as is seen on figures 1 and 2 a few pages ahead–, which is mid-point of the diurnal part of its daily path. This point is called the **region of true zawâl.** As for observers who are at higher places and who (possess the conditions wherein they can) observe the Sun; their **Regions of apparent zawâl** are **circles of regions of zawâl** formed around the celestial region of true zawâl by the points of culmination with respect to the circular lines of apparent horizon peculiar to the heights they occupy. As the Sun moves along its path, it meets with each of these circles at two points. When it reaches the first point, the **time of apparent zawâl** begins. The end of the time of apparent zawâl is when the Sun reaches the second point. As the observer's position becomes higher, dip of horizon takes place and the circles of apparent horizon become larger. And so do the so-called celestial **circles of regions of zawâl**, so that their radii produce arcs subtending angles, equal to the angles, (represented by angle D in fig. 1-A) subtended by their terrestrial counterparts, i.e. arcs produced by the radii of the circles of apparent horizons.

When the observer goes up to the highest point of their location, the circle of celestial region of zawâl becomes the greatest and the outermost. This greatest circle of region of zawâl is called the observer's **Shar'î region of zawâl**. The surface horizon of an observer at the highest point of a location is called the observer's **ufq-i-shar'î**. The altitude of the Sun's (upper) limb with respect to the shar'î horizon is called the **shar'î irtifâ'**. The preceding limb of the Sun enters the circular region of shar'î zawâl when it culminates with respect to the place of sunrise on the shar'î horizon. A hill so far from a location as the shaded and the illuminated regions on it are not distinguishable to the naked eye during the time of isfirâr, (when the Sun's canonical altitude is less than 5° and it is yellow,) is not considered within the limits of that location. The radius of the circle of shar'î region of zawâl subtends an angle equal to the angle of dip of horizon for an observer (supposed to be) on the highest hill of the location. The circles representing times of zawâl are not visible; the Sun's getting in and out of these circles can be determined from the shortening and elongation of the shadow of a vertical rod erected on a level ground.

In the section on the mustahabs to be observed by a fasting Muslim in **Radd al-muhtâr** by Ibn 'Âbidîn and in the annotation to **Marâq al-falâh** by at-Tahtâwî, it is noted, "(Of two Muslims supposed to be fasting,) the one who lives at a lower place, and who therefore observes the apparent sunset earlier, breaks fast earlier than the one living at a higher place, [since Islam recognizes the apparent times, not the true times, as canonically acceptable for those who (can) see the Sun.] For those who are unable to observe the sunset; 'sunset' is when the hills in the east darken." In other words, it is the apparent sunset that would be observed by people living on the highest hill, which in turn means sunset with respect to the shar'î horizon. It is noted also in the book **Majma'al-anhur** and the Shafi'î book **Al-anwâr li-a'mâl-il abrâr** that the **shar'î sunset** is to be taken into account by those who are not able to observe the sunset; and it is determined by calculation.

For easy determination of the times of early and late afternoon prayers, 'Abd al-Haqq as-Sujâdil, who was matured in the suhba of Muhammad Ma'thûm al-Fârûqî as-Sirhindî, describes a method in his Persian book **Masâ'il-i sharh-i Wiqâya**, printed in India in 1294 [1877 A.D.]:

"A circle is drawn on a level ground taking sunlight. This circle is called the **Dâ'ira-i Hindiyya=the Indian circle.** A straight rod, with a length equal to the radius of the circle, is erected at the centre of the circle. The top of the rod must be equidistant from three different points on the circle to make it certain that it is precisely vertical. This vertical rod is called the **miqyâs=gnomon.** Its shadow extends beyond the circle on the western side before noon. As the Sun moves higher up, i.e., as its altitude increases, the shadow shortens. A mark is made at the point where the tip of the shadow enters the circle. Another mark is made at the point where the tip of the shadow exits the circle as it elongates eastwards. A straight line is drawn from the centre of the circle to the midpoint of the arc between the two marks. This straight line is called the **khat nisf-un-nahâr=the meridian line of the location.**" The meridian line extends in the north-south direction. When the preceding limb of the Sun reaches its maximum altitude from the line of apparent horizon of the location, the time of **zâhirî** (apparent) **zawâl** begins. It is no longer possible now to perceive the shortening of the shadow. Next, the centre of the Sun comes to the meridian and is at its maximum altitude from the true horizon. This is **the time of haqîqî** (true) **zawâl.** At the time of true zawâl, the times of zawâl in terms of mean time are not subject to variation on account of latitudinal variation. As the Sun departs from this point, the shadow also departs from the meridian line, though imperceptibly. The apparent zawâl time ends when the following limb descends to its apparent maximum altitude with reference to the sunset spot on the line of apparent horizon. Now the **time of apparent zuhr** begins. The shadow begins observably to lengthen. The middle of the time during which the length of the shadow remains unchanged is the **haqîqî (true) zawâl time.** As the Sun's center transits the meridian, its momentary passage is observed from London with telescopes and thereby zawâlî timepieces are adjusted. At this mer'î haqîqî zawâl time, the haqîqî (true) time is twelve. The algebraic addition of this twelve to the equation of time[1] yields the **meantime** beginning, i.e. twelve, of the day on

---

[1] The modification to be applied to **apparent solar time**, (i.e. the time as shown on a sundial, which records the motions of the real (true) Sun across the sky,) to **mean solar time**, (i.e. the time as shown on timepieces, with the irregularities of apparent solar time, due to elliptic movement of the Earth around the Sun, smoothed out). See Appendix IV.

the local timepiece. The riyâdî times found by calculation show also the mer'î times on timepieces. This **mer'î zawâl time,** which is the beginning for the meantime clocks, is eight minutes and twenty seconds after the **riyâdî zawâl time,** which is the time when the Sun reaches the zawâl. The ratio between the height of anything erected at right angles to the Earth's surface and the length of its shortest shadow, **fay-i-zawâl**, varies with latitude and declination.

A pair of compasses is opened by a length of fay-i-zawâl. The sharp point of the compasses is placed at the point where the meridian line meets the (Indian) circle and a second circle, whose radius is the distance between the centre of the first circle and the point whereon it intersects the extension of the line of meridian beyond the first circle, is drawn. It is the time of **apparent 'asr awwal** when the shadow of the gnomon reaches the second circle. The second circle must be drawn anew daily. Fay-i-zawâl is used only to find the times of early and late afternoon prayers. It is not practicable in finding the times of other prayers.

It is written in the books **Majma'al-anhur** and **Riyâdh-un-nâsihîn:** "The time of zuhr begins when the Sun is at zawâl, i.e., when its following limb begins to descend from the maximum altitude it has ascended with respect to the line of apparent horizon. To determine the time of zawâl, a rod is erected. It is **the time of zawâl** when the shortening of its shadow stops, that is, when it neither shortens nor lengthens. It is not permissible to perform namâz during this time. The time of zawâl is over when the shadow begins to lengthen." The maximum altitude mentioned in the aforenamed books is not the altitude with respect to the true horizon. Two positions are noted: one is when the preceding limb ascends to its maximum altitude from the surface horizon, i.e. with respect to the eastern arc of the line of apparent horizon; and the other is when the following limb begins to descend from its maximum altitude from the surface horizon, i.e. with respect to the western arc of the line of apparent horizon. As a matter of fact, it is written in the annotation to the commentatory book **Imdâd-ul-Fettâh** that the line of apparent horizon, not the true horizon, is to be taken into account in determining the time. The "time of apparent zawâl" commences when the Sun's preceding limb reaches its maximum altitude from the surface horizon, or from (the eastern arc of) the line of apparent horizon. The time of apparent zawâl ends when the following limb begins to descend from its maximum altitude from the surface horizon with respect to the place of sunset on the line of apparent horizon, and thenceforth the time of apparent zuhr commences. At this moment the shadow of the gnomon is imperceptibly longer. The apparent time of late afternoon prayer ('asr) is when the length of this shadow increases by the length of the gnomon. The time of true zawâl is only an instant. On the other hand, the times of apparent zawâl based on the preceding and following limbs are when the respective limbs enter and exit the circles (imagined) on the celestial sphere and termed **Regions of apparent zawâl**, whose centers coexist with the points of true zawâl and radiuses equal the angular value of the **dip of horizon** pertaining to the height of the observer's location. The region of apparent zawâl is not an (instantaneous) point; it is an arc between the two points whereby (each of) the so-called circles intersect(s) the Sun's (apparent daily) path. The greatest of these circles is the **Circle of region of shar'î zawâl**. In Islam, the time of zawâl, i.e. midday, is the period of time between the instant when the Sun's preceding limb enters this shar'î circle and the instant when its following limb exits the circle. The **time of shar'î zawâl** begins when the Sun's preceding limb enters the circle. The shar'î zawâl time ends when the Sun's following limb exits the circle, and then the **shar'î zuhr time** begins. This time is determined by calculation and recorded in calendars.

The six-rak'at salât performed after the fard of evening salât is called the salât (namâz) of **awwâbîn.**

The job of understanding, working out, determining, and explaining the times of acts of worship requires Islamic knowledge ('ulûm ad-dîn). The 'ulamâ' (authorized Islamic scholars) of (the branch of Islamic knowledge termed) **fiqh** wrote in their books of fiqh the teachings which mujtahids (extracted from the Qur'ân al-kerîm and hadîth-i-sherîfs and) explained. It is permissible to exercise oneself in the recalculation of the prescribed times, (which have already been explained by mujtahids.) Results of such calculations, however, are conditional on the aforesaid Islamic scholars' approval. It is noted in the section dealing with (the essentials of) "facing the Qiblâ in salât" in **Radd al-muhtâr** by Ibn 'Âbidîn, and also in **Fatâwâ-i Shams ad-dîn ar-Ramlî**, that it is jâ'iz (permissible) to determine the times of salât and direction of the Qibla by calculation. It is noted in **Mawdû'ât-ul-'ulûm:** "It is fard kifâya to calculate the prayer times. It is fard for Muslims to know the beginning and the end of the prayer times from the position of the Sun or from the calendars approved by Islamic scholars."

The Earth rotates about its axis from west to east. In other words, an overhead view of it, like that of a globe placed on a table (with the North Pole pointing upwards), would reveal that it rotated in a counterclockwise direction. This is called the **true** (direct, prograde) **motion.** The Sun and the fixed stars appear to make a revolution per day from east to west. This is called the **retrograde motion.** The time between two successive meridianal transits of a star at a certain location is defined as **one sidereal day.** One-twenty-fourth of this period is **one sidereal hour.** The time interval between two successive transits of the centre of the Sun across the meridian, that is, the time between successive instants of true zawâl is called **one true solar day.** Meanwhile, the Earth moves from west to east along the **ecliptic** and completes one revolution per year around the Sun. Due to this motion of the Earth, the Sun appears to move from west to east on the ecliptic plane, rotating about the **ecliptical axis** through the Earth's centre perpendicular to the ecliptic plane. The average speed of this translational movement is about 30 kilometres per second, though it is not constant. Since the orbit of the Earth on the ecliptic plane is not circular but **elliptical,** the angles subtended by the arcs travelled in equal intervals are not equal. The smaller its distance to the Sun, the higher its speed. As a result of this movement of the Earth, the Sun is slower than the stars by about 4 minutes per day, thus completing its daily revolution about 4 minutes later than the stars. Therefore, the "true solar day" is about 4 minutes longer than the sidereal day. This extra time slightly varies from day to day around 4 minutes. The second reason for the variation of the lengths of true solar daytimes is that the axis of the Earth is not perpendicular to the plane of ecliptic. There is an angle of about 23°27' between the axis of the Earth and the ecliptical axis. This angle never changes. The third reason is that the maximum altitude of the Sun changes daily. The ecliptic and the equatorial planes intersect along a diameter of the Earth. There is an angle of about 23°27' between these two planes. This diameter of intersection is called the **line of nodes**, (or the nodal line.) This angle never changes. The average direction of the Earth's axis does not change as it revolves round the Sun. It remains parallel to itself. On the 22nd of June, the axis of the Earth is tilted in such a direction as its northern part is inclined towards the Sun with respect to the (upright position of the) axis of the ecliptic, so that more than half of the northern hemisphere takes sunlight. The declination of the Sun is about +23.5°. When the Earth arrives at a point about one-fourth of the length of its yearly round, the projection of axis of the Earth on the ecliptic deviates from the Sun-Earth direction by about 90°. At this time the line of nodes passes through the Sun; and the Sun's declination is zero. When the Earth travels one-half of its yearly orbital round (from the point where it was on 22nd June), the perpendicular projection of the Earth's axis on the ecliptic resumes its former sunward position, (such as it was six months earlier,) with the mere difference that the axis itself, with respect to the (still upright) axis of the ecliptic, is now declined proportionally away from the Sun, whereby the equatorial semi-circle facing the Sun is above (, i.e. to the north of,) the ecliptic plane; less than half of the northern hemisphere and more than half of the southern hemisphere are exposed to sunlight; the Sun is 23.5° below (to the south of) the equator and hence its declination is -23.5°. When the Earth has travelled three-fourths of its yearly orbital route, i.e., on 21st March, the nodal line passes through the Sun and the Sun's declination is again zero. Hasîb Bey notes in his book **Kozmografya**: "The light rays coming nearly parallel to one another are tangent to the Globe around a major circle. This major circle is called the **dâira-i tanwîr=the circle of illumination (the terminator)**. For the first six months during which the Sun is above the equatorial plane, (i.e. north of it,), more than half of the northern hemisphere is on the side of the terminator exposed to the Sun. The plane of illumination defined by this circle passes through the Earth's centre, bisects the Globe, and is perpendicular to the light rays from the Sun. Since the Earth's axis is perpendicular to the equatorial plane, the **angle of illumination** between the plane of illumination and the Earth's axis is equal to the Sun's declination. This is why there are days without nights and nights without daytime at places with latitudes greater than 90°-23°27'=66°33'. Let us assume another and smaller circle sketched parallel to the circle of illumination 19° away from it on the unilluminated side. The phenomena of fajr (morning twilight, dawn, daybreak) and shafaq (evening dusk, evening twilight) take place within the zone between the two circles. At places where the complementaries to the latitudes are less than declination+19°, or, in other words, in situations where regional and seasonal conditions concur in such a way as the sum of latitude and declination, ($\varphi+\delta$), is greater than or equal to 90°-19°=71°, the morning twilight or dawn begins before the evening twilight disappears." In situations when the Sun's declination is smaller than the latitudinal value of a location, the Sun's culmination takes place at a region south of the observer's zenith. The observed paths of the Sun and the stars are circles parallel to the Equator. The Sun's declination is zero when the daily path of the Sun coincides with the equatorial plane on the Gregorian March 21 and on September 23. On these two days, the durations of the night-time and daytime are equal everywhere on the Earth. Since the nisf fadla (excess of semi-diurnal arc, shown as ZL and Z'L' in fig. 2,) is zero, the time of true zawâl in ghurûbî time, and the times of true sunrise and sunset in true solar time are all 06:00 hours everywhere. The shar'î times of zuhr in adhânî time are also shown as 6 in all authentic calendars, because approximately the same amount of time of Tamkin for sunset exists in the time of zuhr as well. Thereafter the Sun's apparent daily paths lapse into an ever-increasing digression from its equatorial course, so that the Sun's declination eventually reaches the angular value of 23°27' on June 22, (i.e. at the end of the three months posterior to the vernal equinox on March 21,) and, conversely, -23°27' on December 22, (i.e. at the end of the three months following the autumnal equinox on September 23). These two dates, (i.e. June 22 and December 22,)[1] are when there begins a gradual decrease in the absolute value of the Sun's declination. During the time when the Sun is below (south of) the Equator, the major part of the northern hemisphere is on the sunless, dark side of the terminator. As the Earth rotates about its axis, the Sun rises when the front edge of the small circle of apparent horizon, (termed 'line of apparent horizon',) of a location touches the illuminated one of the two hemispheres divided by the terminator. The Sun rises exactly in the east when its declination is zero. As the declination increases, the points of sunrise and sunset glide along the line of apparent horizon northwards in summerward months and southwards in winterward months (on the northern hemisphere, and vice versa on the southern hemisphere). The arcs of line of apparent horizon, with their angular value daily changing, are called the **si'a=annual** (sunrise and sunset) **amplitudes**. (The arcs BL and B'L' in figure2.) In northern countries, (in those to the north of Tropic of Cancer,) the Sun, after rising, always appears to gain elevation in a direction

---

[1] The former is termed **Summer Solstice**, and the latter **Winter Solstice**.

with southerly obliquity (with respect to the observer's zenith or plumb level).

One-twenty-fourth of a true solar day is called one **true solar hour.** The lengths of true solar hours change daily. However, the units of time to be adopted (and to be used for civil time-keeping purposes) by using clocks, are required to consist of standardized lengths of days and hours immune to daily fluctuations. Consequently, the **mean solar day** was devised. One-twenty-fourth of a mean solar day is called one **mean hour.** Ibn 'Âbidîn calls the former **mu'awwaj** (crooked, not straight or uniform) and the latter **mu'tadil** (uniform, equable) or **falakî** (celestial) in the chapter dealing with menstruation. The length of one mean solar day is the average of the lengths of true solar days in a year. Since there are 365.242216 true solar days in a madârî (orbital, natural, solar, tropical) year, the [hypothetical] Mean Sun travels an angular distance of 360° within this number of days and 59' 08.33" in a mean solar day. Assume that a Mean Sun which travels that distance per mean solar day along the Equator, and the True Sun (on the ecliptic) start moving on a day with the shortest diurnal period of the year. First the true Sun will be ahead. So the true solar day will be shorter than the mean solar day. Until mid-February the distance (against the Mean Sun) between the two suns will increase every day. Thereafter the True Sun will slow down and they will be on the same meridian around mid-April. After that, the True Sun will lag behind the Mean Sun. Increasing its velocity around mid-May the True Sun will catch up with the Mean Sun around mid-June and they will be on the same meridian. Then it will surpass the Mean Sun. Around mid-July it will slow down, and they will be on the same meridian again around mid-August. Next it will lag behind the Mean Sun. By the end of October it will slow down and the difference between them will gradually decrease. Finally they will resume their concurrence at the start. The time it will take the Mean Sun to travel these differences between the two Suns can be calculated by using Kepler's Laws. The daily difference of time between the two suns is called the **(Solar) Equation of Time.** The equation of time is positive when the Mean Sun is ahead and negative when it is behind. It varies between about +16 minutes and -14 minutes of time throughout a year. It is zero four times a year when the two suns are on the same meridian. A point of time in Mean Solar Time can be converted to True Solar Time by adding to it the equation of time if it is + (positive) and subtracting the equation

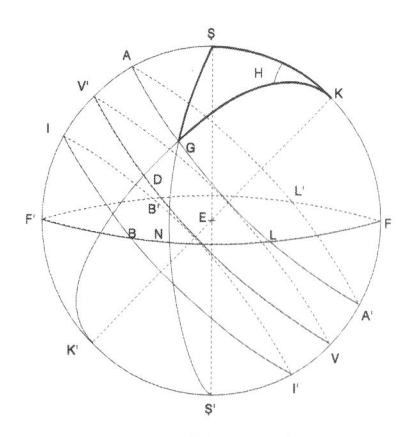

Figure 1

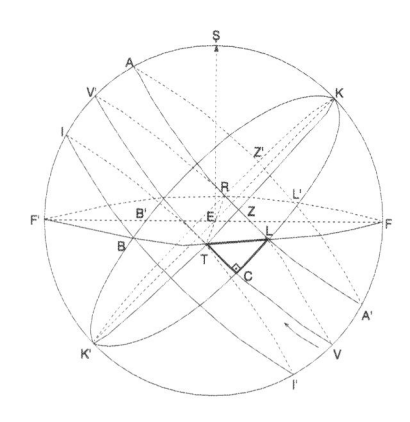

Figure 2

B = Point where the Sun rises on December 22.
T = Point where the Sun rises on March 21 and on September 23.
L = Point where the Sun rises on June 22.
B' = Point where the Sun sets on December 22.
R = Point where the Sun sets on March 21 and on September 23rd.
L' = Point where the Sun sets on June 22.
BI = Semi-diurnal arc (six hours) minus nisf fadla on December 22.
TV' = Semi-diurnal arc on March 21 and September 23.
LA = Semi-diurnal arc (six hours) plus nisf fadla on June 22.
AV' = CL = GD = Declination of the Sun on June 22.
IV' = Minus (southerly) declination of the Sun on December 22.
VTV'R = Celestial equator.
AF', V'F', IF' = The Sun's maximum elevations (at summer solstice, at the two equinoxes, and at winter solstice, respectively).
A = Point where the Sun culminates on June 22.
KLCK' = Semicircle of declination on June 22.
GN = Arc of the Sun's true altitude.

KZK'Z' = Circle of declination on March 21, and September 23.
TC = Arc of the equator equal to nisf fadla at sunrise and sunset on June 22.
FK = F'K' = Arcs of polar distance.
FK = ŞV' = Celestial arc subtending observer's latitude.
H = Angle of fadl-i dâ'ir=hour angle.
GA = Arc of fadl-i dâ'ir.
E = Observer's location.
EŞ = Plumbline direction, (such as that of the observer's upright posture).
TR = East-West diameter of celestial true horizon.
FEF' = Meridian line.
VKV'K' = Meridian circle.
F = Northern point of the true horizon.
ZL = Arc of Nisf fadla, (excess of semi-diurnal arc, or, conversely, complement of semi-nocturnal arc,) at sunrise on June 22.
ZA = Z'A = The semi-diurnal and semi-nocturnal arcs on June 22.
Z'L' = Arc of Nisf fadla, (excess of semi-diurnal arc, or, conversely, complement of semi-nocturnal arc,) at sunset on June 22.
LT, BT = Semi-annual sunrise amplitudes.

of time from it if it is - (negative). The daily variations in the equation of time range between +22 seconds and -30 seconds of time per day. (Please see appendix IV)

Ahmed Ziyâ Bey states, "The value of the dip of horizon in angular seconds is equal to the product of 106.92 and the square root of the elevation in metres of the observer from the tangential horizon of the location." Since the highest hill near the observer in Istanbul is Çamlıca with a height of 267 metres, the greatest angle of dip of horizon is 29' (in Istanbul). In the table of daily Tamkin which Tâhir Efendi, Chairman of the Astronomy Department, calculated, –he prepared it when he assumed office as Director of Cairo Observatory in 1283 A.H. (1866)–; and in the book **Marâsid** by Ismâ'îl Gelenbevî the Virtuous; and in the Turkish book **Mi'yâr-ül-evkât** written by Ismâ'îl Fehîm bin Ibrâhîm Hakkî of Erzurum in the year 1193; and at the end of the calendar for hijrî-solar year 1286 (hijrî-lunar year 1326) prepared by Sayyid Muhammad Ârif Bey, Chairman of the Astronomy Department, it is written: "The angle of dip of horizon in Istanbul is maximally 29', and, at this elevation which is below the true horizon, i.e., below zero, the refraction of light is 44.5'; the apparent radius of the Sun, on the other hand, is at least 15'45"; these three altitudes result in the sighting of the Sun before true sunrise. The solar parallax, however, causes a delay in the sighting of sunrise. Subtraction of 8.8", the angular amount of the solar parallax, from the sum of these three altitudes, yields 1° 29' 6.2", an angular amount termed **the angle of the Sun's altitude**. The period, from the moment when the center of the Sun sets with respect to the true horizon to the moment when its following limb descends by the amount of angular distance (calculated above), so that the following limb dips below the shar'î horizon and daylight reflected on the highest hill (facing the sunset) disappears, is called the **Tamkin**. With the help of the formula used for determining the prayer times on a certain day (in a certain city, say,) in Istanbul, [and a scientific calculator, e.g., Casio], the temporal values of the complements (fadl-i dâir) of the Sun's altitudes, (0° : 0' : 0" and 1° : 29' : 6.2",) at the two times of sunset, i.e., setting of the Sun's center with respect to the true horizon and setting of its upper (following) limb with respect to the cannonical horizon, respectively, are calculated. Since the time of zawâl in terms of true-zawâlî system is zero, the times of two sunsets are the same as the temporal values of their complements thereby determined. The period between the two times of sunset is the **Tamkin**." For instance, on March 21 and on September 23, the angle of the Sun's altitude is 1°29'6.2" and the Tamkin, i.e., the time taken by the center of the Sun to descend that amount of altitude below the true horizon along its trajectory, is 7 minutes 52.29 seconds (for Istanbul). With the variables such as the declination of the Sun and the latitude of the location in the formula of prayer times, period of Tamkin in a certain city varies, depending on the degree of latitude and date. Although the period of Tamkin for a city is not the same for every day or hour, there is a mean period of Tamkin for each city. Please see Appendix V for the table of periods of Tamkin. As a precaution, 2 minutes is added to the Tamkin determined by calculation, and the mean Tamkin for Istanbul is accepted to be 10 minutes (of time). At any place with latitude less than 44°, the difference between maximum and minimum Tamkins in a year is about one or two minutes. A city has only one Tamkin, which is utilized to find the shar'î time of a certain prayer of namâz from the true time. There are not different Tamkins for different prayers of namâz. Nor is there a Tamkin applied to apparent times. If a person, believing that the period of Tamkin is something added with precautionary considerations, continues to eat for 3 to 4 minutes after the imsâk (time to start fasting), his fast becomes fâsid (null), as do his fast and evening prayer when he takes the sunset to be 3 to 4 minutes earlier; this fact is written also in the book **Durr-i Yektâ**. Declination of the Sun, Tamkin and equation of time change every moment at a location, and the unit of haqîqî ghurûbî time, (i.e. the time of true sunset,) is slightly different from the unit of haqîqî zawâlî time, (i.e. the time of true zawâl); and therefore, the calculated prayer times are not precisely exact. To be sure of the beginning of a prayer time, 2 minutes of precaution is added to the period of Tamkin calculated.

There are three kinds of (times of) sunset: the first one is the time when the true altitude of the Sun's centre is zero, called the **true sunset** (haqîqî ghurûb)**;** the second one is the time when it is observed that the apparent altitude of the Sun's following limb with respect to the apparent horizon of the observer's location is zero, i.e. when its upper (following) limb disappears below the line of apparent horizon of the location, called the **apparent sunset** (zâhirî ghurûb); the third one is the time when the altitude of the rear (following) limb is calculated to be zero with respect to the shar'î horizon; this kind of sunset is called the **shar'î sunset** (shar'î ghurûb). A city has only one shar'î horizon. It is noted in all books of fiqh that, of these three kinds of sunset, the sighting of the apparent sunset is to be taken as a basis. However, there are different lines of apparent horizons for different heights. Although the sunset with respect to the shar'î horizon is the apparent sunset observed from the highest hill (of the location), the times of these sunsets and those of true sunsets are mathematical times; that is, they are always determined by calculation. At the time of the calculated true sunset, the Sun is observed not to have set yet below the lines of apparent horizons of high places. This shows that the time for evening prayer and for breaking fast begins not at the moments of the (aforesaid) first and second types of sunset, but at a time somewhat later, i.e. at the time of shar'î sunset. First the true sunset, and then the apparent sunset, and finally the shar'î sunset take place. In his annotation to **Marâq ul-falâh**, Tahtâwî wrote: "Setting of the Sun means sighting of its upper (following) limb disappear below the line of apparent horizon, not below the true horizon." The Sun's setting below the line of apparent horizon means its setting below the surface horizon. If a person, who has failed to perform the late afternoon prayer, (performs the evening prayer and breaks his fast and then) flies west by plane and sees that the Sun has not set yet (at this place he has newly arrived at), he performs the late afternoon prayer and, after sunset, reperforms (i'âda) the evening prayer and, after the 'Iyd, makes qadâ of his fast[1]. At locations where the apparent sunset cannot be seen because of hills, high buildings and clouds, the time of sunset, as is stated in a hadîth-i sherîf, is the time of darkening of the hilltops in the east. This hadîth-i sherîf shows that **"in the calculation of the time of sunset or sunrise, not the true or apparent altitudes but the shar'î altitudes of the Sun with respect to the shar'î horizon are to be used;"** in other words, the Tamkin must be taken into account. This hadîth-i sherîf should be followed, i.e., the Tamkin should be taken into account in calculating the shar'î times of all the other prayers as well because the true riyâdî times are determined by (a single-step astronomical) calculation. There is a difference of time which is as long as the period of Tamkin between the true and canonical times of a prayer. The Tamkin corresponding to the

---

[1] In other words, he reperforms that day's fast after the 'Iyd of Ramadân. Please see the second chapter of the fifth fascicle of **Endless Bliss** for **Fasting in Ramadân** and **'Iyd of Ramadân**, or **'Iyd of Fitra**.

highest hill of a city cannot be changed. If the period of Tamkin is reduced, late afternoon prayer and the prayers following it being performed before their prescribed time, and, for the same matter, (the worship of) fasting being begun after the end of the time of sahur (imsâk), these acts of worship will not be sahîh (valid). Until the year 1982 no one had considered re-arranging the period of Tamkin in Turkey, and for centuries all Scholars of Islam, Awliyâ', Shaikh al-Islâms, Muftîs and all Muslims had performed all their prayers and started their fastings at their shar'î times. (The calendar prepared and published by the daily newspaper Türkiye gives the correct times of prayers and fasting without making any alterations in the period of Tamkin.)[1]

Calculating the early time of any (of the daily five prayers termed) namâz (or salât) requires a definite knowledge of the Sun's altitude pertaining to the prayer in question. First, the true solar time indicating the difference between midday or midnight and the time when [the center of] the Sun reaches the altitude for the prayer with respect to the true horizon on its path at a location of a certain latitude on a given day with a certain declination of the Sun's center, is calculated. This time is called **fadl-i dâir = difference of time** (represented by the arc GA in figure 1). To determine the true altitude specific to a certain prayer of namâz, the altitude of the Sun's upper limb with respect to the mathematical horizon is measured with the help of a **(rub'-i-dâira)** or astrolabic quadrant at the moment when the prayer time written in books of Fiqh begins. From this, the true altitude can be calculated. [The apparent altitude with respect to the apparent horizon is measured by using the sextant.] The arc side GK of the spherical triangle KŞG imagined on the celestial sphere[2] is the complement of the arc of declination, GD; the curvilinear side KŞ is the complement of polar distance KF, or of the observer's latitude, (ŞV'); and the arc ŞG is the complement of the Sun's true altitude, GN. (Figure 1). The angle H at the polar point K of the triangle, as well as the angular value of the arc GA subtending this angle, represents fadl-i dâir (hour angle); this is calculated in angular degrees and multiplied by four to convert it to true time in minutes. The temporal value of hour angle is combined with the

---

[1] Please visit the websites: "**http://www.turktakvim.com**" and "**http://www.namazvakti.com**" and "**www.islamicalendar.co.uk**".

[2] Vertices of this triangle are the Sun (G), the observer's zenith (Ş), and the celestial north pole (K).

time of true or ghurûbî zawâl or midnight; thereby **true time** of the prayer is obtained in terms of true zawâlî or ghurûbî time. Then the ghurûbî time is converted to adhânî by subtracting one unit of Tamkin from it. The zawâlî time is converted to mean time by adding the equation of time to it. Then the **Shar'î time** of the prayer in question is obtained from these adhânî and mean ghurûbî times. While doing this, the **time of Tamkin**, which is the period between the time when the (upper) limb of the Sun has reached the altitude peculiar to this prayer from the shar'î horizon and the time when the center of the Sun has reached this altitude from the true horizon, is taken into consideration. For, the difference of time between the true and shar'î times of a prayer is equal to the difference of time between the true horizon and the shar'î horizon; this difference is the period of **Tamkin**. The shar'î times are found by subtracting one unit of Tamkin from the calculated true prayer times before midday, since (before midday) the Sun passes the shar'î horizon before passing the true horizon. Examples of this are the times of imsâk and sunrise. Ahmad Ziya Bey and Kadûsî say in their books entitled **Rub-i-dâira**: "Fajr begins when the upper (preceding) limb of the Sun has reached a position 19° below the shar'î horizon. The shar'î time of imsâk in terms of true time is obtained by subtracting Tamkin from the calculated true time of fajr (dawn)." Hasan Shawqi Efendi of Hezargrad, senior professor of Islamic sciences at the Fâtih Madrasa and translator of Kadûsî's **İrtifâ'-i şems risâlesi**, (Booklet on the Sun's Altitude), describes the method of finding the time of imsâk in its ninth chapter, and adds: "The times of true imsâk we have obtained by calculation are without Tamkin. A Muslim who will fast must stop eating 15 minutes, i.e. two units of Tamkin, before this time. Thus, they will protect their fast from being fâsid." As is seen, to find the shar'î adhânî time of imsâk, he subtracts twice the Tamkin from the true ghurûbî time and reports that otherwise the fasting will be nullified. [One unit of Tamkin is subtracted from the ghurûbî time to find the Shar'î time, and another unit of Tamkin is subtracted from the ghurûbî time to convert it to the adhânî time.] This we have observed also in the yearly tables of awqât-i shar'iyya (shar'î times) which Hadrat Ibrâhîm Hakki (of Erzurum) arranged for Erzurum, as well as in the book **Hey'et-i-felekiyya**, by Mustafâ Hilmi Efendi in 1307; therein true times of dawn and sunrise are converted to shar'î times in terms of the system of adhânî time by subtracting twice the period of Tamkin. The same method is applied in the book **Hidâyat-ul-mubtadî fî ma'rifat-il-awqât bi-rub'i-d-dâira** by 'Alî bin 'Uthmân; he passed away in 801 [1398 A.D.]. On the other hand, to find the shar'î prayer times within the period after midday, wherein the Sun transits the shar'î horizon after transiting the true horizon, one unit of Tamkin is added to the true times. In this category are the times of early and late afternoon, evening, ishtibâk, and night. Ahmed Ziyâ Bey states as follows in the aforementioned book, in the chapter dealing with the time of Zuhr: "If Tamkin is added to the time of true zawâl in terms of mean time, the time of shar'î Zuhr in terms of mean time is obtained." Always one unit of Tamkin is subtracted from time known in terms of ghurûbî system of time to convert it to adhânî time. To convert time that is known in respect to the ghurûbî horizons belonging of the period covering noontime and thererafter, to the shar'î time with respect to the shar'î horizons, one unit of Tamkin is added; then one unit of Tamkin is subtracted to convert it to the adhânî time. Consequently, the adhânî times of these prayers concur with their ghurûbî times. The shar'î times determined in terms of haqîqî (true) or ghurûbî systems of time are converted to the wasatî (mean) and adhânî times and printed on calendars. The times determined thereby are riyâdî times in terms of riyâdî time system. The riyâdî times, which are calculated in terms of riyâdî time system, also indicate the mer'î times on clocks.

NOTE: To work out the time of zuhr in terms of adhânî-haqîqî (true) time system from the (already known) ghurûbî-haqîqî time of zawâl, Islamic scholars subtracted the Tamkin at sunset from it, and they obtained the ghurûbî-zawâl time again by adding the period of Tamkin, which is the method for finding the shar'î time at zawâl. This fact shows that the Tamkin at the time of zuhr must be equal to the difference of time between the true and shar'î horizons, i.e., to the Tamkin at sunset. Likewise, Tamkins for all the shar'î prayer times are equal to those at sunrise and sunset. As is reported in the book **al-Hadâiq al-wardiyya**, "Ibni Shâtir 'Alî bin Ibrâhîm [d. 777 (1375 A.D.)] describes in his book **an-Naf'ul'âm** the construction of a quadrant practicable at all latitudes. He devised a basîta (sundial) for the Amawiyya Mosque in Damascus. Muhammad bin Muhammad Hânî (d. 306 h.), a khalîfa (disciple and successor) of Hadrat Mawlânâ Khâlid al-Baghdâdî, renewed it in 1293 [1876 A.D.], and wrote a book entitled **Kashf-ul-qinâ' 'an ma'rifat-il-waqt min-al-irtifâ'**."

Two other sources that we have studied and wherein the period of Tamkin was taken into account in the calculations of shar'î times of prayers, are a calendar entitled **'Ilmiyye sâlnâmesi** and prepared by **Mashîhat-i Islâmiyya,** the highest council of the Ottoman 'ulamâ', for the year 1334 [1916 A.D.], and the **Türkiye'ye Mahsûs Evkat-ı Şer'iyye** book no. 14 published by the Kandilli Observatory of the University of Istanbul in 1958. We have seen that the times determined as a result of the observations and calculations carried on by our staff, composed of true men of Islam and specialized astronomers using latest instruments, are the same as those found and reported by Islamic scholars, who used the **rub-i-daira=astrolabic quadrant,** for centuries. Therefore, it is not permissible to change the quantities of Tamkin, for it would mean to defile the prayer times.

One mean solar day on timepieces is twenty-four hours. A period of twenty-four hours which begins when a time measuring instrument, e.g. our watch, shows twelve o'clock at the haqîqî zawâl time and ends at twelve o'clock the following day is called the **mean solar day.** The lengths of mean solar days are all equal. On the other hand, the duration of time that begins when our watch shows twelve at the time of zawâl and ends at the time of zawâl the following day is called the **true solar day.** The length of a **true solar day,** which is the time taken by two successive transits[1] of the center of the Sun, is equal to the length of a mean solar day four times in a year. Except on these days, their daily lengths differ by the amount of daily variation in ta'dîl-i zamân (equation of time). The length of a **ghurûbî day** is the time between two successive settings of the center of the Sun below the true horizon. An **adhânî day** is the time between two successive canonical settings of the upper [following] limb of the Sun below the canonical horizon of a location. When this (second kind of) setting is observed, the adhânî clock is adjusted to 12. Though an adhânî day is equal in length to a ghurûbî day, it begins a period of Tamkin later than a ghurûbî day. Since the Sun culminates only once in a ghurûbî day versus its ascent to and descent from two different altitudes within a true zawâlî day, there is one-or-two-minutes' difference of length between these two days. The

---

[1] When a celestial object is on the observer's meridian, it is at culmination or in transit.

resultant difference of seconds between the horary units of the true zawâlî and ghurûbî times is smoothed out with compensatory modifications manipulated in the period of Tamkin. Timepieces indicate the adhânî or wasatî (mean) times, not the haqîqî (true) or ghurûbî times. Let us set our clock (calibrated to run at the rate of mean time) to 12:00 o'clock at the time of shar'î sunset on any day. The next day, the time of setting of the following limb of the Sun below the shar'î horizon will differ by a little less than one minute from mean solar day, i.e., 24 hours. This alternate difference, which develops against one and the other between the lengths of haqîqî (true) and wasatî (mean) days around (yearly four-time) passing periods of equalization, is termed **equation of time**[1]. Lengths of nights and days have nothing to do with equation of time; nor do ghurûbî or adhânî times. Lengths of days and hours in adhânî hours are equal to lengths of true solar days and hours. For this reason, when timepieces are adjusted to 12 at the time of sunset daily, they indicate the length of true day, not the length of mean day.

Timepieces set to keep the adhânî time must be adjusted to 12:00 at the time of shar'î sunset calculated in mean solar time every evening. Every day, these clocks must be advanced as the time of sunset shifts backwards and taken backwards as it advances. There is not a mean length for an adhânî day, nor a mean equation of time. It is written in the calendar **Mi'yâr-i awqât** prepared in Erzurum in the Hijrî Qamarî year 1193 A.H. (1779): "At the time of true zawâl, when shadows are the shortest, the adhânî clock is taken backwards so as to adjust it to a position one unit of Tamkin behind the time of zuhr written on the calendar." To correct the adhânî clock, when the mean clock comes to a prayer time, the adhânî clock is adjusted to the time of this prayer written on the calendar. A way of adjusting the vasatî and adhânî clocks is as follows: two convergent straight lines are drawn, one in the direction of the observer's meridian and the other towards the Qibla, on a level place. Then, a rod is erected at the point of intersection of these two straight lines. When the shadow of this rod becomes aligned with the line parallel to the meridian the clock is set to the time of zawâl, and when it becomes aligned with the one pointing towards the Qibla, the clock is set to the time of

---

[1] The dates on which the true and mean solar times are equalized, i.e. when the difference between them is zero, are April 15, June 14, September 1, and December 25. Please see Appendix IV.

Qibla. The adhânî clock is not adjusted on days with a variation of sunset time less than 1 minute. In Istanbul, clocks are advanced daily throughout a period of six months, so that they are 186 minutes ahead by the end of this period, and thereafter the process is repeated in the opposite direction for another six-month period at the end of which the 186 minutes gradually added to clocks will have been taken back likewise. These clocks reckon time in reference to the beginning of the adhânî day. Calculation of times of namâz, however, is done in reference to the ghurûbî day. Since an adhânî day begins one unit of Tamkin later than a ghurûbî day, prayer times are converted to adhânî time by subtracting the Tamkin from the ghurûbî times determined by calculation. Equation of time is not used in calculating the ghurûbî or adhânî times.

Since the Earth rotates round its axis from west to east, places to the east see the Sun before those to the west. Prayer times are earlier in the east. There are three hundred and sixty imaginary longitudinal semicircles [meridians] passing through the terrestrial poles, and the semicircle passing through Greenwich, London, (termed prime meridian,) has been accepted as the one for reference. There is one degree of angular distance between two successive semicircles. As the Earth rotates, a city goes fifteen degrees eastwards in one hour. Therefore, of two cities one degree of longitude apart from each other but with the same latitude, prayer times for the one on the east are four minutes earlier. Locations on the same meridian, i.e. with the same longitude, have a common time of true zawâl. Times of zawâl and zuhr on the basis of ghurûbî time system, and also other prayer times, depend on latitude. The greater the latitude of a location, the farther away from noon are the times of sunrise and sunset summer, and vice versa in winter. A quantity is measured in reference to a certain beginning; e.g. zero. The more distant something is from zero the greater is it said to be. To start clocks from zero they are adjusted either to zero or to 12 (or 24). The moment at which a certain kind of work is started is said to be the **time** of that work. The time may mean a moment or a period. Examples of the latter case are the **time of shar'î zawâl**, **prayer times**, and the **time** during which it is **wâjib** to perform the **Qurbân**[1].

---

[1] There is detailed information about **Qurbân** and how to perform the Qurbân in the fourth chapter of the fifth fascicle of **Endless Bliss**.

Clocks adjusted to local (mahallî) times in cities to the east are ahead of those adjusted to the local times in cities to the west on the same day. The time of zuhr, i.e., the shar'î time of early afternoon prayer begins a period of Tamkin later than true zawâl time at every location. Since the adjustments of local clocks vary in direct ratio to their longitudinal degrees, the prayer times on local clocks on the same latitude do not vary with longitudinal variations. The adhânî time clocks are local today, as they were formerly. Since the highest places of different locations are not equal in height, the period of Tamkin applied at different locations differ from one another by about one or two minutes, and so do the shar'î times of (daily five) prayers; yet the precautionary modifications made in Tamkin eliminate such differences. In the present time, clocks adjusted simultaneously to a common mean time in all cities of a country are used. In a country where this **common mean time** is used, time of a certain prayer in standard mean time vary even in cities on the same latitude. Four times the longitudinal difference between a pair of cities with the same latitude shows the difference, in minutes, between the times of the same prayer, in standard mean time, in these two cities. In brief, at locations on the same longitude, the only two things that remain unchanged despite change of latitude are clocks adjusted to local time and those adjusted to standard mean time. As the absolute value of latitude increases, a prayer time moves forwards or backwards, the direction depending on the time's being before or after noon as well as on the season's being summer or winter. Calculation of prayer times from those for the latitude 41° N has been explained in the instructions manual for the **Rub'-i-dâira** (in Turkish). When longitudinal degrees change, i.e. at places with common latitude, the adjustments of timepieces and all the prayer times on the standard timepieces change.

In all places between the two longitudes 7.5° east and west of (the longitude of Greenwich,) London, mean solar time for London (Greenwich Mean Time, GMT, or Universal Time, UT, counted from midnight,) is used. This is called the West European Time. In places between seven and a half degrees and twenty-two and a half degrees east of London, time one hour ahead of it is used, which is called Central European Time. And in places between 22.5° and 37.5° of longitude east, time two hours ahead of GMT is used, which is called East European Time. Times three, four and five hours ahead of GMT are used in the Near,

Middle and Far East, respectively. There are twenty-four such zones of standard time on the Earth, which follow one another by one hour. The **standart time zone** adopted in a country is the one centered on the mean local time of places located on one of the **hourly longitudinal semicircles** imagined to traverse the country with intervals of fifteen degrees. Turkey's standard time zone is the local mean time of the places located on the meridian thirty degrees east of London, which is East European Time. The cities Izmit, Kütahya, Bilecik and Elmalı lie on the meridian 30°. Some countries do not use the time of the geographical zone they are in because of political and economic considerations. For example, France and Spain use the Central European Time. Clocks in countries where different standard times are used are so adjusted as to differ from one another only by multiples of hours at any given moment; the hourhand in a country is in advance of that in one to its west.

The time of a prayer at a given place in Turkey in local solar mean time differs, in minutes, from Turkey's standard time by four times the longitudinal difference between that place and the longitude 30°. To find the time of this prayer in standard time, this difference will be subtracted from or added to the local time if the longitudinal degree of that place is greater or smaller than 30°, respectively. For example, let us say the time of a prayer begins in the city of Kars (41°N, 43°E) at 7 hr 00 minutes in local mean time on May 1. The city's longitude being 43°, which is greater than 30°, local time of Kars is ahead of standard time. Then the time of that prayer begins 13 x 4 = 52 minutes earlier, at 06:08 in standard time.

The sum of M_g (the time of zawâl in ghurûbî time) and S_t (the time of true sunset in true solar time) for the same place is equal to 12 hours [equation (1), below], because this sum is a period of about 12 true hours continuing from 12 o'clock in the morning in ghurûbî time to the time of true sunset. Please see the chart for summer months. The unit of true solar time is approximately equal to that of ghurûbî time.

Time of midday in ghurûbî time+Time of sunset in true time=
=12hours   or

$$M_g + S_t = 12 \text{ hours} \qquad (1)$$

And the sum of half of true daytime and half of true night-time N_t is about 12 hours. Therefore,

Half of true nighttime+Time of sunset in true time=12hours   or

$1/2\ N_t + S_t = 12$ hours (2)

By combining the equations (1) and (2), we obtain:
Time of midday in ghurûbî time=Half of true nigthtime or
$M_g = (1/2)\ N_t$ (3)

The time of midday in ghurûbî time is from the ghurûbî twelve in the morning till true midday. The ghurûbî twelve in the morning is half the daytime later than midnight. It is before sunrise in winter, and after sunrise in summer. The period for morning prayer, as well as that for fasting, begins at the time of fajr-i-sâdiq. Its beginning is known when the adhânî clock, which begins from 12 at the time of sunset, indicates the time of fajr, or when the mean clock, which begins from 12 at the time of midnight, indicates the time of fajr. Sunrise begins half the night-time later than 12 midnight, or a period of night-time later than 12 at the time of sunset, or half the daytime earlier than zawâl. Twelve o'clock in the Ghurûbî morning is 12 hours after 12 at the time of sunset, or half the daytime later than 12 midnight, or half the night time earlier than time of true zawâl. Between the time of sunrise and (the ghurûbî) 12 in the morning there is a difference equal to the difference between halves the lengths of night and day. All these calculations are done using the true solar time. After calculation, true solar time is converted to mean solar time and thence to standard time. Below, we shall see that the time of midday in ghurûbî time is the time of zuhr in adhânî time. For that matter, on May 1, since the time of zuhr in adhânî time is 5:06, the time of shar'î sunrise in standard time in Istanbul is 4:57 (5:57 in one-hour advanced summer time).

If days and nights were always equal in length, the Sun would always rise six hours before midday and set six hours thereafter. Since they are not equal, the period between the times of zawâl and ghurûb (sunset) is somewhat longer than six hours in summer months. In winter months, on the other hand, this period becomes a little shorter. This discrepancy centered around the mean six hours is called the **nisf fadla = excess of semi-diurnal** time. (Please see figure 2). In summer months, true sunsets differ from the time of zawâl by the sum of six and nisf fadla, whereas their difference in winter months is the subtraction of nisf fadla from six. Conversely, the ghurûbî twelve in the morning is transpositionally the same amount different from the time of zawâl.

To find the time of zuhr in adhânî time system and the times of sunrise and sunset in true and mean time systems, the nisf fadla is obtained by using Scottish Mathematician John Napier's (1550-1617) formula. According to this formula, on a spherical right triangle [for example, the triangle TCL in Figure 2] cos of one of the five parts other than the right angle [sin of its complement] is equal to the product of cot values of the two parts adjacent to that part [tag of their complements], or to the product of the sin values of the other two parts not adjacent to it. However, instead of the (angles subtended by the) two perpendicular sides themselves, their complements are included in the calculation. So,

sin (nisf fadla)=tan (declination) x tan (latitude).

Using this formula and with the help of a scientific calculator or a table of logarithms of trigonometric functions, the arc of **nisf fadla** in degrees and, multiplying this by 4, its equivalent in minutes of true solar time are found. If the terrestrial location of a certain city and the celestial position of the Sun are on the same hemisphere, (so that the latitudinal value of the former and the declinational value of the latter share the same sign,) its local solar time of true sunset is obtained by adding the absolute value of nisf fadla to 6 true solar hours (one-fourth of a true day). By subtracting the absolute value of nisf fadla from 6 hours, the time of true midday (zawâl) in ghurûbî time, or the time of true sunrise in true solar time, [beginning with midnight,] is found. That means to say that the ghurûbî 12 in the morning is earlier than the time of true zawâl by the difference obtained by doing this subtraction. Please see appendix IV for the table of declination of the Sun. If the city in question and the Sun are on different hemispheres, the time of true zawâl in ghurûbî time, or the time of true sunrise in true solar time, is obtained by adding the absolute value of nisf fadla to 6 hours; and by subtracting nisf fadla from 6 hours the time of true sunset in true solar time is obtained for that city.

For instance, on May 1, declination of the Sun is +14°55', equation of time is +3 temporal minutes and Istanbul's latitude is +41°; depressing the keys,

14:55 ⊙″′→ tan x 41 tan = arc sin x 4 = →⊙″′

on the scientific calculator (Privilege) gives the resultant 53min 33sec (of time). Nisf fadla is found to be 54min (of time); the calculated true sunset is at 6:54 in true zawâlî time, at 6:51 in local mean zawâlî time, and at 18:55 in standard time or at 19:55 in summer time. Time of canonical sunset is found to be 20:05, in summer time, by adding the Tamkin of 10 minutes for Istanbul. Duration of true daytime is 13 hours plus 48 minutes, and duration of night is its difference from 24 hours, i.e. 10 hours plus 12 minutes; 5:06, which is the difference between nisf fadla and 6 hours, is the time of true sunrise in true time, i.e. from the time of midnight, or the time of zawâl in terms of ghurûbî time. The time of true midday in adhânî time is earlier than that in ghurûbî time by a period of Tamkin; i.e., it is at 4:56. The shar'î time of zuhr in adhânî time begins later than the time of true midday in adhânî time by a period of Tamkin, that is, at 5:06. Twice the time of zuhr in adhânî time, 10 hours and 12 minutes, is the approximate duration of astronomical nighttime, and subtracting 20 minutes (twice the Tamkin) from this gives 9:52 to be the time of shar'î sunrise in adhânî time. If equation of time and Tamkin are subtracted from 5 hours 6 minutes and the result is converted to standard time, the time of shar'î sunset is obtained to be 4:57. Subtraction of the time of adhânî zuhr from 6 hours yields the nisf fadla time. Since the maximum absolute declination of the Sun is 23° 27', the Nisf fadla is 22° maximum by calculation for Istanbul, which makes one hour and twenty-eight minutes, and hence there is a difference of 176 minutes between the latest and earliest times of sunset. And since there is equal difference between the (earliest and latest) times of sunrise, the difference also between the longest and shortest daytimes is 352 minutes, [5 hours and 52 minutes.]

Nisf fadla is zero, always at locations on the equator, and all over the world on March 21st and on September 23rd, because the declination of the Sun, and hence tan. dec., is zero always on the equator and worldover on March 21st and on September 23rd. On April 1, declination of the Sun is 4°20' and the equation of time is -4 minutes. The latitude of Vienna, Austria, is 48°15', and nisf fadla is found, with the use of a scientific (Privilege) calculator by depressing the keys, CE/C 4.20 ︎→ tan x 48.15 ︎→ tan = arc sin x 4= to be about 19.5 minutes. Then, the time of the evening prayer [shar'î sunset] in Vienna begins at 6:33:30 in local mean solar time. Vienna's longitude is 16°25', which is 1°25' east of the (hourly) standard meridian; therefore, the time of evening prayer begins at 6:27:30 in Austria's geographical standard time, which is 1 hour ahead of GMT. Since the latitude of Paris is 48°50', nisf fadla is 20 minutes and the time of the evening prayer in local mean time begins at 6:34; with its longitude +2°20' east, it should normally begin at 6:25 in the geographical standard time, yet the standard time used in France is 1 hour ahead of West European Time; so it begins at 19:25. As for New York; its latitude is 41°, and nifs fadla is 15 minutes; hence the time of evening prayer begins at 6:29 in local mean time; with longitude -74°, it is 1° east of the (hourly) standard meridian -75° which corresponds to the standard geographical time 75/15=5 hours behind that of London; therefore, evening prayer begins at 6:25 in that time zone. For Delhi, latitude is 28°45'; nisf fadla is 9.5 minutes, the time of evening prayer begins at 6:23:30 in local mean time; its longitude is +77°. Since this longitude is 2° east of the standard hourly meridian, which in turn is 5 hours ahead of London, the time of evening prayer begins at 6:15:30 on the standard hourly meridian.

For Trabzon, latitude is the same (41°) as that for Istanbul, and longitude is 39°50'. To find nisf fadla on May 1, the following keys of the CASIO fx- scientific calculator are depressed:

ON 14 [ο,,,] 55 [ο,,,] tan x 41 tan = INV sin x 4 = INV [ο,,,] and the time of nisf fadla is found to be 53 minutes and 33 seconds, which is about 54 minutes[1]. Time of sunset, like in Istanbul, is 7:01 in local mean time, and 39 minutes earlier, i.e. 6:22, in standard time. Al-Mekkat al-mukarrama is on latitude 21°26' and, like Trabzon, on longitude 39°50', and nisf fadla on May 1 is 24 minutes. Time of sunset is 6:31 in local mean time, and 5:52 in standard time, which is 39 minutes before this as adjusted to the standard meridian of longitude 30°. On November 1, declination is -14°16' and the equation of time is +16 minutes. Nisf fadla is 51 and 23 minutes for Istanbul and Mekka, respectively, while the time of sunset in standard time is 5:07 and 4:52 for Istanbul and Mekka, respectively. On November 1, adhân for evening prayer can be heard from a local radio broadcast in Mekka 15 minutes before the same adhân in Istanbul. In the above calculations for sunset at various cities, the Tamkin for Istanbul is used. On the clocks set to adhânî and local mean times in different cities on a common latitude, prayer times differ only by the difference in the periods of Tamkin applied in them.

The time of zawâl in local mean solar time differs from 12 hours (in local true solar time) by the equation of time, i.e. less than one minute, everywhere, and annually ranges, e.g. in Istanbul, from approximately 16 minutes before to 14 minutes after 12. In standard time, however, it is earlier or later than the local time of the place by an amount, in minutes, of four times the longitudinal difference between the place in question and the

---

[1] The use or operation of calculators vary with brand.

standard meridian of longitude 30° for every location in Turkey. And the time of zawâl changes every day for an amount of one or two minutes on the adhânî clocks. The Ottoman administration employed **muwaqqits** (time-keepers), who were in charge of these adjustments in great mosques.

An easy way to determine the equation of time on a certain day is simply to learn the time of early afternoon prayer [zuhr] in terms of standard time on that day in a certain city, e.g. in Istanbul. This time minus 14 minutes is the time of midday in local mean solar time. As the time of midday in true solar time is 12 o'clock everywhere, the difference between these two midday times in minutes is the equation of time. If the time of zawâl (midday) in mean time is short of 12:00, the sign of the equation of time is (+) and, if it exceeds it, it is (-).

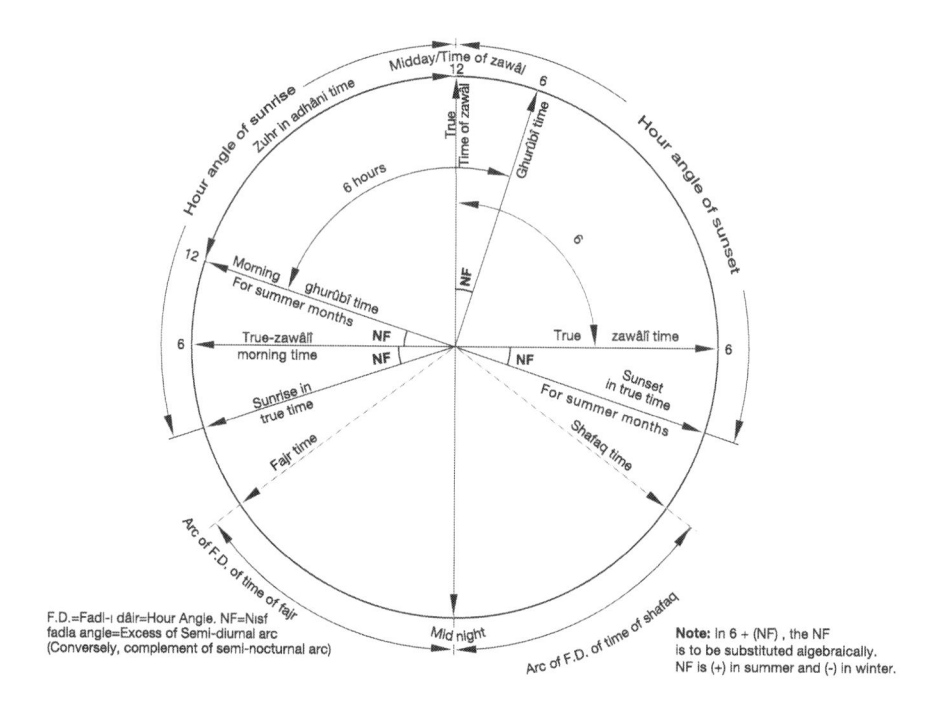

Since the equation of time is -13 minutes on March 1, a place's local time of zawâl in terms of mean solar time is 12:13 everywhere. The time of early afternoon prayer begins later than this by the amount of Tamkin. In Istanbul, for example, it begins at 12:23. At any location, its time in terms of standard time begins either earlier or later than its time in terms of local mean time by an amount, in minutes, equal to four times the longitudinal difference in degrees between the (hourly) standard meridian and the meridian of the place in question. If a location in Turkey is to the east of the standard meridian 30° E, it is earlier, otherwise later. Thus, the time of early afternoon prayer in terms of standard time is about 12:11 in Ankara, whereas it is 12:27 in Istanbul. When a clock adjusted to standard time arrives at the time of early afternoon prayer, the daily adjustment of a clock keeping the adhânî time would have been realized simply by setting it to the time of the early afternoon prayer determined by using the nisf fadla. If the height of the highest place is not known, the **period of Tamkin** of a location is either (1) the period between the moment when sunlight reflected on the highest place disappears and the instant when sunset below the tangential horizon is observed, or (2) the difference between 12 and the time found by combining with equation of time the time shown by a clock set to local mean time when it is the time of zuhr determined by applying nisf fadla to the time shown on an adhânî clock set to 12 when sunlight reflected on the highest place of the location is observed to disappear, or (3) the difference between the time when the reflection of sunlight on the highest place disappears in terms of local mean time and the time of sunset determined by applying nisf fadla; or (4) the period of time determined by adding the equation of time to the difference of time of zuhr in local mean time and 12:00 if the equation of time is positive (+), or by subtracting it if it is negative (-).

It is written as follows in Ibn Âbidîn, as well as in the Shâfi'î book **al-Anwâr** and in the commentary to the Mâlikî book **al-Muqaddamat al-izziyya,** and also in **al-Mîzân ul-kubrâ**: "For a salât (prayer) to be sahîh (valid), one should perform it after its time has begun and know that one is performing it in its correct time. A salât performed with doubtful knowledge as to the arrival of its correct time is not valid (sahîh) even if you realize, after performing it, that you performed it in its correct time. To know that the prayer time has come means to hear the adhân recited by an 'âdil[1] Muslim who knows the prayer times. If the reciter of the

---

[1] A Muslim who never commits a grave sin and who does not commit venial sins continually and whose good deeds are more than his wrongdoings, is called an 'âdil Muslim. On the other hand, fâsiq Muslim means one who is habituated to committing one of the grave sins such as fornication, gambling, consumption of hard drinks, usury (however low the rate of interest), looking at people or things or

adhân is not 'âdil [or if there is not a calendar prepared by an 'âdil Muslim], you should investigate whether the time has come and perform it when you surely believe that it is the time. Information obtained from a fâsiq Muslim or a person who is not known to be an 'âdil Muslim concerning the direction of qibla or other religious matters such as cleanliness or uncleanliness of something, or whether a certain act (or behaviour or thought) is halâl (permitted) or harâm (forbidden), as well as the (call to prayer termed) adhân performed by such a person, is not trustworthy; instead of asking a person of that kind, you have to learn the matter in your own and act in accordance with the result of your personal research."

It is mustahab to perform the morning prayer when it becomes rather light everywhere in every season; this is called **"isfâr"**. It is mustahab to perform the early afternoon prayer in jamâ'a late on hot days in summer and early on winter days. It is mustahab to always perform the evening prayer early. And it is mustahab to perform the night prayer late but till it is the initial one-third of the shar'î night, which is the period of time between ghurûb (sunset) and fajr (dawn). It is makrûh tahrîmî to postpone it till after midnight. In fact, the postponements suggested above apply only to those who perform namâz in jamâ'a. A Muslim who performs namâz alone at home should perform every prayer as soon as its time begins. A hadîth sherîf reported in **Kunûz ad-daqâ'iq** on the authority of Hâkim and Tirmidhî reads: **"The most valuable 'ibâda is the salât performed in its early time."** Another hadîth sherîf, reported in the **Sahîh** of Muslim and also written on page 537 of **Izâlat al-khafâ**[1], declares: **"Such a time will come when directors and imâms will kill the salât; [that is,] they will postpone it till the expiration of its** [prescribed] **time. You should perform your salât within its time! If they perform it in jamâ'a**

---

images that are forbidden for a Muslim to look at, condoning acts of wrongdoing committed by a person under his responsibility such as his wife or daughters, for instance their going out without covering those parts of their body which Islam commands them to cover. Also, a Muslim who habitually neglects one of Islam's open commandments such as the daily five prayers of namâz, etc, as well as one who ignores learning something which is farz or wâjib for a Muslim to learn, is a fâsiq Muslim. Hence, 'âdil and fâsiq are antonymous.

[1] **Izâlat-ul-khafâ an khilâfat-il-khulafâ**, by the great Sunnî Islamic scholar Shâh Waliyyullah Dahlawî (1114 [1702 A.D.]–1176 [1762]; Delhi).

after you [have performed it], **perform it again together with them! The one you perform the second time is nâfila** (supererogatory)." It would be cautious to perform the late afternoon and night prayers according to Al-Imâm al-a'zam's ijtihâd. A Muslim who is afraid he may fail to wake up later should perform the witr prayer immediately after the night prayer. He who performs it before night prayer should reperform it. And he who can wake up should perform it towards the end of the night.

Ahmad Ziyâ Bey provides the following information on page 157: In a city, the algebraic sum of a certain prayer's canonical time known with respect to the local mean time and the equation of time for the day in question is its time with respect to the true solar time. This plus the time of zuhr in adhânî time and minus one unit of Tamkin yields the prayer's shar'î time with respect to the adhânî time. If the result exceeds twelve, the excess indicates the adhânî time. For example, the Sun sets at 18:00 (6:00 p.m.) in standard time in Istanbul on March 1. Since the equation of time at the time of sunset is -12 minutes, the time of shar'î sunset in Istanbul is 5:44 in local true solar time. And since the time of shar'î zuhr in adhânî time is 06:26, the time of sunset is 06:26+05:44-00:10=12:00. In general,

(1) t in adhânî time = t at the same moment in true solar time + t of zuhr in adhânî time - Tamkin of the location

(2) t in true solar time = t in adhânî time + t of shar'î sunset in true solar time

where **t** is time.

In the equation **(2)**, if the time of sunset is in mean time, the zawâlî time obtained is also mean.

The equation **(2)** may also be written as:

(3) t in adhânî time = t in true solar time - t of shar'î sunset in true solar time

If the time of sunset treated is greater than the true time, the subtraction must be done after twelve is added to the true time.

The zawâlî time in the equations **(2)** and **(3)** is given in true solar time; yet, since the same numbers are added and then subtracted while converting standard time to true time and then the true time found to standard time, the computation done without converting standard time to true time yields the same results; as follows:

(4) t in standard time = t in adhânî time + t of shar'î sunset in standard time

(5) t in adhânî time = t in standard time - t of shar'î sunset in standard time

The time of sunset on March 1 as calculated above can also be determined with the help of the last equation: 18:00 - 18:00 = 00:00, which is 12:00 in adhânî time. Likewise, since the time of the late afternoon prayer is 15:34 and the time of sunset is 6:00 in standard time on March 1, the time of the late afternoon prayer in adhânî time is:

15:34 - 6:00 = 9:34.

Similarly, since the time of imsâk in adhânî time on the same day is 10:52, the time of imsâk in standard time is 10:52+6:00=16:52 or 4:52 p.m. by the equation **(4)**.

Let us find the time of sunset in true solar time in Istanbul on 23 June 1982 Wednesday, 1 Ramadan 1402: on that day, the time of the early afternoon prayer in Istanbul is 4:32 in adhânî time, and the equation of time is -2 minutes. The time of sunset in local true solar time in Istanbul is the difference between this and 12 hours; that is, 7:28. The shar'î sunset is at 7:38 in true solar time, at 19:40 in mean solar time, at 19:44 in standard time of Türkey and at 20:44 in summer time.

If the time in standard time is smaller than the time of sunset, 12 or 24 is added to it in the equations **(3)** and **(5)**. Ahmad Ziyâ Bey employs the formulas

(6) t in adhânî time = true time of zawâl + true solar time

and

(7) true solar time = adhânî time-true time of zawâl.

Mustafa Efendi, Chairman of the Ottoman Astronomy Department, wrote in the pocket calendar of 1317 A.H. (1899): "In order to convert ghurûbî and zawâlî times to each other, the time given in one is subtracted from the time of early afternoon prayer if the time in question is before noon (a.m.); then this difference is subtracted from the time of early afternoon prayer in the other time. If it is p.m., the time of early afternoon prayer is subtracted from the time given, and then the difference is added to the time of early afternoon prayer in the other time. For example, the time of imsâk on June 12th, 1989 is 6:22 in adhânî time; the time of zuhr is 4:32. The difference (16:32-6:22)=10:10. Subtracting this from 12:14, which is the time of the early afternoon prayer in standard time, the time of imsâk is found to be 2:04 in standard time.

To determine the time the Sun comes to the altitude for the beginning of the time of a certain salât, first the value of **fadl-i dâir** (time corresponding to the hour angle of the Sun) is calculated. Fadl-i dâir is the interval between the point where the center of the Sun is and the time of zawâl (midday) for the daytime, and it is the interval between that point and midnight for the nighttime. The angle of fadl-i dâir, H, can be calculated from the formula for the spherical triangle: [See figure: 1]

$$\sin \frac{H}{2} = \sqrt{\frac{\sin(M-90°+\delta) \times \sin(M-90°+\varphi)}{\sin(90°-\delta) \times \sin(90°-\varphi)}} \quad (1)$$

where δ is the declination of the Sun and φ is the latitude of the location and M is the half of the sum of the three sides of the spherical triangle and determined with the formula:

$$M = \frac{(90°-\delta) + (90°-\varphi) + (90°-h)}{2}$$

where h is the altitude of the Sun. The sign of altitude is (+) above the true horizon and (-) below it. If declination and altitude have opposite signs, the declination added to 90°, instead of its complementary to 90°, is taken.

The formula for fadl-i dâir is simplified by substituting the value of M as

$$\sin \frac{H}{2} = \sqrt{\frac{\sin \frac{Z+\Delta}{2} \times \sin \frac{Z-\Delta}{2}}{\cos \varphi \times \cos \delta}} \quad (2)$$

Here, the interval represented by the angle H is measured in reference to the meridian (nisf an-nahâr), and:

$\Delta = 90° - \mathbf{GI} =$ (latitude of location) - (declination of the Sun) =
$= \varphi - \delta$,

where **GI** is the acronym of **ghâyat irtifa', which in turn is the maximum altitude of the Sun's centre** (at midday).

Z (angular distance to the zenith) = 90° - (azimuthal zenith), which represents the angle of **Fay-i zawâl** formed by the two straight lines which start from the top of the rod, each extending in the direction of one of the two celestial points, which are the point of culmination and that of azimuthal zenith.

The variables are substituted into the formula with their algebraic signs.

Let us calculate the time of 'asr awwal, i.e. the early time of late afternoon prayer in Istanbul on August 13. Assuming that a rod of 1 m in length is erected on the ground: [The two acute angles of a right triangle are complementary to each other. If one of the sides inscribing an angle is 1 cm. in length, its tangent shows the length of the side subtending it. The Sun's acute angle on the ground, (i.e. the angle formed by the rod's shadow on the ground and subtended by the rod,) is the Sun's altitude.]

tan Z_1 = tan (90° -h_1) = 1 + fay-i zawâl = SAA

where Z_1 represents the angle complementary to the altitude h_1 for 'asr awwal, SAA is the the length of [the rod's] shadow at 'asr awwal, and

fay-i zawâl = tan CGI = tan Δ

where CGI is the angle complementary to ghâyat irtifâ' (altitude of the centre of the Sun at midday). **Ghâyat irtifâ', GI = maximum altitude** of the Sun at the time of zawâl is determined by adding the declination to the angle complementary to latitude if the signs of both are the same, i.e., when both of them are on the same hemisphere, or by subtracting the declination from the latter if they have opposite signs, i.e., when they are on different hemispheres. If the sum of the angle complementary to latitude and declination is more than 90°, its difference from 90° is the GI, and the Sun is in the eastern side of the sky. If latitude and declination are on the same side, their difference or, if they are on different sides, their sum gives the complementary to GI (Δ).

GI = 49°00' + 14°50' = 63°50'
log (fay-i zawâl) = log tan 26°10' = $\overline{1}$.69138
Fay-i zawâl = 0.4913 metres,
tan Z_1 = tan (90° -h_1) = 1.4913   and using the table of logarithms of trigonometric functions,

log tan Z_1 = 0.17357

or with a Privilege calculator, the operations:
1. 4913 arc tan →°,,, give:
90° - h = azimuthal distance = Z_1 = 56°09'

$$M = \frac{75°10' + 49° + 56°09'}{2} = 90°10'$$

$$\sin\frac{H}{2} = \sqrt{\frac{\sin 15°\cdot \sin 41°10'}{\sin 75°10'\cdot \sin 49°}}$$

and using the table of logarithms of trigonometric functions,

$$\log \sin\frac{H}{2} = \frac{1}{2}[(\overline{1}.41300 + \overline{1}.81839) - (\overline{1}.98528 + \overline{1}.87778)]$$

$$= \frac{1}{2}(\overline{1}.23139 - \overline{1}.86306) = \frac{1}{2}(\overline{1}.36833) = \overline{1}.68417$$

(1/2) H=28°54' and H=57°48' and multiplying this by 4 we get 231.2 minutes of time, that is, 3 hours 51 minutes, which is the period of fadl-i dâir (hour angle) for the 'asr awwal on August 13th in Istanbul. Since the true time is 00:00 at the time of true zawâl, it is directly the time of true 'asr awwal in true time and is three hours and fifty-one minutes, which is equal to the time for the rod's shadow to lengthen by a length equal to its height after the time of true zuhr. Shar'î time of 'asr awwal in reference to shar'î zuhr is later than this by the amount of the Tamkin of that location. Since equation of time is -5 minutes, it is 16:10 in standard mean time. If the time of sunset in standard mean time, 7:12, is subtracted from this standard mean time, time for the late afternoon prayer in Istanbul is obtained in adhânî time to be 8:58, using equation (5) a few pages earlier. When the (time termed) fadl-i-dâir is added to the adhânî time of zuhr, i.e. the true time of zawâl with respect to the ghurûbî time, which is five hours and seven minutes, the result is both the true time of late afternoon prayer in ghurûbî time and the shar'î time of 'asr-i-awwal in adhânî time. For, although the shar'î time of 'asr-i-awwal is one unit of Tamkin later than this sum, i.e., than the ghurûbî true time, its shar'î time in adhânî time is one unit of Tamkin earlier than that ghurûbî shar'î time. Similarly, the shar'î times of early afternoon, evening and night prayers in adhânî time are the same as their true times found by calculation in ghurûbî time.

Another method applicable for determining the altitude for the 'asr-i-awwal (the early time for late afternoon prayer) is as follows: the time when the Sun reaches maximum altitude, (i.e. its culmination,) is determined graphically by measuring or calculating, and using the relation

Length of shadow = cot h,

the length of the shadow of a 1 m long (vertical) rod (erected on a level ground) is measured; the maximum altitude and the length of the shadow are recorded daily. Hence, a table of "altitude" versus "shadow length" is obtained. Since the maximum altitude of the Sun is 64° on August 13, the minimum length of shadow is 0.49 m as can be read off from the table. The length of the shadow is 1.49 m and the altitude is 34°. A table of altitude versus length of shadow exists in the appendix of the book **Taqwîm-i sâl** printed in 1924. (Please see Appendix VI.)

The 'asr thânî time of early afternoon prayer (, i.e. the later time for late afternoon prayer,) can be found by utilizing the same formula, yet in this case:

tan Z_2 = 2 + fay-i zawâl = SAT

where Z_2 is the angle complementary to the Sun's altitude for 'asr thânî = azimuthal distance, and **SAT** is the [length of the gnomon's] shadow at 'asr thânî.

Z_2 = 68° 8'. Hence.
M = 96°09' and
H= 73° 43'.

The time of fadl-i dâir is 4 hours 55 minutes. When the Tamkin is added to this, the 'asr thânî comes out to be 5:05 for Istanbul in true solar time.

To determine the time of the 'asr-i-awwal for late afternoon prayer, first the angle Z, complementary to altitude h, and then fadl-i dâir are calculated using the formula:

Z_1 = complementary to the Sun's altitude (bud'-i semt = azimuthal distance) = arc tan (1 + tan Δ),

and for the 'asr-i-thânî:

Z_2 = arc tan (2 + tan Δ),

where tan Δ is fay-i zawâl. The angle whose tangent is equal to the sum of tan Δ and 1 or 2 is the value of Z_1 and Z_2, respectively, (complementary to the altitude) for late afternoon prayer.

At the 'ishâ awwal of night prayer, the center of the Sun is 17° below the true horizon; in other words, its true altitude is -17°. Since the declination plus 90° is taken into account instead of the angle complementary to the declination:

$$M = \frac{104°\ 50' + 49° + 73°}{2} = 113°\ 29'\ \text{and}\ H = 50°\ 53'$$

and the time of fadl-i dâir = hour angle is 3 hours 24 minutes, which is the interval from the time for night prayer in true time to midnight. 10 minutes of Tamkin at the time of 'ishâ for Istanbul is added to the difference between that time [of fadl-i dâir] and 12 hours, since the center of the Sun leaves the shar'î horizon later and naturally its following limb leaves the horizons even later. On August 13, the time for the night prayer is 8:46 in true solar time and 20:55 in standard time. Subtracting the time of fadl-i dâir from the time of adhânî zuhr, which is equal to half the true night-time, one unit of Tamkin is added to it to find the ghurûbî time, which is then converted to adhânî time by subtracting one unit of Tamkin from it. Or, instead of first adding and then subtracting the Tamkin, the time of shar'î 'ishâ awwal in terms of ghurûbî and adhânî times is found to be 1:42, without taking the Tamkin into account.

$$M = \frac{104° 50' + 49° + 71°}{2} = 112° 25' \text{ and } H = 47° 20'$$

On August 13, as the whiteness called fajr-i sâdiq begins to dawn, the center of the Sun is below the true horizon by the sum of 19° and the angle of the Sun's altitude; in other words, the Sun's true altitude exceeds -19°. Hence:

and dividing this by 15, we get the time of fadl-i dâir (hour angle) to be 3 hours 10 minutes, which is the distance between the Sun's center and midnight. This is the time of imsâk in true time since the true time is 00:00 at midnight. The Tamkin, 10 minutes, is subtracted from this, because the Sun's altitude of -19° is closer to the shar'î horizon than it is to the true horizon and naturally the upper (preceding) limb of the Sun is closer than its center to the horizons. Then, the time of imsâk is 3:00 in true solar time of Istanbul and 3:09 in standard time. If fadl-i dâir is added to the time of zuhr, i.e. (5:07), which is equal to half of the night-time, and then 20 minutes of Tamkin is subtracted, the time of imsâk comes out to be 7:57 in adhânî time. The fadl-i dâir found on the programmable CASIO fx-3600p calculator is 8 hours 50 minutes, which is the interval from the fajr (dawn) to the zawâl (midday). To find its difference from midnight, this is subtracted from 12 hours, which yields fadl-i dâir to be 3 hours 10 minutes, again.

The period between dawn and sunrise is called **hissa-i fajr = duration of dawn**, that between dusk and sunset is called **hissa-i shafaq = duration of dusk**. If the fadl-i dâir of dawn or dusk is subtracted from the adhânî zuhr time, [i.e., from midnight,] or if nisf fadla is added (in winter) to or subtracted (in summer) from the complementary to the fadl-i dâir of dawn or dusk, their conversions to time will yield the hissas = durations. Since the signs of the altitudes for fajr and shafaq are (-), their fadl-i dâirs begin from midnight.

Ahmad Ziyâ Bey wrote: "The 'ulamâ' of Islam reported the time of imsâk to be the time of the first sighting of whiteness on the horizon, not the time when it spreads around it." Some European books, however, define the time of dawn as the time when the spread of redness, which begins later than whiteness, along the horizon is completed, thus taking into account the true altitude of the Sun 16° below the horizon. As it has been observed since 1983, some people who publish calendars act under the guidance of those European books and base their calculations of the time of imsâk on the solar position 16° below the horizon. Muslims who begin fasting according to such calendars continue eating sahûr meal till 15 to 20 minutes after the deadlines prescribed by the Islamic scholars. Their fast is not sahîh. On the first and last pages of the pocket calendar **Takwîm-i Ziyâ** for 1926 (Hijrî lunar 1344, solar 1305) by Ahmad Ziyâ Bey, it is stated: "This calendar has been printed after the examination carried out by the Board of Consultation and a certification granted under the authority of the Great Head Office of the Religious Affairs." Prayer times approved by a Board composed of eminent Islamic scholars aided technically by an expert astronomer should not be altered. Some details on this topic have been provided by Elmalılı Hamdi Yazır in the twenty-second volume of the magazine **Sabîl-ur-reshâd**.

Because the Sun's declination changes every moment, its hourly declination should be used in order to obtain accurate results.

For example, let us examine the accuracy of our clock in the afternoon on May 4, in Istanbul. The Sun's declination is 15°49' at 00:00 London time, i.e., at the beginning of the day (the pervious midnight). In Istanbul, with the help of the instrument called **"astrolabic quadrant"**, apparent altitude of the Sun's upper limb with respect to mathematical horizon is measured and, by subtracting the value of the atmospheric refraction of light for this altitude and 16' for the radius of the Sun, true altitude of the Sun's center with respect to true horizon is obtained. We write down the standard zawâlî time of our clock, say, 2:38 pm, at the moment the true altitude is measured, say, +49°10'. Declination of the Sun is

16°06' on May 5. The difference in declination is 17' for 24 hours. Since our clock is 2 hours 38 minutes ahead of the time of zawâl (midday) while the mean solar time in London is 1 hour 56 minutes slower than that in Istanbul, the interval from midnight in London to the time we measure the altitude in Istanbul is 12:00+2:38-1:56=12:42=12.7 hours. The difference in declination for this interval is (17/24)x12.7=9'. Differences of declination must be added to the calculation in determining the prayer times. Accordingly the declination becomes +15°58', since it is on the increase in May.

There is another formula, more suitable to scientific calculators, for finding the angle of fadl-i dâir, the hour angle, H:

$$\cos H = \frac{\sin h \pm (\sin \delta \times \sin \varphi)}{\cos \delta \times \cos \varphi} \qquad (3)$$

where h is the altitude, δ is declination and φ is latitude. Hence

$$\cos H = \frac{\sin 49°10' - [\sin (15°58') \times \sin (41°)]}{\cos 15°58' \times \cos 41°}$$

$$= \frac{0.7566 - (0.2750 \times 0.6561)}{0.9614 \times 0.7547} = \frac{0.7566 - 0.1805}{0.7256}$$

$$= \frac{0.5762}{0.7256} = 0.7940$$

This gives H=37°26' and, dividing this by 15, we get fadl-i dâir to be 2 hours 30 minutes, which is in true solar time. To obtain this result, the following keys of a Privilege calculator are depressed:

CE/C 15.58 [o,,,→] cos x 41 cos = MS 49.10 [o,,,→] sin -

15.58 [o,,,→] sin x 41 sin = ÷ MR = arc cos x 4 = 149.7 minutes of time, which is the result read on the screen.

Since the equation of time is +3 minutes on May 4, it is 2:31 in standard time; hence we see that our clock is approximately 7 minutes fast.

In equation (3), the absolute values of the variables were equated with cos H. If the terrestrial site of the city and the celestial position of the Sun are on the same hemisphere, i.e., if the latitude of the city and the declination of the Sun have the same sign, the (-) sign in the numerator of the formula is used when the Sun is above the horizon, i.e., for diurnal computations, whereas the (+) sign is used in nocturnal calculations. If vice versa, the opposite is done. Fadl-i dâir calculated in this way is the interval between the point where the center of the Sun is and the time of midday (nisf an-nahâr) during the day, or between that point and midnight at night. The same formula may also be used with only the minus sign in the numerator. In that case, all figures will be substituted with their signs and the resultant H will always be reckoned from the meridian (nisf an-nahâr).

Let us find the fadl-i dâir according to the second form of the formula (3): on the Privilege calculator, depressing the keys CE/C 49.10 o,,,→ sin - 15.58 o,,,→ MS sin × 41 sin = ÷ MR cos ÷ 41 cos = arc cos ÷ 15 = →o,,,

gives 2hr 29 min 44.59 sec, showing fadl-i dâir to be about 2 hours and 30 minutes.

To modify the apparent altitude of the upper limb of the Sun with respect to the mathematical horizon measured by using an astrolabic quadrant, the corresponding atmospheric refraction and the apparent radius of the Sun are subtracted from and the solar parallax is added to this altitude, and thus the true altitude of the center of the Sun with respect to the true horizon is obtained. In the book **Rub-i-dâ'ira** by Ahmad Ziyâ Bey, it is written that the times of ishrâq and isfirâr are calculated in the same way as that of checking the accuracy of our clock, (explained a few pages earlier).

We shall now find the time for **salât al-'iyd**[1], i.e., the time of ishrâq, in Istanbul on January 11. This is the time when the following (lower) limb of the Sun is as high as the length of a spear from the line of the apparent horizon, which corresponds to an altitude where its center is 5° above true horizon. The Sun's declination is -21°53', and it is -21°44' the next day. The daily difference of declination is 9'. Because salât al-'iyd is approximately 8 hours later than midnight and the time in Istanbul is two hours ahead of that in London, the difference of declination for 6 hours is 2'. Since the absolute value of declination is on the decrease in this month, the declination at the time of ishrâq is -21°51'. When the following keys are depressed:

ON 5 sin — 21 o,,, 51 o,,, +/− sin × 41 sin = ÷ 21 o,,, 51 o,,,

---

[1] Salât al-'iyd, or namâz of 'iyd, is dealt with in detail in chapter 22.

+/− cos ÷ 41 cos = INV cos ÷ 15 = INV [о,,,]
the calculator (CASIO fx-3600 P) reads 4:07. The difference between the (thereby calculated) fadl-i dâir and midday [12:00], 7:53, is the time of ishrâq with respect to the centre of the Sun in true time. Since the equation of time is -8 minutes, it is 8:05 in standard time. 10 minutes of precaution is added and 8:15 is written in calendars. If fadl-i dâir is subtracted from the adhânî time of zuhr [7:22], the time of ishrâq is found to be 3:15 in ghurûbî time. With a view to safeguarding the correct time of salât al-'iyd, the times of duhâ have been taken forward by an amount equal to the period of Tamkin, and, for this purpose, the time of ishrâq in adhânî time has been written in calendars without subtracting the Tamkin. **Kadûsî** says at the end: "Two units of tamkin [5°] is, in winter subtracted from and, in summer, added to twice the amount of nisf fadla and the angle complementary to the sum is converted to hours and added to 6. The result is the time of sunrise in adhânî time. If two tamkins are added instead of subtracting and subtracted instead of adding and as a precaution a Tamkin is added to the result, the time of **duhâ**, i.e. the time of the prayer of ishrâq is obtained." The treatise by Kadûsî, the booklet **Irtifâ'**, was written in 1268 A.H.[1851] and reprinted in 1311.

The time of **isfirâr-i shams** on the same day is the time when the preceding [lower] limb of the Sun approaches the line of the apparent horizon as near as the length of a spear, i.e., the time when the center of the Sun is at an altitude of 5° from true horizon; the time it spans has been stretched to the length of 40 minutes for precautionary purposes. Since isfirâr is approximately 16 hours later than midnight, and since the difference between the times of Istanbul and London is 1 hour and 56 minutes, declination at that time is 5'16.5" less than that at midnight, that is, it is -21°47' 43.5". Depressing the following keys of the programmable[1] CASIO fx-3600 P calculator:

P₁ 5 RUN 21 [о,,,] 47 [о,,,] 43.5 [о,,,] +/− RUN 41 RUN

fadl-i dâir is easily found to be 4 hours 7 minutes 20.87 seconds. Since the true time is 00:00 at zuhr, the time of isfirâr in true time is at the same time the fadl-i dâir itself; and it is 4:15 in mean solar

---

[1] To make the related programme, for example on the CASIO calculator, this succession is followed:
MODE · P₁ ENT sin — Kin 1 sin × ENT Kin 3 sin = ÷ Kout 1 cos ÷ Kout 3 cos = INV cos ÷ 15 = INV [о,,,] MODE ·

time and 4:19 in standard time. From the sum of the time of zuhr in adhânî time and fadl-i dâir, 11 hours 29 minutes, which is the time of isfirâr in ghurûbî time, a Tamkin is subtracted and the remainder, 11:19, is the time of isfirâr in adhânî time. The time of isfirâr-i shams can also be obtained by subtracting an amount of time one unit of Tamkin shorter than the time of ishrâq written in calendars from the sum of the time of sunset and the time of sunrise in terms of adhânî or local or standard time. The difference of time between the times of isfirâr and sunset is equal to that between the times of ishrâq and sunrise; it is 40 minutes, for precautionary reasons.

The following keys are depressed in order to adjust the CASIO fx - 3600 P calculator so as to use it in the calculation defined above: MODE [0] P₁ ENT sin - ENT Kin 1 sin x ENT Kin 3 sin = ÷ Kout 1 cos ÷ Kout 3 cos = INV cos ÷ 15 = INV [°′″] MODE [·]

Let us find the times ('asr awwal and thânî) of late afternoon prayer in Istanbul as of February the 1st. The Sun's declination is -17°15' (at time 00:00 and -16°58' at 24:00) and the equation of time is -13 min 31 sec (at time 00:00 and -13 min 39 sec at 24:00): Since Fay-i-zawâl = tan (complement of maximum altitude, which in turn is: $\varphi - \delta$), first, the altitudes are found utilizing the formulas:

tan Z_1 = 1 + tan ($\varphi - \delta$)   and
tan Z_2 = 2 + tan ($\varphi - \delta$)

where φ is latitude, δ is declination, Z_1 is the angle complementary to the altitude for 'asr awwal, and Z_2 is the angle complementary to the altitude for 'asr thânî. The series of operations,

CE/C 41 - 17.15 [°′″→] [+/−] = tan + 1 = arc tan MS 90 - MR = [→°′″]

gives the altitude for 'asr awwal to be 20°55', and the series of operations,

20.55 [°′″→] sin - 17.15 [°′″→] - [+/−] MS sin × 41 sin = ÷ MR cos ÷ 41 cos = arc cos ÷ 15 = [→°′″]

gives fadl-i dâir to be 2 hours and 40 minutes on a Privilege calculator. Adding Tamkin of 10 minutes for Istanbul to this result, the time for 'asr awwal comes out to be 2:50 in true solar time, 13:04 in mean solar time, and 3:08 in standard time. Addition of fadl-i dâir to the adhânî time of zuhr (7:03) gives 'asr awwal to be 9:43 in ghurûbî and in adhânî times.

The series of operations,

CE/C 41 - 17.15 [0,,,→] [+/−] = tan + 2 = arc tan MS 90 - MR = [→0,,,]

gives the altitude for 'asr thânî to be 15°28', and the operations,

15.28 [0,,,→] sin - 17.15 [0,,,→] [+/−] MS sin × 41 sin = ÷ MR cos ÷ 41 cos = arc cos ÷ 15 = [→0,,,]

gives fadl-i dâir to be 3 hours 21 minutes. The time for 'asr thânî comes out to be 3:31 in true solar time, 15:45 in mean solar time, 15:49 in standard time, and 10:24 in ghurûbî and in adhânî times.

We can find the time of imsâk on August 13 also with the use of the first form of the equation (3): Depressing the keys

CE/C 19 sin + 14.50 [0,,,→] MS sin × 41 sin = ÷ MR cos ÷ 41 cos = arc cos ÷ 15 = [→0,,,] of the Privilege

gives fadl-i dâir (time of hour angle) to be 3 hours 10 minutes. The time of imsâk for Istanbul in true solar time is obtained to be 3:00 hours in true solar time by subtracting 10 minutes of Tamkin and adding it to midnight.

Since this time of fadl-i dâir calculated for fajr-i sâdiq cannot be subtracted from midnight, [from zero, that is,] it is subtracted from 12 hours and, adding 10 minutes of Tamkin, we obtain the time of 'ishâ thânî for the night prayer to be exactly 9 o'clock in true solar time. Adding the fadl-i dâir to the adhânî time of zuhr corresponding to midnight, [05:07], and subtracting 20 minutes (two Tamkins), we obtain 7:57, which is the adhânî time of imsâk.

Let us defermine the time of 'ishâ'-i-awwal on August 13 (in the solar year 1990+4n). On a programmed CASIO fx-3600 P, keying,

P_1 17 + [+/−] RUN 14 [0,,,] 50 [0,,,] RUN 41 RUN

the fadl-i dâir, FD=H is found to be 08:36 hours. Since true time is 00:00 hours at the time of zawâl, the time of 'ishâ-i-awwal, by adding 10 minutes of Tamkin, is found to be 8:46 pm (or 20:46) in true time, 8:55 (or 20:55) in standard time. As the time of zuhr in adhânî time is 5:07, the adhânî time of 'ishâ'-i-awwal is 13:41 hours or 1:43 pm.

Time for late afternoon prayer found, using the equation with the square root, for August 13 can also be calculated using the electronic calculator (light-operated CASIO); depressing the keys:

ON 26 [₀,,,] 10 [₀,,,] tan

gives 0.4913 as fay-i-zawâl; depressing the keys,

ON 1.4913 INV tan INV [₀,,,]

gives 56°09' as the angle complementary to the altitude for 'asr awwal, and depressing the keys,

75 [₀,,,] 10 [₀,,,] + 49 + 56 [₀,,,] 9 [₀,,,] = ÷ 2 = INV [₀,,,]

gives M to be 90°09'30", and depressing the keys,

ON 15 sin × 41 [₀,,,] 10 [₀,,,] sin ÷ 75 ¨[₀,,,] 10 [₀,,,] sin ÷ 49 sin = √ INV sin × 2 ÷ 15 = INV [₀,,,]

fadl-i-dâir is calculated as 3 hours 51 minutes.

Since the altitude for 'asr-i awwal is 33°51', using a battery operated programmable CASIO fx-3600P calculator, if we depress on the keys

P1 33[₀,,,] 51[₀,,,] RUN 14 [₀,,,] 50 [₀,,,] RUN 41 RUN

the time of hour angle, H is found to be 3 hours 51 minutes.

THERE ARE THREE TIMES WHEN IT IS MAKRÛH TAHRÎMÎ, THAT IS, HARÂM, TO PERFORM SALÂT. These three times are called times of **Karâhat**. A salât is not sahîh (valid) if it is fard and is started at one of these times. If it is supererogatory, it will be sahîh but makrûh tahrîmî. Supererogatory prayers begun at these times must be stopped and performed later (qadâ). These three times are the period of sunrise, that of sunset, and the period when the Sun is at zawâl, i.e. at midday. In this sense, the period of sunrise begins when the upper limb of the Sun is seen on the horizon and ends when it shines too brightly to be looked at, i.e., at the time of **Duhâ;** at the time of Duhâ the altitude of the Sun's center from true horizon is 5°; its lower limb is a spear's length above the üfq-i-mer'î. The time of Duhâ is approximately 40 minutes after sunrise. The period between these times, i.e. between sunrise and Duhâ, is the time of **Karâhat**. It is an act of sunnat to perform two rak'ats of **salât-i-ishrâq**, termed **Kuşluk namâzı** (in Turkish) when the time of Duhâ comes. The salât al 'iyd, or namâz of 'iyd, also is performed at this time. The period of sunset begins when, in a dustfree, smogless, clear sky, the places where sunlight is reflected on, or the Sun itself, become yellow enough to be looked at, and ends as it sinks (below the horizon). This time is termed **isfirâr-i-shams**. In calculations, the time of ishrâq has been taken forward by the addition of Tamkin as a precaution, but the time of isfirâr has not been changed. "To perform salât at midday" means that the first or the last rak'a of it is performed at midday. This fact is written in Ibn 'Âbidîn, and in Tahtâwî's annotation to it, entitled **Marâqil-falâh**.

As is stated above, not the various apparent altitudes relative to the lines of different visible horizons of different heights but the shar'î altitudes relative to the location's established shar'î horizon should be taken into account in calculations of all prayer times. Accordingly, the time of shar'î zawâl is the period between the two times when the preceding and following limbs of the Sun are at their daily ultimate altitudes from the points on the shar'î horizon where it rises and sets, respectively. It is equal to twice the amount of Tamkin for that city. For example, at the time of true zawâl in Istanbul on May 1, the ghâyat irtifâ' = maximum altitude of the center of the Sun from the true horizon is 49°+14.92°=63.92°. This is the same altitude from the (two) true horizons, (one in the east, above which it rises, and the other in the west, below which it sets). The interval of fadl-i dâir is H=00:00 for this altitude. True zawâl in true time is always at 12:00 everywhere. However, the time of shar'î zawâl corresponding to its daily ultimate altitude from the shar'î horizon in the eastern side begins one period of Tamkin earlier than 12:00. And the time of shar'î zawâl corresponding to its daily ultimate altitude relative to the shar'î horizon in the western side comes later than the true zawâl by the amount of Tamkin. In other words, the time of shar'î zawâl for Istanbul begins 10 minutes earlier than 12:00 in true time. In standard time, the shar'î zawâl period begins at 11:51 and ends at 12:11 because the Equation of Time is +3 minutes. The **time of zuhr,** as given in calendars, for those who are unable to see the Sun starts at this time. The interval of 20 minutes between the two is the time of zawâl, or **time of kerâhat**, for Istanbul. [See the initial ten pages of this chapter and the translation of **Shamâil-i Sherîfa**, by Husamaddîn Efendi.]

Since the true altitude, h, of the Sun is zero at the times of true sunset and sunrise, Equation 3 a few pages earlier becomes - tan δ x tan φ = cos H. Hence, on May 1, cos H=-0.23, the angle of fadl-i-dâir = 103.39° and H=6:54, and the time of true sunset is at 6:54 in true time, at 6:51 in local mean time, and at 6:55 in standard time; and the time of shar'î sunset is 07:05. The time of sunrise in true time=12:00-H=05:06, which corresponds to 05:03 in mean time. To find the time of shar'î sunrise, the Tamkin at sunrise for Istanbul, i.e. 10 minutes, is subtracted from this. 04:53 is the remainder, which corresponds to 04:57 in standard time. The time of zuhr in adhânî time is 05:06, from which [or from its sum with 12:00] fadl-i dâir is subtracted to yield the time of true sunrise in ghurûbî time, and subtracting twice the Tamkin from this, the time of shar'î sunrise is obtained to be 09:52 in adhânî time. The time of true sunrise in ghurûbî time and that of shar'î sunset in adhânî time are 12:00 hours, which is, at the same time, the sum of the time of zawâl in ghurûbî time and the time of fadl-i-dâir, i.e. 05.06+06.54=12 hours.

The velocity of light is 300000 kilometres per second. Since the distance between the Sun and the Earth is approximately 150 million kilometres, it takes 8 minutes 20 seconds for the light of the Sun to reach the Earth. Sunrise can be observed only that length of time later than it actually takes place. There are two kinds of solar positions whereby time is reckoned: The first one, **riyâdî** time, begins when the center of the Sun reaches the time of zawâl or the true time of setting. The second one, the **mer'î** time, begins when the Sun can be observed to reach one of these two temporal positions. The mer'î time begins eight minutes and twenty seconds after the riyâdî time. When 8 minutes and 20 seconds is added to the riyâdî time of a certain (daily prayer termed) namâz, which is found by calculation, its mer'î time will be found. When 8 minutes and 20 seconds is subtracted from this, the mer'î time read on timepieces will be found. The times of sunrise, as well as times of all daily prayers, and also the indications of time read as 12 on timepieces, represent the mer'î time. In other words, they correspond to the apparent celestial positions of the Sun. As is seen, the times indicated on timepieces represent also the riyâdî times determined by calculation.

The only prayer that a Muslim is allowed to perform during the period of sunset is the day's late afternoon ('asr) prayer, (which they have somehow failed to perform till then). According to Imâm Abû Yûsuf, it is not makrûh only on Friday to perform a supererogatory prayer when the Sun is at culmination; yet this report is a weak one, (i.e. it falls into the category of reports termed qawl da'îf). At any of these three times, (, i.e. the period of sunrise, that of sunset, and the period when the Sun is at zawâl,) the salât for a janâza[1] that was prepared earlier (than the

---

[1] There is detailed information about death, preparation for death, and salât of janâza in the thirteenth chapter of the fifth fascicle of **Endless Bliss**.

beginning of the makrûh period) or sajda-i tilâwat or sajda-i sahw are not permissible, either. However, it is permissible to perform the salât of a janâza if the preparation for burial is finished within (one of) those (makrûh) times.

There are two periods of time during which only supererogatory salât is makrûh to perform. From dawn till sunrise in the morning no supererogatory other than the sunna of morning prayer should be performed. After performing the late afternoon prayer, it is makrûh to perform any supererogatory prayer within the period between that time and evening prayer. It is makrûh to begin performing the supererogatory, that is, the sunna, when the imâm mounts the minbar on Friday and as the muezzin (or muadhdhin) says the iqâma and while the imâm leads the jamâ'a at any other prayer time; an exception from this is the sunna of morning prayer, and then this must be performed far behind the lines of jamâ'a or behind a pillar. There are some scholars who say that the sunna which has been started before the imâm mounted the minbar must be completed.

If the Sun begins to rise as you are performing morning prayer, the prayer will not be sahîh. If the Sun sets as you are performing late afternoon prayer, the prayer will be sahîh. If a Muslim flies towards west by plane after performing evening prayer and if he sees the Sun, (after arriving their destination in the west), he must perform the evening prayer again when the Sun sets (with respect to their new location).

In the Hanafî Madhhab, two separate prayers must be performed in succession, (an application termed jem',) only by hadjis (Muslims on pilgrimage); and they must do so at two places: at the place called 'Arafât and at the Muzdalifa. In the Hanbalî Madhhab, it is permissible to perform two prayers one after the other during long-distance journeys[1], in case of illness, for a woman during lactation and during istihâda, in case of excuses ('udhr) that break the ablution, for those who have great difficulty in performing ablution or tayammum or cannot know prayer times such as blind people and underground workers, and for a person whose life, property, livelihood or chastity is in danger. For those who cannot leave their duties for performing salât, it is not permissible to postpone it till after its prescribed time in the Hanafî Madhhab. Only on such days, it becomes

---

[1] Namâz during long-distance journeys is explained in detail in the fifteenth chapter.

permissible for them to follow the Hanbalî Madhhab and perform early and late afternoon prayers together or evening and night prayers together by taqdîm (performing the later one in the time of the earlier one) or ta'khîr (performing the ealier one in the time of the later one). When making jem', it is necessary to perform the early afternoon prayer before the late afternoon prayer and the evening prayer before the night prayer, to intend for jem' when beginning the earlier prayer, to perform the two prayers one immediately after the other, and to observe the fards and mufsids of ablution, ghusl and salât prescribed in the **Hanbalî Madhhab**. Please see the last paragraph of the twenty-second chapter!

Definition and estimation of the angle of inihtât (dip of horizon) D for a high place has already been given earlier in the text. This angle is determined by

$\cos D = r/(r+Y) = 6367654/(6367654+Y)$ or

$$D \cong 0.03211 \times \sqrt{Y} \text{ degrees,} \qquad (1)$$

where **r** is the radius of the earth, **Y** is the height in meters, **D** is the dip of horizon in angular degrees.

The fadl-i-dair (hour angle), H, anywhere, can be computed in degrees and converted into hours and minutes as reckoned from midday (nisf-un-nehâr), using a scientific calculator. The operations on a solar Privilege calculator are as follows:

$$\begin{array}{l} h \sin - \varphi \sin \times \delta \sin = \div \varphi \cos \div \delta \cos = \\ \text{arc} \cos \div 15 = \boxed{\rightarrow \circ,,,} \end{array} \qquad (2)$$

where h, the angular altitude of the Sun, is minus (-) during the night; and φ, the latitude of the location and δ, the Sun's declination, are minus (-) if the location in question is on the southern hemisphere.

The adhânî time of imsâk (in hours) = 12 + Zuhr - H - (1 ÷ 3). The time of 'ishâ' (in hours) = H + Zuhr - 12. Prayer times anywhere can be determined in standard time utilizing the following operations[1]:

---

[1] On any day, the declination of the Sun and equation of time and, for locations with latitude 41°, nifs fadla, fadl-i-dâir, and prayer times can be determined easily and rapidly by using the astrolabic quadrant (Rub'-i dâ'ira), which needs no calculation, formula or calculator. It

$$H + S - T = \div\, 15 + 12 - E + N = \text{INV} \;\boxed{\circ,,,} \qquad (3)$$

on a CASIO calculator where

H = hour angle (fadl-ı dâir), in angular degrees,
S = standard meridian, in angular degrees,
T = longitude of the location, in angular degrees,
E = equation of time, hours,
N = Tamkin, hours.

In these operations, the variables are to be substituted in angular degrees for **H**, **S** and **T** and in hours for **E** and **N**. The signs of **H** and **N** are negative in a.m. and positive in p.m. times.

The period of Tamkin should be calculated as explained previously. For any location where the latitude is less than 44° and the height, Y, of the highest place is less than 500 meters, the amount of Tamkin is obtained in hours with the operations,

$$0{,}03211 \times Y\sqrt{} + 1.05 = \sin \div \varphi \cos \div \delta \cos \times 3{,}82 = \text{INV} \;\boxed{\circ,,,} \quad (4)$$

[In the Mâlikî and Shâfi'î Madhhabs, during a long-distance journey and/or in case of illness and/or old age, early and late afternoon prayers, as well as evening and night prayers, may be performed in (a convenience termed) jem', which means to perform each pair in sucession at the time of one or the other making up the pair. (In other words, a Muslim in one of the aforesaid two Madhhabs and undergoing one or all the abovementioned three limiting situations is permitted to perform early and late afternoon prayers in succession within the time allotted to either, and/or to perform evening and night prayers likewise. This, however, should not be vitiated by also joining the two pairs. Nor should one indulge oneself into the eclecticity that all five daily prayers can be performed in succession in the name of enjoying the convenience offered by the aforesaid two Madhhabs.)]

---

is manufactured and distributed along with an instructions manual by Hakîkat Kitabevi in Istanbul. An empty diskette is placed in a computer and prayer times are fed in. The diskette thus programmed can be taken out and stored for years. It is only a matter of seconds to drive it into a computer, feed in the latitudinal and longitudinal degrees of any city, and see a day's or a month's or a year's prayer times on the VDU. Another few seconds' time will suffice to obtain a piece of paper (containing the prayer times) from the computer and fax it to the city in question.

A computer programme can be developed to calculate the prayer times; it can be saved on a magnetic disk, and taken out of the computer and stored for years. The programme on the disk can be run on a compatible computer; if the longitude and latitude of a location are fed in, the prayer times for any given day or month or year can be computed within seconds and displayed on the screen of the monitor or printed as a list on paper. This list can be sent within seconds by fax coupled to a phone to the city where it is required.

WARNING: It is harâm to perform salâts before or after their prescribed times. The time of a salât begins when the relevant limb of the Sun comes to the altitude peculiar to that salât. There are three reasons why the prayer times given by some calendars are different from those given by the calendar published by the daily newspaper Türkiye:

1- They take the altitudes with respect to true horizon, whereas the altitudes should be reckoned from the apparent line of shar'î horizon.

2- The place of the line of apparent horizon of a location changes with the altitude of the location. They convert the times they have determined in accordance to the true horizon to the apparent times calculated in accordance to the altitudes that are taken as per the apparent horizons of the lower points of that location. Therefore, the times thus found are different from the shar'î ones and are disputable. However, they should be converted to the times of the highest place of the location , that is, to the shar'î times based on the shar'î horizon.

3- They calculate the time when the Sun's centre reaches the true altitudes, whereas the time when its relevant limb reaches those altitudes should be calculated, and the true times found thereby should be converted to the shar'î times. The Muslim 'ulamâ have introduced the concept of Tamkin to correct these three errors. The period of Tamkin is ten minutes for Istanbul. Tamkin time is a shield to protect the prayers and fasts against being fâsid (invalid). One single Tamkin is used to convert the calculated true times of all the prayers of namâz to their calculated shar'î times. There are not different Tamkins for different prayers of namâz.

11 – AZÂN (or adhân) and IQÂMAT

The chapter about azân (adhân) has been translated from the book Durr-ul-mukhtâr **and from its commantary,** Radd-ul-muhtâr, **and summarized below**:

Azân means 'public announcement' in certain Arabic phrases in prescribed order. It is not azân to say its translation. It cannot be recited in Persian or else, even though its translation will convey its meaning. The first azân was performed in Mekka on the night of Mi'râj before the Hegira. In the first year of the Hegira, it became a commandment to call the azân to announce the time of salât. At district mosques, it is sunnat to call it at a high place, and the voice must be loud. But one should not exert oneself to shout aloud. [Hence, the required loudness should contain itself within a limit so as to be heard in one's own district. Raising your voice louder is not permitted. There is no need to use a loud-speaker. It is a bid'at to practise the azân or iqâmat through a loud-speaker or radio broadcast. An 'ibâdat done with a bid'at is not acceptable but sinful.] It is sunnat-i muakkada for men to recite the azân for the daily five prayers, for performing the omitted [qadâ] prayers that are fard, and towards the khatîb at Friday prayers. It is makrûh for women to say the azân or the iqâmat. For it is harâm for them to raise their voice. The azân is performed at a high place in order to announce the time to others. But the azân and iqâmat that are recited for the ready jamâ'at or for oneself are performed on the ground. [It is written in **Tanwîr-ul-azhân**: "It is tahrîmî makrûh to say the azân while sitting. It has been understood through tawâtur[1] that it (must) be recited standing"]. The azân or the iqâmat is not recited for the prayers of namâz called witr, 'Iyd, tarâwîh or janâza. It is not sahîh to call the azân before the prescribed time; it is a grave sin. The azân or iqâmat which is recited before the time (of prayer) begins must be repeated after the time begins. It is not permissible to call the azân like a song by adding vowel points or letters or prolong the letters, or to listen to the azân recited or the Qur'ân read in this manner.

[It is written in the section about Medina of the book **Mir'ât-ul-**

---

[1] Information conveyed through an unbroken chain of trustworthy Muslim scholars throughout the centuries since the time of our blessed Prophet, Muhammad 'alaihis-salâm'.

harâmeyn[1]: "Calling the azân commenced in Medîna in the first year of the Hegîra. Before that time only the words Assalâtu jâmi'a were uttered at prayer times. It was Bilâl-i Habashî who said the azân in Medîna first. And Habîb bin Abdurrahmân was first to say it in Mekka. The primary azân for Friday prayer is a sunnat of hadrat 'Uthmân. Formerly this initial azân also was being recited in the mosque. Hadrat Ebbân bin 'Uthmân, governor of Medîna in the time of Abdulmalîk, had it recited on the minaret. In the year 700, Melik Nâser bin Mansûr had the salât-u-salâm called on minarets before the azân of Friday prayer. Prophets of Isrâil would say the tesbîh before the azân of morning prayer. Maslama bin Mahled, one of the Sahâba, as he was governor of Egypt, being commanded by hadrat Mu'âwiyya, had the first minaret built in 58 A.H., and got the muazzin Sharhabîl bin Âmir to say the salât-u-salâm before the morning azân." It is written in **Durr-ul-mukhtâr**: "Saying the salât-u-salâm after the azân was commenced by Sultân Nasser Salâhuddîn's command in Egypt in the year 781." [It is not written in dependable books that deaths must be announced by saying salât-u-salâm on minarets. It is an ugly bid'at. It should not be practised.] It is written in **Mawâhib-i ladunniyya**: "In the first year of the Hegira, Rasûlullah 'sall-Allâhu 'alaihi wa sallam' consulted with the Sahâba. Some of them said, 'Let's ring a bell to announce prayer times as the Nasârâ did.' Some suggested that a horn might be sounded like Jews. And others put forward the idea of making a fire and lifting it up. Rasûlullah 'sall-Allâhu 'alaihi wa sallam' would not accept these. Abdullah bin Zayd bin Sa'laba and hadrat 'Umar told about their dreams in which they had seen the azân being called. Rasûlullah 'sall-Allâhu 'alaihi wa sallam' liked it and commanded that the azân be said at prayer times." So is it written in the books **Madârij-un-nubuwwa**[2] and **Tahtâwî**[3], which inform also that putting lights on minarets, being something like that which was practised by fire-worshippers, is bid'at. [Hence it is inferred that it

---

[1] A history book of five volumes written in the Turkish language by Eyyûb Sabrî Pâsha 'rahmatullâhi ta'âlâ 'alaih', (d. 1308 [1890 A.D.],) one of the admirals of Abd-ul-Hamîd Khân II 'rahmatullâhi ta'âlâ 'alaih', (1258 [1842 A.D.] – 1336 [1918], İstanbul,) the thirty-fourth Ottoman Sultân and the ninety-ninth Khalîfa of Muslims.

[2] A commentary to the book **Mishkât**, written in the Fârisî language by 'Abd-ul-Haqq Dahlawî (958 [1551 A.D.] – 1052 [1642], Delhi.)

[3] An annotation to the book **Durr-ul-mukhtâr**, rendered by Ahmad bin Muhammad Ismâ'îl Tahtâwî, (d. 1231 [1815 A.D.].)

is a grave sin to light lamps on minarets in order to announce prayer times.]

[It is written in the books **Tabyîn-ul-haqâiq**[1] and **Tahtâwî** that, "Rasûlullah 'sall-Allâhu 'alaihi wa sallam' said to Bilâl-i Habashî, **'Put your two fingers on your ears, so that your voice will be louder.'** It is good to put the hands on the ears. Doing so is a sunnat intended to augment the voice, though it is not a sunnat belonging to the performance of azân, since the angel who said the azân in the (above-named Sahâbîs') dream did not do so. It was made a sunnat not in order to beautify the azân but in order to increase the voice. For the causal clause, 'so that your voice will be louder,' points to the reason, the hikmat for doing so. If the fingers are not put on the ears, the azân will be well-performed. If they are put on the ears, making the voice louder will be well-done." It is seen that to put the fingers on the ears is not a sunnat for the azân, although it increases the voice. But, because it has been commanded, it is not a bid'at, either. Hence, the loudspeakers used in some mosques today, although they increase the voice, are not sunnat for the azân and are bid'at, and besides that, they cause the sunnat of raising the fingers to the ears to be omitted. It is seen that minarets are not constructed for some mosques on which loudspeakers are placed. [It is stated in the three hundred and twenty-second page of the fifth volume of **Fatâwâ-yi-Hindiyya**: "It is permissible to build a minaret in order to have the quarter hear the voice. It is not permissible if it is unnecessary." This comes to mean that using a loudspeaker is not permissible.]

It is written in **Radd-ul-muhtâr** and in **'Uqûd-ud-durriyya** (by Ibn-i-'Âbidîn) that, "The azân called by several muazzins together on a minaret or during Jum'a khutba is named the **Azân-i Jawq**. To call it together in order to increase the voice is a **sunnat-i hasana** and jâiz (permissible) because it is mutawârith, i.e. it has been practised for centuries. Allâhu ta'âlâ likes what Muslims like." It is also written in **Berîqa'** on page 94 that, "What Muslims find nice is nice according to mujtahids, too. It makes no difference whether non-mujtahids like it or not." See **Endless Bliss**, 5th fascicle, chapter 1. [Hence it is quite clear that some ignorant trendy avant gardes' recommending the utility of loud-

---

[1] A commentary to Abdullah bin Ahmad Nasafî's book **Kenz-ud-deqâ'iq**, rendered by 'Uthmân bin 'Alî Zeylâ'î, (d. 743 [1343 A.D.], Egypt.)

speakers in calling the azân is of no value. It is a bid'at, and therefore a grave sin, to change the acts of worship with the non-mujtahids' approvals and practices.]

Saying the iqâmat is better than (saying) the azân. The azân and the iqâmat must be said towards the qibla. One must not talk while saying them, nor acknowledge any speech of greeting. If you talk, you will have to say the both again.

What prayers of namâz do we perform the azân and the iqâmat for? We will explain this in three different articles:

1 - For qadâ prayers: When performing qadâ prayers individually or in jamâ'at in the countryside, in fields, it is sunnat for men to say the azân and the iqâmat aloud. People, genies, rocks that hear the voice will bear witness on the Rising Day. He who performs a couple of qadâ prayers one after another should say the azân and the iqâmat first. Then, before performing each of the following qadâ prayers he should say the iqâmat. It will be all right if he does not say the azân for the following prayers of qadâ.

Women do not say the azân or the iqâmat for a namâz; neither for a namâz performed within its prescribed time, nor for one performed as qadâ, i.e. afterwards.

He who makes qadâ in a mosque says the azân and the iqâmat only as loudly as he himself can hear. If a couple of people make qadâ of a namâz in jamâ'at in a mosque, they do not say the azân or the iqâmat. If all the people in a mosque are going to make qadâ of a namâz in jamâ'at, the azân and the iqâmat are said. The fact, however, is that it is makrûh to perform a namâz of qadâ in jamâ'at in a mosque. For, it being a grave sin to leave a namâz to qadâ (to postpone it till after its prescribed time is over), it is not permissible to publicize it. Performing a prayer of qadâ in jamâ'at requires that the imâm and the jamâ'at must be performing the same prayer of the same day. For example, a person who is going to make qadâ of a certain Sunday's early afternoon prayer cannot follow and be jamâ'at for a person who will make qadâ of, say, Tuesday's early afternoon prayer or who performs early afternoon prayer of the present day even if it happens to be another Sunday.

He who makes qadâ in his home says the azân and the iqâmat as loudly as would be heard in the room, so as to increase the number of witnesses. [So does a person who performs qadâ of a fard prayer instead of a sunnat prayer.]

2 - He who performs the time's namâz at home individually or in jamâ'at does not have to say the azân or the iqâmat. For, the azân and the iqâmat said in mosques are counted as being said in homes, too. However, it is better to say them. It is not necessary to hear the muazzin's voice. If the azân is not said in mosques, or if it is not sahîh because they have not observed its conditions, the person who performs namâz individually in his home says the azân and the iqâmat.

After the time's namâz is performed in a local mosque or in a mosque whose jamâ'at are certain people, a person who performs it individually does not say the azân or the iqâmat. After each of daily prayers is performed in jamâ'at with the imâm on the mihrâb in such mosques, other jamâ'ats can be made again. While telling about being an imâm on the three hundred and seventy-first page, it says that if the imâms for the following jamâ'ats stand on the mihrâb, too, the azân and the iqâmat are not said. If the imâms do not stand on the mihrâb the azân and the iqâmat must be said as loudly as to be heard by the (Muslims that make up the) jamâ'ats.

In mosques on roads or in those which have no imâms or muazzins or certain jamâ'ats, various people who come in at various times make various jamâ'ats for the namâz of the same prayer time. They say the azân and the iqâmat for each jamâ'at. Also, he who performs namâz individually in such a mosque says the azân and the iqâmat as loudly as he himself hears.

3 - Musâfirs[1], when they perform namâz in jamâ'at as well as when each performs namâz individually, say the azân and the iqâmat. If a person who is performing namâz individually has friends with him who are performing namâz, too, he may not say the azân. A musâfir says the azân and the iqâmat when he performs namâz individually in a house, too. For, the azân and the iqâmat said in the mosque do not include his namâz. If some of the musâfirs say the azân in a house, those who perform the (same) namâz later at the same place, do not say it. At least three people ought to set out for a long-distance journey, and one of them must be their **emîr** (commander).

The azân said by an **'âqil** (discreet) boy, a blind man, a person illegitimate in birth, or an ignorant villager who knows prayer

---

[1] A person taking a long-distance journey dealt with in chapter 15, is called 'musâfir'.

times and how to say the azân, is permissible without any karâhat (or kerâhat). It is tahrîmî makrûh for a junub person to say the azân or the iqâmat, for a person without an ablution to say the iqâmat, for a woman, a fâsiq or drunk person, a child who is not 'âqil to say the azân, or (for anyone) to say the azân sitting. In such cases, the performance of azân must be repeated. The azân's being sahîh requires the muazzin's being an 'âqil Muslim well aware of the prayer times and an 'âdil Muslim to be trusted. (By 'âqil we mean one who has reached the age of discretion). [Likewise, one must be sure that the calendars giving the prayer times have been prepared by such a Muslim, or at least such a Muslim should witness their accuracy. The prayer times on the calendars which were prepared by sâlih Muslims and followed by all Muslims for centuries should not be altered.] For a namâz being sahîh one should know the exact time for performing it. The reason why the azân of a fâsiq person, – that is, he who consumes alcohol, gambles, looks at nâmahram women, allows his wife and daughter to go out without covering themselves –, is not sahîh, is because his word on worships is not dependable.

[As is seen, it is not permissible to say the azân on the radio or with loudspeakers on minarets or to say it before its prescribed time or to listen to it as azân. Doing these things is both unacceptable and sinful. An azân performed likewise must be said again and compatibly with its conditions. Sounds produced by electricity activated by the voice of an unknown, unseen person, and for the same matter sounds produced by records (or CDs), can by no means be said to be an azân. Moreover, Rasûlullah 'sall-Allâhu 'alaihi wa sallam' stated: **"Those who do not worship as we do are not in our community."** Azân must be said at a high place by a pious Muslim as he (the Prophet) had it performed. For instance, when the azân for the early afternoon prayer is said before its prescribed time, the early sunnat of the early afternoon prayer is performed at a karâhat time. Insisting on venial sins develops into a grave sin.]

It is sunnat for a person who hears the azân to repeat silently what he hears, even if he is junub or reading (or reciting) the Qur'ân al-kerîm. He does not say anything else, does not respond to a speech of greeting, does not do any work. It is wâjib for men to stop working and go to the mosque when they hear the azân. One can make jamâ'at with one's household at home. Yet it is better to go to the mosque [if there is a sâlih imâm in the mosque].

[It is written in the book **Jawhara**[1]: "It is written in the commentary of **Kerhî** that the azân said in the Persian language is not sahîh. This is a clear and a truest statement." It is written in **Marâqifalâh**[2] that it is not permissible to say the azân in any language other than Arabic even if it would be understood that it is the azân.]

The azân is not repeated while listening to the Khutba, while one's awrat parts are exposed, while eating, or studying an Islamic lesson or while reading (or reciting) the Qur'ân al-kerîm in a mosque. But, if the azân is not being said compatibly with the sunnat, e.g. if some of its words are changed or translated or if it is being said partly melodiously, – or if the sound of azân is coming from a loudspeaker –, he who hears it does not repeat any of its words. However, as is written in the twenty-fourth chapter, even so it must be listened to with reverence.

[In the 1031st and 1062nd pages of **Berîqa**, it is written: "A person who is unaware of prayer times of namâz or who says azân melodiously is not eligible for calling the azân. It is not permissible but gravely sinful to appoint such an ineligible person as a muezzin. It is written in **Bezzâziyya** that it is harâm by unanimity to recite the Qur'ân, dhikr or prayer (du'â) melodiously like singing. So is the case with calling the azân melodiously and saying it before its time. Taghannî[3] is permitted in the azân solely while saying the two '**Hayya alâ...**' The taghannî permitted in reciting the Qur'ân al-kerîm means that it should be recited fearing Allâhu ta'âlâ and is done according to the science of tajwîd. Otherwise, taghannî by altering sounds or words or spoiling the meaning or verse is unanimously harâm. Tarjî', that is, recitation by repetitively magnifying and lowering the voice, in the Qur'ân and azân is prohibited in a hadîth-i-sherîf. Listening to such recitations is also harâm."] Also, he who hears an azân said before its

---

[1] **Jawhara-t-un-nayyira**, the abridged version of **Sirâj-ul-wahhâj**, by Abû Bakr bin 'Alî Haddâd Yemenî 'rahmatullâhi ta'âlâ 'alaih', (d. 800 [1397 A.D.].) It should not be mistaken for **Jawhara-t-ut-tawhîd**, a valuable work written in the science of Kelâm by the great scholar and Walî Ibrâhîm Laqânî Mâlikî 'rahmatullâhi ta'âlâ 'alaih', (d. 1041 [1632 A.D.].)
[2] Written by Abul-Ikhlâs Hasan bin Ammâr Shernblâlî 'rahmatullâhi ta'âlâ 'alaih', (994-1069 [1658 A.D.], Egypt.)
[3] Chanting, singing. Please see the twenty-fourth chapter.

prescribed time or melodiously or in a language other than Arabic or or by a junub person or a woman, does not repeat it. If a person hears and repeats the azân said at some place, he does not repeat it again when he hears it said at some other place. Upon hearing the parts of **"Hayya alâ..."**, you do not repeat them, but say, **"Lâ hawla walâ quwwata illâ billâh."** After saying the azân you say the (prayer termed) salawât and then say the prescribed prayer of azân. After saying **Esh' hadu anna Muhammadan Rasûlullah** the second time, it is mustahab to kiss the nails of both thumbs and rub them gently on the eyes. Though a hadîth-i-sherîf stating this fact is written in Tahtâwî's **Hâshiyatu Marâqi'l-falâh**, this hadîth-i-sherîf is reported to be da'îf in **Radd al-muhtâr** and **Hazînat ul-ma'ârif**[1] (page 99). This is not done while saying the iqâmat. It is not sunnat but it is mustahab for a person who hears the iqâmat to repeat it. A person who enters the mosque while the iqâmat is being said sits down. He does not wait standing. He stands up as all the others do as the muazzin says, "Hayya-alal-felâh."

Ibni 'Âbidîn, while explaining the sunnats of namâz, states that it is sunnat for the imâm to raise his voice loud enough to be heard by the jamâ'at when beginning the namâz, when passing from one rukn to another, when performing the salâm (to finish the namâz). It is makrûh to raise it louder. The imâm must say the tekbîr (Allâhu akbar) for the purpose of starting the namâz, and must not think of having it heard by the jamâ'at. Otherwise, his namâz will not be sahîh. When all the jamâ'at do not hear the imâm, it is mustahab also for the muazzin to raise his voice as loud as to be heard by the jamâ'at. If the muazzin does not think of beginning the namâz but shouts only in order to get the jamâ'at to hear, his namâz will not be sahîh, nor will the namâz of those who do not hear the imâm but begin the namâz by the muazzin's voice only. For, in that case they will have followed someone who is not performing the namâz. It is makrûh also for the muazzin to shout more loudly than enough for the jamâ'at to hear. As informed unanimously by the savants of the four Madhhabs, while all the jamâ'at hear the imâm's voice it is makrûh, and a nasty bid'at, too, for the muazzin to repeat the tekbîr aloud. In fact, it is written in **Bahr-ul-fatâwâ**, by Qadizâda, Muftî of Erzurum, in **Fath-ul**

---

[1] Written by Muhammad 'Ubaydullah Serhendî 'rahmatullâhi ta'âlâ 'alaih', (1038 [1628 A.D.] – 1083 [1672], Serhend.)

Qadîr[1], and in the final part of the booklet **Ustuwânî**[2], which is written on the margins of the book **(Miftâh-ul-Cennet İlmihâl)**[3], "In small masjids, if the muazzin says the tekbîr aloud though the imâm's tekbîr can be heard, his namâz will be nullified."

[In addition to the fact that it is sinful to raise the voice more than necessary, what is produced by the loud-speaker is not the imâm's or the muazzin's voice. Their voice turns into electricity and magnetism. So what is heard is the sound produced by electricity and magnetism. It is necessary to follow the voice of a person who is performing the same namâz. The namâz of those who follow the voice of someone who is not performing the same namâz, or the sound produced by any apparatus, is not sahîh. It is written on the five hundred and seventeenth page of the first volume of the book **Radd-ul-muhtâr**: "If a hâfiz's voice spreads out and gets reproduced on mountains, in wilds, in forests or through any other means, the sounds replicated thereby will not be recitation of the Qur'ân al-kerîm. It is not necessary to perform sajda-i-tilâwat[4] with the âyat of sajda heard from them." It is written in **Halabî-yi-kebîr** that these recitals are not human recitals, but they are like human recitals. These clear statements by specialists of Islam show that it is wrong to say or read or listen to the azân or the Qur'ân al-kerîm through radios or loud-speakers or to perform namâz by following them. It is written in detail on page 2361 of the third volume of the book of Tafsîr written by Muhammad Hamdi Efendi of Elmalı that it is not permissible to call the azân or to recite the Qur'ân al-kerîm through a loudspeaker or on the radio. Especially, it is both not sahîh and an abominable bid'at to follow an imâm in another building through a loudspeaker. It is a grave sin. Please see the twentieth chapter for the conditions to be fulfilled to follow the imâm, and please review the second chapter.

The loud-speaker put on minarets has become a means of sloth for some people and caused them to say the azân sitting in dark rooms instead of observing the sunnat. It is written in

---

[1] Written by Ibni Humâm, Kemal-ad-dîn Muhammad bin 'Abd-ul-Wâhid Sivâsî 'rahmatullâhi ta'âlâ 'alaih', (790 [1388 A.D.] – 861 [1456],) as a commentary to the book **Hidâya**.

[2] Written by Muhammad bin Ahmad Ustuwânî 'rahmatullâhi ta'âlâ 'alaih', (d. 1072 [1662 A.D.], Damascus.)

[3] Written by Muhammad bin Qutb-ud-dîn Iznîkî 'rahmatullâhi ta'âlâ 'alaih'.

[4] Please see the sixteenth chapter for kinds of sajda (prostration).

Fatâwâ-yi-Hindiyya: "It is makrûh to call the azân before the prayer time comes, to say it inside the mosque, to say it sitting, to raise the voice more than one's normal puissance, not to say it in the direction of qibla, or to say it melodiously. A person who arrives as the iqâmat is being said, sits down. Then he stands up together with all the others as the muazzin says 'hayya'alal-felah.' " Ibni 'Âbidîn states at the beginning of the subject about namâz: "The azân called at its prescribed time is the Islamic azân. The azân called before its time is no more than a talk. It means to make fun of Islam." And minarets, our spiritual ornaments that have been soaring in the sky for centuries, have been made a mast of loud-speaker because of this atrocious bid'at. Islamic savants have always approved of scientific inventions. So it is doubtless that useful broadcasting via TV's, radios, (satellites, network media,) and loud-speakers everywhere is an invention which Islam not only countenances, but also encourages as a means for its teaching purposes. A meritorious act as it is to exploit all sorts of media as well as loudspeakers for utilitarian broadcasting purposes, –since Islam terms such blessed acts as 'thawâb'–, performance of Islamic acts of worship amidst the lacerating yowls of loud-speakers has been strictly ruled out. It is unnecessary prodigality to install loud-speakers in mosques. When this apparatus did not exist, which clatters as if it were a church bell instead of the voices of pious Believers that would impress hearts with îmân divinely, the azâns said on minarets and the voices of tekbîr in mosques used to move even foreigners to enthusiasm. The jamâ'ats that filled the mosques upon hearing the azâns called at every quarter used to perform their namâz in **khushû'** (deep and humble reverence), as had been in the time of the Sahâba. This heavenly effect of the azân that would move Believers to raptures has been fading away in the metallic ululations of loudspeakers.] [The sixth booklet in the book **Ghâyat-ut-tahqîq**, by Muhammad Hayât-i-Sindî 'rahmatullâhi ta'âlâ 'alaih', (d. 1163 [1749 A.D.], Medîna,) is entitled Hâd-ud-dâllîn. In a hadîth-i-sherîf quoted in this booklet and borrowed from Imâm-i-Abû Nu'aym Isfahânî's book entitled **Hilyat-ul-Awliyâ,** which in its turn quotes it on the authority of Abdullah ibni Abbâs[1],

---

[1] Abdullah ibni Abbâs 'radiy-Allâhu 'anhuma' was the son of Abbâs, who was Rasûlullah's youngest paternal uncle. He was born in Mekka, and passed away in Tâif in 68 A.H. [687]. He was tall, white-complexioned, and handsome. (**Seâdet-i-ebediyye,** p. 1043)

Rasûlullah 'sall-Allâhu 'alaihi wa sallam' stated: **"When Iblîs (the devil) was made to descend to the earth, he asked Allâhu ta'âlâ: 'When Âdam ('alaihissalâm) was made to descend, You gave him Books and Prophets to show Your born slaves the way to Paradise and happiness. What are the Books and the Prophets You are going to give him?' Allâhu ta'âlâ declared: 'They are the Angels, the well-known Prophets, and the four well-known Books.' The devil said: 'What books and prophets are You going to give me so that I may mislead Your born slaves?' Allâhu ta'âlâ declared: 'Your books are poetry and music that provoke the nafs into inordinate behaviour. Your prophets are soothsayers, fortune-tellers and sorcerers, and your food, which undermines people's mental capacity and blackens their hearts, is what they eat and drink without the Basmala,** (i.e. without saying the name of Allah,) **and intoxicating drinks. Your advice is lies, your home is sports fields and public baths, your snares are girls who go out naked, and your mosques are assemblages of fisq** (sinning). **Your muazzins are mizmârs** [musical instruments].' " In other words, the instruments used by muazzins are guides that will lead to Hell. Hence, it is a grave sin to use radios and loudspeakers in religious practices because Allâhu ta'âlâ and our Prophet call them 'the devil's azân and muazzin'.]

He who dislikes or makes fun of any azân said compatibly with the sunnat, or who discredits it by words or actions, becomes a disbeliever. But he who mocks a muazzin (only as a person) does not become a disbeliever[1].

Being an imâm is better than being a muazzin, and saying the iqâmat is better than saying the azân.

> *How fortunate is a lad,*
> *Who reads the Qur'ân;*
> *When he hears azân and iqâmat,*
> *His heart swells with îmân.*

---

[1] It goes without saying, at this point, that it is a grave sin to mock a person. Please see the last paragraph of the first fascicle of **Endless Bliss**, the last three paragraphs of the forty-third chapter of the same book, and the quotation from the book **Jilâ-ul-qulûb** in the twenty-first chapter of the fifth fascicle of **Endless Bliss**.

12 – FIRST VOLUME, 303rd LETTER

This letter (by hadrat Imâm-i Rabbânî), **written for Muazzin Hadji Yûsuf, explains the meaning in the words of azân:**

Be it known that there are seven [with repetitions, fifteen] words in the azân: [Azân (or Adhân) means to say and hear these fifteen words. These words are not heard when the azân is said melodiously through an amplifier. It turns into an unintelligible, humming sound. Thus, an amplifier annihilates the azân rather than help its performance].

ALLÂHU AKBAR: Allâhu ta'âlâ is great. He needs nothing. He is so great that He does not need the worships of His slaves. Worships are of no benefit to Him. In order to settle this well in minds, this utterance is repeated four times. [At the first and the third utterances of the word 'Allâhu akbar', the final consonant 'r' is either made jazm, (which is a rule that must always be observed at the second and fourth utterances,) or you may apply wasl, in which case the final 'r' at the first and third utterances is pronounced 'ra'[1].]

ASH'HADU AN LÂ İLÂHA IL-LAL-LÂH: Though on account of His greatness He does not need anyone's worship, I bear witness and certainly believe that none besides Him is worthy of being worshipped. Nothing is like Him.

ASH'HADU ANNA MUHAMMADAN RASÛLULLÂH: I bear witness and believe that hadrat Muhammad 'alaihi wa 'alâ âlihissalâtu wa sallam' is the Prophet sent by Him, that he is the communicant of the way of the worships liked by Him, that only those ways of worship communicated and shown by him are worthy of Allâhu ta'âlâ.

HAYYA'ALASSALÂH-HAYYA'ALALFALÂH: These are the two words inviting Believers to the namâz, which brings happiness and salvation.

ALLÂHU AKBAR: No one could manage the worship worthy of Him. He is so great, so far from anybody's worship being worthy of Him or suitable for Him.

LÂ ILÂHA IL-LAL-LÂH: He, alone, has the right to be worshipped and for us to humiliate ourselves before. Along with the fact that no one can do the worship worthy of Him, no one

---

[1] 'Jazm' means not to add a vowel to a final consonant, and 'wasl' means to combine a final consonant with the vowel sound of the following word.

besides Him is worthy of being worshipped.

Greatness of the honour in namâz can be understood from the greatness of these words selected for inviting everybody to namâz. A Persian line in English:

How prolific the year will be is predictable by its spring.

O our Allah! Include us among those who perform namâz as Thou likest them to. Âmîn.

[It is written in the tafsîr book **Sâwî**, in its explanation of the **Sûrat-ul-Inshirâh**: "Allâhu ta'âlâ declared: **'I shall raise your name in the East and in the West, all over the world'**." When we travel one degree of longitude toward the west, the times of namâz fall four minutes back. Every twenty-eight kilometres westward carries the time of the same namâz one minute backward and the azân is repeated. Thus, every moment, all over the world the azân is being called and the name of Muhammad 'alaihissalâm is being heard everywhere, every moment. It is written in the commentary of **Shir'at-ul-Islâm**[1]: "When someone came to hadrat Abdullah ibni 'Umar and said, 'I like you very much for Allah's sake,' he answered, 'And for Allah's sake I don't like you at all, because you say the azân melodiously like singing.' "]

13 – IMPORTANCE OF NAMÂZ

The book **Durr-ul-mukhtâr**, at the beginning of its discourse about namâz, and Ibni 'Âbidîn, while explaining it on the two hundred and thirty-fourth page of the book **Radd-ul-muhtâr**, state:

Since Âdam ''alaihissalâm', there was namâz once a day in every sharî'at. All that had been performed were brought together and were made fard for us. Although performing namâz is not one of the principles of îmân, it is essential for îmân to believe that namâz is fard. 'Namâz' means 'duâ'. The 'ibâdat (act of worship) that is commanded by Islam and which we all know has been named 'namâz' **(salât)**. Performing the five daily prayers of namâz is **fard-i 'ayn** for every Muslim who has reached the age of discretion and puberty. That it is fard is openly stated in the

---

[1] Written by Muhammad bin Abî Bakr 'rahmatullâhi ta'âlâ 'alaih', (d. 573 [1178 A.D.].) Its commentary was written by Ya'qûb bin Sayyid 'Alî 'rahmatullâhi ta'âlâ 'alaih (d. 931 [1525 A.D.],) and was published in Istanbul in 1288 [1871 A.D.]. Hakîkat Kitâbevi, Fâtih, Istanbul, reproduced the commentary by way of offset process in 1413 [1992 A.D.].

Qur'ân al-kerîm and hadîth-i-sherîfs. Five daily prayers of namâz became a commandment on the Mi'râj night. The Mi'râj happened on the twenty-seventh night of the month of Rajab a year before the Hegira. Before the Mi'râj, only morning and late afternoon prayers were being performed.

A child must be ordered to perform namâz at the age of seven, and should be disciplined by slightly patting with the hand if it does not perform it at the age of ten. The teacher at the school, too, may pat the student three times with his hands for the purpose of making the student study. He cannot beat him more than that. Nor can he beat him with a stick. [There cannot be bastinados in Islamic schools. Cudgelling may have taken place in a police station or in a jail. For the purpose of estranging younger generations from Islam, the enemies of Islam write film and drama scenarios in which Muslim teachers (khodjas) inflict bastinado on students and which are made to rise to a crescendo fictionalized so as to lead to their fallacious remarks: "Abolition of Islamic lessons and schools has saved the youth from bastinado and cudgelling." It is a deliberate lie, a slander against Islam. It is openly written in Islamic books that Islam proscribes beating the student with a stick. Our Prophet strictly prohibited even beating more than three times with the hand.] It is also necessary to teach other forms of worship to children at this age, to accustom them to doing them, and to prevent them from sinning.

For the purpose of showing the importance of fard namâz, Muhammad Rabhâmî 'rahmatullâhi 'alaih' wrote the Persian book **Riyâd-un-nâsihîn**, a collection from four hundred and forty-four books, in India in 853 A.H.. He says in the twelfth chapter of the first section of the second part of the book:

"In the two fundamental books of Islam called **Sahîhayn**[1] [**Bukhârî** and **Muslim**], Rasûlullah 'sall-Allâhu 'alaihi wa sallam' asked in a hadîth-i sherîf reported by Jâbir bin Abdullah 'radiy-Allâhu 'anh': **'If there were a river before one's house and if he washed himself in this river five times every day, would there be any dirt left on him?'** We [Jâbir ibn 'Abdullah and other Sahâbîs

---

[1] Two great books of hadîth-i-sherîfs. **Bukhârî-i-sherîf** was written by Bukhârî Muhammad bin Ismâ'îl 'rahmatullâhi ta'âlâ 'alaih', (194 [810 A.D.], Bukhâra – 256 [870 A.D.], Samarkand); **Sahîh-i-Muslim** was written by Abul-Husayn Muslim bin Hajjâj Qouraishî, (206 [821 A.D.] – 261 [875 A.D.] – Nîshâpûr.) The two great scholars met at Nîshâpûr.

present there] said, "No, o Rasûlallah." The Prophet said, **'Likewise, minor sins of those who perform the five daily prayers are forgiven.'** [Some ignorant people, upon hearing this hadîth-i-sherîf, say, 'Then, I will both perform namâz and amuse myself as I wish. My sins will be forgiven anyhow.' This thought is not correct, because a namâz that is performed observing its conditions and âdâb and is accepted will cancel sins. In fact, even if minor sins are forgiven, continuing to commit or insisting on minor sins will become grave sins. And insisting on committing grave sins will cause kufr (disbelief.)] Ibn Jawzî wrote in his tafsîr **Almugnî:** Abû Bakr-i Siddîq 'radiy-Allâhu 'anh' said that, when the time of a daily prayer of namâz comes, angels say, 'O the sons of Âdam, stand up! By performing namâz, extinguish the fire prepared to burn human beings.' " In a hadîth-i sherîf, it was stated: **"The difference between the Believer and the unbeliever is namâz,"** that is, the Believer performs namâz, and the unbeliever does not. Munâfiqs, however, sometimes perform it and sometimes do not. Munâfiqs will undergo very bitter torment in Hell. 'Abdullah ibn 'Abbâs 'radiy-Allâhu 'anh', a master of mufassîrs, said that he heard Rasûlullah 'sall-Allâhu 'alaihi wa sallam' say, **"Those who do not perform namâz will find Allâhu ta'âlâ angry on the Day of Resurrection."**

The imâms of hadîth unanimously stated: "A person who does not perform a namâz within its prescibed time intentionally; that is, if he is not sorry for not performing a namâz while its prescribed time is ending, will become a kâfir or will lose his îmân during his death. What will become of those who do not remember namâz or see namâz as a duty?" The Ahl as-Sunnat savants unanimously said, "Ibâdât (worships) are not a part of îmân." But there was not a unanimity concerning namâz. The fiqh imâms Imâm Ahmed Ibn Hanbal, Is'hâq ibn Râheweyh, 'Abdullah ibn Mubârak, Ibrâhîm Nehâî, Hakem ibn Huteyba, Ayyûb Sahtiyânî, Dâwûd Tâî, Abû Bakr ibn Shayba and Zubeyr ibn Harb and many other great savants said that a Muslim who intentionally omits a namâz becomes a kâfir. Then, o Muslim Brother, do not miss any namâz and do not be slack; perform it with love! If Allâhu ta'âlâ punishes according to the ijtihâd of these savants on the Day of Judgement, what will you do? **Tafsîr-i Mugnî** says: "One of the superiors asked the devil what he should do to become damned like him. The devil was pleased and said, 'If you want to be like me, do not pay attention to namâz and take an oath on everything right or wrong, that is, take an oath very much!' That person said, 'I will never neglect namâz and will not take any oath from now on.' " In the Hanbalî Madhhab, a Muslim who does not perform a namâz without an excuse will be put to death like a murtadd, and his corpse will not be washed or shrouded, nor will his janâza namâz be performed. He will not be buried in Muslims' cemetery, and his grave will not be made distinguishable. He will be put in a hollow on the mountain. In the Shâfi'î Madhhab, one who persists in not performing namâz does not become a murtadd, but the punishment will be death. That the Mâlikî Madhhab is the same as the Shâfi'î in this respect is written in **Ibni 'Âbidîn** and on the sixty-third page of the translation of **Milal-nihâl**. And in the Hanafî Madhhab, he is imprisoned until he begins namâz or beaten until bleeding. [However, he who attaches no importance to namâz or who does not know it as a duty will be a kâfir in all four Madhhabs. It is written in the subject of the afflictions incurred by the tongue in **al-Hadîqa** that he becomes a kâfir according to the Hanafî Madhhab, too, if he neglects namâz intentionally and does not think of performing its qadâ and does not fear that he will be tormented for this.] Allâhu ta'âlâ did not command non-Muslims to perform namâz or to fast. They are not honoured with the commandments of Allâhu ta'âlâ. They are not punished for not performing namâz or for not fasting. They only deserve Hell, which is the punishment for kufr. In the book **Zâd-ul-muqwîn,** it is said: "Early savants wrote that he who does not do five things is deprived of five things:

1) He who does not pay the zakât of his property will not get any benefit from his property.

2) In the land and earning of a person who does not pay its **'ushr**, there will be no abundance left.

3) Health will be absent in the body of a person who does not give alms.

4) Person who does not pray will not attain his wish.

5) Person who does not want to perform a namâz when its time comes will fail to say the **kalima-i shahâdat** at his last breath. A person who does not perform namâz because of laziness although he believes that it is the first duty, is a fâsiq. He is not suitable for a marriage partnership with a **sâliha**[1] girl; that is, he does not deserve her and is not suitable for her."

---

[1] Feminine equivalent for the word **'sâlih'**, which in turn is defined in a footnote within the tenth chapter.

As is seen, not performing the fard namâz causes one to die without îmân. Continuing to perform namâz causes the enlightenment of the heart and the attainment of endless bliss. Our Prophet 'sall-Allâhu 'alaihi wa sallam' declared: **"Namâz is nûr,"** that is, it brightens the heart in the world and illuminates the **Sirât** in the Hereafter. Do you know what happens to Allah's beloved ones in namâz and how they attain their wishes in namâz?

Story: 'Abdullah ibn Tâhir, the Governor of Khurasan, was very just. His gendarmes captured some thieves and reported them to the Governor. One of the thieves escaped. A blacksmith from Hirat was caught on his way back from Nîshâpûr at night. He was brought to the presence of the Governor with the thieves. The Governor said, "Imprison them!" The blacksmith performed an ablution and namâz. He stretched his hands and supplicated, "O my Allah! You alone know that I am innocent. Only You can free me from this jail. O my Allah! Protect me!" That night, the Governor woke up just as four strong men were about to turn his throne upside-down in his dream. He immediately made an ablution and performed two rak'ats of namâz. He went to sleep again. He again woke up upon dreaming that those four men were about to pull his throne down. He realized that he had been oppressing someone. As a matter of fact, the poem says:

Thousands of cannons and rifles can never make,
What the tears have made at the time of dawn,

The bayonets that make the enemy flee,
Are usually made into dust by a Believer's plea.

Yâ Rabbî (O our Rabb, Allah)! Only You are Great! You are so great that superiors and inferiors, when in trouble, entreat only You. Those who entreat only You can attain their wish.

The Governor immediately called the director of the jail at that night and asked him whether there was a prisoner kept unjustly. When the director said, "I cannot know him. But there is someone who performs namâz, prays much and sheds tears." The blacksmith was brought to the presence of the Governor, who asked him questions, realized that he was innocent, begged his pardon and said, "Please forgive me for having done an injustice to you, accept my gift of one thousand silver coins and come to me whenever you have a wish!" The blacksmith said, "I forgive you and accept your gift. But I cannot come to you for my problems or wishes." When he was asked its reason, he said, "Does it befit a slave like me, a humble person, to take my wishes to someone other than my Proprietor who several times overturned the throne of a Sultan like you? He made me attain so many wishes of mine. How could I take refuge in someone else? While my Rabb has opened the door of His Treasure of Endless Mercy and spread His Table of Infinite Endowment for everybody, how can I have recourse to others? Who has asked and He has not given? Who has come to Him and returned empty-handed? One cannot attain if one does not know how to ask. If one does not enter His Presence with proper manners, one cannot attain His Mercy. Poem:

Whoever puts his head on the threshold of worship one night;
The Darling's Kindness certainly opens thousands of doors for him.

Râbiat-ul-Adwiyya 'rahmatullâhi 'alaihâ', one of the great Awliyâ, heard a man pray, "O Allah! Open Your Door of Mercy!" She said to him, "O you ignorant person! Has Allâhu ta'âlâ's Door of Mercy been closed up to now so that you want it to be opened now?" [Though the source of Mercy is always open, it is the hearts, the receivers that are not always open. We should pray so that they should open!]

Yâ Rabbî! You, alone, are the One who rescues everybody from distress. Do not leave us in distress in this world and the next! Only You are the One who sends everything to the needy! Send auspicious, useful things to us in this world and the next! Do not leave us in need of anybody in this world and the next! Âmîn." Translation from **Riyâd-un-nâsihîn** is completed here.

While beginning its discourse about namâz, the book **Kitâb-ul-fiqh 'alal-madhâhib-il-arba'a** says: "Namâz is the most important of the arch-stones of Islam. Allâhu ta'âlâ made namâz fard so that His slaves would worship Him only. The hundred and third âyat of Sûrat an-Nisâ' purports that namâz, with its daily times pronounced, became fard for the Believers. A hadîth-i sherîf declares: '**Allâhu ta'âlâ has made it fard to perform namâz five times daily. Allâhu ta'âlâ has promised that He will send to Paradise a person who performs namâz five times daily esteeming it highly and observing its conditions.**' Namâz is the most valuable of worships. A hadîth-i-sherîf declares: '**He who does not perform namâz has no share from Islam!**' A hadîth-i sherîf quoted in **Mishkât,** and in **Kunûz-ud-daqâiq,** and in the **Sahîhayn,** and in **Halabî** declares: "**Discrepancy between man and disbelief is to** give up namâz!"** It does not mean, "Man and disbelief are two separate beings. Between them lies not to perform namâz. When not to perform namâz goes away from between them, that is, when a person performs namâz, the connection between him and disbelief goes up, the two can not be united, and man will not be a disbeliever." But it means, "Disbelief is a property. It does not exist alone. It exists with some people. People who have disbelief have '(not performing namâz)'. But people who do not have disbelief do not have '(not performing namâz)'. Difference between a person who has disbelief and one who does not have disbelief is not performing or performing namâz." This hadîth-i sherîf is like the statement, "Difference between man and death is 'not to breathe.' " A person who has death does not breathe. But a person who does not have death, does not have (the state of) "not breathing." When a person does not breathe, it will be understood that he is dead. This hadîth-i-sherîf vehemently threatens those who are lazy in performing namâz. To perform namâz is to realize one's inferiority before Allâhu ta'âlâ, thinking of His greatness. A person who realizes this always does what is good. He can never do evils. The namâz which is performed by a person who follows his nafs is fruitless, even if it may be sahîh. The heart of a person who intends that he is in the Audience of his Rabb five times each day gets filled with ikhlâs. Every action that one has been commanded to do in namâz provides uses for one's heart and body. Performing namâz in jamâ'at in mosques attaches Muslims' hearts to one another. It provides love between them. Thus they realize that they are brethren. The elder become merciful towards the younger. And the younger become respectful towards the elder. The rich become helpers for the poor and the powerful for the weak. The healthy ones, whenever they do not see their acquaintaces in the mosque, visit them in their homes, thinking that they may be ill. They race with one another for attaining the glad tidings in the hadith-i-sherîf, **'Allâhu ta'âlâ is the helper of a person who runs to the aid of his brother in Islam'."**

A hadîth-i sherîf, quoted in the book **Qurratul'uyûn,** declares: **"If a person does not perform namâz though he has no good excuse, Allâhu ta'âlâ will give him fifteen kinds of plague. Six of them will come in the world, three will come at the time of death, three will come in the grave, and three will come when rising from the grave. The six plagues in the world are:**

**1 - Person who does not perform namâz will not have barakat in his lifetime.

2 - He will not have the beauty, the lovableness peculiar to those who are loved by Allâhu ta'âlâ.

3 - He will not be given thawâb for any good he does. [This hadîth-i sherîf shows that the sunnats of those who do not perform the fard prayers in time are not acceptable. That is, they will not be given thawâb for their sunnats.]

4 - His prayers (duâs) **will not be accepted.**

5 - No one will like him.

6 - Blessings that (other) **Muslims invoke on him will do him no good.**

Kinds of torment he will suffer when dying are:

1 - He will expire in an abhorrent, unsightly, repugnant manner.

2 - He will die hungry.

3 - Much water as he may have, he will die with painful thirst.

Kinds of torment he will suffer in the grave are:

1 - The grave will squeeze him. His bones will intertwine.

2 - His grave will be filled with fire, which will scorch him day and night.

3 - Allâhu ta'âlâ will send a huge serpent to his grave. It is not like terrestrial serpents. It will sting him at every prayer time daily. It will never leave him alone any moment.

Kinds of torment he will suffer after rising are:

1 - Angels of torment that will drag him to Hell will never leave him alone.

2 - Allâhu ta'âlâ will meet him with wrath.

3 - His account will be settled in a very vehement manner, and he will be flung into Hell."

14 – HOW DO WE PERFORM NAMÂZ

When beginning namâz, men raise both hands. Tips of thumbs touch earlobes. Palms must be turned towards the qibla. Saying **Allâhu akbar** is started as hands leave ears and finished as they are folded under navel.

NIYYAT (intention) is made while saying the takbîr of iftitâh (beginning). It is permissible to make niyyat before that, too. In fact, it is permissible if a person who has left his home in order to perform namâz in jamâ'at follows the imâm without niyyat. But on the way he mustn't do one of the things that would nullify namâz. Walking or making ablution does not give harm.

To make niyyat for namâz means to pass through heart its name, time, qibla, to wish to follow the imâm (when performing namâz in jamâ'at), to mean to perform namâz. Knowledge only, that is, knowing what is to be done will not be niyyat. In the Shafi'î Madhhab it is necessary to remember the rukns of namâz, (i.e. actions that are fard during the performance of namâz.) If a person who arrives for the jamâ'at in the middle of namâz cannot make out whether they are performing the fard of night prayer or the tarâwîh, he makes niyyat for the fard and follows the imâm. If the tarâwîh is being performed, his namâz becomes nâfila (supererogatory) because it has been performed before the fard. For, the tarâwîh cannot be performed before the fard. He performs the fard individually at once and then performs some of the tarâwîh together with the jamâ'at. Next he performs the remaining rak'ats individually. Then he performs the namâz of witr.

The niyyat made after the takbîr of iftitâh is not sahîh and namâz performed thereby is not acceptable. When making niyyat for prayers that are fard or wâjib, it is necessary to know which fard or wâjib they are. For example, it is necessary to know the name of the fard and to say, for instance, "To perform today's early afternoon prayer," or, "the present time's fard." When performing the namâz of 'Iyd, witr, or nazr, it is necessary to think of its being wâjib and its name. It is not necessary to make niyyat for the number of rak'ats. When performing a sunnat the niyyat "To perform namâz" will suffice. The niyyat for the namâz of janâza is made as "To perform namâz for Allah's sake and to pray for the deceased." If a person makes niyyat for the fard of early afternoon prayer when performing the first sunnat of early afternoon prayer, he will have performed the fard of early afternoon prayer. The namâz that he performs after that becomes nâfila. The imâm does not have to make niyyat to be the imâm for men. But (if he does not) he will not attain the thawâb of namâz in jamâ'at. If he makes niyyat to be the imâm he will attain this thawâb, too. While a person is performing namâz individually, it is permissible for someone else to come on and begin to follow him. The jamâ'at must also make the niyyat as "I follow the present imâm." The imâm has to make the niyyat as "To become the imâm for women," (when he is to conduct the jamâ'at of women). It is not necessary for the jamâ'at to know the imâm. As the imâm says the takbîr they must make the niyyat to follow him and begin the namâz immediately. It is good as well to make niyyat to follow the imâm when he takes his place and to begin the namâz together.

As you perform a namâz that you have started considering that it is the present time's namâz and with the intention to perform the fard of the present time's namâz, if the time becomes over without you knowing (that it is over), the namâz will not be sahîh. If you intended to perform 'today's fard', it would be sahîh and you would have made qadâ. Namâz performed before its time comes is supererogatory. If it is performed after its time has been over, it becomes qadâ. That is, the person who makes his niyyat as "To perform today's early afternoon prayer" will have made qadâ of the early afternoon prayer if its time has been over. Likewise, if he thinks that the time is over and makes his niyyat as "To make qadâ of today's early afternoon prayer" he will have made adâ[1] of the early afternoon prayer when he finds out (later) that its time was not over. In both cases he has made his niyyat for the same prayer but has been wrong in the time's being over. However, a prayer which he performs with the intention of making qadâ of his past early afternoon prayer does not stand for the present day's early afternoon prayer. For, he has not made his niyyat "for today's prayer." By the same token, (today's) early afternoon prayer performed with the intention of adâ does not stand for any past early afternoon prayer that was omitted. Likewise, if a

---

[1] To make adâ of a certain daily prayer means to perform it within its prescribed time. To make qadâ of a certain daily prayer, on the other hand, is to perform it afterwards. To leave a certain daily prayer to qadâ means to omit it, i.e. not to perform it within its prescribed time. It is one of the gravest and worst sins to leave a fard prayer to qadâ without one of the good reasons (termed 'udhr) dictated by Islam.

person makes his niyyat to follow the imâm and thinks that the imâm is, say, Zayd, whereas the imâm is not Zayd but someone else, his namâz will be accepted. But if he makes his niyyat to follow Zayd and if the imâm is someone else, his namâz which he performs by following him will not be accepted. If a person has performed early afternoon prayer before its time has begun for many years and each time has made his niyyat as "To perform the early afternoon prayer which is fard for me" without thinking of the present day's early afternoon prayer, each day he has performed the previous day's early afternoon prayer. In this case the only early afternoon prayer he will have to reperform is the last day's early afternoon prayer. If each day he has made his niyyat for the present day's early afternoon prayer, regardless of whether or not he has used the word "adâ" in his niyyât, he has performed the present day's early afternoon prayer; but because he has performed them all before the beginning of their time, none of them has been the fard of early afternoon prayer. They all have been nâfila. He has to make qadâ for them all. As is seen, it is necessary to know the times of namâz and to know also that you have performed them in their prescribed times.

Niyyat is not something to be confined to certain words uttered in the name of intention. All four Madhhabs are unanimous in that acts of worship performed without the niyyat made by heart are not sahîh. No one heard Rasûlullah, the Sahâba, the Tâbi'în, or even the four imâms, make niyyat verbally. [Please see chapter 2, par. 15.] Hadrat Imâm-i Rabbânî 'rahmatullâhi 'alaih' says in the hundred and eighty-sixth letter of the first volume of **Maktûbât**: "Niyyat is made by heart. It is bid'at to make niyyat verbally. This bid'at has been called hasana (good, useful). But this bid'at annihilates not only the sunnat but also the fard. For, many people have been making niyyat only by tongue, without passing the niyyat through their heart. Thus niyyat through heart, one of the fards (principles) of namâz, has been neglected, and namâz has been nullified. This faqîr (hadrat Imâm-i Rabbânî means himself) do not recognize any bid'at as 'Hasana'. I see no beauty in any bid'at." It is sunnat to make niyyat (also) orally in Shafi'î and in Hanbalî Madhhabs. It is stated in Ibni 'Âbidîn: "That it is fard to make niyyat when beginning namâz has been stated unanimously. Niyyat is made only with the heart. It is bid'at to make it only in words. It is permissible for a person who makes niyyat with his heart to make niyyat verbally also in order to be safe against doubts."

TAHRÎMA means to say **Allâhu akbar** when beginning namâz, and is fard. No other word to replace it is acceptable. See chapter 21. This takbîr of iftitâh is one of the essentials of namâz. It is not a rukn.

Women raise their both hands as high as their shoulders and say the takbîr of iftitâh. Then they put their hands on their breasts, right hand on top of the left. They do not grasp their wrist. If the takbîr is said too long, like AAAllâhu in the beginning or akbaar at the end, namâz will not be accepted. A person's namâz will not have started if he utters the word 'akbar' before the imâm does, (when performing namâz in jamâ'at.) When standing, it is sunnat (for men) to put right hand on left hand; to form a ring around left wrist with the thumb and the small finger of right hand; to say the Subhânaka and; when performing individually, to say the A'ûdhu and the Basmala after the Subhânaka. He who is late for the jamâ'at, (that is, who arrives in the mosque after the congregational prayer has started,) says the Subhânaka if the îmâm is reciting silently, and says the Subhânaka again when he stands up after the imâm makes the finalizing salâm.

He who performs namâz individually says the Fâtiha. After the Fâtiha it is not necessary to say the Basmala. But it will be good if he does. Those Hanafîs who imitate the Shâfi'î Madhhab have to say this Basmala. Then he says one sûra or three âyats. After the Fâtiha both the imâm and the jamâ'at say "Âmîn" silently. A person who performs namâz together with the imâm does not say the Fâtiha or the sûra. "Âmîn" means "(Please do) accept (this invocation)."

QIYÂM is the first of the five rukns of namâz. Qiyâm means to stand. He who is too ill to stand performs namâz sitting, and if too ill to sit he lies down on his back and performs it with his head (by moving, nodding, etc., his head). A pillow must be put under his head so that his face will be towards the qibla instead of towards the sky. He bends his knees, with his legs towards the Qibla. It is written in **Ibni 'Âbidîn**: "According to Imâm-i a'zam, it is permissible for a healthy person to perform namâz that is fard sitting on board a ship or on a train when it is in motion. However, the Imâmeyn said that it would not be permissible when there is no 'udhr. The (conclusive scholarly instruction termed) fatwâ is in favour of the second ijtihâd. [Please see the fifteenth and twenty-third chapters.] When standing, the two feet must be four times a finger's width apart from each other. A person who is too ill to stand, or who will feel dizzy or have a headache or toothache or pain at some other part of his body or cannot control his urination or wind-breaking or bleeding when he stands, or who fears that his enemy may see (and harm) him or his belongings may be stolen when he stands, or whose fast will break or speech will be slurred or awrat parts will be exposed in case he stands, performs namâz sitting. Also, if an ill person infers from his own experiences or is told by a specialized Muslim doctor that standing will make his illness worse or delay his healing, he performs namâz sitting. Yet the doctor who tells him so should not be a fâsiq person committing sins or harâms floutingly. Such people may sit on the floor in a manner that comes easy to them; cross legged, or knees drawn up with arms folded round the legs or elsewise. A person incapable of sitting in that manner on its own, does so with someone else's help. For the rukû' they bend forward a little. For the sajda they put their head on the ground. A sick person who cannot put his head on the ground puts his head on something hard and less than 25 centimetres high. It is sahîh to do the sajda in this manner. If it is higher (than 25 centimetres) or soft, the performance turns into **îmâ** (signs). If a person cannot even put his head on something hard, he sits and performs namâz by signs, even if he could stand. In other words, performing namâz sitting, he bends a little for the rukû' and bends even more for the sajda. If his bending for the sajda is not more than his bending for the rukû', his namâz will not be sahîh. If he himself or someone else holds something up, and he makes the sajda on it, his namâz will be sahîh, but it is tahrîmî makrûh. In fact, if that thing is not lower than his bending for the rukû', his namâz will not be sahîh." Please see chapter 23, par. 14.

QIRÂAT: Means to recite orally. Reciting only as loud as one can hear is called **khafî**. It is called **jahrî**, that is, loud if it is audible by one's company. [It is stated as follows in the book of Tafsîr by Hamdi of Elmalı: "Sound produced by instruments such as tape recorders, (DVD players), and loud-speakers, is by no means the reading (or recitation) itself. It is mere noise." Azân or Qur'ân al-kerîm recited through them is not sahîh. In fact, it is sinful to use them for this purpose.] It is fard to say an âyat of the Qur'ân al-kerîm while standing at every rak'at of sunnats and of the witr, and at two rak'ats of the fard when performing namâz individually. It brings more thawâb to say a short sûra. As qirâat, it is wâjib to say the Fâtiha sûra at these parts of prayers and to say also a sûra or three âyats at every rak'ât of sunnats and of witr prayer and at two rak'ats of the fard. In the fard, (i.e. prayers of namâz that are obligatory), it is wâjib or sunnat to say the Fâtiha and the (other) sûra at the first two rak'ats. Additionally, it is wâjib to say the Fâtiha before the sûra. Furthermore, it is wâjib to say the Fâtiha once at every rak'at. If one of these five wâjibs is forgotten, it is necessary to make sajda-i-sahw. According to some more dependable information, at third and fourth rak'ats of the fard, it is sunnat for the imâm as well as for a person who performs namâz individually to say the Fâtiha. It will be all right whether he says the additional sûra, too, or says nothing (**Ibnî 'Âbidîn,** page 343). Please see chapter 17. In the other three Madhhabs, it is fard to say the Fâtiha in every namâz and at every rak'at.

A settled person who follows a travelling one stands up when the imâm makes the salâm after the second rak'at, and performs two more rak'ats, but he does not make the qirâat. That is, he does not say the Fâtiha or the other sûra. He does not say any prayer as if he were performing namâz behind the imâm. It is written on the seventy-third page of **Jâmî'-ur-rumûz**[1] and on page 106 of **Tâtârhâniyya**[2]: "According to some savants, a settled person who performs namâz behind a travelling imâm does not make the qirâat, does not say any prayer in the third and fourth rak'ats. But according to Shams-ul-aimma Abdul'azîz Halwânî and other 'ulamâ he has to make the qirâat. Then, he had better be prudent and say them." Because the qiyâm (standing in namâz) is the place for qirâat, there is no harm in making the qirâat. It is written at the end of **Halabî-yi kebîr**: "If the medicine which you have to use to diminish (your) toothache impedes (your) recital (of the Qur'ân) and if it is nearly the end of the time of namâz, you follow an imâm. If you cannot find an imâm you perform the namâz alone without reciting anything." For, toothache is a difficulty that cannot be helped.

---

[1] Written by Shams-ad-dîn Muhammad bin Husâm-ad-dîn 'rahmatullâhi ta'âlâ 'alaih', (d. 962 [1555 A.D.], Bukhârâ,) as a commentary to the book **Nikâya**, which itself is an abridged version that 'Ubaydullah bin Mas'ûd bin Tâj-ush-sharî'a 'Umar 'rahmatullâhi ta'âlâ 'alaih', (d. 750 [1349 A.D.], Bukhârâ,) wrote as a commentary to the book **Vikâya**, which in turn had been written by his grandfather Burkhan-ush-sharî'a Mahmûd bin 'Ubaydullah 'rahmatullâhi ta'âlâ 'alaih', (martyred by the Mongolian hordes in 673 [1274 A.D.].)

[2] A book of fatwâs written by 'Âlim bin 'Alâ 'rahmatullâhi ta'âlâ 'alaih', (d. 688 [1289 A.D.].) The book is also known with the title **Zâd-ul-musâfir**.

When making the qirâat, it is not permissible to recite translations of the Qur'ân.

As is written in the three hundred and sixty-fourth page of **Ibni 'Âbidîn**, in every prayer of namâz except Friday prayer and 'Iyd prayer, it is sunnat for the imâm that the sûra he says in the first rak'at (after the Fâtiha) be twice as long as the one he says in the second rak'at. A person who performs namâz individually may say a sûra of the same length in each rak'at. In every prayer of namâz, it is makrûh to say a sûra in the second rak'at three ayâts longer than the sûra said in the first rak'at. It is makrûh for the imâm to form it a habit to say the same âyats in the same rak'ats of the same prayer of namâz. It is said (by savants) that this is so for those who perform namâz individually to do so in every prayer. From time to time one ought to say some other âyats. It is tanzîhî makrûh to say in the second rak'at the same âyats that you have said in the first rak'at. If you say the Qul a'ûdhu bi-Rabbinnâs, (the last sûra of the Qur'ân al kerîm,) in the first rak'at, you say it again in the second rak'at, since it would be worse to say the previous sûras. In the second rak'at it is best to say the âyat that is immediately after the one said in the first rak'at. In the second rak'at it is makrûh to skip the short sûra following the sûra said in the first rak'at, and say the one immediately after it. It is not makrûh to say several successive sûras in one rak'at, yet it is best to say one sûra. In the second rak'at it is makrûh to say the âyats or sûras that are before the ones you have said in the first rak'at. It is always wâjib to read the Qur'ân's sûras or âyats in the order as they are written in the Qur'ân. Only, at the end of a **khatm**[1] it produces much thawâb to read the initial five âyats of the sûras of **Fâtiha** and **Baqara** immediately after reading the two âyats beginning with the phrase Qul-a'ûdhu. Saying three âyats as long as a short sûra each is better than saying a long sûra. That is, there is more thawâb in it.

RUKÛ': After the sûra you bend for the rukû' saying the takbîr. In the rukû' men open their fingers and put them on their knees. They keep their back and head level. In the rukû' you say **Subhâna rabbiyal-'adhîm** at least thrice. If the imâm raises his head before you have said it three times you must raise your

---

[1] To read the Qur'ân from beginning to end. There is much thawâb in it, especially in the holy month of Ramadân. Imâm-i A'zâm Abû Hanîfa, leader of Hanafî Madhhab, often made the khatm in one or two rak'ats of namâz. That is, he recited the whole Qur'ân.

head, too, immediately. In the rukû' your arms and legs must be straight. Women do not open their fingers. They do not keep their head and back level, or their arms and legs straight. It is sunnat for the imâm as well as for a person who is performing namâz by himself to say **Sami' Allâhu liman hamideh** while straightening up from the rukû'. The jamâ'at do not say it. Immediately after saying it, a person who is performing namâz by himself, and the jamâ'at, upon hearing the imâm recite it, must say: **Rab-banâ lakal hamd,** and stand upright, and then, saying **"Allâhu akbar"** while kneeling down for the sajda, put first the right knee and then the left knee, followed by the right and left hands, on the floor[1]. Finally, the nose and the forehead bones are put on the floor.

SAJDA: At the sajda, fingers must be closed, pointing towards the qibla in line with the ears, and the head must be between hands. It is fard that the forehead be touching something clean, such as stone, soil, wood, cloth, and it is said (by savants) that it is wâjib to put the nose down, too. It is not permissible to put only the nose on the ground without a good excuse. It is makrûh to put only the forehead on the ground. In the sajda you must say **Subhâna rabbiyal-a'lâ** at least thrice. The Shi'îs say that it is better to make the sajda on a brick made from the clay of Kerbelâ[2]. It is either fard or wâjib to put two feet or at least one toe of each foot on the ground. There are also some savants who say that it is sunnat. That is, if two feet are not put on the ground, namâz will either not be sahîh or it will become makrûh. If, during the sajda, the forehead, nose, or feet are raised from the ground for a short while, it will cause no harm. At the sajda, it is sunnat to bend the toes and turn them towards the qibla. It is written in **Radd-ul-muhtâr** that those who say that it is fard or wâjib are wrong. Men must keep their arms and thighs away from their abdomen. It is sunnat to place the hands and the knees on the ground. It is sunnat to keep the heels a four-finger-width away from each other at the qiyâm, but at the rukû', qawma, and sajda they must be kept together. It is written in the three hundred and fifteenth page of **Halabî-yi kebîr** and also in the book **Durr-ul-mukhtâr:** "One of the sunnats at the rukû' is to keep the heel-bones together." For doing this, when bending for the rukû, the heel of the left foot is brought near the right foot.

---

[1] Or on the ground, if they are performing it outdoors.
[2] The town of Kerbelâ, Iraq.

They are separated again when standing up for the qiyâm after the sajda.

Although it is sahîh to prostrate on the winding cloth of one's turban, or on the edges of one's skullcap, or on one's hair hanging down one's forehead, or on the lowest parts of one's sleeves or skirts, or on one's hands, it is tanzîhî makrûh to do so in the absence of an excuse. Women also should keep their forehead uncovered during namâz. It will be sahîh to prostrate on a carpet, a mat, some wheat or barley, on a couch, on a sofa, or on a vehicle that is on the ground on condition that you will press on them until you feel their hardness, that is, until your forehead cannot move downward any more. However, prostrating on an animal, on a swing stretched between two trees, or on rice or millet not packaged, is not sahîh. Because something one is wearing is considered part of one's body, the surface under it should be clean. For this reason, as a person without an ablution is not permitted to hold the Qur'ân with his hands, likewise, he is not permitted to hold it with the end of his sleeves. He is permitted to hold it with things such as clothes he is not wearing or with a towel or a handkerchief. Namâz can be performed on them when they are spread on a najs place. Likewise, a janâza namâz should not be performed while wearing shoes with najs soles or while standing on a najs place. But it will be sahîh if you take off your shoes with najs soles, step on their clean upper parts, and thereafter start performing the namâz.

It is written in **Halabî**: "When getting down for sajda it is makrûh to pull up the skirts of your loose long robe or your trousers, and it is makrûh to fold them before beginning namâz. It is makrûh to perform namâz with folded [or short] sleeves, cuffs, or skirt." It is makrûh to perform namâz with a bare head because of laziness or for lack of realization of the importance of performing namâz with a covered head. And it causes disbelief to slight namâz. It is not makrûh not to cover one's head in order to show one's inferiority and incapability and because one fears Allâhu ta'âlâ. [In other words, if a person who turns pale, trembles, forgets himself and everything for fear of Allâhu ta'âlâ and does not cover his head, it will not be makrûh.] However, even such people had better cover their heads. For, not to cover one's head means to disobey the âyat-i-kerîma that purports: **"Take your ornamented clothes and put them on for namâz!"** It is mustahab to wrap a white turban round the head. The fact that Rasûlullah 'sall-Allâhu 'alaihi wa sallam' used even a black turban is written in the book **Ma'rifatnâma**[1]. He would allow two spans from the end of his turban hang down between his two shoulderblades.

A person who is too ill to prostrate for the sajda, or a healthy person who cannot find an empty place in the mosque, must not prostrate on anything higher than twenty-five centimetres. However, the person who cannot find an empty place can make the sajda on the back of another person who is performing the same prayer of namâz and who is making the sajda on the ground. But his knees must be on the ground (or on the floor). However, it is mustahab for that healthy person to perform the namâz after the crowd thins out, or to go to another mosque that is not crowded and perform his namâz there. It has been informed (by savants) that it is permissible to make the sajda on something less than twenty-five centimetres high when there is no crowd, but it is makrûh. For, Rasûlullah 'sall-Allâhu 'alaihi wa sallam' never made the sajda on anything higher than floor level. [**Ibnî 'Âbidîn**, page 338]. It is written on the right hand margin of the sixty-ninth page of **Jâmi'ur-rumûz** and in the annotation of **Tabyîn** by Shalbî 'rahmatullâhi ta'âlâ 'alaih' that it is not permissible to make the sajda even on something which is only a little higher than floor level. [For this reason, those who do not have a good excuse must not make the sajda even on something a little higher than floor level. To say that we must make the sajda on a high place and not on the ground means to change the (prescribed) way of worshipping. He who wants to change worships becomes a disbeliever. Disbelievers, enemies of Islam, enemies of Rasûlullah want to turn mosques into churches. Like in churches, they are trying to get people to sit at tables and put their heads on tables in the name of sajda, and also to initiate music and musical instruments in mosques. First they are accustoming people to making the place of sajda a little higher and to performing the worships with loud-speakers.] Ibn-i 'Âbidîn 'rahmatullâhi 'alaih' says: "**Istikbâl-i qibla** is fard for namâz. That is, namâz is performed by turning towards the direction of the Ka'ba. Namâz is performed for Allah. Sajda is done for Allâhu ta'âlâ only. It is performed towards the direction of Ka'ba, but not for the Ka'ba. One who makes sajda for the Ka'ba becomes a disbeliever."

QA'DA-I-ÂKHIRA: In the last rak'at it is fard to sit as long

---

[1] Written by Ibrâhîm Haqqi 'rahmatullâhi ta'âlâ 'alaih', (d. 1195 [1751 A.D.], Si'rid-Tillo.) This great Islamic scholar is one of those great Awliyâ and scholars called **Sôfiyya-i-aliyya**.

as it would take to say the tahiyyât. It is written in **Durr-ul-mukhtâr:** "You do not make a sign with your fingers while sitting. The fatwâ says so, too." When sitting, men put their left foot flat on the ground with its toes pointing towards the right. They sit on this foot. The right foot should be upright, with the toes touching the ground and pointing towards the qibla. It is sunnat to sit in this manner. Women sit by **tawarruk**. That is, they sit with their buttocks on the ground. Their thighs should be close to each other. Their feet should jut out from their right.

While explaining the nature of ezkâr, it is written in **Marâqilfalâh** and in its commentary by **Tahtâwî:** "It is sunnat in the Hanafî Madhhab to stand up and perform the sunnat right after the fard without saying anything in between. After performing the fard, our Prophet used to sit as long as it took him to say **Allâhumma Anta-s-salâm wa minkas-salâm tabârakta yâ dhal jalâli wa-l-ikrâm;** then, he would begin to perform the sunnat outright. He would not say the Âyat-al-kursî or the tesbîhs between the fard and the sunnat. Saying them after the final sunnat produces the same thawâb as would be attained by saying them after the fard. The same rule applies for the sunnat before the fard; saying any prayers between the fard and the sunnat diminishes the thawâb of namâz. It is makrûh for the imâm to perform the final sunnat at the same place where he performed the fard. It is not makrûh for the jamâ'at, but it is mustahab for them to perform it at some other place (in the mosque). The namâz of a person who neglects the mustahab will not be deficient, but he will be deprived of its thawâb. After performing the fard if there is no final sunnat after the fard, or after the final sunnat, it is mustahab for the imâm to turn right or left or towards the jamâ'at. He may as well leave the mosque at once if he has some work to do. It is stated in a hadîth-i-sherîf: **'If a person says, "Astaghfirullâh-al'azîm allazî lâ ilâha illâ huw-al-hayy-al-qayyûma wa atûbu ilayh", after every prayer of namâz, all his sins will be forgiven.'** Also it is mustahab (for the imâm and for the jamâ'at) to say the Âyat-al-kursî, to say, **"subhân-Allah,"** thirty-three times, **"al-hamd-u-l-illâh,"** thirt-three times, and **"Allâhu akbar,"** thirty-three times, and then to say the kalima-i-tehlîl once, and then to say, **"lâ ilâha il-l-Allâhu wahdahu lâ sherîka leh-ul mulku wa leh-ul hamdu wa huwa 'alâ kulli shay'in qadîr,"** and then to raise their hands as high as their chest and invoke blessings on themselves and on all Muslims. A hadîth declares: **"Invocations offered after the five daily fard namâz will be** accepted.' But the prayers must be done with a vigilant heart and silently. It is makrûh to pronounce invocations only after namâz or at certain times or to memorize certain invocations and say them repetitively like poems. After offering your invocations, it is sunnat to rub the hands gently on the face. Rasûlullah 'sall-Allâhu 'alaihi wa sallam' used to pronounce invocations during namâz, during the tawâf (visiting the Ka'ba), after meals, and when going to bed. In these invocations of his he would not raise his arms, nor would he rub his hands on his face. Invocations and all other types of dhikr are best when they are pronounced silently. According to the unanimity (of savants), it is harâm to do as some men of tarîqat do, such as to dance or whirl, to clap hands, to play stringed instruments, tambourines, small drums, flutes." As is seen, it is best if the jamâ'at and the imâm pronounce their invocations together silently. It is also permissible for them to pronounce their invocations separately or to leave the mosque without pronouncing their invocations. After the invocations, the (sûra) Ikhlâs is said eleven times and the two sûras beginning with the phrase **"Qul-a'ûdhu..."** are said once. Muhammad Ma'thûm 'rahmatullâhi 'alaih' stated in the eightieth letter of the second volume that after this prayer he said only **Astaghfirullah** sixty-seven times. Finally, the (three) âyats beginning as **"Subhâna Rabbika..."** are said.

    The book **Durr-ul-mukhtâr,** after explaining the **Namâz of Tahiyyat-ul-masjid,** says: "Talking between the sunnat and the fard does not nullify the sunnat, but it diminishes the thawâbs. Such is the case when saying any prayer. According to some savants, the sunnat will not be accepted and it will be necessary to perform the sunnat again." After explaining that it is permissible for a person to follow an imâm who is conducting the namâz while sitting, the book states: "When the imâm's voice does not reach everywhere, it is permissible for muazzins to repeat loudly so the jama'at can hear, but shouting too loudly nullifies their own namâz. Saying the prayers too loudly resembles a worldly conversation. The imâm's saying the prayers more loudly than necessary in a namâz does not nullify the namâz, yet it is harâm." Hence, it is harâm for muazzins to distract the other worshippers by shouting too loudly. It is written in the book **Ma'ârij-un-nubuwwa**:[1] "Hadrat Awzâ'î was asked about what invocations were offered in order to make tawba after making the salâm. 'Say

---

[1] Written by Molla Mithkîn Muhammad Mu'în, (d. 954.)

astaghfirullah three times', he said." [The fact that it is bid'at to say prayers loudly is written on the fifty-ninth page of the 1375 (1956) edition of the book **al-Ibdâ'**, by Shaikh Alî Mahfûz, a member of the assembly of Kibâr-i-ulamâ in Egypt]. Our Prophet 'sall-Allâhu 'alaihi wa sallam' stated: **"Say the Âyat-al-kursî also when going to bed."** He also stated that we should say prayers after namâz.

Invocations to be offered after namâz: When saying duâs (invocations after namâz), men raise their arms up to the level of their chest. The arms should not be bent very much at the elbows. After offering their invocations, they should recite the âyat, Subhâna rabbika......, and rub their hands gently on their faces. A person who cannot lift his hands because of an illness or cold weather, makes a sign with his pointing finger. Fingers are turned towards the qibla. Arms are not opened apart in the right-left direction. They are held parallel to each other, forward.

[After each fard namâz, it is mustahab for the imâm and the jamâ'at to say the istighfâr completely three times, to recite the Âyat al-kursî, to make the tesbîh ninety-nine times, then to offer invocations and then to recite the (sûra called) Ikhlâs eleven times and the two sûras beginning with the phrase, "Qul-a'ûdhu..." and to say, "Astaghfirullah" sixty-seven times. The hadîth-i-sherîf commanding to recite the Ikhlâs eleven times is on the last page of the first volume of **Berîqa**. It is stated in a hadîth-i-sherîf that a person who says the following prayer ten times after morning prayer will be given much thawâb: **"Lâ ilâha il-l-Allah wahdahu lâ sherîka leh lehul-mulku wa lehul-hamdu yuhyî wa yumît wa huwa 'alâ kulli shey'in qadîr." (Imdâd)**[1]. The Âyat-al-kursî and the tesbîhs must never be omitted, (as is mostly the case) when there is a janâza (a dead Muslim that must be interred according to prescribed Islamic rituals). Cannot a janâza that is delayed for hours for various reasons be delayed a few minutes longer in order to say these prayers? Those who prevent the jamâ'at from saying these prayers must fear very much being placed among those cruel people who are declared in the one hundred and fourteenth âyat of Baqâra sûra to be those who will be tormented bitterly in Hell. How lucky for those pious imâms

---

[1] Abul-Ikhlâs Hasan bin Ammâr Shernblâlî 'rahmatullâhi ta'âlâ 'alaih', (994-1069 [1658 A.D.], Egypt,) wrote a book entitled **Nûr-ul-îdhâh**, and another book, entitled '**Marâqilfalâh**', which was a commentary to the former, and which is also known with the title **Imdâd-(ul-Fattâh)**.

and muazzins who do not prevent the jamâ'at from saying these prayers! At each prayer of namâz they get the blessings for a hundred martyrs. For, our Prophet 'sall-Allâhu ta'âlâ 'alaihi wa sallam' declared: **"He who recovers one of my forgotten sunnats will attain the blessings for a hundred martyrs."** In order to be safe against bid'ats, muazzins should say the azân loudly on minarets and the iqâmat inside the mosques, and they should say the takbîrs of namâz loudly only when necessary, without using loud-speakers. The Âyat al-kursî, the tesbîhs and the Kelima-i-tehlîl should be said silently, after the final sunnat in the Hanafî Madhhab and immediately after the fard in the Shâfi'î and Mâlikî Madhhabs. While offering an invocation, the fact that it is mustahab to say salât and salâm for Rasûlullah 'sall-Allâhu ta'âlâ 'alaihi wa sallam' is written in the chapter about Witr prayer in **Tahtâwî's** commentary to the book **Imdâd-ul-Fettâh**.

The fact that it is harâm (forbidden) to prostrate (to make sajda) after namâz, (which is a malpractice rife among some Muslim communities,) is written in the book **Durr-ul-mukhtâr,** in its chapter about the sajda of tilâwat. It is bid'at for the imâm and the jamâ'at to greet each other by putting their hands on their chests. Islam does not recognize any kind of greeting done by moving the hands or the body. Ibni Nujaym Zaynal 'Âbidîn Misrî 'rahmatullâhi ta'âlâ 'alaih', (926-970 [1562 A.D.], Egypt,) states that such greetings are sinful. Please read the final part of the fifteenth chapter of the fifth fascicle of Endless Bliss.

It is written in the (book **Mafâtih-ul-jinân**, which is a) commentary to the book **Shir'at-ul-islâm**: "A hadîth-i sherîf declares: **'Any duâ made at the time of dawn and after the prayers of namâz, will be accepted.'** It is sunnat to begin the duâ with **hamd-u-thanâ**[1] and **salawât**[2] and to rub both palms gently on the face after the duâ." It is written in the fifth chapter of **Fatâwâ-i Hindiyya:** "While making duâ, both hands should be opened towards the sky, apart from each other, and on a level with the chest." It is written in **Bezzâziyya** that performing a namâz which is sunnat is better than making duâ. [Shiites and Wahhabîs make duâ by raising their hands as high as the chest turning the palms towards the face, bringing them together with their fingers closed.]

---

[1] Thank, pray, and laud Allâhu ta'âlâ.
[2] Prescribed blessing invoked on the Prophet's blessed soul.

It is written in **Ni'mat-i Islâm**:[1] "When beginning to perform namâz, a woman raises both hands up to the level of her shoulders. While standing she puts her right hand on the left hand. But she does not grasp her left wrist with the fingers of her right hand. She puts her hands on her breast. While making rukû, her hands are placed on her knees, but she does not grasp them. She does not keep her fingers wide apart. She does not keep her legs straight, nor her back level. While making sajda, she lowers herself, bringing her arms to her sides while she keeps her abdomen placed over her thighs. She sits on the buttocks, her feet jutting out towards right. A woman cannot be an imâm for men. It is makrûh for a woman to be an imâm for other women. If they follow a man as imâm, they should be in the last line of the jamâ'at. If a woman is kissed (while performing namâz), her namâz will be nullified. While performing namâz in jamâ'at, if a woman stands beside or in front of a man, the man's namâz will be fâsid (nullified). The man should signal to the woman to move behind. If she does not do as she is beckoned, in that case, only the woman's namâz will become fâsid. In case of a baby crying or of food boiling over the fire, leaving the namâz is permissible for a woman." A woman does not stretch her hands forward while making duâ, but she keeps them inclined towards her face.

---

[1] Written by Hâdji Muhammad Zihnî 'rahmatullâhi ta'âlâ 'alaih', (1262-1332 [1914 A.D.], Beylerbeyi, Istanbul.)

15 – NAMÂZ DURING LONG–DISTANCE JOURNEYS

Safarî or **Musâfir** means (a person) making a long-distance journey. If a person intends to go to a place that would take a man three days on foot or by camel's pace during the short days of the year, he becomes a musâfir as soon as he reaches beyond the last houses of the place he lives in or on one or both sides of his way. If he sets out without intending to go to a place that is three days' way, he does not become a musâfir even if he travels all over the world. An example of this is the case of soldiers in quest of the enemy. But he will become a musâfir on his way back. If a person who has started off with the intention of going to a place that is two days' way, intends on the way or after reaching the place to go to another place which is two days' way from his first destination, he does not become a musâfir when he is on the way to the place which is four days' way. Suppose a person set out for a place three days' walk from his home, made a temporary stay somewhere on his way, and then left that place with the intention of going to another place three days' walk away; this person becomes a musâfir as soon as he passes beyond the last houses on both sides on his way. The last house does not have to be out of sight. He does not have to have reached beyond the houses that are only on one side of the way. Nomads camping at the seaside or near a forest become musâfirs when they leave their tents. If there are villages the road between which and the city is lined with houses on one side or both, these villages also must have been left behind. It is not necessary to have gone beyond empty fields, vineyards, pastures, or vegetable gardens adjacent to the city. Even if there are farmers' or watchmen's houses in the fields or vegetable gardens, they or the villages beyond them are not counted as parts of the city. Of the empty fields, those large cemeteries that are close to town and called **finâ**, grounds which the townsfolk use for threshing grain, for horse-riding, for diversion, and parts of a lake or sea which they use for hunting etc., [factory buildings, schools, and barracks] are counted as part of the town. That is, they must have been passed. If a finâ is more than two hundred metres away from the town or if there is a field in between, it is not a part of the town. But it is sahîh to perform the prayers of Friday and 'Iyd at a finâ that is far away. Villages and cities between which and the city is a finâ are not counted as parts of the city. It is not necessary to have passed beyond such villages. One becomes safarî when one reaches beyond the finâ only. With large cities, a finâ is still counted as a part of the town when it is more than two hundred metres from the town. It is written in Tahtâwî's commentary to **Imdâd-ul-Fettâh** that according to a narration (report) called Mukhtâr, even if there are houses or a finâ in between, having gone beyond the villages is not a condition.

The walk (to meet the three-day standard established in this Islamic rule) does not necessarily have to be a continuous walk till late evening. On a short day, a walk from the time of morning prayer until the time of the early afternoon prayer will suffice. This journey is called, merhala, manzîl, or **qonaq** (stage). An intervening wayside halt is permissible. Even if one goes on a journey of three days on a fast vehicle, such as a train, which will naturally take much less time, one still becomes a musâfir. [**Majalla**[1], 1664] If there are two ways of going to a place, one of the ways being shorter than the other, the person who goes the shorter way does not become a musâfir. If the longer way takes three days by walking, a person who goes by that way on any vehicle becomes a musâfir.

Ibn-i 'Âbidîn says: "All 'ulamâ have described the "way of three days" by a unit called **farsâh** (parasang), the distance travelled in one hour. Some of them said a way of three days was 21 farsâhs; some said it was 18 farsâhs; and others said it was 15 farsâhs. The fatwâ has been given according to the second judgement." In the fatwâ of the majority, one marhâla, the distance travelled in one day, is six farsâhs on a smooth route. One farsâh is equal to 3 miles. One marhâla is equal to 18 miles, so three times marhâla is 54 miles. It is written in **Ibn-i 'Âbidîn**, within the subject of tayammum, that one mile is equal to 4,000 dhrâ's, that the report saying that it is 4,000 steps is weak and that 1 dhrâ' is a length equal to the total width of as many as the number of letters in the Kalima at-tawhîd, i.e. twenty-four, fingers. A finger is about 2 cm wide. Hence, one dhrâ' is 48 cm, and one mile is 1920 m. Thus 1 fersâh is 5760 m. Then, 1 marhâla is 34,560 m, and a way of three days is about 104 km (103,680 m). [A Geographical mile is a length equivalent to one (angular)

---

[1] A world-famous book on Islamic jurisprudence written by Ahmad Jawdat Pâsha 'rahmatullâhi ta'âlâ 'alaih', (1238 [1823 A.D.], Lowicz – 1312 [1894], Istanbul.) Two other valuable books written by that scholarly personage are **Qisâs-i-Anbiyâ** (A History of Prophets), and **(Ma'lûmât-i-nâfi'a** (Useful Information), which was translated into English and added to the book **The Sunni Path**, one of the publications of **Hakîkat Kitâbevi**, Istanbul.

minute of equatiorial arc, i.e. 1852 m.] A person who goes from Küçükçekmece, a suburb of Istanbul, to Tekirdağ becomes safarî. It is written in **al-Fiqhu 'ala'l-madhâhib:** "In the Shâfi'î, Mâlikî and Hanbalî Madhhabs the distance for becoming safarî is equal to 2 marhâlas (qonaq). This is 16 farsâhs, which makes 48 miles. For, 1 farsâh (league) is 3 miles. One mile is equal to 6,000 dhrâ' [the length of a man's arm]. Distance (to be gone) for becoming safarî is 80,640 m." In that case, one mile should equal 4,000 dhrâ' and one dhrâ' should equal 42 cm. As a matter of fact, it is written in an annotation to the Shâfi'î fiqh book **al-Muqaddimatu'l-hadramiyya**[1] (second ed., 1404/1984): "In the Shafi'î Madhhab, the distance for becoming safarî is equal to 4 barîds, i.e. 2 marhâlas. 1 barîd is equal to 4 farsâhs; 1 farsâh is equal to 3 miles; 1 mile is equal to 1,000 bâ's [qolaches ≃ 1.050 fathoms]. 1 bâ' is 4 dhrâ's [forearms]. 1 dhrâ' is 2 qarishes (≃ 2.1 spans)." According to this annotation, the distance for becoming safarî is equal to 16 farsâhs, i.e. 48 miles, and 1 mile is equal to 4,000 dhrâ's. On page 523, **Mir'ât-i Medina**[2] states: "In this text, the unit dhrâ' is the length of a man's forearm, which is equal to 7/8 of the iron measure used in Egypt and in the Hijâz today. It is about 2 spans." This unit of iron measure is the dhrâ' used in the Hanafî fiqh books and is the total width of 24 fingers. It is 48 cm., and so 7/8 of it makes 42 cm. As is seen, in the Shafi'î Madhhab, one mile is equal to 4,000 dhrâ's, which means 1,680 m. 48 times a mile is 80 km. and 640 m. Distance of safar does not necessarily have to reach exactly this number in kilometres. It will be enough if the distance is known to be so or if one strongly estimates it to be so.

In the sea, the speed of a sailing-boat that sails in a weather with a medium wind is essential. Accordingly, a person who goes to Mudanya from Istanbul does not become safarî. Yet a person who goes from Istanbul to Bursa becomes safarî. One who flies on a plane is supposed to have gone on the road or sea below the plane. Supposing three people set out for a long distance journey from Istanbul; the first person on a bus from Fâtih, the second

---

[1] Written by 'Abdullah bin 'Abd-ur-Rahmân 'rahmatullâhi ta'âlâ 'alaih'.

[2] The book **Mir'ât-ul-Harameyn**, written in Turkish by Eyyûb Sabri Pâsha 'rahmatullâhi ta'âlâ 'alaih', (d. 1308 [1890],) consists of five volumes. The quotation above is from the Medîna section of the book.

one from Aksaray, and the third person from Üsküdâr; and a fourth person left Istanbul with the intention of going to a place that is in Anatolia and 104 kilometres away; the first person becomes safarî when he reaches beyond the cemetery of Edirnekapı, as of today the second person when he gets beyond the cemetery of Topkapı or, if he goes by the coastal route, beyond the Yedikule gate, the third one when he has passed the area between the great military building named Selimiye Kışlası and the Karaca Ahmed cemetery, and the fourth person as soon as he sets foot on the other side of the Bosphorus. Performing two rak'ats of those prayers of fard namâz that contain four rak'ats is wâjib for a safarî person in the Hanafî Madhhab, sunnat-i-muakkada in the Mâlikî Madhhab, and preferrable in the Shâfi'î Madhhab. Following a muqîm[1] imâm is permissible only when making adâ according to the Hanafî Madhhab, permissible both when making adâ and when making qadâ according to the Shâfi'î Madhhab, and makrûh in either case according to the Mâlikî Madhhab. It is explained in the previous chapter how a settled (muqîm) person performs namâz behind a safarî imâm. For three days plus three nights, he can make masah on his mests. He can break his fast (within time). It is not wâjib for him to perform the Qurbân. If a musâfir is comfortable enough, he should not break his fast. Even a person who sets out on a journey for sinful purposes becomes a musâfir. Please see 9th chapter!

Anybody, whether settled or safarî [on a long distance journey], whether with an excuse or not, may perform a supererogatory namâz while sitting on the back of an animal as it walks as well as when it stands still, as long as they are outside of a town or village. The sunnats that are before and after the five daily prayers of fard namâz are supererogatory. Only the sunnat of morning prayer is not supererogatory. Although it is very good to put the hands under the navel with the right hand clasping on the left when saying the Fâtiha and the other sûras, they might as well be put on the thighs. Any kind of sitting posture is permissible. – No one is permitted to perform namâz while he himself is walking; walking nullifies namâz [**Jawhara**]. See chapter 19! – He can perform namâz in that manner as he goes through the cities on his way. However, it is makrûh for him to perform it in that manner in his hometown. He bends for the rukû' and makes the sajda by signs. He does not put his head on something. It is not necessary to

---

[1] 'Muqîm' means 'settled', 'not safarî'.

turn towards the qibla when beginning or while performing namâz. He has to perform it in the direction towards which the animal is walking. Even if there is a great deal of najâsat on the animal or on its halter or saddle, the namâz will be acceptable. Yet it will not be acceptable if he sits on the place smeared with the najâsat. Also, it is necessary to take off the shoes if they are najs. Controlling the animal with small movements such as spurring it with the feet or by pulling its reins does not nullify the namâz. It is permissible for a person who has begun his supererogatory namâz on an animal to dismount quickly and finish the namâz on the ground. Yet it is not permissible to begin it on the ground and finish it on the animal.

It is not permissible to perform a namâz that is fard or wâjib on an animal unless there is a darûrat. The book **Halabî** says: "Performance of farz prayers on an animal is the same as performing the sunnats (on an animal). Yet it is permissible only when the excuses making tayammum permissible are present." Hence it is understood that when you are settled or travelling you can perform the fard prayers on an animal outside of town when there is a darûrat for doing so. Examples of a darûrat that makes up a good excuse are: hazard to one's belongings, life, or animal, likelihood that one's animal or one's belongings that one is keeping on one's animal or on oneself may be stolen in case one dismounts the animal, perils such as wild animals and enemy attacks, inconveniences such as mud on the ground and heavy rain, illness that may worsen or linger on account of the physical toil of dismounting and remounting the animal, an exposed position wherein one will be left by one's companions in case they should not wait for one, and an apprehension of inability to remount the animal without a helping hand if one should dismount it. A little mud does not suffice for an excuse. It becomes an excuse when it is deep enough for one's face to go in and become covered. A person without an animal performs namâz standing and by making signs when there is a great deal of mud. The Imâmeyn said that if a person who cannot mount an animal has someone to help him, inability to mount the animal will no longer be a valid excuse. When performing a namâz that is fard or wâjib, it is necessary to get the animal to turn towards the qibla. If one cannot manage it, one must do one's best at least.

If a musâfir[1] expects that his excuse will be gone towards the end of the prayer time, he had better wait and perform his namâz

---

[1] 'Musâfir' is the noun form of the adjective 'safarî'.

on the ground; however, it is still permissible for him to perform it on the animal as well. Likewise, a person who expects to find water is permitted to perform namâz at its early time by making a tayammum. Performing namâz on the two chests called **Mahmil** (litter) that are on an animal is like performing it on the animal itself. A person who is able to dismount cannot perform the fard namâz on a mahmil. If the legs of the mahmil are lowered down to the ground, it serves as a divan. In that case it becomes permissible for him to perform the fard standing on it. But he cannot perform it sitting.

Since a two-wheeled cart cannot remain level on the ground unless it is tied to an animal, it is like an animal both when moving and when still. Any carriage with three or four wheels that can remain level [such as a bus, a train] is like a divan, if it is not in motion. It is permissible to perform the fard namâz, standing, on it. If the carriage is moving it is like an animal. It is not permissible to perform the fard on it without a good excuse. You must stop it and perform namâz standing towards the qibla. [If you cannot stop it, or if you are on a vehicle which you ride by paying some fare, you get off at a convenient place. If the vehicle leaves you, take the next one or another vehicle that starts from that town. When getting on the first vehicle you should negotiate accordingly. If this is not possible, either, it is permissible to perform namâz by making signs, sitting, as you would do in namâz, and you must turn towards the qibla as well as possible.]

It is not permissible for an ill or travelling person to perform the fard namâz by signs while sitting on a divan or on a chair with his legs hanging down. An ill person should perform his namâz on the floor or on a divân positioned lengthwise in the direction of qibla, turning himself towards the qibla. See chapter 23. It is better for a person who is safarî to imitate the other three Madhhabs and perform the early and late afternoon prayers together and the evening and night prayers together, standing towards the qibla when the vehicle stops on the way. According to the Mâlikî and Shâfi'î Madhhabs, in a safar (long distance journey) that is not sinful and which is a distance of more than eighty kilometres, taqdîm, which means to perform late afternoon prayer immediately after early afternoon prayer in the time of early afternoon prayer or to perform night prayer immediately after evening prayer in the time of evening prayer, and ta'khîr, which means to postpone early afternoon prayer till the time of late afternoon prayer and perform them together or to perform evening and night prayers likewise, are permissible. This practice is not permissible before the journey starts. A place where one intends to stay for less than four days becomes a safarî place. When at a place of this sort, one can make qasr (performing early and late afternoon prayers together); and in case of haraj, jem' (performing evening and night prayers together) is permissible. Making jem'i taqdîm in jamâ'at in a mosque on account of rain is permissible, yet there are seven conditions to be fulfilled. There is no unanimity among scholars as to whether it is permissible for an ill person to make jem'. [To imitate another Madhhab does not mean to change your Madhhab. A Hanafî person who imitates Imâm-i Shâfi'î 'rahmatullâhi ta'âlâ 'alaih' does not leave the Hanafî Madhhab.] It is stated in the fatwâ of Shamsuddîn Muhammad Remlî, a Shafi'î savant, and also in the book **I'ânat-ut-tâlibîn 'alâ-hall-i elfâz-i Fath-il-mu'în**[1], that before starting the journey and when the journey is over one cannot perform two rek'ats of those prayers of fard namâz that contain four rek'ats and that two prayers of namâz cannot be performed within the period of time allotted for either one of them. This fatwâ is printed in the margins of the book **Fatâwâ-i Kubrâ**[2].

Namâz cannot be performed in jamâ'at on different animals. It can be performed on a mahmil, carriage, or bus, in jamâ'at, like performing it in a room, provided all the Muslims in the jamâ'at be on the same motionless mahmil, carriage, or bus.

It is written in **Halabî-i kebîr**: "As Shamsul'aimma Halwânî 'rahmatullâhi ta'âlâ 'alaih', (d. 456 [1064 A.D.], Bukhâra,) said, if you start performing namâz standing towards the qibla on an animal and then the animal turns away from the qibla, the namâz, if it is fard, will not be accepted. You must not remain deviated from the direction of qibla as long as the duration of one rukn. [So is the case when on a bus or train.]

According to the Imâmeyn, when on a sailing ship it is not permissible to perform the fard namâz sitting without a good excuse. Dizziness is a good excuse. Imâm-i a'zam 'rahmatullâhi 'alaih' said that even a dizzy person had better perform it standing. If possible, it is better to get off the ship and perform the prayer on land. A ship anchored out in the sea is like a sailing ship if it is rolling badly with the wind. If it is rolling slightly, or if it is

---

[1] Written by Abû Bakr Shatâ 'rahmatullâhi ta'âlâ 'alaih', (d. 1310).
[2] Written by Ibni Hajar-i-Mekkî 'rahmatullâhi ta'âlâ 'alaih', (899 [1494 A.D.] – 974 [1566], Mekka.)

alongside the shore, it is not permissible to perform the fard namâz sitting. If a ship has run aground, it is always permissible to perform namâz standing on it. If the ship is not stranded, majority of Islamic scholars say that it is not permissible to perform the fard namâz on it if it is possible to get off. Such a ship is like an animal. A stranded ship, [a bridge or a wharf built on masts in water or fastened with chains to the bottom] is like a table or divan on land. When beginning namâz on a sailing ship it is necessary to stand towards the qibla and, as the ship turns, to turn towards the qibla during the namâz. For, turning towards the qibla on a ship is compulsory like when you are in a room. It is not permissible for a person who is able to make the rukû' and the sajda to perform even the supererogatory namâz by signs on a ship."

It is written in **Marâqilfalâh**: "It is permissible to perform the supererogatory prayers in sitting posture even without an excuse. But the sunnat of morning prayer you must perform standing. If you perform supererogatory prayers sitting you will be given only half of the thawâbs. When doing so you bend for the rukû' and place your head on the ground for the sajda. Or you stand up to make the rukû' and then bend into the rukû'. He who cannot perform it standing performs it sitting. He bends for the rukû', and places his head on the ground for the sajda. He who cannot place his head on the ground for the sajda performs namâz by making signs."

It is written in **Hidâya**[1] and in **Nihâya**:[2] "It is permissible to perform the fard namâz on a docked ship. But it is better to get out and perform it on land." It is written in **Bahja**:[3] "When going from Istanbul to Üsküdar on a small sailing ship, if the time of the early afternoon prayer is about to end, it is permissible to perform early afternoon prayer sitting, since it is impossible to get off the ship." Since a Muslim on board that ship is not safarî, he cannot perform the early afternoon prayer together with the late afternoon prayer by imitating the Shâfi'î Madhhab.

On the night of the Mi'râj,[4] evening prayer was arranged as

---

[1] A book of Fiqh written by Burhân-ad-dîn Merghinânî 'rahmatullâhi 'alaih', (martyred in 593 [1197 A.D.] by the hordes of Dzengiz Khân.
[2] Written by Husayn bin 'Alî 'rahmatullâhi 'alaih'.
[3] **Bahja-t-ul-fatâwâ**, by Abdullah Rûmî 'rahmatullâhi 'alaih', (d. 1156 [1743 A.D.], Kanlıca, Bosphorus.)
[4] Hadrat Muhammad's ascent to heaven. There is detailed information about Mi'râj in the first fascicle of **Endless Bliss** and in **Belief and Islam**.

three rak'ats and the other fard prayers as two rak'ats. A second commandment in the blessed city of Medina increased all five prayers, except morning and evening prayers, to four rak'ats. In the fourth year of the Hegira these prayers were reduced again to two rak'ats for a musâfir. In the Hanafî Madhhab it is sinful for a musâfir to perform them as four rak'ats **(Durr-ul-mukhtâr)**.

If a musâfir performs the fard as four rak'ats, the last two rak'ats become supererogatory prayers. But he becomes sinful because he has disobeyed the commandment, because he has omitted the takbîr of iftitâh (beginning) for the supererogatory prayer, because he has omitted the salâm of the fard, and because he has mixed the supererogatory prayer with the fard. He may go to Hell if he does not make tawba. A person who forgets and performs four rak'ats must make the sajda-i sahw. If a musâfir conducts a namâz in jamâ'at as the imâm and performs four rak'ats by mistake, the namâz of a settled person who has followed him becomes fâsid. If he does not sit in the second rak'at, his fard namâz will not be accepted. If, before making the sajda of the third rak'at, he intends to stay for fifteen days in that city, he will have to perform that fard namâz as four rak'ats. But it will be necessary for him to repeat the qiyâm and the rukû' of the third rak'at because he has performed those two (the qiyâm and the rukû') as parts of a supererogatory prayer. An act of worship performed as supererogatory cannot take the place of a fard. [Hence, supererogatory prayers or the sunnats of daily prayers cannot take the place of those fard prayers that have been left to qadâ.] Please see the twentieth chapter. A musâfir says short sûras. He makes the tesbîhs no less than three times. During the journey, i.e. at times of difficulty, he can omit the sunnats except the sunnat of morning prayer. It is permissible to omit the sunnats because of an 'udhr. [Hence, the sunnats can be performed with the intention of performing the qadâ of the omitted fard prayers.]

If a person intends to go back before having gone a distance of three days, he automatically goes out of the state of being a musâfir. He becomes muqîm. If a person who has left the city with the intention of going a way of three days enters his own city after having gone more or less than a three days' journey, or if he intends to stay for fifteen days at some other place, he becomes muqîm again. If he intends to stay there less than fifteen days, or if he stays there for years without intending at all, he is a musâfir. If a soldier in the dâr-ul-harb intends to stay at some place even for fifteen days, he does not become settled (muqîm). Also a musâfir who intends to stay for fifteen days on a ship out in the sea or on an uninhabited island does not become settled. A sailor does not become settled even if his possessions, wife and children are on the ship. A ship is not a home. Those who intend to stay for fifteen days altogether in different places such as Mekka, Minâ and Arafât, do not become settled. Those who are under orders, such as women, students, soldiers, officers, workers, and children act not upon their own intentions, but upon their husbands' or mahram relatives', teachers', commanders', or employers' commands. If their commander intends to stay at some place for fifteen days, they remain safarî until they hear of the commander's intention. Upon knowing the intention, they become settled. Soldiers who invade an enemy country or who besiege a fortress from land or sea become safarî even if they intend for fifteen days. Those who go to an enemy country, but not for war, become safarî or muqîm, depending on their intention. A person who has newly become a Muslim in the **Dâr-ul-harb** is settled if he is not under persecution. Those who live in tents become settled when they intend to stay in a wilderness for fifteen days. Others do not become settled in a wilderness.

He who sets out for a journey towards the end of the time of a certain namâz performs that namâz in two rak'ats if he did not perform it (before setting out). He who arrives at his home towards the end of a prayer time performs four rak'ats if he did not perform it (during the journey).

The place where a person is settled or where he has settled his home is called a **Watan** (home). There are three kinds of watans in the Hanafî Madhhab. The first one, **Watan-i aslî**, a person's real home, is the place where the person was born or made a marriage or where he established his home with the intention of living there permanently. If he intends to leave the place years later or when something he expects happens, he has not settled there even if he lives there for years. If a person gets married at a place, even if without intending to stay there for fifteen days, that place becomes his watan-i aslî. He becomes settled there. When a person who has wives living in two different cities goes to one of those cities, it becomes his watan-i-'aslî. He becomes settled in those cities. If his wife dies, that place is no longer his watan-i-'aslî, even if he has houses or land there. If he goes to a place where he did not get married and intends to establish his home there, the place becomes his watan-i aslî. Even if the place where the parents of a boy at the age of puberty live is at the same time the place where he was born, if he leaves the place and settles in some other place where he intends never to leave, or if he gets married there, that place becomes his watan-i aslî. When he visits his parents, their residence does not become the boy's watan-i-'aslî unless he intends to re-establish his home there. His watan-i-'aslî is where he got married or where he finally settled. When settling at a place, his former watan-i-'aslîs, where he settled before and where he was born, become invalid, even if the distance between them is less than three days or even if he did not set out with the intention of being safarî. If a person who has left his watan-i-'aslî in order to settle in another place changes his way to settle at some other place, he performs (those prayers of) namâz (consisting of four rak'ats) in their origional length, i.e. four rak'ats, as he goes through his first place; (he does not shorten them to two rak'ats) because he has not acquired a new home yet. If he makes his wife settle in one place and then he himself settles in another place, both places become his watan-i-'aslî. When a person enters his watan-i aslî he becomes settled. He does not need to intend to stay there for fifteen days.

The second watan is called **Watan-i iqâmat,** transient home. A place where one intends to stay continuously for fifteen days or more in the Hanafî Madhhab and for four days or more in the Shâfi'î and Mâlikî Madhhabs, excluding the days of arrival and departure, and then leave, is called a **Transient home**. If a person, while intending to stay at a place for the aforesaid number of days, intends also to go to some other place and then return there within these days, that place does not become his transient home. If he intends to spend the nights there and the days at some other place, the former becomes his watan-i iqâmat. If he intends to stay at a place for years in order to receive an education or to do some job there and then leave after finishing it, the place becomes his watan-i iqâmat. If he settled there with the intention of never leaving, it would become his watan-i-'aslî. Three things invalidate the watan-i iqâmat: When one goes to another watan-i iqâmat the first watan-i iqâmat becomes invalid, even if one did not set off with the intention of a safar (long-distance journey), even if the distance between both places is less than three days' walk. Secondly, going to one's watan-i-'aslî invalidates it. If a person in the Hanafî Madhhab stays in the blessed city of Mekka for fifteen days and then goes to Minâ and gets married there, Minâ becomes his watan-i aslî. The blessed city of Mekka is no longer his watan-i iqâmat. The third cause is to set out on a long-distance journey (with the intention of a safar). That is, if a person leaves his watan-i iqâmat with the intention of going to a place of three days plus three nights' way, the first place is no longer his watan-i iqâmat. If he went and came back with the intention of a shorter journey, his watan-i iqâmat would not become invalid. If he leaves his watan-i iqâmat without an intention (for safar) but at another place intends to go to a place that is three days' way away and then enters his watan-i iqâmat again before having walked for three days, his being safarî becomes invalid, and he becomes settled. If he entered there after having walked a distance of three days following the time he had made his intention (for a safar), or if he never went through his watan-i iqâmat, he would not become settled. In the Shâfi'î Madhhab, if a person (going on a safar) knows that the business he is going to do there is going to take no less than four days, he becomes muqîm (settled) as soon as he reaches his destination even if he does not make niyyat. If he does not know well how long it will take, he becomes settled eighteen days later.

Suppose two Muslims in the Hanafî Madhhab, one travelling from Istanbul to Baghdad and the other from the blessed city of Mekka to Kûfa, both intend to stay at their respective destinations for fifteen days and later leave those places, which have now become their respective watan-i iqâmats, and then go to a place called Qasr; neither of them becomes safarî on their way to Qasr. For, the place called Qasr is between Baghdad and Kûfa and is a two days' walk from either place. If they intend to stay in Qasr for fifteen days, Baghdad and Kûfa are no longer their watan-i iqâmats. For, the city called Qasr has now become their new watan-i iqâmat. If they go from Qasr to Kûfa fifteen days later, they do not become safarî. If they leave Kûfa a day later and go to Baghdad through Qasr, they never become safarî on their way because Qasr is the watan-i iqâmat for both of them. When they leave there without intending for a journey of three days and then come back, they do not become safarî. When they first left Baghdad and Kûfe, if they intended for a way of four days, meeting in Qasr and then going to Kûfa together and staying there one day and then leaving for Baghdad, they would be safarî the entire time because they would have intended for a journey of three days. The one from Istanbul would have walked that entire distance. And when the one from the blessed city of Mekka set off on the journey, Kûfa would have no longer been his watan-i iqâmat. Since the city of Qasr is not their hometown, their going through it would not cause them to become settled. If the one from Istanbul, after staying in Kûfa for fifteen days, left with the intention of going to Mekka and then returned to Kûfa for some business before having gone a way of three days, he would not have become settled. For, upon his leaving the city with the intention of going a three days' way, the city of Kûfa would have lost the state of being his watan-i iqâmat. Kûfa is south of Baghdad and Kerbelâ.

The third kind of home, **Watan-i suknâ,** is the place where one has stopped, intended to stay less than fifteen days, or where one has lived for years though one may have intended to leave there a day after one's arrival. A safarî person must always perform two rak'ats of the fard prayers in the watan-i suknâ. If a person arriving in a city or a village intends to stay there ten days and if after ten days he intends again to stay there seven days longer, he does not become settled.

Being in one's watan-i iqâmat or watan-i suknâ does not invalidate one's watan-i aslî. Setting out for a journey does not invalidate one's watan-i aslî, either. Being in a watan-i suknâ does not invalidate one's watan-i iqâmat. But it invalidates one's former watan-i suknâ.

A safarî person does not become settled when he is in a watan-i suknâ. A person who is not safarî is settled in a place where he makes his watan-i-suknâ. If a person who has left his town in order to go to a village that is not so far as a **safar**[1] from his town stays in the village for less than fifteen days, the village becomes his **watan-i suknâ**. He does not become safarî there. He performs the fard prayers completely. Then, if he leaves the village without intending for a safar and intends for a safar on the way before arriving in his own town or in another watan-i suknâ, he must perform two rak'ats of the fard prayers on the way. If he enters the village he becomes settled. For, his watan-i-suknâ has not become invalid because he has not entered his watan-i-aslî or another watan-i-süknâ and because he did not intend for a safar. As is seen, invalidation of the watan-i suknâ is similar to the invalidation of the watan-i iqâmat. One's being settled in the watan-i suknâ requires that the watan-i suknâ be within a distance less than a safar [three days' walk] from one's watan-i aslî or watan-i iqâmat.

A person is going, say, from Kûfa to Qadsiya. The distance between them is less than three days' walk. He leaves Qadsiya for

---

[1] A journey that would take three days plus three nights by walking.

Hira. Also the distance between these two is less than a way of three days. Then he returns to Qadsiya before arriving in Hira. He will pick up something he has forgotten and then go to Damascus. He does not go through Kûfa. He must perform the fard namâz completely in Qadsiya because when leaving there he did not intend to be safarî, nor did he enter Hira; hence, Qadsiya is still his watan. Hira is five kilometres southeast of Kûfa, and Qadsiya is a little farther down south.

If a person sets off for a journey of three days' walk and stays at a village less than fifteen days before having gone a way of three days but leaves the village and then returns there again, he does not become settled. This is because he was safarî when he first arrived there, too. If a menstruating woman who does not have her husband or a mahram relative with her sets off for a journey with the intention of a safar, this intention is of no value. She does not become safarî at a place where she stays before travelling for three more days after her menstruation is over.

It is written in the books **Berîqa** and **Hadîqa:** "It is harâm [in the three Madhhabs] for a free woman to go on a journey of three days alone or with other women, or with her mahram (and male) relative unless he is a sâlih Muslim at the age of discretion and puberty, without her husband or one of her eternally mahram (and male) relatives to accompany her. In the Shâfi'î Madhhab, women may join other women and go out for a hajj that is fard without any one of their mahram (and male) relatives with them. It is makrûh for one man or two men to go on a safar. It is not makrûh for three men. It is sunnat for four men to travel together and for them to choose one from among themselves to be the commander." The book **Hindiyya**, in its chapter about nafaqa, and the books **Tahtâwî, Durr-ul-mukhtâr**, and **Durr-ul-munteqâ**, in the chapters dealing with hajj (pilgrimage), state: "A woman can set off on a safar with a **murâhiq,** that is, her mahram relative who is twelve years old and who has almost reached the state of puberty." The book **Qâdî-Khân** states: "A woman can set off on a safar with a group of sâlih Muslims" [It is permissible to act upon

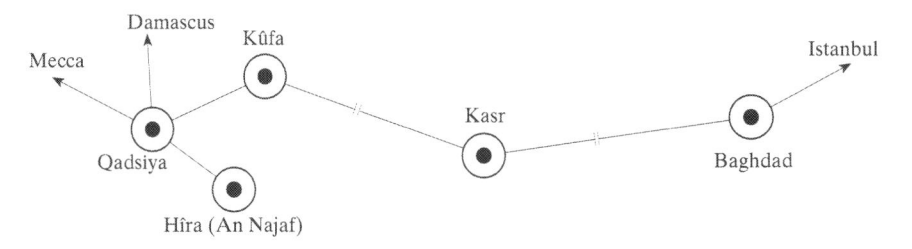

— 245 —

these two judgements when there is a darûrat.] The book **Majalla,** in its 986th article, states: "The age of puberty virtually begins when a boy is over twelve and when a girl is over nine. The extreme limit is fifteen for both of them. When the age of fifteen is transcended, they are said to have reached the age of puberty. Those who have transcended the ages of twelve and nine, respectively, but who have not experienced the state of puberty are called **murâhiq**."

Aggrieved I am, from Khudâ I demand remedy for my distress;
Incapable I am, from true Forgiveness I demand favour and kindness.

With a black face, sins teeming, I've always been disobedient;
From the Janâb-i Kibriyâ I demand pardon and forgiveness.

Heartfelt resolved I am to keep in the right path,
And so I demand a chance to attain His grace.

A diver I have been into the ocean of Islam;
From ocean I demand pearls, corals at each dive into deepness.

16 – WÂJIBS of NAMÂZ, SAJDA-I SAHW

The wâjibs of namâz are: to say (the sûra of) Fâtiha; to say one additional sûra or âyat after the Fâtiha; to say the additional sûra in the first and second rak'ats of the fard prayers and in every rak'at of the sunnats; to make the (two) sajdas one immediately after the other; to sit as long as the tashahhud in the second rak'at; to say the **Attahiyyâtu** during the sitting posture in the last rak'at; to make the **ta'dîl-i arkân**, i.e. to be still as long as (it would take) to say 'Subhânallah'; [It is sunnat for it to be still longer than that;] to say "essalâmu..." at the end of namâz; to say the qunût prayer; for the imâm to say the âyats loudly in the prayers of morning, Friday, 'Iyd, Tarawih, Witr, and in the first two rak'ats of evening and night prayers; and finally to recite, for the imâm as well as for a person performing namâz by himself, the âyats on the level of a whisper in the early and late afternoon prayers, in the third rak'at of the evening prayer and in the third and fourth rak'ats of the night prayer. It is written is **Bezzâziyya** that it is not makrûh for one's recitation to be in a whisper that would be heard by one or two people and that 'reciting loudly' means doing so as loudly as to be heard by several people.

It does not break namâz to omit one of the wâjibs of namâz knowingly. Yet it is sinful. He who forgets or omits one of them must make the **sajda-i sahw**. He who forgets the **zamm-i sûra** (additional sûra) in the first and second rak'ats of a fard prayer of namâz must say it in the third and fourth rak'ats, and he must make the sajda-i sahw (at the end of the namâz). If you remember during the rukû' that you have forgotten to make the qirâat, you immediately straighten up, make the qirâat and then make the rukû'. Also, a person who has made a fard or wâjib before or after its prescribed time has to make the sajda-i sahw. For example, if a person says one part of the additional sûra in the rukû' or delays the third rak'at by saying a small prayer after the Attahiyyâtu, or if the imâm recites âyats very softly instead of loudly or vice versa, the sajda-i sahw becomes necessary. The sûras that are wâjib for the imâm to recite loudly are permissible for a person who performs namâz by himself to recite loudly as well as softly. In case several sajda-i sahws are necessary, making one will be enough. When the imâm makes the sajda-i sahw, the jamâ'at also have to do it. If one person in the jamâ'at makes a mistake he does not make the sajda-i sahw. A person who arrives for the jamâ'at after the first rak'at makes the sajda-i sahw together with the imâm, and then completes his namâz. When a person (performing namâz individually) forgets to sit (at the end of the second rak'at) and then remembers it while standing up for the third rak'at, if his knees have already left the ground, he does not sit down, but instead makes the sajda-i sahw. When a person stands up instead of sitting at the end of the last rak'at, if he remembers before prostrating, he immediately sits down and (at the end) makes the sajda-i sahw because he has delayed the sitting posture. If he remembers after prostrating, (the extra part of) his namâz which is fard becomes supererogatory. Making one more rak'at, he sits for the sixth rak'at and then completes it. If he sits for the fourth rak'at as long as the tashahhud and then stands up for the fifth rak'at instead of making the salâm and then remembers this before going down for the sajda, he sits down, recites what he has not recited of the tashahhud and then makes the salâm and thereafter the sajda-i sahw. If he has already prostrated for the sajda, he completes the sixth rak'at and makes the sajda-i sahw. Thus he has completed the fard, the last two rak'ats being supererogatory. But, as is declared (by savants), these two rak'ats do not replace the final sunnat of the early afternoon, evening or night prayer. For, the sunnats are started with the takbîr of tahrîma. It is permissible for a late comer to the mosque to begin following the imâm even as the imâm makes the sajda-i sahw. It is wâjib for a person to repeat the namâz in which he has knowingly omitted the sajda-i sahw, or has knowingly omitted one of the wâjibs of the namâz, e.g. reciting the Fâtiha. If he does not perform it again he becomes sinful. In Friday and 'Iyd prayers, the imâm had better not make the sajda-i sahw.

To make the sajda-i sahw; after making the salâm to one side (at the end of the namâz), you make two sajdas and then sit down to complete the namâz. It is also permissible to make the sajda-i sahw after making the salâm to both sides as well as without making the salâm at all.

If a person forgets how many rak'ats he has performed, and if this is the first time it has happened, he must make the salâm and perform the namâz again. If it is his habit to get confused, he thinks and performs it as he strongly guesses to be correct. If he cannot guess strongly, he must judge from the point of view that he has performed less of the namâz than he should have, and complete it. If a person doubts whether he has performed a namâz, he performs it if the time is not over yet. If the time is over, he does not perform it.

If a person, getting confused on how many rak'ats of namâz he has performed, thinks and thus extends one rukn by one additional rukn and thereby delays the next rukn, he has to make the sajda-i sahw, even if he said some âyats or tesbîhs in the interim. The fard (rules that must be observed) in namâz are called **rukn**. Saying one âyat, the rukû, the two sajdas, and sitting in the last rak'at are each a rukn. Thinking, when it delays a fard or wâjib, necessitates a sajda-i sahw. For instance, if a person sitting at the end of the last rak'at thinks and delays the salâm, the sajda-i sahw will be necessary. When the extra salawâts and duâs which one says are not intended to be sunnats but are due to wandering thoughts and reveries, delaying the wâjib becomes a guilt. If one wonders whether one has performed some other prayer of namâz, or if one thinks of a worldly affair, the sajda-i sahw will not be necessary, even if it delays one rukn. If after finishing a namâz you have doubts as to how many rak'ats you have performed, this state is called having doubts. Just ignore it. If, after you have finished a namâz, an 'âdil[1] Muslim says that you have performed it wrongly, you had better perform it again. If two 'âdil Muslims witness the same, it is wâjib for you to perform it again. If the Muslim is not an 'âdil one, you must disregard what he says. If the imâm says that they performed the namâz correctly while the jamâ'at says that they performed it wrongly, if the imâm trusts himself or if he has a witness, the namâz does not have to be performed again.

If it is doubtful whether doing something is wâjib or bid'at, it is better to do it. If the doubt is on whether it is bid'at or sunnat, it must not be done. [See chapter 1].

If you doubt whether you said the takbîr of iftitâh, whether you made an ablution, whether your clothes are clean, or whether you have made masah on your head, and if this doubt happens for the first time, you break the namâz and perform it again. But you do not have to perform an ablution, nor do you have to wash your clothes. However, if this happens all the time, you do not break the namâz, but go on and complete it.

SALÂT-I WITR — It is written in **Mawqûfât**: "Imâm-i a'zam 'rahmatullâhi 'alaih' said that the namâz of witr is wâjib, but the two imâms said that it is sunnat. [It is sunnat in the Mâlikî and Shâfi'î Madhhabs, too.] Neither the azân nor the iqâmat is said before it. Before bowing for the rukû' in the third rak'at, it is, always, wâjib to say an Arabic prayer. He who does not perform it

---

[1] Please see chapter 10 for a definition of 'âdil Muslim.

during its appointed time has to make qadâ of it. It is necessary to make its niyyat (intention) as 'the Witr'. The namâz of witr consists of three rak'ats. You make the salâm after the third rak'at is finished. You say the Fâtiha and the additional sûra in all three rak'ats. In the third rak'at, after saying the zamm-i sûra (additional sûra), you raise both hands up to your ears without hanging them down along your sides, and say 'Allâhu akbar.' Then, after fastening your hands without hanging them down along your sides, you say the two well-known prayers of **Qunût,** performance of which is wâjib. A person who does not know these prayers of Qunût recites the istighfâr three times. For instance, he says, 'Allahummaghfir lî.' Or he says the âyat of 'Rabbanâ âtinâ...' up to the end once. Prayers of Qunût are not said in any namâz other than the Witr namâz. Only in Ramadân, the Witr namâz is performed in jamâ'at. In Ramadân, those who have not performed the fard of the night prayer in jama'at may not perform the tarâwih and the witr in jamâ'at. For, the Muslims who are to perform the tarâwih in jamâ'at have to be the same people who have performed the (fard of the) night prayer in jamâ'at. It is written in **Hindiyya**: "A person who performed the fard individually joins the jama'at performing the tarâwih. Later he completes those rak'ats of tarâwih that he missed. A person who was not able to perform the tarâwih in jamâ'at may perform the witr behind the imâm with whom he performed the fard. According to a report, it is sahîh for a person who goes to another mosque after performing the witr in jamâ'at to follow another imâm by intending for the fard or tarâwih while the imâm is performing the fard or tarâwih, respectively. If he sees that the tarâwih is being performed, and if he has not performed the fard, he performs the fard individually in a recess and then follows the imâm. If the imâm bows for the rukû' too early (for him to recite the Subhânaka...), he must catch up with the imâm in the rukû' by saying (the Subhânaka...) quickly or by leaving it half-finished. He who forgets the qunût (as he performs the witr individually does not say it after the rukû', but makes the sajda-i sahw at the end of the namâz. If the imâm does not say the qunût, the jamâ'at does not say it, either. When an imâm in the Shâfi'î Madhhab says the qunût after straightening up from the rukû' in the morning prayer, a person in Hanafî Madhhab who has been following him does not say the qunût, but waits standing. Though it is very blessed to perform the witr namâz after midnight, he who will not be able to wake up must perform it early, immediately after the final sunnat of the night prayer." It is not sahîh to perform the namâz of witr before the fard of the night prayer. To perform them in this order is wâjib according to Imâm-i a'zam. A person who performed it before the fard by mistake does not perform it again. According to the two Imâms, however, the namâz of witr is contingent on the night prayer. It should be performed again by the person who performed it before the fard of the night prayer.

SAJDA-I TILÂWAT — There are âyats of sajda at fourteen places in the Qur'ân al-kerîm. For anyone who reads or hears one of them, even if he does not understand its meaning, it is wâjib to make one sajda (prostration). If a person is in a place where someone else is reading it, but does not hear it, he does not make the sajda. A person who writes or spells an âyat of sajda does not make the sajda. A person who hears or reads its translation makes the sajda if he understands that it is an âyat of sajda.

It is wâjib for those people for whom it is fard to perform namâz to make the sajda upon hearing an âyat of sajda-i tilâwat. For this reason, even a drunk or junub person who hears an âyat of sajda has to make sajda when he performs an ablution (later). If a person is so drunk that he is unconscious, it is not wâjib for him to make the sajda neither when he himself says the âyat nor when he hears it. According to (some) scholars, when a sleeping, unconscious or mad person says an âyat of sajda, it is wâjib for those who hear him to make the sajda. But it is more acceptable that when such people or birds recite the âyat, the sajda should not be made. The reason for this is that their reading (or reciting) is not real, correct reading (or reciting). Real reading (or reciting) is that which you are doing in a state of realization that you are reading (or reciting) the Qur'ân al-kerîm. If a child is old enough to realize what he is doing, those who hear his reciting the âyat have to make the sajda. If he is smaller, it is not necessary. To be exempted from performing namâz, a mad person must have been mad for (a duration of time covering) at least six prayer times. To be exempted from fasting, he must have been insane day and night for a month, and exemption from paying zakât requires him having been insane continuously for one year. However, no matter what time, if he reads the âyat while he is insane, the sajda is not necessary. If he says it while he is sane, the sajda is necessary. The sajda is not wâjib for those who hear the echo of the âyat reflected from mountains, wildernesses, or elsewhere, or for those who hear it from birds. When the âyat of sajda is read or written syllable by syllable, the sajda is not necessary. It is wâjib for Muslims to make the sajda when they hear a disbeliever read the âyat. It is written in **Durr-ul-muntaqâ**[1] that "It must be a human voice." The sound that is heard on the radio, as it will be explained with more detail later, is not human voice, but it is the reproduction of lifeless metal which sounds similar to the voice of the person reading (or reciting) the Qur'ân al-kerîm. Therefore, it is written in **al-Fiqh-u-'alal-Madhhâhib-il-erba'a** that "It is not wâjib for a person hearing the âyat of sajda read on a phonograph [gramophone, tape recorder or radio] to make the sajda of tilâwat."

To make the sajda of tilâwat, with an ablution, you stand towards the qibla, say **Allâhu akbar** without lifting your hands to your ears, and prostrate for the sajda. In the sajda you say **Subhâna rabbiyal-a'lâ** three times. Then while standing up you say **Allâhu akbar** to complete the sajda. It is necessary to make the niyyat first. Without the niyyat it is not acceptable. In case you have to say (an âyat of tilâwat) while performing namâz, you immediately make an additional rukû' or sajda, and then stand up and go on with your recitation (of the Qur'ân). If you bow for the rukû' of namâz after saying a couple of normal âyats after the âyat of sajda and if you intend for the sajda of tilâwat while doing so, the rukû' or the sajdas of the namâz will stand for the sajda of tilâwat. When performing namâz in jamâ'at, in the event that the imâm says an âyat of sajda, you make an additional rukû' and two sajdas together with the imâm, even if you did not hear the imâm say the âyat. The jamâ'at must make niyyat in the rukû'. Outside of namâz, the sajda of tilâwat may be postponed until some other time. Also, a person who is junub or without an ablution or drunk has to make it after purifying himself. When a woman in her monthly period hears the âyat it is not wâjib for her to make the sajda. He who reads the same âyat of sajda several times at one sitting, or who hears it read, makes one sajda for all the readings. So is the case with saying the prayer of salawât upon saying or hearing the blessed name of Hadrat Muhammad 'sall-Allâhu 'alaihi wa sallam'. If two âyats of sajda are read in one gathering, two sajdas are necessary. A person who hears an âyat of sajda being read while he is performing namâz makes the sajda after namâz. It is not permissible to make the sajda-i-tilâwat during one of the three periods of time, (defined in tenth chapter,) during

---

[1] Written by 'Alâ'uddîn Haskafî 'rahmatullâhi ta'âlâ 'alaih', (1021, Haskaf – 1088 [1677 A.D.].).

which it is harâm to perform a namâz.

It is written at the end of the chapters concerning the sajda-i tilâwat in the books **Durr-ul-mukhtâr** and **Nûr-ul-îzâh:** "Imâm-i Nasafî 'rahmatullâhi ta'âlâ 'alaih' says in his book **Kâfî** that if a person, in order to relieve himself from sorrow and distress, entreats Allâhu ta'âlâ by heart, recites the fourteen âyats of sajda [standing], and prostrates for the sajda immediately after reciting each, Allâhu ta'âlâ will protect him against troubles and disasters." When standing up after the last sajda, he holds out his hands, and prays so that he himself and all Muslims will be rescued and protected from the disasters and troubles falling upon their world and upon Islam.

The **Sajda of Shukr** (gratitude) is like the sajda of tilâwat. It is mustahab for a person who has been given a blessing or who has been rescued from a calamity to make the sajda of shukr for Allâhu ta'âlâ. In the sajda he first says, **"Al-hamd-u-lillâh."** Then he says the tesbîhs of sajda. It is makrûh to make a sajda of shukr after namâz. It is written in the hundred and twenty-fourth letter of the first volume of **Maktûbât-i Ma'thûmiyya**. Also, it is tahrîmî makrûh to do those mubâhs (things, actions permitted by Islam) which the ignorant may think sunnat or wâjib. It causes further invention of **bid'ats**.

While describing the namâz of Witr, the book **Radd-ul-muhtâr** states: "Commandments that are fard (necessary, compulsory) both to believe and to do are called **fard**. He who denies a fard becomes a disbeliever. He who does not perform it will be tormented in Hell if he does not repent and make his tawba. Those commandments that are not fard but wâjib to believe and fard to do are called **wâjib**. He who denies the fact that something is wâjib does not become a disbeliever. He who does not do a wâjib will be tormented in Hell, too, if he does not make his tawba. He who denies the fact that the wâjib is an act of worship and necessary to perform, becomes a disbeliever. For, it has been declared unanimously and indispensably (by Islamic scholars) that it is wâjib. Those commandments that are declared in the Qur'ân al-kerîm clearly and which all Islamic scholars have understood unanimously and by way of **definite documentation** are called fard. Those commandments that are declared by doubtful documentation, i.e. unclearly, in the Qur'ân al-kerîm or which have been communicated by only one Sahâbî are called wâjib.

There are four groups of witnesses and documents teaching

the Ahkâm-i-Islâmiyya. The first group are definite both in thubût and in delâlat. In this group are those âyats that are understood clearly and those hadîths that have been communicated by **tawâtur,** that is, unanimously, and which are clearly understood. The second group are definite in thubût but inferred in delâlat. Those âyats that cannot be understood clearly are in this category. The third group are inferred in thubût but definite in delâlat. Those clear hadîth-i-sherîfs reported by only one Sahâbî are in this group. The fourth group are inferred both in thubût and in delâlat. In this group are hadîth-i-sherîfs that are reported by one Sahâbî and which cannot be understood clearly. The first group includes the fards and the harâms; the second and the third groups include the wâjibs and the tahrîmî makrûhs, and the fourth group includes the sunnats, the mustahabs and tanzîhî makrûhs. It is **bid'at** to refuse a report from one Sahâbî, or a qiyâs, without a scientifically sound explanation."

Come on, let's make namâz, and wipe the rust off our hearts;
There's no approach to Allah, unless namâz is performed!

Where namâz is performed, sins are all dumped;
Man can never be perfect, unless namâz is performed!

Allâhu ta'âlâ praises namâz much in Qur'ân al-kerîm;
"I won't love thee," He says, "unless namâz is performed!"

A hadîth-i-sherîf reads: Symptom of îmân will not
Manifest itself on man, unless namâz is performed!

To omit one single namâz is a sin, a gravest one;
Tawba will not absolve thee, unless qadâ is performed!

He who slights namâz will lose his îmân, outright;
One cannot be a Muslim, unless namâz is performed!

Namâz'll purify thine heart, and keep thee from evils;
Thou canst never be enlightened, unless namâz is performed!

17 – THINGS THAT NULLIFY NAMÂZ
The following writing is translated from Durr-ul-mukhtâr:

Things that nullify namâz are called its **mufsids**. An act of worship's being fâsid or bâtil is the same; it means it is broken, nullified. In mu'amalât[1], however, they are not the same. The following are the thirty-one mufsids of namâz:

1 - To talk. Even one word nullifies namâz. It always nullifies namâz regardless of whether it is said intentionally or inadvertently or under duress or by forgetting. However, it does not nullify namâz to say the salâm at the end of the first sitting posture, mistaking it for the second sitting. Yet if you say, "Assalâmu," thinking that the namâz is of two rak'ats, or if you say it while standing, your namâz becomes nullified. To respond to someone's greeting, in any manner whatsoever, nullifies namâz.

2 - Without a good excuse, coughing through the throat nullifies namâz. If it happens involuntarily, it does not nullify namâz. If you do it in order to facilitate your recitation, it is harmless.

3 - To say prayers in namâz that do not exist in âyats or hadîths nullifies namâz. It is written in **Durr-ul-mukhtâr**: "The prayer to be said before making the salâm has to be in Arabic. It is harâm to pray in any other language during namâz." At this point Ibni 'Âbidîn explains: "Imâm-i Abû Yûsuf and Imâm-i Muhammad said that namâz performed in any language other than Arabic would not be sahîh. Imâm-i a'zam's 'rahmatullâhi 'alaihim' later ijtihâd tallies with it."

4 - To moan or to say "Ouch!" etc. nullifies namâz.

5 - To say, "Ugh!" in order to express annoyance nullifies namâz.

6 - Crying for reasons such as a pain or sorrow nullifies namâz. If you weep silently, or cry loudly because of the thought of Paradise and Hell, your namâz does not become nullified. If a sick person cannot help saying "Ouch, ugh!" or crying, their namâz does not become nullified.

7 - It nullifies namâz to say, **"Yerhamukallah,"** to a person who sneezes and says, **"Al-hamdulillâh."** When not performing namâz, it is fard kifâya to say the former immediately after each of the three instances of the latter, and it is mustahab after the third time [**Riyâd un-nâsihîn**].

---

[1] The fifth fascicle of **Endless Bliss**, from its twenty-eighth chapter onwards, deals with 'mu'amalât'.

8 - To say, **"Innâ lillâh wa...,"** upon hearing bad news nullifies namâz. It is sunnat to say it while not performing namâz.

9 - To say **"Jalla Jalâluh"** and **"Sall-Allâhu 'alaihi wa sallam,"** upon hearing the names of Allâhu ta'âlâ or the Prophet 'sall-Allâhu 'alaihi wa sallam', respectively, nullifies namâz. Outside of namâz, saying or writing them is wâjib for the first time and mustahab for those times afterwards of saying, hearing or writing their names.

10 - To say "Âmîn" for a prayer said by anyone but the imâm nullifies namâz. [For this reason, if the imâm is conducting a namâz in jamâ'at (see chapter 20) with a loudspeaker, when he says, **"Walad'dâllîn,"** there is the danger that the namâz of those who say, "Âmîn" may become nullified. For, the sound produced by the loud-speaker is not the imâm's voice. It is some other sound produced by a metal plate that vibrates because of the magnetic power activated by electricity. Such sounds, which are originally caused by the human voice, are indistinguishable from their producers' voices; but in actual fact they are not their voices, as will be explained in detail in Chapter 24]. When the imâm finishes reciting the Fâtiha, it is makrûh for the imâm and for the jamâ'at to say "Âmîn" loudly. They must say it in a whisper.

11 - To change your place or to make room for a newcomer with someone else's warning nullifies namâz. But your moving of your own will a little some time later does not nullify it.

12 - To correct an error made by anyone except the imâm you follow nullifies the namâz (of the person who makes the correction).

13 - Even if a little, or by forgetting, eating or drinking by something that you put into your mouth (after starting to perform namâz) nullifies namâz. It does not nullify namâz to swallow something smaller than a chick-pea that has remained between the teeth. It does not break a fast, either. To chew something small in your mouth three times or to swallow it after melting it nullifies namâz.

14 - To say the prayers by reading and learning them from the Qur'ân al-kerîm or from some other paper nullifies namâz. To do so would mean to learn the prayers from someone else. Imâm-i Muhammad and Imâm-i Abû Yûsuf said that it would be makrûh. They added that it would not even be makrûh if it is not intended to imitate a disbeliever with a Heavenly Book.

Looking at a piece of writing [or something or its picture on the wall] without understanding it, does not nullify namâz. You would have committed an act of makrûh if you understood it (when you looked at it). It would not be makrûh if it only met your eyes by chance.

[Doing the customs of disbelievers, if not with the intention of being like them, if they are not harâm or evil customs, and if they are useful, is permissible. Eating and drinking like them is an example of this. It is harâm if it is done in order to become like them, or if they are harâm and bad customs.

It is written in **Uyûn-ul-basâir**[1]: "If a person draws a portrait or makes a statue of a man and says or does something to express his reverence to the picture or the statue, e.g. prostrates himself before it because he believes that the man represented in the picture or by the statue possesses one of the attributes of divinity, although he knows that that person is an unbeliever, or if he wears a girdle like the one which has been worn by Jews and Christians, or uses something representing their religious tenets, he becomes a disbeliever. If a person wears clothings peculiar to disbelievers in order to trick them in warfare, he does not become a disbeliever." Attributes that exclusively belong to Allâhu ta'âlâ are called attributes of divinity. It is excusable if he wears them only long enough to save his life, property, and sustenance. It is disbelief to wear them any longer. As is written in most of the books of Aqâid (belief) and fiqh, particularly in **Durer**[2], in its chapter preceding the subject of Nikâh: "If a person, replete with îmân as his heart may be, says a word causing disbelief willingly and without a darûrat, he becomes a disbeliever. The îmân in his heart will be of no use then. For, a person's disbelief is judged from his words. When he says a word causing disbelief, he becomes a disbeliever both among people and in the view of Allâhu ta'âlâ." It is written in the third chapter of the sixth section of the book **Sharh-i mawâqif** that the case is the same with the **kufr-i hukmî** (judged disbelief) caused by actions and ways of dressing.]

It is disbelief to do things which disbelievers practise as

---

[1] Written by Ahmad Hamawî, (d. 1098 [1686 A.D.]). It is a commentary to **Eshbâh**, a valuable book written by Ibni Nujaym Zeyn-ul-'âbidîn bin Ibrâhîm ibni Nujaym-i-Misrî 'rahmatullâhi 'alaih', 926 – 970 [1562 A.D.], Egypt.)

[2] Durer ve Ghurer, a splendid book of Fiqh written by the third Ottoman Shaikh-ul-Islâm, Molla Husrev 'rahmatullâhi ta'âlâ 'alaih', (d. 885 [1480 A.D.], İstanbul, buried in Bursa.)

worships, e.g. to play organs, to ring bells in mosques as Christians do in churches, or to use things that Islam judges to be symptoms of disbelief; using such things removes îmân unless there is a darûrat or compulsion to do so. [Please see the final part of the fifty-eighth chapter of the third fascicle of **Endless Bliss**.]

15 - Extra movements that are not parts of namâz nullify namâz. Making the rukû' or the sajdas more than the prescribed number or going out to make ablution does not nullify it. Excusable extra movements such as killing a scorpion or a snake does not nullify it, either. [See the seventeenth and the twenty-sixth makrûhs!] If a hand moves less than three times, it does not nullify namâz. It has been said (by savants) that one movement with both hands nullifies namâz. Raising the hands up to the ears for the takbîrs in namâz does not nullify namâz. Yet it is makrûh.

16 - To stand or to make the sajda at a najs place nullifies namâz. If you spread something over the najs place, your namâz will not become nullified. Shoes and clothes that you are wearing are like parts of your skin. You cannot make the **sajda** by placing the skirt of your overcoat over a najs place. You must take it off and spread it on the ground. [You cannot perform a janâza namâz if the shoes you are wearing are smeared with najâsat.]

17 - If your awrat parts remain open long enough for you to say "Subhân-Allâh" three times in one rukn, if there exists a prescribed amount of najâsat to nullify namâz on your skin or clothes, if you perform namâz ahead of the imâm, or if you are in the same line with a woman [who has been following the same imâm], your namâz becomes nullified. If you yourself do all these, your namâz will be broken immediately. [See chapter 20, Namâz in Jamâ'at!]

18 - To perform namâz on something that you have spread on a najs place and which lets colour, odor and moisture through, nullifies namâz. If it does not let them through, namâz will not become nullified. Performing it after covering the place with plenty of earth does not nullify namâz.

19 - Turning your chest away from the qibla without a good excuse breaks namâz immediately. Turning your face or any other limb away does not nullify namâz, yet it is makrûh. If you cannot help turning away, it nullifies namâz if you remain so as long as one rukn. Walking one line (one metre and half) towards the qibla, does not nullify namâz. If not in the direction of the qibla, or if you walk more than that continuously in the direction of the qibla, it nullifies

namâz. Hence, it is not permissible to perform namâz walking.

20 - When a woman is kissed or held lustfully, her namâz becomes nullified.

21 - The namâz of a person who apostates by heart becomes nullified. [That is, if he says through his heart, "If such and such a thing happens, so and so's word proves true, and the Qur'ân al-kerîm proves to be –may Allâhu ta'âlâ protect us against such thoughts!– untrue," or if a girl decides to marry a disbeliever, he, (in the first example,) or she, (in the second example,) becomes a disbeliever immediately.] A person who intends to become a disbeliever in the future or who believes something causing disbelief becomes an unbeliever, i.e. a renegade, immediately.

22 - While performing namâz, it is harâm to do something that will break your ablution or ghusl. If a person does any one of them before having sat as long as the tashahhud in the last rak'at, his namâz immediately becomes nullified. If he does it after having sat as long as the tashahhud, his namâz will be all right. If his ablution breaks by itself, he may renew it and then continue with his namâz, but it is better to perform it again from the beginning. [In case it should break (by itself) again, and in case of difficulty in renewing your ablution, (it is recommended that) you imitate the Mâlikî Madhhab as you start performing namâz. For, according to the Mâlikî Madhhab, the namâz of an invalid or aging Muslim will not become nullified. After having sat as long as the tashahhud, if your ablution breaks by itself, and if upon this you make an ablution at once and then make the salâm, which is wâjib, or, without making an ablution, if you yourself do something breaking the namâz, e.g. make the salâm, your namâz will remain unimpaired.

23 - If a person omits one rukn and does not perform it during the (same) namâz, his namâz becomes nullified.

24 - If a person begins and finishes a rukn before the imâm begins it, his namâz becomes nullified. But if the imâm begins the rukn later and they finish it at the same time, or if he withdraws before the imâm begins the rukn and then, when the imâm begins the rukn, makes the rukn again together with the imâm, his namâz will not become nullifed, yet it is makrûh. If a person begins a rukn after the imâm has finished it, his namâz will be acceptable.

25 - A person who misses the first rak'at of a namâz in jamâ'at is called a **masbûk**. If a masbûk, after having sat as long as (to say the prayer called) the tashahhud and before the imâm having

made the salâm, stands up and, after making the sajda of the rak'at he has missed, sees the imâm making sajda-i sahw and he, too, makes the sajda-i sahw with the imâm, his namâz will be nullified. Instead of resuming following the imâm (upon seeing the imâm making the sajda-i-sahw), he should have completed his namâz and the sajda-i-sahw on his own. If he stood up but did not make sajda, in that case it would be wâjib for him to sit back and make the sajda-i sahw with the imâm.

26 - If a person who forgot to make the sajda remembers it during the rukû', he prostrates himself outright from the position of rukû' and makes the sajda, instead, and (if he remembers it) during the (following) sajda, he makes the sajda (that he forgot) after sitting after the regular sajda (wherein he remembered about the forgotten sajda); then, (in both cases,) he reperforms the rukû' and the sajda that he performed. Then he makes the sajda-i sahw. Or, at the end of or during the final sitting he makes the sajda which he remembered or which he remembers during the final sitting, then he sits again and says the Tahiyyât, and then makes the sajda-i sahw. If he does not sit again, his namâz becomes nullified.

27 - If a person does not perform again the rukn that he performed sleeping, his namâz becomes nullified.

28 - If during the takbîrs in namâz a person prolongs the first **hamza**[1] (A) when saying "Allâhu," his namâz becomes nullified. If he prolongs it when beginning namâz, his beginning the namâz is not sahîh.

29 - If saying the âyats melodiously defiles the meaning, it defiles your namâz, too. To recite the Qur'an melodiously means to prolong its letters in order to tune them to musical notes. For example, it defiles the meaning to prolong the letter (a) as in "Alhamd-u-lillâhi râbbil." (The fourth 'a' in this example.) Likewise, saying "Râbbanâlakalhamd," (the first 'a' in this example,) as some muazzins do, defiles the meaning. For, **râb** (with a prolonged 'a') means stepfather; so instead of saying, "Praise and gratitude be to our Allah," they say, "Praise and gratitude be to our stepfather." If the meaning is not defiled namâz does not become nullified. But if you extend such vowels as Elif, Waw and Yâ too long, namâz becomes nullified, even if the meaning is not defiled. As is seen, if saying the words

---

[1] Elif, the first letter of the Arabic alphabet.

melodiously does not defile their meaning, if the letters are not prolonged by a length of two vowels, and if it is intended to beautify the voice and to embellish the recitation, it is permissible. In fact, it is mustahab to do so when performing namâz as well as when not performing namâz.

It is written in the fatwâ of Abussu'ûd Efendi[1] 'rahmatullâhi ta'âlâ 'alaih': "If the imâm's singing becomes **'amal-i kethîr**[2], or if he prolongs one letter as long as three vowels, his namâz becomes nullified. 'Teghannî' means to resonate your voice in your larynx so as to produce various sounds."

30 - An incorrect recitation nullifies namâz. The error may happen in four different ways. The first error involves i'râb, that is, it takes place in vowel points or signs of quiescence. For instance, when you don't double the letter with the **shadda**[3] or when you shorten the prolonged ones, and vice versa.

The second kind of error takes place in the letters themselves. For example, you change the place of a letter, add or deduct a letter, or move a letter forward or backward.

The third error involves confusion of words or sentences. And finally, the fourth error concerns the **waqf-wasl**[4]; that is, when you go on where you must pause or pause where you must go on. This fourth kind of error does not nullify namâz even if the meaning is changed.

If the first three kinds of errors change the meaning and produce a meaning that causes disbelief, namâz becomes nullified. On the other hand, when you change the place of a sentence, if you pause for a while, namâz does not become nullified. If some newly produced meaning does not cause disbelief but if it does not have a likeness in the Qur'ân al-kerîm, namâz becomes nullified. To say 'gubâr' instead of 'gurâb,' to

---

[1] The thirteenth Ottoman Shaikh-ul-Islâm.

[2] Kethîr means many. 'Amal means action, movement. 'Amal-i kethîr means more than one movements. Doing 'amal-i-kethîr in namâz nullifies namâz.

[3] Germination mark. When you see that mark above an Arabic consonant letter, you double the consonant.

[4] Waqf means pause. When reading or reciting the Qur'ân al-kerîm, you have to pause when you see certain symbols. These symbols are called Waqf. Wasl means to link the final consonant of an Arabic word to the first vowel of the word following it. Symbols indicating such linkage are called Wasl.

say 'Rabinâs' instead of 'Rabbinnâs,' to say 'zalelnâ' instead of 'zallelnâ,' to say 'emâratun' instead of 'emmâratun,' to add the word "wa kefera" by saying "amila sâlihan wa kefera fa lehum ejruhum," to say 'mesânîna' instead of 'mesânî', or, according to a dependable report, to say "essirâtellezîna" or "iyyâ kena'budu," [that is, to divide one word and add its final part to the following word], to forget "wa" when saying "wa mâ khalaqazzekera," nullifies namâz. If the word becomes meaningless and if it does not have a likeness in the Qur'ân al-kerîm, it nullifies namâz. For instance, to say 'serâil' instead of 'serâir,' to say 'laqnâ,' instead of 'khalaqnâ', to say 'alnâ' instead of 'ja'alnâ.' If the word has a likeness in the Qur'ân but if its meaning is different, namâz does not become nullified according to Imâm-i Abû Yûsuf's ijtihâd. But it becomes nullified according to the **Tarafain**, [i.e. Imâm-i a'zam and Imâm-i Muhammad.] The fatwâ agrees with the second ijtihâd. If the word has no likeness but if its meaning is not changed, they judged it the other way round. The fatwâ agrees with the Tarafain's. For example, when you say "ihdinelsirâta" or "Rabilâlemin" or "İyâka," or when you say "yâ mâlî" instead of "yâ mâlik," or when you say "ta'al" while saying "ta'âlâ jeddu Rabbinâ," namâz does not become nullified. [When you say "ahat" instead of "ahad" namâz becomes nullified. **(Bezzâziyya)**.]

Savants of the later generation said that errors in the i'râb would not nullify namâz. The first is a way of prudence, and the second is a way of latitude.

Pronouncing one letter like another letter, if the two letters are quite different, nullifies namâz. An example of this is to pronounce the letter "Ta" instead of the letter "Sât," as in "tâlihât" instead of "sâlihât." If there is a small difference between the letters and if the meaning is changed, "namâz becomes nullified if you did it intentionally," said most savants. But if it slipped out inadvertently, "namâz does not become nullified," they said. Examples of this are to pronounce the letter "Zı" instead of "Dat," "Sât" instead of "Sin," or "Tı" instead of "Te." Though the fatwâ says so, one must be cautious. So is the case with saying "zâllîn" instead of saying "dâllîn." [For more details see chapter 20, **Namâz in Jamâ'at**.]

When you add a word, if the meaning does not change and if the word added exists in the Qur'ân al-kerîm, namâz does not become nullified. An example of this is to say "wa bilwalideynî ihsânan wa berren." Namâz does not become nullified even if that word does not exist in the Qur'ân al-kerîm. An example is to say, "wa nahlun wa tuffâhun wa rum'mân." But Abû Yûsuf 'rahmatullâhi ta'âlâ 'alaih' said that adding a word that does not exist in the Qur'ân al-kerîm makes your namâz null and void.

When a word is forgotten, if the meaning is not deflected namâz does not become nullified. For instance, while saying "wa jazâu seyyiatin seyyiatun misluhâ," if you omit "seyyiatun" your namâz does not become nullified. If the meaning is deflected, namâz becomes nullified. For example, when saying "lâ yu'minûn," if you omit "lâ," it becomes nullified.

When you change a letter itself or its place, if the meaning is not changed and if the new word has a likeness in the Qur'ân al-kerîm, namâz does not become nullified. For instance, if you say "innelmuslimûna" instead of "innelmuslimîna," your namâz does not become nullified. If it does not have a likeness in the Qur'ân al-kerîm "namâz does not become nullified" according to the two imâms. For example, when you say "kayyâmîne" instead of "kawwâmîne," your namâz does not become nullified. If the meaning is deffected, "it becomes nullified," said the two imâms. Imâm-i Abû Yûsuf said that namâz would become nullified if the word had no likeness in the Qur'ân. According to that great scholar's (Abû Yusûf's) ijtihâd, your namâz becomes nullified if you say, for instance, "eshâbeshshaîr" instead of "es-hâbessa'îr"; and not if you say, for instance, "inferejet" instead, of "infejeret" or "eyyâb" instead of "awwâb".

When you repeat a word, namâz becomes nullified if the meaning is changed. Your namâz becomes nullified when you say, "Rabbi Rabbil'âlemîn, mâliki mâliki yawmiddîn." But if you do not know that the meaning is changed or if you let the word out inadvertently or if you repeat the word in order to pronounce a letter more correctly, your namâz does not become nullified.

If changing a word changes the meaning, too, namâz becomes nullified even if the new word has a likeness in the Qur'ân al-kerîm. It does not become nullified if the meaning is not changed.

The following is a poem written by Ahmad Ibni Kemâl Pâsha 'rahmatullâhi ta'âlâ 'alaih' on the **sejâwands** (marks of pause) in the Qur'ân al-kerîm.

>*Jim: Permissible to pass by it, and proper, too;*
>*Better stop when you see it, though.*

*Ze: You are free to stop, and so have they[1] done.
But they have deemed it better to read on.*

*Ta: It is an absolute sign of stop;
Wherever you see it be sure to stop!*

*Sat: "Stopping is permissible," they[1] have said;
So they have allowed you to take a breath.*

*Mim: Absolutely necessary to stop for it;
Fear of disbelief is in passing by it!*

*Lâ: "No pause!" is its meaning, everywhere;
Never stop! Nor breathe, anywhere!*

*Now perfect your reading with this recipe,
And gift its thawâb to Muslims before thee!*

[Letter "'ayn" means rukû'. It means that when conducting namâz in jamâ'at, Hadrat 'Umar Fârûq 'radiy-Allâhu 'anh' used to discontinue his standing position in namâz (when he came to the end of an âyat terminated with this mark, and he would presently bow for the rukû'. This sign, 'ayn, always comes at the end of âyats. If you stop at the place where the sign lâ is, you must resume reading (or reciting) by beginning with the last word of the part you have read (or recited). When you stop at the end of an âyat terminated with sign 'lâ', you do not have to repeat the previous final word. Please see the twenty-first chapter of the second fascicle of **Endless Bliss**!]

31 - If a person who has omitted fewer than five prayers of namâz remembers that he did not perform the previous prayer, his namâz becomes nullified. [For detailed information see the beginning of the twenty-third chapter!]

Whether outdoors or at any place within a big or small mosque, if a woman or a man or a dog passes close by or far in front of a person who is performing namâz, his namâz never becomes nullified. He who passes between the worshipper's feet and the place of sajda outdoors or in a big mosque, or between his feet and the wall of the qibla in a room or small mosque, becomes sinful. Any mosque between whose qibla wall and back wall is less than twenty metres is called a small mosque. If a person below the level of a bank or sofa where another person is

---

[1] The early savants, who knew how to read the Qur'ân al-kerîm correctly.

performing namâz passes before the worshipper, he becomes sinful if his head is above the worshipper's feet.

When performing namâz at places where others may pass before the worshipper, it is sunnat for the imâm or for the individual worshipper to erect a stick longer than half a meter before himself in line with his left eyebrow. If he cannot set the stick upright he may lay it on the ground towards the qibla or only draw a line. It is permissible to prevent a person from passing before you by making a gesture or by raising your voice; yet, it is better not to prevent them.

It is written in **Halabî-i-kebîr**: "Swallowing blood oozing out from between the teeth does not nullify namâz unless it equals (or exceeds) a mouthful." One's ablution is not broken even if one swallows mouthfully.

How to deal with situations when there are women among the jamâ'at is written in chapter 20. It is fard to perform again a fard namâz that was fâsid. It is wâjib to perform again any prayers in which tahrîmi makrûhs took place and also those sunnats and supererogatory prayers that have become fâsid. Please see the twenty-third chapter.

"So you have reached that age; what deeds have you done?
"Now you reproach yourself, for your life is gone?
"Fie upon you, after all that you have done!"
If Allah says so, how will you answer Him?

"I showed you two choices, and gave you wisdom;
"To pick one of choices, I gave you freedom.
"Behind your nafs, you ignored Islam's dictum!"
If Allah says so, how will you answer Him?

"Hot as well as cold kept you from ablution.
"To namâz you preferred mundane delusion.
"Lingering junub, you ignored ablution."
If Allah says so, how will you answer Him?

"Why didn't you make wudû and perform prayer?
"What kept you from begging and praying Creator?
"Making ghusl was binding summer and winter!"
If Allah says so, how will you answer Him?

18 – MAKRÛHS OF NAMÂZ

Most of the following information has been translated from **Durr-ul-mukhtâr,** and from its commentary entitled **Radd-ul-muhtâr.**

The makrûhs of namâz are of two kinds. When used alone, the word makrûh means **Tahrîmî makrûh**, which is a prohibition that has been determined by deduction (zann) from its dalîl (proof-text). Something for whose prohibition there is no proof-text or witness but which it is good not to do is called **Tanzîhî makrûh**. It is (Tahrîmî) makrûh not to do the wâjibs [and the muakkad sunnats] and (tanzîhî) makrûh not to do the [sunnats that are not muakkad] within namâz. Tanzîhî makrûh is closer to (being) halâl and Tahrîmî makrûh is closer to (being) harâm. Though the namâz performed in a (mediocre) manner termed makrûh is sahîh, it will not be accepted (maqbûl); that is, one will not receive the blessings promised. Please review the final part of the previous chapter. Below are the forty-five makrûhs of namâz:

1 - It is makrûh to drape your coat over your shoulders instead of properly wearing it. It is not makrûh to leave the front of your coat buttoned or unbuttoned.

2 - When prostrating for the sajda, it is makrûh to pull up your skirts or your trouser cuffs.

3 - It is makrûh to begin namâz with your skirts (or cuffs) or sleeves rolled up. If you made an ablution in a hurry in order to catch the imâm and as a result left them rolled up, you should unroll them slowly during namâz. Likewise, if a person's headgear falls off as he performs namâz, he had better put it back on his head. [Hence, it is makrûh to begin namâz with short sleeves that only go down to the elbows, with a flannel, or with short trousers that are just below the knees. It is wrong to say: "It is makrûh to perform namâz with a shirt with long sleeves that are rolled up, but it is not makrûh with a short sleeved shirt." Every fiqh book refers to: "pulled up cuffs and sleeves." For, cuffs are not rolled up. But they are lifted up so as to uncover the legs. The book **Ni'mat-i islâm** says concerning the eleventh of the makrûhs of namâz: "It is makrûh for a man to begin namâz with bare arms." Also, it is written on the two hundred and sixty-eighth page of the book **Ma'rifatnâma** that it is makrûh to perform namâz with bare arms.] Sleeves that are above the elbows are even worse. If a person rolls up his trouser-cuffs or sleeves during namâz, his namâz becomes nullified.

4 - Useless movements, such as playing with your clothes, are

makrûh. But useful movements do not bring harm upon your namâz, e.g. wiping the sweat off your forehead with your hand. When your trousers or loose robe stick on your skin, it is not makrûh to pull them away from your skin lest the shape of your awrat parts should be seen. It is makrûh to shake off dust. There is a hadîth prohibiting useless movements in namâz and laughing in a cemetery. It is not useless to scratch yourself during namâz, but raising your hand three times within one rukn nullifies your namâz.

5 - It is makruh to perform namâz clad in clothes that you wear at work or which you could not wear if you were to see your superiors. Yet it is not makrûh if you have no other clothes. [If you have enough money you should buy extra clothes.] It is not makrûh to perform namâz in pyjamas or any other clothing that you wear when going to bed.

6 - It is makrûh to have something in your mouth that will not prevent you from reciting the Qur'ân al-kerîm correctly. If it prevents you from pronouncing the Qur'ân al-kerîm correctly your namâz becomes nullified.

7 - To perform namâz bare-headed. If a person does not cover his head because he slights the importance of covering his head in namâz, it is makrûh. But if he ignores it because he means to slight namâz itself, he becomes a disbeliever. Kesel (indolence) means not to do something because you do not want to do it. But inability means not to do something because you cannot do it though you want to do it. If your headgear falls off your head, it is recommendable to put it back on your head with a single action. There is no harm in performing namâz bare-headed when it is intended to show your humbleness, yet you still had better cover your head. It is also makrûh to uncover your head seeking comfort and relief from heat. [You can cover your head with a headgear of any colour when performing namâz. Islamic books of Fiqh do not contain the statement that the black headgear is worn by Jews in synagogues. It is sunnat to wear a black headgear. Please see the twenty-seventh chapter of the third fascicle, and also the eighth chapter of the sixth fascicle, of **Endless Bliss**!]

[Rasûlullah and the Sahâba performed namâz with their blessed na'ls [pattens] on. Na'ls are shoes with leather soles. It is written in the book **Terghîb-us-salât**: "It has been said by savants that a person sitting in namâz barefooted, without socks on, should use his right hand to cover the sole of his foot. For, it is bad manners to show your soles to other Believers at any time. In namâz it is even more distasteful. According to some other savants, one must not cover one's bare foot with one's hand during namâz. For, it is sunnat to keep one's hands on one's thighs during the sitting posture in namâz. And the person sitting behind you, in turn, should look down at his own lap in adherence to the sunnat. When both individuals sit in accordance with the sunnat no bad manners will occur." As it can be seen, even according to those savants who say that one should not cover one's foot with one's hand when sitting, being barefooted is repugnant. According to those savants, since it is makrûh to take one's hands away from one's thighs while sitting, one should not commit a second makrûh in order to make up for the makrûh of being bare-footed. If the person behind you looks at his lap, you will become secure against annoying the person sitting behind you. As is written in **Halabî kabîr**, it is makrûh not to keep the hands in the position specified as sunnat when standing, in the rukû, in the sajdas, and when sitting. And it is for this reason that it is written: "It is makrûh to omit a wâjib or a sunnat. Therefore it is makrûh for men to cover their bare feet with their hand as they make the sajda," in the beginning of the makrûhs of namâz in the book **Marâq-il-falâh** and at the end of the makrûhs in **Halabî**. The book **Bahjat-ul-fatâwâ,** which corroborates its every fatwâ with proofs from books of fiqh, has been unable to provide any proof for this wrong fatwâ and has left the space for a proof blank. **Ibni 'Âbidîn** says at the end of the makrûhs of namâz: "It is better to perform namâz with na'ls or mests than doing so bare-footed. Observing this sunnat would also be a wordless expression of disagreement with a Jewish rite, for a hadîth-i sherîf declares: **'Perform namâz with na'ls on, lest you be like Jews.'** Rasûlullah and the Sahâba would perform namâz with na'ls which they wore outdoors. Their na'ls were clean, and the floor of Masjid-i Nebî was covered with sand. It was not for them to enter the Masjîd with dirty na'ls." When your shoes are smeared with najâsat, you must not enter a mosque with them on. You can observe the sunnat by wearing socks. And a person whose socks are najs or who does not have any socks to wear should perform namâz with a loose robe that hangs down to his heel-bones. Also, it is written in the books **Halabî**, **Berîqa**, and **Hadîqa** that there are numerous blessings in the namâz that is performed with covered feet.

It is not permissible to perform namâz with bare head and feet, to make the sajda on a higher place, or to force those who are under your command to perform namâz in this manner by saying, "Non-Muslims pray with bare head and feet in churches. As they do, we must pray in a civilized manner." It is makrûh to imitate disbelievers in manners of worship. And he who disapproves of the manners dictated by Islam becomes a disbeliever.]

8 - It is makrûh to begin namâz when you need to urinate, defecate, or when you need to break wind. If the need happens during namâz, you must break the namâz you are performing. Otherwise, you will become sinful. It is better to break the namâz even if it will cause you to miss the jamâ'at. Rather than performing namâz in a manner that is makrûh, it is better to miss the jamâ'at, which is sunnat. But it is not makrûh (not to break the namâz) lest the prayer time will expire or lest you will miss the namâz of janâza.

9 - It is makrûh for men to begin namâz with their hair tied in a knot on the back of their neck, wound round their head, or gathered on the top of their head and fastened with thread. If a man does so during namâz, his namâz becomes nullified. Namâz is performed bareheaded when you are in the ihrâm in Mekka[1].

10 - During namâz, it is makrûh to sweep stones or soil away from the place of sajda. If such things are giving you trouble making the sajda, it is permissible to get rid of them with one movement. The wiser choice, however, would be to clean them away before namâz.

11 - When joining a line of worshippers in order to perform namâz in a mosque, when beginning namâz, or during namâz, it is makrûh to crack your fingers by bending them or by inserting the fingers of both hands between each other. If it is necessary, it is not makrûh to crack your fingers before getting ready for namâz.

12 - It is makrûh to put your hand on your flank during namâz. Incidentally, inserting the fingers of both hands between each other is tahrîmî makrûh as you perform namâz, as you listen to a religious sermon or a mawlid, and as you sit in a mosque; and it is tanzîhî makrûh elsewhere.

13 - It is makrûh to turn your head (face) around and tanzîhî mekrûh to look around by turning your eyes. If you turn your chest away from the qibla, your namâz becomes nullified.

14 - In the tashahhuds (sitting and reciting certain prayers

---

[1] Please see the seventh chapter of the fifth fascicle of **Endless Bliss** for Hajj.

during namâz), to sit like a dog, that is, to sit on your buttocks with erected thighs while bringing your knees in touch with your chest and putting your hands on the floor, is makrûh.

15 - In the sajda it is makrûh for men to lay their forearms on the floor. But women must lay their forearms on the floor.

16 - It is makrûh to perform namâz toward a person's face. It is makrûh even if the person is far away from you. It is not makrûh if there is someone in between whose back is turned towards you.

17 - It is makrûh to acknowledge someone's greeting with your hand or head. It is not makrûh to answer someone's question with your hand or head. An example of this is, when someone asks you how many rak'ats you have performed, to answer using your fingers. But if you change your place or move to the line in front immediately upon someone's demand, your namâz becomes nullified. [See the eleventh of the mufsîds of namâz!]

18 - It is stated in **Terghîb-us-salât** that it is makrûh to yawn outside of namâz as well as during namâz. The lower lip must be squeezed between the teeth. If you cannot help it, you should cover your mouth with the outer part of your right hand when standing in namâz and with your left hand in the other rukns or when not performing namâz. Unnecessary yawning is caused by Satan. Prophets 'alaihimussalâm' did not yawn.

19 - It is tanzîhî makrûh to close your eyes during namâz. It is not makrûh if you do it lest your mind will be distracted.

20 - It is makrûh for the imâm to stand in the mihrâb. The hollowed out part in the wall of the qibla is called the mihrâb. When his feet are outside of the mihrâb, it is not makrûh for him to make the sajda in the mihrâb. A person is considered to be located in a place if their feet are within that place. This limitation is intended to keep (Muslims) clear of Christian rituals wherein priests conduct public worships by staying alone in an isolated room. In a mosque, it is makrûh for the imâm of the first jamâ'at not to conduct the namâz by standing on the mihrâb.

21 - It is tahzîhî makrûh for the imâm to begin namâz alone at a place half a metre higher than the floor where the jamâ'at are. This prohibition is intended to eliminate the possibility of an imâm resembling Christian priests.

22 - Also it is makrûh for an imâm to begin namâz alone at a lower place.

23 - It is makrûh to perform namâz in the back line while there

is room in the front line or to perform it alone in the back line because there is no room in the front line. When there is no room in the front line, you wait for a probable newcomer until the rukû' instead of performing it alone. If no one comes you make your way gently into the front line. If you cannot go into the front line you get someone you trust in the front line to move back to the rear line with you. If there is no one you can trust, then join the jamâ'at by standing alone.

24 - It is tahrîmî makrûh to perform namâz with clothes that have a picture or pictures of living things on them, [such as pictures of human beings or animals.] It is not makrûh if there are pictures of lifeless things on them. Whether for reverence or for execration, whether small or big, it is harâm to draw or paint pictures or make statues of living things. See the sixtieth and eighty-fifth letters in the book **Mekâtîb-i sherîfa**![1] Translation of the eighty-fifth letter exists in fifty-eighth chapter of the third fascicle of **Endless Bliss**.

[It is written in the section dealing with the afflictions incurred by hands in the book **Hadîqa**: "It is always makrûh to wear clothes with a picture of a living creature on them, even if you take them off when you are to perform namâz. It is permissible to carry pictures with you, provided they are encased." It is understood from this information as well as from the (Warning) on the two hundred and thirty-eighth page of the fifth volume of **Ibni 'Âbidîn** that it is permissible to have your picture taken for identity papers, documents, essential deeds, and other necessities provided you will keep them covered. A hadîth-i-sherîf on the twenty-sixth page of **Zawâjir** declares: **"When you find pictures tear them, destroy them!"** However, if it involves meddling with others' business, which in turn would cause fitna and hostility, we should refrain from doing so. None of the Prophets, the Sahâba, or the great men of Islam had a photograph. Pictures that are shown in newspapers and in motion pictures and which are meant to represent those blessed people, are all false. They are fashioned in order to earn money and to deceive Muslims. Along with the fact that it is harâm also to hang pictures of blessed people high on walls, it is hâram to put them at low places. Since it is harâm to draw pictures of living things anywhere, whether with bare awrat parts or with covered awrat parts, whether small or big, likewise,

---

[1] Written by Sayyid Abdullah Dahlawî 'rahmatullâhi ta'âlâ 'alaih', (1158 [1744 A.D.], Punjab – 1240 [1824], Delhi.)

the money received in return for them is also harâm. This prohibition has been intended to forestall idolatry. It is written in the Tahtâwî's annotation to the book **Imdât-ul-Fettâh** that when you are not performing namâz also, it is makrûh to wear clothes with pictures of living things on them.

Sayyid Abdulhakîm-i Arwâsî 'quddîsa sirruh' says in one of his letters: "It is permissible to use things such as handkerchiefs and coins that have pictures of living things drawn on them. For, such things are earthly, profane; they are not esteemed." This fact is written also in the third volume of **Al-fiqh-u-alal-Madhâhib-il-erba'â**. Hadrat Ibni Hajar-i Haytamî Mekkî 'rahmatullâhi 'alaih' says in his fatwâ:

"Existence of pictures of living things on such articles as handkerchiefs and coins is not harmful. For, it is not permissible to use pictures of living things on respected articles, yet it is permissible to use them on non-spiritual things." Then, it is permissible to have them on the floor, on things laid on the floor, on cushions, mats, handkerchiefs, bills, stamps, in closed places, such as pockets, bags, closets, on those parts of one's clothes that are below one's navel; yet it is harâm to keep them or to hang them above the navel. It is harâm to use pictures of women or pictures with exposed awrat parts even without lust at any place or to look at them lustfully.

It is written on the six hundred and thirty-third page of the second volume of **Hadîqa**: "It is tahrîmî makrûh to put or lay on the floor any piece of paper or cloth or prayer rug that has some writing or even one letter on it. For, it is insulting to use them for any purpose whatsoever or to lay them on the floor. And it is disbelief to lay them on the floor or to use them for the sheer purpose of insulting them. It has been said that it is permissible to write them on walls or to hang framed pieces of writing on walls." Hence, it is not permissible to lay prayer rugs with pieces of writing or pictures of the Ka'ba or mosques on them on the floor in order to pray on them. However, it is permissible to hang them on walls for decoration.

As is seen, Islam has prohibited pictures and statues of human beings that serve as instruments to ridicule human beings, which are used for worshipping living things, and which drift youngsters towards fornication and cause seduction of married people. However, Islam permits pictures of the anatomical parts of living things, of plants, and all kinds of pictures as practical aids in physics, chemistry, astronomy and engineering. It has commanded drawing and utilization of pictures that are necessary for knowledge and science. Islam, as always, has classified pictures into two groups: useful and harmful, and has commanded use of the useful ones while prohibiting the harmful ones. Then, it is a blind claim and a slander for the enemies of the religion to say, "Muslims say that pictures are prohibited; this is retrogression."]

25 - If a picture of a living thing is drawn on the wall or on pieces of cloth or paper hanging or put on a wall just above the head, in front, or immediately to the right or left of a person who is performing namâz, it is makrûh. Even if not in a living form, a picture of the cross is like the picture of a living thing. For it means to imitate Christians. It is makrûh to imitate their evil practices, even if not in order to be like them, or to imitate their unharmful habits with the intention of resembling them. [In fact, it is written in the books **Terghîb-us-salât** and **Nisâb-ul-ahbâr**, (the latter by Muhammad 'Ushî,) that it is makrûh to perform namâz at such places as well as places where people are consuming alcohol, gambling or playing musical instruments, and invocations offered at these places will not be accepted. Apparatuses through which musical instruments are heard and pictures that are harâm to look at are watched, are like musical instruments.] If the picture of a living or lifeless thing is on something upon which a person is standing, sitting or leaning, his namâz does not become makrûh. If the picture is on the walls behind the person performing namâz or on the (part of the) ceiling (remaining behind the location overhead the worshipper), it is **khafîf** (light) makrûh.

It is not makrûh to perform namâz on prayer rugs or mats possessing pictures of living things on the parts other than where prostration is made, since laying them on the floor means belittling them **(Durer)**. [Hence, it is not permissible to lay the carpets with pictures of the Kâ'ba, mosques or pieces of holy writing on the ground, or to use them, or other things containing pictures or embroideries liable to cause mental distraction, as prayer rugs.]

If the picture is under the foot of the person performing namâz, on the place where he is sitting, on his body or in his hand, it is makrûh. [Hence, pictures in one's pocket do not make one's namâz makrûh.] For, the place where one stands or sits is like the clothes one is wearing. A picture hanging on one's wrist is makrûh. For it prevents one from placing one's hands as prescribed by the sunnat.

If the picture on a coin or ring or elsewhere is small, that is, if when it is put on the floor, a person standing cannot make out its limbs, namâz does not become makrûh. When covered, it is not makrûh even if it is big. If the head of the living thing (in the picture) has been cut off, or if its face, chest or belly has been erased or covered with something, namâz does not become makrûh.

With pictures of lifeless things, such as trees and sceneries, no matter where they are, namâz does not become makrûh. For, small or headless pictures or pictures of lifeless things have never been worshipped. There were people who worshipped the sun, the moon, the stars, green trees, but they worshipped those things themselves. They did not worship their pictures. It is also makrûh to perform namâz towards these things.

Angels of compassion do not enter a house where there is a big picture of a living thing placed at a respected place, a dog, or a person who is junub. But the angles of **Haphaza** leave a person only during sexual intercourse and when he goes into the restroom. The two angels called **Kirâman kâtibîn**, who are on a person's shoulders and who write down his good and bad deeds, and those angels who protect a person against genies are called **Angels of Haphaza**. Allâhu ta'âlâ informs the angels of what a person does in the restroom, and the angels write down his actions when he comes out of the restroom. The angels do not write on anything or in letters. As we gather information in our mind and memory, likewise they keep a record of a person's actions at some place. Today there are various ways of writing, such as the recording of voices on an apparatus that we call a tape recorder, on sound films, (or on CDs.) In the heavens there are angels writing with pens (tools) that are unknown to us. As for disbelievers, only their evil deeds are recorded. There are genies around everyone who try to harm them while angels protect them against those genies.

It is permissible according to Imâm-i Abû Yûsuf to buy dolls for children to play with.

26 - It is tanzîhî makrûh to count âyats, or tasbîhs with the hand during namâz. It is permissible to count them through the heart or by moving the fingers. Outside of namâz it is permissible to count them with fingers or to use beads. Once Rasûlullah 'sall-Allâhu 'alaihi wa sallam' saw a woman counting the tasbîhs with seeds and did not forbid her. It is makrûh to use beads for ostentation.

It does not nullify namâz, nor is it makrûh, to kill a snake or a scorpion that is slithering or crawling towards you and may sting you. It is mustahab to kill it with your left shoe. A white snake that crawls straight without twisting is a genie. You must not kill him if he does not harm you. But it is permissible to kill him, too. For genies promised Rasûlullah 'sall-Allâhu 'alaihi wa sallam' that they would not enter Muslims' homes. Entering a home, they will have gone back on their word. First you should warn him by saying **"Irji' bi-idhnillâh."** Then, if he will not go away, you should kill him. But you cannot warn him if you are performing namâz. Not killing a genie disguised as a snake immediately is not intended to respect them but, to prevent their harm.

27 - It is not makrûh to perform namâz against the backs of sitting or standing people, even if they are talking. It is makrûh to perform it against a person's face or against the backs of people who are talking loudly.

28 - It is not makrûh to perform namâz against the Qur'ân al-kerîm, a sword, a candle, a candle-lamp, any lamp, flames, against instruments of war such as pistols, or against a person who is lying asleep. For, none of these creatures has ever been worshipped. Magians worship fire, not flames. However, it is makrûh to perform it against a fire, also when it has flames.

29 - It is tahrîmî makrûh to perform namâz by wrapping yourself in a towel from head to foot.

30 - It is tahrîmî makrûh to perform namâz with the top of your head bare by winding a turban round your head.

31 - It is tahrîmî makrûh to perform namâz by covering your mouth and nose. Magians worship in that manner. [You must not perform namâz with a mask, gloves, or spectacles that prevent your forehead from touching the floor. Unless there is a darûrat you must not perform namâz with anything that prevents your forehead, nose or hands from touching the floor, that is, from doing any fard or sunnat. There is no necessity for wearing such things during namâz, even for women.]

32 - It is makrûh to cough up phlegm from the throat without a strong necessity. If blood formed in your mouth is not a mouthful, neither its formation nor swallowing it nullifies your ablution or namâz. So is the case with vomitting. [**Halabî-i kebîr** and **Fatâwâ-i-Hindiyya**.]

33 - **'Amal-i qalîl**, that is, moving one hand once or twice, is makrûh. [See the fifteenth of things that nullify namâz!] It is permissible to kill a louse or flea with amal-i qalîl, but it is makrûh

to catch or kill it if it is not biting you. It is harâm to leave such insects in the mosque, alive and dead ones alike.

34 - It is makrûh to omit one of the sunnats of namâz.

There are two groups of sunnat. The first group is **Sunan-i hudâ**. They are the **muakkad** [emphasized] **sunnats**. The second group is **Sunan-i zawâid**. They are the sunnats that are not muakkad. The mustahabs and the mandûbs are in this (second) category, according to an authentic scholarly report.

It is tahrîmî makrûh to omit a muakkad sunnat in namâz. It is tanzîhî makrûh to omit a sunnat that is not muakkad. It is not makrûh but khilâf-i awlâ to omit a mustahab. That is, it is a blessing to do the mustahabs, and it is not sinful not to do them; only, in that case you will be deprived of their blessings.

35 - Without a darûrat, it is makrûh to begin namâz with your child in your arms. It is not makrûh if there is a darûrat to do so, provided the child's clothes are clean.

36 - Unless there is a darûrat it is makrûh to perform namâz against things that distract your heart and prevent your khushû', such as ornamented things, plays, musical instruments, or any food that you desire. It is makrûh to leave your shoes behind you when you are to perform namâz. This last makrûh is written on the one hundred and eighty-sixth page, within the subject of Hajj, in the book **Durr-ul-mukhtâr**, at the end of **Halabî-yi kebîr**, and in **Bezzâziyya**. It is also written in detail within the subject of suspicion in tahârat, at the end of each of the books **Berîqa** and **Hadîqa**.

37 - It is makrûh to lean on a wall or mast when performing the fard namâz if there is not a darûrat to do so. It is not makrûh to do so while performing the supererogatory namâz.

38 - It is makrûh to raise your hands up to your ears when bowing for the rukû' or when straightening up from the rukû'.

39 - It is makrûh to complete the qirâat after bowing for the rukû'.

40 - When making the sajdas and the rukû', it is makrûh to put your head down or to raise your head before the imâm does so.

41 - It is makrûh to perform namâz at places that are likely to be najs, such as in a cemetery, in a public bath or church; but it is not makrûh to perform it after cleaning or washing such places, or in the dressing room of a bath or in a mosque within the cemetery. In case you cannot perform namâz at another place because of cold weather or for some other reason, or if you cannot find

another place, it is permissible to perform it in a church individually or in jamâ'at. But you must leave the place immediately after namâz. For, a church is a place where devils meet together. If you purge a church of the symbols of disbelief, it will never be makrûh to perform namâz there. It is makrûh to perform it against najâsat that is not covered.

42 - It is makrûh to perform it against a grave. Wahhabis say that it is **shirk** (to attribute a partner to Allâhu ta'âlâ).

[It is written on the six hundred and thirtieth page of the second volume of **Hadîqa**: "A hadîth-i-sherîf declares: **'Curse be upon those who perform namâz on a grave!'** To perform namâz on a grave is to imitate a Jew. Therefore it has been said to be makruh. It is written in the books **Khâniyya**[1] and **Hâwî**[2] that it is not makrûh to perform it at those parts of a cemetery where there are no graves. If the grave is behind the worshipper, or in front of him but so far that it would be permissible for someone else to pass before him within such a distance, it is not makrûh, either. Also, to turn the graves of Prophets or pious Muslims into mosques is to imitate Jews. Because it is like attributing a partner to Allâhu ta'âlâ while worshipping, our Prophet prohibited it and entreated: **'Yâ Rabbî** (O my Rabb, Allâhu ta'âlâ)! **Do not make my grave an idol that is worshipped!'** But if a mosque is built at a place close to a (dead) pious Muslim or if you perform namâz at a place close to his grave thinking that you will attain Allah's compassion through him or that your worship will be useful to him also, and if you do not think of worshipping him or performing namâz towards him, it is not harmful at all. For, Hadrat Ismâîl's ''alaihissalâm' grave is in a place called **Hâtîm**, which is close to Ka'ba. Because the most valuable namâz performed in Mesjîd-i harâm is the one performed at that place, hajjis vie to perform namâz there. It is written in the explanation of **Masâbih** that this is so. It is written on the two hundred and sixty-eighth page of **Ma'rifatnâma**: 'It is makrûh to perform namâz against a grave that is not curtained.' It is written on the three hundred and twentieth page of the fifth chapter of **Fatâwâ-i Hindiyya:** "It is not

---

[1] **Fatâwâ-i-Khâniyya**, or **Majmu'â-i-Khâniyya**, by Qâdî Khân Hasan bin Mansûr Ferghânî 'rahmatullâh ta'âlâ 'alaih', (d. 592 [1196 A.D.].). It was printed on the margins of the book **Fatâwâ-i-Hindiyya** in Egypt in 1310 A.H., and was reproduced by way of offset in 1393 [1973 A.D.].

[2] Written by 'Alî bin Muhammad Wâwerdî 'rahmatullâhî ta'âlâ 'alaih', (364 [974 A.D.], Basra – 450 [1058], Baghdâd.)

makrûh if there is a curtain between the qibla of the mosque and the grave or if the grave is on one side or behind you."

It is written in **Fatâwâ-i Fayziyya**[1]: "There are three kinds of pious foundations: those that are only for the poor; those that are primarily for the rich and next for the poor; and those that are both for the rich and for the poor. Schools, inns, hospitals, cemeteries, mosques and fountains have been established both for the rich and for the poor." The prohibition against making tombs in those cemeteries established by pious foundations is intended so as not to occupy the places belonging to the poor. Therefore, it cannot be said that such prohibitions are enforced because they are harâm.]

43 - It is tanzîhî makrûh not to sit in accordance with the sunnat in the **tashahhuds** (sitting postures). But it is not makrûh if you have an excuse.

44 - It is tanzîhî makrûh to recite in the second rak'at the same âyat you have recited in the first rak'at. It is tahrîmî makrûh to recite an âyat previous to it. These errors are not makrûh if they are done as a result of forgetfulness. It is makrûh in the second rak'at to say three âyats longer than what was said in the first rak'at. [See fourteenth chapter!].

45 - It is makrûh not to stand up for the final sunnat immediately after the fard **[Terghîb-us-salât]**.

THE FOLLOWING ARE REASONS FOR WHICH IT IS PERMISSIBLE TO BREAK NAMÂZ:

1 - In order to kill a snake;

2 - In order to catch an a runaway animal;

3 - In order to rescue a flock from wolves;

4 - In order to take food that is boiling over away from the fire;

5 - In order to protect your or someone else's property that is worth no less than one dirham of silver from destruction; [See the expression **dirham-i shar'î** in the first chapter of the fifth fascicle.]

6 - In order to urinate or to break wind;

7 - When there is no fear that the prayer time may expire or that you may be late for the jamâ'at, in order to rid yourself of something that mullifies namâz according to another Madhhab, e.g. to clean the najâsat that is less than one dirham or to make an

---

[1] Written by Fayzullah Efendi 'rahmatullâhi ta'âlâ 'alaih', (martyred in Edirne in 1115 [1703 A.D.],) forty-sixth Ottoman Shaikh-ul-Islâm.

ablution when you remember that you have touched a woman who is a nâmahram, you can break your namâz.

THERE ARE TWO REASONS THAT MAKE IT FARD (NECESSARY) TO BREAK ANY NAMÂZ:

1 - Namâz must be broken in order to save a person who screams for help, to save a blind person who is about to fall down into a well, to save a person who is about to burn or drown, or to put out a fire.

2 - When your mother, father, grandmother or grandfather calls you, it is not wâjib for you to break a fard namâz, but it is permissible; yet, you must not break it if it is not necessary. But supererogatory namâz [even the sunnats] must be broken. If they call for help, it is necessary to break the fard namâz, too. If they call you although they know that you are performing namâz, you may not break even the supererogatory namâz. But if they call you and do not know that you are performing namâz, you have to break it.

THERE ARE FIVE THINGS THAT ARE MAKRÛH TO DO WHEN NOT PERFORMING NAMÂZ:

1 - It is tahrîmî makrûh to turn your front or back towards the qibla when emptying the bowels or urinating in a restroom or elsewhere. It is not makrûh if you forget or if there is the danger that you may dirty your clothes or if there is some other danger.

2 - It is tanzîhî makrûh to turn your front or back towards the qibla when cleaning yourself after relieving nature, or to urinate or empty the bowels towards the sun or the moon.

3 - To make a small child relieve itself by holding it towards one of these directions is makrûh for the adult who holds it. Likewise, to have a small child do something that is harâm for adults is harâm for the adult who has the child do it. For example, a person who makes a boy wear silk clothes or ornaments it with jewels or makes it drink alcohol commits a harâm by doing so.

4 - It is tahrîmî makrûh to stretch your legs or only one leg towards the qibla without a good excuse. Yet it is not makrûh to do so with an excuse ('udhr) or by mistake.

5 - Also it is makrûh to stretch your legs toward a Qur'ân or other Islamic books. It is not makrûh if they are on a higher level. [It is written in the fifth chapter of **Hindiyya**: "It is permissible and even advisable to keep the Qur'ân in your house only for blessings and abundance without ever reading it. It is makrûh to

write in Arabic letters a disbeliever's name and insult it, for Islamic letters have to be respected."]

It is written on the thirteen hundred and sixty-eighth page of the book **Berîqa**: "It is written in the book **Tâtârhâniyya**[1] that an old and torn copy of the Qur'ân that cannot be used must not be burned, but it can be wrapped in a clean piece of cloth and buried, or it can be put in a clean place that never becomes dusty. The book **Fatâwâ-i-Sirâjiyya**[2] says that it can be buried or burned. The same is written also in the book **Munyatul-muftî**[3]. The book **Mujtabâ**[4] says that burying it is better than leaving it in flowing water. And the book **Minhâj-ud-dîn**, written by Huseyn Jurjânî, a Shafi'î scholar, says that it is not forbidden to burn it; when Hadrat 'Uthmân 'radiy-Allâhu 'anh' burned the copy of the Qur'ân that contained mansûkh[5] âyats none of the Sahâba 'radiy-Allâhu ta'âlâ 'alaihim ajma'în' expressed their disapproval of it. Burning it is better than removing the writing by washing it. For, the water used in washing it will be trodden on sometime later, according to savants. Qâdî Huseyn said that it was harâm to burn it because it would be sacrilege. And Nawawî said that it would be makrûh. As we infer from all of these, it is better to remove the writing by washing it or to bury it than to burn it. Translation from **Berîqa** has come to an end. As is understood from all of these citations, it is insulting and harâm to leave old copies of the Qur'ân al-kerîm that cannot be used any more in places where they will be trampled underfoot, to wrap or cover things with them or to use them in making paper bags or other things of this sort. It is necessary to bury them in places where they will not be dug up until they rot and turn back into earth or, if this is impossible, to burn them and bury the ashes or throw them in the sea or river. In order to save them from being disrespected, it is permissible and even necessary to burn them. This is understood also from **Fatâwâ-i-Sirâjiyya**, from **Minyatul-muftî**, and from **Hâlimî**.

---

[1] That book, also known with the title Zâd-ul-musâfir, was written by 'Âlim bin 'Alâ 'rahmatullâhi ta'âlâ 'alaih', (d. 688 [1289 A.D.].)

[2] Written by 'Alî 'Ûshî bin 'Uthman 'rahmatullâhi ta'âlâ 'alaih', (d. 575 [1180 A.D.])

[3] Written by Yûsuf bin Ahmad Sijstânî 'rahmatullâhi ta'âlâ 'alaih', (638 [1240 A.D.], Sivas.)

[4] Written by Mukhtâr bin Mahmûd Zâhidî 'rahmatullâhi ta'âlâ 'alaih', (d. 658 [1259 A.D.].)

[5] Âyat means verse of the Qur'ân. Some âyats were changed by other âyats that were revealed later. Such changed âyats are called **Mansûkh**. Those âyats that changed them are called **Nâsikh**.

19 – THE NAMÂZ OF TARÂWÎH and REVERENCE DUE TO MOSQUES

THE NAMÂZ OF TARÂWÎH – It is written in the commentary of the book **Nûr-ul-izâh**[1] and also in its annotation: "It is sunnat-i muakkada for men and women to perform the tarâwîh, which consists of twenty rak'ats. A person who denies this is a heretic and his testimony is not to be accepted. Rasûlullah 'sall-Allâhu 'alaihi wa sallam' performed eight rak'ats of the tarâwîh in jamâ'at for several nights. [Thereafter he would go home and complete the set of twenty rak'ats.] According to another report, when alone he performed twenty rak'ats of tarâwîh. [It consists of twenty rak'ats in all four Madhhabs.] Hence, it was understood that it is a sunnat. The three Khalîfas and all the Sahâba of that time performed twenty rak'ats of the tarâwîh in jamâ'at. And a hadîth commands us to adapt ourselves to those Khalîfas and to the ijmâ' (unanimity) of the Sahâba."

The tarâwîh is performed after the final sunnat of night prayer and before the witr. [A person cannot perform the tarâwîh before performing the night prayer. (**Ibni Âbidîn,** p. 295) It can be performed after the witr. It can be performed any time until morning prayer. It cannot be performed after dawn. It cannot be performed as a qadâ prayer, either. (That is, it cannot be performed later at some other time.) For, the tarâwîh is an emphasized sunnat, but not as strongly as the final sunnats of the evening and night prayers. And those sunnats, despite their value, are not performed as qadâ. Qadâ is necessary only for those prayers of namâz that are fard and for the witr. The tarâwih is performed as a qadâ prayer in the Shâfi'î Madhhab. It is sunnat-i kifâya to perform the tarâwîh in jamâ'at. That is, when it is performed in jamâ'at in a mosque, others may perform it alone in their homes, which is not sinful. Yet in that case they will be deprived of the blessings of jamâ'at in the mosque.] If they perform it in jamâ'at with one or more people in their homes, they will earn twenty-seven times the blessings they would attain if they performed it individually. To perform tarâwîh, they stand up for the following rak'at after making the salâm at the end of

---

[1] This book, and also its commentary entitled **Imdâd-ul-Fettâh**, or **Merâq-il-felâh**, were written by the scholar of Fiqh in the Hanafî Madhhab Abul-Ikhlâs Hasan bin Ammar Shernblâlî 'rahmatullâhi ta'âlâ 'alaih', (994-1069 [1658 A.D.], Egypt.) Ahmad bin Muhammad Ismâ'îl Tahtâwî 'rahmatullâhi ta'âlâ 'alaih', (d. 1231 [1815 A.D.],) wrote an annotation to the commentary **Imdâd-ul-Fettâh**.

every two rak'ats. Or they can make the salâm at the end of every four rak'ats. They sit for a period equaling the time it takes to perform four rak'ats between every four rak'ats and they should recite the salawât or the tasbîhât or the Qur'ân-al kerîm. They might as well sit silently. It is better to make the salâm after every two rak'ats and to make the niyyat (intention) before each takbîr of iftitâh (beginning). People who did not perform the night prayer in jamâ'at cannot come together and perform the tarâwîh in jamâ'at. For, the jamâ'at performing the tarâwîh have to be the same jamâ'at that performed the fard. A person who did not perform the night prayer in jamâ'at can perform the fard alone and then join the jamâ'at who are performing the tarâwîh. [See the twenty-third chapter.]

The prayer to be said before standing up to begin the namâz of tarâwih:

Subhâna zi-l-mulki wa-l-melekût. Subhâna zi-l-'izzeti wa-l-'azameti wa-l-jelâli wa-l-jemâli wa-l-jeberût. Subhâna-l-meliki-l-mevjûd. Subhâna-l-meliki-l-ma'bûd. Subhâna-l-meliki-l-hayyillezî lâ yenâmu wa lâ yemût. Subbûhun quddûsun Rabbunâ wa Rabb-ul-melâiketi wa-r-rûh. Merhaben, merhaben, merhabâ yâ shehr-a-Ramadân. Merhaben, merhaben, merhabâ yâ shehr-al-bereket-i-wa-l-ghufrân. Merhaben, merhaben, merhabâ yâ shehr-et-tesbîhi wa-t-tehlîli wa-dh-dhikri wa tilâwa-t-il-Qur'ân. Awwaluhû, âkhiruhû, zâhiruhû, bâtinuhû yâ men lâ ilâha illâ huw.

The prayer to be said at the end of the namâz of tarâwih:

Allâhumma salli 'alâ sayyidinâ Muhammadin wa 'alâ Âl-i-sayyidinâ Muhammad. Bi'aded-i-kull-i-dâin wa dewâin wa bârik wa sellim 'alaihi wa 'alaihim kethîrâ. This prayer is recited three times. At the third time the following prayer is added: **"wa salli wa sellim wa bârik 'alaihi wa 'alaihim kethîran kethîrâ." Yâ Hannân, yâ Mennân, yâ Deyyân, yâ Burhân. Yâ Zel-fadli wa-l-ihsân nerjul-afwa wa-l-ghufrân. Wa-j-'alnâ min utekâ shehr-i-Ramadân bi hurmet-il-Qur'ân.**

THERE ARE TWENTY-TWO THINGS THAT ARE NOT PERMISSIBLE TO DO IN A MOSQUE:

Places where people come together in order to worship are called **temples** or **places of worship**. Jewish temples are called **Synagogues** or **Hawras**. Christian temples are called **Churches** or **Bî'as** or **Sawme'as**. Muslim temples are called **Masjîds** or **Jâmî's**. In temples methods of worship and religious commandments and prohibitions are taught. People who are responsible for making speeches in today's temples dwell upon two things:

1 - Through bright, squinned sermons, tragic stories, melodious, touching recitals enhanced with musical instruments and loud-speakers, today's preachers try to stir the audience to a level of enthusiasm and compassion and to conquer their hearts so that they will give themselves up and be driven towards a certain purpose.

2 - To teach the commandments and the prohibitions of the religion, and to get people to obey them.

Today in Christian churches and Jewish synagogues only the first aim is being accomplished, which results in the unity of egos and thoughts, rather than in the unity of hearts and souls. And in the name of religious obligations, tenets that were put forward by ancient men of religion are being taught, but these things vary with time and place. Consequently, churches and synagogues are no longer temples but places for politics and conferences, where people are benumbed and dragged behind the desires and thoughts of leaders and chiefs.

Mosques also have many a time and aft been sullied by impostors who infiltrate religious institutions and speak for political and financial purposes. They are religiously ignorant people **(yobaz)** who have not read books written by Islamic scholars, but have been deceived by false books written by lâ-Madhhabî and heretical people. They are poor people who, let alone teaching religious tenets and having them practised, have not even learned them for themselves. These ignorant and schismatic people do not even know how to make an ablution or ghusl properly or how to perform namâz suitably with its conditions; they have misled Muslims and harmed Islam and people in every century. They are mere orators and lecturers, who, wearing long loose gowns and big turbans, impress the audience under a rootless and transient influence by reciting melodiously, pronouncing falsely adorned words, and telling exciting stories on minbars and preaching pulpits. Like speakers for political parties, dictatorial and fascist administrators and churches, they have deceived pious people by dosing them with ephemeral enthusiasm. Islamic scholars have referred to them not as men of religion but as thieves of faith and îmân, **yobazes**. Those true men of religion, who have always preached from the books of Islamic scholars and whose words, manners and deeds have always been in conformity with those books, have protected Islam against their harms.

Abussu'ûd Efendi 'rahmatullâhi ta'âlâ 'alaih' says in his fatwâ: "If there is not a mosque in a village or district and if the inhabitants do not perform namâz in jamâ'at, the government has to force them to make a mosque, and chastise those who neglect the jamâ'at. In the year 940 (Hijrî) [1533 A.D.] an edict (firman) commanding this course of action was sent to every province by the Khalîfa." It is written in **Majmû'at-i jadîda**[1]: "If an old mosque cannot contain the entire jama'at, it is permissible for the people living in that quarter to demolish it and build a larger one at their own expense."

It is written on the six hundred and thirteenth page of **Halabî-i kebîr**: "Performing namâz in a local masjîd is better than performing it in larger mosques, even if the people making the jamâ'at are fewer than that in larger ones. It is better for someone who is late for the jamâ'at in his local majsîd to go to another mosque in order to perform the time's prayer with the jamâ'at therein. If it is not possible for him to join another jamâ'at in another mosque, it will be better for him to prefer his own local masjîd and perform the prayer individually. If there is not an imâm or a muazzin (to conduct the namâz in jamâ'at) in a local mosque, one of the Muslims in the jamâ'at must assume this task. They should not go to another mosque. If the imâm of your local masjîd performs the night prayer too early, i.e. during the time when the redness in the sky where the sun has set has disappeared, instead of waiting for the whiteness also to disappear, it will be better for you not to perform namâz with that imâm in jamâ'at, but to perform it alone when the whiteness has disappeared as well. [Nowadays, the azâns for night prayers are being called rather early in big cities. Thus, the ijtihâd of Imâm-i a'zam is not being followed. Yet, because they are called in compliance with the qawl of the Imâmeyn, it is better to join these jamâ'ats.] If the imâm of your local masjid is notorious for fisq, that is, if he is known to commit any one of the grave sins, [for instance, if he does not perform the azân in conformity with the Sharî'at], it will be better for you to go to another mosque to perform the prayer in jamâ'at. For, abstaining from something that is makrûh is given priority when compared with doing

---

[1] Written by Hasan Khayrullah Efendi 'rahmatullâhi ta'âlâ 'alaih', (d. 1316). Please review the final part of fourth chapter.

something that is sunnat.

Ibni 'Âbidîn states:

1 - It is makrûh to lock the doors of a mosque. It is not makrûh if there is a danger of burglars.

2 - Sexual intercourse on a mosque is tahrîmî makrûh. Also it is makrûh to step on the Ka'ba or on a mosque. It is harâm for a person who is junub to mount the mosque.

3 - It is tahrîmî makrûh to relieve nature on a mosque. [It is written in **Terghîb-us-salât** that it is makrûh to build a toilet under a mosque or in front of the Mihrâb wall]. For, the area over the mosque is a mosque all the way up to heaven. So is the area below the mosque. However, it is permissible to make a shadirvan or a public bath under a mosque.

4 - It is permissible to walk through a mosque sometimes. But it is makrûh to make it your regular route. It is not makrûh if there is a good reason to do so. At your first passing daily you should perform the namâz of **Tahiyyatulmasjîd**. You do not have to perform it during your subsequent passings. Hamawî states in his (book **Uyûn-ul-besâir**, which is a) commentary to the book **Eshbâh**: "It is a unanimously-reported sunnat that anybody entering a mosque should perform two rak'ats of **Tahiyyat-ul-masjîd**. Sometimes the word mustahab means sunnat. If the Qur'ân-i kerîm is being recited aloud in the mosque, then the tahiyyat-ul-masjîd must not be performed because it is fard to listen to the Qur'ân al-kerîm being read or recited aloud. It is **awlâ** (better) to omit a sunnat even for (the sake of doing) a fard-i kifâya. Reading the Qur'ân al-kerîm melodiously and, in turn, listening to it, are harâm. [Hence, it is necessary to perform the sunnats of the four daily prayers of namâz with the intention of qadâ.] It is stated in **Qâdî-Khân**: "If the imâm recites melodiously, it is recommendable to go to another mosque. If he is a fornicator or a usurer, [or if it is known that he commits another harâm or allows his wife or daughters to go out without covering themselves properly as prescribed by Islam,] it becomes a must to go to another mosque." A person who makes it a habit to walk through a mosque without a good excuse becomes a fâsiq. How one should step in and out of a mosque is written at the beginning of chapter 20.

5 - It is makrûh to bring najasât into a mosque. A person who has najâsat on his person cannot enter a mosque. It is permissible to burn a lamp with najs oil. It is written in **Fatâwâ-i fiqhiyya**: "A person who sees najâsat in a mosque has to clean it immediately.

It is sinful to delay the cleaning without an excuse. A person who sees najâsat on another person who is performing namâz or on the place where he is making the sajda should let him know. Letting him know it or waking up a person who is about to miss namâz (because he is sleeping) is not wâjib, but it is sunnat."

6 - It is makrûh to plaster a mosque with mortar or mud made with najs water. It is not makrûh to plaster it with mud mixed with the dung of a cow. This is because there is a darûrat in doing so **(Hindiyya)**. Please see chapter 6.

7 - It is makrûh to relieve one's nature in a container in a mosque. The same applies for cupping. It is not makrûh to break wind inadvertently.

8 - It is harâm to let mad people or small children who will bring najâsat into a mosque enter the mosque. It is makrûh if there is no danger of najâsat.

9 - It is tahrîmî makrûh to set up markets, to talk loudly, to make speeches, to quarrel, to take up arms, and to punish others in a mosque. [It is harâm to say the khutbas of Friday and 'Iyd prayers as though one is making a speech.]

10 - It is makrûh to enter a mosque with na'ls, i.e. shoes worn outdoors. It is much better for men to perform namâz with clean mests or na'ls than to perform it with their bare feet. This preference sustains a disapproval against imitating Jews. Please see the fifty-fourth chapter of the third fascicle of **Endless Bliss**. [Na'ls or na'layn are shoes with leather soles and straps. It is makrûh to walk around wearing na'layn with wooden soles.]

It is not makrûh to relieve one's nature or to have sexual intercourse on a house where one room has been made a masjîd or on a room containing a copy of the Qur'ân al-kerîm. So is the case with those places where namâz of 'Iyd or namâz of janâza is performed; yet the jamâ'at in the mosque can follow the imâm (who is conducting the namâz) at one of those places. A menstruating woman or a person who is junub can enter such places as well as mosque-yards, madrasas and tekkes.

11 - It is permissible to decorate the walls of a mosque, except the wall of the qibla. However, it is better to spend the money for the poor. It is makrûh to decorate the wall of the qibla with valuable things or with colours. Also, excessive decoration of the side walls is makrûh.

The book **Durr-ul-mukhtâr** says at the end of the section

dealing with the makrûhs of namâz: "The best of mosques is the Ka'ba-i mu'azzama, next comes **Masjîd-i-harâm**, which surrounds it, and next comes **Masjîd-i-Nebî**, which is in Medîna-i munawwara. Then comes **Masjîd-i-aqsâ** in Jerusalem, which is followed by the masjîd of **Kubâ**, which is near the blessed city of Medîna-i munawwara. Masjîd-i Nebî used to be a hundred dhrâ' long and a hundred dhrâ' wide. One dhrâ' is half a metre. Later it was widened in the course of time. Its present size is good, too."

[The most valuable soil is the soil which is in contact with the Prophet's 'sall-Allâhu 'alaihi wa sallam' blessed body in the Qabr-i Sa'âdat (the Prophet's grave); it is more valuable than the Arsh and than Gardens of Paradise. Times, places, his children, and also all other things that are closer to him, are more valuable and better than those that are farther from him. Mosques and Prophets are exempt from this.]

12 - It is harâm to beg [importunately] in a mosque.

13 - It is makrûh to give alms to a beggar who annoys people in a mosque.

14 - It is makrûh to look for lost things in a mosque.

15 - It is tahrîmî makrûh to read (or recite) a poem containing a lampoon against a Believer, a love affair or indecency. It produces thawâb to read poems containing preaches, advice, hikmat, blessings of Allâhu ta'âlâ, eulogies praising Believers [i.e. ilâhîs, mawlids] without melodies, and it is permissible to read (or recite) historical poems occasionally; yet, it is not something esteemable to busy oneself with poetry. It is permissible to say ilâhîs and mawlîds in mosques sometimes [provided you will not prevent others from performing namâz]. It is not permissible to do so very often or to make it a habit.

16 - It is fard-i kifâya for people without an excuse to listen to the Qur'ân al-kerîm being read (or recited) aloud. It is sinful to begin reading the Qur'ân al-kerîm aloud in a place where people are working, sleeping, performing namâz, or if there is someone preaching. [By the same token, a person who turns up the volume of the radio or the tape recorder (or the CD player) being used in one of these places, and the person, (e.g. the hafiz,) who has allowed his voice to be recorded, share the sin for not having properly respected the Qur'ân al-kerîm.]

17 - It is makrûh to splash the water used for making an ablution in a mosque, to dirty a mosque with phlegm or mucus.

However, it is permissible to make an ablution at a place specially prepared (for ablution) in a mosque.

It is not permissible to make an ablution or a ghusl around the well of Zamzam. For, it is within the area of a mosque. Also, it is not permissible for a person who is junub to enter there.

18 - It is makrûh to plant unnecessary trees in a mosque. It is permissible if they give public benefits, such as absorbing the moisture in the mosque or making shades. It is makrûh to plant them for one's personal use.

19 - It is makrûh to eat something or to sleep in a mosque. A musâfir is exempted from this. When entering a mosque, a musâfir must intend for **i'tikâf** and perform the namâz of tahiyyatulmasjîd first. Thereafter he can eat and talk about worldly matters. A person who makes i'tikâf can eat and sleep. I'tikâf is sunnat-i muakkada. It is written in **Berîqa** that neglecting the i'tikâf without a good excuse is like omitting the sunnats of five daily prayers.

A person who eats strong smelling things, such as onions and garlics [or who smokes], in the mosque, must be prohibited. Butchers, fishermen, sellers of livers, oil sellers, – if their clothes are dirty or if they smell badly – those with bad smelling clothes and those who verbally hurt the jamâ'at must be turned out of the mosque. A person who has eaten something smelling for a medical reason or as a result of inattention should not go to a mosque because he has an excuse. A bad smell annoys men and angels.

20 - Making a contract for buying and selling in a mosque is makrûh. Yet it is mustahab to establish a contract for a nikâh.

21 - It is tahrîmî makrûh to busy with worldly conversations instead of worshipping in a mosque. As fire consumes wood, likewise worldly conversations in a mosque removes one's blessings. After worshipping, it is permissible to talk on permissible matters softly. It is never permissible to talk about matters not approved of by the Sharî'at.

22 - It is makrûh to reserve a certain place for yourself in a mosque. But if you leave your coat in your place lest someone else will sit there when you go out of the mosque, you can sit there again when you come back. The same rule applies in public places, in Minâ, on Arafât [on ships, buses]. That is, if someone else is sitting in the place where it is your habit to sit, you cannot force him to stand up. If you reserve more seats than you need, someone

else may take the extra seat. If two people ask for the extra seat, the one whom you give the seat can sit there. If before either of the two people asks for the seat one of them sits there, you cannot take it back and give it to the other person. If you swear to tell the truth and say, "I reserved this seat for him with his instructions and not for myself," you can make the person leave the seat. The same applies to cases involving places where sellers set up in a market place; a late comer cannot force an early comer to leave his place. In all these public places, if the first occupant has been causing harm to others, he can be forced to leave his place.

If those who are performing namâz are too closely pressed together, they can make those who are not performing namâz leave their places.

If a district mosque is too small for a large jamâ'at, those who do not live in that district can be made to leave the mosque.

It is permissible [and necessary] for the people in a district to appoint a mutawallî [administrator] who will collect income for the mosque and who will take care of its maintenance and other expenditures.

If a hâfiz is reciting the Qur'ân al-kerîm on one side of the mosque and a pious Muslim of the Ahl as-Sunnat Madhhab is preaching on another side, it is better to listen to the preacher. [In fact, if the hâfiz is a fâsiq and is reciting the Qur'ân melodiously, it is not permissible to listen to him. A 'mosque' does not mean a 'building with a dome on top and a minaret adjacent to it'. It means a 'building wherein namâz in jamâ'at is performed five times daily'. It is also permissible to preach to the Muslims making up the jamâ'at before or after the prayers. The preaching is performed by a pious Muslim holding the belief of Ahl as-sunnat; he performs it by reading a passage from a book written by a scholar of Ahl as-sunnat, or by reciting a statement that was made by that scholar, and by explaining what he has read or recited. Speeches made by people without a certain Madhhab or by English spies or by missionaries are not called preaches; they are called orations or conferences. It is not permissible to make speeches or conferences in mosques or to listen to such speeches therein. Each and every statement made by a scholar of Ahl as-sunnat is an explanation based on the Qur'ân al-kerîm and hadîth-i-sherîfs.]

It is permissible to scare away bats and pigeons in a mosque and to throw out their nests. Otherwise they will dirty the mosque. They are expelled so that the mosque will remain clean. It is written in

Fatâwâ-i qâri-ul-Hidâya[1] and **Jawâhir-ul-fatâwa**[2]: "It is permissible to kill the birds that dirty a mosque if it is impossible to expell them. Animals that give trouble to people can be killed anywhere." It is not permissible to destroy birds' nests outside of a mosque.

It is written in the fatwâ of **Qâdî-Khân** 'rahmatullâhi 'alaih': "If the adhân (azân) is not performed in a city or village or neighborhood, the government has to ensure that it is performed even by using force." It is written in **Fatâwâ-i Hindiyya**: "The azân is performed outside of the mosque, or on the minaret. It is sunnat to say it at an elevated place and not to exert oneself to make one's voice loud." Hence, it can be easily understood that there is no need to say the adhân (azân) or the iqâmat through a loud speaker. For, the azân is said in every neighborhood. It is bid'at to perform acts of worship with tape recorders, (C.D. players,) radios, or loudspeakers. Bid'ats are grave sins. [The azân said by the muazzin and qirâ'at (recital of a sûra or three âyats of the Qur'an al-kerîm during the standing position in a namâz) performed by the imâm should be made in their natural voices and loud enough to be heard by the Muslims around the mosque and by the jamâ'at therein. It is makrûh for them to exert themselves so that they will be heard from afar. This should suffice to show the pointlessness of using loudspeakers in mosques. It is written as follows in **Munjid**: "Any instrument that is used to produce sound is called a **'mizmâr'**. A drum, a tambourine, a woodwind instrument such as a reed flute, a violin, a lute, a loud-speaker, a tape recorder, and a television set are a mizmâr each." Ibni Hajar-i-Mekkî 'rahmatullâhi ta'âlâ 'alaih', (899 [1494 A.D.] – 974 [1566], Mekka,) states in his book **Keff-ur-reâ' an muharremât-ilâ lehw-i-wa-s-simâ'**: "A hadîth-i-sherîf reads: **'I have been commanded to annihilate the drum and the mizmâr.'** And another one reads: **'A time will come when the Qur'ân al-kerîm will be read** (and recited) **through mizmârs. Allâhu ta'âlâ will damn those who do so and their listeners.'** " Also in this category is to say the azân or the mawlid (by using a loudspeaker). Please see the twenty-fourth chapter.]

No knowledge is so good as knowing your own shortcomings!

False is all your blessings; oh, world, you are so base;
Cold wind called 'death' destroys all your gifts in highness!

---

[1] Written by 'Umar bin Is-haqq 'rahmatullâhi ta'âlâ 'alaih'.
[2] Written by Rukn-ud-dîn Abû Bakr Muhammad bin Abd-ur-Reshîd 'rahmatullâhi ta'âlâ 'alaih', (d. 565 [1169 A.D.].)

20 – NAMÂZ IN JAMÂ'AT

You step in a mosque with your right foot. When leaving a mosque you step out with your left foot first. It is written in **Uyûn-ul-basâir:** "When entering a mosque, you take off your left and then right shoe before entering. Then you step in with your right foot first. You put on your right shoe after [or before] leaving with your left foot first." While explaining the afflictions incurred by one's hands and feet, the book **Hadîqa** says: "As imâm-i Nawawî says in his commentary to **Muslim**, it is mustahab to begin with your right side when doing blessed, honoured and pure deeds. You begin with your right when putting on your shoes, trousers, shirt, when cutting or combing your hair, when trimming your moustache, when using a miswâk, when cutting your nails, when washing your hands and feet, when entering a mosque, a Muslim's house, a Muslim's room, when going out of a rest room, when giving alms, when eating, and when drinking. When doing the opposites of these; for example, when taking off your shoes, socks, clothes, when going out of a mosque, or a Muslim's house, a Muslim's room, when entering the restroom, when expelling mucus from your nose, when cleaning yourself after relieving nature, it is mustahab to begin with your left. It is tanzîhî makrûh to do them conversely, because it means omitting the sunnat in **hey'et** (form)." [To shave the beard in order to follow the local regulations is an example of this. Please see the final explanations at the end of the following eleventh paragraph!]

Ibni Âbidîn 'rahmatullâhi ta'âlâ 'alaih' says: "There are two types of being an imâm. Let us discuss **Imâmat-i-kubrâ** first. This will be mentioned again in the explanation of bâghîs (rebels) on the three hundred and tenth page of the third volume. It is also written on the one hundred and forty-third, two hundred and ninety-fourth, and three hundred and fifty-first pages of the book **Al-Hadîqat-un-nediyya**, written by Abdulghanî Nablusî 'rahmatullâhi ta'âlâ 'alaih'. The second type of being an imâm is called **Imâmat-i sugrâ**, which means being an imâm to conduct a namâz that is fard. It is sunnat for men in the Hanafî and Mâlikî Madhhabs to perform the fard of the five daily prayers of namâz in jamâ'at. And it is obligatory (fard) for the prayers of Friday and 'Iyd. It is makrûh to perform the supererogatory prayers of namâz in jamâ'at. In the five daily prayers even one person will suffice as a jamâ'at. A person whose **qirâat** (recitation of the Qur'ân) is beautiful, that is, who knows the letters of the Qur'ân al-kerîm and who knows how to read the Qur'ân al-kerîm with tajwîd, becomes the imâm, and not a person whose voice is good and who recites the Qur'ân al-kerîm melodiously! It is makrûh for a fâsiq to become the imâm. It is tahrîmî makrûh to follow him even if he is deeply learned. A hadîth-i-sherîf declares: **"A person who performs namâz with a savant who is muttaqî has performed namâz as though he were with the Prophet** 'sall-Allâhu 'alaihi wa sallam'."

It is written in the one hundred and thirty-fifth page of the book **Uyûn-ul basâir**: "A person who does not go to the mosque [though he does not have an excuse], but instead makes the jamâ'at with his wife at home, cannot attain the blessings of the jamâ'at in the mosque. That is, he cannot get the extra blessings that are peculiar to the mosque. But he gets the blessings of the jamâ'at, e.i. the blessings that are twenty-seven times the number of those received for performing namâz individually. However, we must add that this is so when both of the jamâ'ats fulfill the conditions and sunnats. If the jamâ'at at home is more acceptable, it is necessary to perform it at home." The same is written on the four hundred and second, the six hundred and thirteenth, and the six hundred and nineteenth pages of **Halabî-i kebîr**.

[As it can be understood, we must not perform namâz behind those imâms who do not observe the conditions of namâz properly. Their namâz is not sahîh. It is permissible but makrûh to perform namâz behind an îmâm who knows and respects the fards of ablution and namâz though he commits sins, e.g. drinks alcohol, takes interest for the money he has lent, looks at women and girls, and gambles. It is written in the fatwâ of Ebussu'ûd Efendi that the hadîth **"Perform namâz behind a fâjir as well as behind a pious Muslim!"** is meant not for the îmâms of mosques but for Emîrs and governors who conduct Friday prayers, so that they will be followed and obeyed. We must not perform namâz behind those imâms who we know are committing sins. We must not follow an imâm who does not have the conditions that an imâm must have and who reads the Qur'ân al-kerîm melodiously. We must go to the mosque of an imâm who is devoted to his faith. We must go to the mosque for every namâz, but when meeting with an imâm who is sinful, ignorant, lâ-Madhhabî, or who is a reformer of Islam, we must not follow him. We must not stop attending the mosque only because we think that there may be such an imâm. It is written in the fatwâ of Ebussu'ûd Efendi, which exists in the library of Molla Murâd (in Istanbul) with number 1114: "It is wâjib to dismiss an imâm who makes a living through harâm and who takes interest by lending money. It is fard to know how to read the Qur'ân al-kerîm with tajwîd. He who does not know the tajwîd cannot observe the rules concerning **makhârij-i hurûf** (parts of the mouth, tongue, velum, and pharynx where letters and sounds are articulated). The Qur'ân al-kerîm read (or recited) and the namâz performed by a person who cannot observe the places of the letters in the articulatory organs are not acceptable." [See Endless Bliss, II, chapter 21.] It is every Muslim's duty to strive so that a person who fulfills the conditions for being an imâm will become the imâm.

It is written in the annotation to the commentary of **Nûr-ul-îzâh**: "**Being an imâm requires fulfilling six conditions.**" Namâz should not be not performed behind an imâm who is known not to fulfil one of these conditions:

1 - To be a Muslim. He who disbelieves the fact that Abû Bakr Siddîq and 'Umar Fâruq were Khalîfas, or who does not believe in the Mi'râj or the torment in the grave cannot be an imâm unless he is knowledgeable about the te'vîl (explanation, documentation) of the matter.

2 - To have reached the age of puberty.

3 - To be discreet. A drunk or senile person cannot be an imâm.

4 - To be a man. A woman cannot be an imâm for men.

5 - To be able to recite at least the Fâtiha-i sherîfa and one more âyat correctly. A person who has not memorized one ayât or who cannot recite with tajwîd the âyats he has memorized or who recites the âyats melodiously cannot be an imâm.

6 - To be without an 'udhr. A person who has an 'udhr cannot be imâm for those who do not have an 'udhr. 'Udhrs are: continuous bleeding at some part of the body, incontinence in wind-breaking or urination, repeated pronunciation of the letters "te" and "fe", lisping, that is, pronouncing the letter "sin" as "se" (a letter which is pronounced with **"th"** sound), or dyslalia, i.e. pronouncing the letter "ra" as "ghayn" (that is, voiced post-alveolar fricative instead of voiced post-alveolar trill), being without an ablution or being smeared with najâsat in excess of one dirham, and being with bare awrat parts. A person who has an eye sore becomes a person with an 'udhr if he cannot control his tears. Any liquid coming out of the ears, navel, nose, nipples because of some pain is an 'udhr if it exudes continuously. The same is the

case with blood, filth, yellow liquid exuded by the above-named parts or by a cut or sore even without pain. Those who share the same 'udhr can be imâm for each other, and a person who has one 'udhr can be imâm for a person who has two. In the Shafi'î and Mâlikî Madhhabs, a person who has an 'udhr can be imâm for those who do not have an 'udhr. [A person who makes a masah on the ointment on a wound or on a bandage, or who has had his teeth crowned or filled and therefore imitates the Shafi'î or Mâlikî Madhhab 'rahmatullâhi ta'âlâ 'alaihimâ', is not considered to have an 'udhr.]

It is written in the three hundred and seventy-sixth page of **Durr-ul-mukhtâr**: "It is makrûh for those who are religiously ignorant [even if they are professors], for fâsiqs, that is, for those who (habitually) commit grave sins, – drink alcohol, commit fornication, take interest, allow their wives and daughters to go out without covering themselves properly – and for blind people, to become imâm. [It is not sahîh for a fâsiq (person who sins frankly) to be imâm, according to the Mâlikî Madhhab **(Halabî)**.] We have given the fatwâ of Ebussu'ûd Efendi 'rahmatullâhi 'alaih' above. If a blind person is deeply learned he can be imâm. Also, it is makrûh for a bastard, that is, one who was born out of a relation between a couple who had not performed (the marriage contract prescribed by Islam and termed) nikâh, to be imâm. It is makrûh for a beardless person who has just reached the age of puberty to be imâm, even if he is deeply learned. For it causes fitna. It is not makrûh to perform namâz behind a person whose beard does not grow but who is not attractively good looking." [Therefore, being an imâm does not require having a beard. Namâz may be performed behind a person who shaves because of a good excuse. A person whose beard does not have the shape prescribed by the sunnat is a bid'at holder. A person who slights the fact that one's beard must be in compliance with the sunnat becomes a disbeliever. See twenty-first chapter!]

There are ten conditions to be fulfilled to follow the imâm correctly:

1 - When beginning namâz, you must make the niyyat (intend) to follow the imâm before saying the takbîr. It is not necessary to intend with the name of the imâm.

2 - The imâm has to intend to become the imâm for women (if he is to conduct a jamâ'at of women). [Ibni Âbidîn says while stating the makrûhs of namâz: "It is not permissible for girls,

women or old women to go to a mosque for the five daily prayers, for prayers of Friday or 'Iyd, or to listen to sermons. Of old, only old women were allowed to go to mosques for evening and night prayers, but now it is not permissible for them, either." It is harâm for women to go to mosques with bare heads, arms and legs for the purpose of listening to mawlids, sermons and hâfizes. It is a grave sin. Even Christian women are not so freely dressed when they go to church. Places where freely dressed women are mixed with men are not called mosques. One does not go to such places even to perform namâz. An imâm does not have to make intention to be imâm for men. Yet if he does he will attain the blessings of the Jamâ'at, too. It is written in the hundred and forty-eighth page of the book **Hadîqa**: "Savants of Fiqh said that if the imâm does not make his niyyat to become imâm for Muslims who will follow him when beginning namâz, it is sahîh to follow him, but he himself will not be given the blessings for conducting namâz as imâm. He will be given the blessings of his own namâz as if he performed it individually, since his niyyat (intention) did not include 'conducting namâz in jamâ'at'. When he makes his niyyat to conduct the namâz he will also be given the blessings for being imâm, and the blessing will vary, depending on the number of people in the jamâ'at."]

3 - Heels of the people making up the jamâ'at must take up the rear with respect to the imâm's heels.

4 - The imâm and the jamâ'at must be performing the same fard namâz. When a person who has already performed the fard of the time follows the imâm, he will have performed a supererogatory namâz.

5 - There must not be a line of women between the imâm and the jamâ'at. If the women are fewer than enough to form a complete line and there is a curtain in between or if they are at a lower or higher place, it will be permissible. [It is stated in **Terghîb-us-salât**: Four women standing side by side (for the performance of the same fard namâz by following the same imâm being followed by the rest of the jamâ'at), will have made a complete line. In this case the namâz performed by all the men (making up all the lines) behind that line of women, will become fâsid, (i.e. null and void.) If there are three women in the line in question, only the namâz performed by five of the men, three of them on the line immediately behind that of the women, each of the three men standing right behind one of the three women; and two of them on either side of the line of three women, will

become fâsid. If there were a pillar or a curtain or a wall separating any of the men from the woman immediately before him or beside him, then his namâz would not become fâsid. The same rule applies to relations between both sexes concerning matters of being mahram. It is makrûh for women at home to perform namâz in jamâ'at among themselves without (at least) one of their male (mahram) relatives (to conduct the namâz as the imâm).]

6 - A wall (between the imâm and the jamâ'at) is not a hindrance as long as the jamâ'at see or hear the imâm. However, there must not be a road or a river whereby a cart or a boat could pass through, which is a hindrance. When two more lines on the road or on a bridge over the river follows the imâm the namâz of the jamâ'at behind will be accepted. Please scan the twenty-fourth chapter!

7 - Following the imâm in jamâ'at is not acceptable unless you can hear the imâm's or the muazzin's voice, or see the acts of other people who can hear them. There must not be a wall between the imâm and the jamâ'at without a window convenient for seeing or hearing the imâm.

[We have already written in the section concerning the adhân (azân) that the voice coming out of a radio, a television or a loud-speaker is not a human voice. The image of an imâm that is seen to be conducting namâz in jamâ'at on a movie screen or television is not the imâm himself. As it is not permissible to follow that image, likewise an act of worship performed in accordance with sounds coming thereof is not sahîh (valid); into the bargain, it is an act of bid'at and a grave sin.]

It is written in **al-Muqaddimat-ul-hadramiyya, al-Anwâr li-a'mâl-il-ebrâr, al-Fiqh-u-'alal-madhâhib-il-erba'a,** and **Misbâh-un-najât**: "In the Shafi'î Madhhab, if someone outside of the mosque follows the imâm who is inside, it will be necessary for him to sense the actions of the imâm either by seeing the imâm or someone who sees him in the jamâ'at, or by hearing the imâm's or the muazzin's voice. Moreover, the distance between him and the last line of the jamâ'at should not be more than three hundred dhrâs [300x0.42=126 meters] approximately." It is stated in **Terghîb-us-salât**: "If a person is outside of the mosque, his following the imâm is sahîh only when the mosque is full. If the mosque is not full or if it is full but there is a distance large enough for a cart (or car) to pass between the last line and the person outside of the mosque, his following the imâm will not be sahîh." The fact that those prayers performed by following the voice in a loud speaker or the image of the imâm on television are not sahîh, is written in the twelfth issue of the magazine **al-Mu'allim**, dated Rabî'ul-awwal, 1406 [December, 1985], and published by the Indian Muslim scholars of the city of Malappuram, Kerala, India. It is written explicitly in the fifth page of the book **Suyûfullâh-il-ejilla**[1], (1401 [1981 A.D.], Pakistan,) that it is not permissible to join a jamâ'at conducted through a loudspeaker by the imâm. The book was published as an appendage to the book **Fitna-t-ul-Wahhâbiyya**[2] by **Hakîkat Kitâbevi**, Istanbul. See the fatwâ of Yahyâ Efendi!

8 - The imâm must not be on an animal while the jamâ'at are on the ground or vice versa.

9 - The imâm and the jamâ'at must not be aboard two different ships that are not adjacent to each other.

10 - The jamâ'at that is following an imâm who is in another Madhhab must not know that something that nullifies namâz according to their own Madhhab exists in the imâm. For example, because it is not permissible for the imâm to bleed or to have made a masah on less than one-fourth of his head (when making an ablution) according to the Hanafî Madhhab, a Shâfi'î imâm who is known to have done so must not be followed, according to a good majority of scholars. This report is (authentic and) sahîh. If the Shafi'î imâm is seen bleeding, then if he disappears for a while and then comes back, he can be followed. For he may have made an ablution in the meantime. It is good to have (a good opinion called) **husn-i-zân**. [Also, according to the same scholars, a Hanafî person must not follow a Shâfi'î imâm who has been seen to have crowned or filled teeth.] As it is written in **Radd al-muhtâr**, in Tahtâwî's annotation to **Imdâd-ul-Fettâh** and in the two hundred and seventeenth page of the second volume of Ahmad Hamawî's annotation to **Eshbâh** (v.2, p.217): "There are also savants such as Muhammad Hinduwânî who say that a Shâfi'î imâm whose namâz is sahîh according to his own Madhhab can be followed." The book **Nihâya** writes that this report is more conformable to qiyâs, adding: "According to this report a Shâfi'î imâm on whom something not permissible in Hanafî Madhhab is seen may be followed." And that this report is sahîh (valid) is written in

---

[1] Written by Muhammad Âshiq-ur-Rahmân.
[2] Written by Ahmad bin Sayyid Zeynî Dahlân 'rahmatullâhi ta'âlâ 'alaih', (1231 [1816 A.D.], Mekka, – 1304 [1886], Medîna.)

Halabî-i kebîr. It is permissible in the Mâlikî Madhhab, too. According to those savants, it is permissible to follow a Shâfi'î or Mâlikî imâm who has been seen to have crowned or filled teeth. This means that a person who is in the Hanafî Madhhab but who follows the Shâfi'î or Mâlikî Madhhab because he has crowned or filled teeth can also, according to those savants, be an imâm for those Hanafîs who do not have crowned or filled teeth. This is because he is like an imâm who himself is in the Shâfi'î or Mâlikî Madhhab. Into the bargain, he adapts himself to the other conditions of his Madhhab and performs, for instance, the witr prayer in a state of awareness of the fact that it is wâjib (in his Madhhab, i.e. in the Hanafî Madhhab.). It is not permissible to ask or inquire if he has a crowning or filling, or, supposing he has (a crowning or filling), whether he is imitating Shâfi'î or Mâlikî. If an imâm in another Madhhab observes the conditions in the Hanafî Madhhab, too, following him is better (for people in the Hanafî Madhhab) than performing namâz individually, and still, following a Hanafî imâm is better than following him. [One who has crowned or filled teeth should not assume a duty that will require his conducting namâz in jamâ'at as imâm.]

If the jamâ'at is made up of only one person, he stands on the right-hand side of the imâm. It is makrûh to stand on his left. It is makrûh also to stand behind him. Unloss his heel is ahead of the imâm's heel, his namâz will be sahîh. When there are two or more people they must stand behind the imâm. In a jamâ'at the first one stands right behind the imâm, the second one on the right of the first one, the third one on the left of the first, the fourth one on the right of the second, the fifth one on the left of the third, and so on. If the second person arrives after the imâm has started, he stands behind the imâm, and the first person must move backwards and stand behind the imâm without breaking his namâz. The imâm does not move forward. Please see the twenty-third paragraph of the eighteenth chapter.

If there is a space large enough to include two lines or a large pond between the imâm and the jamâ'at, it is permissible for the people behind it to follow the imâm; yet it is makrûh to perform it alone in this case. It is not required for there to be jamâ'at (people performing the same namâz and following the same imâm) on both sides of the pond or the space. So is the case with open or closed places or rooms adjacent to a mosque. [Tahtâwî's annotation to the commentary entitled Imdâd-ul-Fettâh]. Please see the twenty-fourth chapter.

A person who made an ablution can follow[1] an imâm who made a tayammum; a person who performs namâz standing can follow an imâm performing it sitting; and one performing a supererogatory namâz can follow an imâm performing a fard. One must search for an imâm who knows and loves Islam and follow him.

In a mosque belonging to a certain quarter, the azân and the iqâmat are said before only one of the performances in jamâ'at of each of the (five) daily prayers. However, in mosques along roads and in mosques that do not have appointed imâms and muazzins, namâz is performed with a new azân and iqâmat for each jamâ'at. A genie can be an imâm. An angel cannot be an imâm because an angel has not been enjoined (to perform namâz). An angel, a genie or a child can make up a jamâ'at even if it is only a jamâ'at of one, (i.e. even if there is no one else in the jamâ'at.) When a person who is performing a supererogatory namâz follows a person who is performing the fard, both attain the blessing for a jamâ'at.

There are many savants who say that it is wâjib to perform namâz in jamâ'at. According to the (past) savants of Iraq 'rahmatullâhi ta'âlâ 'alaihim ajma'în', it is sinful to omit a wâjib even once without a good excuse. And according to the unanimity of savants, one becomes sinful if one makes it a habit to omit a wâjib. Yet it is not sinful to omit a sunnat. It is mustahab for a person who is late for the jamâ'at in one mosque to try and catch a jamâ'at in another mosque.

It is not necessary for a sick or paralytic person, for a person whose one foot has been cut off, for a person too old to walk, and for a blind person to go out for the jamâ'at. It is not necessary even if he (one of these people) has helpers and vehicles. Rain, mud, very cold weather and darkness are excuses, too. A strong wind is an excuse only at night. Fear of losing one's possessions because of thieves or other reasons, a poor person's fear of the person to whom he owes, having trouble with the gas in one's stomach or bowels, one's fear of an evildoer who may cause harm to one's life and property, a traveller's fear of missing the vehicle, constant attendance on an invalid person, fear of missing the food which one longs for, and fear of missing an opportunity to learn knowledge of fiqh are excuses for not attending the jamâ'at. Also it is an excuse to know that the imâm is a bid'at holder or that he does not observe the principles of ablution, ghusl and namâz. A person who

---

[1] It would be prudent to remind at this point that to follow an imâm means to perform namâz as the jamâ'at conducted by him.

knows and observes these principles has precedence over others in being preferred as the imâm. After this the one who reads the Qur'ân al-kerîm with tajwîd is preferable. It is not necessary to be a hâfiz. If there are a few hâfizes, the one who has more wara' must be chosen. **Wara'** means to avoid things that are doubtful (that might be sinful). After this, the one who is older must be preferred. The next qualities that are preferable in choosing the imâm are: a good nature, a beautiful face, noble descent, a nice voice, and good clothes. If there are a few such people, the one who has much property and a high rank must be chosen. If these qualities are also common, a settled person becomes imâm for a safarî one. If there cannot be an agreement about choosing the imâm, the one chosen by the majority becomes imâm. While there is someone superior, it is unpleasant to choose someone else. But it is not sinful. So is the case with electing a commander or a governor. However, in an election of Khalîfa, it is sinful not to elect the most superior one. In a house or feast, the host or the one who is giving the feast becomes imâm regardless of choice. Or the person chosen by him becomes imâm. A tenant is the host in this respect. It is makrûh for a disliked person to become imâm.

It is tahrîmî makrûh for a bid'at holder to become imâm. A holder of a belief disagreeing with the belief of the Ahl as-Sunna is called a lâ-Madhhabî. If a lâ-Madhhabî disbelieves or doubts something clearly declared in the Qur'ân al-kerîm and the hadîth-i-sherîfs, it will be an act of **kufr** (disbelief). And it will be **bid'at** to make wrong interpretations of those indefinite facts that are not declared clearly. It is kufr to deny the fact that the world was created and to say that it will go on so forth. It is bid'at to disbelieve that Believers will see Allâhu ta'âlâ in Paradise. However, denial of (the proof-texts termed) Nass is bid'at only when it happens in consequence of misunderstanding. Otherwise, if a person abhors the fact by saying, "It is impossible. My mind does not accept it," he becomes a kâfir. The hadîth-i sherîfs about bid'at exist in the initial pages of the books **Hadîqa** and **Berîqa** and in the hundred and twenty-fifth page of the Persian book **Eshi'at -ul-Leme'at**[1]. The

---

[1] A commentary to Muhammad bin Abdullah Tebrîzî's 'rahmatullâhi ta'âlâ 'alaih', (d. 749 [1348 A.D.],) book entitled **Mishkât-ul-mesâbih**, –which in turn was an annotationally commentated version of the book of Hadîth entitled Mesâbih, written by Muhy-is-sunna Huseyn bin Mes'ûd Baghâwi 'rahmatullâhi ta'âlâ 'alaih', (d. 516 [1122 A.D.], Bâg, Khorasan,)– was written by 'Abd-ul-Haqq Dahlawî 'rahmatullâhi ta'âlâ 'alaih', (958 [1551 A.D.] – 1052 [1642], Delhi.)

ones existing in Eshi'at-ul-Leme'at have been transferred into our book **Maz-hariyya**[1]. The **Ahl-i qibla**, that is, a person who performs namâz, cannot be called a **kâfir** unless he says or does something that causes disbelief. But a person who says or does something that is disagreeable with something that is declared clearly in the Qur'ân al-kerîm and in hadîth-i-sherîfs and which Muslims have been believing for centuries, is called a **kâfir**, even if he performs namâz and does all kinds of worship throughout his life. For example, if he says, "Allâhu ta'âlâ does not know every tiny mote, the number of leaves, or secret things," he becomes a kâfir. A person who speaks ill about a Sahâbi except Abû Bakr and 'Umar 'radiy-Allâhu anhumâ' for some religious reason becomes a bid'at holder[2]. A person who says mubâh (permissible) about a harâm does not become a kâfir, if he says so sincerely depending on an âyat-i-kerîma or a hadîth-i-sherîf. If he says so capriciously without depending on Nass (âyats and hadîths with clear meanings), he becomes a kâfir. It is bid'at to say that it was unjust to elect Abû Bakr and 'Umar for the caliphate. But it is an act of disbelief to say that they had no rights to become Khalîfas.

A fatwâ has been given that if a person who fulfills the conditions for being an imâm does the duty of an imâm for a wage or salary it is permissible to perform namâz behind him. It is written at the end of **Halabî-i kebîr** that it is necessary to re-perform a namâz performed behind an imâm who mispronounces or recites melodiously as well as one performed before its time. [One must do one's best to be sure that an imâm who holds the belief of the Ahl as-Sunnat be appointed to the office. This will prevent one who does not fulfill the conditions for being an imâm and who is known to be a lâ-Madhhabî or a religion reformer from getting that position.]

---

[1] **Maqâmât-i-Maz-hariyya** is a valuable book which Abdullâh-i-Dahlawî 'rahmatullâhi 'alaih' wrote, mostly about his valuable Murshîd, Shems-ud-dîn Habîbullah Maz-har-i-Jân-i-Jânân 'rahmatullâhi 'alaih', (1111 [1699 A.D.], India-martyred in 1195 [1781],) and which was reproduced by Hakîkat Kitâbevi in Istanbul.

[2] This scholarly statement should not be misconstrued. It does not mean that it is something less criminal to speak ill of the Shaikhayn, (i.e. Abû Bakr as-Siddîq and 'Umar ul-Fârûq 'radiy-Allâhu 'anhumâ'.) On the contrary, it is much more dangerous even to doubt their superiority. For that matter, the afore-quoted statement shows that speaking ill off the blessed Shaikhayn 'radiy-Allâhu 'anhuma' incurs a degradation and squalor far worse than becoming a bid'at holder.

It is tahrîmî makrûh for the imâm to say the qirâat and the tesbîhs beyond the measure prescribed by the sunnat when conducting the fard namâz, even if the jamâ'at want him to do so. It is tahrîmî makrûh for a woman to become imâm and conduct a namâz in jamâ'at made up of women. When there are no men it is not makrûh for them to perform a namâz of janâza in jamâ'at. For, if they perform it individually, the woman who performs it first will have performed the fard, and the ones who perform it later will have performed a supererogatory prayer. It is makrûh as well to perform a namâz of janâza as a supererogatory prayer. It is fard to perform a namâz of janâza once. If a woman becomes imâm for men in a namâz of janâza, the men do not perform it again. This is because only the woman's namâz has been accepted and the fard has been performed by one person. If a woman becomes imâm for women, she stands in the middle of the first line. It is sinful for her to stand ahead of the first line.

At home a man can be imâm for women who are his mahram. He cannot be imâm for women who are nâmahram to him. For it would be halwat. If there is another man or the imâm's mahram among the jamâ'at, the nâmahram women can join the jamâ'at. In this event as well as in cases of halwat, it is makrûh for those mahram relatives who are related to the imâm through milk (having been breastfed by the same mother) or through nikâh to be young. Halwat does not occur in a mosque. A woman stands behind the imâm, not by his side. If there is a man, the woman stands behind the man and performs namâz with the imâm.

In Masjîd-i harâm, it is best for the imâm to stand in the Maqâm-i Ibrâhîm. A newcomer to the mosque should not walk to the front lines lest he should disturb the jamâ'at. (As all the jamâ'at stand up) to begin the fard, he can move to a vacant space in the line ahead. In the namâz of janâza the back lines are more blessed than the front lines. A person who finds the imâm making the rukû' stands in the last line lest he will miss the rak'at. He should not walk to the front lines. If there is no place in the last line he must not stand alone; and this interdiction applies even in cases that involve his missing the rak'at. If there is an empty space in the first line and if there is no space available in the second line, he can make his way through the second line in order to reach the first line. In this case, it is not sinful to pass before the jamâ'at, that is, those who are performing namâz in the back.

If a man performing namâz in jamâ'at remains as long as one rukn in the same line with a woman who is following the same imâm and if there is not a thick curtain or a pole more than one finger (2 cm.) thick or an open space wide enough to accommodate one person between them, the man's namâz becomes nullified. When a woman (joins the jamâ'at and) performs namâz in a line, only the namâz of the three men, two of them on her either side, and one right behind her, becomes nullified. If the one behind her is farther back by more than nine feet, his namâz does not become nullified. It is makrûh for a man and a woman who are not following the same imâm to perform namâz in the same line. When a man sees a woman by his side who is preparing (to join the jamâ'at and) to follow the imâm, he must give her a warning with his hand to stand behind him. If she does not move back, the woman's namâz will not be accepted. But the man's namâz will not become nullified. If the woman is in the same line but on a level higher or lower by an average man's stature, there is no harm.

A person who cannot make the rukû' or the sajdas cannot be imâm for a person who can make them. A person who is performing a supererogatory prayer cannot be imâm for someone who is performing a fard.

A person who is **alsagh** cannot be imâm for one who is not alsagh. An alsagh (lisper) is a person who pronounces the letter sin (voiceless alveolar fricative) as se (voiceless dental fricative) (which is pronounced like voiceless "th"). Also, a person who cannot pronounce other letters correctly cannot be imâm for one who prononuces them correctly. It is fard for such people to exercise themselves day and night to acquire an ability to pronounce the letters correctly. If a person cannot pronounce them try hard as he may, his individual namâz will be acceptable. If he does not try to pronounce them, his namâz becomes fâsid. If he performs his namâz individually while it is possible for him to perform it in jamâ'at by following an imâm who pronounces the letters correctly, in this case also his namâz is not acceptable because he has not pronounced the letters correctly. If there is an âyat with no letters that he cannot pronounce correctly, he must memorize it or a few âyats of that nature, and recite them in namâz. While there is an âyat that he can pronounce correctly, if he does not memorize it but recites one that he cannot pronounce correctly, his namâz will not be acceptable. Since it is obligatory to recite the Fâtiha in every namâz, he must try to pronounce it well. [As is seen, if one letter is not articulated correctly the Qur'ân al-kerîm will not be correct and the namâz will not be accepted. Because letters are not produced correctly in sounds sent through radios or loud-speakers, it is not right, not acceptable to read (or

– 303 –

recite) the Qur'ân al-kerîm through them, to listen to âyats read (or recited) through them, or to perform namâz (by following an imâm reciting) through them; it is sinful.]

A person who makes masah on his mests or on a bandage can be imâm for a person who washes the limbs involved, and one who is performing a fard can be imâm for one who is performing a supererogatory prayer. It is written in Ibni 'Âbidîn that the same rule applies to all sunnats including the tarâwîh. When a person who is performing a sunnat namâz consisting of four rak'ats follows an imâm who is performing a fard, he performs a namâz as if it were the fard namâz. Reciting the additional sûra in the third and fourth rak'ats, which is wâjib, becomes supererogatory now. A person who is performing a supererogatory namâz can become imâm for another person who also is performing a supererogatory namâz.

A person going to perform a namâz that is fard in jamâ'at has to intend by also passing the thought **"I am following the imâm who is present"** through his heart. He performs it together with the imâm as though he were performing it individually. But, when standing he does not say a prayer, regardless of whether the imâm says the sûras in a whisper or aloud. Only in the first rak'at he says the **Subhânaka**. It is tahrîmî makrûh in the Hanafî Madhhab to recite the Fâtiha sûra behind the imâm. It is fard in the Shafi'î Madhhab. In Mâlikî, on the other hand, it is tahrîmî makrûh as the imâm recites it loud, and it is mustahab as the imâm recites it in a whisper. When the imâm finishes saying the Fâtiha aloud, he says "Âmîn" in a whisper. He must not say it loudly. When the imâm says, **"Semi'-Allâhu liman hamidah"** while straightening up from the rukû', he says, **"Rabbanâ lakal hamd."** Then, he prostrates for the sajda together with the imâm, saying, **"Allâhu akbar"** (in a whisper) while doing so. In the rukû', in the sajdas, and while sitting, he says the prayers as he would if he were performing namâz individually.

A person who finds out that the imâm has something (or is doing something) that nullifies a namâz, performs the namâz again. If the imâm remembers it during the namâz or if something nullifying namâz happens while performing the namâz, the imâm must immediately inform the jamâ'at. If he notices it after the namâz, he writes, tells, or sends somebody to inform the ones he remembers to have joined the jamâ'at. The ones who learn it have to perform the namâz again. Those who do not hear it will be pardoned. According to an authentic report and in the Shâfi'î Madhhab, the imâm does not have to inform the jamâ'at. If the imâm's ablution breaks while performing namâz, it is permissible for him to put somebody in his place by pulling on his shirt. Then he performs an ablution outside and completes the namâz by following his deputy. If he performs an ablution within the mosque, a deputy is not needed. If he leaves the mosque without assigning a deputy, the namâz becomes invalid if the jamâ'at are composed of more than one people.

The namâz of witr is performed in jamâ'at during Ramadân. It is performed individually at all other times.

It is makrûh to perform the prayers of Raghâib, Ber'ât and Qadr[1] in jamâ'at. The namâz of Raghâib is a supererogatory namâz performed on the first Friday night[2] of the blessed month of Rajab. It was invented in 480 A.H. Many scholars have written that it is an unpleasant bid'at. We must not think it is sunnat only because we see many people perform it.

If other people begin performing a fard namâz in jamâ'at in the presence of a person who is performing the same fard individually, if that person has not made the sajda of the first rak'at he breaks his namâz by making salâm to one side while standing and begins to follow the imâm. If he has made the sajda of the first rak'at, he makes the salâm after completing two rak'ats in those fard prayers that have four rak'ats in them. If he has not made the sajda of the third rak'at he breaks his namâz by making the salâm to one side while standing and then joins the jamâ'at. If he has made the sajda of the third rak'at he completes the four rak'ats. Thereafter it is good if he follows the imâm and performs four (more) rak'ats; the namâz he performs thereby is a supererogatory prayer. But he cannot perform late afternoon prayer ('Asr) in jamâ'at in this manner. In the fard of morning and evening prayers, he breaks the namâz even if he has made the sajda of the first rak'at. However, if he has made the sajda of the second rak'at, he must complete the namâz. After that he does not perform supererogatory prayer by (joining the jamâ'at and) following the imâm. If they begin to perform the fard or if the khutba of Friday prayer begins as he performs qadâ of an omitted fard prayer instead of the sunnat, he does not break the namâz. He completes its two or four rak'ats. A person who has made the salâm after performing two rak'ats of the sunnat of the early afternoon or of Friday prayer completes it to four rak'ats by performing two more rak'ats after the fard. But he had better perform the entire four rak'ats again. If the namâz in jamâ'at begins while he is making qâda, he does not break the

---

[1] See third fascicle of Endless Bliss chapter 60. Sacred Nights.
[2] The night between Thursday and Friday

namâz if he has to observe the tertîb[1]. The same applies in the Mâlikî Madhhab.

When the azân is said it is tahrîmî makrûh for a person who is in a mosque to go out without a good excuse before performing the namâz in jamâ'at. Examples of good excuse are: habituation, i.e. that person may leave that mosque in order to go to a certain other mosque if it is his habit to perform his daily prayers in jamâ'at with the Muslims who are the habitual congregation of that other mosque; congenial company, i.e. he may leave if he wants to join the jamâ'at in the mosque of his own quarter; learning, i.e. he may leave in order to join the jamâ'at in a mosque attended by his master or another Islamic scholar lest he should miss their lecture; business, i.e. he may leave for the purpose of joining the jamâ'at in a mosque close to his work. Also, a person who has performed the fard individually before the jamâ'at can leave the mosque. Yet it is makrûh to perform it individually: Once the recital of iqâmat has started, none of the aforesaid excuses is valid, and the person who has any one of these excuses can no longer leave the mosque. A person who has performed the fard individually performs the supererogatory prayer with the jamâ'at performing early afternoon and night prayers. It is wâjib for a person who has performed any of the other three prayers individually to leave the mosque even while the namâz is being performed in jamâ'at. For, it is a grave sin not to join the jamâ'at. If a person who has not performed the sunnat of morning prayer apprehends that he will fail to catch up with the jamâ'at at least as they perform the final sitting posture of the namâz in case he performs the sunnat, he does not perform the sunnat, but immediately (joins the jamâ'at and) begins following the imâm. If he estimates that he will be able to make the last sitting together with the jamâ'at he performs the sunnat quickly in the ante-room of the mosque. If there is not an ante-room he performs it behind a pillar in the mosque. If there is not such an empty place, he does not perform the sunnat. For, it is makrûh to begin a supererogatory namâz while a fard namâz is being performed in jamâ'at. It is necessary to omit a sunnat in order not to commit a makrûh. [Since it is necessary to omit even the sunnat of morning prayer in order not to commit a makrûh, it must be realized that it is necessary to make qadâ of omitted fard prayers instead of performing the sunnat prayers.] A person who arrives in a

---

[1] What 'observing the tertîb' means, is explained in the twenty-third chapter.

mosque while early afternoon or Friday prayer is being performed in jamâ'at does not perform the sunnat if he has the apprehension that he may be too late for the first rak'at. He begins following the imâm immediately. He performs the sunnat of the early afternoon prayer after the fard. It is not right to begin the sunnat and to break it by making the salâm immediately thereafter lest you should miss the jamâ'at for morning or early afternoon prayer and thereafter to begin following the imâm and thereafter to make qadâ of the sunnat after the fard. For, it is harâm to break a namâz without a good excuse. Furthermore, a namâz of nazr[1], for instance, cannot be performed after the fard of morning prayer. Reperforming a sunnat prayer that has been broken is not as important as performing a namâz of nazr. It is wâjib to reperform supererogatory prayers of namâz that have been broken. It is fard to reperform broken fard prayers [**Uyûn-ul-basâir**]. For, once you have started a supererogatory namâz it becomes wâjib to complete it. A person who has not been able to perform morning prayer makes qadâ of it together with its sunnat before noon of that same day. But if he performs it after noon, he makes qadâ of the fard only. A person who arrives in the mosque during the performance of the fard of Friday or early afternoon prayer performs the first sunnat after the fard. A person who has not caught the rukû' (of a rak'at) has not performed that rak'at together with the imâm. A person who arrives when the imâm is in the rukû' makes his niyyat, says the takbîr standing, joins the namâz, and immediately begins following the imâm by bowing for the rukû'. If the imâm straightens up from the rukû' before the newcomer has bowed for the rukû', he has not caught the rukû'. Though he has not caught the rak'at he has to make the sajdas together with the imâm. If he does not do so his namâz does not become nullified. But he will have omitted a wâjib. If a person has begun following the imâm as the imâm stands but has not bowed for the rukû' together with the imâm, it is acceptable if he makes the rukû' individually after the imâm and catches up with the imâm in the sajda. Yet he is sinful because he has been late. It is tahrîmî makrûh to bow for the rukû', to prostrate for the sajda, or to get up from the sajda before the imâm does. Please see the twenty-fourth paragraph in the seventeenth chapter.

[It is necessary to imitate the imâm's movements. It is not necessary to follow his voice. If a person who cannot see the imâm

---

[1] A namâz that was vowed. Please see the fifth chapter of the fifth fascicle of **Endless Bliss**.

imitates the movements of those who see the imâm, he will have followed the imâm. Since the imâm's takbîrs and the actions of those who are following the imâm signify the imâm's actions, it is permissible to imitate them. It is not necessary to install television screens at various places in the mosque so that people who cannot see the imâm should follow his actions. Likewise, those who cannot hear the imâm's voice have to follow the actions of those who see the imâm and the voices of muazzins. In existence of these facilities, to install television screens or amplifiers in mosques means to despise Islam's prescription and adapt the acts of worship to one's own personal thoughts. This, in its turn, is not an attitude that a Muslim would assume. So is the case with installing loudspeakers on minarets.] It is makrûh for the imâm to perform the final sunnat at the same spot where he performed the fard. He should perform it after moving a little bit to the right or left of his former position. Also, it is makrûh for him to sit towards the qibla after namâz. If there is no one in the first line performing namâz towards the imâm, he should sit facing the jamâ'at. If there is a person performing namâz, he should turn to his right or left. All these things (that are makrûh for the imâm) are not makrûh for the jamâ'at or for a person performing namâz individually. It is written before the subject concerning the azân in the book **Imdâd-ul-Fettâh** that it is better for them to perform the final sunnat at some other spot; in fact, it is better to perform it back at home. It is mustahab to undo the lines after the fard namâz.

While describing the namâz of witr, the book **Mawqûfât** says: **"If the imâm does not do five things the jamâ'at do not do them, either**:

1 - If the imâm does not say the prayers of Qunût the jamâ'at do not say them, either.

2 - If the imâm does not say the takbîrs of 'Iyd the jamâ'at do not say them, either.

3 - If the imâm does not sit in the second rak'at of a namâz that has four rak'ats, the jamâ'at do not sit, either.

4 - If the imâm does not make the sajda-i-tilâwat though he said an âyat of sajda, the jamâ'at do not make the sajda-i-tilâwat, either.

5 - If the imâm does not make the sajda-i sahw the jamâ'at do not, either.

If the imâm does four things the jamâ'at do not do them:

1 - If the imâm makes more than two sajdas the jamâ'at does not do so.

2 - If the imâm says the takbîr of 'Iyd more than three times in one rak'at the jamâ'at do not do so.

3 - If the imâm says more than four takbîrs in the namâz of janâza the jamâ'at do not do so.

4 - If the imâm stands up for the fifth rak'at the jamâ'at do not stand up. Instead, (they wait for the imâm, and) they make the salâm together.

There are ten things which the jamâ'at must do even if the imâm does not do them:

1 - Raising the hands for the takbîr of iftitâh (beginning namâz).

2 - Saying the Subhânaka. According to the Imâmeyn, (i.e. Imâm Abû Yûsuf and Imâm Muhammad,) the jamâ'at do not say it, either.

3 - Saying the takbîr when bowing for the rukû'.

4 - Saying the tasbîhs in the rukû'.

5 - Saying the takbîr when prostrating for the sajdas and when getting up from the sajdas.

6 - Saying the tasbîhs in the sajda.

7 - Even if he does not say "Sami' Allâhu," the jamâ'at say, "Rabbanâlakal hamd."

8 - Saying the Attahiyyâtu up to the end.

9 - Making the salâm at the end of namâz.

10 - During the 'Iyd of Qurbân, saying the takbîr immediately after making the salâm after every one of the twenty-three fard prayers.

A **masbûk,** that is, a person who has not caught up with the imâm in the first rak'at, stands up after the imâm has made the salâm to both sides, and makes qadâ of the rak'ats which he missed. He recites in an order as he would do if he were performing the first rak'at, then the second, and then the third rak'at. But he does the sitting postures in a backward order, as if he were performing the fourth, third, and second rak'ats, that is, as if he began with the last rak'at, and so on backwards. For example, a person who arrives during the last rak'at of night prayer stands up after the imâm makes the salâm, says the fâtiha and the additional sûra in the first and second rak'ats. However, he sits in the first rak'at, but does not sit in the second rak'at.

Umdat-ul-Islâm quotes from **Fatâwâ-i-Attâbî**[1]: "If the Masbûk, i.e. person who has not caught up with the imâm in the first rak'at, finishes reciting the 'At-tahiyyâtu' before the end of the final sitting posture, he reiterates the Kalima-i-shahâdat until the imâm makes the salâm. He does not sit without reciting anything. It is harâm to remain mute at places where it is necessary to recite during namâz. He does not recite the Salawât, either. For, the Salawât is recited by people doing their final sitting posture. If he says the Salawât at the first sitting, sajda-i-sahw will be necessary. If he says 'Allâhumma selli' during the Qa'da-i-ûlâ, his namâz will become fâsid." A settled (muqîm) person may follow a musâfir when making adâ[2] as well as when making qadâ. [See chapter 15!] A musâfir may follow a settled person only when making adâ of those fard prayers of namâz that have four rak'ats. If there should be any rak'ats that he has not caught, he performs them after the imâm makes the salâm, and thus completes the rak'ats. For, if a musâfir follows a settled imâm within a prayer time his namâz changes to four rak'ats like the imâm's namâz. On the other hand, because he would have to perform only two rak'ats of the prayers of qadâ, he could not follow a settled imâm; otherwise, a person for whom it is fard to sit and recite would have followed another person for whom it is supererogatory to sit and recite. It is written in the 15th chapter how a settled person performs namâz behind a musâfir imâm. A person who misses one rak'at of the namâz in jamâ'at has not performed that namâz in jamâ'at. But he will be given the blessings of the jamâ'at. If a person who misses the last rak'at catches up with the imâm during the tashahhud, he will be given the blessings of the jamâ'at. There are a lot of additional blessings in saying the Takbîr of iftitâh together with the imâm.

It is stated in **Umdat-ul-Islâm**: "If a person arriving for the jamâ'at sees the imâm bowing for the rukû', he makes the Takbîr (iftitâh) standing and then bows for the rukû'. If he says the Takbîr as he bows, his namâz will not be sahîh. If the imâm straightens up before this person has bowed, he has not caught up with the rak'at."

---

[1] Written by Ahmad Attâbî, (d. 586.)
[2] To make adâ of a certain prayer means to perform that prayer within its prescribed time. To make qadâ of a prayer means to perform it after its prescribed time. We make qadâ of prayers that are fard or wâjib and which we failed to perform within their prescribed time.

21 – FRIDAY (JUM'A) PRAYER

Friday prayer consists of sixteen rak'ats. It is fard-i 'ayn for every man to perform its two rak'ats. He who denies or slights it becomes a kâfir. It is a fard more emphatic than the early afternoon prayer. Friday prayer depends on two groups of conditions for being fard: The first group are the **conditions of wujûb**, and the second group are the **conditions of adâ**. If any one of the conditions of adâ does not exist, the namâz will not be sahîh. If the conditions of wujûb do not exist, the namâz will still be sahîh. There are seven conditions of adâ:

The first condition is to perform the namâz in a **shahr** (city). A shahr is a place whose jamâ'at cannot be accommodated by the largest mosque. The majority of Fiqh savants in the Hanafî Madhhab 'rahmatullâhi ta'âlâ 'alaihim ajma'în' are unanimous in this definition. Also it is written in **Welwâlijiyya**[1] that this ijtihâd is sahîh. Also, a place that has a Muslim governor or commander powerful enough to enforce the commandments of Islam is called a shahr. Even if he cannot enforce all the commandments of the Sharî'at, it will be sufficient if he can protect the people's rights and freedom, prevent faction and mischief, and can take back the rights of the oppressed from their oppressors. It is an excuse if a governor cannot enforce the performance of some of the fards because of the government's oppression.

[Those villages that have headmen confirmed and ratified by today's governments or that have gendarmes, and the regions that are in today's large cities are each a different city for Friday prayer according to both of the above definitions. It is permissible to perform Friday and 'Iyd prayers in such villages and regions. Moreover, according to the Shâfi'î Madhhab, forty people can perform Friday prayer anywhere. When the government gives permission for something permissible in one Madhhab, it becomes permissible in another Madhhab, too. When the government commands a mubâh (something permitted by Islam), it becomes wâjib to do it; and a mubâh prohibited by the government becomes harâm. Unaware of this fact, those who think only of today's large cities when they hear the name shahr (city) speak ill of religious books. By way of simplistic arguments such as: "There is no need to explain that all the people in one city cannot go into one mosque. We are pointing out the fact that

---

[1] A book of fatwâs written by Zahîruddîn Is-hâq Abul Mekârim Welwâlijî, (d. 710 [1310 A.D.].)

the points of view concerning Friday are incompatible with the religion and that there are some misstatements on the conditions of Friday prayer," they attempt to blemish books of fiqh. Shame on these people, whose ignorance has overwhelmed their awareness in such a vulgar complacency as to coax them into traducing Islamic scholars! Even more wretched, though, are those who believe the falsely adorned and enthusiastic articles of such people and who think of these writers as religious men.]

Also, places which the people of a city have reserved as fields, cemeteries or for recreation, are counted as parts of a city.

The second condition is to perform it with the permission of the president of the state or government, or of the governor. A khatîb appointed by them can appoint someone else as his deputy. No one other than those who have been deputizing one another in the process of time can conduct Friday prayer. When a person conducts it without permission, the namâz will be accepted if someone who has permission to conduct it performs the namâz by following him. If the governor of a city dies or cannot come to the mosque for one of such reasons as fitna or chaos, it is permissible for his deputy, assistant or for the judge of the law court to conduct the namâz. For, these people as well as the governor are permitted by the government to conduct the people's religious and worldly affairs. While they are present, an imâm elected by the jamâ'at cannot conduct the Friday prayer. However, if they cannot come to the mosque or if they are not permitted to administer religious affairs, the imâm elected by the jamâ'at can conduct the namâz. Likewise, if the Sultan oppresses the people and prevents the jamâ'at from coming together without a good reason, they may meet together at some place and their imâm may conduct the namâz. But they cannot perform it if the Sultan intends to abrogate the status of the city. If the governors and judges in cities captured by disbelievers are administering them compatibly with the Sharî'at, such cities are not **Dâr-ul-harb**. They are **Dâr-ul-Islâm**. In such cities the governor or the judge elected by the Muslims or any imâm elected by them or by the jamâ'at can conduct the Friday prayer.

While describing the Qâdîs, i.e. judges, the book **Durr al-mukhtâr** says on the three hundred and eighth page of its fourth volume: "Those Islamic countries that are controlled by disbelievers are not dâr-ul-harb; they are dâr-ul-Islâm. For, rules of disbelief have not yet been established in those places. Judges in such places are Muslims and their presidents are Muslims, too. They are obeying the disbelievers unwillingly. If Muslim administrators obey the disbelievers willingly they become fâsiq. In such countries it is permissible for the Muslim governors appointed by disbelievers to conduct the Friday and 'Iyd prayers, to collect kharâj[1], to appoint judges and to see about marriages of orphans. This is because the people are Muslims. The governor's obeying the disbelievers is compulsory and tricky. In such countries, if the governor presiding over the Muslims is a disbeliever, too, the Friday and 'Iyd prayers conducted by an imâm elected by the Muslims and the religious decisions given by the judge chosen by them are acceptable. Or, the Muslims elect a governor from among themselves. That governor appoints the judge and the khatîb (the imâm who will conduct the Friday prayers). If the Muslims like the Muslim judge appointed by a governor who is a disbeliever, it is permissible for him to make religious decisions and to conduct namâz. If a Muslim has revolted against the Sultan, captured a few places and established a government, it is permissible for him to appoint a judge and an imâm."

In the village of Minâ near the blessed city of Mekka, Friday prayer can be performed during the time of Hajj. For, during that time it becomes a city and the governor or the Amîr of Mekka is there, too. To facilitate the affairs of the hadjis, the namâz of 'Iyd in Minâ has been forgiven. The official who is administering the duties of Hajj cannot conduct the Friday prayer if he does not have special permission for doing so, too. It cannot be performed on Arafât because Arafât is an empty plain. It cannot become a city.

In any kind of city Friday prayer can be performed in several mosques. But some of the scholars of the Hanafî Madhhab and the majority of the scholars of the other three Madhhabs have said that Friday prayer cannot be performed in more than one mosques. And, since the acceptableness of Friday prayer is doubtful in a place that is doubtfully a city, we must perform four more rak'ats between the final sunnat of Friday prayer and the sunnat of the time by intending to perform the namâz of **zuhr-i âkhir**, that is, the **latest early afternoon prayer**. When performing these four rak'ats we must add the phrase "which is fard for me" to our intention. We must not say, "which is fard to perform." For, although early afternoon prayer is fard at the time of noon it is not fard to perform it immediately. It becomes fard to perform it when there is only time enough to perform four rak'ats of namâz before late afternoon prayer. Performing it [adâ] does not become fard before that time.

---

[1] Please see the first chapter of the fifth fascicle of **Endless Bliss**.

If a Friday prayer is not accepted, those four rak'ats do not become the fard of Friday's early afternoon prayer when you say, "which is fard to perform." They become the fard of the previous day's early afternoon prayer. And since you already performed it on Thursday the four rak'ats become supererogatory. But when you say, "the last early afternoon prayer which is fard for me," they count for the fard of Friday's early afternoon prayer. However, if the Friday prayer is accepted you will have performed also the fard of the early afternoon prayer, in which case those four rak'ats will become supererogatory. For, a sunnat can be performed with the intention of a fard. If you have any na'mâz of qadâ, you will not have performed it. If it should be argued that when the Friday prayer is accepted the early afternoon prayer lapses, then you will have made your niyyat for Thursday's early afternoon prayer, in which case, again, it will be supererogatory. If there is any early afternoon prayer which you have not performed before, you will not have made qadâ of it. If you intend, **"To perform the last early afternoon prayer that is fard upon me, but which I have not performed,"** and if the Friday prayer is accepted, the namâz stands for the qadâ of a namâz, so this intention is suitable. A person who does not have any namâz of qadâ must say additional sûras in all four rak'ats of the zuhr-i âkhir. If the Friday prayer is not accepted and the namâz stands for the fard of the early afternoon prayer, and then it is not harmful to say sûras in the fard. A person who has debts of early afternoon prayers does not say additional sûras (in the last two rak'ats). For, if the Friday prayer is not accepted the namâz stands for the fard of the early afternoon prayer; if it is accepted the namâz stands for a namâz of qadâ.

The third condition is to perform it during the time of early afternoon prayer. As soon as the azân for early afternoon prayer is performed a namâz of four rak'ats, (the initial sunnat of Friday prayer), is performed. Second, the second azân is performed inside the mosque. Third, the khutba is performed. Fourth, two rak'ats, (the fard of Friday prayer), are performed in jamâ'at. Fifth, four rak'ats, (the final sunnat), are performed, and then the zuhr-i âkhir is performed by intending, "to perform the last early afternoon prayer that is fard upon me but which I have not performed." Finally, two rak'ats (the time's sunnat) are performed. If the Friday prayer is not accepted these ten rak'ats become the early afternoon prayer. Next the Âyatalkursî and the tesbîhs are said, and then the duâ is made. Our Prophet 'sall-Allâhu 'alaihi wa sallam' used to perform six rak'ats of sunnat after the two rak'ats of the fard of Friday prayer.

It is written in the five hundred and fifth page of **Ashi'at ul-leme'ât**: "Amîr al-mu'minîn Hadrat Alî 'radiy-Allâhu 'anh' used to tell people to perform six more rak'ats after the fard namâz of Friday; and Abdullah ibn 'Umar 'radiy-Allâhu 'anhumâ' is reported to have performed six additional rak'ats after the fard of Friday." al-'Allâma ash-Shâmî Sayyid Muhammad Amîn ibn 'Âbidîn 'rahmatullâhi 'alaih' writes on the subject of "i'tikâf" in the second volume of **Radd al-muhtâr**: "After the fard namâz of Friday, as communicated in **Badâyi'**, four rak'ats of sunnat namâz shall be performed according to Imâm-i â'zam, or six rak'ats according to the Imâmeyn. According to scholars who said that the Friday prayer should be performed in a single mosque, four rak'ats of namâz, called **zuhr-i âkhir**, should be performed in addition. According to scholars who said that the performance of the Friday prayer in every mosque is permissible, these four rak'ats become a nâfila, a mustahab; though it is not obligatory to perform them, no one has said they should not be performed. It is better if they are performed."

It is written in **Fatâwâ-i Hindiyya**: "It is not fard for slaves, women, musâfirs, and invalids to perform Friday prayer. There should be at least one man to listen to the khutba. The khutba is not permitted if there are no listeners or if all the listeners are women. It is obligatory that the jamâ'at should comprise of at least three men who have the qualifications to act as imâms. Friday prayer is not sahîh if they are women or children."

The fourth condition is to say the khutba within the time of early afternoon prayer. After the khutba, the person who said the khutba may appoint one of those who listened to the khutba to conduct the namâz on his behalf. He who has not listened to the khutba cannot conduct the namâz.

Our scholars have said that saying the khutba is like saying "Allâhu akbar" when beginning namâz, which means to say that both must be said only in Arabic. There are also savants who have said that it can be said in Persian as well as those who have said that it is permissible to say it in any language, but then it is tahrîmî makrûh according to those savants. It is makrûh for the khâtib to say things other than amr-i ma'rûf in the khutba, even in Arabic. The khatîb first says the "A'ûdhu" silently, then says the "hamd-u-thenâ," the kalima-i shahâdat, and the salât-u-salâm loudly. Afterwards he preaches, that is, admonishes about things that bring rewards and torment, and then recites âyat-i-kerîmas. He sits down and stands up again. After saying the second khutba, he invokes benedictions on the Believers instead of preaching. It is necessary (mustahab) for him to mention the names of the four Khalîfas (Hadrat Abû Bakr, Hadrat 'Umar, Hadrat 'Uthmân, Hadrat Alî). It is not permissible to mention the name of the Sultan or those of the state authorities. It is harâm to praise them with attributes they do not actually have. It has been said by savants that it is permissible to say prayers for them so that they will be just, benevolent, and victorious over their enemies, but when praying nothing must be said that might cause disbelief or harâm. It is harâm to insert a worldly speech into the khutba. The khutba must not be turned into a speech, a conference. He who praises cruel rulers and says that they are just, or who prays for enemies of religion when they are dead or alive, becomes a disbeliever. Also it is harâm to lie in the name of praising a Muslim. To preach in the khutba means to perform amr-i ma'rûf and nahy-i anilmunkar. It does not mean to tell stories or to talk about politics, economics, or other worldly affairs. [Our Prophet 'sall-Allâhu 'alaihi wa sallam' declared: **"There will come such a time that monkey-natured, human-figured people will climb the minbar and teach you what is against the religion and their irreligiousness in the name of the religion."**] Khatîbs, preachers, must be careful not to be among those people who are described in this hadîth-i-sherîf and not to serve as means for irreligiousness. Muslims must not listen to the khutbas and preachings of such people. It is written in the two hundred and eighty-first page of **Tahtâwî**'s annotation to the commentary of the book **Nûr-al-izâh**: "It is sunnat to make a short khutba, and it is makrûh to make a long one."

While explaining the khutba, the takbîr of iftitâh, and reciting prayers in namâz, **Ibni 'Âbidîn** says: "Saying the khutba in any language other than Arabic is like saying the takbîr of iftitâh in another language when beginning namâz. And this, in its turn, is like the other dhikrs of namâz. It is tahrîmî makrûh to say the dhikrs and the prayers within namâz in any language other than Arabic. It was prohibited by Hadrat 'Umar." He also says while explaining the wâjibs of namâz: "Committing tahrîmî makrûh is a venial sin, but a person who keeps doing it loses his 'adl[1]." It is written in **Tahtâwî**: "A person who keeps committing venial sins becomes fâsiq. We must not perform namâz behind those imâms who are fâsiq or who commit bid'ats; instead, we must perform namâz in another mosque." The Sahâba and the Tâbi'în always said the khutbas in

---

[1] To lose one's 'adl means to become 'fâsiq', which, and its antonym, ''âdil', (adjectival form of 'adl,) are defined in tenth chapter.

Arabic both in Asia and in Africa. For, it is bid'at and makrûh to say the khutba in another language. This was done even when those who listened did not know Arabic and did not understand the khutbas. Nor did they have any religious information. It was necessary to teach them. But still they said the khutbas in Arabic. It is said in the book **al-Adillatul-kawâti'** written by Muhammad Viltorî, an Indian scholar, and published in 1395 [1975]: "It is bid'at to say the khutbas of Friday and 'Iyd in any language except Arabic, either completely or partially. It is tahrîmî makrûh. An imâm who continuously does so should not be followed when performing namâz in jamâ'at." This fatwâ is in Arabic. It was printed in Istanbul in 1396 [1976]. For six hundred years, Islamic savants in Turkey had been desiring to have the khutba said in Turkish so that the people could understand it, yet apprehending that the khutba might not be accepted, they had to ban it despite themselves. On second thoughts they appointed Friday preachers who explained the meaning of the khutba before or after the namâz. Thus the jamâ'at learned what was said during the khutba.

Hadrat Sayyid Abdulhakîm Arwâsî 'quddisa sirruh' said: "To worship means to do the commandments. It is worship to read the Qur'ân al-kerîm and to say the khutba. We have not been commanded to understand their meanings. Therefore, it is not something within the worship to understand them. Understanding the Qur'ân al-kerîm requires learning the seventy-two subsidiary branches of knowledge along with its eight main branches. Thereafter, only, will one develop an aptitude towards understanding the Qur'ân al-kerîm. And then one can understand it only if Allâhu ta'âlâ graces one with the lot. To say that everyone must understand the Qur'ân al-kerîm is to belittle the religion. For understanding the **Qur'ân al-kerîm**, a person with great talents has to work for ten years and one with average talents has to work for fifty years. Therefore, we with little ability can not understand it even if we study for a hundred years. In the Sharî'at, what is called knowledge is useful information. Useful information is the information that serves as a means for obtaining endless bliss, i.e. for attaining grace of Allâhu ta'âlâ. This information is called **Islamic knowledge**."

The fifth condition is to say the khutba before the namâz. It must be said in the presence of discreet men who have reached the age of puberty. But it is not a condition for the jamâ'at to hear it or to understand it.

[It is written in **Hindiyya**, in **Durr-ul-mukhtâr**, and in **Imdâd-ul-**

Fettâh: "One man's presence during the khutba is sufficient. If the entire jamâ'at is deaf or asleep, the khutba will be accepted. But the khutba listened to by women without a man being present is not sahîh." As we have discussed earlier, it is not necessary for the jamâ'at to understand the khutba, and it is not even necessary for them to hear it. It is written in **Durr-ul-mukhtâr**: "Saying the khutba in any other language is like saying **Allâhu akbar** (in another language) when beginning namâz. The same applies to the prayers and tesbîhs in namâz." Ibni 'Âbidîn says: "According to Imâm-i A'zam, it is permissible for an imâm who can recite them in Arabic to recite them in any other language. Yet it is makrûh. According to the Imâmeyn, however, it is not permissible for an imâm who can recite them in Arabic to recite them in any other language. [It is written in **Majmâ'ul-Anhur** that Imâm-i A'zam later recanted his former ijtihâd and agreed with the ijtihâd of the Imâmeyn.] It is written in **Welwâljiyya** that it is an act of worship to say the takbîr of namâz and that Allâhu ta'âlâ does not like its being said in another language. Therefore, even in cases where it is permissible to say it wholly or partially in another language, it is tahrîmî makrûh within worships and tanzîhî makrûh outside of worships. It is unanimously reported that during the standing position in salât to recite the âyat-i kerîmas in other languages is not jaîz (permissible). This unanimity has been endorsed in the fatwâ given thereon." So did the blessed imâms of the other three Madhhabs say, because their ijtihâds, like the ijtihâds of our blessed 'Imâmeyn', indicated the result that a khutba said in a language other than Arabic by a person who could read Arabic would not be sahîh. It is written in **Badâyi'**[1]: "Saying the khutba partly in Arabic and partly in another language spoils the Arabic verse, which is makrûh." A person who says it in another language has deviated from the way of the Salaf-i-sâlihîn and has committed a bid'at. It is declared in the hundred and fourteenth (114) âyat of Nisâ sûra that the deviated people will go to Hell. And those who use a television or a loudspeaker in their worships should take this âyat into account.]

According to Imâm-i A'zâm, by only saying "Alhamdu lillâh" or "Subhânallah" or "Lâ ilâha il-l-Allah" the khutba will have

---

[1] **Badâyi'-us-sanâyi fî-tertîb-ish-Sharâyi'**, by Abû Bakr bin Mes'ûd Alâuddîn-i-Shâshî Kâshânî 'rahmatullâhi ta'âlâ 'alaih', (d. 587 [1191 A.D.], Aleppo,) the son-in-law of Muhammad Samarkandî 'rahmatullâhi ta'âlâ 'alaih', (d. 1117 A.D., Karaca Ahmed, İstanbul.) The book is a commentary to his father-in-law's work **Tuhfa-t-ul-fuqahâ**.

been performed; however, it is tanzîhî makrûh. According to the Imâmayn, it is necessary to prolong it long enough to say the prayer of Attahiyyâtu. It is sunnat to make two short khutbas. It is sinful not to sit between the two khutbas. Our Prophet 'sall-Allâhu 'alaihi wa sallam' would say an âyat or a sûra at the Friday khutba. At the khutba or on any other occasion the A'ûdhu and the Basmala is said before saying a sûra. According to the majority of the 'ulamâ, only the A'ûdhu is said before saying an âyat. The Basmala is not said. It is sunnat for the khatîb to wear a black robe and to perform the sunnat on the right hand side of the minbar before the khutba. It is sunnat to say the khutba standing.

The sixth condition is to perform the Friday prayer in jamâ'at. Three men other than the imâm in the Hanafî Madhhab, forty in the Shâfi'î Madhhab, and twelve in the Mâlikî Madhhab, are sufficient. It is acceptable if the entire jamâ'at listening to the khutba leave and other people come and perform the namâz. The jamâ'at may also be formed by musâfirs or by invalids in the Hanafî Madhhab.

The seventh condition is for the mosque to be open for the public. If the namâz is performed inside the mosque with its door locked, it will not be accepted. However, it does not hurt the namâz not to allow women into the mosque in order to prevent fitna.

There are nine **conditions of wujûb** for Friday prayer. That is, for it to be fard for a person requires the existence of the nine conditions that follow: 1- To live in a city or town. It is not fard for musâfirs or for villagers. It is fard for a villager who is in a city and who hears the azân. It is fard for a person whose house is one fersakh, that is, one hour [six kilometres], from the outskirts of a city. 2- To be healthy. It is not fard for an invalid person, for a person who looks after a an invalid whom he cannot leave alone, or for a very old person. 3- To be free. Friday prayer is fard for workers, for civil servants, for soldiers. Their bosses and directors cannot prohibit them from namâz. If the way is long so that they cannot work for a few hours, it is their own wages that will suffer the loss. 4- To be a man. Friday prayer is not fard for women. 5- To be discreet and at the age of puberty. 6- Not to be blind. It is not fard for a blind person even if he has someone to lead him. However, it is fard for a blind person, and for an invalid or squint-eyed person, who can walk along streets without anyone to help him. 7- To be able to walk. Even if there are vehicles, it is not fard for a paralysed person or for a person without feet. 8- Not to be in prison, not to have fear of an enemy, the government, or evildoers.

9- There must not to be too much rain, snow, or mud. And the weather must not to be too cold.

A man who does not have one of these conditions may still perform Friday prayer if he wants to. The hadîth-i-sherîfs declaring that Friday prayer is not fard for women are written in **Tafsîr-i Mazharî** and in **Mishkât-ul-masâbih.**

A musâfir or an invalid person may conduct Friday prayer. It is harâm for a person who has neglected a Friday prayer without a good excuse to perform the early afternoon prayer in a city before the Friday prayer is performed. Thereafter, however, it becomes fard for him to perform the early afternoon prayer[1]. It is makrûh for those who have omitted the Friday prayer with a good excuse to perform the early afternoon prayer in a jamâ'at in a city.

A person who arrives while the imâm is sitting or making the sajda-i sahw joins the jamâ'at. When the imâm makes the salâm he stands up and completes the two rak'ats of Friday prayer. The same applies for a person who arrives late for the namâz of 'Iyd.

After the imâm climbs the minbar, it becomes harâm for the jamâ'at to perform namâz or to talk. As the khatîb prays the jamâ'at must not say "âmîn" loudly. They say it silently. Also, they say the salawât not loudly but silently through their hearts. In short, everything that is harâm to do while performing namâz is harâm while listening to the khutba, too. It is harâm also for those who are far behind and cannot hear the khutba. It is permissible to warn and save those who are in danger of a scorpion, a thief, or a well. It is good to warn such people by signalling with the hand or head. It is makrûh for muazzins to shout prayers during the khutba.

It is fard for every Muslim who hears the first azân for the Friday prayer to stop his work, shopping, or whatever he is doing, and to go to the mosque for the namâz. The first azân did not exist during the time of our Prophet 'sall-Allâhu 'alaihi wa sallam'. The azân used to be said only before the minbar. Hadrat 'Uthmân 'radiy-Allâhu 'anh' ordered the first azân during his caliphate. Rasûlullah's 'sall-Allâhu 'alaihi wa sallam' minbar was on the left hand side of the mihrâb and had three steps. [A person who stood towards the qibla before the mihrâb would have had the minbar on his right hand side and the **Hujra-i sa'âdat** on his left.] It is a loathsome bid'at to say the second part of the khutba after descending on the lower step and then to ascend back to the higher step.

---

[1] It goes without saying that it should be performed before the arrival of the time of late afternoon prayer.

It is tahrîmî makrûh for the khatîb to talk about worldly affairs between the khutba and the namâz. He may advise to follow the commandments and to avoid the prohibitions. If he delays the namâz by talking about things that are not a part of the khutba, his khutba will not be accepted. He will have to say the khutba again. It is permissible for a child to say the khutba, yet the namâz must be conducted by the imâm. On Friday it is permissible to set out on a journey before noon. However, after noon it is makrûh (to do so) before performing the Friday prayer.

In cities conquered by warfare, such as blessed Mekka and Bursa, the khatîb holds a sword in his left hand when he mounts the minbar. He says the khutba leaning on the sword.

If the azân is said while a person is eating, he stops eating if otherwise the prayer time will expire. If he will only be late for the jamâ'at he does not stop eating. He performs namâz alone. But he must not miss the jamâ'at if it is a Friday prayer.

If a villager comes to the city for Friday prayer and to shop, if his intention for the namâz is stronger (than his intention for shopping) he attains the blessings of coming for the Friday prayer. The blessings of namâz are another matter. He will attain those blessings anyway. Likewise is the case with every kind of worship mixed with some worldly intentions. [See the beginning of Hajj in the fifth fascicle.]

Before the khutba begins, it is permissible to pass through the lines (of Muslims) in order to be closer to the minbar and the mihrâb, provided that you will not step on others' shoulders and clothes. While the khutba is being said, it is harâm to change your place or to vex those sitting beside you by pressing against them. It is harâm to beg among the jamâ'at or to give alms to a person who does so. Such a beggar must be sent out of the mosque.

On Friday there is a moment at which any duâ (prayer) will be accepted. There are many savants who say that that moment is between the khutba and the Friday prayer. During the khutba all prayers must be sent through the heart. It is not permissible to utter them in sounds. That moment is different for every city. Friday itself is more valuable than Friday night. During the day or at night there are many blessings in reciting **Sûra-i Kahf. [Tafsîr-i Mazharî]**.

It is sunnat to make a ghusl ablution, to put on fragrant scents, to wear new, clean clothes, to have a haircut, to cut the nails, to burn incense in the mosque, to make **Tabkîr** [to come to the mosque early] for Friday prayer. It is written in the fifth volume of **Durr-ul-mukhtâr**: "It is sunnat for every Muslim to have a haircut and to cut his nails before or after Friday prayer on Fridays. It is better to do these after the prayer. Likewise, these are done after the hajj. He who does not cut them on Friday has to cut them some other day. He must not wait until next Friday to cut them. In warfare it is mustahab to grow the nails and moustache. It is mustahab to get clean by bathing and shaving the hairs in the arm-pits and pubes every Friday. It is permissible to clean the hairs with a chemical [with a razor blade, or Rosma powder] or by plucking. It is permissible as well to clean them every fifteen days. It is tahrîmî makrûh not to clean them for more than forty days." It is written in the annotation made to Imdâd-ul-Fettâh by Tahtâwî 'rahmatullâhi ta'âlâ 'alaih' that it is mustahab to remove the hairs around the anus.

The sustenance of a person with long nails comes with difficulty, with trouble. A hadîth-i-sherîf reads: **"A person who cuts his nails on Friday becomes safe from calamities for one week."**

It is bid'at to shave the moustache. It is sunnat to clip the moustache so as to shorten it to the length of the eye-brows. It is sunnat to grow the beard as long as a small handful, [as measured so as to include its part on the chin,] and to cut the parts longer than that. It is permissible to pull out the white hairs among the beard and moustache. It has been said by savants that the beard longer than one small handful is a sign of a weak mind.

[It is written within the subject concerning the fards of ghusl in **Tabyîn-ul-haqâiq**, and in its commentary rendered by Ahmad bin Muhammad Shelbî, (d. 1031 [1621 A.D.], Egypt,) 'rahmatullâhi ta'âlâ 'alaih': "A hadîth-i sherîf, which exists in **Muslim**, declares: **'Ten acts are sunnat: To clip the moustache, to grow the beard, to use miswâk, madmada,** (or mazmaza, to rinse out the mouth with water when making an ablution), **istinshaq.** (snuffing up water into the nostrils when making an ablution), **to cut the nails, to wash the toes, to clean the arm-pits, to clean the pubes, and istinjâ with water.'** " It is declared clearly in the hadîth-i sherîf that it is sunnat to grow a beard. It is sunnat to grow a beard as long as one handful and to cut it when it is longer than one handful. To shave the cheeks and to grow a beard only on the chin, as some people do, is to change the sunnat. Nor is it compatible with the sunnat to grow a beard less than a handful. Maintaining a short beard with the intention of following the sunnat is bid'at. It is harâm. It becomes wâjib to grow such a short beard as long as a handful. It is makrûh to shave a beard just because it is customary and in order to do as all other people do. But when you live among disbelievers it is permissible and even necessary to shave it altogether for fear you will be mocked, oppressed, or lest you will commit an act of disbelief or harâm, in order to carry out Islam's commandments, earn your living, perform amr-i ma'rûf and nahy-i anilmunkar to youngsters, serve Islam, help the oppressed, or to prevent fitna. These reasons above are excuses for not doing the sunnat. But they are not excuses for committing bid'at.

It is written in the book **al-Halâl wal-harâm**: "A hadîth-i sherîf declares: **'Act contrary to polytheists. Grow your beard!'** [The author of that book, Yûsuf Qardâwî, proclaims himself to be a lâ-Madhhabî in its preface. Therefore, his statements cannot be witnesses. Yet he explains this hadîth-i sherîf correctly and compatibly with the Ahl-as-sunnat.] Ibni Taymiyya said that this hadîth shows that it is harâm to shave a beard. The book **Fath-ul-qadîr**, quoting from Qâdî 'Iyâd 'rahmatullâhi ta'âlâ 'alaih', (476-544 [1150 A.D.], Marrakesh,) says that it is makrûh. There are also savants who say that it is mubâh. The truth is that the hadîth-i sherîf does not show that it is wâjib to grow a beard. No savant has inferred that it is wâjib to dye the beard from the hadîth: **'Jews and Christians do not dye their beard. Act contrary to them and dye** (your beard)!' These hadîth-i sherîfs show that it is mustahab. The Salaf-i sâlihîn did not shave their beards; at that time it was customary to grow a beard." He who slights the beard becomes a disbeliever. It is harâm to shave in order to look pretty or to make your face bright like that of a woman or to shave the chin and grow hair on the cheeks. For, it is harâm for men to imitate women and for women to imitate men. It is written in **Kimyâ-i sa'âdat**, at the end of the chapter dealing with wudû that it is makrûh to shave the beard in order to look young and handsome, without thinking of resembling a woman. It is makrûh for women to shave their hair without an **'udhr** (excuse). It is harâm for women to cut their hair like a man's hair. Women have been prohibited by a hadîth-i sherîf to shave their head or to gather their hair together to make a knot like the lump of a camel on top of the head or on the neck. This hadîth-i sherîf is quoted in **Berîqa** and **Hadîqa**, and in Yûsuf Qardâwî's **al-Halâl wal-harâm fil-islâm**. If it is difficult for a woman to cover her long hair, or if it would cause fitna, it is permissible for her to shorten it by having its part extending down below the ear lobes cut off.

It is written in **Hadîqat-un-nadiyya**[1], in the hundred and forty-first page: "Sunnats are of two kinds: **sunnat-i hudâ** and **sunnat-i**

---

[1] Written by Muhammad Baghdâdî.

zawâid. **Sunnat-i hudâ** are like i'tikâf in a mosque, calling the azân or iqâmat, and performing salât in jamâ'at. They are the characteristic traits of Islam, properties peculiar to this Ummat. [It is written in Ibni 'Âbidîn, at the end of the last volume that circumcision of children is also a sunnat of this kind.] If the inhabitants of a city abandon any one of these sunnats, they are to be fought against. The **rawâtib**, that is, the muakkad sunnats, of three of the daily five prayers are of this kind, too. **Sunnat-i zawâid** involve the actions which Rasûlullah, 'sall-Allâhu 'alaihi wa sallam', habitually did in clothing, eating, drinking, sitting, housing, sleeping, walking, beginning the good deeds with the right-hand side, eating, and drinking with the right hand." It is written in the second volume, page five hundred and eighty-two: "In some hadîth-i-sherîfs, dyeing the beard has been ordered. In some others, it has been prohibited. It has been declared: **"Christians dye. You must not dye. Do not be like them!"** That is why some of the Salaf-i sâlihîn dyed their beard, and others did not. For, it is not wâjib to obey this order or prohibition. Therefore, in this respect, the custom of the city in which one is living is to be followed. It is an act of notoriety not to follow the local customs and usage. It is makrûh." In the second volume, page three hundred and twenty-four of the book **at-Tafhîmât**, Shâh Waliyyullah-i Dahlawî 'rahmatullâhi ta'âlâ 'alaih', a scholar of India, quotes from the great scholar Muhammad Thanâullah Pâniputî: "Rasûlullah 'sall-Allâhu 'alaihi wa sallam' used to cover his head with a head-scarf, wear an antârî (loose long robe), strapped shoes and the like. The Khalîfa 'Umar 'radiy-Allâhu 'anh' also ordered his soldiers in Azerbaijan to clothe themselves in this way. But, today, this kind of attire is not customary. It brings opprobrium to wear things not customary in a country. It causes one to be pointed out, and fitna. A hadîth-i sherîf declares: **"Being singled out is an evil enough for any person."** Therefore, it is necessary to follow the Muslims' customary usage in clothing. It was customary among Believers in the time of Hadrat 'Umar to wear loose long robes, head-scarfs and strapped shoes. Wearing them in this way did not cause distinction, fame or being singled out." But it would cause trouble today. Imâm-i Rabbânî 'quddisa sirruh' states in his three hundred and thirteenth letter: "It is understood from valuable Hanafî books that Muslim women used to wear antârîs (long robes) open in the front. It is necessary for men to wear antârîs closed in the front in places where women wear them open, and open in the front where women wear them closed. Fame brings calamities. It causes disasters." In the two hundred and eighty-eighth letter, he states: **" 'May Allah's curse be upon the one who arouses fitna!'** in a hadîth-i sherîf."

The book **Eshi'at-ul-leme'at**, as it explains the hadîth-i-sherîf, "**Ten beautiful things are Prophets' sunnats**," in the two hundred and twelfth page of its first volume, states that there is not a consensus (among the Islamic authorities) that growing a beard is one of the ten things referred to in the hadîth-i-sherîf. These ten things are written in the forty-second chapter of the book **Terghîb-us-salât**, wherein it is stated also that they are (among the group of sunnats termed) **sunnat-i-hudâ**. It is written in **Eshi'at-ul-leme'at** that growing a beard as long as an amount that can be grasped with the fingers is wâjib. The reason why he says wâjib about growing a beard, distinguishing it from the ten things clearly classified as sunnats in the hadîth-i sherîf, is because it will cause fitna to shave your beard or to grow it shorter than a handful in places where it is customary to grow a beard with the length dictated in the sunnat. For, a person who causes notoriety or arouses fitna has been cursed in a hadîth-i-sherîf. As shaving the beard will cause fitna in a place where it is the vogue to grow a beard, likewise it may arouse fitna to grow a beard in places where it has become customary to shave the beard. Growing a beard shorter than a handful, on the other hand, is a bid'a. Hence, it is wâjib to shave your beard if it is customary in your environment, thereby bracing yourself against the danger of falling into the pit of fitna and staying clear of the worse guilt of joining bid'at holders. It is written on the one hundred and forty-eighth page of **al-Hadîqa**: "Committing a bid'a is more harmful than abandoning a sunnat. A bid'a should be avoided while a sunnat need not be done." It is necessary to follow the custom of a country in order not to cause fitna concerning the mubâhs and the things that are permissible, and in the sunnat-i-zawâids. But, in doing things that are fard, wâjib, sunnat-i hudâ, and in keeping away from harâms, makrûhs and bid'ats, customs are not to be followed. These may be altered only in cases involving appropriate excuses and to the extent prescribed in the fiqh books. This hadîth-i sherîf shows clearly that growing a beard is not Islam's characteristic sign, that it is not peculiar to Islam, and therefore, that it is not sunnat-i hudâ. Hence, it is seen that growing a beard is sunnat-i zawâid. As for people who are in charge of religious duties; it is never permissible for them to omit the sunnat-i-zawâids or the mustahabs, not even with the excuse of having to follow the customs. Such people should always grow a beard as long as a handful. It is an alteration of the sunnat to keep a beard shorter than a handful. Calling the short beard a sunnat is bid'at, which is a grave sin. It is written in fiqh books that no savant said it is mubâh to keep a beard shorter than a handful, [as measured by including the part on the chin.] A handful is four fingers in width. Measuring it is done by clasping the part of your chin beginning from the lower edge of your lower lip. It is fard for a person who keeps a beard to wet the skin under the beard when performing a ghusl. If he does not wet it, his ghusl and his ablution and consequently his namâz will not be sahîh.

It is permissible for men to dye their hair or beard any colour except black. Also there are savants who have said that it is permissible to dye it black, too. It is not permissible for them to dye their hands, feet, or nails. For, it would be an act of imitating a woman. It is permissible for a woman to dye those parts with a dye, provided that it will not prevent them from being washed in an ablution and in a ghusl, and provided they will not show them to men.

It is written in the twelve hundred and twenty-ninth page of the second volume of the 1284 - Istanbul edition of the book **Berîqa** by hadrat Muhammad Hâdimî 'rahmatullâhi ta'âlâ 'alaih': "It is not permissible for women to shave their hair and for men to shave their beard. If a woman has a beard she is permitted to shave it. A hadîth-i sherîf declares: **"Shorten your moustache! Grow your beard."** According to this command, it is against the sunnat to shave the beard. If this hadîth-i sherîf denoted wujûb, it would be harâm to shave the beard. The book **Tâtârhâniyya** says, borrowing from **Tajnîs**[1], that this hadîth-i sherîf means: 'Do not shave your beard, nor grow it shorter than a small handful'. Such statements as, 'A person who shaves his beard or who grows it shorter than a handful is not permitted to (conduct namâz in jamâ'at as) imâm. Also the namâz which he performs alone becomes makrûh. He is accursed and rejected both in this world and in the next,' which are said to have been derived from **Tahtâwî**, or statements to this effect that are said to have been derived from **Tafsîr-i Qurtubî**[2], do not have any foundation, nor have they been proven to be true." It is written in the thirteen hundred and thirty-sixth page: "It is also harâm for women to slenderize their eye-brows by plucking them, and it is permissible for them to pull out or to shave the hairs

---

[1] Written by Burhân-ad-dîn Alî bin Abî Bakr Merghinânî 'rahmatullâhi ta'âlâ 'alaih', (martyred by the hordes of Dzengiz Khân in 593 [1197 A.D.].)

[2] Written by Abû Abdullah Muhammad bin Ahmad Qurtubî (of Cordova) 'rahmatullâhi ta'âlâ 'alaih', (d. 671 [1272 A.D.].)

growing on their foreheads, cheeks, and chins." After cutting the hair, the beard or other hairs, the hairs cut must be buried or put on a grave or on a place that is not trodden upon, or in the sea. It is not sinful to throw them away. It is makrûh to throw them into toilets or into wash-basins where kitchen utensils are washed. It is makrûh to cut the nails with the teeth. It causes the disease called speckles. It is harâm for women to let men (nâ-mahram to them) see the parts cut off (from their body).

It is sunnat for men to shave their head or to grow their hair and comb it by parting it into two. It is makrûh for them to curl or plait their hair. It is written in the book **Bahr-ur-râiq**, in the chapter **el-Kerâhiyya**: "It is permissible for a man to shave the top of his head and grow the surrounding hair. Yet it is makrûh to curl and plait the hanging hair. To plait the hair is to be like some kafirs (disbelievers.)" That means also that it is makrûh, not harâm to do something forbidden because it is like the customs of disbelievers. Therefore, the hadîth-i sherîfs **"Do not be like mushriks** (polytheists). **Grow a beard!"** and **"Perform your salât with na'ls on. Do not be like Jews!"** show that it is makrûh, not harâm to shave the beard and to perform salât with bare feet. See chapter 18 for **makrûhs of namâz**, article 25!

It is makrûh to fast only on Fridays or to perform the namâz of tahajjud (the namâz performed after midnight) only on Friday nights. It is harâm to perform any namâz when the sun is overhead, [that is, during the period of time between the moment as long before the time of early afternoon prayer as the time called Tamkin and the time of early afternoon prayer.] A more dependable statement is that of those savants who say that it is harâm to perform any namâz during that time even on Fridays.

On Fridays souls come together and meet one another. Graves are visited. Torment in graves is suspended on that day. According to some savants, Believers' torment does not begin again. But a disbeliever's torment continues until Rising Day except on Fridays and in Ramadân. Those Believers who die on that day or during that night are never tormented in their graves. Hell is not very hot on Friday. Hadrat Adam 'alaihissalâm' was created on Friday. He was taken out of Paradise on Friday. People who will be in Paradise will see Allâhu ta'âlâ on Fridays.

The following passage is a translation from **Riyâd-un-nâsihîn**:

Allâhu ta'âlâ has assigned Friday to Muslims. He declares at the end of Jum'a Sûra: **"O My slaves who have been honoured with imân! When the adhân** (azân) **of early afternoon prayer is** said on Friday run to the mosque to listen to the khutba and to perform Friday prayer. Stop buying and selling! Friday prayer and the khutba are more useful to you than your other businesses. After performing Friday prayer you may leave the mosque and disperse so that you can resume your worldly transactions. You work, and expect your sustenance from Allâhu ta'âlâ. Remember Allâhu ta'âlâ very often so that you will be saved!" After the namâz those who want to work may go out to work, and those who want to spend their time reading the Qur'ân al-kerîm and praying may stay in the mosque. Buying and selling is sahîh during the prayer time, yet it is sinful. Rasûlullah 'sall-Allâhu 'alaihi wa sallam' declared: **"If a Muslim makes a ghusl and goes to the mosque for Friday prayer, the sins he has committed during the week will be forgiven and he will be given blessings for each step."** A hadîth-i sherîf declares: **"The most valuable of days is Friday. Friday is more valuable than the days of 'Iyd and the day of Ashûra** (the tenth day of Muharram). **Friday is the Believers' day of feast in this world and in the next."** Another hadîth-i sherîf declares: **"Allâhu ta'âlâ seals the hearts of those who do not perform the Friday prayer. They sink back into oblivion."** Another hadîth declares: **"If a person does not perform three Friday prayers though there is no hindrance, Allâhu ta'âlâ seals his heart. That is, he can never do any good."** A person who does not perform a series of three Friday prayers without a good excuse becomes a munâfiq. Abû Alî Daqqaq 'rahmatullâhi 'alaih'[1] advised three things as he died: "On Friday perform a ghusl! Every night go to bed with an ablution! Remember Allâhu ta'âlâ every moment!" A hadîth-i sherîf declares: **"On Fridays there is a moment when any prayer a Believer sends is not refused."** Some savants said that that moment is between the late afternoon and evening azâns. Another hadîth-i-sherîf, which exists in the Fârisî book **Terghîb-us-salât**, declares: **"If you say the prayer, 'Estaghfirullâh-al-'azîm-allazî lâ ilâha illâ Huwal hayyal qayyûma wa atûbu ilayh,' three times before the morning prayer of Friday all your sins will be forgiven."** [But this is conditional upon your having paid all your (material and spiritual) debts which you owe to creatures, performed the prayers of namâz which you have omitted, and ceased from committing harâms.] Another hadîth-i-sherîf declares: **"If a person says the sûra of Ikhlâs and the sûras**

---

[1] His name is Hasan bin Muhammad, (d. 405 [1014 A.D.], Nishâpûr.) He was the father-in-law and master of Abul-Qâsim Qushayrî 'rahmatullâhi ta'âlâ 'alaih', (376 [986 A.D.] – 465 [1072], Nishâpûr.)

of Mu'awwazatayn seven times after Friday prayer Allâhu ta'âlâ protects him against calamities, troubles and evil deeds for one week." Worships done on Friday are given at least twice as many blessings as those that are given for worships done on other days. And sins committed on Friday are registered two-fold. A hadîth-i sherîf declares: **"As Saturday was given to Jews and Sunday to Christians, Friday has been given to Muslims. On this day there are uses, barakats and goodnesses for Muslims."**

The following **prayer of istighfâr** must be said on Fridays and every day: "**Allâhummaghfirlî wa li âbâî wa ummahâtî wa li ebnâî wa benâtî wa li ihvetî wa ahawâtî wa li-a'mâmî wa ammâtî wa li ahwâlî wa hâlâtî wa li zawjatî wa abawayhâ wa li-esâtizetî wa li-l-mu'minîna wa-l-mu'minât wa-l-hamdu-li-llâhi Rabb-il-'âlemîn!**"

22 – THE NAMÂZ OF 'IYD

The first of the month of Shawwâl is the first day of the 'Iyd of Fitr and the tenth of Zilhijja is the first day of the 'Iyd of Qurbân. On these two days it is wâjib for men to perform two rak'ats of 'Iyd namâz at the time of **ishrâq**, that is, after the time of karâhat[1] has passed following the sunrise. The conditions for the namâz of 'Iyd are like the conditions for Friday prayer. But in the former, the khutba is sunnat and is said after the namâz. In the 'Iyd of Fitr it is mustahab to eat something sweet [dates or candy], to make a ghusl, to use the miswâk, to wear the newest clothes, to pay the fitra before the namâz, and to say the takbîr softly on the way.

In the 'Iyd of Qurbân it is mustahab not to eat anything before the namâz, to eat the meat of Qurbân first after the namâz, to say the **takbîr-i teshrîq** loudly, but softly by those who have an excuse, when going for the namâz.

It is written in **Halabî-yi kebîr**: "The namâz of 'Iyd consists of two rak'ats. It is performed in jamâ'at. It cannot be performed individually. In the first rak'at, after the Subhânaka the **takbîr-i zawâid** is said three times; that is, the hands are lifted up to the ears three times; in the first and second times, they are let down hanging on both sides, and after the third time they are clasped under the navel. After the imâm says the Fâtiha and the additional sûra aloud, they (the imâm and the jamâ'at) bow for the rukû'. In the second rak'at the Fâtiha and an additional sûra are said first, then the hands are lifted up to the ears again, three times, and after

---

[1] Period of time wherein it is not permissible to perform namâz. Times of karâhat are explained in detail in the tenth chapter.

each time they are let down hanging on both sides. In the fourth takbîr you do not lift your hands up to your ears but instead bend for the rukû'. In the first and second rak'ats five and four takbîrs are said respectively. And in order not to forget where you will put your hands after those nine takbîrs, you memorize this procedure as follows: "Hang them twice and clasp them once. Hang them thrice and then bend." It is stated in **Mâ-lâ-budda**[1]: "A person who misses the jamâ'at does not make qadâ of 'Iyd prayer. If the entire jamâ'at have failed to perform a namâz of 'Iyd because of some excuse, the namâz of 'Iyd of Fitr can be performed on the second, (and not on the third,) and the namâz of 'Iyd of Adhâ can be performed on the third day as well (as on the second).

'Iyd means bayram. Those days are called **'Iyd** because every year Muslims' sins are forgiven in the month of Ramadân and on the 'Arafa Day and their joy and felicity come back on those days. If the first day of 'Iyd is a Friday, both the namâz of 'Iyd and the namâz of Friday will be performed according to the Hanafî Madhhab. They are performed at their appointed times. If there is a janâza on the morning of the 'Iyd the namâz of 'Iyd is performed first. The namâz of janâza is performed after that because the namâz of 'Iyd is wâjib for everybody. However, the namâz of janâza is to be performed before the khutba of the 'Iyd.

It is makrûh for those who are not on the Arafât to assemble at some place and do as the hadjis do on the 'Arafa day. But it is permissible to assemble in order to listen to some Islamic preaching or for doing any other worship. [Please see the seventh chapter in the fifth fascicle of Endless Bliss.]

According to the Imâmeyn, from morning prayer on the 'Arafa day, that is, the day preceding the 'Iyd of Qurbân, until after late afternoon prayer on the fourth day, which amounts to twenty-three prayers of namâz in all, it is wâjib for everyone, men and women alike, for **hadjis** and for those who are not making the **hajj**, for those who are performing namâz in jamâ'at and for those who are performing it alone to say the **Takbîr-i teshrîq (Allâhu akbar, Allâhu akbar. Lâ ilâha illallah. Wallâhu akbar. Allâhu akbar wa lillâhil-hamd)** once immediately after making the salâm in any namâz that is fard or when making qadâ of any fard namâz for the days of this 'Iyd. This (takbîr) is said after Friday prayer as well. It

---

[1] It was written by Thenâullah Dahlawî 'rahmatullâhi ta'âlâ 'alaih', (1143 [1730 A.D.] – 1255 [1810].) The book was reproduced by Hakîkat Kitâbevi in 1409 [1989 A.D.].

is mustahab to recite it after 'Iyd prayer. It is not said after the namâz of janâza. It is not necessary to say it after leaving the mosque or if you have talked (after the namâz). If the imâm forgets the takbîr, the jamâ'at must not omit it. Men may say it loudly. The second, third and fourth days of the 'Iyd of Qurbân are called **Ayyâm-i teshrîq**.

It is written in the book **Ni'met-i Islâm**: "It is sunnat to do the following things on the 'Iyd days: to get up early; to make a ghusl; to clean the teeth with miswâk; to put on perfume; to wear new and clean clothes; to manifest that you are happy; to eat sweetmeat before the prayer of the 'Iyd of Fitr; to eat dates; to eat an odd number of them; for one who performs the qurbân, to eat first the meat of qurbân; to perform morning prayer in the masjid of one's quarter and to go a large mosque for the 'Iyd prayer; to wear a ring on that day; to go to the mosque early and to go on foot; to say the takbîrs of 'Iyd in whispers on the 'Iyd of Fitr and audibly on the 'Iyd of Adhâ; to take a different route on one's way back [from the mosque]. This is because the places where one offers one's ibâdat and the routes that one takes when going for 'ibâdat will stand as witnesses on the Day of Judgement; to welcome the Believers [Muslims] with a smiling face and by saying 'Salâmun 'alaykum'; to give alms generously to the poor [and to give help to those who are working to disseminate true Islam]; to give the sadaqa-i fitr before the 'Iyd prayer." It is sunnat also to reconcile those who are cross with one another; to visit one's relatives and brothers-in-Islam, and to give them presents. Finally, it is sunnat for men to visit graves.

[It is stated as follows in hadîth-i sherîfs: **"Man takes to those who do him favours,"** and **"Give presents to one another and you will love one another."** The most valuable and the most useful present is a smiling face and honeyed words. You should always treat everybody with a smiling face and soft words, whether they are friends or enemies, Muslims or disbelievers, unless they are bid'at holders. You should not quarrel with anybody. Quarreling will destroy friendship. It will aggravate hostilities. You should not become angry with anybody. A hadîth-i-sherîf admonishes: **"Do not become angry!"** At times of fitna, mischief, when you see people worshipping a cow, feed straw to the cow lest you should anger them.

In the Hanbalî Madhhab, it is permissible to make jem' of evening and night prayers, (i.e. to perform one immediately after the other,) at home for reasons such as cold weather, winter, mud, and storm, as well as the excuses stated towards the end of the ninth chapter, during a journey of 80 kilometres. The sunnats are not performed when making jem'. You make niyyat (intention) for jem' when beginning the earlier one of the two salâts. People with duties and jobs inconvenient for them to perform early and late afternoon and evening prayers within their prescribed periods should imitate the Hanbalî Madhhab and make jem' of early and late afternoon prayers and evening and night prayers instead of resigning from office. If they resign from office, they will share the responsibility for the persecutions and irreligious activities likely to be perpetrated by people who will fill the vacancies they have occasioned. In the Hanbalî Madhhab, there are six fards (compulsory acts) for ablution: to wash the face together with inside of the mouth and the nostrils; to make niyyat (intention); to wash the arms; to make masah (rub the wet hands gently) on the entire head, on the ears, and on the piece of skin above them; [masah is not made on hanging parts of long hair. In the Mâlikî Madhhab, on the other hand, masah is compulsory on the hanging parts as well;] to wash the feet together with the ankle-bones on the sides; tertîb, [i.e. to observe the prescribed order;] muwâlât [quickness]. (If the person imitating the Hanbalî Madhhab is a male Muslim,) his ablution will be broken if he feels lust in case he touches anyone of the opposite sex on the bare skin, or if he touches his male organ. When a woman touches him, however, his ablution will not be broken even if he feels lust. Anything emitted by the skin will break the ablution if it is in a big amount. Eating camel's meat will break an ablution. Situations in which a person has an 'udhr are the same as those in the Hanafî Madhhab, (which are explained in the last six paragraphs of the third chapter.) In ghusl, (which is explained in the fourth chapter,) it is fard to wash inside the mouth and the nostrils and the hair, and for men to wash their plaited hair, (if they have plaited hair). It is sunnat (if ghusl is made for purification from janâbat), and fard (if it is made for purification from the state of menstruation), for women to undo their plaited hair. It is fard to sit as long as a (duration of time that would enable a person to say a certain prayer termed) tashahhud (during the sitting posture in namâz) and to make the salâm by turning the head to both sides (at the end of namâz). (These are the essentials that people who imitate the Hanbalî Madhhab have to learn and observe.)

23 – THE QADÂ NAMÂZES [PRAYERS NOT PERFORMED WITHIN THEIR PRESCRIBED PERIOD]

Being an **'Ibâdat-i badaniyya** (physical worship), namâz cannot be performed on behalf of someone else. Everyone has to perform it themselves. A person who is seriously ill or very old cannot give fidya [money] to the poor in place of performing namâz. However, he can pay fidya as a substitute for fasting when he is not able to fast.

It is written in **Halabî-i-kebîr**: "A person who has omitted a namâz with an excuse or without an excuse has to make qadâ of it (has to perform it later). Since only in the Hanbalî Madhhab a person who omits a namâz without an excuse becomes a renegade, he does not have to make qadâ of his namâz. He has to make his tawba for disbelief first." It is written on its sixth page: "Because it is fard to perform namâz, he who disbelieves it becomes a kâfir. A person who believes it but does not perform it becomes fâsiq. This rule applies to all the fards that are declared clearly in the Qur'ân al-kerîm, by the sunnat (the Prophet's hadîths), and by the ijmâ (unanimity of the Sahâba). Those fards that have been inferred through ijtihâd are called **muqayyad**. A person who denies them does not become a kâfir." [However, a person who slights these fards, who follows his own mind, and who despises the word of a mujtahid becomes a kâfir.]

Master Ibrâhim Muhammad Neshât 'rahmatullâhi ta'âlâ 'alaih', representative of **Jâmi'ul azhar** in the Republic of Cameroon, says on the twenty-fifth page of the sixth of the series of books entitled **Islamic Culture**: "All savants have declared that it is a grave sin to omit namâz and that it is necessary to make qadâ of it. Ibn-i Taymiyya said that a person who omitted namâz without a good reason would not have to make qadâ of it, that it was not sahîh to make qadâ of it, that the person would have to perform many supererogatory prayers, do many favours, do many good things, and recite istighfâr a great deal, instead. These heretical thoughts had been put forth earlier, too, namely by ibn Hazm." Attaching wrong meanings to âyat-i-kerîmas and hadîth-i-sherîfs, ibn Taymiyya and ibn Hazm disagreed with the **Ahl as-Sunna** in this respect too, and fanned the flames of the heretical idea that good deeds could replace namâz. This was one of the most harmful wounds that they inflicted on Islam.

It is written on the two hundred and fifty-sixth page of **Durr-ul-mukhtâr**: "It is harâm to postpone a fard namâz till after its prescribed time is over, that is, to leave it to qadâ, without a good excuse." It is written on its four hundred and eighty-fifth page: "It is a grave sin to perform a fard namâz after its prescibed time without an excuse, [that is, without one of the good reasons dictated by Islam.] This sin is not forgiven when the namâz is performed later. In addition to making qadâ of it, (i.e. paying the debt by performing it aftenwards,) it is necessary to make tawba or to make a hajj. When the qadâ is made, only the sin of not having performed the namâz is forgiven. If you make tawba without making qadâ of the namâz, neither the sin of omitting the namâz nor the sin of delaying it is forgiven. The basis for this is that acceptance of the tawba requires eliminating the sin."

[Some preaching books say that a namâz of four rak'ats is performed in the name of **Kaffârat-i namâz** after the last Friday prayer of the blessed month of Ramadân. They even prescribe the recitations to be made at each rak'at and after the salâm. This namâz, they say, will serve as the kaffârat for all the prayers of namâz that you have omitted previously, and all of them will be forgiven. This statement is true. But this namâz, like all other acts of worship performed at sacred times, is for the admittance of the tawba that you make for the forgiveness of the sin of not having performed the fard prayers of namâz during their appointed times, provided that you should have made qadâ of them. The omitted prayers of namâz will never be forgiven unless you make qadâ of them. Likewise, the kaffârat for fasting does not make up for the debt of fasting; it is necessary also to make qadâ for as many days as you did not fast.]

The following extract has been translated from **Durr-ul-mukhtâr**:

When performing the fard part of the five daily prayers and the namâz of Witr and when making qadâ of them, it is necessary to observe the **tertîb**. That is, when performing namâz it is necessary to pay attention to the order of time. Also the fard of Friday prayer must be performed at the time of the day's early afternoon prayer. A person who cannot wake up for morning prayer has to make qadâ of it as soon as he remembers it, even if he remembers it during the khutba (of Friday prayer). Unless a person performs a prayer or makes qadâ of it, it is not permissible for him to perform the five prayers following it. A hadîth-i sherîf declares: **"If a person who has over-slept or forgotten a prayer remembers it while performing the following prayer in jamâ'at, he must finish the prayer together with the imâm and then make** qadâ of the previous prayer! Then he must perform again the one that he has performed with the imâm!"

Performing any kind of namâz in its prescribed time is called **adâ**. Once you have started to perform a supererogatory prayer, it it has become its time, and it has now become wâjib to complete it. If it becomes fâsid (null and void) before being completed, it is wâjib to make qadâ of it. Performing any namâz for the second time before its time is over is named **iâda**. If a namâz is not performed in its time, performing it after its prescribed time is over is named **qadâ**. It is fard to make qadâ of a fard. It is wâjib to make qadâ of a wâjib. We are not commanded to make qadâ of a sunnat namâz that we have failed to perform within its correct time. If a person makes qadâ of a sunnat, the namâz that he has performed becomes supererogatory and he does not get the blessings of the sunnat.

[It is written in a Shiite book: "If a person who has not performed his prayers of namâz with good excuses dies, his protector performs them or has them performed by someone else in return for money. It is permissible to save a dead person from his debts by hiring someone to perform his other worships as well."]

The qadâ can be performed at any time except the three times cited in the tenth chapter. If a person remembers that he did not perform the witr before he begins the morning prayer or as he performs it, his morning prayer will not be accepted. The morning prayer will be accepted only in case there is only enough time for him to perform the witr namâz before sunrise. This means to say that if at the end of a prayer time there is not enough time to make the qadâ also, the necessity to make the qadâ first lapses. If a person who performed the fard of the time's namâz because he misjudged that there was very little time left finds out later that there is enough time, he makes the qadâ and then performs the time's fard again. If he forgets that he has a namâz of qadâ as he begins the time's namâz or as he performs the namâz, the namâz that he performs is accepted even if he remembers the qadâ after the namâz. For it is an excuse to forget.

Another reason that excuses the necessity of performing the prayers of qadâ in order of time is when the number of the prayers of qadâ equals six. A person who omitted six successive fard prayers, or performed them but they were unacceptable, is not a person with tertîb. In this case he does not have to pay attention to the sequence of time between the prayers of qadâ themselves or between the qada prayers and the daily prayers that he is to perform in time. For example, if a person who has not performed a fard prayer performs the five daily prayers coming after it though he remembers it, the five prayers will not be accepted and as a result the number of prayers that he has not performed will be six. The namâz of witr is not included in this calculation. But those fard prayers that have not been performed before are added into the calculation.

The fourth reason that eliminates the necessity of observing the order of time among the prayers of namâz is not to know the fact that time order is necessary. It is excusable not to know something on which there is no Nass or ijmâ'. For example, if a person who did not perform the morning prayer performs the early afternoon prayer though he remembers (that he did not perform the morning prayer), the early afternoon prayer is not acceptable. Then if he makes qadâ of the morning prayer and performs the late afternoon prayer, the late afternoon prayer is acceptable. For, he thinks that the early afternoon prayer that he performed has been accepted. If a person has more than five prayers of qadâ and if, as he makes qadâ of them, the number of prayers which he did not perform becomes fewer than six, the necessity of observing the time order does not reapply. He may perform the remaining prayers without paying attention to their sequence.

If a person has fewer than six prayers that he did not perform, the daily prayers that he performs without observing this time order are not accepted. But this, according to Imâm-i a'zam 'rahmatullâhi ta'âlâ 'alaih', depends on a condition. When the number of prayers that he has performed later and the number of prayers left to qadâ add up to six, the prayers that he has performed later become acceptable again. For example, if a person does not perform one fard prayer or the witr, the prayers that he performs later are not accepted. If he makes qadâ of the prayer which he has omitted before having performed the fifth prayer, the prayers that he has performed become supererogatory prayers. If the time of the fifth prayer is over before he performs the omitted prayer, the number of prayers not accepted, when added to the omitted prayer, becomes six. In this case, the five prayers which he has performed become acceptable again. However, during each prayer that he performs he must remember that he has a prayer of qadâ. If he has not remembered during a few of them, they are not added into the calculation. If a person who has not performed the morning prayer performs the following prayers, at the time of sunrise the following morning, all the five prayers he has performed become acceptable.

According to the Imâmeyn, the unacceptability of the prayers that are performed with no regard to time order does not depend on any conditions; it is categorical.

A person who cannot stand, or who may suffer harm or feels dizzy if he stands, performs the fard prayers sitting at the place where he makes the sajda. He bows for the rukû' and places his head on the floor for the sajda. For a person who can stand for a little while by leaning on a wall, on a stick or on a person, it is fard to say the takbîr (of iftitâh) while standing up and to remain standing at least long enough for that. A person who is unable to prostrate for the sajda must make the sajda on something hard that is less than 25 cm high and which has been put on the floor beforehand. A person who has a wound on his forehead puts only his nose on the floor, and a person with a wound on his nose puts only his forehead on the floor, for the sajda. A person who has excuses both on his nose and on his forehead, and who therefore cannot put his head down on the floor or on a similar hard thing, performs the namâz sitting, with signs, even if he could stand. That is, he bends a little for the rukû', and bends even more for the sajda. To make the sajda, it is tahrîmî makrûh for him or for someone else to lift up something from the floor in order to make sajda on it. As is written in the books **Fath-ul-qadîr, Marâqîl-falâh, Halabî**, and **Majmâ'ul anhur**, one day Rasûlullah 'sall-Allâhu 'alaihi wa sallam' visited an invalid person. When he saw that the person lifted up a pillow and made the sajda on it, he removed the pillow. This time the sick person picked up a piece of wood and made the sajda on it. Rasûlullah removed the piece of wood, too, and stated: **"Make the sajda on the floor if you can! If you cannot bend down to the floor do not lift something up to your face to make sajda on it! Perform the namâz by signs and for the sajda bend more than you do for the rukû'!"** If a person bends more than he does for the rukû' when making the sajda on something propped up, he will have performed the namâz by signs, and his namâz will become sahîh. Therefore, it is unnecesary to lift up something with hands.

Ibrâhîm Halabî 'rahmatullâhi ta'âlâ 'alaih' says in the six hundred and eighteenth page of **Halabî-i kebîr**: "If the medicine put on a person's tooth in order to stop vehement pain prevents him from saying the prayers, he follows the imâm if the time is running short. If there is not an imâm he performs the namâz without saying the prayers."

A person who cannot sit properly because of some pain in one of his limbs, sits as he likes. He may even stretch his legs towards the qibla in order to sit. He leans against a pillow or something else, or someone may support or hold him and prevent him from falling. It is not permissible for him to sit on something high and perform the namâz with signs. [The namâz of a person who performs it sitting on a chair is not acceptable. For, there is no darûrat for sitting on a chair. He who can sit on a chair can sit on the floor as well, and therefore he has to perform namâz sitting on the floor. If a person is too ill to get up from the floor after the namâz, whereas it would be easier for him to stand up if he sat on a chair, then someone should help him to his feet. Or, the sick person can perform the namâz sitting without hanging his feet down from a divan laid towards the qibla. After namâz, he can hang down his feet from one side of the divan and stand up as he would from a chair.] A sick person who cannot sit up on the floor, lean up against something, or be held up by someone else, must perform namâz lying on his back. He stretches his feet towards the qibla. He puts a pillow under his head, thus his face being turned towards the qibla, or he lies on his right or left with the front of his body towards the qibla. He makes signs with his head for the rukû' and the sajda. A conscious but sick person who cannot perform his prayers of namâz even by such signs does not make qadâ of any of them, if he cannot perform namâz for more than a day. So is the case with a person who, for some reason not caused by himself or due to an illness, remains unconscious or oblivious so as to forget the number of sajdas or rak'ats for more than a period comprising five salâts. One who becomes unconscious by taking alcoholic drinks, narcotics or a medicine has to make qadâ of all the prayers he has not performed even if they stretch over a period of several days.

A person who finds himself on his death-bed before having performed his prayers, though he could have performed them at least with signs, must order that the kaffârat for his prayers be made. The kaffârât of namâz is to give half a sâ' [1750 gr.] of wheat to a poor Muslim for each namâz. The person whom he has enjoined it upon or one of his heirs must pay it. It must be paid out of one-third of the property which the person who enjoined it has left behind. If he did not order it while dying, it is not necessary for anyone to pay it.

Even if the number of prayers that have not been performed is more than five, they must be performed as soon as possible. There is no need to hurry for the sajda-i tilâwat or for the qadâ of fasting. It is not sinful to delay them.

A person who became a Muslim in (a country which Islam categorizes as a) dâr-ul-harb does not make qadâ of the prayers of namâz which he did not perform between the time he became a Muslim and the time when he heard that namâz is fard. When a renegade becomes a Muslim again he does not have to make qadâ of the prayers of namâz or the fasts that he had performed before he turned a renegade or those that he did not perform after becoming a renegade. But he has to make hajj again. He makes qadâ of those fard prayers which he did not perform before turning a renegade. It is a grave sin for a Muslim not to do the fard. His sins are not pardoned when he becomes a renegade.

During an illness it is permissible to make qadâ of the prayers you did not perform while you were healthy, by making a tayammum or with signs. When you recover you do not have to perform them again. A person who is making qadâ must not let others know of it. It is sinful to omit namâz, and must be kept secret.

There are two justifiable reasons for leaving a namâz that is fard or wâjib to qadâ knowingly. The first one applies in case of a direct confrontation with the enemy. The second one applies for a travelling person – a person who is on a journey even if he did not intend to go a distance of three days – who fears a thief, a wild animal, a flood, or a storm. When such people cannot perform namâz even with signs, by sitting, by turning towards a direction, or on an animal, they can leave it to qadâ. It is not sinful to leave the fards to qadâ for one of these two reasons or to miss them as a result of falling asleep or forgetting. After stating that it is mustahab to delay night prayer until one-third of the time allotted for it has passed, they (scholars) add: "It is not harâm to go to sleep after a prayer time has begun and thus to miss the prayer, yet it is tahrîmî makrûh. If you do something to make sure that you will wake up, e.g. ask someone to wake you up or set an alarm clock, it will not be makrûh to go to sleep after the prayer time has begun; and it is not makrûh anyway to do so before the beginning of a prayer time. It is written in the commentatory to **Eshbâh** by Kara Çelebizâde: "It is acceptable to perform namâz after its appointed time if you have to do so to save someone who is about to drown or because you are up against a situation of equally vital importance." But it is fard to make qadâ of it [as soon as the excuse ceases to exist]. It is permissible to delay the prayers of qadâ long enough to earn sustenance for your household and to supply your indispensable needs; however, you will have to perform the qadâ prayers in your earliest free time, unless that free time coincides with one of the three periods of time during which it is harâm to perform a namâz. You become sinful if you delay them any longer. As a matter of fact, Rasûlullah 'sall-Allâhu 'alaihi wa sallam' performed the four prayers, which they had failed to perform because of the severity of the war of Handak (Trench), in jamâ'at on the same night although the Sahâba 'radiy-Allâhu 'anhum' were wounded and debilitated.

As the savants of the Hanafî Madhhab unanimously declare, "Obligation to perform prayers of namâz that are in the category of sunnat is binding only within their dictated periods of time. Those sunnat prayers not performed within the time allotted to them are not debts that must be paid. So, we have not been commanded to make qadâ of them. However, since the sunnat of morning prayer verges on to wâjib, when it cannot be performed in time, it is performed together with its fard before noon the same day. The sunnat of the morning prayer cannot be made qadâ of in the afternoon, and the sunnats of other prayers can never be made qadâ of. If you make qadâ of it you do not get the blessings (that you would get) for having performed a sunnat, but you get the blessings of supererogatory prayer."

As is stated concurrently in the books **Durr-ul-mukhtâr** and **Ibni 'Âbidîn** and Tahtâwî's annotation to **Marâq-il-falâh**, and also in the books **Durr-ul-muntaqâ** and **Jawhara-t-un-nayyira**: "There are two kinds of a Muslim's not performing a namâz within its prescribed time:

"1 - His not performing it due to some excuse. It is called **fawt** to miss a namâz due to some excuse. A sunnat is omitted in order not to commit a harâm, a makrûh or a bid'at, not to miss or even not to delay a fard or a wâjib. It is permissible, and even necessary, to omit the sunnats for these reasons and purposes. In fact, it is sinful not to omit them in such cases. It is not sinful to miss a fard prayer because of an excuse, either, but its qadâ must be made immediately.

"2 - His omitting namâz because of laziness though he knows

that namâz is his duty and esteems it highly." It is not sinful to omit the sunnats insistently without an excuse, but it will incur questioning and scolding in the Hereafter. Kamâladdîn ibni Humâm said: "It is sinful not to perform a fard or a wâjib, whereas not performing the sunnats would cause one to be deprived of their blessings and high grades." Likewise is stated in **Halabî-i-saghîr**: "It is not sinful to omit the sunnat of morning prayer and other muakkad sunnats. However, it will cause one to be deprived of their blessings, high grades, and one will be scolded." However, omitting the fard prayers without an excuse is a very grave sin. Therefore, in explaining the prayers of qadâ, religious books state: "A Muslim omits his prayer of namâz only when he has an excuse to do so. For this reason, every book refers to the qadâ of prayers termed **Fâita**, that is, prayers missed (for reasons justified by Islam)." For, Muslims of the past would miss their namâz only for reasons they could not help. None of them would omit it without an excuse. It is written in the books **Umdat-ul-islâm** and **Jâmi'-ul-fatâwâ**[1]: "In cases of direct confrontation with the enemy, omitting a namâz while it is possible to perform it, is as sinful as committing seven hundred grave sins." As is seen, fâita namâz means namâz that has been left to qadâ involuntarily; (in other words, they are prayers that you have failed to perform within their correct time for reasons that you could not help.) Omitted namâz, on the other hand, means namâz that you have left to qadâ voluntarily, (although you could have performed it within its allotted time.) Namâz that has been left to qadâ can be expressed with the word 'fâita' as well as with the word 'omitted'. Using these two words interchangeably for this purpose does not indicate that rules to be applied to fâita namâz are the same as those to be applied to omitted namâz. Fâita namâz is a namâz that is not sinful, (that is, one does not become sinful on account of fâita namâz). Omitted namâz, on the other hand, incurs a grave sin. For example, a fighter for Islam is a human being. A murderer is a human being, too. That both of them are human does not eliminate the fact that the murderer is sinful. Nor does it abrogate the thawâb that the fighter for Islam deserves.

As scholarly information (that we have inherited via basic Islamic books) shows, a person who missed a few of his daily prayers of namâz for reasons which Islam classifies as valid

---

[1] Written by Abu-l-Qâsim Semerkandî 'rahmatullâhi ta'âlâ 'alaih', (d. 556 [1161 A.D.].) The book is also called **Jâmi'-ul-kebîr**.

excuses, is accredited to keep on with their ordinary routine of performing the sunnats of their daily prayers, rather than substituting them with the fards of the missed prayers. Yet the basic Islamic books were written in those good old days when a Muslim not regularly performing the daily five prayers could not even be conceptualized in any Islamic country. Nor would anyone omit any of the daily prayers without an excuse. And there were few people, if any, who missed one or two of the daily prayers with an excuse. But now, these people have omitted their prayers without any excuse and have become very sinful. Seeing these facts, in order not to die with debts of namâz, and to escape the torment in Hell, those who have omitted their prayers without an excuse should, at least, intend to make qadâ when performing the sunnats of four of the daily five prayers. Yet, because the sunnat of morning prayer is strongly emphasized, the sunnat of morning prayer must be performed still with the intention of sunnat.

Hadrat Sayyid Abdulhakîm Arvâsî 'rahmatullâhi 'alaih', who was an expert in the knowledge of fiqh in all four Madhhabs, said: "Those who do not perform namâz because of laziness, and those who have years of debts of namâz, when they begin to perform their daily prayers of namâz, concurrently with the sunnat of each of the daily prayers of namâz, should make their niyyat (intention) to make qadâ of the fard of the (missed or omitted) earliest daily prayer in serial correspondence with the namâz they are currently performing. All four Madhhabs are unanimous on that they should perform the sunnats by making their niyyat for the namâz of qadâ. In the Hanafî Madhhab it is a grave sin to leave a namâz (that is fard) to qadâ, (i.e. to omit it,) without an excuse. This very grave sin becomes double as each free time that is long enough to perform namâz passes. For, it is fard also to make qadâ of namâz in your free time as soon as possible. To get rid of this terrible sin, which cannot be calculated or measured, and for escaping its torment, it is necessary to perform the sunnats of four daily prayers, – with the exception of the morning prayer – and also the initial and final sunnats of Friday prayer, and also the (namâz that consists of four rak'ats and which is termed) sunnat of the time (of Friday), by making the niyyat to make qadâ of the omitted fard prayers, and to perform the Witr namâz instead of the final sunnat of night prayer. Books written by Hanafî scholars contain many evidences to prove that this is true.

"It is a grave sin to omit a namâz that is fard. It is necessary to make tawba immediately. And worse is the sin of postponing the tawba [by postponing the performance of qadâ]. This grave sin becomes twice itself in wickedness at each length of time wherein one could perform the qadâ, i.e. six minutes, spent at leisure. It is fard to make tawba also for postponing the performance of qadâ. Once you have performed the qadâ for the earliest prayer of namâz that you omitted, all the sins incurred by postponing the qadâ for such a long time, (i.e. since the correct time you should have performed it,) will be forgiven. Therefore, it is necessary to perform the prayers of qadâ, and thereby to pay off your debts, as soon as possible.

"**FARDS and SUNNATS**: [Taking away someone else's property secretly is termed **sirqat** (theft). Outright seizure by way of extortion, violation and usurpation is termed **ghasb** (plunder, pillage). Both of them are harâm. In either case the rightful owner suffers deprivation; so the sinfulness thereby incurred lasts as long as the deprivation lasts, till the owner is given back what he has been stripped of. It becomes a permanent kind of wrongdoing that demands an extra, continuous, and daily performance of tawba. Supererogatory worship done by a person who does not perform the worship that is fard within its correct time is not acceptable. For, that person is satisfying the desires of his nafs instead of performing the command of Allâhu ta'âlâ. When zakât is not paid the poor people's right has been expropriated. A rich person who does not pay zakât has robbed thousands of poor people of their right and has disobeyed the command of Allâhu ta'âlâ; therefore all his acts of charity and supererogatory donations will be rejected. Likewise, a person who does not pay his debts is under heavy responsibility laden with similar rights.

"To perform namâz is a debt that one owes to Allâhu ta'âlâ. Not to perform a certain namâz within the time allotted to it means to run up this debt along with the debt of benedictions that Muslims invoke on one another during the performance o namâz. Negligence of this divine and civic duty causes rejection of all the supererogatory and sunnat prayers of namâz performed until the (payment of debt termed) qadâ of the omitted namâz is performed. It is a deadly sin to leave a (fard) namâz to qadâ, (i.e. not to perform it within the time Islam dictates.) A person who does not make qadâ of an omitted or missed namâz, (i.e. who does not perform it as soon as possible,) will be subjected to fire (in Hell) for a period of time as long as eighty huqba. At each additional six minutes, the torment incurred becomes worse by twice. With this speed of aggravation it becomes ten times worse in an hour and two hundred and forty times worse in a day. So, the retribution that has been decreed to be eighty huqba for the posponement of each of the prayers of qadâ for the first day, is multiplied by two at each sixth minute, beginning on the day immediately afterwards. Every Muslim who did not begin to perform their daily prayers of namâz as soon as they reached the age of puberty, which is twelve for boys and nine for girls according to the criteria established by Islam, should make qadâ instead of the sunnats of their daily prayers for as long as the number of years between the beginning of pubescence and the time when they began to regularly perform their daily prayers. As it is a grave sin not to perform namâz (five times daily), likewise it is a sin even more grave not to make qadâ of one's missed or omitted prayers of daily namâz, and the sin entangled in continues taking a turn for the worse for days on end. A person who leaves a certain daily prayer to qadâ has to make tawba, not only once for having omitted the prayer, but also at the end of each duration of time, [six minutes,] long enough for the accomplishment of qadâ and yet not spent doing so. Among the components making up a consummate tawba to be made for a certain prayer missed or omitted, is to have performed the qadâ, i.e. to have paid the debt by performing the missed or omitted prayer. For this reason, whenever Muslims with many debts of namâz perform one of the daily prayers of namâz, they should perform the fard of the earliest omitted namâz instead of the sunnat of the namâz they are currently performing. For, the sunnats of a namâz are not acceptable before its fards omitted have been performed. As they are making qadâ of a certain prayer (not performed within its correct time) instead of the sunnat of the prayer (they are currently performing,) they are at the same time performing the sunnat of the current prayer.

"Depending on the number of the standard [six-minute] periods long enough to perform a namâz and spent in leisure after the earliest daily prayer omitted, a person who omitted that prayer has gone into a debt of qadâ with a multiplier to be expressed in terms of millions. By the time that person makes qadâ of the earliest one, all the sins thereby accumulated (and multiplied by two at each stage of deferment) will be forgiven. The importance of performing prayers of qadâ must be realized well. A person who dies without îmân will find no mercy in the Hereafter; what such people will find is eternal fire in Hell. A Muslim who committed grave sins and died without having made tawba will be forgiven either by way of shafâ'at (intercession) or in return for his efforts to spread Islam. As a matter of fact, a hadîth-i-sherîf purports: '**A pious deed that Allâhu ta'âlâ loves best is hubb-i-fillâh** (love for the sake of Allah) **and bughd-i-fillâh** (dislike for the sake of Allah).' A Believer who loves the scholars of Ahl as-sunnat and the Awliyâ will attain the blessings imparted in this hadîth-i-sherîf. And, attaining the blessings purported in the hadîth-i-sherîf, '**A person who recovers one of my forgotten** (or distorted) **sunnats will be given thawâbs** (blessings) **equal to the total sum of the blessings that will be given to a hundred martyrs**,' requires selling, (distributing, dispensing, promulgating) books written by scholars of Ahl-as-sunnat and thereby contributing to the fortunate deed of spreading Islam in its pristine purity as it had when it was conveyed and taught by Muhammad 'alaihis-salâm'. All the books published by **Hakîkat Kitâbevi** in Istanbul are facsimiles of works written by scholars of Ahl as-sunnat.]

"To perform the sunnat with the intention of making qadâ, you must perform the initial sunnat of the early afternoon prayer, which has four rak'ats, by intending also to make qadâ of the fard of the earliest early afternoon prayer that you did not perform. When performing the final sunnat of the early afternoon prayer you must intend also to make qadâ of the fard of the earliest omitted morning prayer. When performing the sunnat of the late afternoon prayer you must make qadâ with the intention also of the fard of the earliest late afternoon prayer. When performing the sunnat of the evening prayer you must also make qadâ with the intention of the three-rak'at fard of the earliest evening prayer. When performing the initial sunnat of night prayer you must intend also to make qadâ of the fard of the earliest night prayer, and when performing the final sunnat of the night prayer you must intend also to make qadâ of the earliest omitted Witr prayer and perform three rak'ats. Thus each day you will pay the debt of a day's qadâ. Also when performing the namâz of tarâwîh you must make qadâ by intending also to make qadâ. You must go on doing this for as many years as the number of years during which you left your prayers to qadâ. After finishing your prayers of qadâ you must begin performing only the sunnats as usual." [See chapter 13!]

[Instead of performing the namâz of tarâwîh you must make qadâ in your home. For, it is written in Islamic books that a person who omits the fard prayers will not be given blessings for his sunnat prayers. When certain people perform the namâz of tarâwîh in jamâ'at in the mosque of a quarter or in a house, a person who has debts of qadâ namâz or who cannot trust that the imâm's namâz is acceptable performs the namâz of tarâwîh in jamâ'at in the mosque in order to guide the young beginners of namâz and to accustom them to performing namâz and to prevent gossip or fitna. Yet he does not intend to follow the imâm. He pretends to follow the imâm. He makes qadâ at the same time. If the imâm is making the salâm after every two rak'ats, this person intends also to make qadâ of the fard of morning prayers, and if the imâm is making the salâm at the end of four rak'ats, this person intends also to make qadâ of the fard of other prayers of namâz. If he cannot synchronize his actions with the imâm's actions, he intends to perform the tarâwih and follows the imâm.

The number of prayers that could not be performed and were left to qadâ for the defined two reasons or because of sleeping and forgetting is very small, so their qadâ can be made up in a day. In this case it is not necessary to perform the sunnats with the intention of qadâ. Moreover, since it is not sinful to miss them with an excuse, delaying their qadâ long enough to perform the sunnats does not initiate the state of sinfulness.

It is a grave sin not to perform a fard namâz in its prescribed time without an excuse or because of laziness. After commiting a grave sin, it is necessary to make **tawba** so that one can be forgiven. A sincere **tawba** requires four conditions: feeling deep penitence; deciding not to commit it again; invoking Allâhu ta'âlâ to forgive you and expressing istighfâr; repaying the rights of Allâhu ta'âlâ and His slaves. If any one of these four conditions is absent, that sin will not be forgiven. Such people must pay the rights of Allâhu ta'âlâ as soon as possible by performing the sunnats of four daily prayers with the intention of qadâ every day. The additional sûra is not recited in the third and fourth rak'ats of a qadâ namâz.

It is written in **Imdâd-ul-Fettâh** and in the four hundred and fiftieth page of **Ibni 'Âbidîn:** "The sunnat is omitted in order not to delay the wâjib." After saying the same thing in its three hundred and sixteenth page, it goes on: "When performing namâz in jamâ'at, it is fard to follow the imâm in actions that are fard. It is wâjib to follow him in the wâjibs. And it is sunnat to follow him in the sunnats. Following the imâm means doing the actions with him or after him, or waiting for the imâm if you have begun before the imâm. For example, it means to follow the imâm to bow for the rukû' together with the imâm or to bow after the imâm and catch up with him in the rukû' or to bow after the imâm straightens up from the rukû' or, after bowing and straightening before the imâm (if you have done so), to bow again together with the imâm or after him. If you do not bow again you will not have followed the imâm; you will have omitted the fard, and your namâz will be nullified. Independent of this taxonomy of rulings, it is wâjib to act together with the imâm in the fards and in the wâjibs. If the imâm straightens up from the rukû' before a person has said the tasbîh of rukû' three times, it is wâjib for him to straighten up together with the imâm instead of completing the tasbîhs. A sunnat must be omitted if it is necessary to do so lest you should delay a wâjib." In other words, the act of completing the repetition of the tasbîhs three times, which is sunnat, must be omitted lest you should delay in acting together with the imâm, which is wâjib. The sunnats that are inside namâz are more important than any sunnat outside namâz. For example, reading (or reciting) the Qur'ân al-kerîm is sunnat and there are innumerable blessings in doing it. But it has been declared in a hadîth-i sherîf that there are more blessings in reciting the Qur'ân-i kerîm during namâz. The hadîth-i sherîf is written in the twenty-second page of **Khazinat-ul-asrâr** together with its proofs. This also should make us realize that it is necessary to omit the sunnats in order to get rid of a grave sin by making qadâ of those prayers of namâz that have been omitted without an excuse. Nevertheless a person who performs the sunnats with the intention of making qadâ has not omitted the sunnats by doing so.

As we have explained while describing the namâz in jamâ'at in the twentieth chapter, a person who comes to the mosque as the imâm begins conducting the morning prayer performs the sunnat outside the mosque or behind a pillar inside the mosque. Then he joins the jamâ'at following the imâm. If he cannot find such a place that is apart from the jamâ'at, he must not perform the sunnat behind the jamâ'at. He must begin to follow the imâm immediately. For, it is makrûh to begin performing namâz individually as namâz is being performed in jamâ'at. The sunnat of morning prayer is omitted in order not to commit a makrûh. As will be inferred also from this piece of writing from **Durr-ul-mukhtâr,** it is necessary to make qadâ instead of the sunnats. Since even the most emphatic sunnat, the sunnat of the morning prayer, is omitted in order to avoid a makrûh, then a fortiori a sunnat must be omitted to avoid a harâm. Thus, the namâz of qadâ performed instead of a sunnat saves one from a grave sin.

Some people, particularly people who are religiously ignorant and who pass themselves as men of religion, attempt to distort the words of great authorities of Islamic knowledge. Yet, because they know nothing, and all the worse to provide proofs from a book, they say whatever occurs to their minds in the name of an objection. With the vanity flattered by their own ignorance, they make gratuitous assertions. For instance, there are those who say, "No, sir, qadâ of the fards cannot be made in place of the sunnats. I cannot accept it. Instead of wasting time sitting for hours in a coffee-house, let them perform their prayers of qadâ. Why should one omit the sunnats!" Yes, the statement, "Let them perform their prayers of qadâ instead of sitting for hours in the coffee-house," is right. But it is wrong to say, "One must not omit the sunnats in order to make the qadâ." Delaying the qadâ of omitted prayers and wasting time are two separate grave sins. Yet to ask a person who has already committed the so-called sins not to make the qadâ instead of the sunnats means to ask him to commit a third sin. It is like asking a person who has debts of qadâ and who wastes his time insead of performing his qadâ prayers to gamble or to drink alcohol, too, since he has already sinned. The great saying of our superiors is well-known: "If something cannot be done perfectly, one should not entirely give it up." Then, a person who has omitted his prayers without an excuse should not miss the opportunity of making qadâ instead of the sunnats and thus ridding himself of this grave sin. Likewise, a person who does not perform namâz should not give up fasting too.

It is written in the same page of **Tahtâwî:** "The sunnat of morning prayer is very virtuous. It is enjoined in many hadîth-i sherîfs to perform it. There are countless blessings in it. But there is no punishment declared even for a person who omits the sunnat of the morning prayer. However, it is declared that a person who performs the fard not in jamâ'at but alone will go to Hell. This means to say that the value of jamâ'at is very much greater than even the sunnat of the morning prayer."

Ibni 'Âbidîn says: "If a person comes to the mosque when the imâm is in the second rak'at of the morning prayer he must omit the sunnat and follow the imâm. For the sunnat cannot equal even one of the twenty-seven blessings of the fard caused by the jamâ'at." Since the most emphatic sunnat, the sunnat of morning prayer, is omitted in order to catch up with the jamâ'at, it must a fortiori be omitted in order to perform the fard. Hence, also, it is understood that in order not to die with debts of qadâ it is necessary to perform the sunnats with the intention of qadâ.

Hadrat 'Abdulqâdir-i Geylânî says in the forty-eighth article of his book **Futûh-ul-ghayb**, which was printed in India in 1313 [1896]: A Believer must do the fards first. When the fards are finished the sunnats must be done. Next he goes on with the supererogatory. It is idiocy to perform the sunnats while one has debts of fard. The sunnats of a person who has debts of fard are not acceptable. 'Alî ibni Abî Tâlib 'radiy-Allâhu 'anh' reports: Rasûlullah "sall-Allâhu 'alaihi wa sallam" stated: **"If a person has omitted his fard prayers and has debts of qadâ, his performing the supererogatory is useless trouble. Unless he pays his qadâ, Allâhu ta'âlâ will not accept his supererogatory prayers."** 'Abdulhaq-i Dahlawî, one of the savants of Hanafî Madhhab, (in his commentary to the book,) explains this hadîth quoted by 'Abdulqâdir-i Geylânî as follows: "This information shows that the sunnats and the supererogatory prayers of those who have debts of fards will not be accepted. We know that the sunnats complement the fards. This means that while doing the fard if something is omitted which would otherwise have caused the fard to reach perfection then the sunnats will cause the fard performed to reach perfection. The unacceptable sunnats of a person who has debts of fards are good for nothing." This commentary to **Futûh-ul-ghayb** is in Persian and exists at number 3866 in the State Library at Bâyezîd in Istanbul. Also Ibni 'Âbidîn says on the subject of supererogatory prayers: "A hadîth-i sherîf declares that **'The incomplete namâz, zakât and other fard worships are completed with the supererogatory.'** Imâm-i Bayhaqî remarks that this hadîth-i sherîf means that if the sunnats within fards remain incomplete they will be completed with the supererogatory, and that it does not mean that the supererogatory will replace the fards that have not been performed. As a matter of fact, another hadîth-i sherîf declares: **'If a person has not completed his namâz, his supererogatory prayers of namâz are added to that namâz until it is completed.'** He remarks that this hadîth shows that the supererogatory prayers will complete not those prayers of fard namâz that have not been performed but those which have been performed incompletely. This hadîth-i-sherîf is cited also in the two hundred and forty, seventh page of **Tahtâwî**'s annotation to (Shernblâlî's) **Imdâd-ul-Fettâh**, and it is added that the sunnats will make up for the defects in the performed fards. And the savants who are not in the Hanafî Madhhab, such as Imâm-i Ghazâlî and Ibni 'Arabî, say that the supererogatory prayers will replace those fards that have been missed because of good excuses."

It is written in **Uyûn-ul-basâir** that Imâm-i Bayhakî said that the prayers of namâz performed as acts of sunnat would compensate for the faults committed in the acts of sunnat within the prayers of namâz performed as acts of fard, since none of the sunnats could ever be comparable to an act that is wâjib. As a matter of fact, in a hadîth-i qudsî Allâhu ta'âlâ declares: **"A person can approach Me with none as he approaches Me by doing the worship which I have enjoined as a fard upon him."** Please see the sixtieth chapter in the first fascicle of Endless Bliss.

As is seen, according to some Islamic savants, the supererogatory prayer will make up for the defects in those fard prayers that have been performed. And some of them say that they will also replace those fard prayers that have been missed with an excuse. But even those savants do not say that those who have committed a grave sin by not performing their namâz because of laziness can benefit from the hadîth-i sherîf quoted above. The fact is, the supererogatory prayers of those who do not perform the fard prayers are not acceptable. How can they ever be good for completing the fard, then? It is not permissible for us muqallids to set aside these two different ijtihâds of our savants, which we have explained, and to say a third one. Ibni Melek 'rahmatullâhi ta'âlâ 'alaih' says in his commentary to **Menâr**: "It has been declared unanimously by savants that when mujtahids' statements concerning an Islamic matter disagree with one another it is pointless for later savants to propound a solution disagreeing with both parties." According to this ijmâ' (unanimity of savants), it would be silly to say that the supererogatory prayers will replace those fard prayers that have not been performed because of laziness. A lâ-Madhhabî person who cannot understand the words of mujtahîds or who slights them though he understands them may talk any twaddle that occurs to him.

In explaining the prayers that are to be recited after each fard namâz, the book, **Marâqil-falâh** and **Imdâd-ul-fattâh** state: "The imâm turns towards the jamâ'at after the fard if there is no supererogatory prayer to be performed after the fard, or after performing the supererogatory prayer (if there is any)." **Durr al-**

mukhtâr writes: "It is makrûh for the imâm to perform the supererogatory prayer where he performed the fard. He should perform it after moving somewhat to his left." These statements and the explanation in the book **Khazînat-ul-esrâr** show clearly that the prayers that are performed in the name of the sunnat with the five daily prayers are supererogatory.

Again, it is written in the same book as well as in its commentary by **Tahtâwî**: "All sunnats are called supererogatory. Supererogatory means a worship that is neither fard nor wâjib. A supererogatory prayer is either a sunnat or any worship that a person performs by his own wish. A hadîth-i sherîf declares: **'On the day of Judgement the first question will be asked concerning namâz. If one has performed namâz properly one will be saved. If namâz has been badly performed one will be in a very bad situation. If there are any defects in one's fard namâz it will be made up for by one's supererogatory prayers.'** A man cannot do something perfectly no matter how high his grade is. The supererogatory prayers make up for the mistakes made in the fards."

Shernblâlî says in his **Durer**, which is an annotation to his **Merâq-is-sa'ada**: "The term supererogatory namâz includes the sunnats, too. Qâdî Imâm-i Abû Zayd said that performing supererogatory namâz was commanded so that the defects in the fard prayers would be compensated for. If a person can perform the fard without a defect he cannot be blamed for not performing the sunnats." **Ibni 'Âbidîn** writes in the introduction to the section about 'the Witr namâz and performing nâfila namâz on an animal' that **sunnats**, whether **muakkada** or **ghayr-i muakkada**, are called **nâfila**.

The book **Jawhara-t-un-nayyira** says quoting from **Hidâya-t-ul-mubtedî fî ma'rifat-ul-awqât**: "It is permissible to perform the sunnats of five daily prayers sitting, without a good excuse. For, these sunnats are supererogatory worships." Ibni Melek says in his annotation to **Majmâ'ul-bahreyn**[1]: "If a person comes to the mosque and sees that any of the daily prayers, except morning prayer, is being performed in jamâ'at, he does not perform the first sunnat but begins following the jamâ'at outright. For it is mekrûh to perform a supererogatory prayer after the iqâmat has

---

[1] Written by Ibn-is-Sâ'atî Ahmad bin Alî Ba'lebekî 'rahmatullâhi ta'âlâ' 'alaih', (d. 694 [1294 A.D.].)

been said for the fard prayer. If the iqâmat is said as he performs the sunnat, he makes the salâm after completing two or four rak'ats of it, and then begins following the imâm. If the iqâmat is said as he performs the fard of the morning or evening prayer, he stops his fard prayer and follows the imâm. For a prayer that is fard can be stopped in order to perform it better. It is like demolishing a mosque in order to build a better one. But the case is not so with stopping a sunnat in order to catch the jamâ'at."

It is written in the book **Al-hikam-ul-Atâiyya**[1]: "Of two jobs do the one that comes harder to your nafs! For a job that is right (liked by Allâhu ta'âlâ) comes difficult to the nafs[2]. To try to do the supererogatory good deeds while being slack in doing the wâjibs is one of the signs of following the desires of the nafs." This statement provides an answer to ibni Taymiyya's assertion that it is "unnecessary to perform qadâ of prayers."

As is stated in the forty-sixth chapter of the first fascicle of **Endless Bliss**, Hadrat Imâm-i Rabbânî says: "When compared to those worships that are fard, the supererogatory worships are of no value. They are not even a drop of water compared with an ocean. The accursed satan is deceiving Muslims by misrepresenting the fard as insignificant. [He is preventing them from making their prayers of qadâ.] He is misleading them towards the supererogatory worships. He is preventing them from paying zakât, and misrepresenting the supererogatory alms as beautiful. In fact, to give one gold coin to a poor (Muslim) with the intention of zakât is much more blessed than giving a hundred thousand gold coins as alms. For, paying the zakât is performing the fard. But giving without the intention of zakât is a supererogatory worship." He says in his two hundred and sixtieth letter: "The value of supererogatory worship, when compared with the fard, is not even like that of a drop of water compared with an ocean. In fact, so is the value of supererogatory worships in comparison to the sunnats. However, the vaule of a sunnat compared with a fard is not even like that of a drop of water compared with an ocean." As is understood from all these statements quoted from Islamic savants, those who have omitted their prayers of namâz without an excuse must look for ways of

---

[1] Written by Ahmad bin Muhammad ibni Atâullah Tâj-ud-dîn Iskenderî 'rahmatullâhi ta'âlâ 'alaih', (d. 709 [1309 A.D.], Egypt).

[2] Nafs is a malignant force in man that lures him to do what Allah prohibits and prevents him from doing what Allah commands.

escaping Hell's torment by making qadâ of them as soon as possible. It does not save one from Hell to make qadâ from time to time by saying, "I intend to make qadâ of all my omitted prayers." Islamic savants teach the Sharî'at. We must follow not the factious and corrupt words of kâfirs and bid'at-holders, but the 'Ulamâ of Ahl-as-sunnat.

Hadrat 'Abdulqâdir-i Geylânî 'qaddas-Allâhu sirrahul 'azîz' says in the same chapter: "A person performing the sunnats while he has debts of qadâ is like a debtor taking a present to the person to whom he owes, which, normally, is not acceptable. A person who performs the sunnats while he has debts of qadâ is like a person who spends his time with the Sultân's servant while the Sultân himself has invited him. A Believer is like a businessman. The fard prayers are his capital of which the supererogatory prayers are the profit. Unless the capital is rescued they will give no profit."

Observed with due attention, both the hadîth-i sherîfs and the statements quoted from savants declare that the sunnats and the supererogatory prayers of a person who has debts of fard prayers are not acceptable. Not acceptable does not mean not sahîh. They are sahîh, but they produce no blessings, no use. The book **Radd-ul-muhtâr** explains this very well within the subject of Qurbân. In explaining the hadîth, **"The hajj and the jihâd of a person who commits bid'ats are not acceptable,"** the books **Hadîqa** and **Berîqa** say that: "Their worships are sahîh, but they are given no rewards." [See the hadîth which is quoted at the end of the thirteenth chapter!]

Some people say, "Performing the sunnats with the intention of qadâ is in the Shâfi'î Madhhab. We are Hanafîs, not Shâfi'îs." It would be pertinent to remind them that the compiler of this book, **Endless Bliss**, is in the Hanafî Madhhab, too. Those Shâfi'îs who miss a namâz that is fard because of some excuse make qadâ of it together with its sunnat. But the Hanafîs make qadâ of only the missed fard. The case is not so with a namâz that has been omitted because of laziness. A Shafi'î or a Hanafî who omits the namâz has to make qadâ of it immediately. If he does not make its qadâ immediately he will be punished with **hadd**, and killed if he is in the Shâfi'î Madhhab. But if he is in the Hanafî Madhhab he will be put into jail, and will be kept in the dungeon until he makes his qadâ or dies. Hadrat Ibni Hajar-i Mekkî, one of the savants of the Shafi'î Madhhab, says on the hundred and eighty-ninth page of his book **Fatâwâ-i fiqhiyya**: "A person who does not perform a namâz that is fard makes its qadâ together with its supererogatory prayer, i.e. its sunnat. For, in the Shâfi'î Madhhab it is sunnat to make qadâ of supererogatory prayers, i.e., the sunnats, which are performed together with the fards of five daily prayers. If a person has omitted the fard without an excuse he cannot perform any supererogatory prayer before making its qadâ because he has to make qadâ of the fard immediately. Otherwise, he will have delayed the qadâ of the fard by a length of time equal to the time he has spent performing the sunnats. To say that one has to make its qadâ means to say that one has to spend all one's time making the qadâ. That is, with the exception of the time that one may reserve for earning one's sustenance and the sustenance of those who it is wâjib for one to support, it is not permissible for one to delay the qadâ for any other reason, or else one will become sinful." As is seen, it is necessary to make qadâ of the prayers of namâz omitted without an excuse immediately in the Shafi'î Madhhab as well as in the Hanafî Madhhab. There is no difference between the two Madhhabs. On things that are declared clearly in the Qur'ân al-kerîm and in hadîth-i sherîfs, Madhhabs do not disagree with one another. They may disagree on things that are not declared clearly but which are inferred through ijtihâd. It is declared clearly in a hadîth-i-sherîf reported by Hadrat 'Alî that the supererogatory worships of those who have debts of fard will not be accepted. When mentioned with the word fard, the word **nâfila** (supererogatory) includes the muakkad sunnats, too. This fact not only is shown by Hadrat Abdulqâdir-i Geylânî's statement, but also is written clearly in the books of Hanafî savants, e.g. in **Halâbî-i kebîr**.

Some other people say, "Qadâ is not made instead of the sunnats. For, qadâ can be made any time. But a sunnat cannot be compensated for. To say that qadâ is made instead of a sunnat is the word of those who cannot realise the importance of the sunnats." It is wrong to delay the qadâ of omitted prayers of namâz by saying that qadâ can be made at any time. For, it is a grave sin to delay the performance of qadâ. We have not been commanded to compensate for the omitted sunnats. Why, then, should there be the question of whether or not it will be possible to compensate for them? Ibni 'Âbidîn says on the four hundred and thirty-third page: "A wâjib is omitted for reasons prescibed by Islam. Then *a fortiori* a sunnat must be omitted for reasons prescribed by Islam."

It is written in the book **Marâqilfalâh** and in its commentary by, **Tahtâwî**: "It is tahrîmî makrûh to perform a supererogatory namâz after the fard of the morning prayer until sunrise. If you have not performed the sunnat of the morning prayer beforehand, its performance also is included in the same prohibition. This time is alloted to perform the fard only. That is, a person who does not perform namâz after the fard until sunrise is considered to be performing the fard all the time. And this is better than performing any supererogatory namâz even if it is the sunnat of the morning prayer. Yet it is not makrûh to make qadâ prayers during that time. For, being considered to be performing the fard is better than performing the sunnat. Making qadâ, on the other hand, is an act of actually performing a fard, which is much better." These statements support the fact that the sunnats are supererogatory prayers. It is written clearly in **Jawhara** that the sunnats are supererogatory prayers and can be performed on an animal without an excuse.

It is written on the same page: "When there is very little time left for a certain daily fard namâz, it is tahrîmî makrûh to perform a supererogatory namâz because it causes one to miss the fard. This would mean to miss a namâz that is necessary by performing a namâz which is not necessary, which is something that a reasonable person would not prefer. So is the case with performing a supererogatory prayer as the sun rises, when it is right on top, or as it sets, even if the supererogatory prayer performed is one of the sunnats of the five daily prayers." It is written on the hundred and forty-ninth page of **Hadîqa**: "If performing the sunnat which is before the fard while there is little time left will cause the fard to be left to qadâ, it is harâm to perform the sunnat." It is written in the subject concerning the afflictions incurred by the tongue: "It is not permissible to omit something that is fard in order to do something which is not fard."

As is written in many Hanafî books, e.g. in **Durr-ul-mukhtâr**, in **Ibni 'Âbidîn**, in **Durr-ul-muntaqâ**, a commentary to the book **Multaqâ**, and in **Ni'mat-i Islâm**: "A judge or a pupil may omit the sunnat of any namâz except the sunnat of the morning prayer, the former in order to do his duty and the latter not be late for his religious class." While a judge's duty, which is not fard-i-'ayn, is counted as an excuse for omitting the sunnats, why should it not be an excuse to pay the debts of qadâ, which are fard-i 'ayn and for which there will be vehement punishment?

There are countless blessings for those who perform the sunnats and some supererogatory prayers. Yet these blessings are for those who do not have any debts of qadâ. It is not sensible to perform the prayers of qadâ only when you have free time while performing the supererogatory prayers continuously mercy because there are many blessings in them. The book of tafsîr entitled **Rûh-ul-beyân** explains the hundred and sixty-fifth âyat-i-kerîma of An'âm Sûra as follows: "To encourage His slaves to doing good deeds, Allâhu ta'âlâ has promised many blessings. That it has been declared that innumerable rewards will be given for them does not show that they are better than those worships that are commanded but for which not so many blessings have been promised. As declared unanimously by savants, the fards are superior to the wâjibs and to the sunnats, and there are more blessings in them. Supererogatory worships do not substitute for those fard worships that have not been done. The debts for the fards cannot be paid by doing the supererogatory prayers. The ignorant set aside the fard prayers and do the supererogatory prayers. Saying that there are limitless blessings in the supererogatory, they suppose they will pay their debts of fard by performing supererogatory prayers. To say as they do is incompatible with Islam." Zerqânî says in his explanation of **Mawâhib**: "He who performs the fards instead of the sunnats has made a good gain (by doing so). He who performs the sunnats instead of the fards has cheated himself." As written on the two hundred and twelfth page of **Tahtâwî**'s commentary to **Nûr-ul-îzâh, Qâdî-Khân** says that performing the sunnat before the fard has been commanded in order to frustrate Satan, to make him sorry. Satan becomes sorry because he thinks that he can never dupe man into not doing the fards which Allâhu ta'âlâ commands since he cannot mislead him even in the sunnats which Allâhu ta'âlâ does not command. This fact is also written in **Durr-ul-mukhtâr** and in **Radd-ul-muhtâr**.

In explaining how to make qadâ of omitted prayers in his book **an-Nawâdir-ul-fiqhiyya fî Madhhab-il-aimmat-il Hanafiyya**, copies of which exist at number 1037 in the Es'ad Efendi 'rahmatullâhi ta'âlâ 'alaih' section and at number 1463 in the Yahya Tevfîk Efendi section of the public library of Süleymâniyye in Istanbul, Muhammad Sâdiq Efendi, the (then) Qâdî of Jerusalem, says: "The great savant Ibni Nujaym was asked: If a person has left some of his prayers of namâz to qadâ and if he performs the sunnats of the morning, early-afternoon, late-afternoon, evening, and night prayers with the intention of making their qadâ, will he have omitted the sunnats?

"His answer was: He will not have omitted the sunnats. For,

the purpose in performing the sunnats of the five daily prayers is to perform namâz in addition to the fard of each prayer time. Satan will always try to prevent you from performing namâz. By performing one more prayer in addition to the fard you will have resisted, disgraced Satan. It is written in **Nawâdîr**[1] that by making qadâ instead of the sunnats you will have performed the sunnats, too. To fulfill the sunnat by performing one more prayer in addition to the fard of each prayer time, those who have debts of qadâ must make qadâ. Many people are performing the sunnats instead of making qadâ. They will go to Hell. But a person who makes qadâ instead of the sunnats will be saved from Hell."

Ibni Nujaym 'rahmatullâhi ta'âlâ 'alaih' states in **Eshbâh**: "Avoiding prohibitions and harâms has precedence over doing good and useful things. A hadîth-i-sherîf reads: **'Do my commands as well as you can. Avoid what I have prohibited!'** Another hadîth-i sherîf reads: **'Not to do a mote of something prohibited is more blessed than the worships of all people and genies.'** For this reason, a wâjib may be omitted when there is great difficulty. Yet permission is never given for doing the prohibitions, especially if they are grave sins." While explaining the istinjâ, **Ibni 'Âbidîn** says: "If it is impossible for you to clean najâsat without exposing your awrat parts you must perform namâz in that state. For it is a command to clean (the najâsat), but it is a prohibition to expose your awrat parts. Avoiding sins has priority. The sunnats come even after the commands. The sunnats are observed in order to receive blessings. A sunnat cannot be performed at the cost of committing an act that is makrûh. But a fard can be performed, so that the debt will be paid. For example, it is makrûh to make an ablution with someone else's water, but by doing so the tahârat, which is fard, will have been made. When a person without an ablution makes an ablution with someone else's water he will not get the blessings of the sunnat." This adds further proof to our rightful argument that absolving yourself from a grave sin by making qadâ has priority over performing the sunnats.

Hadrat Imâm-i Rabbânî 'rahmatullâhi ta'âlâ 'alaih' says in his hundred and twenty-ninth letter: "A hadîth-i sherîf declares: **'A**

---

[1] Written by 'Abd-ul-'Azîz bin Ahmad Shems-ul-eimma Hulwânî 'rahmatullâhi ta'âlâ 'alaih', (d. 456 [1064 A.D.], Bukhârâ.

person's spending his time on mâ-lâ-ya'nî signifies that Allâhu ta'âlâ does not like him.' Mâ-lâ-ya'nî means useless deeds. Doing supererogatory worships instead of doing one fard is spending time on mâ-lâ-ya'nî." And he says in his two hundred and sixtieth letter: "Compared with the fard, the supererogatory worships are not as valuable as a drop of water compared to an ocean. Likewise is the value of the sunnat when compared to the fard." Please see the first chapter in the first fascicle.

It is written in the four hundred and fifty-eighth page of **Durr-ul-mukhtâr**: "A person who wants to perform a supererogatory namâz must first vow to perform a namâz, and then perform the vowed namâz instead of making the supererogatory namâz. There are also savants who say that the supererogatory prayers must be performed without making a vow. A person who performs prayers of namâz that are sunnat after vowing them will have performed the sunnats themselves." Explaining these lines, Ibni 'Âbidîn 'rahmatullâhi ta'âlâ 'alaih' says: "Those savants who say that prayers of namâz must be performed without vowing mean that they must not be vowed by stipulating a condition, for otherwise the condition stipulated will have been made equivalent to a worship. A hadîth-i sherîf prohibits any vow being dependent upon such a condition, such as: 'I shall fulfill my such and such worship if Allahu ta'âlâ restores my (father, etc.) to health.' Not so is the case with vowing worships without stipulating a condition. It is wâjib to perform a vowed prayer; you will be given the blessings of a wâjib. When you perform the vowed namâz instead of the sunnat you will have performed the sunnat, too." That it is better to vow the sunnats in advance and then to perform them as vowed namâz is written at the end of the subject concerning supererogatory prayers in the book **Halabî** and in Tahtâwî's annotation to **Merâqil-felâh**. Thus, if a person says, "May it be my vow to perform a namâz of four rak'ats," before performing the sunnat of the early afternoon prayer and then performs it with the intention of a vowed namâz, he will both get the reward of a wâjib and will have performed the sunnat of early afternoon prayer. Since a born slave will not have omitted the sunnat when he performs the namâz which he has made wâjib for himself, then a fortiori he will not have omitted the sunnat when he performs the namâz that has been made fard by Allâhu ta'âlâ. He will both have made the qadâ and have performed the sunnat. For, it is a grave sin to omit the fard prayers because of laziness. It is fard to make tawba for every sin immediately. See the final three pages of the sixth-seventh letter of the second volume (of **Maktûbât**) in the first chapter of the third fascicle of **Endless Bliss**!

Those who assert that one cannot intend for prayers of qadâ while performing the sunnats cannot cite any valuable books as proofs to support their antithesis when they are asked why not. Instead, they say that it is written in **Ibnî 'Âbidîn**, in **Halabî**, and in Tahtâwî's annotion to **Imdâd-ul-fettah** that "The qadâ of those prayers that have been missed with fawt must be made up as soon as possible. Making qadâ of prayers missed with fawt is better and more important than performing supererogatory prayers, but the case is not so with performing the sunnats of the five daily prayers and certain prayers that have been praised by hadîth-i sherîfs, such as the namâz of Duhâ, the namâz of Tesbîh, the namâz of Tahiyyatulmesjîd, the four rak'ats of sunnat before late afternoon prayer and the six rak'ats of sunnat after evening prayer. These must be performed with the intention of a supererogatory prayer." These statements concern those who have failed to perform the fard of the five daily prayers with fawt[1], that is, for reasons that could not be helped. It says that the qadâ of those prayers that have been missed thus must not be performed instead of the sunnats, but they must be performed separately. We agree with this entirely. We accept that there is no need to make the qadâ of a few fard prayers missed with an excuse instead of the sunnats. For, it is not a guilt or sin, we say, to leave namâz to qadâ because of an excuse, nor is it sinful to postpone its qadâ until you have performed the sunnats. But being unable to perform namâz because of an excuse is different from omitting it knowingly, which means not performing it because of laziness. The former is not a sin. But the latter is a grave sin. It is quite wrong to confuse the two cases with each other. Reading in books that the fard prayers missed with an excuse cannot be performed instead of the sunnats, and to suppose thereby that the fard prayers that have been omitted because of laziness cannot be performed instead of the sunnats either and, furthermore, to attempt to adduce the former as a proof for the latter, is not worthy of a man of knowledge. This statement in Hanafî books does not say that "those who have

---

[1] To fail to perform a certain prayer with fawt, means to be unable to perform it within its time for reasons justified by Islam.

committed a grave sin by not performing the fard prayers because of laziness cannot perform the sunnats with the intention of qadâ." In fact, it says that the sunnats are supererogatory prayers and are to be performed with the intention of a supererogatory worship. As is written in **Jawhara-t-un-nayyira**, books of fiqh in the Hanafî Madhhab state: "Qadâ of the namâz missed with fawt." They do not say, "Qadâ of the namâz omitted." For, a Muslim does not omit his namâz knowingly. He misses it with such excuses as unawareness, sleep, or forgetfulness. The two situations must not be confused with each other.

Importance of the fard prayers has been stated clearly in the Qur'ân al-kerîm and in hadîth-i sherîfs. For instance, it is written in the sixth page of the book **Terghîbussalât**, which is in Persian: "Our Prophet 'sall-Allâhu 'alaihi wa sallam' stated: **'It is a grave sin to bring two prayers of fard namâz together.'** That is, it is a grave sin not to perform a fard in its prescribed time and to perform it later. Another hadîth-i sherîf declares: **'Allâhu ta'âlâ will keep a person who performs a namâz after its time is over in Hell for eighty hukbas.'** This is the punishment for performing one namâz after its prescribed time. We must try to imagine the retribution for never performing namâz."

The book **Umdat-ul-islâm** exists in the section of Muhammed Es'ad Efendi in the library of Süleymâniyye. This book, along with the book **Menâhij-ul-'ibâd**, was reproduced by Hakîkât Kitâbevi in 1989. It is written in that book: "Our Prophet 'sall-Allâhu 'alaihi wa sallam' stated: **'Namâz is the arch-stone of faith. He who performs namâz has built up his faith. He who does not perform namâz has demolished his faith.'** He stated in a hadîth-i sherîf: **'On the Day of Judgement, after îmân the first question will be on namâz.'** Allâhu ta'âlâ will declare: **'O My slave, if you get over your account of namâz, safety is yours. I shall facilitate your other accounts!'** Our Prophet 'sall-Allâhu 'alaihi wasallam' stated: **'A person who omits one namâz knowingly without an excuse will remain in Hell for one hukba.'** One **hukba** is eighty years, and one day in the next world is as long as a thousand worldly years. At is seen, a person who omits one fard without an excuse will burn in Hell for eighty times three hundred and sixty-five thousand years. [It is written on the five hundred and tenth page of **Medârij-un-nubuwwa** and on the one hundred and eighteenth page of **Ma'rifatnâma**: "The purpose of giving such foregrounded examples is not to give numerical values but to demonstrate the importance of the matter and the graveness of the horrifying situation that would be incurred, by way of numerical evaluation."] Then, shame upon those who do not perform namâz because of laziness or without an excuse! Our savants say unanimously that "A person who does not perform namâz is not acceptable as a witness. For, a person who does not perform namâz is a fâsiq one. The fard namâz is a debt which a Believer owes to Allâhu ta'âlâ. He cannot rid himself of the debt unless he performs it during its prescribed time." It is written in the book **Aqîdatunnejâh**: "If a person makes tawba-i nasûh his sins will be pardoned. Unless he makes qadâ of his prayers of namâz they will not be pardoned only by making tawba. If he makes tawba after making qadâ of his prayers, there is the hope that he will be pardoned."

Ibni Nujaym Zayn-ul-'Âbidîn says in his book **Kabâir wa saghâir**: "It is a grave sin to perform the fard namâz [by trusting the time-table arranged incorrectly on a false calendar] before its time begins or after its time is over. A grave sin is pardoned only by making tawba. There are a number of things that will have small sins pardoned. When making tawba, one has to make qadâ for the prayers of namâz which one has omitted. Those savants who said that an accepted hajj would clear away grave sins did not mean that the qadâ of the omitted prayers would not be necessary. They meant that the sin of delaying namâz without an excuse until its time was over would be pardoned. It is necessary to make the qadâ, too. If one does not make the qadâ though one is able to do so, one will have committed another grave sin." Namâz will be deemed to have been performed during its prescribed time if a Hanafî Muslim says takbîr of tahrîma before the time is over. But a Shafi'î or Malikî Muslim is not considered to have performed the namâz unless one rak'at of namâz has been completed before the time is over. It will be considered a venial sin if namâz can not be completed within its prescibed time.

It is written in **Durr-ul-muntaqâ**: "A person who does not recognize namâz as a duty, who disbelieves the fact that it is fard, becomes a disbeliever. Those who convert to Islam in a country of renegades and disbelievers do not have to make qadâ of the prayers of namâz which they had not performed until they learned that it is fard to perform namâz."

It is written in the subject concerning the intentions of namâz in Ibni 'Âbidîn and on the twenty-sixth page of **Fatâwâ-i kubrâ**: "If a person performs prayers of namâz for years but does not know which ones are initial sunnats and which are final sunnats and if he performs every one them all with the intention of a fard, all of them will be accepted. For, if a certain prayer of namâz is performed with the intention of fard although it is in the category of sunnats, the sunnat thereby performed is acceptable." The one which he has performed first in every prayer time becomes the fard. The one which he has performed next becomes the sunnat. It is written in **Halabî-i saghîr**: "If a person realizes that there has been a defect in all the prayers of namâz which he has been performing for years, – that is, if one of the twelve conditions of namâz is missing – it will be good if he makes qadâ of them all. If there has not been any defects in them, to make qadâ of them is makrûh according to some savants and not mekrûh to other savants. Those savants who said that it would not be makrûh said that one must not perform those prayers of qadâ after morning and late afternoon prayers or else all of them would be supererogatory [if one did not have any prayers of qadâ to perform]."

It is written in the book entitled **Eshbâh**: "The fatwâ which is sahîh, dependable, shows that it is not necessary to intend for a sunnat when performing the first and final sunnats of the five prayers, that is, the muakkad sunnats. The rawâtib (prescribed) sunnats will be sahîh when performed with the intention of a supererogatory namâz or even only with the intention of namâz. That is, they will be the sunnats of the times within which they are performed. It is not necessary to intend specially for the sunnats. Imâm-i Zaylâ'î 'rahmatullâhi ta'âlâ 'alaih' said likewise. For example, if you perform two rak'ats of namâz before dawn with the intention of tahajjud (midnight prayer) and then later find out that dawn had already broken before you performed it, this namâz stands for the sunnat of morning prayer. It is not necessary to perform another namâz (of two rak'ats) as the sunnat of morning prayer. If after sitting for the fourth rak'at of the fard of early afternoon prayer you forget (to make the salâm) and stand up for the fifth rak'at, you make the salâm after making the sixth rak'at. The two additional rak'ats will become a supererogatory prayer. The reason why these two rak'ats do not make up for the final sunnat is not because you have not intended to perform the sunnat, but because you have not begun the sunnat with a separate takbîr. Also, there is a dependable report that it is not necessary to intend for tarâwih when you are performing the tarâwîh. Likewise, if a person who does not have any early afternoon prayers left to qadâ intends 'to perform the last early afternoon prayer which he has not performed though he has reached its time' as he performs the four rak'ats after Friday prayer and if he finds out later that the Friday prayer has been sahîh, these four rak'ats, according to a dependable and sahîh report, become the sunnat of Friday prayer." It is written in its fifty-ninth page: "We have already stated that when supererogatory prayers and the prescribed sunnats are performed with the intention of namâz only, or of any kind of namâz other than the sunnats, they will be sahîh.' As is seen, any namâz, [e.g. a namâz of qadâ,] performed during the time of one of the five daily prayers of namâz in addition to the time's fard namâz, is (at the same time) the sunnat of the time's namâz.

It is written on the fifty-fourth page of the book **Uyûn-ul-basâir** and in **Ibni 'Âbidîn**, in the chapter dealing with the intention of namâz: "According to profoundly learned savants, a sunnat performed only with the intention of namâz becomes sahîh. For, the sunnats of five daily prayers means the namâz performed by our Prophet 'sall-Allâhu 'alaihi wa sallam'. It was afterwards that those prayers of namâz were named sunnats. When performing the sunnats of the five daily prayers, Rasûlullah 'sall-Allâhu 'alaihi wa sallam' used to intend, 'To perform namâz for Allah's sake.' He did not intend, 'To perform the sunnat.' Any namâz performed so in every prayer time becomes the namâz which is called sunnat." Likewise is written in Halabî-yi kebîr, too. It is written in its fifty-second page that, as it is communicated in the book **Tajnîs**, the sunnats of the five daily prayers are supererogatory namâz and can be performed with the intention of a supererogatory worship, too. It is written in **Durr-ul-mukhtâr**, and also in the book **Durer** by Molla Husraw: "The sunnats of five daily prayers and the namâz of tarâwih are originally supererogatory prayers. When performing them an intention for namâz only will suffice."

It is written in **Ibni 'Âbidîn** and in the annotation to **Nûr-ul-îzâh**: "It is sunnat to perform two rak'ats of namâz before you sit down after entering a mosque. This is called the namâz of **Tahiyyatulmasjid**. When you enter a mosque, if you perform the fard, the sunnat, or any other namâz, you will have performed the tahiyyatulmasjid, too. The namâz that is performed does not need the special intention of tahiyyatulmasjid. For, the purpose of performing the tahiyyatulmasjid is to respect Allâhu ta'âlâ, Who is the Owner of the mosque. And the namâz which you perform serves this purpose."

While explaining the namâz of **Tahiyyatulmasjid**, Ibni 'Âbidîn 'rahmatullâhi ta'âlâ alaih' says: "When beginning the fard of the early afternoon prayer, if you make two intentions, one for the fard and one for the sunnat, you will have performed the fard only according to the two Imâms. But according to Imâm-i Muhammad the namâz will not be accepted. For the fard and the sunnat are two different kinds of namâz. [Prayers of namâz performed within a prayer time are either the time's fard namâz, or any namâz other than that fard. The sunnats of the time and prayers of qadâ are of this second kind. On the other hand, since prayers of qadâ and the sunnats are of the same kind, one single prayer of namâz can be performed with double intentions.] According to the two imâms, you have performed the more important one. On the other hand, since any namâz which you perform after you enter a mosque stands for the namâz of tahiyyatulmasjid, it is permissible to intend for the namâz of tahiyyatulmasjid while performing a fard prayer, according to Imam-i Muhammad as well. When you intend for the fard, too, you will have been deemed to have performed both the fard and the sunnat." Even though the time's fard and sunnat are different from each other, because of the fact that the sunnat means all the other prayers except the fard, the similarity between the sunnat and the qadâ prayer is identical with the similarity between tahiyyatulmasjid and the fard.

It is stated in the thirtieth page of **Eshbâh**: "A worship's causing thawâb requires not only its being sahîh, but also, and more essentially, the worshipper's having a true and sincere intention. If a worship performed with a sincere and true intention becomes fâsid inadvertently, it will not be sahîh. However, because one has made niyyat (true intention), it will cause much thawâb. For instance, a namâz performed without an ablution though one thinks one has had an ablution will not be sahîh. Yet one will be given much thawâb in return for one's niyyat (intention). If a person finds some najs water and yet thinks it is clean and makes an ablution with it and performs namâz, his namâz will not be sahîh because one of its conditions has not been fulfilled; however, he will be given thawâb owing to his intention. On the other hand, a namâz that is sahîh because it has been performed with all its conditions fulfilled will not be given any thawâb if it has been performed for ostentation." A person who makes qadâ instead of a namâz that is sunnat will not have omitted the sunnat; yet, for attaining thawâb for the sunnat as well, he should make niyyat, that is, pass through his heart the intention to perform the sunnat as well, as he makes the qadâ. Because a namâz that is fard is different from one which is sunna, it is not permissible to make niyya also to perform a namâz that is sunnat as you perform a namâz that is fard. The sunnat performed in this way is not sahîh. Yet, since a (fard) namâz being performed (after its prescribed time is over and which therefore is known) as qadâ and a namâz that is sunnat are not different from each other, (for they are in the same category,) it is sahîh to add the performance of a namâz that is sunna to your intention as you perform a namâz of qadâ.

Let us take a Muslim who has not performed his daily prayers of namâz for years, and eventually decides to make qadâ of the prayers which he has omitted. There are three ways whereby he can do so:

1– He can always perform namâz of qadâ instead of the sunnats of five daily prayers as well as during his leisure time daily.

2– He can perform qadâ only instead of the daily sunnats.

3– He can perform qadâ always, but only, during his daily leisure time, and not instead of the daily sunnats. The first choice is the best of all three of them. Thereby the debts of qadâ will have been paid in the fastest way. The second way is not preferrable in so far as his main concern is to wipe out his debts of qadâ soon. Into the bargain, as long as a person has debts of qadâ, the sunnats he performs will not be given any thawâb. However, he will be wiser to perform prayers of qadâ instead of the sunnats than to not perform them at all. For, it is advised by our superiors that "when you cannot do all of something good you should at least do as much of it as you can, instead of foregoing your gain altogether." As for the third choice; it is for someone who has failed to perform a certain prayer or prayers of namâz within its or their time for (reasons which Islam recognizes as excuses and terms) 'udhr. For, it is not sinful for that person to delay the performance of qadâ for as long as the time he is to spend performing the sunnat(s). Some people think and talk better of the third choice than the second choice. However, if a person would be able to make the third choice, then he would be capable of the first choice as well. Hence, people who omitted their prayers of namâz for months should calculate the prayers that they omitted, and perform them in the first way described above, or at least in the second way, and thereby pay their debts of qadâ as soon as possible, which in turn will save them from Hell.

If a person without any debts of qadâ makes qadâ instead of a namâz which is sunnat, his namâz becomes supererogatory. We have stated earlier that the thawâb for a supererogatory namâz is quite insignificant when compared to the thawâb for a namâz that is sunnat.

Shaikh-ul-Islâm Ahmad bin Suleymân bin Kemâl Pâsha 'rahmatullâhi ta'âlâ 'alaih', in his book **Sharh-i hadîth-i arbaîn,** explains the hadîth-i sherîf, **"My shafâ'at has become harâm for one who omits my sunnat,"** as follows:

In this hadîth-i sherîf the word sunnat means the path of Islam. For even if a Believer commits a grave sin he will not be deprived of (the Prophet's) shafâ'at. A hadîth-i-sherîf reads: **"I shall do shafâ'at** (intercede) **for those who have committed grave sins."** It is necessary to obey the religion which Rasûlullah 'sall-Allâhu 'alaihi wa sallam' brought from Allâhu ta'âlâ. A person who abandons this cannot attain shafâ'at. It is written in the book **Shir'at-ul-Islâm**: "The sunnat in this hadîth-i sherîf denotes things that are wâjib to do. And this is the way followed by the Sahâba, by the Tâbi'în and by the Taba'i tâbi'în 'rahmatullâhi ta'âlâ 'alaihim ajma'în'. Those who hold fast to this sunnat are called the **Ahl-as-Sunnat**. Then, the meaning of the hadîth-i-sherîf is that those who disagree with the Ahl-as-Sunnat in facts to be believed and in actions to be done or to be avoided, will not attain the shafâ'at." See Second Volume, 19th letter, in the fourth chapter of the third fascicle of **Endless Bliss**.

[Also, the hadîth-i sherîf, **"At a time when fitna and depravity are rife among my Ummat, a person who holds fast to my sunnat will attain the blessings of a hundred martyrs,"** means: "A person who adapts himself to the tenets of îmân and rules of Islam as they were taught during the time of the Salaf-i sâlihîn will attain the blessings of a hundred martyrs."] It is written in **Riyâd un-nâsihîn** while explaining the importance of namâz: "Imâm-i Nasîr-ud-Dîn Sayyid Abul-Qâsim Samarkandî says: 'This hadîth-i sherîf means that when fitna and depravity are widespread among the Ummat, a person who has the i'tiqâd (belief) of Ahl-i sunnat wal jamâ'at and who performs the daily five prayers in jamâ'at will attain the blessings of a hundred martyrs.' " For this reason, one must first have îmân agreeing with that of the Ahl-as-Sunnat, then avoid the harâms, then do the fards, then avoid the makrûhs, then do the muakkad sunnats, and then do the mustahabs. If a person does not do something which is earlier in this order it will be futile for him to do something which is later; in fact, if doing something that is earlier in this order is impossible unless something later in this order is omitted, then it is permissible, nay, compulsory, to do so. For example, it will be useless in the Hereafter for a person without îmân to avoid sinning and for a person who keeps committing harâms to do the fard. And it is useless for a person who is negligent in any one of these to grow a beard. For, growing a beard is the last in the order mentioned above. Nor can one say that it is bid'at to shave your beard. For, bid'at means to do something in the name of worship, that is, in order to get blessings, though it has not been commanded by Islam. No Muslim shaves his beard in order to get blessings. A Muslim knows that it is makrûh to shave one's beard. He knows that it is permissible to shave one's beard in order to do a more important religious duty, and thus he obeys the rules of Islam, the Sunnat.

It is written in **Bahr-ur-râiq** and in the chapter about things that will not break a fast in **Tahtâwî**'s annotation to **Durr-ul-mukhtâr**: "It is makrûh to put some ointment on your moustache or beard in order to ornament yourself. It is not makrûh when you do it for jamâl, that is, to remove any ugliness or to protect your dignity and honour. If adornment takes place when you do something for jamâl though you do not intend for adornment, it will be acceptable. Also, it is mubâh (permitted) and good to wear new, lovely clothes for jamâl. Yet it is harâm to wear them for arrogance. If your behaviour does not change when you wear them, it will be understood that they are not for arrogance. If the length of your beard is as prescribed by the sunnat, it is tahrîmî makrûh to put ointment on it in order to grow it longer. The length of the beard as prescribed by the sunnat is a small handful. It is wâjib to clip off that part of the beard exceeding a small handful, the part on the chin included. The hadîth-i sherîf, **'Grow your beard!'** does not mean, 'Grow it longer than a small handful.' It means, 'Do not grow your beard shorter than a handful', or, 'Do not shave it altogether.' The narrator of this hadîth, 'Abdullah Ibni 'Umar 'radiy-Allâhu 'anhumâ', clipped off that part of his beard exceeding a small handful. Not one single savant said that it was mubâh to have a beard shorter than a small handful. Shaving the beard is a custom of fire-worshippers and Indian Jews. It is harâm to make yourself look like disbelievers." As is seen, savants say that it is sunnat to grow a beard. Those who say that it is wâjib are contradicting the Jumhûr (Islamic savants' consensus) by saying so. It is harâm to keep your beard shorter than a small handful or to shave it entirely in order to be like disbelievers or women. It is makrûh if you do so not to be like them but to follow the custom in your country. It is bid'at to say that a beard that is shorter than a small handful is sunnat. If a person slights the sunnat he becomes a disbeliever. It is written in Islamic books that it is permissible, and even necessary, to give up the sunnat when you have a prescribed excuse.]

It is written on the seventy-first, three hundred and nineteenth, four hundred and thirty-third, and four hundred and fifty-third pages of **Ibni 'Âbidîn**: "A person who esteems and values the sunnats of prayers of namâz but omits them often without an excuse or because of laziness will be scolded. But he will not be deprived of shafâ'at." The hadîth-i sherîf, **"He who omits the sunnat which is before the early afternoon prayer will not attain my shafâ'at"** means, "A person who omits it insistently without an excuse will not get my shafâ'at which is for this namâz and which will serve for his promotion." It is written in **Ibni 'Âbidîn** and in the two hundred and third page of **Tahtâwî**'s annotation to **Imdâd-ul-Fettâh** that omitting it with some excuse will not prevent the shafâ'at. Besides, to perform the sunnats of daily prayers of namâz with the intention of qadâ does not mean to omit them.

It is written in the three hundred and ninety-sixth page of **Ibni 'Âbidîn** and in the hundred and twelfth page of **Majma'ul-anhur**: "When a person performing a supererogatory namâz follows the imâm who is performing the fard, it is not fard for him to say the additional sûras in the third and fourth rak'ats; it is supererogatory. For, this namâz of his has taken the shape of a fard." This comes to mean that when making qadâ instead of the sunnats it is not fard to say the additional sûras in the third and fourth rak'ats. It is written in the one hundred and third page of **Uyûn-ul-basâir**: "It is written in **Tâtârhâniyya** that a person who does not know whether or not he has any prayers of namâz left to qadâ had better say the additional sûras in the sunnats of the early afternoon, late-afternoon, and night prayers. The meaning of this is that it is better for him to intend for qadâ when performing the sunnats and to say the additional sûras."

It is written in detail in the 14 Zilqa'da, 1388 [1969] issue of a periodical named **esh-Shihâb** published in Beirut that the virtuous Hadrat Râmiz-ul-mulk, the superintendent of fatwâ in Tripoli, has given a fatwâ that it is permissible to make qadâ instead of the (daily) sunnats when performing the fard.

24 – TAGHANNÎ (SINGING) AND MUSIC

Music, classified as a branch of fine arts, is the art of expressing feelings and thoughts in terms of sounds and movements composed in melody, harmony, and polyphony. All heavenly religions state that there is music in Paradise; and so was it believed by the ancient Egyptians, Chinese and Greek philosophers including Buddhists, and Brahmin kâfirs, who were the followers of distorted forms of Heavenly Religions. The origin of the word "music" has connections with the name Mousa given to the nine statues which were believed to be the statues of the daughters of Zeus, the great idol of the ancient Greeks. It is written in **Durr al-munteqâ** that music is a grave sin according to all revealed religions. That afterwards priests instilled music, which was prohibited by the Injîl, into the Christian religion is written in detail in the fifth volume of Zarqânî's 'rahmatullâhi ta'âlâ 'alaih' commentary to **Mawâhib al-laduniyya**. Since a corrupted religion could not nourish their souls, they thought music had a spiritual affect, whereas in fact it is just a pleasure for the nafs. Today's western music originated from church music. Music became a kind of worship in all corrupt religions all over the world. With music, the nafses are pleased, the voluptuous bestial instincts are soothed, whilst the holy 'ibâdât which nourish the soul and purify the heart are forgotten. It is written at the end of the nineitieth and ninety-ninth letters of **Mekâtîb-i sherîfa**: "Do not listen to songs, to music very much. Music will kill your heart and cause mischief." And the ninety-sixth letter reads: "Listening to poetry increasing love for Allahu ta'âlâ in the heart is permissible provided that there should not be any musical instruments or sinners." Music motivates a man to lead an indolent life like that of alcoholics and drug addicts, and thus causes the kâfirs to be deprived of endless bliss. To protect man against this calamity and endless perdition, Islam has made distinctions between different kinds of music and has prohibited the harmful ones.

In the last chapter of the book **Qurrat al-'uyûn** are quoted some of the hadîths which describe the music in Paradise and the kind of music which is harâm for both men and women in this world. This book is printed on the margin of **Mukhtasar-i**

tedhkira-i Qurtubî[1] published in Egypt in 1302 [1884 A.D.]. The two books were reproduced by Hakîkat Kitâbevi in Istanbul in 1421 [2001 A.D.].

It is written in **Hadîqa**: "It is written in the Fatwâ book **Tâtârhâniyya**: 'It is harâm in every revealed religion to read with taghannî, that is, with a melodious voice, poems that satirize others or describe indecency, alcoholic drinks, and incite lust. Those things that cause acts of harâm to be committed are forbidden by Islam, so they are harâm, too.' One who says, 'How well-done!', for something which is certainly harâm becomes a kâfir. The same rule applies for harâms, such as adultery, usury, hypocrisy and drinking wine. It is permissible to recite with taghannî the poems and ilâhîs that are conveying Islamic preachings, wisdom, good advice, or beautiful moral qualities. It is makrûh to occupy oneself with these continually. It is a more serious harâm for the false tarîqat followers to excite the lust of people by reciting ilâhîs, dhikr or tasbîh in mosques or takkas. One should not attend gatherings that are certainly known to be so. Such places have ceased to be places of 'ibâdat and become gatherings of fisq [immorality, sinning]. However, one should not have a bad opinion of them unless one knows for certain. According to the unanimity [of savants], it is harâm to recite with teghannî the **Qur'ân-al kerîm**, dhikr, prayers or azân. Taghannî distorts the letters and words, and spoils the meaning. It is harâm to change these intentionally, advertently. It is not harâm when it is spoilt by mistake, by taghannî or inadvertently for those who are trying to learn where it will be spoilt and where it will not. Hence, it is necessary to learn tajwîd. It is mustahab to recite the **Qur'ân-al kerîm**, the dhikr and the ilâhîs with a beautiful voice provided that it does not spoil the meaning. And this is done by reciting compatibly with the tajwîd. The effect of this on the heart and the soul is tremendous. Reciting with a beautiful voice does not mean making melody and moving ones chin; it means reciting with the fear of Allah. Anbiyâ 'salawâtullâhi ta'âlâ 'alaihim ajmâîn' and Awliyâ 'rahmatullâhi ta'âlâ 'alaihim ajmaîn' used to

---

[1] An abridged version rendered by Abd-ul-Wahhâb Sha'rânî 'rahmatullâhi ta'âlâ 'alaih', (d. 973 [1565 A.D.] for the book **Tedhkira-i-Qurtubî**, which in turn had been written by an Andalusian Islamic Mâlikî scholar named Abû Abdullah Muhammad bin Ahmad Qurtubî 'rahmatullâhi ta'âlâ 'alaih', (d. 671 [1272 A.D.].

recite with a beautiful voice. It was prohibited by a hadîth-i sherîf to recite with a sad voice and to listen to it like the fâsiqs and the Ahl-i kitâb. To spoil the tajwîd by **elhân**, that is, by keeping up with a musical tune, is an ugly bid'at and to listen to it is a grave sin.

To give a complete explanation of taghannî and music, the eighth article of the first chapter of **Kimyâ-yi sa'âdat** is translated below. There is detailed information on singing on page 182 of the book **Akhlâq-i 'alâ'î** and in the last chapter of **Tibb-un-nabawî** by Muhammad ibn Ahmad Zahabî. Imâm-i-Ghâzâlî's account is as follows:

"There is a force called qalb or inclination in the heart. Beautiful and harmonious sound sets this hidden force into motion, as a spark will be generated when flintstone is struck against a piece of steel [and as a glass or a bakelite rod when rubbed with wool attracts pieces of paper]. Beautiful sounds penetrate into one's heart, despite one's will, because the qalb (heart) and rûh (soul) have a connexion with the **'âlam al-arwâh**, which is above the 'Arsh. This non-material and immeasurable 'âlam is the 'âlam of 'husn al jamâl' or beauty, and the basic element of beauty is tanâsub (harmony). Every kind of beauty in this world comes from the beauty of that 'âlam. Beautiful, rhythmic and harmonious sounds resemble that 'âlam. The hearts of those who obey Islam become pure and strong. Such hearts have a strong connexion with the **'âlam al-amr**, and music influences and sets them into motion in the direction of their inclinations or orientations as the wind sets the glowing fire into flames. If there is love of Allâhu ta'âlâ in the heart, a mellifluous voice causes that love to increase, and, therefore, it is beneficial. Contrary to this is the case of a person whose heart is corrupt and whose nafs has become stronger because he does not obey Islam but follows his nafs, instead. The sick heart of such a person cannot enjoy music because his nafs is excited by music, so music is harmful and harâm for him. Those who cannot understand that there can be love of Allâhu ta'âlâ in a heart say that any beautiful voice is harâm. They say man can love his like and man's heart cannot have any relation with anything which is not of his kind, and, therefore, they do not believe in love of Allâhu ta'âlâ. When they are told that Islam orders man to have love of Allâhu ta'âlâ, they say this means that we should obey His orders lovingly.

"A beautiful sound does not bring to the heart anything from the outside. It excites the halâl 'connections' in the healthy heart, and, therefore, it is halâl to listen to taghannî (singing) for a heart that is not sick. If there is no inclination (or connection) in the heart, his enjoying a beautiful voice is similar to his listening to birds, singing, or his looking at green plants, beautiful streams and flowers. As these refresh the eyes, fragrant scents are pleasurable to the nose, delicious food gives delight to the mouth, scientific knowledge and discoveries are sweet to the intellect, so a beautiful voice is pleasurable to the ears and is mubâh as they are.

"The nafs of a person with a sick heart fancies a nâ-mahram girl or boy. This desire in his or her nafs becomes more intense when he or she listens to music. Since it is harâm for him or her to be with her or him, listening to any kind of taghannî (singing) causes harâm activities.

"He whose heart is not sick does not enjoy hearing the voice which is describing girls, lust and desire; on the contrary, he feels uncomfortable. But if the heart happens to be sick, the nafs enjoys it and is excited towards the harâm. Therefore, it is harâm for such people to listen to music. All young people, both boys and girls, are in this category. Anything that enrages the fire of the nafs, which the Sharî'at has ordered to be extinguished, is harâm. And it is only under certain conditions and within limitations that it becomes mubâh for a healthy heart to listen to the sounds that increase the love for, or the inclination towards, the halâl.

"It is mubâh, even blessed, for the will-be hadjis to listen to songs about Ka'ba, hajj, Mekka and Medina, and for soldiers to listen to songs about warfare and bravery.

"In **al-Mawâhib al-laduniyya**, it is written that when Rasûlullah 'sall-Allâhu 'alaihi wa sallam' entered the city of Mekka, Ibn Rawâha was walking in front of the procession and reciting couplets. 'Umar 'radiy-Allâhu 'anh' said, 'Is it appropriate to recite poems in the presence of Rasûlullah?' Thereupon, Rasûlullah declared: **'Let him carry on, o 'Umar; do not prevent him! These couplets are more detrimental to the kâfirs than arrows.'** This shows that it is jâ'iz (permissible) to read poems that harm the morale of the enemy and make them feel sad, whereas it is not jâ'iz to read poems that excite the nafs.

"It is a blessing to feel sorry and to repent by reading qasîdas and ilâhîs about faults, sins and the torment in Hell. But, it is harâm to feel sorry while listening to poetry against death, qadâ and qadar. [Therefore, we should not read the chapter on death in Mawlîds.]

"It is mubâh to make merry with halâl sounds on happy occasions when it is necessary to be joyful, such as at weddings, feasts, sunnats (circumcision ceremonies), 'Iyds and returns from safars (expeditions). These sounds strengthen not the nafs but the qalb. It is self-deception for those with stained hearts to say there is love of Allah in their hearts and then to listen to songs or ilâhîs. Only a murshid kâmil 'rahmatullâhi ta'âlâ 'alaihim ajma'în' can diagnose whether the qalb is pure, strong and has defeated the nafs or if the qalb is sick and the nafs has overpowered it. [It was for this reason that Imâm-i Rabbânî 'quddisa sirruh' did not approve of young people reciting ilâhîs at meetings, as is written in his 266th letter, –please see the first chapter of the second fascicle of Endless Bliss–.] A beautiful voice or naghma (song) does more harm than good to the devotees of Tasawwuf whose hearts have not attained ahwâl, or whose nafses have not been redeemed from shahwa (lust), though they may have ahwâl," elucidates Imâm-i Ghazâlî in **Kimyâ-yi sa'âdet**.

Hadrat Sa'd ad-dîn al-Kashgârî reports from Khwâja Muhammad Pârisâ 'quddisa sirruhumâ' in **Rashâhât**: "The most harmful of the curtains separating man from Allâhu ta'âlâ is the settling of worldly thoughts in his heart. These thoughts come from bad companions or from watching unnecessary things. One should try very hard to expel them from one's heart. Reading frivolous books [or novels, newspapers, magazines, stories] and talking about unnecessary or trivial subjects increase such thoughts. Watching women or their pictures [in photo-novels, films or on television] and listening to songs and music [with voices of women] cause such harmful thoughts to settle in the heart, all of which take a man away from Allâhu ta'âlâ. Sickness of the heart is its forgetting Allâhu ta'âlâ. Please see the final part of the forty-sixth chapter in the first fascicle! Those who want to approach Allâhu ta'âlâ should avoid this and abstain from anything which incites a malignant imagination. Allâhu ta'âlâ's habit is such that He does not bestow the blessing (of approaching Him) upon those who do not work, endure hardships and give up their joys and desires."

[The qalb (heart) is the home of joy and love. Any qalb without them is said to be dead. Either love of Allâhu ta'âlâ or love of the world is in one's qalb. The word 'world' here means things that are harâm. When you expel love of the world from your qalb by performing dhikr and worship, it will be purified. Love of Allâhu ta'âlâ will be infused into this purified qalb automatically. When you commit sins, the qalb becomes dark and ill. Consequently, love of the world settles in the qalb instead of love of Allâhu ta'âlâ. An example of this is: If you fill a bottle with water, the air in it will be expelled automatically. When the water is poured out, air will come into the bottle again automatically.]

Mahmûd Anjîr Faghnawî 'rahmatullâhi ta'âlâ 'alaih', a great spiritual guide in Tasawwuf, states: "For the dhikr al-'alaniyya (the audible dhikr) to be useful [and therefore, permissible], the heart should be in a state of **lewn** (deep sorrow, bleeding), that is, there should not be the stain of lying or backbiting in the heart, nothing harâm or mushtabih should have passed through one's throat, and one's mind should be free from **riyâ'** (hypocrisy) and **sum'a** (desire for fame) and inclinations towards anything but the sirr-i Hadrat Haqq." For such people only is taghannî (singing) or simâ' beneficial. For those who have not attained such a state, the fiqh ulamâ' (fuqahâ) say, taghannî is harâm. The following couplets, which are translated from Persian, indicate the state of those who practise tasawwuf and taqwâ:

> *Wandering hand-in-hand with my honey,*
> *My eyes caught a flower, unknowingly.*
>
> *'Aren't you ashamed!' she said, and added,*
> *'How can you see the rose while I am with thee?'*

The following five conditions should be observed in order for taghannî to be mubâh.

1 - It is harâm for every [nâ-mahram] man to listen to the voice of women, girls or attractive boys when he is with them and looking at them. A pure heart is distressed at the sight of such scenes, and is stained; the nafs enjoys them, gets stronger and becomes excessive. The Shaytân helps the nafs and shahwa. Although it is jâ'iz to listen to the voice of an unattractive boy, it is harâm to listen to even an ugly girl while near her. Nâmahram men listening to girls or women reading or singing something permissible, such as mawlid or ilâhî, without seeing them [for example, from a record-player or radio-receiver], is similar to their looking at a boy's face. That is, it becomes halâl or harâm depending on the thought or intention; listening to a mawlîd is permissible, while listening to the voice is harâm. One should

avoid doubtful actions.

It is written in **al-Hadîqa** that it is harâm for men to talk with nâmahram women unless there is a darûrat[1]; it is jâ'iz (permissible) to talk only as much as necessary in cases such as buying and selling.

2 - No musical instruments, such as the lute, the violin, the reed, the saxophone or the flute should be played while listening to the voice of the reciter. It is harâm to play or listen to any musical instrument for pleasure or for merry making. It is the habit of those who drink alcoholic beverages. And alcohol incites the malignant desire of the nafs, that is, the shahwa. However, it is permissible for every Muslim to play band music to strengthen the morale of the soldiers in war and to improvise during peacetime to get ready, and to play the drums and tambourines at wedding parties. [Political congresses are regarded as battlefields in this respect.]

Playing musical instruments is harâm, not the instruments themselves.

3 - Muslims should not read with a mellifluous voice or listen to poems about indecency, women or alcoholic drinks. It is harâm to listen to anyone who blames Muslims or the Islamic scholars.

4 - There should not be attractive boys or nâmahram women among an audience. Fisq (debauchery), obscenities, sodomy and adultery are all the lusts, the shahawât, of the nafs; they should not be called love or affection. It is the heart wherein love and affection dwell, so they are valuable.

5 - Although it is permissible to listen to a beautiful voice for pleasure for those who have no worldly love in their hearts or no shahwa of the nafs, this must not become habitual. It is **lahw** (amusement, entertainment), **la'b** (playing, game) and absurdity to do or to use some mubâhs frequently. These are ways of killing time, which is harâm.

[The profound 'âlim in zâhirî sciences and 'ârif (he who has attained the highest degree in the knowledge termed ma'rifa) and kâmil (perfect) Hadrat Mazhar-i Jân-i Jânân 'rahmatullâhi ta'âlâ 'alaih' said: "Simâ', that is, qasîda, ilâhî or mawlîd, fills a heart that is not ill with compassion and make it tender. Allâhu ta'âlâ pities and looks with compassion on people with tender hearts.

---

[1] 'Darûrat' is defined at various places of this book, especially in the chapter dealing with 'Ghusl and Ablution'.

Why should something be harâm while it causes Allâhu ta'âlâ's compassion? It is a fact unanimously stated (by Islamic scholars) that instrumental music is harâm. However, it is said that at wedding parties, playing tambourines [and drums] is mubâh and playing reeds is makrûh. Rasûlullah 'sall-Allâhu 'alaihi wa sallam' plugged his ears with his fingers when he heard the sound of a reed when passing by, but he did not order 'Abdullah bin 'Umar, who was with him, to do so, too. This means that to avoid hearing the sound of a reed is taqwâ' (fear of Allâhu ta'âlâ) and 'azîma (a high moral quality). There is a difference of opinion about simâ' (singing). There are those who say it is permissible, as well as those who say it is not. It is better not to do something on which there is a disagreement. It was for this reason that those who had taqwâ did not perform an audible dhikr; they performed dhikr silently." These words of Hadrat Mazhar-i Jân-i Jânân are written in **Maqâmat-i Mazhariryya**.]

On the fourth page of **Durr al-ma'ârif**[1], it is written: "Simâ' is permissible only for those who have turned towards Allâhu ta'âlâ and who know that everything is from Allâhu ta'âlâ. Involuntary dancing is called **wajd**, and voluntary dancing is called **tawâjud**. There was simâ' in Hadrat Nizâm ad-dîn Awliyâ's 'rahmatullâhi ta'âlâ 'alaih' majlis (lecture, gathering, meeting), but there was no musical instrument, women or boys; there was not even the clapping of hands. A voice without instrumental music is called **simâ'** [that is, **taghannî**]. The human voice accompanied with instrumental music is called **ghinâ'** [that is, **music**]. Ghinâ' is harâm according to the unanimity of the 'ulamâ.' There are 'âlims who said that the 64th âyat of sûrat al-Isrâ declared ghinâ' harâm. The hadîths-i sherîfs, **'Shaytân was the first one to make taghannî,'** and **'Ghinâ arouses discord in the heart,'** prove that ghinâ' is harâm. The 'ulamâ' disagreed on whether simâ' is harâm or not, while there is no dispute that ghinâ' is harâm. The voice of women or young boys is also classified as ghinâ.' The 'ulamâ' who said that simâ' is halâl also stated the conditions for it to be halâl. When these conditions are not fulfilled, simâ' is harâm according to the unanimity." The above extract from **Durr al-ma'ârif** shows that there is no music or musical instrument in Islam. The term **Islamic music**, which has been coined recently, has no connection with Islam. A person who says "halâl" for something harâm

---

[1] Written by Sayyid Abdullah Dahlawî 'rahmatullâhi ta'âlâ 'alaih', (1158 [1744 A.D.], Punjab-1240 [1827], Delhi.)

becomes a kâfir. Moreover, it should be understood that those who mix the harâm into their ibâdât become kâfirs like the zindîqs who try to demolish and corrupt the image of Islam. Therefore, it is a dangerous bid'at to recite the **Qur'ân-al-kerîm**, the takbîr, and the eulogies with musical instruments like reeds, for instance. The Qur'ân al-kerîm should be recited with a beautiful voice and with tajwîd. It is harâm to recite it by modifying the words to keep up with tune.

It is ghinâ', and therefore harâm, for young hâfiz qurrâs to recite the Qur'ân al-kerîm, mawlîds or ilâhis to an audience of young women and girls. If a person looks at something with lust his heart also becomes busy with it; the heart gets stained and falls ill. The nafs gets stronger and becomes impetuously violent.

Although we said it is permissible to listen to a beautiful voice for those with only love of Allah in their hearts, providing they recite in accordance with the above-mentioned conditions, we should also note that the Sahâba 'radıy-Allâhu ta'âlâ 'anhum ajma'în' and the Tâbi'ûn 'rahmatullâhi ta'âla 'alaihim ajma'în' never did such things. Though taghannî is obviously a bid'at, we said it was jâ'iz because it has some uses. Hasan Basrî states at the end of **Siyar-ul-aqtâb**: "A person who listens to simâ' with love of Allah becomes a siddîq. A person who listens to it by following his nafs becomes a zindiq."

When the Qur'ân al-kerîm is recited on the radio or through a loudspeaker, the original sounds, that is, the original articulation of the letters are distorted most of the time and the meanings of the âyats change. The Qur'ân al-kerîm recited then becomes a common composition of a meaningless waves of sound, and a means of sentimental pleasure like the melodies of a song. In addition, as written in **Radd al-muhtâr**, in **Majma' al-anhur**, and in **Durr al-munteqâ**, and also on the 2361st page of the third volume of the tafsîr by Elmalılı Hamdi Efendi 'rahmatullâhi ta'âlâ 'alaih': "Recital of the Qur'ân al-kerîm is its recital by a person conscious enough to recognize what he is reciting is the Qur'ân al-kerîm." Mosques are built primarily to perform salât inside them. There is no quiet corner left for praying when the voice of a wâ'iz or hâfiz qurrâ' fills the whole mosque by means of radios and loudspeakers. Those who are praying in the mosque become confused. Ibni 'Âbidîn wrote that it is sinful for the imâm to be so loud as to disturb others when it is wâjib to recite aloud. Those who recite through loud-speakers are sinning from this point of view as well.

In the beginning of the section where he described a ghusl in his **Fatâwâ' al-kubrâ**, Hadrat Ibni Hâjar al-Makkî 'rahmatullâhi ta'âlâ 'alaih' wrote: "Reciting the Qur'ân al-kerîm in a mosque is a valuable qurba. But, it is necessary to silence the children who recite loudly and who confuse those who are performing salât. If the teacher does not keep the children quiet, the authorities should send the children and the teacher out of the mosque."

[**Question**: A loud-speaker makes it possible for the azân to be heard from distances; Believers can hear the azân. Therefore, is the loud-speaker not useful and beneficial?

Answer: If the assumption that the azân should be heard over a large area were true, this question then would have a meaning and value. If it had been necessary for the azân to be recited with a voice louder than that of a normal human being, Rasûlullah 'sall-Allâhu 'alaihi wa sallam' would have given a solution for this since it was his duty to preach and see that everything necessary in Islam was learnt and done. Although there had been those who proposed that prayer times should be announced by ringing bells like Christians or by blowing horns like Jews to make it heard from distances, he did not accept any of these ideas. **"We shall not do it that way. Mount a high place and call the azân,"** he declared. Thus, it became clear that it was not necessary to make a single azân heard everywhere. We know that any alteration in 'ibâdât is a bid'at and a grave sin, and it is an even more detestable bid'at and a more disgusting sin to mix an 'ibâdat with something which was never approved of and even refused by Rasûlullah 'sall-Allâhu 'alaihi wa sallam'. It is written in the nineteenth letter of the thirty-fourth chapter in the first volume: "Even if bid'ats seem to be bright, glorious and beneficial, all of them must be abstained from. Not one bid'at contains an advantage." The 186th letter in the book **Mektûbât Tercemesi** states: "Since the hearts of today's men have been darkened, some bid'ats appear to be beautiful and useful, but on the Rising Day, when the hearts will be awakened it will be understood that all the bid'ats were harmful without exception. Rasûlullah 'sall-Allâhu 'alaihi wa sallam' declares: **"Any renovation in the religion is harmful. You should throw them out."** In the 216th verse of sûra Baqara, Allâhu ta'âlâ declares: **"It may happen that you love something which is bad for you."** As is seen, (See chapter 4, Endless Bliss, Third Fascicle) it does not befit a Muslim to propound the bid'at of calling the azân through a loud-speaker. In addition to this, in **Durr al-mukhtâr** in the section on yamîn (oath) where the nazr (vow) is

– 378 –

explained, it is declared: "It is wâjib for the government to build a mosque in every town and locality. It is necessary to get it built with funds from the Bayt-ul-mâl. If the government does not build it, then it becomes wâjib for the Muslims to build it." On the 480th page of the first volume, it is written: "It is harâm to leave a mosque while the azân is being called. However, it is permissible to leave it in order to join the jamâ'at of one's own locality because it is wâjib to pray in the mosque of one's own locality." In summary, it is ordered that there should be a mosque in every Muslim ward, that the azân should be called at every mosque, and that one should hear the azân called at the mosque in one's locality or market and join the jamâ'at there. There must be a mosque in every ward of a town; the azân must be called at each and every mosque, and everyone must hear the azân. There is no need to make the azân heard over great distances. If loud-speakers are used, the result is interference and confusion, and the azân will have been made a play-thing. Therefore, it is unecessary and harmful to use loud-speakers to amplify the azân. If, following Islam's command, every muazzin calls the azân in accordance with the Sunnat from a minaret, every Muslim will hear clearly the azân closest to his home without the need of a loud-speaker calling it over a distance. Using loudspeakers to make the azân audible over great distances is a manifestation of the wish to have the azân called at one single mosque only and not at other mosques.

In a hadîth-i-sherîf quoted in **Kunûz ad-daqâiq** on the authority of al-Beyhekî[1], Rasûlullah 'sall-Allâhu 'alaihi wa sallam' stated: **"There will come a time after you when the most miserable and the most debased of Muslims of the time will be the muazzins."** This hadîth-i-sherîf prophesied that there would be people who would do taghannî and would not recite or call the azân in accordance with the Sunnat, and who would mix bid'ats into the 'ibâdât. May Allâhu ta'âlâ protect our muazzin brothers from being like the muazzins condemned in the above hadîth-i-sherîf! Âmîn.

In our time, it is difficult to see any mosque where the azân is being called on the minaret compatibly with the Sunnat. The practice of not calling the azân on the minaret has spread in both towns and villages. Thankfully, the [Turkish] Authority of

---

[1] Abû Bakr Ahmad bin Husayn of Beyhek, Nishâpûr 'rahmatullâhi ta'âlâ 'alaih', (384 [994 A.D.]–458 [1066].)

Religious Affairs has made all Muslims happy by announcing, in the circular sent to the muftîs dated December 1, 1981 and numbered 19, which orders muazzins to call the azân on minarets, that they are resolved to give an end to this ugly bid'at.

It is necessary for Muslims to know that the muazzin is a Muslim, 'âqil (sane) and sâlih (pious). Therefore, the azân on a tape-recorder or radio is not sahîh. It is not compatible with the Sunnat even if an 'âqil and sâlih Muslim calls the azân on the minaret and yet through a loudspeaker. Please see the final part of the eleventh chapter. 'Ibâdât should be distinguished from 'âdât (customs). Radios and loudspeakers are of course used in functions other than 'ibâdât and no one would have any reason to protest simply their being used. But anyone who makes the slightest alteration in 'ibâdât becomes a man without a Madhhab.

It is written in all books of fiqh, e.g. in the Persian book **Terghîb-us-salât**, as follows: "It is makrûh for a person without an ablution or without a ghusl, (for a person who is junub), for a drunk person, for a fâsiq (sinner), for a child, for a woman or for an insane person to perform the azân. There is a consensus (of Islamic scholars) on that it is necessary to reperform an azân called by a drunk or junub or insane person. If a disbeliever calls the azân at a prayer time, it must be concluded that he has become a Muslim. For, the azân is a sign, a characteristic of Islam." Performing the azân knowing, believing and loving its meaning is a symptom of being a Muslim. A person who commits a grave sin is called **fâsiq**. A person who drinks alcohol or gambles or makes friends with (nâmahram) women and girls or does not perform the five daily prayers of namâz, is fâsiq. It is harâm for women to let (nâmahram) men hear their voices by calling the azân, reading or reciting the Qur'ân-al-kerîm, or by performing mawlids or ilâhîs aloud. And it is makrûh if they do it through loudspeakers, radio or television. These instruments are instruments of merriment, (**âlat-i-lahw**), at places where it is customary to use them for pleasure. It is not permissible, therefore, to perform acts of worship with them, e.g. to perform the azân with a loudspeaker, which, in this case, would be like having a fâsiq to perform the azân. It is written in **Durar** that it is harâm to perform the azân in a manner similar to that of people committing fisq (grave sins).

Many examples can be given of the fact that a phonetical distortion made while reciting the Qur'ân al-kerîm results in an alteration of its meaning and thereby causes kufr. One of many such examples is given below to illustrate the subject: The last phrase of the 81st âyat of sûra Yâsîn means: **"Those He has created are very many. He is who knows everything."** He is the Creator of incalculable things. And He has knowledge of all things. However, when this same âyat is recited on a radio or through a loud-speaker the pharyngeal 'kh' of the word "khallâq" is transformed usually into 'h', and the word becomes, "hallâq", which means barber. Then, the new meaning of the phrase becomes "He is the barber, and He has knowledge of all things." Those who read the âyat that way and the ones who hear and approve or like it all become kâfirs. In the Islamic letters (Arabic) the words "Khallâq" and "Hallâq"[1] are two different words both in spelling and in pronunciation; they mean creator and barber respectively. Another example is the three z sounds of the Arabic language. Each one of them requires different sounds. The first is the emphatic "Zı", the second is "Ze", the third is "Zel." Ibni 'Âbidîn, on the 332nd page, wrote: "One should say 'azim' with 'Zı' in the rukû tesbîh which means 'My Rabb is Great.' If, instead, it is pronounced with 'Ze', it means, 'My Rabb is my enemy', and the salât (namâz) is null and void." A Muslim who reads and learns the Qur'ân al-kerîm transliterated into Latin characters will hardly be able to distinguish these three phonemic consonants, and, therefore, his salât will not be sahîh.

It is not permissible to transliterate the Qur'ân al-kerîm into Latin characters. This is noted in the chapter on Najâsa in Ibn Hâjar's **al-Fatâwâ' al-kubrâ** and in the fatwâ on page 62 of the book **al-Hady al-Islâmî** published by Al-Jâmi'at al-Islâmiyya in Libya, in 1966. A fatwâ on this matter in the 1406 [1985] issue of the monthly periodical **al-Muallim** published by the professors of "Bâkıyâtus-sâlihât" madrassa which is one of the great madrasses of the hundreds in India. A copy of this fatwâ is written in the book of khutba titled **al-Adillat-ul-kawâti** published by Hakikat Kitâbevi in Istanbul.

The **Qur'ân al-kerîm** recited on the radio or through a loud-speaker, like the Bibles and Torahs of today's Christians and Jews, is not the Word of Allâhu ta'âlâ. It is written on the 115th page of the book **al-Hadîqa** that it is not permissible to insult or show contempt for, to ridicule or to read or to listen to the Divine Books that have been abrogated by Allâhu ta'âlâ and the texts of

---

[1] The voiceless glottal fricative, /h/, and the voiceless pharyngeal fricative, / ħ /, are two different phonemes in the Arabic language.

which have been interpolated by people. For example, it is kufr to make merry by listening to the **Qur'ân al-kerîm** or Mawlîd on the radio in public houses, gambling-rooms, playgrounds, or in places where sins are being committed. And those who cause kufr become kâfirs.

There may be those who listen reverently to the **Qur'ân al-kerîm** or Mawlîd on a radio and weep as a result of being touched by the naghma (melodious voice) of the qâri' (reciter). The beautiful voice and the naghma influences the nafs of the sick-hearted; it nourishes the nafs, and the nafs makes the person weep. However, reciting the Qur'ân al-kerîm is a sunnat, and it is a basic rule in fiqh that a sunnat which brings about a harâm or even a makrûh should be abandoned. Therefore, it is better not to recite the **Qur'ân al-kerîm** or a Mawlîd on the radio. Nevertheless, it is necessary to broadcast the human word on the radio about the teachings of Islam and the soul-nourishing words of the Ahl as-Sunnat 'ulamâ', which fill with admiration the learned minds of the world. Such broadcast (and publications) are certainly very useful and very blessed.

Question: It is true that the sound on the radio is not clear when tuned to the radio stations in distant countries. But, the reception from a local radio-station is perfectly similar to that of the qâri.' Besides, the meaning also is clear. Would such a sound heard from a radio-receiver, a tape-recorder or a loud-speaker still not be regarded as the Qur'ân?

Answer: Scientifically speaking, the sound heard from a radio-receiver is neither **aqs as-sadâ** (reflection of sound) nor **naql as-sadâ** (transmission of sound). Naql means transmission or the transfer of the sound itself without any transformation. For example, heat may be transferred by conduction as well as by radiation and convection. An iron rod conducts heat without transforming it. Heat is conducted from one iron crystal to the next one and thus from one end of the rod to the other. The voice of the reader is heard by transmission, that is, **Naql as-sadâ,** by the people within earshot. The vocal chords in the larynx in the throat become tense and the air blown from the lungs sets them (the two fleshy chords) into vibration when we talk. Vibrations of these chords set into vibration the air molecules surrounding them, and this vibration is transmitted by other air molecules to our ears, and thus we hear the voice of someone talking. Sound propagates in the form of spherical pressure waves in air. Air transmits sound; it does not transport (or carry sound) itself. Sound travels

340 metres per second in dry air. Water molecules also conduct sound. Velocity of sound in water is about 1500 metres per second. Solids transmit sound much faster. The velocity of sound in steel and glass is approximately 5000 metres per second.

Sound waves propagating in air or water change their direction when they hit a solid smooth surface like a wall or a rocky cliff. The reflected waves give a second sound of similar qualities. This second sound is called **aqs as-sadâ** or "echo." Although the reflected sound, the echo, is similar in quality to the orginal sound, it has been stated that it is not necessary to perform sajdat at-tilâwat (to prostrate) when one hears the echo of an âyat as-sajda even if one understands the âyat clearly. That is, the echo of **Qur'ân** is not the **Qur'ân al-kerîm**. This sound is not called the Word of Allâhu ta'âlâ. The voice on the radio is neither the naql (transmission without transformation) nor even the aqs (echo) of the voice of the qâri'. It is a sound different from and only similar to the voice of the qâri'. Looking at the reflections of women in a mirror or water, or the pictures of women on paper or a screen is not the same as looking at them directly. The sound that reaches the microphone is no longer a sound wave when it is converted into, first, electrical impulses and then into electromagnetic waves. The sound heard from the radio is a reproduction through an inverse process: the electromagnetic waves received by the antenna of the radio-receiver are converted into electrical impulses and then into a new sound. A loudspeaker is defined as an apparatus that converts electrical impulses into audible sound waves. (See, for example, the French dictionary **Larousse** for hautparlour.)[1] How can a transmission of the Qur'ân al-kerîm which involves transformations or conversions into another sound be called the Qur'ân while even an echo of the Qur'ân is not?

Question: The voice on the radio is not the voice of the hâfiz qurrâ', as proved scientifically, but it is still completely similar in all its harmonics. And the meaning is not distorted, either. Why should it not be permissible to listen to it?

Answer: Something similar to something else is not that thing itself. For example, brass bracelets may be similar to gold ones, but they are never the same; brass does not count as gold. The

---

[1] Also 'loudspeaker' in Macmillan Contemporary Dictionary, 1979, Mac Millan Publishing Co. Inc., New York.

sound from a radio-receiver or a loud-speaker may be very similar to that of the qâri', but it is not the human voice. It is a metallic sound. Its quality, pitch, volume and harmonics are different. Picture of a woman may be very similar to her, but it is never the woman herself, nor is it something which has a connection with her. This is why it is not harâm to look without desire at the 'awrat of a woman in her picture, while it is harâm to look at her very body. Nevertheless, because the picture of a woman is like her, it is makrûh to look at the picture. Similarly, it is necessary to respect the like of a respected being because of its close proximity, even if it is not the same.

It is written in valuable books that it is kufr to recite the **Qur'ân al-kerîm** accompanied with instrumental music, like the kâfirs' singing hymns in a church with organ music. Please see the fortieth chapter in the second part of the Turkish version. Also, it is kufr to profane in this manner the Qur'anic recitation on the radio or through a loud-speaker, which is very similar to the **Qur'ân**. If the **Qur'ân al-kerîm** is recited without any instrumental music, and if it is recited with tajwîd on the radio just for a few minutes after hours of music and other shahwa-inciting programmes, and then the usual sinful broadcasting starts again, this case is similar to that of people in a fisq majlis with gambling, drinking, playing and immodestly dressed women reciting some **Qur'ân al-kerîm** in an interval between the harâm; it is sinful. In the commentaries of **Multaqâ**, it is written: "It is sinful to say tesbîh, tahlîl, dhikr, takbîr or to read hadîth, fiqh and the like in a gathering of debauchery or to those who profane." The reason for this is that our Prophet 'sall-Allâhu 'alaihi wa sallam' forbade reciting the **Qur'ân** in such gatherings or without proper reverence. For example, in the book **Kimyâ-i sa'âdat**, it is written: "Rasûlullah 'sall-Allâhu 'alaihi wa sallam' went to Rabî bin Su'ûd's house. Small girls were playing tambourines and singing in the house. They stopped singing [and playing thambourines], and started lauding Rasûlullah. **'Do not mention my name!** [Go on with what you have been reciting already!] **Eulogizing me** [reciting mawlîd or ilâhî] **is an 'ibâdat. It is not permissible to perform 'ibâdat when playing tambourines** [musical instruments], **making merry and playing,'** he stated." It is written in **Jawâhir al-fiqh** that he who recites **Qur'ân al-kerîm** while playing a tambourine or any other musical instrument, or while playing any other thing or game will become a kâfir. It is written in the chapter on ablution in **Mizân-i Sha'rânî**: "The 'ulamâ' of Islam declared that the person who recites the **Qur'ân al-kerîm** after saying unpleasant words is like that person who puts the **Qur'ân al-kerîm** into dirt. There is no doubt about his kufr."

It is written in **al-Hadîqa** in the chapter on the inflictions of the tongue that a hadîth-i-sherîf stated: **"Announce nikâh to the public! For this purpose, perform the ceremony in mosques and play tambourines!"** Imâm Munâwî explains this hadîth-i sherîf and writes: "Tambourines are not to be played in mosques. This hadîth-i-sherîf does not order that the tambourines should be played in mosques; it orders that only nikâh could be done in mosques." It is clear as explained in **al-Hadîqa** that it is never permissible to play any other musical instruments in mosques while it is prohibited to play even tambourines which are otherwise certainly permissible outside the mosque.

In the hadîths quoted in **Mukhtasar at-tadhkîra**, it is stated: **"In the latest time ignorant men of religion and fâsiq hâfiz qurrâ' will be on the increase. There will come such a time that men of religious profession will be more rotten and putrid than a donkey's carcass."** This hadîth-i sherîf prophecies that as the Rising Day nears fâsiq and corrupted men of religion will appear. We have heard that in Russia they put a turban and gown on communist spies and anarchists trained with special methods and call them the muftî of Turkmanistan, Azarbaijan, or hadrat so and so. We have seen their photographs in their periodicals published to further their internationl propaganda. They are sending these spies in the guise of religious men to African and Arabic countries where people are Muslims. Through these spies they are sowing seeds of anarchy and are making brothers enemies to one another. They have thus gotten hold of countries called "Socialist Islamic Republic." We see with gratitude that in our pure country there are no such corrupted men of religion among our honourable nation.

Recording the **Qur'ân al-kerîm** on magnetic tapes or gramophone discs is like writing it on paper. There can be no arguments against doing this based on the objection that tapes and dics are used for recording music, songs, games and amusements, since paper also is used for printing picture-novels, obscene pictures, amusements and pornographic magazines. The **Qur'ân al-kerîm** is called a **Mus'haf** when it is written on paper. A Mus'haf is valuable because it is the cause and means whereby people read and learn and memorize the **Qur'ân al-kerîm**. For this reason, it is very meritorious to write or print Mus'hafs and distribute them as gifts. Tapes and discs are also used as means for learning and memorizing the **Qur'ân al-kerîm** for they sound very much like something it. A tape or a disc on which the **Qur'ân al-kerîm** is recorded should be esteemed like a Mus'haf ash-sherîf, and nothing else should be recorded on them; they should be kept somewhere high, and nothing else should be placed on them; they should not be touched without a wudû', or given to kâfirs or fâsiqs; they should not be put together with tapes and discs on which other things are recorded; and they should not be played at places where there is fisq (debauchery), games, gambling, and entertainment. The record player or the tape-recorder used for listening to the **Qur'ân al-kerîm** should in no circumstance be taken to a fisq majlis (gathering for debauchery), and should never be used for playing harâm and indecent recordings. It is not permissible to play the **Qur'ân al-kerîm** on a record-player or tape-recorder which is used also for playing music because it is like listening to the **Qur'ân al-kerîm** recited by a fâsiq hafîz qâri' who also sings songs and lyrics which are not permissible as stated above. In short, the tapes and discs on which the **Qur'ân al-kerîm** is recorded are held in high regard and valued like Mushaf-i sherîfs, and disrespecting or dishonoring them causes kufr. However, listening to these recordings of the **Qur'ân al-kerîm** is a way of listening to something very much like the **Qur'ân al-kerîm**, but it is not the same as listening to the hâfiz qurrâ' reciting it. One cannot obtain the blessings of listening to the **Qur'ân al-kerîm** from it. For, the tilâwat of al-**Qur'ân al-kerîm** (recital of the **Qur'ân**) is its recital by someone (a Muslim) who is conscious about the fact that he is reciting the **Qur'ân al-kerîm**. This fact is written on the five hundred and sixteenth page of **Radd-ul-muhtâr**. However, it is fard to listen to any recitation which sounds like the Qur'ân al-kerîm. It is written on the three hundred and sixty-sixth page of **Radd-ul-muhtâr** that the **Qur'ân** al-kerîm recited by a small child who is not conscious of what he is reciting should also be listened to respectfully.

If the radio is always used for listening to useful things and things causing thawâb and never used for listening to things prohibited by Islam, it is permissible, for the purpose of learning, to listen to recitals of Qur'ân al-kerîm performed amidst these useful things or performed during the preaches, lessons and other programs on tapes at home, provided these programs be proper and suitable for Muslims. However, it is written in page 2361 of the third volume of the book of Tafsîr by Hamdi Efendi of Elmalı that this does not mean to listen to Qur'ân al-kerîm. It is a worship to recite (or read) Qur'ân al-kerîm as was done by our Prophet 'sallallâhu 'alaihi wa sallam' and the As-hâb-i-kirâm. To recite it in another manner or to listen to such recitals means to change a worship, which is a bid'at. And bid'at, in its turn, is the gravest sin. [Please read the twenty-second chapter in the second fascicle of Endless Bliss!]

It was written in a letter from India that the Wahhâbis in a certain town performed salât without an imâm in some mosques. These mosques were connected with a wire to the central mosque and the jamâ'ats followed the imâm by hearing his voice through loud-speakers. That the salât is not sahîh if performed by following the voice of an imâm through a loud-speaker is written in chapter 19. It is stated in **Fatâwâ-i-Hindiyya**: "One of the hindrances against following an imâm is the existence of a stream as wide as to let a boat pass or a road wide enough for a cart (car) to pass or there being an empty space of two lines (between the imâm and the jamâ'at, or between the last line of the jamâ'at and the people intending to join). In mosques, it is permissible to follow the imâm behind a large empty space. Another hindrance is the existence of a wall big enough to prevent the person performing the namâz in or outside the mosque from hearing the imâm or one of the jamâ'at or from seeing the movements of the imâm or one of the jamâ'at. [The voice heard through a loudspeaker is not the voice of the imâm himself. Likewise, pictures seen on a television screen are not their originals; they are their visions.] It is not permissible for a person performing the namâz in the mosque or behind the wall to follow someone except the imâm or one of the jamâ'at. If the mosque is full to the entrance, it is sahîh for a person performing the namâz at a place adjacent to the mosque to follow the imâm. If it is not full to the entrance, it is sahîh if the distance between him and the last line is not large enough to let a cart (or car) pass. If the distance is larger, his following the imâm is not sahîh [even if he hears the imâm]. It is stated in **Qâdî-Khân** that it is permissible for a person performing the (same) namâz in a building adjacent to the mosque to follow the imâm. It is not permissible if this person is in an upper storey or in a building which is not adjacent to the mosque." This plain fact shows that those men of religion who are making Muslims perform namâz in jamâ'at without an imâm are guiding them not to acts of worship but to acts leading to perdition.

Unbelievers are trying to convert Muslims into Christians and mosques into churches. To do this insidiously, they disguise themselves as Muslims. They attempt to elevate the place of sajda (where the head is laid in prostration) to pave the way for the future introduction of desks into mosques. "A head should not be laid on places trodden on by feet," they say, "for it causes infection." They have in mind a plan of evolving these higher places of sajda into desks by making them higher and higher year by year. To introduce music and an organ into mosques, they start first by introducing loud-speakers and tape-recorders to prepare people gradually for worship accompanied with music and musical instruments. However, it is a basic fiqh rule that doing a mubâh, which is not a sin, becomes harâm if there is the danger of this mubâh being mistaken for an 'ibâdat. Doing such a mubâh then becomes a grave sin. Therefore, Muslims should be very vigilant, indeed, and should be extremely careful to worship like the Sahâbat al-kirâm, as their grandfathers did. Because it is bid'at and will give way to other alterations in 'ibâdât, loud-speakers, tape-recorders and the like should not be allowed in mosques, though they may seem good and useful. Also, Muslims should be careful not to be caught in the traps or used in the plans of enemies of Islam. In the 216th âyat of Sûrat-ul-Baqara, it is declared: **"There are many things that you approve of and like but which are** [in fact] **harmful for you!"** One should abstain from the slightest alteration in 'ibâdât, no matter how useful they may appear. An azân called through a radio or loud-speaker is not sahîh. A salât is not sahîh if it is performed in jamâ'at by following a voice from a radio or loud-speaker, without hearing the voice of the imâm or the muazzin himself. This fact is explained in the nineteenth chapter.

In **Targhîb-us-salât** it is written: "In a hadîth-i-sherîf quoted in the pamphlet **Kitâb al-qirâ'a**, Rasûlullah 'sall-Allâhu 'alaihi wa sallam', describing the signs of the Rising Day, declared: **"Judges will take bribes and decide unjustly. Murders will increase. The younger generation will not care or respect their parents and kin. The Qur'ân will be recited with mizmâr, that is, with musical instruments. People will not listen to those who recite beautifully with tajwîd; they will listen to those who recite with music like songs."** In his book **Musâmara**, Hadrat Muhyiddîn-i 'Arabî 'qaddas-Allâhu sirrahul'azîz' wrote that in a hadîth-i sherîf narrated by Abu Huraira 'radiy-Allâhu 'anh', it is declared: **"There will be such a time that Muslims will disunite, break into groups. They will abandon Islam and follow their own ideas and judgments. They will recite the Qur'ân al-kerîm with mizmârs, that is, with instruments, as if singing songs. They will recite not for Allah's sake but for fun. There will be no blessings for those who recite so. Allâhu ta'âlâ condemns them. He will punish them."** In many such hadîth-i sherîfs Rasûlullah 'sall-Allâhu 'alaihi wa sallam' foretold that the **Qur'ân al-kerîm** would be recited through an apparatus, such as radios, magnetic tapes, records and loud-speakers, which are used for playing music. He declared that it will be sinful to recite in such a manner. In the translation of the collection of the forty hadîths by the profound 'âlim, Shaikh-ul-Islâm Ahmad bin Suleyman bin Kemâl Pâshâ, in the thirty-ninth hadîth it is declared: **"I have been sent to break mizmârs and to destroy pigs."** In the translation, this hadîth is explained: "mizmâr means flute or all musical instruments." By this hadîth he means. "I am ordered to forbid every kind of musical instrument and the consumption of pork." In another hadîth, it is declared: **"Recite the Qur'ân with the Arabic dialect and the Arabic phonetic! Do not recite like fâsiqs and singers!"** It is harâm for a person who recites like singing a song to be imâm (lead the salât). The namâz performed behind him is not sahîh. The reason for this is that in order to tune up or make a melody, he adds syllables, which changes the recitation into human language and not the **Qur'ân al-kerîm**.]

WARNING: All that is explained above is about reciting and listening to the **Qur'ân al-kerîm** on the radio. No mention of using or listening to the radio in general has been made. The general use of a radio should not be confused with its use in 'ibâdât. Comments on the use of a radio in general will be made later.

In **Kimyâ-i sa'âdat**, it is declared: "It is very meritorious to learn how to read the **Qur'ân al-kerîm**. But, those who read and the hâfiz qurrâ' should revere the **Qur'ân al-kerîm**. And to do this, they must obey the **Qur'ân al-kerîm** in every word and action of theirs. They must adopt the âdâb (rules and manners) of the **Qur'ân al-kerîm**. They must keep away from what it prohibits. If they do not act in this manner, the **Qur'ân al-kerîm** will become their enemy (and hate them.). Rasûlullah 'sall-Allâhu 'alaihi wa sallam' declared: **"Most of the munâfiqs of my Ummat will be of those who recite the Qur'ân al-kerîm."** Abû Sulaiman Dârânî said: "The Zebânîs, the angels who will do the tormenting in Hell, will attack the hâfiz qurrâ' who do not obey Islam, before they attack the idolatrous kâfirs. The hâfiz qurrâ' who recite mawlîd for money and those who recite melodiously are of this kind. It should be realized quite well that the **Qur'ân al-kerîm** is not for reciting only; it was sent for man to follow the way, Islam, preached in it." In the commentary of **Shir'at al-Islâm**, it is written: "It is the ugliest and most loathsome bid'at to recite the **Qur'ân al-kerîm** as if singing a song. Those who recite in such a manner are to be punished."

In **Riyâd an-nâsihîn**, it is written: "The **Qur'ân al-kerîm** will intercede for the hâfiz of the **Qur'ân al-kerîm** who obeys the Sharî'at. In a hadîth-i sherîf in the book **Muslim**, it is declared: 'The **Qur'ân al-kerîm will be either the intercessor or the enemy of its reciters.**' In a hadîth-i sherîf it is declared: '**There are many who recite the Qur'ân al-kerîm while the Qûr'ân al-kerîm calls down curses upon them.**' It is necessary for one to have a wudû' (ablution) when reading the **Qur'ân al-kerîm**, to hold it in the right hand, not to keep it lower than one's knees, not to leave it open after reading but to close and put it somewhere high [and clean], not to talk when reading it, and if one does talk, one should say the A'ûdhu again and then start reading or reciting. One should take (or hand) the Mus'haf [and also the tape on which the **Qur'ân al-kerîm** is recorded] standing as one is.

And those who listen to the **Qur'ân al-kerîm** on the radio should at least put the radio-set somewhere high, should not busy themselves with anything else, and should sit facing the Qibla. It is an irreverence to the **Qur'ân al-kerîm** (or the Mawlîd) to listen to music, songs or other kufr and harâms before or after the **Qur'ân al-kerîm**. The **Qur'ân al-kerîm** calls curses upon those who do not revere it when it is recited. Actions and behaviours that are sins for those who are reading or reciting are also sins for those who make or have it read or recited.

Listeners who cause the hâfiz to recite the **Qur'ân al-kerîm** on the radio are, in some respects, like those who watch an acrobat: If the acrobat falls down during the show and dies, the spectators will have committed a sin because the acrobat would not have been in the show and would not have died if the spectators had not been there to watch. It is true that victims die because man is mortal and the time for death has come; however, the killer is punished.

It distorts the meaning and is harmful to recite the **Qur'ân al-**

kerîm, the Mawlîd and the Azân with music (melodiously) and taghannî. For example, "Allâhu akbar" means Allâhu ta'âlâ is the Greatest. If it is recited as 'Aaaallâhu akbar" with a long "A", it means "Is Allâhu ta'âlâ (really) great?" This injects a tone of doubt, which is kufr. Therefore, it is obvious that those who say "Allâhu akbar" with a long initial 'A' become kâfirs.

In fiqh books, e.g. in **Halabî as-saghîr** on page 252, it is written: "The 'ulamâ' said that it is makrûh to recite the Qur'ân al-kerîm with naghma (melodiously), even if it does not cause any phonetical distortion. The basis for this is that it is a simulation of the fâsiqs' singing, and it is harâm if there is phonetical distortion. It is makrûh to listen to something which is makrûh to read, and it is harâm to listen to something which is harâm to read. It is wâjib (necessary) to do amr bi'lma'rûf (to remind someone of the rules of the Sharî'at) to the hâfiz qurrâ' who recite the **Qur'ân al-kerîm** with taghannî (melody). If reminding them is likely to arouse hostility or enmity, one should not listen and should leave that place." **In Halabî** on page 297, it is written: "It is necessary to re-perform those salâts performed behind an imâm who recites melodiously." On another page it is written: "It is a sinful action to recite the **Qur'ân al-kerîm** loudly where people are working (or studying) or lying down resting."

On page 496 of **al-Halabî al-kebîr**, it is written: "It is permissible to recite the **Qur'ân al-kerîm** through one's heart while lying down on one's side with one's legs put together, or to recite when walking, working, taking a bath or sitting beside graves. It becomes a sin to recite the **Qur'ân al-kerîm** loudly near people who are reading, writing or working while they are not listening. It is tahrîmî makrûh for a group of people to recite the **Qur'ân al-kerîm** loudly in a chorus. One of them should recite and the others should listen quietly. It is not fard to listen for those who have work to do. It is fard-i kifâya to listen to the **Qur'ân al-kerîm**, and listening to the **Qur'ân al-kerîm** is more meritorious than reciting it or doing any nâfila 'ibâdât (supererogatory worship). A woman should learn from another woman how to read or recite the **Qur'ân al-kerîm**. A woman should not learn it from a nâ-mahram man, even if he is blind. It is written in **Berîqa** and **al-Hadîqa** that it is sinful to forget the **Qur'ân al-kerîm** after one has learnt it. In **Khulâsat al-fatâwâ**, it is written: "It is permissible to recite the **Qur'ân al-kerîm** in the heart or mind while working or walking."

There is no need to learn music to recite the **Qur'ân al-kerîm** correctly and beautifully. It is necessary to learn the **'ilm at-tajwîd** (the science of reading or reciting the **Qur'ân al-kerîm** correctly). According to the majority of Islamic scholars, the **Qur'ân al-kerîm** cannot be recited correctly, and the azân and salât (namâz) will not be accepted when done without studying the 'ilm at-tajwîd, which teaches the articulation places of the letters (makhârij al-hurûf) or correct pronunciation, the madd, that is, the length of vowels, and many other rules.

In **al-Halabî as-saghîr**, a few lines above the section on sajdat at-tilâwa, it is written: "It is a sin to write the **Qur'ân al-kerîm** in an illegibly small script or to get or own such small-sized copies of **Qur'ân al-kerîm**." Allâhu ta'âlâ sent the **Qur'ân al-kerîm** to be recited, read, listened to and its contents to be learnt and obeyed. It is an insult to the **Qur'ân al-kerîm** to write it in an illegibly small script. Khalîfa 'Umar 'radiy-Allâhu 'anh' punished a man who wrote an illegibly small copy of the **Qur'ân al-kerîm**. Buying such Mus'hafs, carrying them in small golden boxes attached to a string around the neck, as Christians do with their icons or crosses, is useless and very sinful.

It is written in **al-Halabî** that it is tahrîmî makrûh to write âyats or names of Allâhu ta'âlâ' [and also a picture of the Ka'ba] on things spread on the ground or on praying mats (sajjada). It is written in **Tahtâwî's** annotation to **Imdâd** that it is makrûh to write such sacred words on coins or paper bills. The exalted 'âlim as-Sayyid 'Abd al Hakîm Arwâsî 'quddisa sirruh' states in one of his letters that during the time of the Sahâbât al-kirâm and the Tâbi'în 'izâm ''alaihim ar-ridwân' no sacred word was written on money. The reason for this is that money is used in buying and selling, and, therefore, it is not treated with respect. It is permissible to print pictures on it. The non-Sunnite governments, for example, Fâtimîs and the Rasûlîs, who belonged to the Mu'tazila and who bore the name Muslim but who in reality did not obey Islam, had âyats and hadîths printed on money. This was one of the tricks they played to deceive the people and hide in a Muslim guise. The 'ulamâ' of Islam [that is, the Fuqahâ-yî 'izâm] did not permit writing blessed words even on grave-stones, let alone money. It is written in **Al-fatâwâ al-Hindiyya** that it is makrûh to touch such money without an ablution. It is written in the explanation of **Shîr-at al-islâm** that it is necessary to bury or burn the old and ruined Mus'hafs.

'Ibâdât cannot be altered to please men. It is very wrong to think that Allâhu ta'âlâ will be pleased with what man himself is pleased with. If it were so, then there would be no need for Prophets to be sent; everyone would worship in a way they pleased and Allâhu ta'âlâ would be pleased with it, too. However, in reality, for a worship to be acceptable, it must be in conformity with Islam, though the human mind may not see the reason or appreciate the benefit and use of it.

What has been written above may not please those who have made Islam a means to earn earthly possessions. However, it is not intended for them but for those who want to learn the truth.

Question: Is it sinful to listen to the radio and watch television?

Answer: This question is similar to asking whether or not it is sinful to go to the cinema. Let us answer the two questions together.

Question: Is it sinful to go to the cinema?

Radio, cinema, and television are all media for mass communication. They are like books, newspapers and magazines. They are all means or tools like guns. It is sinful to use guns against faultless, innocent, and harmless people, but it is very meritorious to use them against enemy in warfare. Therefore, it would not be correct to make a clear-cut judgement of the matter by saying that it is all sinful or all definitely meritorious.

Similarly, if the radio programmes and films are prepared by decent people and, therefore, their contents are of what Allâhu ta'âlâ approves of, such as the use and application of Islamic teachings, ethics, trade, arts, factories and production, history, military training and other useful religious or secular information, then it is not sinful but mubâh to listen to such radio programmes or watch a television and cinema film. It is even necessary for every Muslim to listen to and to watch them as it is necessary to read useful books and magazines. Please see the eighteenth chapter.

However, if such media are under the control of the enemies of Islam and the programmes are tabled by morally indecent people who propagate such ugly and harmful things as the ideas of enemies of Islam and the promotion of harâm, then it is not permissible to listen to such radio programmes or to watch such television programmes or to go to the cinemas where they show such films. It is harâm like reading publications, books and novels with similar harâm contents.

It is stated in the final sections of **Hadîqa and Berîqa**: "It is sinful to keep tambourines or other sorts of musical instruments in one's home or shop or to sell them or to give them as presents or to hire them out, though one may not be using them oneself.

If **mubâh** (permissible things) and sins are mixed and if there is harâm where the programmes are broadcast or where the radio, television or films are listened to or watched, it is necessary to give up the mubâh or even the thawâb (merits) in it in order to save oneself from the sins. As a matter of fact, although it is sunnat to accept an invitation from a Muslim, one should not accept or attend an invitation wherein there is harâm; one should give up a sunnat to avoid harâm or makrûh.

In the book **Akhlâq-i alâ'î**[1], it is written: "Poetry is metred words in verse form. It is certainly mubâh to listen to a beautiful voice in which there is no melody or singing. Some said it is jâ'iz (permissible) to sing to oneself to rid oneself of boredom or worries. But it is harâm to do so to entertain others or to earn money. There are three kinds of naghma, that is, metred sound:

1 - Human voice. (We have explained this kind of naghma above in detail.)

2 - Animal voice, such as birds' singing, is certainly halâl to listen to.

3 - Sound made by percussion, wind and string instruments [all musical instruments] is certainly harâm to listen to. It is not sinful to listen to a stream of water murmuring, waves splashing, wind blowing and leaves fluttering. It is useful to listen to such sounds, for it helps to dissipate worries."

It is written in **Ashi'at al-leme'ât**, in the chapter **Bayân wa Shî'r**, that a hadîth narrated by Â'isha 'radiy-Allâhu anhâ', stated: **"Poetry is an utterance that makes itself good when it is good and bad when it is bad."** "That is, metre or rhyme does not make a word bad or displeasing; it is the meaning which makes it so."

It is written in **al-Hadîqa**: "Music mixed with harâm pleases the nafses of fâsiqs, in the same way as that taghannî into which no harâm is added pleases the pure hearts and souls of pious men." Neither the former nor the latter enjoy the other's music; they feel uncomfortable. This is because what tastes good to hearts and souls makes the nafs uncomfortable, and what tastes

---

[1] Written by 'Ali bin Emrullah 'rahmatullâhi ta'âlâ 'alaih', (916 [1509 A.D.]–979 [1571], Edirne, Turkey.)

sweet to the nafs gives discomfort to pure hearts. This is why the places that offer a life of Jannat (Paradise) to the kâfirs and fâsiqs are prisons to the Muslims, the pious. The hadîth-i sherîf, **"The Dunyâ** [that is, places where there is harâm, the majlis al-fisq] **is a dungeon to Believers, and Paradise to the kâfirs,"** communicates this unchanging fact. With this fact in view, everyone can judge the quality of his qalb (heart). Because the nafses of most people have become strong by using the 'alâmats (signs) of kufr and by committing harâms their nafses have suppressed their hearts and souls; naghma (singing) excites their nafses causing them to become excessive. And the soul or the heart is not influenced or moved because their talents and attributes have been blunted and made insensible. Thus, people assume the good taste felt by their nafses is also the same taste felt by their hearts and souls, whereas the latter two have no share. As a matter of fact, animals also enjoy naghma."

In the tafsîr books (explanations of the **Qur'ân al-kerîm**), for example, in **Tafsîr-i medârik**[1], it is written that the âyat **Lehw al-hadîth** in the **Sûrat al-Luqmân** is a prohibition against music. In the Persian tafsîr book **Mawâhib-i 'aliyya**[2] this âyat is interpreted: "Some people gossip, tell and write false stories and novels, and pay songstresses to get them to sing for the public. By doing so, they are actually trying to hinder people from listening to the **Qur'ân al-kerîm**, from reading and learning the fard and the harâm, and from performing salât; in short, they are trying to divert them from the way of Islam. Thus, they ridicule Muslims and insult Allâhu ta'âlâ's commandments. They call Islam 'regression' and Muslims abnormal, old-fashioned, sick men who are retrogressive or reactionary. When these so-called intellectuals are told about Allâhu ta'âlâ's commandments or the words of the Ahl as-Sunnat 'ulamâ', they put on an air and turn away their faces haughtily, full of conceit and take no notice as if they do not at all hear what is being said. Give them the news of the fire of Hell and its very bitter torments." This tafsîr has been translated into Turkish under the title **Mawâkib tefsîri**. The book **Durr-al-munteqâ** declares: "It is harâm to recite the **Qur'ân al-kerîm** with taghannî (that is, melodiously) and to listen to it being

---

[1] Written by Abu-l-berekât Hâfiz-ud-dîn, Abdullah bin Ahmad Nesefî 'rahmatullâhi ta'âlâ 'alaih', (d. 710 [1310 A.D.], Baghdâd.)
[2] Written by Husayn Wa'id-i-Kâshifî 'rahmatullâhi ta'âlâ 'alaih', (d. 910 [1505 A.D.], Hirât).

so recited. Burhân ad-Dîn Merginânî 'rahmatullâhi ta'âlâ 'alaih' stated that a person will lose his îmân if he says, 'How beautifully you recite!' to a hâfiz who recites the **Qur'ân al-kerîm** melodiously. He will necessarily have to renew his îmân and nikâh (marriage). Hadrat Quhistâni also wrote the same. If some people say, 'We go into ecstasies by reciting qasîdas and ilâhîs melodiously,' they should not be believed. There is no such thing in Islam. Dances in takkas and melodious recitals [of ilâhîs or mawlids] are all harâm. It is not permissible to go to such places and listen to their un-Islamic practices. The Tasawwuf leaders did not have such practices. They were invented later. Our Prophet 'sall-Allâhu 'alaihi wa sallam' listened to poetry. But this is no implication of a permission to listen to naghma (singing). Those who say our **Nabî** 'sall-Allâhu 'alaihi wa sallam' listened to songs and went into ecstasies are liars." [The taghannî which is harâm is to recite or read (Qur'ân al-kerîm) by tuning it up to musical notes. And the taghannî which is sunnat is to recite or read by observing the rules of Tajwîd.] There is detailed information on raqs and simâ' (dancing and singing) in the last chapter of **'Uqûd ad-durriyya**.

On page 270 of the fifth volume of **Durr al-mukhtâr**, it is written: "It is permissible and beautiful to recite the **Qur'ân al-kerîm** with taghannî provided that no letter is added and the words are not misspelt or mispronounced. Otherwise it is harâm. There is the fear of kufr if one says, 'How nicely you recite!' to someone who performs taghannî in a way that distorts the **Qur'ân al-kerîm**." Ibn 'Âbidîn explaining this statement in his commentary, writes: "It was said that a person will become kâfir if he says, 'How beautifully you recite!' to a hâfiz who recites with taghannî. This is because he who says 'good' for something which is harâm, according to all four Madhhabs, will become a kâfir (disbeliever). Also, he who says, 'You recite beautifully!' referring to the distorted words becomes a kâfir, and certainly not the one who means his voice or his reciting the **Qur'ân al-kerîm** itself is beautiful." Such a person will enjoy listening to the same hâfiz also when he recites without performing taghannî, and will say, 'He recites beautifully.' Nevertheless, one should not listen to a hâfiz who recites with taghannî; it is harâm both to recite and to listen to. In **al-Hadîqa**, in the section on the afflictions incurred by the tongue, it is declared: "It is harâm to recite the **Qur'ân al-kerîm** by keeping up with a tune and, thereby, altering the harakas and meds (the vocalizations and the prolongations), and so is the case with listening to this. Beautifying the recitation of the **Qur'ân al-kerîm** means reciting it in accordance with the rules of tajwîd."

On the 266th page of the book **Kimyâ-i sa'âdat**, in the paragraph concerning child training, it is written: "Children should not be allowed to read or recite poems about women, girls and love affairs, and parents should not let their children go to or learn from a teacher who says such poems are "nourishment for the soul." A teacher who says so [and teaches sex] to his students is not a master but a shaytân because he is spoiling the hearts of children." Our Nabî 'sall-Allâhu 'alaihi wa sallam' stated: **"Ghinâ darkens the heart."** That is, taghannî with human voice and instrumental music stains the heart. [Ibni 'Âbidîn explains this hadîth on page 222, volume five.] One should not fancy music or be taken in by the taste of it. Not the soul but the nafs, who is the enemy of Allâhu ta'âlâ, enjoys its taste. The wretched rûh (soul) has fallen prey to the hands of the nafs and, therefore, thinks it is its taste. The taste of music is like that of honey that is poisoned or the najâsat [dirt] that is sweetened and gilded.

The aim of reporting that music is harâm and harmful is not to brand thousands of music addicts as fâsiq and sinful; it must certainly be pointed out that the sins of the author of these lines are much more than those of his readers. Only Prophets ''alaihimussalâm' are ma'thûm, that is, free from any sin. It is another sin not to know the widespread sins. He who shamelessly commits any harâm which is unanimously said to be a harâm, thinking that it is halâl, becomes a kâfir. Thinking of how we are so sinful, we must always be in supplication with bowed necks before our Rabb. We must make tawba every day!

The great walî Celâleddîn Rûmî 'quddisa sirruh', who was full of love for Allâhu ta'âlâ, never played reeds or any other instrument. He did not listen to music, nor did he ever dance (raqs). Commentaries have been written in every country in many languages to his **Mathnawî** (Mesnevî), which has more than forty-seven thousand couplets that have been spreading nûr (light) to the world. The most valuable and tasteful of these commentaries is the one by Mawlânâ Jâmî which has also been commentated on by many others. And, of these, 56 pages, which covered only four couplets, of the commentary by Suleymân Nesh'et Efendi was published during the time of Sultân 'Abd al-Majîd Khân by the Matba'a-i Âmira in 1263 A.H. In this book, Mawlânâ Jâmî 'quddisa sirruh' wrote: "The word 'ney' in the first couplet of the

Mathnawî [Listen to the reed...] means a perfect and exalted human being brought up in Islam. Such people have forgotten themselves and everything else. Their minds are always busy seeking Allâhu ta'âlâ's ridâ (grace, love). In the Persian language, 'ney' means 'non-existent.' Such people have become non-existent from their own existence. The musical instrument called 'ney' is a plain pipe and the sound from the ney is completely from the player. As those exalted men are emptied of their existence, the manifestation of Allâhu ta'âlâ's Akhlâq, Sifât and Kamâlât (moral qualities, attributes of perfection) are observed in them. The third meaning of the word 'ney' is reed-pen, which again means, or points to, an insân-i kâmil (perfect human). Movements and writings of a pen are not from itself, nor are the actions and words of a perfect human; they are all inspired to him by Allâhu ta'âlâ." 'Abidîn Pasha 'rahmatullâhi ta'âlâ 'alaih', the governor of Ankara during the time of Sultan 'Abd al-Hamîd Khân the Second, gave nine proofs in his **Mesnevî Şerhi** to show that 'ney' meant insân-i kâmil.

Also, the Mawlawî (Mevlevî) Shaikhs were learned and pious persons. Osmân ('Uthmân) Efendi, one of them, wrote a book titled **Tezkiya-i-Ahl-i-Bayt**, in which he refuted the Râfidî book **Husniya** with documents, thus rendering a great service to Islam[1]. Later some ignorant people thought that 'ney' meant 'musical instrument' and began to play musical instruments such as flutes and drums and dance. Musical instruments were placed in the mausoleum of that great master of Tasawwuf (Mevlânâ Celâleddîn Rûmî). Certainly, poeple who have read the explanations of **Mathnawî** (Mesnevî) and know that sun of truth well, will not be misled by such falsifications.

Celâleddîn Rûmî 'quddisa sirruh' did not even perform loud dhikrs (to say Allâhu ta'âlâ's name loudly). In fact he declared:

"Pes zi jân kun, wasl-i jânânrâ taleb,
Bî leb-u-bî-gâm migû, nâm-i Rabb!"

in his **Mathnawî**, which means, "Therefore, with all your heart, you desire to attain to the Beloved. Without moving your lip and tongue, say [in your heart] the name of your Rabb!" Later, people ignorant of Islam entertained their nafses by playing instruments, such as the ney, saz and tambourines and by singing lyrics and

---

[1] Please see the book **Documents of the Right Word**.

dancing. In order to call these sins 'ibâdât and to make themselves known as men of Islam they even lie; they say, "Mawlânâ also used to play and dance like this. We are Mawlâwîs; we are following his path."

Hadrat Abdullâh-i Dahlawî, a specialist in 'ilm az-zâhir, an owner of high ranks in tasawwuf, a profound 'âlim, a great Walî, states in his 74th letter: "Taghannî, sad voice and poetry on the theme of love of Allâhu ta'âlâ and the qasîdas telling the lifestories of the Awliyâ-i kirâm, move the related connections and bonds in the heart. Making dhikr with a low voice and listening to poetry not prohibited by the Sharî'at refines and gives tenderness to the hearts of the followers of the Chishtiyya tarîqat." In the 85th letter, he states: "Tasawwuf masters and leaders listened to beautiful voices. But the voices were not accompanied by instrumental music, and the listeners were not in the company of boys or girls, nor were they in the company of fâsiqs. A great leader of the Chishtiyya tarîqat, Hadrat Sultân al-Meshâyikh Nizâm ud-Dîn-i Awliyâ, listened to beautiful voices, but never to instrumental music, as written in the books **Fawâ'id al-fuâd** and **Siyar al-Awliyâ**. The Awliyâ's listening to **sima'**, that is, to beautiful voices, is for the purpose of converting the heart from the state of discomfort to comfort. The ghâfils' (those devoid of love of Allâhu ta'âlâ) listening to a beautiful voice gives way to fisq. No instrumental music is halâl. Although there were those who, when in a state of sekr (ecstasy), said it was permissible, they are held excusable; one should not say jâ'iz putting forth their word as an evidence. Silent dhikr (dhikr al-khafî) is more meritorious (afdal), though it is permissible to make audible dhikr (dhikr al-'alanî), observing the conditions compatible with Islam. It is not permissible to play an instrument, such as a flute, violin, saz, ney, or to listen to the songs of ghâfils, to dance [raqs], or to watch those who do so." In the 99th letter, he states: "To dissipate the qadb [discomfort] of the heart, the Qur'ân al-kerîm, recited with a beautiful voice and in accordance with the rules of tajwîd, should be listened to. This is what the Sahâbat al-kirâm used to do. It was not their habit to listen to qasîdas or poems. Listening to songs and musical instruments and performing audible dhikr were introduced later. The great Tasawwuf leaders like Abû 'l-Hasan ash-Shâdhilî and Hammâd ad-Dabbâs 'qaddas-Allâhu ta'âlâ esrârahumâ' categorically refused all such things. 'Abd al-Haqq ad-Dahlawî 'rahmatullâhi 'alaihim' relates this in detail. There were also those leaders who, without any accompanying music, fâsiqs or ghâfils, listened to poetry about love for Allâhu ta'âlâ. When they brought the ney and saz to Hadrat Shâh an-Naqshaband al-Bukhârî, he stated: 'We do not listen to these. But we do not deny the mutasawwifs who listen. Rasûlullah 'sall-Allâhu 'alaihi wa sallam' never listened to a musical instrument. In the Tarîqat-i Mujaddidiyya, listening to taghannî does not influence the heart. Listening to the **Qur'ân al-kerîm** gives ease to the heart and increases its peace. To those in (the phase called) the sayr-i qalb, songs and music give pleasure. The dhikr made with a low voice and sad taghannî increases zawq (joy) and shawq (ardour). The dhikr with a loud voice full of pain and sorrow, outside of one's own control and option, is not prohibited. But it should not be made a habit."

In **Ashi'at al-leme'ât**, in chapter **Bayân wa Shi'r**, it is written: "Nâfi', a great Tâbi', said: "Abdullah ibn 'Umar 'radiy-Allâhu 'anhumâ' and I were walking together. We heard the sound of a ney. Abdullah plugged his ears with his fingers. We quickly walked away from that place. 'Is the sound still audible?' he asked. 'No, it can no longer be heard,' I replied. He took his fingers from his ears and, 'Rasûlullah 'sall-Allâhu 'alaihi wa sallam', too, had done so,' he said. Then, Nâfi' added, 'I was only a child then.' This means that he did not order Nâfi' to plug his ears because he was a child. Therefore, it is not correct to deduce from this that listening to the sound of a ney is tanzîhî makrûh and not tahrîmî makrûh, and to think that 'Abdullah 'radiy-Allâhu 'anh' plugged his ears with his fingers out of wara' and taqwâ. Nâfi' added the explanation that he was a child then to prevent such misinterpretations."

Itrî Efendi, who lived in the time of Sultân Muhammad Khân the Third 'rahmatullâhi ta'âlâ esrârahum', was not an Islamic scholar. He was a master of music like Beethoven. By composing the Takbîr in the segâh maqâm (tune), he did not perform a service to Islam but rather introduced a bid'at into Islam. To keep up with a tune, the words are distorted and the meaning is spoilt. People are carried away by the effect of naghma on their ears and nafses, and, therefore, the meaning of the Takbîr and its effect on the heart and the soul is lost. The same distortion of words and the consequent spoiling of the meanings happen when the **Qur'ân al-kerîm** and the Mawlîds are recited with naghma. No desirable effect or blessing is left in such recitations. The **Qur'ân al-kerîm** should be recited with a beautiful voice and tajwîd so that it will be more effective and full of blessings.

In the book **Berîqa**, ghinâ, that is, taghannî is explained and discussed in detail as the seventeenth of the afflictions incurred by the tongue (âfât al-lisân), and Shaikh al-Islâm Abu's-Su'ûd Efendi's 'rahmatullâhi ta'âlâ 'alaih' fatwâ is also quoted. In this fatwâ, a distinction is made between the halâl and harâm kinds of taghannîs only. And there is nothing written in the fatwâ about musical instruments. Despite this fact, some people who play the ney and other musical instruments put this fatwâ forward as a support and thus slander Abu's-Su'ûd Efendi.

Ibni 'Âbidîn, in the fourth volume, within the paragraph concerning people whose testimony is not acceptable, declares: "It is unanimously understood that it is harâm to sing to people to entertain or to earn money. It is a grave sin to play music and dance. It is not a sin to sing to oneself to dissipate one's worries. It is permissible to listen to poetry in which there is wa'z (preaching) and hikmat (wisdom). As for musical instruments, only women are allowed to play tambourines at wedding parties." But both sexes must not intermingle. There is detailed information on taghannî and musical instruments in the last chapter of the second part of **al-Mawâhib al-Ladunniyya**. In **al-Hadîqa**, in the section dealing with the afflictions incurred by the ear, it is written: "It is harâm to play or listen to musical instruments with girls dancing in a function where there are fisq and alcohol. These are the kinds of music and musical instruments prohibited in the Hadîth. Although Rasûlullah 'sall-Allâhu 'alaihi wa sallam' plugged his blessed ears with his fingers upon hearing the shepherd's flute, he did not order 'Abdullah ibn 'Umar, who was with him, to do so. This shows that it is not harâm to hear when passing by." In the section on the afflictions of the hand, it is stated: "It is harâm to play musical instruments for entertainment with alcohol, playing, dancing and women. It was ordered in a hadîth to play tambourines at wedding parties. It is true that this order includes men, too. [But Ibni 'Âbidîn's prohibiting statement quoted above is preferrable.] It is permissible to play drums and similar instruments on the way to hajj and in the army." The last sentence shows that it is permissible to have musical bands play at schools or at national and political functions.

In the last chapters of Imâm-i Zahabî's 'rahmatullâhi ta'âlâ 'alaih' **Tibb-un-nabawî** and Ibni 'Âbidîn's 'rahmatullâhi ta'âlâ 'alaih' fatwâ book **Al-'uqûd ad-durriyya**, the harâm and the permitted kinds of taghannî are explained in detail in Arabic. The whole of the former was printed in the margins of the book **Tas'hil al-manâfi'**, and the chapter on taghannî of the latter was appended to the book **Al-habl al-matin fî ittibâ' as-Salaf as-sâlihîn**. These two books have been published by Hakîkat Kitâbevi in Istanbul.

Oh, do not get lured by the world, the end will be ruination one day,
The moments that you now enjoy will surely be a lie one day.

Do not rely on property and post, only the shroud is what you will take away,
And also that will rot in the soil, and you'll become one with the earth one day.

People will be resurrected from their graves, some unveiled and some naked.
Bare-footed and bare-headed, all will wear their skins one day.

Deed-books will fall like snow, men will shiver when they see them.
All people will sweat to their shin, great council will be held one day.

Some of them are wholly stained, never have they helped Islam.
He who follows Islam will smile happily one day.

25 – SECOND VOLUME, FORTY-SIXTH LETTER

Translation of the forty-sixth letter in the second volume of **Maktûbât**, by Imâm Rabbânî Mujaddid-i-alf-i-thânî Ahmad Fârûqî Serhendî 'quddisa sirruh'. The letter, written to Mawlânâ Hamîd-i-Banghâlî, explains the superiorities in the Kalima-t-tawhîd and emphasizes that being a Walî is impossible without Islam:

"**LÂ ILÂHA IL-L-ALLAH MUHAMMADUN RASÛLULLAH.**" This beautiful statement embodies dhils, haqîqa (truth, reality), and Islam. As long as the sâlik (person at the stage of sulûk as he makes progress in a path of tasawwuf) remains at the position of '**nefy**', [which is the stage of LÂ (NO, NOT),] he is at the position of a tâlib (traveller). By the time he is through with **LÂ**, so that he sees none but Allâhu ta'âlâ, he is also through with his travel, having reached his destination, i.e. the position termed '**Fanâ**'. Next after the stage of '**nefy**', he reaches the position of '**ithbât**, [i.e. the rank of '**haqîqa**', or '**Baqâ**',] which is attained when the person making the progress is transferred from the stage termed '**sulûk**' to the stage termed '**jadhba**' by saying "**IL-L-ALLAH**." With this '**nefy**' and '**ithbât**', [i.e. by saying, "**LÂ ILÂHA İLLALLAH.**"] and by way of this travel and haqîqa, and by way of this '**fanâ**' and '**baqâ**' and '**sulûk**' and '**jadhba**', he attains the grade named '**Wilâya**', [i.e. being a '**Walî**']. The nafs (a malignant creature in man's nature) becomes liberated from its dormant maleficence, wherein it is called '**ammâra**', and attains a state of docility termed '**itmi'nân**'; it becomes cleansed and purified. Hence, wilâya is attainable by way of '**nefy**' and '**ithbât**', which make up the initial half of that beautiful statement. The second half of the statement is the confirmation of the fact that the final Prophet 'alaihi wa 'alaihim-us-salawât' is the Messenger of Allah. This second half makes up Islam and brings it to perfection. Islam at the beginning of seyr (travel) and midway through it is the outward appearance of Islam. It is no more than name and shape. Real Islam, its essence, that is, is obtained after the attainment of wilâya. At this time, those who perfectly follow in the footsteps of Prophets 'alaihim-us-salawât' attain the '**kamâlât-i-nubuwwa**' allotted for them. The travel (seyr) and the haqîqa, which are the two component parts of wilâya, are, as it were, two conditions to be fulfilled for the attainment of Islam's inner essence (Haqîqat of Islam) and the Kamâlât-i-nubuwwa. Wilâyat is, so to speak, the ablution for namâz, Islam being the namâz itself. In the beginning (ibtidâ), real [visible, material] dirts (najâsat) are, sort of, cleansed away; once haqîqa is obtained, hukmî [immaterial, invisible] dirts are gotten rid of. Only after the attainment of this perfect cleanliness is a person capable of performing the ahkâm-i-islâmiyya (commandments and prohibitions of Islam) in the full sense, and only at this level of spiritual perfection can a person adequately perform the namâz which is the acme of the avenues leading towards Allâhu ta'âlâ. The namâz is the pillar of Islam and the Mi'râj of a Believer. And therein lies the way of cultivating oneself so as to perform that namâz.

I see this second half of that beautiful statement as an endless ocean. In comparison to this half, the initial half looks like a drop of water. Yes; the kamâlât (perfections) of wilâyat are a mere nothing when compared with the kamâlât of Prophethood. [What can an atom's weight be in terms of the weight of the Sun?] Subhân-Allah! Some people must be squint-eyed to see things awry, as they do, in that they think more of wilâyat than they do of Prophethood and look on Islam, which is the essence of all essentials, as a mere outer cover. How could they see any better with that extrinsic stance of theirs, since what such onlookers would view in the name of Islam would normally be the outer cover of Islam! What is reflected on their shallow vision is the outer cover of something which itself is the essence of what they see. Prophets' busying themselves with creatures must have led them into thinking less of them. They must have mistaken those prophetic occupations for the social interactions among people.

Their thinking better of wilâyat must be an optical illusion aggrandized by the fact that wilâyat involves progress towards Allâhu ta'âlâ. So, their saying that wilâyat is superior to nubuwwa (prophethood) is simply an expression of their short-sighted syllogism. They do not know something: as there is progress towards Allâhu ta'âlâ in wilâyat, likewise the improvements accomplished in the kamâlât-i-nubuwwa have their specific progress towards Allâhu ta'âlâ. In fact, the progress in wilâyat is only a vision, an appearance of the progress in nubuwwa. During the nuzûl, [i.e. in the course of descent,] there are phases of occupation with the khalq [creatures] both in wilâyat and in nubuwwat. Yet the both types of occupation are unlike each other. In wilâyat the 'Bâtin [the heart, the soul, and the other latîfas]' are with Allâhu ta'âlâ as the 'Zâhir [the body and the sense organs]' are with creatures, whereas in prophethood both the zâhir and the bâtin are busy with creatures during the descent. A Prophet calls the born slaves to Allâhu ta'âlâ with all his existence. This kind of nuzûl (descent) is more thoroughgoing and more perfect than the descent in wilâyat.

Those great people's turning their attention (tawajjuh) to the creation, i.e. their communications with people, is dissimilar to transactions among common people. As common people transact among themselves, they are fond of and attached to one another, which involves a fondness of and attachment to beings other than Allâhu ta'âlâ. Those superior people, however, are not attached to common people as they communicate with them. For, those superiors have freed themselves from all sorts of attachments other than that to Allâhu ta'âlâ, having attached themselves to the Khâliq (Creator) of the khalq (creation, creatures). Their communication with the khalq is intended to attract them to Haqq (Allâhu ta'âlâ), and to bring them round to the path Allâhu ta'âlâ likes and approves of. To communicate with people for the purpose of delivering them from the shameful state of being others' slaves, is certainly preferable to and more valuable than communication carried on for the purpose of keeping oneself attached to Haqq (Allâhu ta'âlâ). Imagine a person murmuring the Name of Allâhu ta'âlâ and a blind man passing by him in the direction of a well quite close by. So urgent is the situation that one more step and the blind man will end up down in the well.

Now, which choice will be more valuable for this person to make; to carry on with his murmuring the Name of Allâhu ta'âlâ, or to stop doing so and save the blind man from falling into the well? Doubtless, saving the blind man is better than the dhikr-i-ilâhî. For, Allâhu ta'âlâ does not need him or his making dhikr. The blind man, on the other hand, is a needy born slave. He has to be saved from the danger. In fact, since it is Islam's commandment to save him, saving him is more important than the dhikr-i-ilâhî. By doing so, he will have obeyed the commandment. Only the right of Allâhu ta'âlâ is involved in making dhikr, whereas two different rights will have been paid by obeying His command and saving the blind man: one of them is the right of a creature, and the other one is the right of the Creator. As a matter of fact, it would be a sinful act to continue dhikring at such an urgency. For, dhikring may not always be good. There are times when it is better not to dhikr. There are certain days and situations during which it is forbidden to perform namâz or to fast; it is better on those days or in those situations to omit the so-called acts of worships than performing them.

[Enemies of religion suppose that Muslims are egoistic, selfish people. They vilify Muslims by saying that they are concerned only about what they should do to attain to the blessings of Paradise without ever thinking of doing favours to others. The facts written above clearly show that those assertions on the part of the enemies of Islam are lies and slanders.]

'Dhikring' means 'liberating oneself from (the state of) ghafla'. ['Ghafla' means 'to forget about Allâhu ta'âlâ'.] Dhikring does not mean only saying the 'Kalima-i-tawhîd' or continuously repeating the Name of 'Allah'. It is 'dhikr' to somehow deliver yourself from the state of ghafla. Then, acts of worship such as performance of Islam's commandments and avoiding its prohibitions, are all dhikr. So is a business transaction such as buying and selling carried out in observance of Islam's dictations. And so is a nikâh (marriage contract performed compatibly with Islam) and a talâq (divorce, dissolution of marriage) performed in a way prescribed by Islam. For, these acts are done in a state of consciousness of the source of the commandments and prohibitions; in other words, the state of ghafla is gone. It is also a fact, however, that a dhikr performed in the accompaniment of a repeated (silent) utterance of the Names and Attributes of Allâhu ta'âlâ is fast to take effect, so that love of Him will be attained in a short time. Not so is the case with the dhikr that is realized by way of strict obedience to the commandments and prohibitions. There have been occasions, however, when dhikrs of this nature were seen to produce rapid results, quite rare as they are. Muhammad Behâ-ad-dîn Bukhârî,

(718 [1318 A.D.] – 791 [1389], Qasr-i-'ârifân, Bukhârâ,) stated: "Mawlânâ Zeyn-ud-dîn Taybâdî, (d. 791 [1388 A.D.],) – So strictly obedient to Islam was this profound scholar that owing to his close adherence to the Sunnat he attained high grades in bâtinî (spiritual) knowledge – 'qaddas-Allâhu ta'âlâ sirrah-ul-'azîz' attained to Allâhu ta'âlâ as a fruit of his adherence." Furthermore, the dhikr performed by way of the Names and Attributes (of Allâhu ta'âlâ) causes the dhikr by way of adapting oneself to Islam. For, unless one perfectly loves the Owner of Islam it will be very difficult for one to observe Islam in everything one does. And obtaining perfect love, in turn, requires the dhikr performed by way of the Names and Attributes. Then, in order to attain the dhikr by way of adapting oneself to Islam, one should first perform the dhikr by way of the Names and Attributes. It is also true, however, that a special lûtf (favour, grace) and ihsân (kindness, blessing) on the part of Jenâb-i-Haqq (Allâhu ta'âlâ) comes gratis. Without any apparent reason, He may bestow anything He likes on anyone He choses. As a matter of fact, He declares, as is purported in the thirteenth âyat-i-kerîma of Shûrâ sûra: "**... Allâhu ta'âlâ chooses to Himself those whom He pleases**," (42:13)

[Mazhar-Jân-i-Jânân, (1111 [1699 A.D.], India – 1195 [1781], martyred,) 'qadda-Allâhu sirrah-ul-'azîz' states as follows in the eleventh letter of his valuable book '**Maqâmât-i-Mazhariyya**': "There are three kinds of dhikr:

"1– Dhikring only with the lips, without the heart partaking in the event. It is useless.

"2– Dhikring only with the heart, without the tongue taking part. How to dhikr is described in, the hundred and fortieth letter in the second volume of '**Maktûbât-i-Ma'thûmiyya**'. [Please see the fortieth chapter, the final four paragraphs of the forty-sixth chapter in the first fascicle, of '**Endless Bliss**', and the nineteenth chapter in the third fascicle. This dhikr is called '**dhikr-i-khafî**'. It is the dhikr of the Dhât-i-Ilâhî (The Person of Allâhu ta'âlâ). Or, it might as well be done by thinking of His Attributes. When one thinks of His blessings as well, one's dhikring becomes '**Tafakkur**' (Meditation).

"3– Dhikring both with the heart and with the tongue. If this dhikr is said loud enough only for the person who says it to hear, it is called a 'dhikr-i-khafî'. It is this dhikr-i-khafî that is commanded in the âyat-i-kerîma. If it is louder, so that it can be heard by others as well, it is termed a 'dhikr-i-jehrî'. Âyat-i-kerîmas and hadîth-i-sherîfs show that the dhikr-i-khafî is more meritorious than the dhikr-i-jehrî. The dhikr-i-jehrî that Rasûlullah 'sall-Allâhu 'alaihi wa sallam' taught Hadrat 'Alî was no louder than enough to be heard by himself; it was a dhikr-i-khafî in its true sense. His having the door shut shows that this was the case." The author of the book '**Tafsîr-i-'Azîzî**' (Abd-ul-'Azîz Dahlawî, 1159 [1745 A.D.], Delhi – 1239 [1824], Delhi,) 'rahmatullâhi ta'âlâ 'alaih' states as follows in his explanation of the Dahr (Time) sûra, (the seventy-sixth sûra, which is also named the Insân [Man] sûra): "Dhikring is intended to expel all sorts of love and fondness except love of Allah from the heart. It is an experiential reality that dhikring is the most potent medication for the elimination of the heart's attachment to creatures. A hadîth-i-sherîf reads as follows: "**By dhikring join the way of those who deliver their hearts from their burden**!" To this end they (Islamic superiors) said: 'In order to attain to Allâhu ta'âlâ and to His love and grace, we should cut the lines attaching our hearts to creatures and eliminate their keenness on worldly pleasures. No other medication is more useful than dhikring in the liberation of the heart.' " [Two kinds of simâ' and raqs are widely known among men of Tasawwuf. The first kind happens during the manifestation of the Attributes of Jemâl and Jelâl, which follows the Fanâ of the heart and the nafs. Mind and nafs do not perform a function in this kind. Examples of this kind are the dhikr, simâ', and raqs supervised by superiors such as Celaleddin (Jelâl-ad-dîn) Rûmî, (604 [1207 A.D.], Belkh – 672 [1273], Konya,) and Sünbül (Sunbul) Sinan Efendi, (d. 936 [1529 A.D.], İstanbul.) Shâh-i-Naqshiband Bahâ-ad-dîn Bukhârî 'rahmatullâhi 'alaih', stated as follows (when he talked about this first kind): "We do not reject it." And about the second kind, which consisted in fits of frenzy, as some ignorant and unconscious dervishes yelled and jumped, and which were no more than acrid illustrations of the shortage of mental range they have been suffering from and their helplessness in the talons of an unbridled nafs, he stated as follows: "We would not do as they do."]

(Some hundred and forty pages, pages from 1059 through 1198, of the Turkish book entitled Se'âdet-i Ebediyye and written by the Islamic scholar and beloved Waliyyullah Hüseyn Hilmi bin Sa'îd Işık 'rahmatullâhi ta'âlâ 'alaih', has been allotted to biographies. The following sample is an abridged and summarized information from the hundred and ninety-fourth article, which is a short biography of Mawlânâ (Mevlânâ) Jelâl-ad-deen Rûmî:

[It is stated as follows in the hundred and seventh page of 'Mekâtib-i-sherîfa: "Mawlânâ Jelâl-ad-dîn Rûmî was among the greater ones of the Awliyâ of the Ahl as-Sunna Muslims." He was in the Qâdirî Tarîqa. His father, Sultân ul-'Ulamâ Muhammad Bahâ-ad-dîn Veled, was a great scholar and Walî. Hadrat Rûmî was only a child when he attained the fayz in his father's heart. He did not play musical instruments such as reeds or drums, nor was he ever seen to whirl. Such absurdities were invented later in the name of Tarîqa by ignorant people.])

An âyat-i-kerîma in Ra'd Sûra purports: "**... It should be known without doubt that in the dhikr of Allâhu ta'âlâ do hearts find satisfaction.**" (13:28). Itmi'nân means satisfaction, calmness, ease? When the word 'dhikr' with a harf-i-jer (preposition) is said before the verb, it expresses hasr (restriction to one purpose). So, it was stated (by scholars) that "in only the dhikr (of Allâhu ta'âlâ) do hearts find satisfaction." Dhikr means remembrance. Remembrance of Allâhu ta'âlâ is possible by saying His Name or by seeing a Walî, a born slave of His whom He loves very much. As a matter of fact, a hadîth-i-sherîf reads as follows: "**When they are seen Allâhu ta'âlâ is remembered**." Other thoughts may occupy your mind as you hear or say His Name, and remembrance of Him becomes dubious. Remembering Him continuously requires saying His Name thousands of times daily. As the good news (in the hadîth-i-sherîf quoted above) asseverates, when you see a Walî and love him, you will definitely remember Allâhu ta'âlâ. As the event of seeing is realized with the nûr (light) of eyes, when you bring the outward appearance and the face of a Walî into your imagination and heart, it will be in effect as if you actually saw that Walî, which in turn will cause your remembering Allâhu ta'âlâ. This kind of seeing a Walî through heart is called '**râbita**'; it is a means to have recourse to, to deliver the heart from loving or thinking of beings other than Allâhu ta'âlâ; it is a way that leads to the attainment of a heart blessed with the ikhlâs imparted in the âyat-i-kerîma and the hadîth-i-sherîf quoted above. Yes, to adhere to Islam, i.e. to perform the commandments and to avoid the prohibitions, will provide one with the grace and love of Allâhu ta'âlâ; but it is a condition that this obedience should be accompained by ikhlâs. Then, we should both adapt ourselves to Islam and obtain ikhlâs.]

Let us return to the point we have been discussing! There is one more thing that is beyond the three entities we have so far been dealing with, i.e. Tarîqa, Haqîqa, and Islam, and when compared with the value of which that of those three entities is a mere nothing. The spiritual state experienced when the sâlik says, "... ill-Allah," at the position of haqîqa, is the appearance, [the vision,] of it, (i.e. haqîqa,) and yet it is the haqîqa, the origin of the other visions experienced enroute to that rank. By the same token, every Muslim possesses Islam's vision in the beginning. After the attainment of Tarîqa and Haqîqa, the Haqîqa of that vision is attained. This subject should be given sobering thought: a sort of haqîqa (reality, truth, essence, origin) whose vision [appearance] is haqîqa and whose beginning is wilâya. How could that haqîqa ever be defined through words? Even if it were possible to define it, who could ever understand it, and what little of it could they understand? This haqîqa is so superb a rarity that very few, nay, very very few of the inheritors of those Prophets called Ulûl''azm, [the six highest ones of Prophets with dispensations,] have been gifted with it. Since there are few Prophets singled out with the attribute Ulûl'azm, then a fortiori there are even fewer people to inherit from them.

QUESTION: The explanations made above lead to the conclusion that an 'ârif who has attained that haqîqa has gone out of Islam. For, he has attained a rank above Islam.

ANSWER: The ahkâm-i-islâmiyya (Islam's commandments and prohibitions) consist of acts of worship to be performed by the zâhir, [i.e. by the discernible limbs]. On the other hand, the haqîqa falls to the lot of the bâtin, [i.e. heart and soul.] The zâhir has been enjoined to always obey the ahkâm-i-islâmiyya (by doing the commandments and avoiding the prohibitions). In the meantime the bâtin is busy with the deeds of that haqîqa. 'Amals, acts of worship are necessary in this world. These acts of worship are very helpful to the bâtin. In other words, the bâtin's improvement and progress are dependent on the zâhir's obedience to the ahkâm-i-islâmiyya. Then, in this world both the zâhir and the bâtin need the ahkâm-i-islâmiyya. The zâhir's business is to adapt itself to Islam, and the bâtin's business is to collect the fruits, the benefits of Islam. Islam is the source of all sorts of perfection, the basis of all ennoblements. Islam's fruitfulness, beneficence, is not confined to this world. The perfections and blessings awaiting in the Hereafter are all products and fruits of Islam. As is seen, Islam is such a 'Shajara-i-tayyiba' [blessed tree] that all creation benefits from its fruits both in this world and in the Hereafter.

QUESTION: That means to say that in the kamâlât-i-nubuwwa (perfections of prophethood) also, the bâtin is with Haqq (Allâhu ta'âlâ) and the zâhir is with the khalk (creation, creatures). In other letters (written by Hadrat Imâm Rabbânî), however, it is stated that both the zâhir and the bâtin are with the khalk, whereby to invite people (to Islam). How can these two statements be reconciled?

ANSWER: What we call the kamâlât-i-nubuwwa are a series of kamâlât (perfections) attained during the stages of urûj (ascent, promotion, improvement). The rank of prophethood, in contrast, involves a process of nuzûl (descent). During the ascent the bâtin is with Haqq (Allâhu ta'âlâ). The zâhir, in the meantime, is with the khalq, paying the rights of the khalq in a way compatible with Islam. During the nuzûl both the zâhir and the bâtin are with the khalq, and thereby the Prophet employs both his zâhir and his bâtin in his mission to call the creatures to Allâhu ta'âlâ.

Then, inconsistency between the two statements is not the case. To be with the khalk, (in this sense,) means to be with Haqq. The hundred and fifteenth âyat-i-kerîma of Baqara sûra purports: "**... Withersoever ye turn, there is the presence of Allâhu ta'âlâ**, (and there will ye find Him,)..." However, this should not be construed as, "creatures will be Allah," or as, "creatures are mirrors that reflect Allâhu ta'âlâ." How could it ever be possible for the mumkin, (i.e. for something whose existence is dependent) to be the Wâjib (Allâhu ta'âlâ, whose existence is independent and indispensable)? How could a creature ever be the Creator? How can it be a mirror to reflect Him? (On the contrary,) it might make sense to say that the Wâjib is a mirror to reflect the (vision of the) mumkin. Yes. During the nuzûl [descent back], the existence can be a mirror for the visions of the Divine Attributes. For, attributes such as hearing, sight, and power that are seen on creatures are the visions of the attributes of hearing, seeing and power, which are themselves mirrors reflecting the creatures. They are the attributes of the mirror that manifest themselves on visible creatures. And the visions seen on the mirror are themselves the mirrors of the attributes and works of the mirror. For instance, if the mirror is long the visions also will look long, and they will be mirrors showing the length of the mirror. If the mirror is small each of the visions will be, so to speak, a mirror showing the smallness of the mirror.

During the urûj, or the ascent, it is felt as if things were being seen in the mirror of Allâhu ta'âlâ. It is like visions seen in the mirror giving the impression as if they were the things themselves in there. In actual fact, however, the visions of things do not exist in the mirror. Likewise, the creatures are not in the mirror of Allâhu ta'âlâ. Nothing exists in the mirror. Visions are not in the mirror;

they are in our imagination. There are no visions in the mirror. Nor can there be a mirror in the place where visions exist. Visions are in our fancy and imagination. If they have a place, it is on the level of fancy; if they have time, it is on the level of imagination. However, because this incorporeal vision of the creatures exists with the power of Allâhu ta'âlâ, it is permanent. It is these visions that will taste the eternal torments or blessings of the Hereafter.

In the world's mirrors, visions are first to come into sight. Seeing the mirror itself requires a specially focused attention. In the mirror of Allâhu ta'âlâ, however, what is seen first is the mirror itself. Seeing the creatures requires special concentration. When the Walî starts to make rujû' (withdrawal, retreat), the creatures' visions in the mirrors of Divine Attributes start to manifest themselves. When rujû' and nuzûl (descent) comes to an end and the state of 'seyr der eshyâ', i.e. progress in things, assumes its motion, the shuhûd-i-ilâhî is gone, so that it gets into a state of ghayb; the îmân-i-shuhûdî changes into îmân-i-ghaybî. When the Walî passes away after the completion of his invitatory mission, the state of shuhûd returns. Yet this state of shuhûd is more close-grained and more immaculate than the shuhûd experienced before the state of rujû'; it is a perfect state of shuhûd. The shuhûd in the Hereafter is more impressive than the shuhûd in the world.

In conclusion, visions seen in a mirror are not in the mirror. Their existence is only a fancy, which can be said to have been enveloped, covered by the mirror, so that we say that the mirror is with them. However, this state of qurb (affinity, closeness), encompassion and togetherness is unlike the state of affinity, encompassion, and togetherness between objects or between an object and its properties, [such as its colour, etc.] Human brain cannot reason on or comprehend the nature of affinity, encompassion and togetherness between visions and a mirror (wherein they are seen). It is for certain that the visions are close to the mirror, that they are with it, that they are enveloped by it. But its nature cannot be defined or described. So is the case with the nature of closeness, encompassion and togetherness between Allâhu ta'âlâ and the creatures. We believe that these states do exist. But we cannot know what sorts of things these states are. For, these Attributes of Allâhu ta'âlâ are quite dissimilar to the attributes of creatures; there is, in actual fact, no resemblance between them and the properties of objects. This universe is a mere visionary sample of reality; so our mention of visions and the mirror in an attempt to exemplify the relations between attributes has been intended for people of wisdom to realize this fact from that example. A stanza:

> *"Make namâz for the sake of Allah five times a day,*
> *Waste no time, winter or summer, be it as it may!*
>
> *If you wish to be close to Haqq,*
> *Perform the sunnat and fard, for it's the only way!*

26 – SECOND VOLUME, THIRTY-SEVENTH LETTER

The thirty-seventh letter in the second volume of the valuable book entitled **Maktûbât**, by the great Walî and profound scholar Imâm Rabbânî 'quddisa sirruh', was written for faqîr and haqîr 'Abd-ul-Hayy 'rahmatullâhi ta'âlâ 'alaih', and tells about the superior merits and virtues inherent in the Kalima-i-tawhîd, LÂ ILÂHA IL-L-ALLAH. Hadrat Abd-ul-Hayy of Safâ, India, (was one of those fortunate people who attended, and served in the blessed sohbat of Hadrat Imâm Rabbânî for years, and thereby attained plenty of fayz. Being commanded by Hadrat Muhammad Ma'thûm 'quddisa sirruh', the third son of Imâm Rabbânî and also his immediate successor in the Mujaddidî order, he compiled the letters making up the second volume of **Maktûbât**. He was sent to the city of Putna to teach Tasawwuf to the lovers living there, and guided them to perfection. He educated and trained many a Walî and Khalîfa. He was honoured with the glad tidings that he was one of the Qutbs.) The following essay is an attempt we have so brazenly made to translate that great letter into English:

Nothing in the world could be more effective than the beautiful utterance "LÂ ILÂHA IL-L-ALLAH" to extinguish the Wrath, the Vengeance of our Rabb, (Allâhu ta'âlâ,) 'jalla sultânuh'. Inasmuch as this pulchritudinous utterance is capable of assuaging the Wrath that is operative enough to drag one to Hell, then *a fortiori* it must bring down His Wrath incurred on account of matters of lesser importance. Why should it not, in the face of the fact that when a born slave repeats this lovely word time and again he shakes off all the occupants other than Him in his cognitive repertory, turns away from all, and directs all his existence to one rightful ma'bûd? The reason for His Wrath is His slaves' turning towards beings other than Him and attaching themselves to those other beings. We observe examples of this state in this world of tokens. Imagine a wealthy person angered by his servant. The servant, a good-hearted one, turns away from others and commits himself thoroughly to the commandments of his overlord. Willy-nilly, his master will soften down, his tender mercies bestirred and his anger appeased. Likewise, this lovable phrase is the key to the ninety-nine treasuries of Rahma (Compassion) reserved for the Hereafter. For the cleansing of the darknesses of kufr (unbelief) and dirts of shirk (polytheism), no aid could be more adequately antidotal than this graceful utterance. Once a person attains belief in this phrase, the earliest mote of îmân blossoms.

If a person, after developing a mote of îmân in his heart on account of his belief in this beautiful word, still imitates disbelievers in their customary and dirty polytheistic rites, he will be taken out of Hell due to the shafâ'a (intercession) of this lovely word; he will be saved from the eternal torment. Likewise, the mightiest saviour bestowed upon this Umma (Muslims) is Muhammad Rasûlullah 'sall-Allâhu 'alaihi wa sallam', who will save them from torment by interceding for their grave sins. We say, "grave sins," because there were very few people to commit grave sins among the previous ummats. And ever fewer were the people who dirtied their îmân with customs of disbelief and polytheism. It is this Umma who are most desperately in need of shafâ'a (intercession). As for the previous ummats; people that one would expect to encounter were either some obdurate heathens or a congregation of true, adherent and devoted believers.

Had it not been for this beautiful word and a treasure of shafâ'at like the Pinnacle of Prophethood 'alaihi wa 'alaihim-us-salawât-u-wa-t-tehiyyat', this Umma would have perished in their own wrongdoings. This Umma are so sinful. Yet, boundless also is the forgiveness, the 'afw and maghfira, of Allâhu ta'âlâ. So profusely will Allâhu ta'âlâ shower His 'afw and maghfira on this Ummat that He is not known to have shown so great magnanimity over any of the previous ummats. It is as if He reserved ninety-nine percent of His Compassion for this Ummat of offenders. Kindness and grace, one feels egged on to say, favour sinners and offenders. Allâhu ta'âlâ loves blessing His slaves with 'afw and maghfira. Nothing will be treated with such abundance of 'afw and maghfira as will be this Ummat, so sinful and guilty as they are. And this is the very reason for which this Ummat has been gifted with the championship of meritoriousness, ahead of all other ummats; this exquisite word, which is their intercessor, has been the most valuable of all words ever said; and likewise their Prophet, their intermediator, has been the highest of Prophets 'alaihi wa 'alaihim-us-salawât-u-wa-t-tehiyyât'. The seventieth âyat-i-kerîma of Furqân sûra purports: "**They are the persons whose evil Allâhu** ta'âlâ will change into good. Allâhu ta'âlâ is oft forgiving, most merciful.**" (25:70)

That is something quite simple for Allâhu ta'âlâ to do. O our Rabb (Allâhu ta'âlâ)! Forgive us our sins, extravagance and excess in our doings. Keep us in the right path! Help us to overcome the faithless! Now, hearken to the merits of this lovely word:

Rasûlullah 'sall-Allâhu ta'âlâ 'alaihi wa âlihi wa sallama wa bâreka' stated: "**A person** who says '**Lâ ilâha il-l-Allâh', will enter Paradise**." Short-sighted people will be astonished at this statement. "How could it ever be possible to enter Paradise by saying, 'lâ ilâha il-l-Allah,' once," they will say. They do not know the barakats, the benefits of this comely word. To the understanding of this faqîr [Imâm Rabânî 'rahmatullâhi 'alaih' means himself], it would be fair if they were to forgive all unbelievers and send then all to Paradise in return for saying that beautiful word only once. I see it that if they were to divide the barakats and benefits of that sacred utterance by the number of all the creatures till the end of the world it would satiate them all. Over and above that, when that sacred and beautiful word is complemented with the addition of "**Muhammad-un-Rasûlullah**', and thereby tabligh and tawhîd are arranged side by side like cultured pearls, whereby Risâlat (Prophethood) and Wilâyat will have been brought nearer to each other, all the superior and high qualities of Wilâyat and Nubuwwa will come together. It is these utterances that make one attain the gateway leading to the two resources of happiness. It is this statement that delivers Wilâya from the glooms of shades and reflections, clarifies it, and raises Nubuwwa to heights of culmination. O our Allah! Do not deprive us from the benefits of this beautiful word! Take our souls out at a time when we are in a state of affirmation of this beautiful word! On the Rising Day, make us among those who affirm this beautiful word! For the sake of this word and for the sake of those who taught us this word 'alaihim-us-salawât wa-t-taslîmât wa-t-tehiyyât, wa-l-barakât', place us into Janna (Paradise)! Âmîn.

When sight and advance are incapacitated, when the wings of himma fall, and once you have gone beyond the boundaries of all sorts of knowledge and exploration, nothing other than the Kalima-t-at-tawhîd, '**Lâ ilâha il-l-Allah Muhammadun Rasûlullah**," will help you make further progress. Unless you find sanctuary in the bosom of this word you will make no progress beyond those heights. One single utterance of that beautiful word makes the 'sâlik' soar and reach those heights. Owing to the haqîqa signified by that highly honourable word he makes an ascent above those heights. He gets further away from himself and draws nearer to Allâhu ta'âlâ. A tiny part of that uplifting path is times and again greater than all the celestial spheres around us. This comparison should suffice to give an idea about the superiority of that word. Existence of all creatures would look a mere nothing, were it possible to place them beside that word. They would be quite imperceptible. They would not even be a drop of water compared with an immense ocean. The superior grades of this beautiful word will manifest themselves depending on the levels of those who utter it. The higher the level of the person who utters it, the higher will the grandeur be wherein that divine word will manifest itself. An Arabic couplet rendered into English reads as follows:

*"The beauty will show itself the more,
As the look comes from deeper in the core."*

No other worldly appetite could be more valuable than or superior to the pleasure and the delicious taste one relishes from uttering this splendid word time and time again, [throughout one's occupations and duties.] Yet there is no help for it, and one cannot get all one's wishes. Talking to others is ineluctable, even at the cost of ghafla.

27 – SECOND VOLUME, THIRTY-NINTH LETTER

This is an attempt to translate into English the thirty-ninth letter in the second volume of the great book **Maktûbât**, by Hadrat Imâm Rabbânî 'quddisa sirruh'. Written for Sayyid 'Abd-ul-Bâqî Sârenkpûrî, the blessed letter explains terms such as 'Ashâb-i-yemîn', 'Ashâb-i-shimâl', and 'Sâbiqûn'.

Hamd (praise and gratitude) be to Allâhu ta'âlâ. Salâm (salutations) be to His chosen slaves. May Allâhu ta'âlâ bless you with making progress in the right path!

People who remain behind zulmânî, dark, gloomy curtains are called '**Ashâb-i-shimâl**'. Those who have passed over those curtains and are therefore behind curtains of nûr (lights, radiations of light), are called 'Ashâb-i-yemîn'. And those who have passed over curtains of nûr, too, are the 'Sâbiqûn'. They have passed over curtains of creatures and curtains of wujûb, and attained to the 'asl (essence of existence). They reject names, attributes, shu'ûns and i'tibârs, [i.e. things considered,] and anything whatsoever other than the Dhât-i-ilâhî (The Person of

Allâhu ta'âlâ). The Ashâb-i-shimâl are disbelievers and shaqîs. The Ashâb-i-yemîn are Muslims and the Awliyâ. And the Sâbiqûn are Prophets 'alahim-us-salawât-u-wa-t-taslîmât'. A few of those who follow in the footsteps of these superior people have been honoured with this grand fortune. The greater ones of the Sahâba hold a majority among those honoured spiritual elites of ummats. And among the non-Sahâba, fewer personages have been honoured with this highest spiritual state. These people are accounted to be among the Sahâba and have attained the kamâlât (perfections) of Prophethood. It might have been in this connection that our Prophet ''alaihi wa 'alâ âlihissalawâtu wa-t-taslîmât' stated: "**Are the earlier ones or the later ones more beneficent? It is not known for certain.**" It is true, on the other hand, that he stated as follows in another hadîth-i-sherîf: "**The most beneficent of all times is the time wherein I live.**" However, whereas ages and times are meant in this latter hadîth-i-sherîf, the former one concerns people. Scholars of Ahl as-Sunna unanimously state that "With the exception of Prophets ''alaihim-us-salawât-u-wa-t-taslîmât', no one is superior to Abû Bakr and 'Umar, and no one is superior to Abû Bakr. He is the highest of the highest ones of this Umma (Muslims)." 'Umar 'radiy-Allâhu 'anh' became superior because he followed in the footsteps of Abû Bakr as-Siddîq; he surpassed others because he adapted himself to the Siddîq. He was therefore called '**Khalîfa-i-Siddîq**', and his name was mentioned as 'Khalîfa-i-Khalîfa-i-Rasûlullah (Successor of the Successor of the Messenger of Allah)," during Khutbas. Hadrat Abû Bakr as-Siddîq is the cavalryman in the lead. Hadrat 'Umar-ul-Fârûq 'radiy-Allâhu 'anhumâ' is his groom, or reservist, so to speak. And such a wonderful groom, too, who has perfectly adapted himself to the cavalryman, so that he has become the cavalryman's partner in his superiorities.

Let us come back to the subject we have been discussing! The Sâbiqûn are dissimilar to the Ashâb-i-yemîn or to the Ashâb-i-shimâl. They are beyond zulmânî and nûrânî matters. Their books, [i.e. deed-books,] are unlike the books of the other two. And their accounts, on the Rising Day, will be unlike the accounts of the others. They will be served a special treatment. They will be shown exceptional courtesy and kindness. For, the Ashâb-i-yemîn, as well as the Ashâb-i-shimâl, are quite far away from the kamâlât that these elite people have been honoured with. The Awliyâ 'qaddas-Allâhu ta'âlâ asrârahum-ul-'azîz', as well as other Believers, are incapable of comprehending their hidden superiorities. The symbols written in different letters in the Qur'ân al-kerîm signify the hidden superiorities allotted for them. The symbolical âyat-i-kerîmas in the Qur'ân al-kerîm are the treasures signifying the high grades they have obtained. Attaining to the 'asl, they have rid themselves of shades and visions. Those who have attained to the dhils are quite unaware of the rank allotted for these superiors. These persons are the (ones called) muqarrabs, the ones who are close to the 'Asl. Comfort and compassion are for these people. It is these people who are safe against the fear of the Rising Day. Unlike others, they will not be frightened by the horror of the Rising Day.

O our Allah, Most Great! Make us lovers of them! For, on that day every person will be with the person they love. As an alms for the Master of all Prophets, do accept this du'â of ours "alaihi wa 'alâ âlihi wa 'alaihim wa 'alâ âli kullin as-salât-u-wa-t-teslîmât-u-wa-t-tehiyyât-u-wa-l-barakât'. Âmîn.

HÜSEYN HİLMİ IŞIK,
'Rahmat-Allahi 'alaih'

Hüseyn Hilmi Işık, 'Rahmat-Allahi 'alaih', publisher of the Hakikat Kitabevi Publications, was born in Eyyub Sultan, Istanbul in 1329 (A.D. 1911).

Of the one hundred and forty-four books he published, sixty are Arabic, twenty-five Persian, fourteen Turkish, and the remaining are books in French, German, English, Russian, and other languages.

Hüseyn Hilmi Işık, 'Rahmat-Allahi 'alaih' (guided by Sayyid 'Abdulhakim Arwâsî, 'Rahmat-Allahi 'alaih', a profound Islamic scholar and perfect in virtues of Tasawwuf and capable to guide disciples in a fully mature manner; possessor of glories and wisdom), was a competent, great Islamic scholar able to guide to happiness, passed away during the night between October 25, 2001 (8 Sha'bân 1422) and October 26, 2001 (9 Sha'bân 1422). He was buried at Eyyub Sultan, where he had been born.

Appendix I

FINDING
THE FIRST DAY OF AN ARABIC MONTH

There are various methods for finding what the first day of an Arabic (lunar) month is. The most valid of them is the one written by Uluğ Bey. According to his method, initially the first day of Muharram, the first month of the Hijrî year, is found. To find the first day of Muharram, the year in question is always divided by 210. The last digit of the remainder of this division is subtracted from the remainder and this second remainder is looked up in the first column of the first table [below left.]. In the other columns of the same table, the number corresponding to the first digit of the remainder written in the first line of the table is obtained to be the number corresponding to the day of the week beginning from Sunday. And it is the first day of Muharram. Let's find the first day of Muharram of the Hijrî year 1316, for example:

$$\frac{1316}{210} = 6\frac{56}{210}$$

The first digit, 6, is subtracted from 56, the remainder, and thus 50 is obtained. Across from the number 50 in the first column, 1 is written in the column headed by 6, the first digit. Thus, the first day of the year is found to be Sunday. After finding the first day of the year, the first day of a mounth is found by the use of the second table. In the line containing Muharram, the number corresponding to the first day of the year is found. The number below this and across from the month in question is the day, as numbered from Sunday, of the month in question. Let's find, for example, the first day of Ramadân in 1316: the first day of this year is Sunday, i.e. the first day of the week, and, in the column headed by 1 in the first line of the second table, 6 is written across from Ramadân. Thus, the first day of Ramadân is the sixth day of the week, i.e. Friday.

Appendix II
ULUĞ BEY'S TABLES FOR LUNAR (QAMARÎ) MONTHS

TABLE I
First digit of the remainder

	0	1	2	3	4	5	6	7	8	9
0		2	6	3	1	5	2	7	4	2	6
10	3	1	5	2	7	4	2	6	3	1
20	4	2	7	4	1	6	3	1	5	2
30	7	4	1	6	3	7	5	2	7	4
40	1	6	3	7	5	2	7	4	1	6
50	3	7	5	2	6	4	1	6	3	7
60	5	2	6	4	1	5	3	7	5	2
70	6	4	1	5	3	7	5	2	6	4
80	1	5	3	7	4	2	6	4	1	5
90	3	7	4	2	6	3	1	5	3	7
100	4	2	6	3	1	5	3	7	4	2
110	6	3	1	5	2	7	4	2	6	3
120	1	5	2	7	4	1	6	3	1	5
130	2	7	4	1	6	3	1	5	2	7
140	4	1	6	3	7	5	2	7	4	1
150	6	3	7	5	2	6	4	1	6	3
160	7	5	2	6	4	1	6	3	7	5
170	2	6	4	1	5	3	7	5	2	6
180	4	1	5	3	7	4	2	6	4	1
190	5	3	7	4	2	6	4	1	5	3
200	7	4	2	6	3	1	5	3	7	4

(The remainder minus its last digit)

TABLE II

MONTHS	DAYS
Muharram	5 6 7 1 2 3 4
Safar	7 1 2 3 4 5 6
Rabi'al-awwal	1 2 3 4 5 6 7
Rabi'al-âkhir	3 4 5 6 7 1 2
Jamâzi'l-awwal	4 5 6 7 1 2 3
Jamâzi'l-âkhir	6 7 1 2 3 4 5
Rajab	7 1 2 3 4 5 6
Sha'ban	2 3 4 5 6 7 1
Ramadân	3 4 5 6 7 1 2
Shawwal	5 6 7 1 2 3 4
Dhu'l-qa'da	6 7 1 2 3 4 5
Dhu'l-hijja	1 2 3 4 5 6 7

'id al-ad'hâ   3 4 5 6 7 1 2

TABLE III

Mîlâdî Year	Hijrî Year	Mîlâdî Year	Hijrî Year
1323	724	607	-14
1356	758	640	20
1388	791	672	53
1421	825	705	87
1454	859	737	120
1486	892	770	154
1519	926	802	187
1551	959	835	221
1585	994	868	255
1617	1027	900	288
1650	1061	933	322
1682	1094	965	355
1715	1128	998	389
1748	1162	1030	422
1780	1195	1063	456
1813	1229	1095	489
1845	1262	1128	523
1878	1296	1160	556
1911	1330	1193	590
1943	1363	1226	624
1976	1397	1258	657
2008	1430	1291	691

TABLE IV

1 2 December	3 4 November	5 6 7 October	8 9 10 September	11 12 13 August	14 15 16 July
17 18 June	19 20 21 May	22 23 24 April	25 26 27 March	28 29 30 February	31 32 33 34 January

Appendix III

FINDING THE MÎLÂDÎ YEAR COINCIDING WITH THE BEGINNING OF THE HIJRÎ YEAR

Every hijrî year begins in the mîlâdî (Christian) year following the year wherein the previous hijrî year began, and approximately eleven days earlier. Every 33.58 hijrî and 32.58 mîlâdî years, the beginning of the hijrî year takes place during the first ten days of January. TABLE III contains the hijrî years beginning in December. The hijrî year beginnings following each of these move backwards from this twelfth month, coinciding with each of the mîlâdî months in rearward order. For finding the mîlâdî equivalent of any one of the hijrî year beginnings that are not written on the table, the hijrî year previous to it and written on the table and the mîlâdî year level with it are found on the table. Difference between the two hijrî years is added to the mîlâdî year found on the table. For example, to find the mîlâdî year coinciding with the beginning of the hijrî year 1344: 1344 - 1330 = 14; hence 1911 + 14 = 1925. When it is checked on the table indicating the months (TABLE IV), it will be seen that it coincided with July, which is the month below number 14 on the table. The mîlâdî year with which a solar month in a certain hijrî year coincides is one year ahead of the number found if the month concerned is previous to the month with which the beginning of the hijrî year coincides.

Appendix IV

TABLE EQUATION OF TIME and DECLINATION OF THE SUN (1986 *)

00:00 in Universal Time (UT, GMT)

DATE	E min.sec.	δ, °'	DATE	E min.sec.	δ, °'	DATE	E min.sec.	δ, °'	DATE	E min.sec.	δ, °'
Jan.	0–02 48	–23 07	Feb.	15–14 12	–12 51	Apr.	1–04 06	+04 20	May	17+03 40	+19 13
	1 03 16	23 03		16 14 09	12 31		2 03 48	04 44		18 03 38	19 26
	2 03 44	22 58		17 14 06	12 10		3 03 30	05 07		19 03 36	19 40
	3 04 12	22 52		18 14 01	11 49		4 03 13	05 30		20 03 33	19 52
	4 04 40	22 47		19 13 56	11 28		5 02 55	05 53		21 03 30	20 05
	5–05 07	–22 40		20–13 51	–11 06		6–02 38	+06 15		22+03 26	+20 17
	6 05 34	22 33		21 13 44	10 45		7 02 21	06 38		23 03 22	20 29
	7 06 01	22 26		22 13 37	10 23		8 02 04	07 01		24 03 17	20 40
	8 06 27	22 19		23 13 29	10 01		9 01 47	07 23		25 03 12	20 51
	9 06 52	22 11		24 13 21	09 39		10 01 31	07 45		26 03 06	21 02
	10–07 17	–22 02		25–13 12	–09 17		11–01 15	+08 08		27+03 00	+21 13
	11 07 41	21 53		26 13 02	08 55		12 00 59	08 30		28 02 53	21 23
	12 08 05	21 44		27 12 52	08 32		13 00 44	08 52		29 02 46	21 32
	13 08 28	21 34		28 12 42	08 10		14 00 28	09 13		30 02 38	21 42
	14 08 51	21 24	Mar.	1 12 31	07 47		15–00 13	09 35		31 02 30	21 51
	15–09 13	–21 13		2–12 19	–07 24		16+00 01	+09 56	June	1+02 21	+21 59
	16 09 34	21 02		3 12 07	07 01		17 00 15	10 18		2 02 12	22 07
	17 09 55	20 51		4 11 54	06 38		18 00 29	10 39		3 02 02	22 15
	18 10 15	20 39		5 11 41	06 15		19 00 43	11 00		4 01 52	22 22
	19 10 34	20 27		6 11 28	05 52		20 00 56	11 21		5 01 42	22 29
	20–10 52	–20 14		7–11 14	–05 29		21+01 09	+11 41		6+01 31	+22 36
	21 11 10	20 01		8–10 59	05 05		22 01 21	12 01		7 01 20	22 42
	22 11 26	19 48		9 10 45	04 42		23 01 33	12 22		8 01 09	22 48
	23 11 42	19 34		10 10 30	04 18		24 01 44	12 42		9 00 58	22 53
	24 11 58	19 20		11 10 14	03 55		25 01 55	13 01		10 00 46	22 58
	25–12 12	–19 05		12–09 59	–03 31		26+02 06	+13 21		11+00 34	+23 02
	26 12 26	18 51		13 09 43	03 08		27 02 16	13 40		12 00 22	23 07
	27 12 39	18 35		14 09 26	02 44		28 02 25	13 59		13+00 09	23 11
	28 12 51	18 20		15 09 10	02 20		29 02 34	14 18		14 –00 03	23 14
	29 13 02	18 04		16 08 53	01 57		30 02 43	14 37		15 00 16	23 17
	30–13 13	–17 48		17–08 36	–01 33	May	1+02 51	+14 55		16–00 29	+23 20
	31 13 22	17 32		18 08 19	01 09		2 02 58	15 13		17 00 42	23 22
Feb.	1 13 31	17 15		19 08 01	00 46		3 03 05	15 31		18 00 54	23 24
	2 13 39	16 58		20 07 44	–00 22		4 03 11	15 49		19 01 07	23 25
	3 13 46	16 40		21 07 26	+00 02		5 03 17	16 06		20 01 20	23 26
	4 13 53	–16 23		22–07 08	+00 26		6+03 22	+16 24		21–01 33	+23 26
	5 13 59	16 05		23 06 50	00 49		7 03 26	16 40		22 01 46	23 27
	6 14 04	15 46		24 06 32	01 13		8 03 30	16 57		23 01 59	23 26
	7 14 08	15 28		25 06 13	01 37		9 03 34	17 13		24 02 12	23 25
	8 14 11	15 09		26 05 55	02 00		10 03 36	17 29		25 02 25	23 24
	9–14 13	–14 50		27–05 37	+02 24		11+03 39	+17 45		26–02 38	+23 23
	10 14 15	14 31		28 05 19	02 47		12 03 40	18 00		27 02 50	23 21
	11 14 16	14 11		29 05 00	03 11		13 03 41	18 15		28 03 03	23 18
	12 14 16	13 52		30 04 42	03 34		14 03 42	18 30		29 03 15	23 16
	13 14 16	13 32		31 04 24	03 57		15 03 42	18 45		30 03 27	23 12
	14 14 14	–13 12	Apr.	1–04 16	+04 20		16+03 41	+18 59	July	1–03 39	+23 09
	15 14 12	–12 51		2–03 48	+04 44		17+03 40	+19 13		2–03 50	+23 05

(Continued)

E: equation of time, δ: declination of the Sun, min: minutes, sec: seconds.

* These values are for solar years 1986+4n (n=0,1,2,3,...). For 1987+4n, values corresponding to 6 hours earlier; for 1988+4n, values corresponding to 12 hours earlier (prior to March) and to 12 hours later (from March on); for 1989+4n, values corresponding to 6 hours later are used. For example, for 0 Jan. 1989 (31 Dec. 1988) the declination is determined as follows; Declination (δ) = –23°27' - [-23°27' - (-23°03')] x 6÷24= -23°06'. Ibrâhîm Fezârî Baghdâdî was the earliest Muslim to devise the quadrant and use it to measure the Sun's altitude. Among the very valuable books that he wrote are **Zeyj-i-Fezârî**, **Amal-i-bi-l-usturlâb**, and **Kitâb-ul-mikyâs-uz-zawâl**. He passed away in 188 [A.D. 803]. Two other extremely valuable books are **Kitâb-ul-usturlâb**, by Usbu' Ghirnâtî (of Granada), who passed away in 426 (hijrî), and **Ridâyat-ul-mubtadî**, by Alî bin Ahmad Baghdâdî (of Baghdâd) who passed away in 801 [A.D. 1398] in Egypt.

Appendix IV (continued)

DATE	E min.sec.	δ ° '	DATE	E min.sec.	δ ° '	DATE	E min.sec.	δ ° '	DATE	E min.sec.	δ ° '
July 1	–03 39	+23 09	16	–04 24	+13 54	Oct. 1	+10 06	–02 59	Nov. 16	+15 21	–18 36
2	03 50	23 05	17	04 12	13 35	2	10 25	03 22	17	15 10	18 51
3	04 02	23 00	18	03 59	13 16	3	10 44	03 46	18	14 58	19 06
4	04 13	22 55	19	03 46	12 57	4	11 03	04 09	19	14 46	19 20
5	04 24	22 50	20	03 32	12 37	5	11 21	04 32	20	14 32	19 34
6	04 34	+22 45	21	–03 17	+12 17	6	+11 39	–04 55	21	+14 18	–19 48
7	04 45	22 39	22	03 03	11 57	7	11 57	05 18	22	14 03	20 01
8	04 54	22 32	23	02 47	11 37	8	12 14	05 41	23	13 48	20 14
9	05 04	22 25	24	02 32	11 17	9	12 31	06 04	24	13 31	20 27
10	05 13	22 18	25	02 16	10 56	10	12 47	06 27	25	13 14	20 39
11	–05 21	+22 11	26	–01 59	+10 36	11	+13 03	–06 50	26	+12 55	–20 51
12	05 29	22 03	27	01 42	10 15	12	13 19	07 12	27	12 37	21 02
13	05 37	21 54	28	01 25	09 54	13	13 34	07 35	28	12 17	21 13
14	05 44	21 46	29	01 07	09 33	14	13 48	07 57	29	11 57	21 23
15	05 51	21 37	30	00 49	09 11	15	14 02	08 20	30	11 35	21 34
16	–05 57	+21 27	Sept. 31	–00 31	+08 50	16	+14 16	–08 42	Dec. 1	+11 14	–21 43
17	06 03	21 17	1	–00 13	08 28	17	14 29	09 04	2	10 51	21 53
18	06 08	21 07	2	+00 06	08 06	18	14 41	09 26	3	10 28	22 02
19	06 12	20 57	3	00 25	07 45	19	14 53	09 48	4	10 04	22 10
20	06 16	20 46	4	00 45	07 23	20	15 04	10 09	5	09 40	22 18
21	–06 20	+20 34	5	+01 05	+07 00	21	+15 15	–10 31	6	+09 15	–22 26
22	06 23	20 23	6	01 24	06 38	22	15 24	10 52	7	08 50	22 33
23	06 25	20 11	7	01 45	06 16	23	15 33	11 13	8	08 24	22 40
24	06 27	19 59	8	02 05	05 53	24	15 42	11 34	9	07 58	22 46
25	06 28	19 46	9	02 26	05 31	25	15 50	11 55	10	07 31	22 52
26	–06 28	+19 33	10	+02 46	+05 08	26	+15 57	–12 16	11	+07 04	–22 57
27	06 28	19 20	11	03 07	04 45	27	16 03	12 36	12	06 36	23 02
28	06 28	19 06	12	03 28	04 23	28	16 08	12 57	13	06 09	23 07
29	06 26	18 53	13	03 49	04 00	29	16 13	13 17	14	05 40	23 11
30	06 25	18 38	14	04 11	03 37	30	16 17	13 37	15	05 12	23 15
31	–06 22	+18 24	15	+04 32	+03 14	31	+16 20	–13 56	16	+04 43	–23 18
Aug. 1	06 19	18 09	16	04 53	02 51	Nov. 1	16 23	14 16	17	04 14	23 20
2	06 16	17 54	17	05 15	02 27	2	16 24	14 35	18	03 45	23 22
3	06 12	17 39	18	05 36	02 04	3	16 25	14 54	19	03 15	23 24
4	06 07	17 23	19	05 58	01 41	4	16 25	15 13	20	02 46	23 25
5	–06 02	+17 07	20	+06 19	+01 18	5	+16 24	–15 31	21	+02 16	–23 26
6	+05 56	16 51	21	06 41	00 54	6	16 22	15 50	22	01 46	23 27
7	05 49	16 34	22	07 02	00 31	7	16 20	16 08	23	01 16	23 26
8	05 42	16 17	23	07 23	+00 08	8	16 17	16 25	24	00 47	23 26
9	05 34	16 00	24	07 44	–00 16	9	16 13	16 43	25	+00 17	23 25
10	–05 26	+15 43	25	+08 05	–00 39	10	+16 08	–17 00	26	–00 13	–23 23
11	05 17	15 25	26	08 26	01 02	11	16 02	17 17	27	00 43	23 21
12	05 08	15 08	27	08 46	01 26	12	15 55	17 33	28	01 12	23 19
13	04 58	14 50	28	09 07	01 49	13	15 48	17 50	29	01 42	23 16
14	04 47	14 31	29	09 27	02 12	14	15 40	18 06	30	02 11	23 12
15	–04 36	+14 13	30	+09 47	–02 36	15	+15 30	–18 21	31	–02 40	–23 08
16	–04 24	+13 54	Oct. 1	+10 06	–02 59	16	+15 21	–18 36	32	–03 09	–23 04

E = (true time)-(mean time).

The above values are determined when it was 00:00 in London i.e. at 24:00 (the previous midnight). They are used after correction in direct proportion to a given longitude. The time t in standard time is calculated from $\delta = \delta_2 + (\delta_2 - \delta_1) \times (t-(S/15))/24$ where δ_1 and δ_2 are the values on that day and on the following, respectively; S is the degree of the meridian determining standard time; all used with their algebraic signs.

Appendix V
TABLE of TAMKINS

(With latitudes zero through sixty by threes and heights zero through five hundred by twenty-fives)

HEIGHT (m)	L 0 min.sec.	3 min.sec.	A 6 min.sec.	9 min.sec.	T 12 min.sec.	15 min.sec.	I 18 min.sec.	21 min.sec.	T 24 min.sec.	27 min.sec.	U 30 min.sec.	33 min.sec.	D 36 min.sec.	39 min.sec.	E 42 min.sec.	45 min.sec.	48 min.sec.	51 min.sec.	S 54 min.sec.	57 min.sec.	60 min.sec.
0	3.49	3.49	3.51	3.53	3.55	3.58	4.02	4.06	4.12	4.20	4.29	4.42	4.57	5.13	5.33	5.57	6.28	7.09	8.06	9.25	11.44
25	4.38	4.38	4.39	4.41	4.45	4.49	4.54	5.01	5.08	5.19	5.31	5.41	5.59	6.20	6.42	7.13	7.52	8.40	9.54	11.20	14.20
50	4.58	4.58	5.00	5.02	5.06	5.10	5.16	5.23	5.31	5.42	5.54	6.08	6.27	6.48	7.14	7.46	8.28	9.19	10.38	12.19	15.27
75	5.16	5.16	5.18	5.21	5.24	5.29	5.36	5.43	5.52	6.03	6.12	6.27	6.50	7.10	7.38	8.12	8.59	9.54	11.11	13.05	16.26
100	5.27	5.27	5.29	5.30	5.35	5.40	5.47	5.55	6.05	6.15	6.27	6.44	7.04	7.28	7.56	8.33	9.19	10.16	11.39	13.39	17.06
125	5.38	5.39	5.40	5.42	5.46	5.53	6.00	6.07	6.17	6.27	6.41	6.58	7.19	7.44	8.14	8.51	9.38	10.39	12.05	14.08	17.42
150	5.49	5.50	5.52	5.54	5.58	6.03	6.11	6.19	6.29	6.40	6.54	7.12	7.34	7.59	8.30	9.08	9.57	11.00	12.28	14.35	18.17
175	5.58	5.59	6.01	6.03	6.08	6.14	6.21	6.29	6.40	6.52	7.06	7.24	7.47	8.13	8.45	9.24	10.14	11.18	12.51	15.00	18.49
200	6.08	6.09	6.10	6.13	6.17	6.23	6.31	6.39	6.50	7.03	7.18	7.36	7.59	8.26	8.59	9.39	10.30	11.36	13.11	15.23	19.21
225	6.17	6.17	6.18	6.22	6.26	6.32	6.40	6.48	7.00	7.13	7.28	7.46	8.10	8.38	9.12	9.53	10.45	11.53	13.31	15.45	19.51
250	6.25	6.25	6.26	6.30	6.35	6.41	6.49	6.57	7.09	7.22	7.38	7.57	8.21	8.49	9.24	10.06	10.59	12.09	13.49	16.06	20.20
275	6.31	6.33	6.34	6.38	6.41	6.47	6.57	7.06	7.18	7.32	7.48	8.06	8.31	9.00	9.35	10.18	11.13	12.25	14.06	16.26	20.48
300	6.40	6.41	6.42	6.46	6.51	6.57	7.05	7.14	7.26	7.40	7.57	8.16	8.41	9.12	9.46	10.30	11.26	12.40	14.23	16.46	21.15
325	6.47	6.48	6.49	6.53	6.58	7.05	7.12	7.22	7.34	7.49	8.05	8.25	8.52	9.21	9.57	10.41	11.39	12.54	14.38	17.05	21.41
350	6.54	6.55	6.56	7.00	7.05	7.13	7.20	7.30	7.42	7.57	8.13	8.32	9.01	9.31	10.07	10.52	11.51	13.07	14.53	17.25	22.05
375	7.01	7.02	7.04	7.07	7.12	7.19	7.27	7.37	7.49	8.05	8.22	8.42	9.10	9.40	10.17	11.03	12.03	13.20	15.08	17.44	22.31
400	7.08	7.09	7.11	7.14	7.19	7.25	7.34	7.45	7.57	8.12	8.30	8.51	9.18	9.49	10.27	11.14	12.15	13.32	15.23	18.03	22.55
425	7.14	7.15	7.17	7.20	7.25	7.32	7.41	7.51	8.04	8.20	8.37	8.58	9.26	9.58	10.34	11.24	12.26	13.44	15.38	18.22	23.17
450	7.20	7.21	7.23	7.26	7.32	7.38	7.47	7.58	8.11	8.26	8.44	9.06	9.34	10.07	10.42	11.34	12.37	13.56	15.53	18.40	23.38
475	7.26	7.27	7.29	7.32	7.38	7.44	7.54	8.04	8.18	8.34	8.52	9.13	9.42	10.15	10.50	11.44	12.48	14.08	16.08	18.58	23.59
500	7.32	7.33	7.35	7.39	7.44	7.51	8.00	8.11	8.25	8.41	8.59	9.20	9.50	10.23	10.58	11.53	12.58	14.20	16.18	19.15	24.20

Height is the elevation of the highest place of a location above its lowest place. Information about Tamkin is given in the tenth chapter, **Prayer Times**, of this book. Muhammad bin Mûsâ Baghdâdî and Abû Bakr Muhammad bin 'Umar Munajjim Baghdâdî explained how to determine the time by using the Rub'-i dâira [quadrant] in their books **al-'Amal-u bi-l-usturlâb**. The former passed away in 205, and the latter in 320 [A.D. 932]. Another valuable source is the book **Rubu'i muqantarât** by Abdullah bin Alî Mardînî. He passed away in 779 [A.D. 1377].

Captain Mustafâ Hilmi Efendi, a teacher of fann-i hey'et (astronomy) in the Mekteb-i-bahriya-i-shâhâna (Royal Naval Academy), gave perfect calculations of prayer times and of the beginnings of Arabic months in his book **Hey'et-i felekiyye**, printed in 1306 [A.D. 1888].

Appendix VI

Sun's Altitudes at Time of Late Afternoon Prayer for Any Latitude

Ghâyat Irtifâ'	Fay-i-zawâl	Ghâyat Irtifâ'	Fay-i-zawâl	Ghâyat Irtifâ'	Fay-i-zawâl	Ghâyat Irtifâ'	Fay-i-zawâl	Ghâyat Irtifâ'	Fay-i-zawâl
0.15	229.182	10.30	5.395	25.30	2.097	40.30	1.171	61	0.554
0.30	114.589	11.00	5.145	26.00	2.050	41.00	1.150	62	0.532
0.45	76.390	11.30	4.915	26.30	2.006	41.30	1.130	63	0.510
1.00	57.290	12.00	4.705	27.00	1.963	42.00	1.111	64	0.488
1.15	45.829	12.30	4.511	27.30	1.921	42.30	1.091	65	0.466
1.30	38.188	13.00	4.331	28.00	1.881	43.00	1.072	66	0.445
1.45	32.730	13.30	4.165	28.30	1.842	43.30	1.054	67	0.424
2.00	28.636	14.00	4.011	29.00	1.804	44.00	1.036	68	0.404
2.15	25.452	14.30	3.867	29.30	1.767	44.30	1.018	69	0.384
2.30	22.904	15.00	3.732	30.00	1.732	45.00	1.000	70	0.364
2.45	20.819	15.30	3.606	30.30	1.698	45.30	0.983	71	0.344
3.00	19.081	16.00	3.487	31.00	1.664	46.00	0.966	72	0.325
3.15	17.611	16.30	3.376	31.30	1.632	46.30	0.949	73	0.306
3.30	16.350	17.00	3.271	32.00	1.600	47.00	0.933	74	0.287
3.45	15.257	17.30	3.172	32.30	1.570	47.30	0.916	75	0.268
4.00	14.301	18.00	3.078	33.00	1.540	48.00	0.900	76	0.249
4.15	13.457	18.30	2.989	33.30	1.511	48.30	0.885	77	0.230
4.30	12.706	19.00	2.904	34.00	1.483	49.00	0.869	78	0.213
4.45	12.035	19.30	2.824	34.30	1.455	49.30	0.854	79	0.194
5.00	11.430	20.00	2.747	35.00	1.428	50.00	0.839	80	0.179
5.30	10.385	20.30	2.675	35.30	1.402	51.00	0.830	81	0.158
6.00	9.514	21.00	2.605	36.00	1.376	52.00	0.781	82	0.141
6.30	8.777	21.30	2.539	36.30	1.351	53.00	0.754	83	0.123
7.00	8.144	22.00	2.475	37.00	1.327	54.00	0.727	84	0.105
7.30	7.596	22.30	2.414	37.30	1.303	55.00	0.700	85	0.087
8.00	7.115	23.00	2.356	38.00	1.280	56.00	0.675	86	0.070
8.30	6.691	23.30	2.300	38.30	1.257	57.00	0.649	87	0.052
9.00	6.394	24.00	2.246	39.00	1.235	58.00	0.625	88	0.035
9.30	5.976	24.30	2.194	39.30	1.213	59.00	0.601	89	0.017
10.00	5.671	25.00	2.145	40.00	1.192	60.00	0.577	90	0.000

For instance, the Sun's declination on February 2 is -16.48° in Istanbul; hence, ghâyat irtifâ' (point of solar culmination, the Sun's maximum altitude) is -16.48° +49° = 32.12°; fay-i-zawâl (the shortest shadow) of a one-metre-long perpendicular rod is 1.58m.; and the length of its late-afternoon shadow is 2.58m.; and the Sun's late-afternoon altitude is 21.20°. The fadl-i-dâir (temporal value of the arc of complement of the Sun's true altitude) is 2 hours and 41 minutes, which will be found by using a calculator. Thereby the time of late afternoon will be found to be 9.42 hours, adhânî, and 3.09 hours, in standard time, since the equation of time is -13.39; (please see Appendix IV.) A method to be used in the absence of the chart above is to get a privileg calculator, touch the buttons for the computation: 90-32.12 ⟶ = tan + 1 = arc tan MS 90-MR = ⟶, and find the Sun's altitude at the time of 'asr-i awwal (the earlier time of late afternoon) to be 21.08°. There is yet another method: The Rub-i-dâira (quadrant). Its khayt, (thread that represents the daily rotation,) is brought over the number representing the ghâyat irtifâ'; the number on the arc of zill-i-mebsût and crossed by the khayt shows the length of the shortest shadow termed fay-i-zawâl.

GLOSSARY

Adâ: performing namâz within its appointed time.

Adab: there is a special adab in doing everything. The adab of doing something means to follow the conditions necessary for doing it in the best way.

Aqîqa: animal killed (by cutting its throat) to thank Allahu ta'âlâ for a newly born child. Two are killed for a son, while one is killed for a daughter. It is not fard. It is mustahab to kill it. That is, it is not sinful not to kill it. Please see the fourth chapter of the fifth fascicle.

Alastu: Allah's declaration: Alastu bi-rab-bikum? "Am I not your Allah?" which, when He created Hadrat Adam, He asked to all the souls of Hadrat Adam's descendants that would come until the end of the world.

Ansâr: those Muslims who lived in Madîna and helped Rasûlullah when he migrated to Madîna. Those companions of the Prophet who migrated to Madîna from Mekka are called **Muhâjir**.

Arsh: end of the world of matter surrounding the seven heavens.

As'hâb-i kahf: seven great people who survived in a cave in Tarsus. One pious action they did – they migrated to another country when their country was invaded by enemies – made them so beloved by Allahu ta'âlâ.

Awliyâ: a person whom Allahu ta'âlâ loves is called **Walî**. **Awliyâ** is the plural form of **Walî**, though we sometimes use the word for both singular and plural.

Âyat: a verse in the Qur'ân al-kerîm. There are 6236 âyats in the Qur'ân al-kerîm.

Âyat-al-kursî: one of the âyats in the Qur'ân. It explains the greatness of Allahu ta'âlâ and the fact that His power is infinite.

Azân: at each prayer time, a Muslim goes up the minaret and calls all Muslims to prayer. He has to recite prescribed words. Meanings of these Arabic words are explained in the eleventh chapter.

Bid'at: wrong, false information about the dîn; an action or word that did not exist in the Dîn originally but which was concocted later. All bid'âts are corrupt.

Dhikr: to mention the name of Allahu ta'âlâ through the

– 425 –

heart, to remember.

Faqîr: a poor person who has property more than his subsistence but less than what will make him rich in comparison with the level of richness (nisâb) prescribed by Islam. 'Nisâb' is the amount of money or property a person has, excluding what he needs for his subsistence. Nisâb is equivalent to 96 grams of gold or 672 grams of silver (in the Hanafî Madhhab). Faqîr also means a person who does not regard worldly property and who does not hesitate to give his property in the way of Allah. Also, a faqîr is a person who knows that he needs everything and who expects what he needs from Allahu ta'âlâ only. He asks from men, but expects from Allahu ta'âlâ.

Fard: an action, word or thought which Allahu ta'âlâ clearly commands in the **Qur'ân al-kerîm**. There are two kinds of fard: 1- **Fard-i ayn** has to be done by everybody, e.g. performing namâz. 2- **Fard-i kifâya** lapses from other Muslims when one Muslim does it. For example, it is sunnat to greet a Muslim when meeting him by saying the prescribed Arabic word: "Salâmun alaikum." And it is fard (Allah's command) to respond to a Muslim who greets you. That is, you say, "Wa 'alaikum salâm." If no one acknowledges the greeting they all will become sinful. If one of them greets back the duty will lapse from the others.

Fâtiha: first sûra in the **Qur'ân al-kerîm**. It is recited during every standing position when performing namâz. It is also recited for the souls of dead Muslims.

Fitra: alms that must be given when the month of Ramadân is over. About two kilograms of wheat or equivalent silver is given. Please see third chapter of fifth fascicle.

Hadîth: any blessed word or tradition of the Prophet.

Hadîth-i qudsî: a hadîth inspired by Allahu ta'âlâ but said by the Prophet.

Hâl: continuous variation of the kashfs and manifestations that come to the heart. Also see **Kashf**.

Halâl: action, word or thought permitted by Allahu ta'âlâ.

Hamd: thanking, praising and lauding. Also **Hamd-u thanâ**.

Harâm: an action, word or thought prohibited by Allahu ta'âlâ.

Hubb-i fillâh: loving for Allah's sake. Hating, being hostile for Allah's sake is called **Bughdh-i fillâh**.

Ibni Âbidîn: Sayyed Muhammad Amîn bin 'Umar bin Abdul'azîz is one of the savants of fiqh. He was born in Damascus in 1198 and died there in 1252 A.H. He became mature with the tawajjuh of Mawlânâ Khâlid-i Baghdâdî, keeping company with him. When that sun of wilâyat set in Damascus, he conducted his janâza namâz as the îmâm. He wrote many books. His explanation of **Durrulmukhtâr** consists of five volumes and has been printed several times with the title **Raddulmuhtâr**. It is the most dependable book of fiqh in the Hanafî Madhhab. The major parts of the information concerning fiqh covering 130 chapters of the Turkish version of **Endless Bliss** has been translated from its five volumes that were printed in Egypt in 1272 A.H.

Ijtihâd: ability to understand the symbolic, hidden meanings in the **Qur'ân**. Work of this kind. It is explained in more detail in **Religion Reformers in Islam**.

Iftâr: the act of breaking a fast. Fasting is done for thirty days in Ramadân. Iftâr is done when the sun sets. Please see the second chapter in the fifth fascicle.

Ijtibâ: Means to choose, to like.

Ikhlâs: quality and intention of doing everything for Allah's sake.

Imâm: (pl. a'imma) 1- Profound savant, **Imâm-al-Madhhab**, leader, founder of a Madhhab; **twelve a'imma** (imâms), three male members of the Ahl-i bayt and their nine successors; **Imâm-i a'zam** (the greatest leader), title of Abû Hanîfa, leader of the Hanafî Madhhab. 2- Leader in public salât (namâz in jamâ'at).

Inâbat: to repent for having sinned. It has been used to mean to get attached and to adapt oneself to an Islamic savant.

Irâdat: to wish; to wish to get attached to an Islamic savant.

Ism-i a'zam: a Name of Allahu ta'âlâ which He likes best among His Names which He has communicated. He will positively accept a prayer sent by mentioning this Name. We do not know this Name.

Istighfâr: prayer for repentance; prescribed prayer recited in order to entreat Allahu ta'âlâ for forgiveness.

Jadhba: means the murîd's progress with the fayd that flows into his heart from the Murshid's heart.

Jalîs-i ilâhî: jalîs means to stay together. A person who thinks of Allah every moment is called so.

Jamâ'at: a congregation of Muslims. One person performs namâz in the front; the others, behind him, preform it like him by adapting themselves to him. The person who performs it in the front is called the imâm. Those who perform it behind him are called the jamâ'at.

Janâza namâz: a namâz performed when a Muslim dies. His relatives, neighbors and acquaintances make a line in front of his dead body. They beg Allah for his forgiveness. It is necessary to beg by saying the prayers prescribed by the Dîn.

Junub: a person who needs a ghusl ablution. What causes a person to become junub is prescribed by Islam. The causes are explained in the fourth chapter.

Kalâm: its lexical meaning is a word, speech.

Kashf: manifestation, appearing of Allah's attributes.

Kayfiyyat: peculiarity of something, showing how it is.

Khutba: the speech made in the mosque by the îmâm during Friday prayer or 'Iyd prayer.

Latâfat: fineness.

Latîfa: See first fascicle, Fanâ and Baqâ in 38th chapter.

Lawh: a smooth surface.

Mekrûh: things which our Prophet did not like and said were unpleasant. It is not a guilt to do them, but it dirties the heart.

Mashhûr: known by the majority of people.

Mubâh: action, word of thought permitted by Allahu ta'âlâ.

Muhâjir: See **Ansâr**.

Mujaddid: restorer. Hadrat Muhammad informed that every hundred years there will be an Islamic savant restoring Islam.

Mujaddidî: a great savant who follows the path of the great Islamic savant Hadrat Imâm-i Rabbânî and who educates youngsters with his methods.

Mulhid: he who goes out of the Dîn by misunderstanding one or more parts of Islam.

Murâd: chosen person to whom the deeds causing Allah's love has been shown and facilitated.

Murâqaba: paying attention, thinking always of one thing only.

Murshid-i kâmil: a great savant who has reached perfection and can make others attain it, too.

Mushâhada: a word used by men of tasawwuf. We may say it is to see through the heart's eye.

Mustahab: action, word or thought that brings a lot of thawâb.

Nafs: (Nafs-i ammâra). Nafs is ammâra by creation, that is, it always wishes evil and harmful deeds to be done. It is reluctant to obey the Sharî'at. The nafs of a man who obeys the Sharî'at and makes progress in the way of tasawwuf becomes mutmainna. It wishes to obey the Sharî'at.

Najâsat: any kind of dirt, filth, that prevents one from performing namâz. It is explained in more detail in the sixth chapter.

Rak'at: In performing namâz, the actions of standing, bowing and putting the head on the ground twice are altogether called a rak'at. Most prayers of namâz consist of two or four rak'ats. One of them contains three rak'ats.

Sahâba: if a Muslim has seen the Prophet, or talked to him, at least once when the Prophet was alive, he is called **Sahabî**. Plural form of Sahabî is **Sahâba** or **As'hâb**. The word **Sahâba-i kirâm** includes all those great people each of whom has seen the Prophet at least once. The lowest of the Sahâba is much higher than the highest of other Muslims. If a person has not seen the Prophet but has seen or talked to one of the Sahâba at least once, he is called **Tâbi'**. Its plural form is **Tâbi'în**. In other words, the Tâbi'în are the successors of the Sahâba. If a person has not seen any of the Sahâba but has seen at least one of the Tabi'în, he is called **Taba'î Tâbi'în**. The Sahâba, the Tâbi'în and the Taba'i tabi'în altogether are called the **Salaf-i sâlihin** (the early savants).

Sahabî: See Sahâba.

Sahîh: 1- Valid, lawful; 2- A kind of hadîth. Kinds of hadîth are explained in the sixth chapter of the second fascicle of Endless Bliss.

Sajda-i sahw: two sajdas (prostrations) done as soon as namâz is over in order to have some errors forgiven that may have been done while performing namâz.

Salâtan tunjînâ: the word **salât** means both prayer and namâz. Muslims send their prayers to Allahu ta'âlâ so that the Prophet's grade will go up and he will be given more goodness. Such prayers are called salât, too. Allahu ta'âlâ loves those who pray so. He rescues them from troubles. Salâtan tunjînâ means to invoke a blessing on the Prophet in order to get rid of troubles.

Sayr: to go, travel.

Sayyid: title given to the Prophet's descendants. When they are through Hadrat Husayn, Hadrad Ali's second son, they are called Sayyid, and when they are through Hadrat Hasan, Hadrat Ali's elder son, they are called Sherîf.

Shar'an makrûh: things which our Prophet disliked and said to be loathsome. It is not a guilt to do them, but it dirties the heart.

Sherîf: See **Sayyid**.

Silsila-i aliyya: a valuable chain. It is the chain of Islamic savants beginning with our Prophet up to today, each of whom saw the one previous to him, and followed his path, footsteps.

Sohbat: to make friends, to stay together for a long time; to talk to one another and to derive use from one another.

Shuhûd: a word used by men of tasawwuf. See **Mushâhada**.

Sulûk: to make progress by striving in the way shown by men of tasawwuf.

Sufiyya-i aliyya: Great men of tasawwuf.

Sunnat: 1- (when used alone) The **Sharî'at;** 2- (when used together with the name **Book**) The hadîth of the Prophet. 3- (when used together with the word **Fard**) Any action, word or thought liked and commanded by the Prophet.

Sûra: a chapter of the **Qur'ân**.

Tab'an makrûh: anything that one is loath to do although it is not comething that our Prophet disapproved of.

Tâbi'în: see Sahâba.

Ta'dîl-i arkân: see first and second fascicles of Endless Bliss.

Tahrîmî makrûh: of those things that are Shar'an mekrûh, the ones that are loathsome and harmful. Those that are not loathsome and harmful, but should not be done are called **tenzîhî mekrûh**.

Takbîr: the word **Allâhu akbar,** means: Allahu ta'âlâ is the greatest.

Taqdîth: to declare to be without defects or faults.

Tasbih: may be used for the word taqdîth, though there is a very subtle difference between their meanings.

tawâtur: to be known by Muslims all over the world.

Tawba: (after committing a sin) to repent, to promise Allah not to do it again, to entreat Him for forgiveness. Everyone does his tawba by himself.

Tawhîd: oneness of Allahu ta'âlâ; a word describing oneness of Allahu ta'âlâ.

Thawâb: Muslims will be rewarded in the Hereafter for all their pious actions which they have done in the world. The rewards which Muslims will be given in the Hereafter are called **thawâb**. The word is used as an adjective as well as a noun. For example, when we say that an action is very thawâb we mean that Allahu ta'âlâ will give many rewards for the action.

Tumânînat: see first and second fascicles of Endless Bliss.

'Ushr: a kind of zakât.

Wahy: see **Belief and Islam**.

Wâjib: see **Belief and Islam**.

Walî: see **Awliyâ**.

Wilâyat: the grade reached by a Muslim who has managed the very hard job of adapting his every word, every action and every thought to the Sharî'at. Such a person is called a **Walî**.

Wilâyat-i khâssa: see first and second fascicles of Endless Bliss.

Wudû': Ablution.

Yâddâsht: To become accustomed to thinking of Allahu ta'âlâ all the time. If one wants to think of anything besides Allahu ta'âlâ one will not be able to do it.

Yaqîn: belief without any doubt.

zâhid: a person who does not set his heart on worldly things.

Zakât: to give every year a certain amount of one's property to the people prescribed by the Qur'ân.

Zî-rahm: One's relative through lineage, through one's parents.

Zî-rahm-i mahram: those zî-rahm relatives of a woman or girl who she is permitted to talk to with a bare head and arms, to stay alone in a room and to go on a trip with, but not permitted to get married to.

Zuhd: not to set one's heart on worldly things. Person who has this quality is called zâhid.

BOOKS PUBLISHED BY HAKİKAT KİTABEVİ

ENGLISH:
1– Endless Bliss I, 304 pp.
2– Endless Bliss II, 400 pp.
3– Endless Bliss III, 336 pp.
4– Endless Bliss IV, 432 pp.
5– Endless Bliss V, 512 pp.
6– Endless Bliss VI, 352 pp.
7– The Sunni Path, 128 pp.
8– Belief and Islam, 128 pp.
9– The Proof of Prophethood, 144 pp.
10– Answer to an Enemy of Islam, 128 pp.
11– Advice for the Muslim, 352 pp.
12– Islam and Christianity, 336 pp.
13– Could Not Answer, 432 pp.
14– Confessions of a British Spy, 128 pp.
15– Documents of the Right Word, 496 pp.
16– Why Did They Become Muslims?, 304 pp.
17– Ethics of Islam, 240 pp.
18– Sahaba 'The Blessed', 384 pp.
19– Islam's Reformers, 320 pp.
20– The Rising and the Hereafter 112 pp.
21– Miftah-ul-janna, 288 pp.

DEUTSCH:
1– Islam, der Weg der Sunniten, 128 Seiten
2– Glaube und Islam, 128 Seiten
3– Islam und Christentum, 352 Seiten
4– Beweis des Prophetentums, 160 Seiten
5– Geständnisse von einem Britischen Spion, 176 Seiten
6– Islamische Sitte, 288 Seiten

EN FRANÇAIS:
1– L'Islam et la Voie de Sunna, 112 pp.
2– Foi et Islam, 160 pp.
3– Islam et Christianisme, 304 pp.
4– L'évidence de la Prophétie, et les Temps de Prières, 144 pp.
5– Ar-radd al Jamil, Ayyuha'l-Walad (Al-Ghazâli), 96 pp.
6– Al-Munqid min ad'Dalâl, (Al-Ghazâli), 64 pp.

SHQIP:
1- Besimi dhe Islami, 96 fq.
2- Libri Namazit, 208 fq.
3- Rrefimet e Agjentit Anglez, 112 fq.

ESPAÑOL:
1- Creencia e Islam, 112

ПО РУССКИ:
1- Всем Нужная Вера, (128) стр.
2- Признания Английского Шпиона, (144) стр.
3- Китаб-ус-Салат (Молитвенник) Книга о намазе, (224) стр.
4- О Сын Мой (256) стр.
5- Религя Ислам (256) стр.

НА БЪЛГАРСКИ ЕЗИК:
1- Вяра и Ислям. (128) стр.
2- НАМАЗ КИТАБЪ (256) стр.

BOSHNJAKISHT:
1- Iman i Islam. (128) str.
2- Odgovor Neprijatelju Islama, (144) str.
3- Knjiga o Namazu, (192) str.
4- Nije Mogao Odgovoriti. (432) str.
5- Put Ehl-i Sunneta. (128) str.
6- Ispovijesti Jednog Engleskog Spijuna. (144) str.

Printed in Germany
by Amazon Distribution
GmbH, Leipzig